Expert ASP.NET Web API 2 for MVC Developers

Adam Freeman

Apress®

Expert ASP.NET Web API 2 for MVC Developers

ISBN-13 (pbk): 978-1-4842-0086-5

ISBN-13 (electronic): 978-1-4842-0085-8

Publisher: Heinz Weinheimer
Lead Editor: James T. DeWolf
Development Editor: Douglas Pundick
Technical Reviewer: Fabio Claudio Ferracchiati
Editorial Board: Steve Anglin, Mark Beckner, Ewan Buckingham, Gary Cornell, Louise Corrigan, Jim DeWolf, Jonathan Gennick, Jonathan Hassell, Robert Hutchinson, Michelle Lowman, James Markham, Matthew Moodie, Jeff Olson, Jeffrey Pepper, Douglas Pundick, Ben Renow-Clarke, Dominic Shakeshaft, Gwenan Spearing, Matt Wade, Steve Weiss
Coordinating Editor: Kevin Walter
Copy Editor: Kim Wimpsett
Compositor: SPi Global
Indexer: SPi Global
Artist: SPi Global
Cover Designer: Anna Ishchenko

Distributed to the book trade worldwide by Springer Science+Business Media New York, 233 Spring Street, 6th Floor, New York, NY 10013. Phone 1-800-SPRINGER, fax (201) 348-4505, e-mail orders-ny@springer-sbm.com, or visit www.springeronline.com. Apress Media, LLC is a California LLC and the sole member (owner) is Springer Science + Business Media Finance Inc (SSBM Finance Inc). SSBM Finance Inc is a Delaware corporation.

For information on translations, please e-mail rights@apress.com, or visit www.apress.com.

Apress and friends of ED books may be purchased in bulk for academic, corporate, or promotional use. eBook versions and licenses are also available for most titles. For more information, reference our Special Bulk Sales–eBook Licensing web page at www.apress.com/bulk-sales.

Any source code or other supplementary material referenced by the author in this text is available to readers at www.apress.com. For detailed information about how to locate your book's source code, go to www.apress.com/source-code/.

Dedicated to my lovely wife, Jacqui Griffyth

Contents at a Glance

About the Author xxiii

About the Technical Reviewer xxv

■Part I: Getting Ready.. 1

■Chapter 1: Getting Readys 3

■Chapter 2: Your First Web API Application 9

■Chapter 3: Essential Techniques 35

■Chapter 4: Understanding HTTP Web Services 57

■Chapter 5: SportsStore: Preparation 69

■Chapter 6: SportsStore: A RESTful Application..99

■Chapter 7: SportsStore: Creating the Clients...131

■Chapter 8: SportsStore: Deployment 169

■Part 2: Results and Parameters.. 179

■Chapter 9: The Anatomy of ASP.NET Web API 181

■Chapter 10: Creating and Configuring a Web API Application 191

■Chapter 11: Action Method Results 215

■Chapter 12: Creating Media Type Formatters...243

■Chapter 13: Using the Built-in Media Formatters...267

■Chapter 14: Understanding Parameter and Model Binding 297

■Chapter 15: Binding Simple Data Types...325

■Chapter 16: Binding Complex Data Types Part I 351

v

■**Chapter 17: Binding Complex Data Types Part II**...**389**

■**Chapter 18: Model Validation** **427**

■**Part 3: Dispatching Requests** **449**

■**Chapter 19: Dispatching Requests** **451**

■**Chapter 20: URL Routing: Part I**...**483**

■**Chapter 21: URL Routing: Part II**..**511**

■**Chapter 22: Controllers and Actions**...**535**

■**Chapter 23: Filters Part I** **567**

■**Chapter 24: Filters Part II** **599**

■**Chapter 25: Error Handling**...**623**

■**Chapter 26: Using OWIN**...**645**

Index...**651**

Contents

About the Author xxiii

About the Technical Reviewer xxv

■Part I: Getting Ready 1

■Chapter 1: Getting Readys 3

What Do You Need to Know? 3

What Does *Expert* Mean? 3

What Is the Structure of This Book? 3

    Part 1: Getting Ready 4

    Part 2: Results and Parameters 4

    Part 3: Dispatching Requests 4

Are There Lots of Examples? 4

Where Can You Get the Example Code? 5

How Do You Set Up a Development Environment? 5

    Getting Visual Studio 6

    Getting Google Chrome 6

Summary 7

■Chapter 2: Your First Web API Application 9

Preparing the Example Project 9

    Creating the Visual Studio Project 10

    Adding and Updating NuGet Packages 11

    Setting the Port and Start URL 12

Creating the MVC Application 12

Creating the Model 12

Creating the MVC Controller 14

Creating the Views 16

Using the MVC Application 18

Creating the Web Service 20

Creating the Web API Controller 20

Testing the Web API Controller 23

Implementing the Single-Page Client 25

Setting Up JavaScript IntelliSense 26

Defining the Client-Side Data Model and Controller 26

Registering the JavaScript File 29

Appling Data Bindings 30

Testing the Single-Page Client 32

Measuring the Single-Page Implementation 33

Summary 33

■Chapter 3: Essential Techniques 35

Preparing the Example Project 35

Adding and Updating NuGet Packages 37

Creating the Web API Controller 37

Creating the MVC Framework Controller 39

Setting the Port and Start URL 41

Testing the Web Service 41

Understanding Asynchronous Methods 42

Understanding the Problem Asynchronous Methods Solve 42

Implementing an Asynchronous Interface 44

Creating a Self-Contained Asynchronous Method Body 47

Returning a Task from a Synchronous Method Body 48

Making Ajax Requests with jQuery 49

Making an Ajax Request 50

Understanding the $.ajax Method 52

Using Knockout 54

    Applying the Bindings 54

Summary 56

■ Chapter 4: Understanding HTTP Web Services 57

Understanding ASP.NET Web API 57

    Understanding Single-Page Applications 58

    Understanding Native Applications...59

    Understanding Shared-Model Applications 59

    Understanding Service Applications 60

Understanding Simple Web Services 61

Understanding RESTful Web Services 62

    Embracing HTTP 63

    Adding Data Discovery 65

Summary 67

■ Chapter 5: SportsStore: Preparation 69

Preparing the Example Project...69

    Adding and Updating NuGet Packages 72

    Creating a Prep Controller 73

    Creating a Razor Layout 73

    Creating the OWIN Startup Class..74

    Setting the TCP Port...75

Creating the Product and Order Models 75

    Defining the Model Classes 75

    Creating the Repository Classes 77

    Testing the Repository 82

    Checking the Database Schema...86

Configuring ASP.NET Identity 87

    Defining the User and Role Classes 87

    Creating the Database Context Classes..88

    Creating the Manager Classes...90

Adding the Configuration Statements...92

Testing ASP.NET Identity 93

Removing the Application Cookie 97

Summary...98

■Chapter 6: SportsStore: A RESTful Application...99

Creating a RESTful Web Service..99

Testing the Products Web Service 101

Putting the Web Service in Context...102

Working with Regular C# Objects 102

Using the RESTful Action Method Convention 103

Configuring Serialization 104

Adding Basic Data Validation...106

Securing the Product Web Service...109

Restricting Access to Action Method 110

Authenticating Requests 111

Adding Model Validation...118

Applying Validation Attributes 119

Validating the Model 120

Adding Simple Dependency Injection..121

Recapping the Problem 121

Creating the Dependency Resolver 121

Using the Dependency Resolver in the Controller Class 123

Creating a Non-RESTful Web Service...124

Preparing the Routing Configuration 124

Preparing the Model Objects...125

Preventing Formatting Loops 126

Defining the Web API Controller 127

Completing the Product Controller..128

Summary...129

■Chapter 7: SportsStore: Creating the Clients 131

Preparing the Example Project 131

Setting Up JavaScript IntelliSense 132

Updating the Layout 132

Implementing the Common Code 133

Defining the Ajax Layer 133

Defining the Model 135

Defining the Authentication Controller 136

Defining the Products Controller 138

Defining the Orders Controller 142

Creating the Customer Client 145

Creating the Customer Model 145

Creating the Customer Controller 146

Creating the Views 149

Creating the Administration Client 159

Creating the Admin Model 159

Creating the Admin Controller 159

Creating the Views 160

Testing the Admin Client 165

Summary 167

■Chapter 8: SportsStore: Deployment 169

Preparing the SportsStore Application 169

Preventing the Product Database from Resetting 169

Adding Database Connection Strings 171

Preparing Azure 172

Creating the Databases 172

Creating the Web Site 175

Downloading the Publish Profile 175

Deploying the Application 176

   Configuring the Databases 177

Publishing the Application 177

Summary 178

■Part 2: Results and Parameters 179

■Chapter 9: The Anatomy of ASP.NET Web API 181

Understanding the Web API Namespaces and Types...181

Understanding the Web API Context Objects 183

   Getting Information About the Request 184

   Getting Information About the Controller 185

   Getting Information About Everything Else 186

Understanding the Web API Components 186

   Application Configuration 187

   Controllers, Actions, and Results 187

   Services 187

   Dispatchers and Handlers 189

Summary 190

■Chapter 10: Creating and Configuring a Web API Application 191

Preparing the Example Project...191

   Creating the Model and Repository 192

   Creating an HTTP Web Service 193

   Creating the Browser Client...194

   Testing the Example Application...197

Configuring a Web API Application 199

   Configuring Web API Through the ASP.NET Platform...199

   Understanding the Configuration Object..201

Configuring Web API Dependency Injection 202

   Preparing for Dependency Injection 203

   Understanding the Web API Dependency Interfaces..204

   Installing the Dependency Injection Container 206

Implementing the Dependency Interfaces...206

Configuring Web API..209

Configuring Dependency Injection for Web API and MVC 210

Declaring the Dependency..210

Installing the Dependency Injection Packages 211

Adding MVC Support to the Resolver..211

Configuring the MVC Framework..213

Summary..214

■Chapter 11: Action Method Results 215

Preparing the Example Project..215

Understanding Action Method Results 217

Returning No Result 218

Consuming a No Result Action Method 219

Returning an Action Result 222

Understanding the IHttpActionResult Interface 223

Using the ApiController Action Result Methods 224

Returning Other Status Codes 226

Creating a Custom Action Result 228

Returning Model Data 230

Understanding the Default Behavior 230

Understanding the Content Negotiation Process 231

Implementing a Custom Content Negotiator 232

Bypassing Content Negotiation 238

Returning Negotiable Action Results 239

Creating Negotiable Action Results 239

Summary..241

■Chapter 12: Creating Media Type Formatters..................................243

Preparing the Example Project..244

Creating a Media Type Formatter 245

Implementing a Basic Media Type Formatter 246

Refining the Custom Formatter 252

    Supporting Content Encodings 252

    Setting the HTTP Response Headers 255

Participating in the Negotiation Process 257

    Creating a Media Type Mapping 258

    Using the Mapping Extension Methods 261

Creating Per-Request Media Type Formatters 263

    Creating the Formatter Instance 264

    Testing the Per-Request Formatter 265

Summary 266

■Chapter 13: Using the Built-in Media Formatters 267

Preparing the Example Project 268

Working with the Built-in Media Type Formatters 269

    Listing the Built-in Media Type Formatters 269

    Dealing with Type Matching During Negotiation 272

Working with the JSON Media Type Formatter 281

    Configuring the JSON Media Type Formatter 282

    Configuring Json.Net 284

Using the XML Media Type Formatter 293

    Configuring the XML Media Type Formatter 293

    Getting the Xml Media Type Formatter Working 294

Summary 296

■Chapter 14: Understanding Parameter and Model Binding 297

Preparing the Example Project 298

    Creating the Controller 298

    Creating the Client 298

    Adding a New Route 300

    Testing the Example Application 301

Understanding the Default Binding Behavior 302

Understanding Parameter Binding 303

Understanding Model Binding 307

Performing Binding Customizations 312

Binding Complex Types from the Request URL... 312

Binding Simple Types from the Request Body 314

Defining a Binding Rule 316

Manually Obtaining Request Values 318

Handling POST Requests 322

Summary..324

■Chapter 15: Binding Simple Data Types..325

Preparing the Example Project...325

Preparing the Common Code 328

Working with Value Providers and Value Provider Factories 329

Understanding Value Providers and Value Provider Factories 330

Creating a Custom Value Provider and Factory 332

Applying a Custom Value Provider and Factory 334

Understanding How Web API Looks for Values 334

Applying a Value Provider Factory with an Attribute 335

Extending the Default Behavior 340

Creating a Parameter Binding Rule 344

Summary..350

■Chapter 16: Binding Complex Data Types Part I 351

Preparing the Example Project...351

Using the Built-in Model Binders..354

Binding Objects 355

Broadening the Source of Binding Values 359

Binding Collections and Arrays.. 362

Binding Key-Value Pairs 366

Working with Custom Model Binders 368

Preparing the Application 368

Understanding Model Binders 370

Creating a Custom Model Binder..372

Applying a Custom Model Binder 376

Using Type Converters..382

Understanding Type Converters 382

Creating a Type Converter..383

Applying a Type Converter 384

Summary..387

■**Chapter 17: Binding Complex Data Types Part II** 389

Preparing the Example Project..390

Testing the Application 392

Creating a Custom Media Type Formatter 393

Preparing the Client..394

Creating the Media Type Formatter 395

Registering and Testing the Media Type Formatter 400

Using the Built-in Media Type Formatters 401

Handling URL-Encoded Data..402

Handling JSON Requests...411

Handling XML Requests 414

Customizing the Model Binding Process 420

Changing the Behavior of the Default Action Value Binder 421

Creating a Custom Action Value Binder 424

Summary..425

■**Chapter 18: Model Validation** 427

Preparing the Example Project..427

Testing the Changes 430

Understanding Common Data Problems 431

Understanding Under-Posting...431

Understanding Over-Posting...433

Understanding Bad Data..434

Using Web API Model Validation 436

Understanding Model State...436

Testing the Model State...438

Removing the Debug Output Code...439

Using the Binding Control Attributes 439

Performing Validation with Validation Attributes 441

Using the Built-in Validation Attributes...441

Creating a Self-validating Model Class 443

Performing Validation in a Media Type Formatter 444

Creating a Validating Media Type Formatter...445

Registering and Using the Custom Media Type Formatter 447

Summary...448

■Part 3: Dispatching Requests 449

■Chapter 19: Dispatching Requests 451

Preparing the Example Project..451

Creating the Model Class...452

Creating the Web API Web Service 452

Creating the MVC Controller and View...453

Testing the Example Application...456

Understanding Request Dispatching 457

Understanding the HttpServer Class 459

Understanding the HttpRoutingDispatcher Class...460

Understanding the HttpControllerDispatcher Class 463

Customizing the Dispatch Process...467

Creating Custom Message Handlers 468

Customizing Other Dispatch Components 474

Summary...481

■Chapter 20: URL Routing: Part I 483

Preparing the Example Project 483
Testing the Application Changes 486

Understanding URL Routing 486
Understanding the Routing Classes and Interfaces 488

Working with Convention-Based Routing 492
Using Route Templates 493
Routing to the New Controller 494

Controlling Route Matching 499
Using Routing Data Default Values 500
Using Routing Constraints 504

Summary 509

■Chapter 21: URL Routing: Part II 511

Preparing the Example Project 511

Understanding Direct Routing 512
Creating a Direct Route 513
Creating a Controller-wide Direct Route 523

Customizing URL Routing 525
Using a Route-Specific Message Handler 525
Applying Custom Constraints to Direct Routes 529

Summary 533

■Chapter 22: Controllers and Actions 535

Preparing the Example Project 535

Understanding Controllers 537
Creating a Controller 538
Using Built-in Services and Features 541

Understanding the ApiController Dispatch Process 543
Preparing the Example Controller 545
Understanding the Action Selection Process 547

Understanding the RESTful/Non-RESTful Routing Problem 554

Understanding Filters 558

Understanding the Action Method Execution Process 559

Customizing the Controller Dispatch Process 559

Creating a Custom IHttpActionInvoker Implementation 560

Creating a Custom IHttpActionSelector Implementation 562

Creating a Controller-Specific Configuration 563

Summary 565

■Chapter 23: Filters Part I 567

Preparing the Example Project 567

Understanding Filters 567

Working with Action Filters 569

Creating an Action Filter by Implementing IActionFilter 570

Using the Convenience Action Filter Base Class 574

Creating a Short-Circuiting Action Filter 577

Understanding the Filter Pipeline 582

Displaying the Filter Pipeline 582

Understanding Filter Scope 584

Working with Authentication Filters 587

Preparing for Authentication 588

Understanding Authentication Filters 590

Creating an Authentication Filter 591

Viewing the Filter Pipeline 596

Summary 598

■Chapter 24: Filters Part II 599

Preparing the Example Project 599

Reviewing Filters in the Dispatch Process 599

Working with Authorization Filters 600

Understanding Authorization Filters 601

Creating an Authorization Filter 601

Appling the Authorization Filter 603

Removing the Authentication Filter 604

Using the Built-in Authorization Filter Attributes 607

Reworking the Authentication Filter 609

Working with Exception Filters..611

Understanding the Default Behavior 611

Understanding Exception Filters 613

Creating an Exception Filter 614

Deriving the Filter from the ExceptionFilterAttribute Class 615

Working with Override Filters..617

Overriding Built-in Filter Types 618

Redefining Filter Policies... 620

Summary..621

■Chapter 25: Error Handling...623

Preparing the Example Project...623

Dealing with Errors..626

Relying on the Default Behavior 626

Using an Implementation of the IHttpActionResult Interface... 629

Using the HttpError Class...629

Using an Error Response and an HttpError Object... 630

Adding Extra Information to the HttpError Object 632

Including Model State Errors in the HTTP Response 632

Controlling Error Detail.. 635

Displaying HttpError Information in the Client... 636

Responding to Errors Globally 637

Handling Exceptions.. 637

Logging Exceptions 641

Summary..644

■Chapter 26: Using OWIN...645

Understanding OWIN 645

Creating a Self-hosted Web API Application 646

    Creating the Project 646

    Installing the Packages 646

    Creating the Model and Repository 646

    Defining the Configuration Classes 648

    Creating the Web API Controller...649

    Testing the Self-hosted Web API Application 650

Summary...650

Index...651

About the Author

Adam Freeman is an experienced IT professional who has held senior positions in a range of companies, most recently serving as chief technology officer and chief operating officer of a global bank. Now retired, he spends his time writing and running.

About the Technical Reviewer

Fabio Claudio Ferracchiati is a senior consultant and a senior analyst/developer using Microsoft technologies. He works at BluArancio SpA (`www.bluarancio.com`) as Senior Analyst/Developer and Microsoft Dynamics CRM Specialist. He is a Microsoft Certified Solution Developer for .NET, a Microsoft Certified Application Developer for .NET, a Microsoft Certified Professional, and a prolific author and technical reviewer. Over the past ten years, he's written articles for Italian and international magazines and coauthored more than ten books on a variety of computer topics.

Getting Ready

CHAPTER 1

■ ■ ■

Getting Readys

Web API 2 is the latest evolution of Microsoft's web services toolkit, which allows you to create RESTful applications built on the ASP.NET platform. It provides a standards-based approach and a high-productivity development model that makes it easy to deliver services to a wide range of clients, including mobile devices.

In this book, I take you right from creating your first Web API web services to the most advanced techniques and features. No prior knowledge of HTTP web services or Web API is required. I start with the basics and explain everything you need to know. In short, this book will give you expert insight and understanding of how to create, customize, and deploy complex, flexible, and robust HTTP web services.

Web services don't exist in isolation, so I also show you how to write browser-based single-page applications to consume them. I demonstrate how these clients influence the way that Web API web services respond and how you can adapt your web service to different client types.

What Do You Need to Know?

You should be familiar with using the ASP.NET MVC framework to create web applications. This means you are able to use Visual Studio to write C# classes and know how to use Razor and HTML to create views. The term *Expert* in the title refers to the degree of depth that I cover in this book, and you don't need any knowledge of Web API or HTTP web services; however, if you don't know how to use ASP.NET MVC, then you will struggle to follow many of the examples. If you want to brush up on your knowledge of MVC, then read my *Pro ASP.NET MVC 5* and *Pro ASP.NET MVC Platform* books, both published by Apress.

What Does *Expert* Mean?

This book is for programmers who want to understand every aspect of web services development using ASP.NET Web API. Or, put another way, you want to be an expert in Web API. I dig deeply into the details of how Web API works behind the scenes in this book and give you a warts-and-all view of how Web API can be used to create sophisticated and secure RESTful web services. You don't have to know anything about Web API or HTTP web services before you start. I build on your existing knowledge of the MVC framework to give you all the information you need.

What Is the Structure of This Book?

This book is split into three parts, each of which covers a set of related topics.

Part 1: Getting Ready

Part 1 of this book provides the information you need to get ready for the rest of the book. It includes this chapter and a primer for the techniques you will need to follow the examples in this chapter. I also show you how to build your first web service and single-page client and take you through the process of building a more realistic application, called SportsStore.

Part 2: Results and Parameters

Part 2 of this book focuses on the aspect of Web API that you will spend most of your time on during your first real projects: the data sent from clients and the responses that you produce in return. I explain how to create different kinds of HTTP responses using Web API, how to master the data binding process that Web API uses to process request data, and how to ensure that the data you receive from clients is valid.

Part 3: Dispatching Requests

Part 3 of this book explains how Web API dispatches HTTP requests from the moment they arrive from the client until the response is generated. I describe all of the steps that a request goes through and show you how to configure and customize just about every class and interface that Web API relies on to get fine-grain control over how your web services operate. I show you how Web API uses the URL routing system to support RESTful web services, how controllers and action methods are selected, and how to deal with errors and cross-cutting concerns. Many of these techniques are similar to the ones you know from MVC framework development, but Web API uses its own namespaces and classes and has a different approach than the one you are used to using.

Are There Lots of Examples?

There are *loads* of examples. The best way to learn Web API is by example, and I have packed as many of them as I can into this book. To maximize the number of examples in this book, I have adopted a simple convention to avoid listing the contents of files over and over again. The first time I use a file in a chapter, I'll list the complete contents, just as I have in Listing 1-1.

Listing 1-1. A Complete Example Document

```
using System;
using System.Collections.Generic;
using System.Linq;
using System.Web.Http;

namespace SportsStore {
    public static class WebApiConfig {
        public static void Register(HttpConfiguration config) {

            config.MapHttpAttributeRoutes();

            config.Routes.MapHttpRoute(
                name: "DefaultApi",
                routeTemplate: "api/{controller}/{id}",
                defaults: new { id = RouteParameter.Optional }
            );
```

```
        config.Formatters.Remove(config.Formatters.XmlFormatter);
    }
  }
}
```

This listing is taken from Chapter 6. Don't worry about what it does; just be aware that the first time I use a file in each chapter there will be complete listing, similar to Listing 1-1 shown here. For the second and subsequent examples, I show you just the elements that change, in a *partial listing*. You can spot a partial the listing because it starts and ends with ellipsis (...), as shown in Listing 1-2.

Listing 1-2. A Partial Listing

```
...
public Product GetProduct(int id) {
    Product result = Repository.Products.Where(p => p.Id == id).FirstOrDefault();
    if (result == null) {
        throw new HttpResponseException(HttpStatusCode.BadRequest);
    } else {
        return result;
    }
}
...
```

This is a subsequent listing from Chapter 6. You can see that just the GetProduct method is shown and that I have highlighted a number of statements. This is how I draw your attention to the part of the example that shows the feature or technique I am describing. In a partial listing like this, only those parts shown have changed from the full listing earlier in the chapter.

This convention lets me pack in more examples, but it does mean it can be hard to locate a specific technique. To this end, all of the chapters in which I describe Web API features in Parts 2 and 3 begin with a summary table that describes the techniques contained in the chapter and the listings that demonstrate how they are used.

Where Can You Get the Example Code?

You can download all of the examples for all of the chapters in this book from www.apress.com. The download is available without charge and includes all of the supporting resources that are required to re-create the examples without having to type them in. You don't have to download the code, but it is the easiest way of experimenting with the examples and cutting and pasting them into your own projects.

If you do want to re-create the examples from scratch, then you will find that every chapter contains detailed listings of all the files I create and modify. I never refer you to an external file or hand-wave about leaving the rest of the example as an exercise; every detail you need to re-create every example is contained within this book.

How Do You Set Up a Development Environment?

The most important software you need for this book is Visual Studio 2013, which contains everything you need to get started, including a built-in application server for running and debugging Web API applications, an administration-free edition of SQL Server for developing database-driven applications, and, of course, a code editor compiler and debugger.

Getting Visual Studio

There are several editions of Visual Studio, but I will be using the one that Microsoft makes available free of charge, called Visual Studio Express 2013 for Web. Microsoft adds some nice features to the paid-for editions of Visual Studio, but you will not need them for this book, and all of the figures that you see throughout this book have been taken using the Express edition, which you can download from www.visualstudio.com.

There are several versions of Visual Studio 2013 Express, each of which is used for a different kind of development. Make sure you get the Web version, which supports ASP.NET applications.

■ **Note** All of the examples in this book will work with Visual Studio Express 2013 for Web, except those in Chapter 26 where I use Visual Studio Express 2013 for Windows Desktop, which allows me to create a console application.

I follow a specific approach to creating ASP.NET projects: I don't use the predefined templates that Microsoft provides, preferring to explicitly add all of the packages I require. This means more work is required to get set up, but the benefit is that you end up with a much better understanding of how an application fits together. I provide a primer in Chapter 2 that gives an example of what you can expect.

■ **Tip** Visual Studio includes NuGet for downloading and installing software packages. I use NuGet throughout this book and always specify the version of each NuGet package so that you are sure to get the results that I demonstrate. If you are in doubt, download the source code for this book from www.apress.com, which contains complete projects for each chapter.

Preparing Visual Studio

Visual Studio Express contains all the features you need to create, test, and deploy Web API applications, but some of those features are hidden away until you ask for them. To enable all of the features, select Expert Settings from the Visual Studio Tools ➤ Settings menu.

■ **Tip** Microsoft has decided that the top-level menus in Visual Studio should be all in uppercase, which means that the menu to which I just referred is really TOOLS. I think this is rather like shouting, and I will capitalize menu names like Tools is here throughout this book.

Getting Google Chrome

In this book, I use the Google Chrome browser. In part this is because it has some excellent F12 developer tools (so-called because they are accessed by pressing the F12 key) but also because using Chrome allows me to use Postman, an outstanding HTTP client that makes it easy to test web services by manually crafting HTTP requests.

You can download Chrome from https://www.google.com/chrome/browser and, once it is installed, get the Postman client from www.getpostman.com. Both are available without charge, but I encourage you to donate to the Postman developers if you find it useful.

You will also need the Postman Interceptor extension, which increases the functionality and is available through the Google Chrome Extension Store as a zero-cost installation. Click the Chrome settings button (the one with three horizontal lines at the right side of the screen) and select Tools ➤ Extensions. Search for *Postman Interceptor* and follow the installation instructions.

Selecting Chrome for Debugging

You can select Chrome as the browser that Visual Studio will start when you debug a project by selecting it from the drop-down list of browsers, as shown in Figure 1-1.

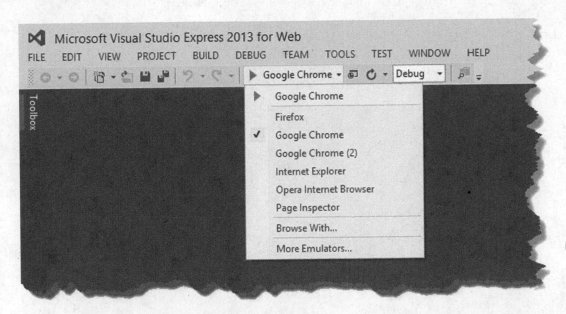

Figure 1-1. *Selecting Google Chrome in Visual Studio*

Summary

In this chapter, I outlined the content and structure of this book and outlined the software that is required for Web API web development. As I said earlier, the best way to learn Web API is by example, and in Chapter 2 I jump right in and show you how to create your first web service and client application.

■ ■ ■

CHAPTER 2

Your First Web API Application

The best way to get a feel for a new technology is by applying it, so in this chapter I jump right in and demonstrate one of the most common uses for Web API: adding an HTTP web service to an existing MVC framework application.

This is nowhere near as awkward as it might sound, not least because the MVC framework and Web API share a common heritage and can use the same data models. In fact, you may be surprised at how little time I spend in this chapter creating the web service compared with building the example MVC framework application and writing the JavaScript code that consumes the web service in the browser.

You don't need to retrofit an HTTP web service to an existing application, of course, and in Chapters 5–8 I build a more complex example that begins with Web API and puts the HTTP web service right at the heart of the development process.

■ **Note** I start slowly in this chapter and spell out every detail. I'll pick up the pace—and the depth of detail—in later chapters, but I want to make clear the process by which I create projects and emphasize the relationship between the components in the application.

Preparing the Example Project

Visual Studio includes templates for different kinds of projects. The basic starting point is the Empty project, which can be set up to include just the files and references required for an MVC or Web API application. Other options add models, views, and controllers to help kick-start a project by providing commonly used features.

I prefer to work with the Empty template and just have Visual Studio add the minimum initial content—and I recommend you do the same. This approach gives you greater insight into how an application is put together and where you need to start looking when something goes wrong. Throughout this book, I'll be creating projects in the way that I describe here, so I'll walk through the process step-by-step in this chapter so you know what to expect.

■ **Note** The example projects that I created in this chapter and in Chapters 5–8 are derived from the ones I used in *Pro ASP.NET MVC 5*. You don't need to have any of my other books to understand the examples, but if you already have a copy, then you may find it interesting to compare the different approaches required for creating a pure MVC framework application and one that integrates Web API.

Creating the Visual Studio Project

To get started, I created a new Visual Studio project. Select New Project from the File menu to open the New Project dialog window. Navigate through the Templates section to select the Visual C# ➤ Web ➤ ASP.NET Web Application template and set the name of the project to PartyInvites, as shown in Figure 2-1.

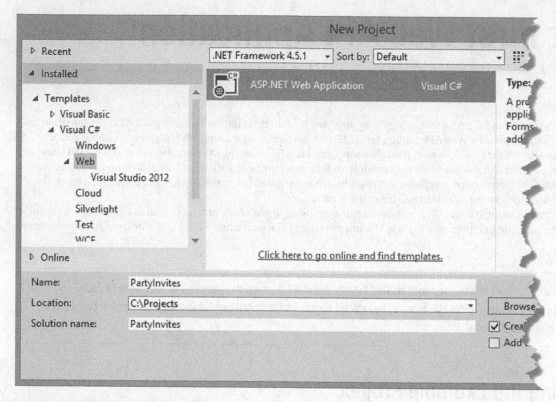

Figure 2-1. *Creating the new project*

Click the OK button to move to the New ASP.NET Project dialog window. Ensure that the Empty option is selected and check the MVC and Web API options, as shown in Figure 2-2. Click the OK button, and Visual Studio will create a new project called PartyInvites.

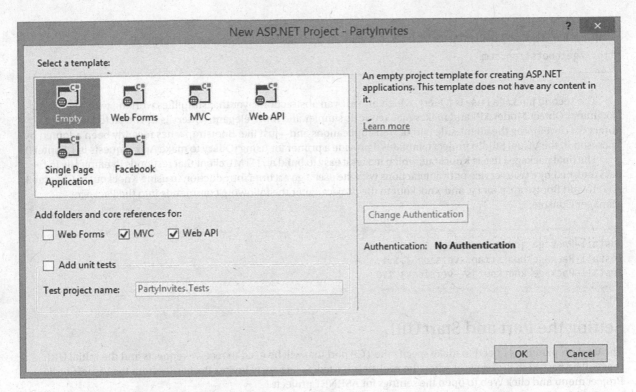

Figure 2-2. Selecting the ASP.NET project type

Adding and Updating NuGet Packages

One of the most useful enhancements to Visual Studio in recent years has been the addition of NuGet, which makes it easy to download, install, and update software packages in a project.

I am going to be working with specific versions of NuGet packages in this book to make sure you are able to re-create the examples and get the same results. The days where Microsoft made enormous releases of the entire .NET stack every 18 months have passed, and each piece of technology receives more frequent small updates. This means the versions of the MVC and Web API that are added to projects by Visual Studio may not be the latest versions available.

Select Package Manager Console from the Visual Studio Tools ➤ NuGet Package Manager menu and enter the following commands to update the MVC and Web API packages, as well as the package that is used to process JSON data (I describe JSON in more detail in Chapter 3):

```
Update-Package microsoft.aspnet.mvc -version 5.1.1
Update-Package microsoft.aspnet.webapi -version 5.1.1
Update-Package Newtonsoft.json -version 6.0.1
```

There are two other packages that I rely on for the example application in this chapter and those in later chapters. The first is Bootstrap, which is a CSS package that makes it easy to style the HTML generated by MVC views. I have no visual design skills at all—to the extent that I was excused from art lessons at school and allowed to do extra math— but even I can hack together something that looks appealing with Bootstrap. I prefer to work with a real designer on complex projects, but for simple applications, Bootstrap works just fine.

■ **Tip** I don't describe Bootstrap in this book, but you can get details of the CSS classes I apply at
http://getbootstrap.com.

The second package I use is jQuery, which provides an abstraction layer that simplifies working with the HTML Document Object Model API and makes Ajax requests simpler and more elegant. jQuery is the de facto JavaScript library for developing the client-side part of web applications and—just like Bootstrap—has recently been adopted by Microsoft in the Visual Studio project templates. I provide a primer for using jQuery to make Ajax requests in Chapter 3.

The final package I use is Knockout, which makes it easy to build an HTML client that responds dynamically to the data returned by a web service or by interactions with the user. I give a brief introduction to using Knockout in Chapter 3.

To add Bootstrap, jQuery, and Knockout to the project, enter the following commands into the Package Manager Console:

```
Install-Package jquery -version 2.1.0
Install-Package bootstrap -version 3.1.1
Install-Package knockoutjs -version 3.1.0
```

Setting the Port and Start URL

The final preparations I need to make specify the TCP port that will be used to receive requests and the initial URL that will be passed to the browser when the project is started. Select Party Invites Properties from the Visual Studio Project menu and click Web to open the settings for ASP.NET projects.

Enable the Specific Page option and enter Home/Index in the field. On the same page, change the value in the Project Url field to http://localhost:37993/ and click the Create Virtual Directory button.

The first change prevents Visual Studio from trying to work out what URL should be shown when the application starts based on the file you edited most recently, and the second change means that requests will be received on TCP port 37993.

Creating the MVC Application

In this section, I create a simple MVC framework application that gathers responses from invitees to a party. This is a variation on the project with which I start the *Pro ASP.NET MVC 5* book, and I chose it to emphasize the ease with which Web API can be applied to MVC framework applications. I spend much of the rest of the book explaining the differences, so it is good to start with something that focuses on just how much you already know how to do.

Creating the Model

Now that I have created the project, I can add the model. The structure of a Web API application shares a lot with the MVC framework, which is one of the reasons that both technologies can coexist so well. I created a file called GuestResponse.cs in the Models folder and used it to define the class shown in Listing 2-1.

Listing 2-1. The Contents of the GuestResponse.cs File

```
using System.ComponentModel.DataAnnotations;

namespace PartyInvites.Models {
    public class GuestResponse {
        [Required]
        public string Name { get; set; }
        [Required]
        public string Email { get; set; }
        [Required]
        public bool? WillAttend { get; set; }
    }
}
```

To create a simple model repository, I created a class file called `Repository.cs` in the `Models` folder and used it to define the class shown in Listing 2-2.

Listing 2-2. The Contents of the Repository.cs File

```
using System.Collections.Generic;

namespace PartyInvites.Models {
    public class Repository {
        private static Dictionary<string, GuestResponse> responses;

        static Repository() {
            responses = new Dictionary<string, GuestResponse>();
            responses.Add("Bob", new GuestResponse {Name = "Bob",
                Email="bob@example.com", WillAttend=true});
            responses.Add("Alice", new GuestResponse { Name = "Alice",
                Email = "alice@example.com", WillAttend = true });
            responses.Add("Paul", new GuestResponse { Name = "Paul",
                Email = "paul@example.com", WillAttend = true });
        }

        public static void Add(GuestResponse newResponse) {
            string key = newResponse.Name.ToLowerInvariant();
            if (responses.ContainsKey(key)) {
                responses[key] = newResponse;
            } else {
                responses.Add(key, newResponse);
            }
        }

        public static IEnumerable<GuestResponse> Responses {
            get { return responses.Values; }
        }
    }
}
```

The repository for this application is simple and stores its data objects as a collection in memory that is exposed through static properties. This means the model state will be lost when the application is restarted, but it does allow me to keep the example simple. (I show a more persistent model in Chapter 5 when I create a larger and more realistic MVC/Web API application that stores its model in a database.) In the static constructor, I add some default data so that the model is populated with responses.

Creating the MVC Controller

My next step is to create an MVC controller that will generate content and receive form data from my application clients. Web API also has controllers—as you will see in the "Creating the Web Service" section—and I will be clear about which kind of controller I am using throughout this book. I created an MVC controller by right-clicking the Controllers folder and selecting Add ➤ Controller from the pop-up menu. Figure 2-3 shows the options that Visual Studio presents for creating controllers for both MVC and Web API.

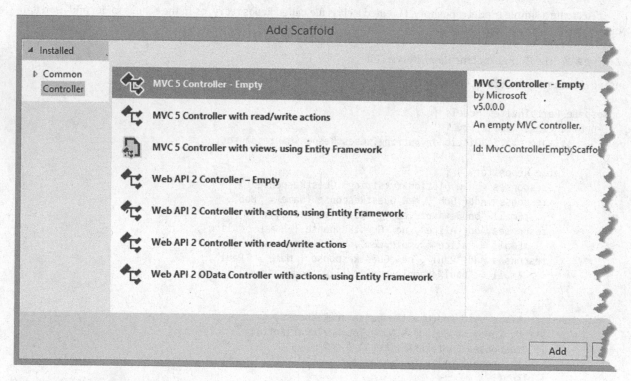

Figure 2-3. *Selecting a controller type*

Visual Studio is able to generate a templated set of action methods for controllers, but I will be using empty controllers for both MVC and Web API throughout this book. Just as with the project template, I prefer to define just the code I need for my applications, and I follow the same approach for the examples in this book so that you know where every action methods comes from and why I have added it.

I selected the MVC 5 Controller – Empty option from the list, clicked the Add button, and set the name to HomeController, as shown in Figure 2-4.

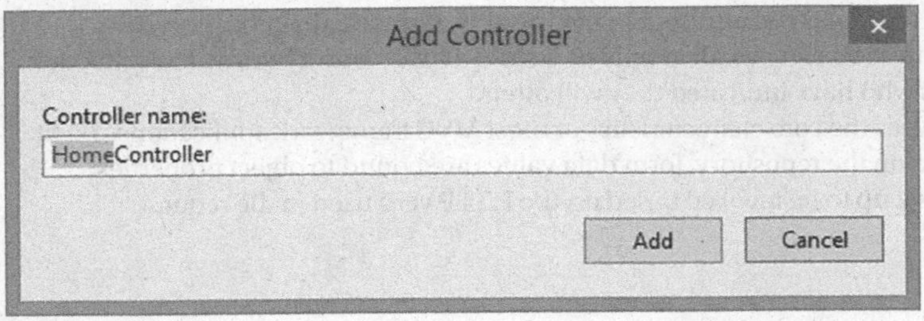

Figure 2-4. *Creating an MVC controller*

Clicking the Add button creates the `Controllers/HomeController.cs` file, which I used to define the controller shown in Listing 2-3.

Listing 2-3. The Contents of the HomeController.cs File

```
using System.Web.Mvc;
using PartyInvites.Models;
using System.Linq;

namespace PartyInvites.Controllers {
    public class HomeController : Controller {

        public ActionResult Index() {
            return View();
        }

        public ActionResult Rsvp() {
            return View();
        }

        [HttpPost]
        public ActionResult Rsvp(GuestResponse response) {
            if (ModelState.IsValid) {
                Repository.Add(response);
                return View("Thanks", response);
            } else {
                return View();
            }
        }

        [ChildActionOnly]
        public ActionResult Attendees() {
            return View(Repository.Responses.Where(x => x.WillAttend == true));
        }
    }
}
```

The controller defines four action methods. The `Index` action simply renders a view that welcomes the user to the application. The `Rsvp` methods allow the user to populate the fields of a `GuestResponse` model object through model binding and validate using the model state feature. When the user submits a complete set of values for the

15

GuestResponse object (enforced by the use of the Required attribute in Listing 2-1), I update the repository and render a view called Thanks. The final action method can be called only as a child action, and it returns the collection of GuestResponse objects that represent users who have indicated they will attend.

This is a pretty basic controller, but it captures the core characteristics of most MVC framework applications, albeit on a simplified basis. Operations are performed on the repository, form data values are bound to object properties using model binding, and action methods are set up to be invoked based on the HTTP verb used in the request.

Creating the Views

I need to create a layout and four views for my example application. I created the Views/Shared folder, and Listing 2-4 shows the _Layout.cshtml file I added to it, which contains references for the Bootstrap, jQuery, and Knockout files.

Listing 2-4. The Contents of the _Layout.cshtml File

```
<!DOCTYPE html>
<html>
<head>
    <meta name="viewport" content="width=device-width" />
    <script src="~/Scripts/jquery-2.1.0.min.js"></script>
    <script src="~/Scripts/knockout-3.1.0.js"></script>
    <link href="~/Content/bootstrap.css" rel="stylesheet" />
    <link href="~/Content/bootstrap-theme.css" rel="stylesheet" />
    <title>@ViewBag.Title</title>
    <style>
        body { padding-top: 10px; }
    </style>
</head>
<body class="container">
    @RenderBody()
</body>
</html>
```

Listing 2-5 shows the Index.cshtml file that I created by right-clicking the Index action method in the Home controller and selecting Add View from the pop-up menu. I set View Name to Index, ensured that the Use a Layout Page option is checked, and clicked the Add button to create the view file. (Visual Studio also creates the Views/_ViewStart.cshtml file, which ensures that the _Layout.cshtml file I created in Listing 2-4 is applied.)

Listing 2-5. The Contents of the Index.cshtml File

```
@{ ViewBag.Title = "Party!";}
<div class="text-center">
    <h2>We're going to have an exciting party!</h2>
    <h3>And you are invited.</h3>
    @Html.ActionLink("RSVP Now", "Rsvp", null, new { @class="btn btn-success"})
</div>
```

This view doesn't contain any model data, but it does use the routing system to generate a link element that targets the Rsvp action method on the same controller. Listing 2-6 shows the view that the Rsvp action renders, which is the Rsvp.cshtml file I added to the /Views/Home folder.

Listing 2-6. The Contents of the Rsvp.cshtml File

```
@model PartyInvites.Models.GuestResponse
@{ ViewBag.Title = "Rsvp"; }

<div class="panel panel-success">
    <div class="panel-heading"><h4>RSVP</h4></div>
    <div class="panel-body">
        @using (Html.BeginForm()) {
            <div class="form-group">
                <label>Your name:</label>
                @Html.TextBoxFor(x => x.Name, new { @class = "form-control" })
            </div>
            <div class="form-group">
                <label>Your email:</label>
                @Html.TextBoxFor(x => x.Email, new { @class = "form-control" })
            </div>
            <div class="form-group">
                <label>Will you attend?</label>
                @Html.DropDownListFor(x => x.WillAttend, new[] {
                        new SelectListItem() {Text = "Yes, I'll be there",
                            Value = bool.TrueString},
                        new SelectListItem() {Text = "No, I can't come",
                            Value = bool.FalseString}
                    }, "Choose an option", new { @class = "form-control" })
            </div>
            <div class="text-center">
                <input class="btn btn-success" type="submit" value="Submit RSVP" />
            </div>
        }
    </div>
</div>
```

This view contains a standard HTML form that collects values from the user via input and select elements. When the user submits the form with valid data, the Thanks.cshtml view in the Views/Home folder is rendered. You can see the contents of the Thanks.cshtml file in Listing 2-7.

Listing 2-7. The Contents of the Thanks.cshtml File

```
@model PartyInvites.Models.GuestResponse
@{ ViewBag.Title = "Thanks";}
<h1>Thank you, @Model.Name!</h1>
<div class="lead">
    @if (Model.WillAttend == true) {
        @:It's great that you're coming. The drinks are already in the fridge!
        @Html.Action("Attendees", "Home")
    } else {
        @:Sorry to hear that you can't make it, but thanks for letting us know.
    }
</div>
```

If the user has indicated that they will attend the party, then I use the `Html.Action` helper to invoke the Attendees child action method, which renders the /Views/Home/Attendees.cshtml view file, whose contents are shown in Listing 2-8.

Listing 2-8. *The Contents of the Attendees.cshtml File*

```
@model IEnumerable<PartyInvites.Models.GuestResponse>

@if (Model.Count() == 1) {
    <p>You are the first to accept! Hurrah!</p>
} else {
    <p>Here is the list of cool people coming: @string.Join(", ",
        Model.Select(x => x.Name))</p>
}
```

Using the MVC Application

To test the basic functionality, start the application and navigate to the /Home/Index URL. Click the RSVP Now button, fill out the form, and click Submit RSVP. Figure 2-5 shows the different views rendered by the application.

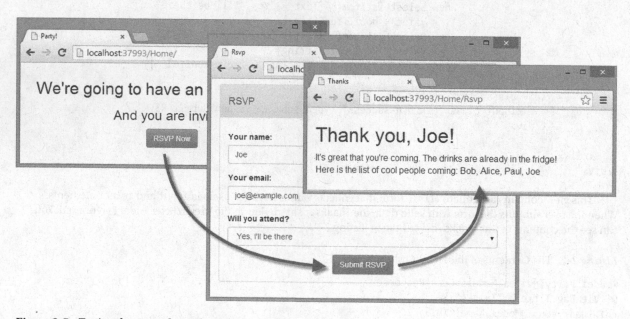

Figure 2-5. *Testing the example application*

■ **Tip**   If you get an error telling you that the Attendees action is accessible only as a child request, it is because Visual Studio has tried to be helpful and has told the browser to navigate to the /Home/Attendees URL because that is the last view you were editing. Navigate to /Home/Index, and everything will be fine.

Google Chrome, like all modern browsers, contains some useful developer tools, known as the *F12 tools* because they are opened by pressing F12 on the keyboard. Before adding Web API to the application, I am going to use the F12 tools to measure the number of requests and the total amount of data sent from the server.

Getting an honest assessment of the requests required to go through the RSVP process entails some specific steps, switching between the browser window that displays the applications and the F12 tools. Here is the sequence:

1. Open the F12 tools, click the Network tab and check the Preserve Log option so that the list of network requests isn't cleared for each new request.

2. Ensure that the first icon in the toolbar, which is a circle, is red, indicating that Chrome will record the network requests it makes. If the circle isn't red, then click it so that it is.

3. Ensure that the browser window is showing the /Home/Index URL.

4. Click the Clear button on the F12 toolbar (it is next to the red circle button).

5. Right-click the Reload icon in the browser window and select Empty Cache and Hard Reload from the pop-up menu, as shown in Figure 2-6.

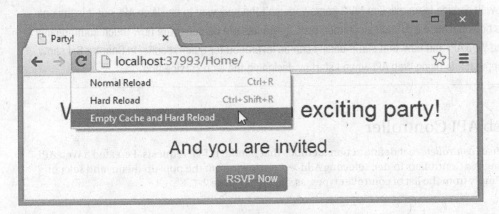

Figure 2-6. *Clearing the cache and reloading the page*

6. Click the RSVP Now button in the browser window, complete the form, and click the Submit RSVP button to send the form data to the server.

■ **Tip** The menu shown in Figure 2-6 is available only when the F12 tools window is open.

The F12 Network tab will detail requests that the browser makes as you work through the example application. Not all of these are for action methods—I added link and script elements to the _Layout.cshtml file, which is used as the layout for all the views and so the Bootstrap and JavaScript files have to be loaded from the server. (This happens just for the initial request so that the files are in the browser cache. You can see which requests are cached by the browser by looking at the Size column.) At the bottom of the F12 window, Chrome displays a summary of the requests it has made, and I have put my results in Table 2-1. Don't worry if you get different numbers; I just want to give an illustrative reference.

Table 2-1. *The Request Summary from Google Chrome*

Description	Value
Total number of requests	21, of which 13 were made to the server and 8 were satisfied using the browser cache
Total amount of data	247KB

Creating the Web Service

Now that I have a basic MVC framework application in place, I can add some Web API functionality to create a web service that exposes my RSVP model to HTTP clients. In the sections that follow, you will see just how easy it is to use MVC and Web API side-by-side.

■ **Tip** Adding an HTTP web service to an existing MVC framework isn't the only way to use Web API, but it is the one I have started with in this book because it is such a common task. It also lets me demonstrate how much commonality there is between MVC and Web API and how that commonality can be leveraged for quick results. In Chapter 6, I show you a more considered approach to using Web API when I start by designing the web service first.

Creating the Web API Controller

Just like MVC, Web API uses *controllers* that define action methods that handle HTTP requests. I created a Web API controller by right-clicking the Controllers folder, selecting Add ➤ Controller from the pop-up menu, and selecting Web API 2 Controller – Empty from the list of controller types, as shown in Figure 2-7.

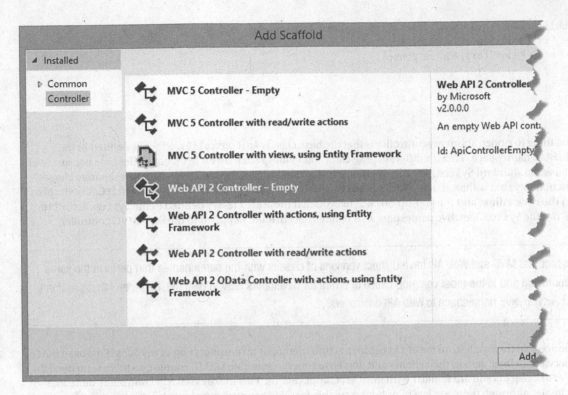

Figure 2-7. *Adding a Web API controller*

Just as with MVC controllers, Visual Studio can create controllers with templated content. I'll be using the empty controller for Web API throughout this book so that I can explain the purpose of all the code statements I use. Click the Add button once you have selected the type, set the name of the new controller to RsvpController, and click the Add button to create the Controllers/RsvpController.cs file. Listing 2-9 shows the action methods that I added to the RsvpController class to create a simple web service.

Listing 2-9. The Contents of the RsvpController.cs File

```
using System.Collections.Generic;
using System.Linq;
using System.Web.Http;
using PartyInvites.Models;

namespace PartyInvites.Controllers {

    public class RsvpController : ApiController {

        public IEnumerable<GuestResponse> GetAttendees() {
            return Repository.Responses.Where(x => x.WillAttend == true);
        }
    }
```

```
        public void PostResponse(GuestResponse response) {
            if (ModelState.IsValid) {
                Repository.Add(response);
            }
        }
    }
}
```

The first thing to notice about my controller is that the base class is ApiController, which is defined in the System.Web.Http namespace. This is a different base class and namespace than an MVC controller uses because Web API doesn't use the standard System.Web and System.Web.Mvc namespaces. Instead, Web API uses separate classes, even for functionality that is shared with MVC, such as filter attributes. Hover the mouse over the HttpGet or HttpPost attributes in the code editor, and the pop-up box will tell you that these are classes defined in the System.Web.Http namespace, not the System.Web.Mvc namespace that defines the attribute I applied to the Home MVC controller.

■ **Tip** The fact that MVC and Web API have distinct versions of classes with the same names that perform the same function is confusing and is the most common cause of errors for developers new to Web API. Be careful that you don't add the System.Web.Mvc namespace to Web API controllers.

Next, notice that the result from the GetAttendees action method is an enumeration of my GuestResponse model class. Web services deliver data to their clients and don't use views to generate HTML content, so there is no need for the ActionResult objects you are familiar with from MVC applications. This makes Web API controllers more like regular C# classes, although there are lots of options available for taking control over how the data returned from a Web API action method is formatted and sent to the client, which I explain in Part 2 of this book.

IS THAT IT?

The RsvpController class is the only one I need to add to the project to create an HTTP web service. The rest of this chapter is given over to checking that the web service works and implementing the client-side jQuery code that consumes the service.

You might be asking yourself, is that it? The answer is yes and no. Yes, because you can create a basic HTTP web service just by adding a Web API controller to the project. In this example, I was able to minimize the amount of work I had to do by reusing the model that I created for the MVC framework application and relying on the default conventions and configuration of a Web API application.

And no, that isn't it because this is a trivially simple example that I designed specifically to emphasize how easy it is to get started with Web API. Creating sophisticated and robust HTTP web services requires more knowledge about how Web API works and how to consume web services in the browser. Happily, I explain everything you need to know in the rest of this book, starting with the SportsStore application in Chapter 5, where I define an equally simple Web API controller and show its transformation as I enable more features.

Testing the Web API Controller

As simple as the RsvpController is, it is all that I need to add a basic HTTP web service to my application. I am relying on some convention and default configuration settings, of course—which I'll explain in depth in Part 2, but with the addition of one simple class I have a web service that is capable of delivering data over HTTP.

There are different levels of testing that you can perform on a web service created with Web API. There is unit testing, which can be applied in much the same way as for MVC framework application. And, of course, you can perform system-level testing once the web service is integrated into the client. For this chapter, I am going to use the Postman tool that I described and installed in Chapter 1. To recap, Postman is a Chrome application that provides excellent support for testing web services, even the basic kind that I have created here. It is free to use, although donations are accepted, and it makes it easy to explore a web service without having to write any code at all.

■ **Tip**   If you have not installed Google Chrome and Postman, then now is the time to do so. I provided instructions and URLs in Chapter 1.

Start the application and then start Postman by opening a new Chrome tab, clicking the Apps icon in the top-left corner of the toolbar, and clicking the Postman icon. Postman will open a new window. Replace the "Enter request URL here" text with, the following URL:

---

http://localhost:37993/api/rsvp

Once you have entered the URL, click the Send button, and Postman will send a request to the web service and display the data that it gets, as shown in Figure 2-8.

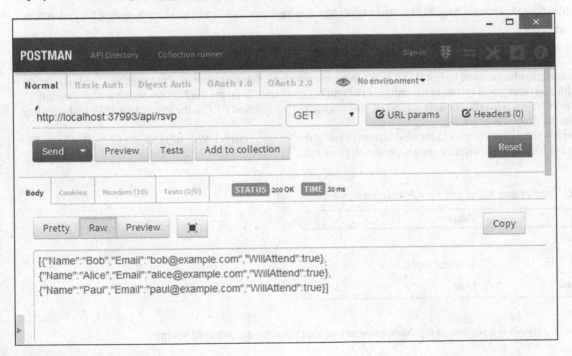

Figure 2-8. Making a request using Postman

■ **Tip**   Web API uses the ASP.NET routing system to match requests to controllers and action methods, which means that URLs can be customized. The default convention is that all URLs for Web API web services are prefixed with /api, followed by the controller name. The selection of the action method is made using the HTTP verb from the request, matched to an action method whose name begins with the verb—so the GET request sent by Postman to /api/rsvp is mapped to the GetAttendees action method in the RsvpController class. I explain more about how this mapping works in Chapter 22.

The URL I specified targeted the GetAttendees action method on the Web API Rsvp controller, and the data that is returned represents the responses from potential guests. It can be hard to make out from the figure, but here is the data that Postman receives from the web service:

```
[{"Name":"Bob","Email":"bob@example.com","WillAttend":true},
 {"Name":"Alice","Email":"alice@example.com","WillAttend":true},
 {"Name":"Paul","Email":"paul@example.com","WillAttend":true}]
```

This is the JSON data format, which is especially easy to work with in JavaScript—as you'll see when I implement the client-side part of the application in the "Implementing the Client" section. I describe JSON in a little more detail in Chapter 3, but the initial [and final] characters indicate an array of objects—just like in C# each set of braces (the { and } characters) denotes a single object. Each object in this array has Name, Email, and WillAttend properties, and the values correspond to the initial model data that I defined in the Repository class in Listing 2-2.

■ **Tip**   Notice that Web API automatically converted the result from the GetAttendees action method from IEnumerable<GuestResponse> to a JSON array. I explain how this happens—and show you how to control the conversion process—in Part 2.

Postman can also be used to test HTTP POST requests, which allows me to test my PostResponse action method as well, although care must be taken to configure the request correctly. To target the PostResponse action method, change the HTTP verb for the request to POST by clicking the button marked GET to the right of the URL and selecting POST from the drop-down list.

Now click the x-www-form-urlencoded button to select the format in which Web API expects to receive form data and enter key/value pairs to define the properties in Table 2-2.

Table 2-2. *The Key and Value Pairs for Testing the Web Service*

Key	Value
name	Jane
email	jane@example.com
willattend	true

Figure 2-9 shows the section of the Postman interface that displays the required settings.

Figure 2-9. *Preparing a POST request*

Click the Send button to send the POST request to the application. The PostResponse action method doesn't return any data, so the response area of the Postman interface doesn't show any data, but if you send a GET request to the GetAttendees method (which you can easily do from the Postman History area), you will see that a new RSVP object is included in the JSON data, like this:

```
[{"Name":"Bob","Email":"bob@example.com","WillAttend":true},
 {"Name":"Alice","Email":"alice@example.com","WillAttend":true},
 {"Name":"Paul","Email":"paul@example.com","WillAttend":true},
 {"Name":"Jane","Email":"jane@example.com","WillAttend":true}]
```

Implementing the Single-Page Client

Using Postman allows a web service to be tested by manually composing requests. It is a nice way to test the web service separately from the MVC framework part of the application, but that isn't good for users, who generally don't want to type URLs and read JSON strings. In this section, I will update the MVC part of the application to use jQuery to consume the HTTP web service I created using Web API. My goal is to create a simple *single-page application*, where a single HTML document is requested by the browser and then manipulated and populated using JavaScript and data obtained via Ajax requests.

For this example, I am also going to ensure that non-JavaScript clients can still use the application. JavaScript is remarkably prevalent these days, but there are still devices that don't support it and a substantial minority of users who disable JavaScript in their browsers, mostly for reasons of security.

■ **Tip** Don't worry if you are unfamiliar with some of the techniques I use here. Chapter 3 contains a primer to get you started, focused on what you need to follow the examples in this book and create clients that can consume web applications.

Setting Up JavaScript IntelliSense

Visual Studio is capable of providing the same kind of IntelliSense editor support for JavaScript like it does for C#. This makes working with libraries such as jQuery quicker and less error-prone, especially since JavaScript code doesn't go through a compiler in the same that that C# does—any errors in the code are not revealed until runtime. To enable JavaScript IntelliSense, add a new JavaScript file called _references.js (don't forget the leading underscore character) in the Scripts folder. Listing 2-10 shows the additions I made to the new file to set up IntelliSense for the jQuery file present in the project.

Listing 2-10. Adding IntelliSense References to the _references.js File

```
/// <reference path="jquery-2.1.0.js" />
/// <reference path="knockout-3.1.0.debug.js" />
```

A reference element has a path attribute that refers to one of the JavaScript files in the Scripts folder.

■ **Tip** You don't have to type the resource elements by hand—you can just drop JavaScript files from the Solution Explorer onto the editor window for the _resources.js file, and Visual Studio will create the reference element for you.

Defining the Client-Side Data Model and Controller

The basic model for creating single-page applications with jQuery and Knockout is to follow the same approach taken on the server side: a data model that is manipulated by a controller, which selects the views to be displayed and responds to user input. To get started, I added a JavaScript file called rsvp.js to the Scripts folder, the contents of which are shown in Listing 2-11.

Listing 2-11. The Contents of the rsvp.js File

```
var model = {
    view: ko.observable("welcome"),
    rsvp: {
        name: ko.observable(""),
        email: "",
        willattend: ko.observable("true")
    },
    attendees: ko.observableArray([])
}

var showForm = function() {
    model.view("form");
}
```

```
var sendRsvp= function () {
    $.ajax("/api/rsvp", {
        type: "POST",
        data: {
            name: model.rsvp.name(),
            email: model.rsvp.email,
            willattend: model.rsvp.willattend()
        },
        success: function () {
            getAttendees();
        }
    });
}

var getAttendees = function () {
    $.ajax("/api/rsvp", {
        type: "GET",
        success: function (data) {
            model.attendees.removeAll();
            model.attendees.push.apply(model.attendees, data.map(function(rsvp) {
                return rsvp.Name;
            }));
            model.view("thanks");
        }
    });
}

$(document).ready(function () {
    ko.applyBindings();
})
```

The PartyInvites application is sufficiently simple that I have defined the data model and the functions that comprise the controller in the same JavaScript file. For more complex projects (like the SportsStore application I created in Chapters 5–8), I use several files. In the sections that follow, I describe the contents of the JavaScript file.

Defining the Model

The data model is at the heart of the client-side part of the application, just as it is in the server. I have defined a JavaScript object called model that has properties that correspond to the data items I need in the application, as follows:

```
...
var model = {
    view: ko.observable("welcome"),
    rsvp: {
        name: ko.observable(""),
        email: "",
        willattend: ko.observable("true")
    },
    attendees: ko.observableArray([])
}
...
```

There are two Knockout-specific features in the model object. The first is the use of the ko.observable method, which is used to create a data value that can be used to automatically update HTML elements when it changes. I use the view property, for example, to keep track of which client-side view should be displayed to the user, and I don't have to write any additional code to change the view—I just set the value for the view property. The hard work is done by a Knockout *binding*, which I apply to the HTML in the "Adding Data Bindings" section. Data values that are created with the ko.observable method are known as *observables*. The other Knockout feature is similar; the ko.observableArray method performs the same role as ko.observable but for an array of objects, creating what is known as an *observable array*.

To help you understand what is happening as I apply the data model in the application, Table 2-3 explains the purpose of each property in the model.

Table 2-3. The PartyInvites Data Model Properties

Name	Description
view	This property is used to keep track of which part of the client interface is shown to the user.
rsvp	This property is set to an object that I use to capture the user's response to the party invitation. The object has fields for name, e-mail address, and attendance. The name and willattend properties are observable.
attendees	This property is an array of the names of the other attendees, which are obtained from the web service after the user has responded to the invitation.

Defining the Controller

The showForm, sendRsvp, and getAttendees functions collectively form the client-side controller. JavaScript isn't as structured as C#, and I want to keep the example simple, but these are the functions that are used to manipulate the data model and select the content shown to the user, just like an MVC framework controller. The main difference—language aside—is that the data is obtained from the web service using Ajax, rather than from a local repository. I am not going to explain these functions in detail in chapter, but I explain how to make changes to a Knockout data model and how to use jQuery to make Ajax requests in Chapter 3. To help provide context, Table 2-4 describes the purpose of the functions.

Table 2-4. The PartyInvites Controller Functions

Name	Description
showForm	This function shows the user the HTML form that gathers their responses to the invitation and allows the response to be sent to the web service.
sendRsvp	This function sends a POST request to the web service to submit the RSVP data.
getAttendees	This function sends a GET request to the web service to get the list of attendees, and it is called after a successful POST request.

Initializing Knockout

Knockout requires initialization to associate the observables and observable arrays in the data model with the bindings attached to the HTML elements (which I define shortly). Here is the code that starts the initialization process:

```
...
$(document).ready(function () {
    ko.applyBindings();
})
...
```

The ko.applyBindings method is called to initialize Knockout but should not be called until the browser has loaded and processed all of the HTML and JavaScript files. The call to $(document).ready is a common incantation in a JavaScript web application. The ready function is provided by jQuery, and when called in this way, it defers execution of the function it is passed until the browser is ready. In this case, it allows me to defer initializing Knockout until the elements that it will operate on have been processed by the browser.

Registering the JavaScript File

Listing 2-12 shows the script element I added to the _Layout.cshtml file so that the browser will request the contents of the rsvp.js file and execute the code it contains.

■ **Tip** You don't have to type script elements into the editor. You can just drag and drop the JavaScript files from the Solution Explorer to the code editor, and a script element will be created automatically. Visual Studio shows a cursor so you can control where the element is added.

Listing 2-12. Adding a script Element to the _Layout.cshtml File

```
<!DOCTYPE html>
<html>
<head>
    <meta name="viewport" content="width=device-width" />
    <script src="~/Scripts/jquery-2.1.0.min.js"></script>
    <script src="~/Scripts/knockout-3.1.0.js"></script>
    <link href="~/Content/bootstrap.css" rel="stylesheet" />
    <link href="~/Content/bootstrap-theme.css" rel="stylesheet" />
    <title>@ViewBag.Title</title>
    <script src="~/Scripts/rsvp.js"></script>
    <style>
        body { padding-top: 10px; }
    </style>
</head>
<body class="container">
    @RenderBody()
</body>
</html>
```

Appling Data Bindings

Now that I have a model and controller in place, I can update the HTML so that it responds dynamically to data changes. Knockout uses a system of bindings, which are applied to elements through the data-bind attribute. Listing 2-13 shows the changes I made to the Index.cshtml file to apply the bindings I need for the application. I have also taken the opportunity to combine the HTML into one file.

■ **Tip** A single-page application doesn't have to be defined in a single HTML page—the principle of updating the content with data obtained via Ajax requests. For large applications, it often makes sense to have several HTML hub pages that represent each major area of the application, which is what I do with the SportsStore application in Chapters 5–8. As with all patterns, don't let the ideal interfere with pragmatic implementation.

Listing 2-13. Creating a Dynamic Client in the Index.cshtml File

```
@{ ViewBag.Title = "Party!";}

<div class="text-center" data-bind="visible: model.view() == 'welcome'">
    <h2>We're going to have an exciting party!</h2>
    <h3>And you are invited.</h3>
    <button class="btn btn-success" data-bind="click: showForm">RSVP Now</button>
</div>

<div data-bind="visible: model.view() == 'form'">
    <div class="panel panel-success">
        <div class="panel-heading"><h4>RSVP</h4></div>
        <div class="panel-body">
            <div class="form-group">
                <label>Your name:</label>
                <input class="form-control" data-bind="value: model.rsvp.name" />
            </div>
            <div class="form-group">
                <label>Your email:</label>
                <input class="form-control" data-bind="value: model.rsvp.email" />
            </div>
            <div class="form-group">
                <label>Will you attend?</label>
                <select class="form-control" data-bind="value: model.rsvp.willattend">
                    <option value="true">Yes, I'll be there</option>
                    <option value="false">No, I can't come</option>
                </select>
            </div>
            <div class="text-center">
                <button class="btn btn-success"
                    data-bind="click: sendRsvp">Submit RSVP</button>
            </div>
        </div>
    </div>
</div>
```

```
<div data-bind="visible: model.view() == 'thanks'">
    <h1>Thank you, <span data-bind="text: model.rsvp.name()"></span>!</h1>
    <div class="lead">
        <span data-bind="visible: model.rsvp.willattend() == 'true'">
            It's great that you're coming. The drinks are already in the fridge!
            <br />
            Here is the list of cool people coming:
                <span data-bind="text: model.attendees().join(',')"></span>
        </span>
        <span data-bind="visible: model.rsvp.willattend() == 'false'">
            Sorry to hear that you can't make it, but thanks for letting us know.
        </span>
    </div>
</div>
```

There are three sections to the HTML, each of which represents a view. I control which view is shown to the user through a Knockout binding, like this one:

```
...
<div class="text-center" data-bind="visible: model.view() == 'welcome'">
...
```

This is an example of the visible binding, which controls whether an element is shown to the user. There are a range of bindings including text (which sets the text content of an element), value (which sets a model value based on the contents of a form element), and click (which calls a function when an element, such as button, is clicked). I describe the available bindings in more detail in Chapter 3.

Some bindings—including the visible binding—evaluate expressions to figure out what they need to do. In this case, the element to which the binding has been applied will be shown to the user if the value of the model.view property is welcome. The other views have their own visible bindings that are looking for different model.view values.

■ **Tip** Observable values are functions, which means you have to invoke them to read their value—like model.view()—and pass values as arguments to set them, such as model.view(newView).

To change the view, I need to change the value of the model.view property. You can see an example of how I do this on a button element, like this:

```
...
<button class="btn btn-success" data-bind="click: showForm">RSVP Now</button>
...
```

This is an example of the click binding, and I have configured it to invoke the showForm controller function when the button element is clicked. The showForm function is defined as follows:

```
...
var showForm = function() {
    model.view("form");
}
...
```

The only other binding I have used in the example is value, which synchronizes the contents of a form element, such as an input, with a model value. Here is an example:

```
...
<input class="form-control" data-bind="value: model.rsvp.name" />
...
```

The value that is entered into the input element is synchronized with the model.rsvp.name property, which I use to generate the Ajax POST request to submit the RSVP to the web service.

Testing the Single-Page Client

Start the application to see the effect of the changes I made. There is little obvious difference when using the application, other than being a little snappier, because I have implemented the same application model that the round-trip version of the application used, as illustrated by Figure 2-10. To make sure everything is working, you will need to use the browser F12 tools to see the Ajax requests that are being sent.

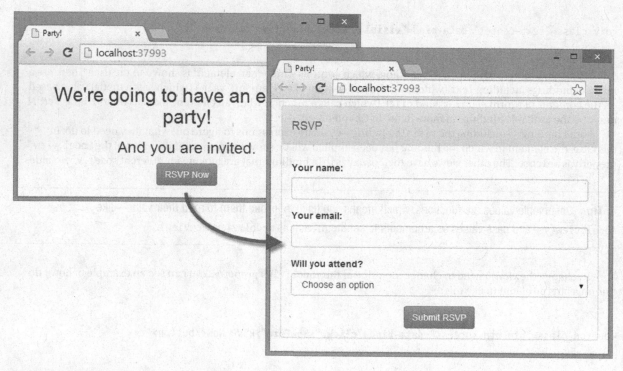

Figure 2-10. *The single-page application*

Measuring the Single-Page Implementation

With the addition of a simple Web API controller, some changes to the views, and a little JavaScript code, I have created an application that requests a single HTML document from the server and uses Ajax requests to take the user through the RSVP process.

I want to confirm that my application is working the way that I expect, and a good way to do this is to repeat the tests I performed in the "Using the MVC Application" section earlier in the chapter and use the browser F12 tools to record the requests made by the browser. Table 2-5 shows the results I received.

Table 2-5. *The Request Summary from Google Chrome*

Description	Value
Total number of requests	10, all of which were made to the server (none was cached)
Total amount of data	246KB

The effect of using Web API has been to eliminate several requests to the server, which is always a good thing. But the amount of data that has been sent by the server remains the same. This is to be expected because all I did in this example was move the content around so that it was all contained in the Index.cshtml file or obtained through Ajax requests. The application does the same things, using the same content; it just does them in a different way.

The main advantage of adding a simple HTTP web service to an application like this is that it improves the user experience because the application responds immediately to user input, rather than needing to send a request to the server and wait for an HTML response that must then be parsed and displayed.

■ **Tip** More complex applications, especially those that have the user perform the same task repeatedly, can obtain some serious bandwidth savings—something that will become apparent in later examples in this book.

Summary

In this chapter, I showed you how to use Web API to add an HTTP web service to an MVC framework application and consume that web service in the browser. The example in this chapter is rather simple, but it does emphasize the fact that ASP.NET Web API is easy to work with and works happily alongside the MVC framework. It also demonstrates that creating a web service is only part of the story. You must also create the client-side functionality that consumes the web service. Throughout this book, I show you not only how to create and configure web services but how to use them, too. As with most web application technologies, context and integration are important. In the next chapter, I provide a primer on some important techniques that you need to understand to get the best from this book.

CHAPTER 3

■ ■ ■

Essential Techniques

As I explained in Chapter 1, this book is targeted at MVC framework developers, which means you already know C# and key components such as Razor and action results. In this chapter, I provide a quick primer for three topics that you may not be as familiar with: using C# async methods, making Ajax requests using jQuery, and using the Knockout library. Understanding all three will help you get the most from this book.

Asynchronous methods are important in Web API development, especially once you go beyond creating action methods and start to customize the way that requests are processed using the techniques I describe in Part 3 of this book.

jQuery and Knockout are not part of Web API, but I use them throughout this book to create client applications that demonstrate different kinds of interactions with web services that I create using Web API. jQuery and Knockout are both packages with a rich range of functionality, but I describe only the features that I use in examples.

Preparing the Example Project

For this chapter, I created a new Visual Studio project by following the same process that I used in Chapter 2 and that I use throughout this book. Select New Project from the File menu to open the New Project dialog window, and locate the ASP.NET Web Application template in the Visual C# ➤ Web section. Set the name of the project to Primer, as shown in Figure 3-1.

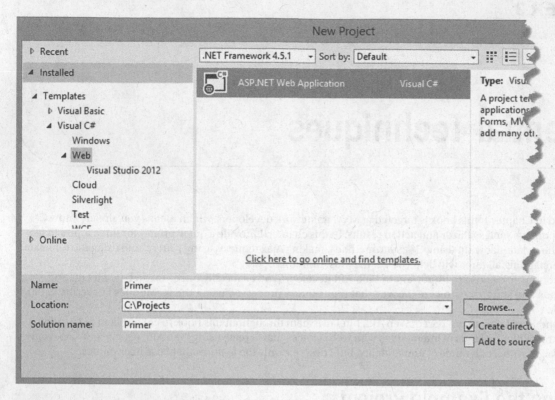

Figure 3-1. *Creating the Primer project*

Click the OK button to move to the New ASP.NET Project dialog window. Ensure that the Empty option is selected and check the MVC and Web API core references options, as shown in Figure 3-2. Click the OK button, and Visual Studio will create the project.

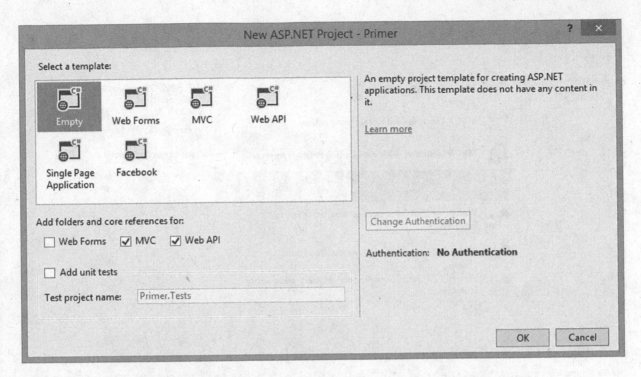

Figure 3-2. Selecting the ASP.NET project type

Adding and Updating NuGet Packages

Select Package Manager Console from the Visual Studio Tools ➤ NuGet Package Manager menu and enter the following commands to update the MVC and Web API packages and install the jQuery Bootstrap and Knockout packages:

```
Update-Package microsoft.aspnet.mvc -version 5.1.1
Update-Package microsoft.aspnet.webapi -version 5.1.1
Update-Package Newtonsoft.json -version 6.0.1
Install-Package jquery -version 2.1.0
Install-Package bootstrap -version 3.1.1
Install-Package knockoutjs –version 3.1.0
```

Creating the Web API Controller

I need a simple web service for this chapter, which means creating a Web API controller class. The controller I create in this chapter is basic, rather like the one I created in Chapter 2, and it exists only so I can demonstrate essential techniques. You can see a more complete example in Chapter 6, when I create a more realistic Web API application, and I explain how controllers fit into Web API in Chapter 22.

To create the controller, right-click the Controllers folder and select Add ➤ Controller from the pop-up menu. Select Web API 2 Controller – Empty from the list of controller types, as shown in Figure 3-3.

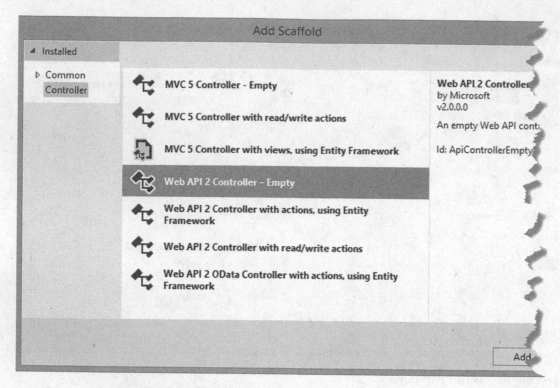

Figure 3-3. Adding a Web API controller

Click the Add button once you have selected the type, set the name of the new controller to PageSizeController, and click the Add button to create the Controllers/PageSizeController.cs file. Listing 3-1 shows the action method I added to the controller.

Listing 3-1. Adding an Action Method to the PageSizeController.cs File

```
using System.Net;
using System.Web.Http;
using System.Diagnostics;

namespace Primer.Controllers {

    public class PageSizeController : ApiController {
        private static string TargetUrl = "http://apress.com";

        public long GetPageSize() {
            WebClient wc = new WebClient();
            Stopwatch sw = Stopwatch.StartNew();
            byte[] apressData = wc.DownloadData(TargetUrl);
            Debug.WriteLine("Elapsed ms: {0}", sw.ElapsedMilliseconds);
            return apressData.LongLength;
        }
    }
}
```

The action method is called GetPageSize, and it makes HTTP requests for the Apress home page and returns the number of bytes returned. I use the Stopwatch class from the System.Diagnostics namespace to measure how long the requests take and use the Debug class to write out the duration to the Visual Studio Output window.

■ **Tip** Getting the number of bytes returned by a URL isn't something you will often need in a real project, but it is a helpful demonstration of a task that can be performed synchronously and asynchronously without requiring me to write any code beyond the Web API controller. If you are keen to see a more realistic example, then skip ahead to Chapter 5, where I begin the development of the SportsStore application.

Creating the MVC Framework Controller

I will be using the MVC framework to deliver HTML and JavaScript to the browser so that I can explain how to send Ajax requests back to the web service and use Knockout to respond to the data that is received. To create an MVC controller, right-click the Controllers folder and select Add ➤ Controller from the pop-up menu. Figure 3-4 shows the options that Visual Studio presents for creating controllers for both MVC and Web API.

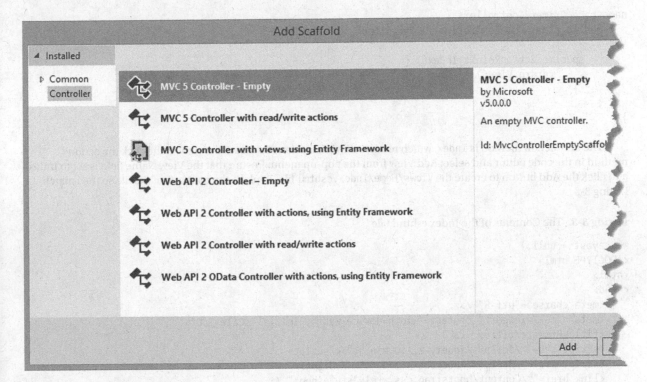

Figure 3-4. Selecting a controller type

Select the MVC 5 Controller – Empty option from the list, click the Add button, and set the name to HomeController, as shown in Figure 3-5.

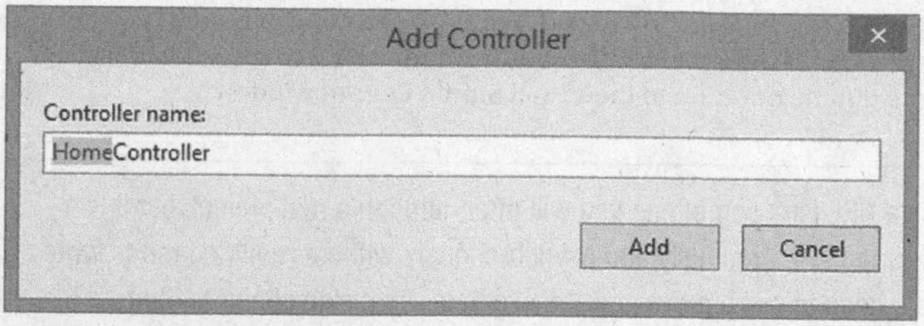

Figure 3-5. *Creating an MVC controller*

Clicking the Add button creates the `Controllers/HomeController.cs` file, the contents of which are shown in Listing 3-2.

Listing 3-2. The Contents of the HomeController.cs File

```
using System.Web.Mvc;

namespace Primer.Controllers {
    public class HomeController : Controller {

        public ActionResult Index() {
            return View();
        }
    }
}
```

The only action method is `Index`, which renders the default view. To create the view, right-click the action method in the code editor and select Add View from the pop-up menu. Ensure that the View Name field is set to Index and click the Add button to create the `Views/Home/Index.cshtml` file. Replace the contents of the file so they match Listing 3-3.

Listing 3-3. The Contents of the Index.cshtml File

```
@{ Layout = null;}
<!DOCTYPE html>
<html>
<head>
    <meta charset="utf-8" />
    <meta name="viewport" content="width=device-width, initial-scale=1.0">
    <title>Primer</title>
    <script src="~/Scripts/jquery-2.1.0.min.js"></script>
    <script src="~/Scripts/knockout-3.1.0.js"></script>
    <link href="~/Content/bootstrap.css" rel="stylesheet" />
    <link href="~/Content/bootstrap-theme.css" rel="stylesheet" />
</head>
<body>
    <h2>Content will be added here</h2>
</body>
</html>
```

The view contains script elements for jQuery and Knockout and link elements for the Bootstrap files. I have left a placeholder within the body element that I will replace when I start to demonstrate client-side features later in the chapter.

Setting the Port and Start URL

The final preparations I need to make specify the TCP port that will be used to receive requests and the initial URL that will be passed to the browser when the project is started, just as I did in Chapter 2. Select Primer Properties from the Visual Studio Project menu and click Web to open the settings for ASP.NET projects.

Enable the Specific Page option and enter Home/Index into the field. On the same page, change the value shown in the Project Url field to `http://localhost:38000/` and click the Create Virtual Directory button.

The first change prevents Visual Studio from trying to work out what URL should be shown when the application first starts based on the file you edited most recently, and the second change means that requests will be received on TCP port 38000.

Testing the Web Service

Start the application by selecting Start Debugging from the Visual Studio Debug menu. Ignore the browser window that is opened; I will not add any useful content to the view until the "Making Ajax Requests with jQuery" section.

Instead, start the Postman client (which I described in Chapter 1 and used in Chapter 2) and send a GET request to the following URL:

```
http://localhost:38000/api/pagesize
```

The default behavior for the Web API controller is to use the HTTP verb to select the action method, and the GET request will target GetPageSize. The action method will request the content from Apress.com and return the number of bytes received, as shown in Figure 3-6.

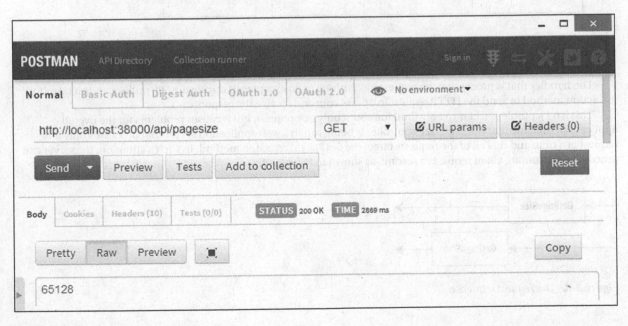

Figure 3-6. *Testing the Web API web service*

■ **Note**   The Apress web site changes often to reflect new releases and special offers. The number of bytes you receive is likely to be different from the result I show here.

Understanding Asynchronous Methods

Asynchronous methods have been part of ASP.NET for a while, but as something of an afterthought. Web API adopts asynchronous methods throughout its API. They are optional in controllers, but many of the classes that customize the way that Web API processes requests define only asynchronous methods.

Asynchronous methods are one of the most misunderstood aspects of web application development. In the sections that follow, I'll explain the benefit they offer, dispel a commonly held misconception, and demonstrate the patterns you will need to deal with asynchronous methods in Web API.

Understanding the Problem Asynchronous Methods Solve

When writing action methods—or any part of a web application—the natural tendency is to think about the path that a single request follows through the code. In the case of the GetPageSize action method in the PageSize controller, the path is simple: a request arrives at the action method, I make a request to the remote web server, and 500 milliseconds later, I get the data I need and can return the result, as illustrated by Figure 3-7. (The actual elapsed time will differ, but I am going to assume a constant 500 milliseconds.)

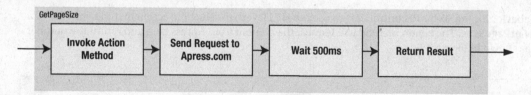

Figure 3-7. *The request path for the GetPageSize action*

The handler that is processing the request has nothing to do except wait during the 500 milliseconds it takes for the action method to send the HTTP request to Apress.com and receive the response.

This isn't a problem when you are thinking about only one request, but it causes problems for the overall application. Imagine that the PageSize controller is being run in a web application server that processes only one request at a time and that all of the requests target the GetPageSize action method. In such a situation, the server can process two incoming client requests a second, as shown in Figure 3-8.

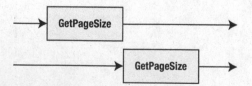

Figure 3-8. *The request sequence*

■ **Tip** An application server that handles only one request at a time isn't as unlikely as it may seem, as the success of Node.js has demonstrated.

The handler can start processing a request only when it has finished processing the previous one, and for the majority of the time, the handler is sitting idle. The problem isn't the work that the action method is performing—it is the way that the handler and the action method work together.

The solution is to perform the request to Apress.com asynchronously, which frees up the handler to process other incoming client requests instead of waiting for the Apress.com response. Listing 3-4 shows the application of the async and await keywords to the GetPageSize action method.

Listing 3-4. Creating an Asynchronous Action Method in the PageSizeController.cs File

```
using System.Net;
using System.Web.Http;
using System.Diagnostics;
using System.Threading.Tasks;

namespace Primer.Controllers {

    public class PageSizeController : ApiController {
        private static string TargetUrl = "http://apress.com";

        public async Task<long> GetPageSize() {
            WebClient wc = new WebClient();
            Stopwatch sw = Stopwatch.StartNew();
            byte[] apressData = await wc.DownloadDataTaskAsync(TargetUrl);
            Debug.WriteLine("Elapsed ms: {0}", sw.ElapsedMilliseconds);
            return apressData.LongLength;
        }
    }
}
```

The async keyword is applied to the method definition, and the result is changed to a Task<long>, which means a Task object that will yield a long value when it completes. Within the action method, I have used an asynchronous implementation of the method that gets the HTTP data, and I apply the await keyword to indicate that this is an asynchronous operation and that the statements that follow can be packaged up by the complier to generate the Task<long> result required as the method result.

This arrangement doesn't change the work that the action method performs, but it does mean that the handler is free to handle other client requests while the action method is waiting for the response from Apress.com. Figure 3-9 illustrates the effect.

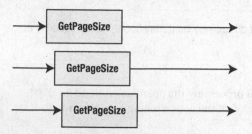

Figure 3-9. *The effect of an asynchronous action method*

Instead of waiting for the action method as it waits for `Apress.com`, the handler can process the next request or process the results when `Apress.com` responds.

Using asynchronous methods increases the overall throughput of the web application, but it can degrade the performance for each individual request. This is because there is only one handler, and it is now responsible for managing several concurrent requests. In the synchronous model, the handler was able to deal with the result from the action method immediately because it had been waiting for it to arrive, but in the asynchronous model, the handler may be doing something else and not be available to process the result immediately. Or, put another way, asynchronous methods increase the overall performance of the application by reducing the performance of individual requests.

■ **Tip**   The amount of delay will depend on how the application server is configured and what kind of requests are being processed—and, of course, how many handlers are available to process those requests (because single-handler servers are great for describing theory but are not often used in ASP.NET projects).

Implementing an Asynchronous Interface

You can choose between asynchronous and synchronous action methods in Web API controllers, but once you start using some of the advanced features, you will need to implement interfaces that are written explicitly for asynchronous execution. As an example, I created a folder called `Infrastructure` and added to it a class file called `ICustomController.cs` that I used to define the interface shown in Listing 3-5.

Listing 3-5. The Contents of the ICustomController.cs File

```
using System.Threading;
using System.Threading.Tasks;

namespace Primer.Infrastructure {
    public interface ICustomController {

        Task<long> GetPageSize(CancellationToken cToken);
    }
}
```

You will see this pattern of interface method a lot in Part 3 of this book, when I describe the end-to-end dispatch process: a return type of `Task` or `Task<T>` and a `CancellationToken` parameter. In the sections that follow, I'll show you how to deal with some common patterns of asynchronous method you will need to write.

If the method you are going to write calls another asynchronous method, then you can use the `async` and `await` keywords, just as I did in Listing 3-4 and receive the `CancellationToken` parameter, as shown in Listing 3-6.

Listing 3-6. Implementing the Interface in the PageSizeController.cs File

```csharp
using System.Net;
using System.Web.Http;
using System.Diagnostics;
using System.Threading.Tasks;
using Primer.Infrastructure;
using System.Threading;

namespace Primer.Controllers {

    public class PageSizeController : ApiController, ICustomController {
        private static string TargetUrl = "http://apress.com";

        public async Task<long> GetPageSize(CancellationToken cToken) {
            WebClient wc = new WebClient();
            Stopwatch sw = Stopwatch.StartNew();
            byte[] apressData = await wc.DownloadDataTaskAsync(TargetUrl);
            Debug.WriteLine("Elapsed ms: {0}", sw.ElapsedMilliseconds);
            return apressData.LongLength;
        }
    }
}
```

I come back to the CancellationToken parameter in the next section, but implementing the Web API asynchronous interface pattern is simple when you are relying on other asynchronous methods to do your work, something that is often the case in action methods that access services like the Entity Framework and ASP.NET Identity, both of which I use in Chapter 5 when I prepare for the more realistic SportsStore application.

■ **Tip** If you define a CancellationToken parameter on an action method, Web API will provide one for you that is triggered when the request is terminated.

Not all methods can use this approach, however, either because they are going to perform the work directly or because the implementation of the method is so simple that the overhead of creating and managing Task objects does not justify the benefit of freeing the handler to process other requests. In the sections that follow, I show you how to handle the most common scenarios you are likely to encounter.

■ **Note**   I don't go into detail about what is happening behind the scenes in this chapter. If you want more information about .NET asynchronous programming, then see my *Pro .NET 4 Parallel Programming in C#* book or *Pro Asynchronous Programming with .NET*, written by Richard Blewett and Andrew Clymer. Both books are published by Apress.

Dealing with Cancellation

The CancellationToken parameter is used to signal when the request has been cancelled. You can ignore cancellation in your asynchronous methods, but it is good practice to stop the work you are performing if you can, not least because you know that the result you produce is going to be discarded. In Listing 3-7, I have changed the implementation of the GetPageSize method in the PageSize controller so that it does more work and monitors its cancellation token.

Listing 3-7. Using a Cancellation Token in the PageSizeController.cs File

```
using System.Net;
using System.Web.Http;
using System.Diagnostics;
using System.Threading.Tasks;
using Primer.Infrastructure;
using System.Threading;
using System.Collections.Generic;
using System.Linq;

namespace Primer.Controllers {

    public class PageSizeController : ApiController, ICustomController {
        private static string TargetUrl = "http://apress.com";

        public async Task<long> GetPageSize(CancellationToken cToken) {
            WebClient wc = new WebClient();
            Stopwatch sw = Stopwatch.StartNew();

            List<long> results = new List<long>();

            for (int i = 0; i < 10; i++) {
                if (!cToken.IsCancellationRequested) {
                    Debug.WriteLine("Making Request: {0}", i);
                    byte[] apressData = await wc.DownloadDataTaskAsync(TargetUrl);
                    results.Add(apressData.LongLength);
                } else {
                    Debug.WriteLine("Cancelled");
                    return 0;
                }
            }

            Debug.WriteLine("Elapsed ms: {0}", sw.ElapsedMilliseconds);
            return (long)results.Average();
        }
    }
}
```

This implementation gets the content from the Apress web site ten times and averages the result. (Ignore the fact that there is unlikely to be any variation between requests.) Before I send each request to Apress.com, I check the value of the CancellationToken.IsCancellationRequested property to see whether the request has been cancelled. If it has been cancelled, I know that the request has been terminated and do not perform any further work. I return zero as the result from the method, although I could have returned any value from the method because it will be discarded.

■ **Tip**   Use the browser to test request cancellation by requesting the URL http://localhost:38000/api/pagesize and then clicking the Cancel button. Don't use Postman because the current version as I write this doesn't terminate the HTTP request when its Cancel button is clicked—and this means that the Web API application will not trigger the cancellation token and all ten requests to Apress.com will be performed.

Creating a Self-Contained Asynchronous Method Body

A common scenario in Web API development is where you have a series of synchronous statements that you want to execute asynchronously. This is done by creating and starting a Task that wraps around the statements you need to execute and return the Task as the result from the method, as shown in Listing 3-8.

Listing 3-8. Creating a Task in the PageSizeController.cs File

```
using System.Net;
using System.Web.Http;
using System.Diagnostics;
using System.Threading.Tasks;
using Primer.Infrastructure;
using System.Threading;
using System.Collections.Generic;
using System.Linq;

namespace Primer.Controllers {

    public class PageSizeController : ApiController, ICustomController {
        private static string TargetUrl = "http://apress.com";

        public Task<long> GetPageSize(CancellationToken cToken) {

            return Task<long>.Factory.StartNew(() => {
                WebClient wc = new WebClient();
                Stopwatch sw = Stopwatch.StartNew();

                List<long> results = new List<long>();

                for (int i = 0; i < 10; i++) {
                    if (!cToken.IsCancellationRequested) {
                        Debug.WriteLine("Making Request: {0}", i);
                        results.Add(wc.DownloadData(TargetUrl).LongLength);
                    } else {
                        Debug.WriteLine("Cancelled");
                        return 0;
                    }
                }

                Debug.WriteLine("Elapsed ms: {0}", sw.ElapsedMilliseconds);
                return (long)results.Average();
            });
        }
    }
}
```

I have returned to calling the synchronous WebClient.DownloadData method in this example, which lets me demonstrate using a set of synchronous statements. I call the static Task<long>.Factory.StartNew method to create and start the Task and pass the statements I want executed through a lambda expression. You must create and start the Task in the action method; if you just create and return the Task without starting it, then the work will never be performed, and eventually the client times out waiting for a response.

■ **Tip**   Notice that the method definition does not include the `async` keyword. This is required only when using the `await` keyword.

Returning a Task from a Synchronous Method Body

There is nothing about the method definition I created in Listing 3-5 that forces you to create an asynchronous method—just an opportunity to create one if it would be advantageous to your application. For simple methods, the overhead of creating a `Task` is greater than simply executing the method statements synchronously. As a demonstration, I have added a new method to the `ICustomController` interface, as shown in Listing 3-9.

Listing 3-9. Adding a New Method in the ICustomController.cs File

```
using System.Threading;
using System.Threading.Tasks;

namespace Primer.Infrastructure {
    public interface ICustomController {

        Task<long> GetPageSize(CancellationToken cToken);

        Task PostUrl(string newUrl, CancellationToken cToken);
    }
}
```

The new method is written so that it can be implemented asynchronously, but my implementation in the controller, as shown by Listing 3-10, can do its work in a single statement.

Listing 3-10. Implementing a Simple Method in the PageSizeController.cs File

```
using System.Net;
using System.Web.Http;
using System.Diagnostics;
using System.Threading.Tasks;
using Primer.Infrastructure;
using System.Threading;
using System.Collections.Generic;
using System.Linq;

namespace Primer.Controllers {

    public class PageSizeController : ApiController, ICustomController {
        private static string TargetUrl = "http://apress.com";

        public Task<long> GetPageSize(CancellationToken cToken) {

            return Task<long>.Factory.StartNew(() => {
                WebClient wc = new WebClient();
                Stopwatch sw = Stopwatch.StartNew();

                List<long> results = new List<long>();
```

```
            for (int i = 0; i < 10; i++) {
                if (!cToken.IsCancellationRequested) {
                    Debug.WriteLine("Making Request: {0}", i);
                    results.Add(wc.DownloadData(TargetUrl).LongLength);
                } else {
                    Debug.WriteLine("Cancelled");
                    return 0;
                }
            }
            Debug.WriteLine("Elapsed ms: {0}", sw.ElapsedMilliseconds);
            return (long)results.Average();
        });
    }

    public Task PostUrl(string newUrl, CancellationToken cToken) {
        TargetUrl = newUrl;
        return Task.FromResult<object>(null);
    }
    }
}
```

The static `Task.FromResult<T>` method is used to create a `Task` that is a wrapper around a specific value. The version I used in the listing is helpful when the method doesn't return a value. If I had a similar method that returned an int value, for example, then I might use the following statements:

```
...
int x = 100;
int y = 200;
return Task.FromResult<int>(x + y);
...
```

`Task.FromResult` allows you to generate `Task` wrappers around results that you generated synchronously; in this case, the evaluation of x+y happens synchronously and is wrapped in the `Task` that yields this value immediately. There is no asynchronous work performed when you use the `FromResult` method.

Making Ajax Requests with jQuery

The jQuery library is one of my favorite pieces of software. It makes manipulating HTML and CSS simple, easy, and consistent, and it has so many features that it took me more than 1,000 pages to describe them all in my *Pro jQuery 2* book.

In *this* book, I use jQuery only to make Ajax requests. This is a small fraction of what jQuery is capable of, but Ajax is a theme that runs throughout this book, and jQuery Ajax is robust, is reliable, and has some helpful convenience features. In the sections that follow, I show you the pattern I used to make jQuery Ajax requests in this book.

■ **Note** You don't need to be able to send Ajax requests to use Web API. In fact, for projects that involve third-party developers, you may not have to write a client at all. Most projects, however, will involve some form of client development, and this is likely to be a browser-based client if you are also using the MVC framework. So, while Ajax isn't part of Web API, it is the way that most clients will access your web services.

Making an Ajax Request

jQuery provides a range of different ways to make Ajax requests, but the one that I have used in this book is the $.ajax method (that is a dollar sign, followed by a period, followed by ajax). There are some higher-level alternatives available, but the $.ajax method lets me make a complete range of HTTP request types and take control over the way that the request is formatted, sent, and processed.

Before I start using jQuery, I am going to change the implementation of the GetPageSize action method in the PageSize controller. The implementation I defined in Listing 3-8 makes ten requests to Apress.com and averages the responses, which was useful for demonstrating how to deal with asynchronous methods but is not helpful when you are waiting for a response to test a client feature. Listing 3-11 shows how I have simplified the action method so that it makes only a single request.

Listing 3-11. Simplifying an Action Method in the PageSizeController.cs File

```
using System.Net;
using System.Web.Http;
using System.Diagnostics;
using System.Threading.Tasks;
using Primer.Infrastructure;
using System.Threading;
using System.Collections.Generic;
using System.Linq;

namespace Primer.Controllers {

    public class PageSizeController : ApiController, ICustomController {
        private static string TargetUrl = "http://apress.com";

        public async Task<long> GetPageSize(CancellationToken cToken) {
            WebClient wc = new WebClient();
            Stopwatch sw = Stopwatch.StartNew();
            byte[] apressData = await wc.DownloadDataTaskAsync(TargetUrl);
            Debug.WriteLine("Elapsed ms: {0}", sw.ElapsedMilliseconds);
            return apressData.LongLength;
        }

        public Task PostUrl(string newUrl, CancellationToken cToken) {
            TargetUrl = newUrl;
            return Task.FromResult<object>(null);
        }
    }
}
```

To get started with jQuery, I have updated the Index.cshtml file so that I can send a basic request to the web service. Listing 3-12 shows the changes I made.

Listing 3-12. Making a Simple Ajax Request in the Index.cshtml File

```
@{ Layout = null;}
<!DOCTYPE html>
<html>
<head>
    <meta charset="utf-8" />
    <meta name="viewport" content="width=device-width, initial-scale=1.0">
    <title>Primer</title>
    <script src="~/Scripts/jquery-2.1.0.min.js"></script>
    <script src="~/Scripts/knockout-3.1.0.js"></script>
    <script src="~/Scripts/primer.js"></script>
    <link href="~/Content/bootstrap.css" rel="stylesheet" />
    <link href="~/Content/bootstrap-theme.css" rel="stylesheet" />
</head>
<body>
    <div class="alert alert-success">
        <span data-bind="text: modelData"></span>
    </div>
    <button class="btn btn-primary"data-bind="click: sendRequest">
        Send Request
    </button>
</body>
</html>
```

Within the body element, I have added HTML elements and applied Knockout bindings. I touched on Knockout bindings in Chapter 2, and I return to them in the "Using Knockout" section of this chapter. My emphasis in this section is on how to use jQuery, so I'll skip over the detail and just summarize: the text data binding displays the value of a JavaScript variable called modelData in a span element, like this:

```
...
<span data-bind="text: modelData"></span>
...
```

The text content of the span element will change automatically when the modelData value changes. The other binding I have used is click, which invokes a JavaScript function when the button element it is applied to is clicked.

```
...
<button class="btn btn-primary" data-bind="click: sendRequest">
...
```

The function is called sendRequest, and I defined it—and the modelValue variable—in a JavaScript file called primer.js, for which I added script element in Listing 3-12. I created the primer.js file in the Scripts folder, and Listing 3-13 shows its contents.

Listing 3-13. The Contents of the primer.js File

```
var modelData = ko.observable("(Ready)");

var sendRequest = function () {
    $.ajax("/api/pagesize", {
        type: "GET",
        success: function (data) {
```

```
            modelData("Response: " + data + " bytes");
        }
    });
}

$(document).ready(function () {
    ko.applyBindings();
});
```

The interesting part of the primer.js file—at least for this section of the chapter—is the call to the $.ajax method. To test the example, start the application and click the Send Request button. After a brief pause, the response from the server will be displayed in the browser window, as shown by Figure 3-10.

Figure 3-10. *Sending a Simple Ajax Request*

Understanding the $.ajax Method

The $.ajax method accepts two arguments: the URL that the request will be sent to and a JavaScript object that contains the settings for the request. The URL is expressed relative to the URL of the document that has loaded the JavaScript code, which is why I am able to specify the URL like this:

```
...
$.ajax("/api/pagesize", {
...
```

The URL of the web page is http://localhost:38000/Home/Index, and by specifying a relative URL that starts with a / character, I am specifying that the request be directed to http://localhost:38000/api/pagesize, which is the URL for my web service.

The second argument provides control over how the request is made. The properties of the object correspond to request settings. I have specified the HTTP verb for the request with the type property and a callback function that will be invoked for successful requests with the success property. The argument to the function assigned to the success property is an object that jQuery automatically decodes from the serialized data that the web service sends in the request. The success function that I specified in Listing 3-13 uses the data argument to set the value of the modelData property, which Knockout uses to update the content of the span HTML element.

UNDERSTANDING JSON DATA

JavaScript Object Notation (JSON) has become the de facto data format for web apps. JSON is simple and easy to work with in JavaScript code, which is why it has become so popular and has displaced XML. (The *x* in Ajax stands for XML, but it is a format that is used less and less.)

JSON supports some basic data types, which neatly align with those of JavaScript: Number, String, Boolean, Array, Object, and the special type null. You don't have to work directly with JSON when writing Web API web services or when using jQuery to handle Ajax requests; Web API will automatically encode your data as JSON, and jQuery will automatically decode it. I explain how Web API deals with JSON in Part 2 of this book and demonstrate how to take control of the serialization and deserialization processes.

A lot of configuration properties are available for jQuery, all of which are detailed at http://api.jquery.com/jQuery.ajax. Table 3-1 describes the properties that I use most often in this book to configure the Ajax requests I sent to my web services.

Table 3-1. *The jQuery Ajax Properties Used in This Book*

Name	Description
accepts	This property sets the content types that the client will tell the server it is willing to accept. This is part of a process called *content negotiation*, which I describe in Part 2.
complete	This property registers a callback function that is invoked when the Ajax request is complete, regardless of whether the request was successful or failed.
contentType	This property sets the value of the Content-Type header, which tells the server how the data in the request has been formatted.
data	This property specifies the data that will be sent to the server. jQuery will automatically serialize a JavaScript object to produce a JSON string.
dataType	This property specifies the type of data that the client should expect the web service to return.
error	This property specifies a callback function that is invoked when the Ajax request fails.
headers	This property is set to a JavaScript object used to define headers for the request. The object properties specify the headers to be set.
success	This property registers a callback function that is invoked when the Ajax request succeeds. jQuery deserializes the data sent by the web service and presents the callback function with a JavaScript object.
type	This property specifies the HTTP verb for the Ajax request.

■ **Tip**   jQuery also provides the $.ajaxSetup method that configures all subsequent Ajax requests. I use this method in Chapter 7 to configure client-side authentication for the SportsStore example application. The $.ajaxSetup method uses the same configuration properties as the $.ajax method.

Using Knockout

I use Knockout in this book to create example clients that respond automatically to the data that is returned by web services. There are other libraries and frameworks that perform the same task, including AngularJS, which I use for my most complex projects. Knockout, however, is perfect for simpler projects and has the benefit of being one of the libraries that Microsoft has started including in the ASP.NET example application and templates, giving it a semi-blessed status. In the sections that follow, I show you how I use Knockout in this book.

■ **Tip**   Knockout has more functionality than I describe here. See `http://knockoutjs.com` or my *Pro JavaScript for Web Apps* book for more details.

There are two major Knockout components: the model and the bindings. The model consists of one or more *observable* data items. An observable data item is monitored by Knockout, and when it changes, the new value is used to update the content of HTML elements that have been annotated with the bindings. Bindings are also used to respond to user input and update the model values. You saw a simple example of a model in Listing 3-13, where I defined an observable called `modelData`, like this:

```
...
var modelData = ko.observable("(Ready)");
...
```

I called the `ko.observable` method to set up a new observable and passed the initial value as the method argument. I assigned the result to a JavaScript variable called `modelData`, and in doing so, I created a simple Knockout data model.

Knockout can also create observable arrays, through the use of the `ko.observableArray` method. Here is an example of a model from Chapter 7 that mixes standard observables with observable arrays:

```
...
var customerModel = {
    productCategories: ko.observableArray([]),
    filteredProducts: ko.observableArray([]),
    selectedCategory: ko.observable(null),
    cart: ko.observableArray([]),
    cartTotal: ko.observable(0),
    cartCount: ko.observable(0),
    currentView: ko.observable("list")
}
...
```

Applying the Bindings

Knockout defines a range of bindings. The simplest bindings insert model values into HTML elements, but there are also bindings for generating HTML elements for each item in an array and even responding to user input. Here is an example of a binding from Listing 3-12 that applies a binding to a span element:

```
...
<span data-bind="text: modelData"></span>
...
```

Bindings are applied to HTML elements using the data-bind attribute, the value of which is set to the binding name, followed by a comma, followed by an expression that the binding uses to do its work. In this case, the value of the attribute is text: modelData, meaning that I have applied a binding called text with the expression modelData. Bindings interpret their expressions in different ways, but the effect of this binding is to set the text content of the span element to the value of the modelData variable. Table 3-2 describes the bindings that I have used in this chapter.

Table 3-2. *The Knockout Bindings Used in This Book*

Name	Description
click	This binding is used to invoke functions when an element, typically a button, is clicked. If you just want to invoke the function without arguments, then specify the function name: data-bind="click: myFunction". If you want to provide arguments to the function, then you have to use a different approach, like this: data-bind="click: myFunction.bind($data, "hello"). This will have the effect of invoking the function with a single hello argument because the $data value is not passed to the function. I use the click binding throughout this book to invoke functions that send Ajax requests.
css	This binding is used to assign CSS classes to an element when the expression evaluates as true. The CSS classes are removed from the element when the expression is false. I use this binding to change the style of HTML elements when an Ajax request fails.
foreach	This binding is used to generate HTML elements for each item in an array. The content of the element to which the binding is applied is treated like a template with its own data bindings. The current item is referred to using $data within the template. I use this binding to display data received from web services, usually as tables.
text	This binding sets the text content of an element to the value of the expression. I use this binding throughout the book to display the results obtained from web services.
value	This binding is used with input and select elements and synchronizes an observable value with the contents of the element. I use this binding to obtain user input so that I can send it to web services.
visible	This binding changes the visibility of the element it is applied to. The element is visible if the expression evaluates to true and hidden otherwise. I use this binding to treat sections of the HTML document as views and show only one to the user at a time.

■ **Tip** You can also define JavaScript functions that are invoked when an observable or observable array is changed. I use this feature in Chapter 7 to derive data values from the model so that I have to perform complex calculations only once but display the results several times.

There isn't always a convenient HTML element to which you can apply a Knockout binding. In Chapter 7, I encounter such a problem when creating a complex table layout with the foreach binding and solve it by applying the binding to a specially formatted comment.

Activating the Bindings

Knockout has to process the HTML elements in a document to locate and activate its data bindings. Here are the statements that perform this initialization from Listing 3-13:

```
...
$(document).ready(function () {
    ko.applyBindings();
});
...
```

The initialization is performed by the ko.applyBindings method. I don't want to call the method until the browser has finished loading all of the HTML elements; otherwise, there may be bindings that are not activated. To ensure that all of my bindings are activated, I call the ko.applyBindings method from within a function passed to the jQuery ready function, which I introduced in Chapter 2.

Summary

In this chapter, I described the essential techniques you will need to get the most from this book. I showed you different ways of dealing with asynchronous methods and described how I use jQuery to make Ajax requests and Knockout to create dynamically updating applications. In Chapter 4, I put HTTP web services in context and explain the role of Web API in the ASP.NET world.

CHAPTER 4

■ ■ ■

Understanding HTTP Web Services

In this chapter, I explain the different ways in which ASP.NET Web API can be used to deliver an HTTP web service and the kinds of clients that each arrangement best suits. I build on this foundation to describe the two broad categories of web service that you can create: simple web services (like the one I created in Chapter 2) and RESTful web services, which are more complex but are easier to maintain.

The choice between simple and RESTful web services echoes themes that run through MVC framework development: an initial investment of design and development time that is paid back through a loosely coupled system that is easier to change over time.

To explain RESTful web services, I describe the process for designing and evolving an API that allows a client to consume the service in a loosely coupled way. The result is a description of a RESTful API that may strike you as rather abstract, but don't worry because I back this up with implementation examples in Chapter 5–8, as well as detailed explanations of the ASP.NET Web API features throughout this book.

Understanding ASP.NET Web API

ASP.NET Web API solves a simple problem: it creates services that deliver data from ASP.NET applications to clients over HTTP requests, known as *HTTP web services*. This may sound similar to the MVC framework, but the difference is that MVC usually delivers content that mixes the data with presentation instructions to the client. Figure 4-1 shows the standard arrangement of components in an MVC framework application.

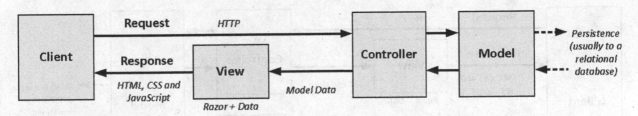

Figure 4-1. *The components in an MVC application*

The MVC framework view combines Razor markup with model data to generate content that can be presented to the user, typically as a combination of HTML, CSS, and JavaScript.

ASP.NET Web API also uses a controller and a model, but it doesn't have views. Instead, it sends just the data, as illustrated in Figure 4-2.

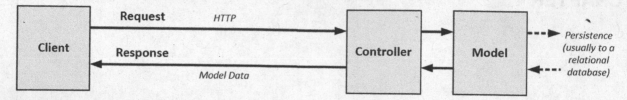

Figure 4-2. *The components in a Web API application*

Sending just the data means that presenting the data to the user becomes the responsibility of the client that made the HTTP request. There are four different types of Web API client, each of which benefits from a data-only service in a different way: *single-page applications*, *native applications*, *shared-model applications*, and *service applications*. I describe each of the client types in the sections that follow.

The decision about which model to use is driven largely by where raw data is processed and combined with presentation elements to show to the user. The presentation need not be HTML; native clients use their own UI toolkits, and service applications may not present the data to a user at all.

Understanding Single-Page Applications

Browser-based web applications can be broken into two broad categories. The first is round-trip applications, which is where every request to the server returns a complete page of HTML content. The other category, *single-page applications*, starts with an HTML document and uses JavaScript to make Ajax requests to the server for additional data or fragments of HTML in order to response to user interaction. In Chapter 2, I created a simple single-page application to introduce you to ASP.NET Web API.

These round-trip and single-page categories are the ends of a spectrum, and most modern web applications fall somewhere in the middle such that some requests return complete HTML documents, while others are just for data.

For most MVC framework developers, single-page applications are the reason that ASP.NET Web API is interesting, allowing an HTTP web service to be used alongside the MVC framework components of an application, and it is this model that I focus on for most of the book. The MVC framework is used to deliver the initial content, which is then supplemented or updated using Ajax requests to an ASP.NET Web API web service, as shown in Figure 4-3.

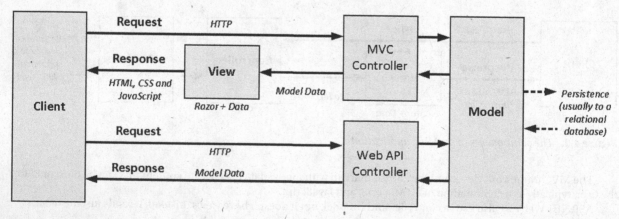

Figure 4-3. *Using MVC and Web API in a single-page application*

The model data is processed in two places: in the view when the initial content for the application is requested from the MVC controller and in the browser when the data is received from the Web API controller. ASP.NET makes it easy to create a data model that is exposed to clients through MVC and Web API controllers, as I demonstrated in Chapter 2.

Understanding Native Applications

The rise of smartphones and tablets means that many applications are delivered as native clients, rather than as HTML content in a browser window. Native applications still require data and perform operations on that data, which is readily supported through Web API. Web API delivers the data, and the native applications are responsible for processing the data they receive and displaying it to the user. Figure 4-4 shows a mix of client types being supported by an ASP.NET application.

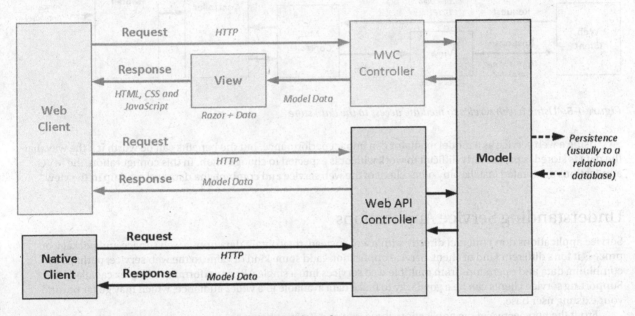

Figure 4-4. Supporting mixed client types in an ASP.NET application

Smartphones and tablets are not the only kinds of native application, and just about any application that can send HTTP requests and process common data formats can consume a web service. Smartphones are the most numerous native clients, especially if you are creating an Internet-facing application, but you can also use Web API to support desktop clients, embedded devices, and smart TVs. I don't describe native applications in this book, but the web services that I create with Web API can easily be consumed by any kind of client.

Understanding Shared-Model Applications

The implicit assumption in Figure 4-4 is that the model state is stored persistently and that all of the applications that need to access the model will do so through the data store, which is typically a database of some kind.

The problem with this approach is that databases are good at managing data but do not have means to consistently enforce features such as authorization or logging in a way that makes sense for the application. For example, it may be possible to log a particular SQL query but not what application function the user was performing that led to the query.

In addition, if there are multiple applications that need to share the model data, it can be difficult to manage schema and data changes without upgrading the database and all of the applications in lock-step, which requires careful planning and testing.

An alternative approach is to use a web service to mediate access to the data store from multiple applications, providing an abstraction from the storage implementation and isolating the applications from changes in the way that data is stored. Figure 4-5 shows this approach.

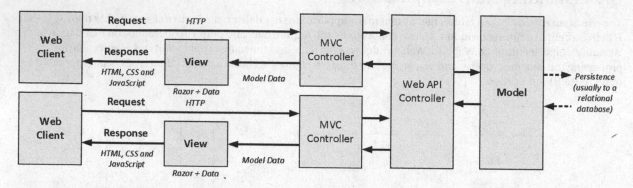

Figure 4-5. *Using a web service to mediate access to the data store*

Using a web service as a model mediator can impact performance, but the benefits can be worth it if the way that the data is stored is particularly difficult to work with or is expected to change often. In this configuration, the MVC applications are treated just like any other client of the web service and combine the data and markup in the view.

Understanding Service Applications

Service applications don't interact directly with users. Instead, they obtain data from a web service and package or process it for a different kind of client. Service applications add some kind of value to the web service, perhaps by combining data and operations from multiple web services into a single API or performing complex calculations. Supporting service clients can be a good way to make data available to a wider audience, which may go far beyond your existing user base.

From the perspective of the application, there is little difference between supporting a native application and a service application; the same HTTP requests are received and processed to retrieve data or update the model, and the way in which the data is processed or presented is not known to the web service.

■ **Tip** You can see a good example at `http://fitbit.com` of an API that reaches a wider audience through service applications. Fitbit sells hardware devices that monitor activity levels and provides a web application that collects the activity data. The data and user information are exposed through an API, which has allowed a substantial ecosystem of other sites and services to thrive. Supporting service clients can be useful if your business model isn't tied to drawing users into your application.

Understanding Simple Web Services

The HTTP web service that I created with ASP.NET Web API in Chapter 2 is what is referred to as a *simple web service* or, to use a term that has more resonance for an MVC framework developer, a *tightly coupled* web service. The tight coupling refers to the fact that the client has to have prior knowledge of how the web service has been designed in order to consume the web service.

As an example of prior knowledge, the client in the PartyInvites application needs to know that new RSVP responses are submitted as POST requests to the /api/rsvp/add URL. There is nothing in the responses sent by the Web API controller to indicate that the /api/rsvp/add URL exists; the client needs to have this information ahead of time. This isn't hard to arrange when the client code is delivered from an MVC framework application because you can embed the information in a view, it becomes more of a problem for native clients of a web service, such as iPhone and Android applications.

As you may expect if you are familiar with the MVC pattern, the problem with tight coupling is that it makes it hard to maintain the application because changes have to be made to the Web API controller and the client JavaScript code at the same time.

It also makes it difficult to use the Web API controller beyond its original purpose because controllers for simple web services tend to offer only action methods for the specific functions that the original client requires. As an example, if I needed to add an administration-type client that allows me to list, edit, and delete guest responses, then I need to extend the functionality of the controller—something that prevents clients from being created without the coordination of the web service developer.

The alternative is to create a web service that doesn't require the client to have any prior knowledge of the web service, which is the essence of what REST is all about. I describe REST and RESTful web services in the next section and demonstrate how ASP.NET Web API can be used to create them, but before I move on, I want to emphasize that you should not dismiss simple web services out of hand.

Despite the problems that arise from tight coupling, simple web services can transform a round-trip MVC framework application to the single-page model with just a few lines of C# and JavaScript code. You saw this in Chapter 2, where I created the following Web API controller.

```
using System.Collections.Generic;
using System.Linq;
using System.Web.Http;
using PartyInvites.Models;

namespace PartyInvites.Controllers {

    public class RsvpController : ApiController {

        [HttpGet]
        public IEnumerable<GuestResponse> Attendees() {
            return Repository.Responses.Where(x => x.WillAttend == true);
        }

        [HttpPost]
        public void Add(GuestResponse response) {
            if (ModelState.IsValid) {
                Repository.Add(response);
            }
        }
    }
}
```

It is hard to beat the level of return for such little investment of effort. Simple web services are perfectly acceptable for situations where you are confident that the only client will be delivered by the MVC framework and you know that the rate of change will be low and not driven by third parties (in other words, you are not trying to create an API that can be consumed by a wider audience outside the scope of the MVC framework application). Table 4-1 summarizes simple web services and the situations in which they can be usefully applied.

Table 4-1. *Putting Simple Web Services in Context*

Question	Answer
What is it?	Simple web services support just the features required for the client of a single application.
When should I use it?	Simple web services are quick to set up and are useful when you don't expect to add additional types of clients or need to significantly enhance the functionality that the existing client delivers.
What do I need to know?	Simple web services are tightly coupled to their clients, which makes it more difficult to add additional types of client or to change existing clients without also modifying the web service and the supporting MVC framework application.

Understanding RESTful Web Services

The most commonly used pattern to create loosely coupled web services is Representational State Transfer (REST). REST is a general-purpose pattern that, when applied to a web service, creates what is known as a *RESTful web service*.

THE DANGER OF DESIGN PATTERNS

Like just about all useful design patterns, REST is the subject of endless arguments about what is really RESTful and what is not. These arguments are a waste of time, and you should ignore them. Patterns are templates that you can customize for your own needs. The goal behind RESTful web services is to ensure that the client and ASP. NET Web API controller are loosely coupled, and only you know which aspects of the REST pattern will help you achieve that goal. I stopped arguing with pattern zealots when I realized that the least-skilled programmers are the ones who shout the loudest. My advice is to focus on delivering good software and borrow from and adapt patterns any way you need to get the job done.

In the sections that follow, I describe how to design a RESTful web service API using the GuestResponse model class that I defined for the PartyInvites application in Chapter 2. As a reminder, Listing 4-1 shows the definition of the model class.

Listing 4-1. The Definition of the GuestResponse Model Class

```
using System.ComponentModel.DataAnnotations;

namespace PartyInvites.Models {
    public class GuestResponse {
        [Required]
        public string Name { get; set; }
        [Required]
```

```
        public string Email { get; set; }
        [Required]
        public bool? WillAttend { get; set; }
    }
}
```

As a reminder, here is how instances of the GuestResponse class are rendered as JSON:

```
[{"Name":"Bob","Email":"bob@example.com","WillAttend":true},
 {"Name":"Alice","Email":"alice@example.com","WillAttend":true},
 {"Name":"Paul","Email":"paul@example.com","WillAttend":true}]
```

I am not going to implement the web service in this chapter; I will just define the API that I need. You can see how I implement a RESTful web service in Chapter 6, where I build the more realistic SportsStore application to show the end-to-end implementation process for working with ASP.NET Web API.

■ **Tip** Although I use JSON throughout this chapter, ASP.NET Web API is capable of generating different data formats to suit different client requirements. See Chapters 11–13 for details.

The reason I don't write the code in this chapter is that I want to focus on the design of an effective and useful web service API free of the details of its implementation. Understanding why RESTful web services are useful is important, not least because they are more complex and complicated to design. As you will learn, decoupling the client from a web service requires more of an investment of time and effort, which is then paid back through increased flexibility and maintainability, much like the initial investment required to lay the foundation for an MVC framework application. Table 4-2 summarizes RESTful web services and the situations in which they can be usefully applied.

Table 4-2. *Putting RESTful Web Services in Context*

Question	Answer
What are they?	RESTful web services are useful for decoupling clients and the web services they consume. They require more design and development effort, but they make it easier to maintain the web service.
When should I use them?	You should use RESTful web services when clients are being developed by third parties or when you expect a high rate of change in the API delivered by the web service.
What do I need to know?	You have several choices about how RESTful you make your web service and, as a consequence, how loosely coupled the client and web service are. The less prior knowledge a client requires to consume a web service, the more RESTful that service is.

Embracing HTTP

The core foundation of RESTful web services is to define operations on the model using a combination of HTTP verbs and unique URLs to refer to individual data objects and collections of those objects.

■ **Tip** The terms *verbs* and *methods* are equivalent when referring to HTTP and can be used interchangeably. I tend to refer to *methods* when I am writing MVC framework views (because the `form` element defines a `method` attribute) and *verbs* when writing web services.

Here is an example of a URL that uniquely represents the RSVP response from a user called Bob (I have left out the part of the URL that specifies the protocol, hostname, and port because all of these are going to be constant for my example):

```
/api/rsvp/bob
```

In a RESTful web service, I use this URL whenever I want to perform an operation on the GuestResponse object that describes Bob's attendance at the party. To tell the web service what kind of operation I want to perform, I make an HTTP request that targets the URL and specify one of the HTTP verbs in the request.

■ **Note** REST is a general-purpose pattern that has found a home in the world of web services, but since this is a book about web services, I am going to treat REST and RESTful web services as being the same thing so that I don't get tied up in making fine-grained distinctions that don't have any real impact on Web API development.

You are already familiar with at least two of the HTTP verbs from their use in the MVC framework: GET and POST. What you might not know is that the HTTP specification contains additional verbs and that, in a RESTful web service, these are used to indicate what kind of operation is being requested on the data object identities by the URL in the request. Table 4-3 shows how combining an HTTP verb with a URL can be used to request that a web service perform an operation. Some operations require the client to send data to the server or the server to send data to the client, and I have included this information in the table.

Table 4-3. Combining HTTP Verbs with URLs to Specify a Web Service API

Verb	URL	Description	Client Sends	Server Sends
GET	/api/rsvp/bob	Gets the data object that represents Bob's RSVP	Nothing	The GuestResponse for Bob
POST	/api/rvsp/bob	Creates a new RSVP object for Bob	The GuestResponse to be saved	The saved GuestResponse object
PUT	/api/rsvp/bob	Updates the existing RSVP for Bob	The modified GuestResponse to be saved	The saved GuestResponse object
DELETE	/api/rsvp/bob	Deletes the RSVP for Bob	Nothing	Nothing

■ **Tip** A web service doesn't have to support all the verbs listed in Table 4-3. It wouldn't make sense for a read-only web service to support the DELETE, POST, and PUT verbs, for example, and you need to implement support only for the verbs you require.

The contents of the table define the web service API, and a client-side developer can use this information to consume the web service. This kind of API embraces HTTP by combining URLs and HTTP verbs, which feels exciting and dynamic and like a definite improvement over URLs derived from arbitrary methods names in a controller class, but the truth is somewhat different because the client and server are still too tightly coupled for comfort. I explain why in the following sections.

USING SAFE AND IDEMPOTENT HTTP VERBS

There is no standard mapping of HTTP verbs to web service operations, although the one I describe in Table 4-3 is common. You can use any HTTP verb that you like for your web services, as long as you understand the importance of the *safe* and *idempotent* HTTP verbs.

Safe verbs have no side effects. The most commonly used safe verb is GET, and when you receive a GET request, you may not perform any action that alters the state of the data model. All you may do is return the data that has been requested and, optionally, perform cross-cutting activities such as logging and caching.

Idempotent verbs, such as PUT and DELETE, are allowed to modify the data model, but multiple requests with the same verb to the same URL should have the same effect as a single request. The practical effect of this is that you should use URLs to uniquely identify resources, rather than relying on the relationship between data items. For example, if you support a URL such as /api/rsvp/first that refers to the first data object in the repository, accepting a DELETE request for that URL should not cause the data items to shuffle so that there is a new "first" object. You must also write your web service so that it doesn't generate an error when receiving multiple requests such as a DELETE request for a data object that has already been removed from the repository.

Be careful with the POST verb; it is not necessarily safe or idempotent, and you have some flexibility about how you respond to multiple requests that target the same URL. Most web services will treat a POST request as a PUT request if there is already a matching data item, but you can choose to create a new object or report an error depending on the needs of your data model.

Adding Data Discovery

Uniquely identifying each data object—more properly known as a *resource* in REST—with a URL is an excellent idea, but it presents a problem: how does the client discover the set of data objects and the URLs that refer to them?

The solution is to create a *collection URL*, which returns all of the data objects in the model. The convention is that the collection of data objects is retrieved using the root URL that identifies individual objects. In my API, this means that the URL /api/rsvp would return all of the data objects in the model. Table 4-4 shows the addition of the collection URL to the web service API.

Table 4-4. *Adding a Collections URL to the Web Service API*

Verb	URL	Description	Client Sends	Server Sends
GET	/api/rsvp/bob	Gets the data object that represents Bob's RSVP	Nothing	The GuestResponse for Bob
POST	/api/rvsp/bob	Creates a new RSVP object for Bob	The GuestResponse to be saved	The saved GuestResponse object
PUT	/api/rsvp/bob	Updates the existing RSVP for Bob	The modified GuestResponse to be saved	The saved GuestResponse object
DELETE	/api/rsvp/bob	Deletes the RSVP for Bob	Nothing	Nothing
GET	**/api/rsvp**	Gets the collection of data objects	Nothing	The collection of all GuestResponse objects in the repository

Filtering the Collection

Most clients don't need to retrieve all of the data in the model, so the convention is to allow clients to narrow the data returned by the collection URL by using query string parameters. For example, to obtain the set of attendees, for which I added a specific action method in Chapter 2, the client would send a GET request to the following URL:

```
/api/rsvp?WillAttend=true
```

The web service can ignore the query string and return all of the data objects in the model, but it is generally a good idea to support this convention so that you are not transferring endless amounts of data that clients don't require and that will be discarded. Table 4-5 shows my revised API.

Table 4-5. *Adding Collections Filtering to the Web Service API*

Verb	URL	Description	Client Sends	Server Sends
GET	/api/rsvp/bob	Gets the data object that represents Bob's RSVP	Nothing	The GuestResponse for Bob
POST	/api/rvsp/bob	Creates a new RSVP object for Bob	The GuestResponse to be saved	The saved GuestResponse object
PUT	/api/rsvp/bob	Updates the existing RSVP for Bob	The modified GuestResponse to be saved	The saved GuestResponse object
DELETE	/api/rsvp/bob	Deletes the RSVP for Bob	Nothing	Nothing
GET	/api/rsvp	Gets the collection of data objects	Nothing	The collection of all GuestResponse objects in the repository
GET	**/api/rsvp?prop=val**	Gets a filtered collection of data objects	Nothing	The collection of all GuestResponse objects in the repository for which the property prop is set to val

---

■ **Tip**   A common variation on this pattern is to build the filter into the URL, rather than relying on the query string. For example, in Chapter 6, I define a web service that returns all of its model objects when the URL `/api/products` is requested. The object that has the unique identifier 100, for example, would be accessed via the URL `/api/products/100`. Web API makes it easy to support both URL formats.

This is an example of what I mean about pragmatism in design patterns—even as I am trying to minimize the amount of prior knowledge that the client requires, I am extending my web service API using a convention that both the client and the server need to understand. There is a balance to be found between client-server coupling and applying sensible optimizations, which differs for each project. There is no universal right approach, and you should use your judgment to decide when following a design pattern doesn't make sense.

Summary

In this chapter, I described the ways in which ASP.NET Web API can be used to deliver web services to a set of different and disparate clients. I also described the two main categories of web services: simple web services, like the one I created in Chapter 2, and RESTful web services, which I demonstrate in the next chapter. I explained that RESTful web services require more design and development effort but produce loosely coupled software systems that are easier to manage and maintain.

This chapter has been a little abstract in nature because I wanted to separate the design of a RESTful web service API from the implementation detail. But don't worry if you have found it hard going because in the next chapter I revert to showing you code examples to implement the concepts that I have described in this chapter.

■ ■ ■

CHAPTER 5

SportsStore: Preparation

In this chapter, I set the foundations for a more realistic project that incorporates all of the key aspects of Web API development and shows them working together. Later chapters zoom into specific features, which is a good way of getting into the detail, but it doesn't provide any end-to-end context.

My application, called SportsStore, will follow the classic approach taken by online stores everywhere. I will create an online product catalog that customers can browse by category and page, a shopping cart where users can add and remove products, and a checkout where customers can enter their shipping details. I will also create an administration area that includes create, read, update, and delete (CRUD) facilities for managing the catalog, and I will protect it so that only logged-in administrators can make changes.

In this chapter, I create the database that contains the product information and configure the ASP.NET identity system so that I can restrict access to administrators in Chapter 6.

If you have read my other books—including *Pro ASP.NET MVC 5* and *Pro AngularJS*—then you will have seen different versions of the SportsStore application. I use it in many of my books to show how key features and functions fit together and to demonstrate different technologies and to show how different development frameworks and toolkits can be used to solve common problems, such as database access and user security.

■ **Note**   The goal of the SportsStore project is to show a more realistic use of Web API, rather than accurately re-creating all of the aspects of an online store—many of which have nothing to do with HTTP web services at all. To that end, I use a simple product database and don't address details such as card payments or order tracking.

This chapter is all preparation, and I don't describe any Web API features. If you are already familiar with how Entity Framework Code First and ASP.NET Identity are set up and configured, you can skip to Chapter 6.

■ **Tip**   You don't have to re-create the code yourself; you can download Visual Studio projects organized for every chapter in this book without charge from Apress.com.

Preparing the Example Project

To begin the process of creating the SportsStore application, I need to create the Visual Studio project and use NuGet to add the packages that I will rely on.

Select New Project from the File menu to open the New Project dialog window. Navigate through the Templates section to select the Visual C# ➤ Web ➤ ASP.NET Web Application template and set the name of the project to SportsStore, as shown in Figure 5-1.

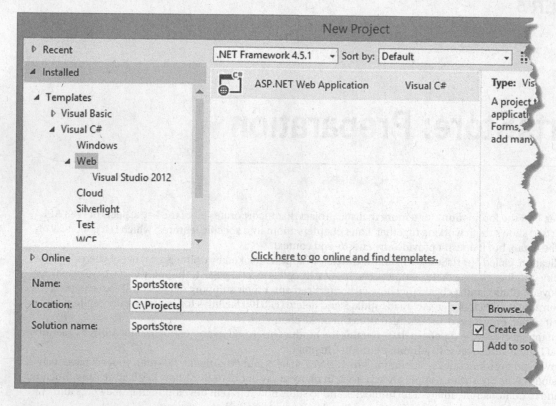

Figure 5-1. *Creating the new project*

Click the OK button to move to the New ASP.NET Project dialog window. Ensure that the Empty option is selected and check the MVC and Web API options, as shown in Figure 5-2. Click the OK button, and Visual Studio will create a new project called SportsStore.

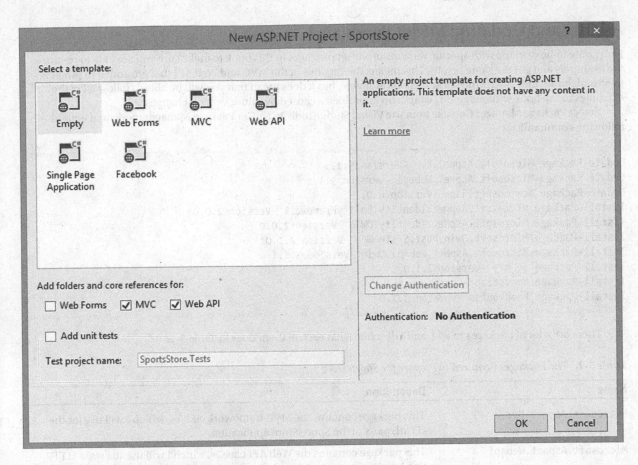

Figure 5-2. Selecting the ASP.NET project type

At this point, the Solution Explorer will have the basic folder structure for a web application, as illustrated by Figure 5-3, and it will soon become populated as I build out the foundations for the application.

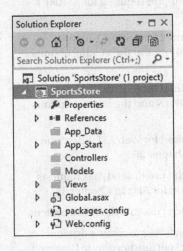

Figure 5-3. The Solution Explorer

Adding and Updating NuGet Packages

I am going to be working with specific versions of NuGet packages in this book to make sure you are able to re-create the examples and get the same results. This means the versions of the MVC and Web API that are added to projects by Visual Studio may not be the latest versions available, but it does mean that you will be able to follow all of the examples in the book without getting caught up in problems caused by minor version changes.

Select Package Manager Console from the Visual Studio Tools ➤ NuGet Package Manager menu and enter the following commands:

```
Update-Package Microsoft.Aspnet.Mvc -version 5.1.1
Update-Package Microsoft.Aspnet.Webapi -version 5.1.1
Update-Package Newtonsoft.Json -version 6.0.1
Install-Package Microsoft.AspNet.Identity.EntityFramework –Version 2.0.0
Install-Package Microsoft.AspNet.Identity.OWIN -Version 2.0.0
Install-Package Microsoft.Owin.Host.SystemWeb -Version 2.1.0
Install-Package Microsoft.AspNet.WebApi.Owin -Version 5.1.1
Install-Package jquery -version 2.1.0
Install-Package bootstrap -version 3.1.1
Install-Package knockoutjs –version 3.1.0
```

There are a lot of packages to add, and I describe what each of them does in Table 5-1.

Table 5-1. *The Packages Required to Prepare for SportsStore*

Name	Description
Microsoft.Aspnet.Mvc	This package contains the MVC framework classes, which I will use for the HTML parts of the SportsStore application.
Microsoft.Aspnet.Webapi	This package contains the Web API classes, which I will use to create HTTP web services.
Newtonsoft.Json	This package contains classes used to serialize and deserialize JSON data. I describe the JSON serialization process in detail in Chapter 13.
Microsoft.AspNet.Identity. EntityFramework	This package contains the Entity Framework support required for ASP.NET Identity, which I use for user management.
Microsoft.AspNet.Identity.OWIN	This package contains the OWIN support required for ASP.NET Identity, which I use for user management. I describe OWIN and the hosting options it supports in Chapter 26.
Microsoft.Owin.Host.SystemWeb	This package contains the OWIN support required for ASP.NET Identity, which I use for user management. I describe OWIN and the hosting options it supports in Chapter 26.
Microsoft.AspNet.WebApi.Owin	This package contains the OWIN support required for Web API. I describe OWIN and the hosting options it supports in Chapter 26.
jquery	This package contains the jQuery library, which I use to send Ajax requests from the browser. I described the jQuery support for Ajax in Chapter 3.
bootstrap	This package contains the Bootstrap library, which I use to style HTML content.
knockoutjs	This package contains the Knockout package, which I use to create a dynamic client-side application. I described the basic Knockout functionality in Chapter 3.

You can create applications that consist of just web services created with Web API, in which case you would not need many of the packages that I have listed in the table. But Web API is rarely used in isolation, and most applications need to create a client, deliver HTML and JavaScript content, and apply some sort of security. As you will see, creating web services with Web API is relatively simple; it is the integration of those web services into a wider application that takes time, skill, and effort.

Creating a Prep Controller

I need to test the preparations that I made for the SportsStore application. I don't want to get into Web API itself prematurely, so I am going to use a simple MVC framework controller to generate some basic diagnostic web pages. I right-clicked the Controllers folder, selected Add ➤ Controller, picked the MVC 5 Controller – Empty template, and clicked the Add button. I set the controller name to PrepController in the Add Controller dialog box and clicked the Add button, which caused Visual Studio to create the Controllers/PrepController.cs class file, the contents of which are shown in Listing 5-1.

Listing 5-1. The Contents of the **PrepController.cs** File

```
using System;
using System.Collections.Generic;
using System.Linq;
using System.Web;
using System.Web.Mvc;

namespace SportsStore.Controllers {

    public class PrepController : Controller {

        public ActionResult Index() {
            return View();
        }
    }
}
```

This is the default content, as created by Visual Studio, but I will add action methods (and views for them to render) as I build out the foundation for the SportsStore application.

Creating a Razor Layout

Although this book is about Web API, I use the MVC framework to generate the HTML content that creates the browser-based client. To make sure I generate consistent HTML that contains all the JavaScript files I need, I created the Views/Shared folder and added a file called _Layout.cshtml to it, which I then used to create the layout shown in Listing 5-2. I will use this layout for the views I create throughout the SportsStore application.

Listing 5-2. The Content of the _Layout.cshtml File

```
<!DOCTYPE html>
<html>
<head>
    <meta name="viewport" content="width=device-width" />
    <script src="~/Scripts/jquery-2.1.0.min.js"></script>
    <script src="~/Scripts/knockout-3.1.0.js"></script>
```

```
    <link href="~/Content/bootstrap.css" rel="stylesheet" />
    <link href="~/Content/bootstrap-theme.css" rel="stylesheet" />
    <title>SportsStore</title>
    <style>
        body { padding-top: 10px; }
    </style>
    @RenderSection("Scripts", false)
</head>
<body class="container">
    @RenderBody()
</body>
</html>
```

■ **Tip** The easiest way to create the view is to add the Views/Shared folder, right-click it, and select Add ➤ MVC 5 Layout Page (Razor). Enter _Layout.cshtml as the file name and click the OK button, and Visual Studio will create and open the layout file.

Creating the OWIN Startup Class

The ASP.NET Identity packages look for a configuration class when the application starts. I will explain the role of this class in the "Configuring ASP.NET Identity" section, but I am going to define it here so that the SportsStore application will start without errors even though I won't be setting up user accounts immediately. Listing 5-3 shows the content of the IdentityConfig.cs file, which I added to the App_Start folder.

Listing 5-3. The Contents of the IdentityConfig.cs File

```
using Microsoft.Owin;
using Owin;

[assembly: OwinStartup(typeof(SportsStore.IdentityConfig))]

namespace SportsStore {
    public class IdentityConfig {
        public void Configuration(IAppBuilder app) {}
    }
}
```

The important part of this file is the OwinStartup attribute, which specifies that the SportsStore.IdentityConfig class should be used for configuration. I'll return to this class when I configure ASP.NET Identity later in the chapter.

■ **Tip** When Visual Studio adds the outline for the class to the new file, it sets the namespace to SportsStore.App_Start, reflecting the location of the file. The convention is to define configuration classes in the top-level namespace of the project, which is why I changed the namespace to SportsStore.

Setting the TCP Port

I will be building the web services part of the SportsStore application before I create an HTML/JavaScript client, and that means I will have to test URLs directly using the browser and the Postman tool. To make life easier, I am going to change the TCP port that the IIS Express server uses to listen to requests to a value that is easy to remember. IIS Express is a cut-down version of the Internet Information Services (IIS) product that is traditionally used to host ASP. NET applications and is included with Visual Studio so you can run and test applications during development.

■ **Tip** IIS is no longer the only choice for deploying ASP.NET applications. In Chapter 8, I demonstrate how to deploy the SportsStore application to the Microsoft Azure cloud service, and in Chapter 26, I describe one additional hosting option for Web API applications.

Select SportsStore Properties from the Visual Studio Project menu and click the Web button on the left side of the screen. In the Servers section, change the Project Url value as follows:

```
http://localhost:6100
```

Click the Create Virtual Directory button and close the settings document. IIS Express will listen for HTTP requests on port 6100 when the application is running.

Creating the Product and Order Models

At the heart of the SportsStore application is the database that stores details of the products that are available for sale and the orders that have been placed. Web API relies on model classes in just the same way as the MVC framework, and the model classes I create in this chapter will be used by both frameworks.

The glue that will connect the model classes to the database is the Entity Framework (EF), and I will create the database by using the Code First feature, which uses model objects to create the database schema. In the sections that follow, I'll create the model classes and use EF Code First to set up the database.

Defining the Model Classes

My starting point is to define the model class that I will use to represent each product. I added a class file called `Product.cs` to the `Models` folder and used it to define the class shown in Listing 5-4.

Listing 5-4. The Contents of the Product.cs File

```
namespace SportsStore.Models {

    public class Product {
        public int Id { get; set; }
        public string Name { get; set; }
        public string Description { get; set; }
        public decimal Price { get; set; }
        public string Category { get; set; }
    }
}
```

This is a simple class that describes a basic description of a product. A real online store would have a more complex product model, of course, but the Product class shown in Listing 5-4 is sufficient for this book because I don't need to get into the details of suppliers, inventory levels, returns, and all of the other issues that would have to be addressed for a real business.

I am also going to store orders that customers place. Listing 5-5 shows the contents of the Order.cs file, which I added to the Models folder.

Listing 5-5. The Contents of the Order.cs File

```
using System.Collections.Generic;

namespace SportsStore.Models {
    public class Order {

        public int Id { get; set; }
        public string Customer { get; set; }
        public decimal TotalCost { get; set; }
        public ICollection<OrderLine> Lines { get; set; }
    }

    public class OrderLine {
        public int Id { get; set; }
        public int Count { get; set; }

        public int ProductId { get; set; }
        public int OrderId { get; set; }

        public Product Product { get; set; }
        public Order Order { get; set; }
    }
}
```

The Order class defines Id, Customer, and TotalCost properties, which are simple types. The Lines property is an ICollection<OrderLine> object, which is a signal to the Entity Framework that there is a relationship between the Order and OrderLine classes. I will use the OrderLine class to represent an individual product selection, and the way I have defined the OrderLine class allows me to take advantage of some clever EF Code First features.

EF Code First will recognize that these two properties are to be used as foreign keys to reference Product and Order objects:

```
...
public int ProductId { get; set; }
public int OrderId { get; set; }
...
```

EF will recognize these as navigation properties:

```
...
public Product Product { get; set; }
public Order Order { get; set; }
...
```

Navigation properties allow for navigation around the data model without having to request separate objects from the database. I'll configure their use when I create the classes that will manage the database in the next section.

Creating the Repository Classes

The *repository pattern* allows the complexity of how model objects are stored and retrieved to be isolated from the rest of the application. In the sections that follow, I will define the interface that describes the repository, create the database implementation classes, and then use them to define a repository class that implements the interface.

■ **Caution**   These classes are interdependent, and you won't be able to compile and run the project until you have created all of them.

Defining the Repository Interface

Listing 5-6 shows the contents of the IRepository.cs file, which I added to the Models folder and used to define a repository interface. This is the interface that I will implement shortly to provide access to data through the Entity Framework.

Listing 5-6. The Contents of the IRepository.cs File

```
using System.Collections.Generic;
using System.Threading.Tasks;

namespace SportsStore.Models {

    public interface IRepository {

        IEnumerable<Product> Products { get; }
        Task<int> SaveProductAsync(Product product);
        Task<Product> DeleteProductAsync(int productID);

        IEnumerable<Order> Orders { get; }
        Task<int> SaveOrderAsync(Order order);
        Task<Order> DeleteOrderAsync(int orderID);
    }
}
```

The Products and Orders properties provide access to all of the Product and Order objects in the repository, and the methods that I have defined—SaveProductAsync, DeleteProductAsync, SaveOrderAsync, and DeleteOrderAsync—will allow me to store and remove objects from the model.

Creating the Database Context and Initializer Classes

The database context class provides the link between the application and the database, and the initializer specifies when the schema will be created and provides the initial data added to the database when it is created. Listing 5-7 shows the contents of the ProductDbContext.cs file, which I added to the Models folder.

Listing 5-7. *The Contents of the ProductDbContext.cs File*

```
using System;
using System.Collections.Generic;
using System.Data.Entity;
using System.Linq;
using System.Web;

namespace SportsStore.Models {

    public class ProductDbContext : DbContext {

        public ProductDbContext() : base("SportsStoreDb") {
            Database.SetInitializer<ProductDbContext>(new ProductDbInitializer());
        }

        public DbSet<Product> Products { get; set; }
        public DbSet<Order> Orders { get; set; }
        public DbSet<OrderLine> OrderLines { get; set; }
    }
}
```

The ProductDbContext class is derived from DbContext, which is the Entity Framework class that does all the heavy lifting in accessing the database and translating C# model objects to and from SQL rows. The Products, Orders, and OrderLines properties return strongly typed DbSet objects, which provide access to the data in the database, expressed as a collection of model objects.

The constructor for the ProductDbContext class calls the base constructor, like this:

```
...
public ProductDbContext() : base("SportsStoreDb") {
...
```

The argument passed to the base constructor is the name of the connection string that is used to create the database. As you will see, when using EF Code First, I don't have to create a connection string in the Web.config file, but the name I have specified—SportsStoreDb—will be important when I deploy the application in Chapter 8.

Within the constructor, I register the initializer class, as follows:

```
...
public ProductDbContext() : base("SportsStoreDb") {
    Database.SetInitializer<ProductDbContext>(new ProductDbInitializer());
}
...
```

This statement specifies that the ProductDbInitializer class will be used to initialize the database. To create the initializer, I added a ProductDbInitializer.cs file to the Models folder and defined the class shown in Listing 5-8.

Listing 5-8. The Contents of the ProductDbInitializer.cs File

```csharp
using System.Collections.Generic;
using System.Data.Entity;

namespace SportsStore.Models {

    public class ProductDbInitializer : DropCreateDatabaseAlways<ProductDbContext> {

        protected override void Seed(ProductDbContext context) {

            new List<Product> {
                new Product() { Name = "Kayak", Description = "A boat for one person",
                    Category = "Watersports", Price = 275m },
                new Product() { Name = "Lifejacket",
                    Description = "Protective and fashionable",
                    Category = "Watersports", Price = 48.95m },
                new Product() { Name = "Soccer Ball",
                    Description = "FIFA-approved size and weight",
                    Category = "Soccer", Price = 19.50m },
                new Product() {
                    Name = "Corner Flags",
                    Description = "Give your playing field a professional touch",
                    Category = "Soccer", Price = 34.95m },
                new Product() { Name = "Stadium",
                    Description = "Flat-packed 35,000-seat stadium",
                    Category = "Soccer", Price = 79500m },
                new Product() { Name = "Thinking Cap",
                    Description = "Improve your brain efficiency by 75%",
                    Category = "Chess", Price = 16m },
                new Product() { Name = "Unsteady Chair",
                    Description = "Secretly give your opponent a disadvantage",
                    Category = "Chess", Price = 29.95m },
                new Product() { Name = "Human Chess Board",
                    Description = "A fun game for the family",
                    Category = "Chess", Price = 75m },
                new Product() { Name = "Bling-Bling King",
                    Description = "Gold-plated, diamond-studded King",
                    Category = "Chess", Price = 1200m },
            }.ForEach(product => context.Products.Add(product));

            context.SaveChanges();

            new List<Order> {
                new Order() { Customer = "Alice Smith", TotalCost = 68.45m,
                    Lines = new List<OrderLine> {
                        new OrderLine() { ProductId = 2, Count = 2},
                        new OrderLine() { ProductId = 3, Count = 1},
                    }},
                new Order() { Customer = "Peter Jones", TotalCost = 79791m,
                    Lines = new List<OrderLine> {
                        new OrderLine() { ProductId = 5, Count = 1},
```

```
                            new OrderLine() { ProductId = 6, Count = 3},
                            new OrderLine() { ProductId = 1, Count = 3},
                }}
            }.ForEach(order => context.Orders.Add(order));

            context.SaveChanges();
        }
    }
}
```

Database initializers are derived from one of three base classes, which determine when the database contents are dropped and the schema is re-created. Table 5-2 describes the classes available, where T is the type of the database context class, which is ProductDbContext for the SportsStore application.

Table 5-2. *The Database Initializer Base Classes*

Name	Description
DropCreateDatabaseAlways<T>	The database is dropped and re-created every time the database context is initialized.
DropCreateDatabaseIfModelChanges<T>	The database is dropped and re-created when any of the model classes are changed.
CreateDatabaseIfNotExists<T>	The database is created only if it does not already exist.

I have used the DropCreateDatabaseAlways<T> base class, which means that the SportsStore database will be dropped and re-created every time the application starts. This is useful during the early stages of development because it allows me to make changes to the contents of the database and then reset them by simply restarting the application. I will change the base class for the initializer before I deploy the application in Chapter 8.

■ **Caution**　Do not deploy an application using the DropCreateDatabaseAlways class because all of your data will be lost each time the application is restarted.

I want to populate the database when it is created with some useful data, which I do by overriding the Seed method. I create a set of Product, Order, and OrderList objects and store them in the database using the ProductDbContext argument. Since my database will be reset each time, having some default data helps in the early stages of development, where I like to write small amounts of code and test their effect.

Defining the Repository Class

The final step in creating the repository is to create the repository class, which will implement the IRepository interface and use the Entity Framework context classes to provide the application with data. Listing 5-9 shows the contents of the ProductRepository.cs file, which I added to the Models folder.

Listing 5-9. The Contents of the ProductRepository.cs File

```
using System.Collections.Generic;
using System.Threading.Tasks;

namespace SportsStore.Models {

    public class ProductRepository : IRepository {
        private ProductDbContext context = new ProductDbContext();


        public IEnumerable<Product> Products {
            get { return context.Products; }
        }

        public async Task<int> SaveProductAsync(Product product) {
            if (product.Id == 0) {
                context.Products.Add(product);
            } else {
                Product dbEntry = context.Products.Find(product.Id);
                if (dbEntry != null) {
                    dbEntry.Name = product.Name;
                    dbEntry.Description = product.Description;
                    dbEntry.Price = product.Price;
                    dbEntry.Category = product.Category;
                }
            }
            return await context.SaveChangesAsync();
        }

        public async Task<Product> DeleteProductAsync(int productID) {
            Product dbEntry = context.Products.Find(productID);
            if (dbEntry != null) {
                context.Products.Remove(dbEntry);
            }
            await context.SaveChangesAsync();
            return dbEntry;
        }

        public IEnumerable<Order> Orders {
            get { return context.Orders.Include("Lines").Include("Lines.Product"); }
        }

        public async Task<int> SaveOrderAsync(Order order) {
            if (order.Id == 0) {
                context.Orders.Add(order);
            }
            return await context.SaveChangesAsync();
        }

        public async Task<Order> DeleteOrderAsync(int orderID) {
            Order dbEntry = context.Orders.Find(orderID);
```

```
            if (dbEntry != null) {
                context.Orders.Remove(dbEntry);
            }
            await context.SaveChangesAsync();
            return dbEntry;
        }
    }
}
```

This is the class that controllers will call to retrieve model data and store new objects in the database. The Products and Orders properties return a collection of model objects from the database context and the implementations of the SaveProductAsync, DeleteProductAsync, SaveOrderAsync, and DeleteOrderAsync methods use the database context to modify the data store.

■ **Note** I have added support for modifying and saving Product objects, but only for saving Order objects; I am not going to allow SportsStore orders to be modified once they are saved.

Testing the Repository

To test the repository, I am going to add some simple action methods to the Prep controller I created at the start of the chapter so that I can read, save, and delete model objects, as shown in Listing 5-10.

Listing 5-10. Adding Action Methods in the PrepController.cs File

```
using System.Threading.Tasks;
using System.Web.Mvc;
using SportsStore.Models;

namespace SportsStore.Controllers {

    public class PrepController : Controller {
        IRepository repo;

        public PrepController() {
            repo = new ProductRepository();
        }

        public ActionResult Index() {
            return View(repo.Products);
        }

        public async Task<ActionResult> DeleteProduct(int id) {
            await repo.DeleteProductAsync(id);
            return RedirectToAction("Index");
        }

        public async Task<ActionResult> SaveProduct(Product product) {
            await repo.SaveProductAsync(product);
            return RedirectToAction("Index");
        }
```

```
        public ActionResult Orders() {
            return View(repo.Orders);
        }

        public async Task<ActionResult> DeleteOrder(int id) {
            await repo.DeleteOrderAsync(id);
            return RedirectToAction("Orders");
        }

        public async Task<ActionResult> SaveOrder(Order order) {
            await repo.SaveOrderAsync(order);
            return RedirectToAction("Orders");
        }
    }
}
```

These are standard MVC framework actions that operate on the repository and pass data objects to Razor views so they can be rendered as HTML and sent to a browser. I need two views to test the repository: one for testing products and one for testing orders. Listing 5-11 shows the contents of the Index.cshtml file, which I added to the /Views/Prep folder.

■ **Tip**   Notice that I instantiate the ProductRepository class directly. This is poor practice in real projects, and dependency injection (DI) should be used instead. I explain how Web API handled DI in Chapter 10, but I don't want to get distracted by the MVC framework, which works in a different way. See my *Pro ASP.NET MVC 5* book for details if you are unfamiliar with DI within an MVC framework application.

Listing 5-11. The Contents of the Index.cshtml File

```
@model IEnumerable<SportsStore.Models.Product>

<div class="panel panel-primary">
    <div class="panel-heading">Products</div>
    <table class="table table-striped">
        <tr><th>ID</th><th>Name</th><th>Category</th><th>Price</th></tr>
        @foreach (var p in Model) {
            <tr>
                <td>@p.Id</td><td>@p.Name</td><td>@p.Category</td><td>@p.Price</td>
            </tr>
        }
    </table>
</div>

@using(Html.BeginForm("SaveProduct", "Prep")) {
    <input type="hidden" name="Name" value="Zippy Running Shoes" />
    <input type="hidden" name="Category" value="Running" />
    <input type="hidden" name="Description" value="Set a new Record Time" />
    <input type="hidden" name="Price" value="159.99" />

    <button class="btn btn-primary" type="submit">Create</button>
    <a href="/prep/deleteproduct/2" class="btn btn-primary">Delete</a>
}
```

The view generates a Bootstrap-formatted table element that contains details of the Product objects contained in the repository. I have also added a Create button that invokes the SaveProduct action to save a new Product to the repository and a Delete button that invokes the DeleteProduct action to remove the Product whose Id is 2. (The Create and Delete buttons use hardwired values, so once you have clicked them, you will need to restart the application to reset the database; otherwise, the Delete operation will fail, and the Create operation will create a duplicate product.)

To test the repository support for products, start the application by selecting Start Debugging from the Visual Studio Debug menu and use the browser to navigate to the /Prep/Index URL. You will see a list of the products available, as shown in Figure 5-4, and can click the buttons to check that changes can be made to the database.

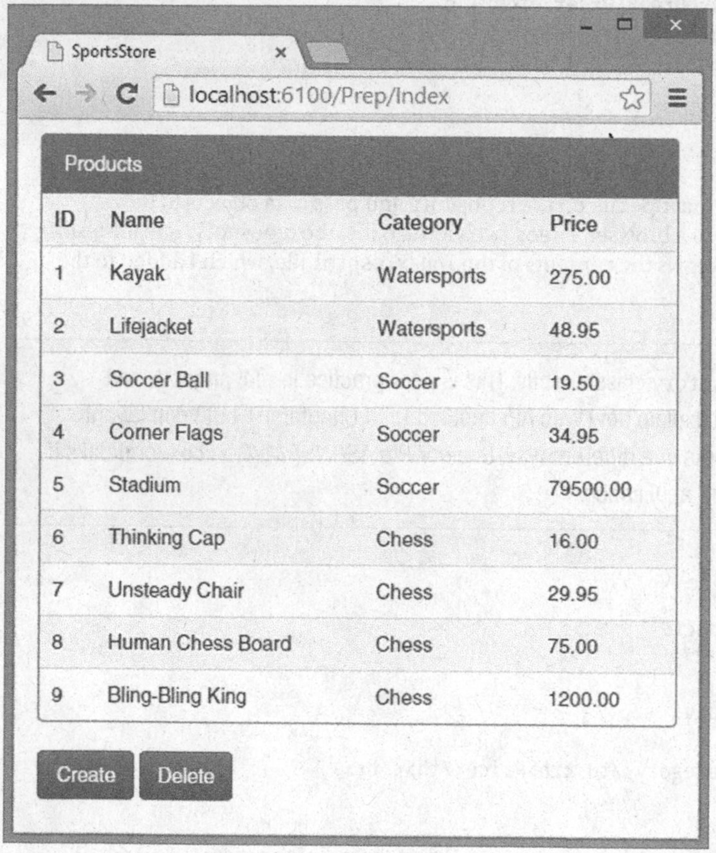

Figure 5-4. *Testing the repository for products*

■ **Tip** The data that is displayed is created in the Seed method of the database initializer class, which I defined in Listing 5-8. Don't forget that, at the moment, the data in the database is reset every time the application is started.

■ **Caution** The database isn't initialized and populated until the database context class is instantiated. This means you won't see any database, schema, or data if you are using a tool like SQL Server Management Studio or the Visual Studio SQL Server Object Explorer until after the /Prep/Index or /Prep/Orders URL has been requested.

The second view I need to create will allow me to perform a similar test on the repository support for Order objects. Listing 5-12 shows the contents of the Orders.cshtml file, which I added to the Views/Prep folder.

Listing 5-12. The Contents of the Orders.cshtml File

```
@model IEnumerable<SportsStore.Models.Order>

<div class="panel panel-primary">
    <div class="panel-heading">
        Orders
    </div>
    <table class="table table-striped">
        <tr>
            <th>ID</th>
            <th>Customer</th>
            <th colspan="3"></th>
            <th>Total Cost</th>
        </tr>
        @foreach (var o in Model) {
            <tr>
                <td>@o.Id</td>
                <td>@o.Customer</td>
                <td colspan="3"></td>
                <td>@string.Format("{0:c}", o.TotalCost)</td>
            </tr>
            <tr>
                <th colspan="2"></th>
                <th>Product</th>
                <th>Quantity</th>
                <th>Price</th>
                <th></th>
            </tr>
            foreach (var ol in o.Lines) {
                <tr>
                    <td colspan="2"></td>
                    <td>@ol.Product.Name</td>
                    <td>@ol.Count</td>
                    <td>@string.Format("{0:c}", ol.Product.Price)</td>
                    <td></td>
                </tr>
            }
        }
    </table>
</div>

@using (Html.BeginForm("SaveOrder", "Prep")) {
    <input type="hidden" name="Customer" value="John Poet" />
    <input type="hidden" name="TotalCost" value="91" />
    <input type="hidden" name="lines[0].productid" value="6" />
    <input type="hidden" name="lines[0].count" value="1" />
```

```
<input type="hidden" name="lines[1].productid" value="8" />
<input type="hidden" name="lines[1].count" value="1" />

<button class="btn btn-primary" type="submit">Create</button>
<a href="/prep/deleteorder/2" class="btn btn-primary">Delete</a>
}
```

This view is more complex because I need to deal with the OrderLine objects that are associated with each Order. To test the repository, start the application and navigate to the /Prep/Orders URL.

Checking the Database Schema

It is worth taking a moment to reflect how I created the SportsStore database. I defined my model classes and then defined the Entity Framework context and initializer classes that operate on them. Finally, I implemented my repository interface to act as the bridge between the application and the Entity Framework.

I didn't have to create the database or define its schema. These tasks were performed automatically based on the structure of the model classes, following a set of well-defined conventions, which you can learn about here: http://msdn.microsoft.com/data/ef.aspx. Figure 5-5 shows a diagram of the schema that Entity Framework created for me, which I created using the SQL Server Management Studio tool (which is a free download from Microsoft).

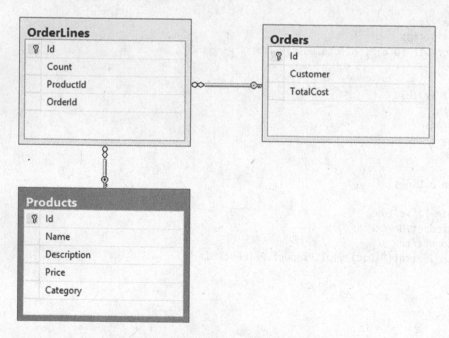

Figure 5-5. *The structure of the SportsStore Products and Orders databases*

This is, admittedly, a simple schema, and using Entity Framework Code First is no substitute for a professional data architect on complex projects, but it is an excellent tool for getting started and is entirely sufficient for simple databases.

Configuring ASP.NET Identity

ASP.NET Identity is the user management system for ASP.NET applications and has replaced the Membership system that Microsoft provided for the last few years. Identity is more flexible, is easier to extend, and relies on the same Entity Framework Code First features that I used in the previous section to set up the product database. In the sections that follow, I'll create a simple ASP.NET Identity system that will allow me to authenticate users, check the membership of roles, and restrict some SportsStore features to administration users.

■ **Note** I need only a simple ASP.NET Identity configuration to authenticate users and authorize access to the SportsStore web services. The Identity system has many features that go well beyond what I need for this book, including the ability to authenticate users through third parties (including Facebook, Twitter, and Google) and the ability to authorize users based on *claims*, which allows external data to be taken into consideration. I describe both features in my *Pro ASP. NET 5 Platform* book, which is published by Apress.

Defining the User and Role Classes

The starting point when working with Identity is to create the class that will represent a user, known as the *user class*. This is a key part of how Identity works because it allows you to define custom properties that can be used to store application-specific data. I created the `Infrastructure/Identity` folder in the Solution Explorer and added the `StoreUser.cs` file, the contents of which are shown in Listing 5-13.

Listing 5-13. The Contents of the StoreUser.cs File

```
using Microsoft.AspNet.Identity.EntityFramework;

namespace SportsStore.Infrastructure.Identity {

    public class StoreUser : IdentityUser {
        // application-specific properties go here
    }
}
```

User classes are derived from the `IdentityUser` class, which is defined in the `Microsoft.AspNet.Identity.EntityFramework` namespace. The user class can be defined with application-specific properties that correspond to the user profile features of the old ASP.NET Membership system and which are added automatically to the database schema when it is created. I am going to create a basic Identity configuration and don't need any custom properties, so I just have to create a class that is derived from `IdentityUser` but adds no new properties of methods. My `StoreUser` class inherits a number of useful properties, however, which I have described in Table 5-3. There are other properties, but these are the ones I need for the SportsStore application.

Table 5-3. Useful Properties Inherited from the IdentityUser Class

Name	Description
Email	Returns the e-mail address of the user
Id	Returns the unique ID of the user
Roles	Returns a collection containing the roles to which the user has been assigned
UserName	Returns the name of the user

I also need to define a class that will represent a role. Once again, Identity provides a base class—called IdentityRole—from which an application-specific role class is derived. Listing 5-14 shows the contents of the StoreRole.cs file, which I added to the Infrastructure/Identity folder.

Listing 5-14. The Contents of the StoreRole.cs File

```
using Microsoft.AspNet.Identity.EntityFramework;

namespace SportsStore.Infrastructure.Identity {
    public class StoreRole : IdentityRole {

        public StoreRole() : base() { }
        public StoreRole(string name) : base(name) { }
    }
}
```

I don't have any customizations to make for the SportsStore application, so the SportsStore class is derived from IdentityRole but doesn't add any additional properties.

Creating the Database Context Classes

The next step is to create Entity Framework context classes that will be used to manage the storage of user and role records in the database. Listing 5-15 shows the contents of the StoreIdentityDbContext.cs file, which I added to the Infrastructure/Identity folder.

Listing 5-15. The Contents of the StoreIdentityDbContext.cs File

```
using Microsoft.AspNet.Identity.EntityFramework;
using System.Data.Entity;

namespace SportsStore.Infrastructure.Identity {

    public class StoreIdentityDbContext : IdentityDbContext<StoreUser> {

        public StoreIdentityDbContext() : base("SportsStoreIdentityDb") {
            Database.SetInitializer<StoreIdentityDbContext>(new
                StoreIdentityDbInitializer());
        }

        public static StoreIdentityDbContext Create() {
            return new StoreIdentityDbContext();
        }
    }
}
```

This is similar to the context class I created for the products database, but there are a couple of important differences. First, the class is derived from IdentityDbContext and not DbContext, which is why I don't need to define any properties to expose the data in the database—everything is provided by the base class.

The second difference is that I have defined a Create method. Identity uses a convention of instantiating the classes it needs through static methods that are specified in the configuration file, and the Create method performs that task.

■ **Tip** The StoreIdentityDbContext constructor calls the base class constructor with a string argument whose value is SportsStoreIdentityDb. This string specifies the connection string used for the database. I will need this name when I deploy the SportsStore application in Chapter 8, but I don't need to create the database explicitly at the moment because the default setting is to create the database using LocalDb, which is a zero-configuration edition of SQL Server included with Visual Studio specifically intended to make it easy for developers to work with databases.

The constructor for the StoreIdentityDbContext class registers an initializer class that I use to specify the initial data for the database and to control when the database will be dropped and re-created. Listing 5-16 shows the contents of the StoreIdentityDbInitializer.cs file, which I added to the Infrastructure/Identity folder.

Listing 5-16. The Contents of the StoreIdentityDbInitializer.cs File

```
using System;
using System.Collections.Generic;
using System.Data.Entity;
using System.Linq;
using System.Web;
using Microsoft.AspNet.Identity.EntityFramework;
using Microsoft.AspNet.Identity;

namespace SportsStore.Infrastructure.Identity {
    public class StoreIdentityDbInitializer :
        CreateDatabaseIfNotExists<StoreIdentityDbContext> {

        protected override void Seed(StoreIdentityDbContext context) {

            StoreUserManager userMgr =
                new StoreUserManager(new UserStore<StoreUser>(context));
            StoreRoleManager roleMgr =
                new StoreRoleManager(new RoleStore<StoreRole>(context));

            string roleName = "Administrators";
            string userName = "Admin";
            string password = "secret";
            string email = "admin@example.com";

            if (!roleMgr.RoleExists(roleName)) {
                roleMgr.Create(new StoreRole(roleName));
            }

            StoreUser user = userMgr.FindByName(userName);
            if (user == null) {
                userMgr.Create(new StoreUser {
                    UserName = userName, Email = email
                }, password);
                user = userMgr.FindByName(userName);
            }
```

```
            if (!userMgr.IsInRole(user.Id, roleName)) {
                userMgr.AddToRole(user.Id, roleName);
            }

            base.Seed(context);
        }
    }
}
```

I have set the base class for the initializer to CreateDatabaseIfNotExists, which means that, as I described in Table 5-2, the schema will be created only if it doesn't already exist in the database. It is especially important not to drop and re-create the database for user data because it will usually contain accounts, preferences, passwords, and other profile data that cannot be reseeded. For the SportsStore application, it doesn't really matter because the Seed method creates the only user account that will be used and for which the password is fixed.

Creating the Manager Classes

In the database initializer class shown in Listing 5-16, I used the StoreUserManager and StoreRoleManager classes to check whether the database contained the administration user and role and created them if needed. The StoreUserManager class is used to perform operations on StoreUser objects. I added a StoreUserManager.cs file to the Infrastructure/Identity folder and used it to define the class shown in Listing 5-17.

Listing 5-17. The Contents of the StoreUserManager.cs File

```
using Microsoft.AspNet.Identity;
using Microsoft.AspNet.Identity.EntityFramework;
using Microsoft.AspNet.Identity.Owin;
using Microsoft.Owin;

namespace SportsStore.Infrastructure.Identity {
    public class StoreUserManager : UserManager<StoreUser> {

        public StoreUserManager(IUserStore<StoreUser> store)
            : base(store) {}

        public static StoreUserManager Create(
                IdentityFactoryOptions<StoreUserManager> options,
                IOwinContext context) {

            StoreIdentityDbContext dbContext = context.Get<StoreIdentityDbContext>();
            StoreUserManager manager =
                new StoreUserManager(new UserStore<StoreUser>(dbContext));
            return manager;
        }
    }
}
```

The base class is UserManager, which provides the methods and properties required for common user management tasks, as described in Table 5-4. I don't need any application-specific functionality for the SportsStore application, but I do have to follow two important patterns. The first is that the constructor to the StoreUserManager class is passed an IUserStore<StoreUser> parameter, which is used to access user data, and it is important to pass this on to the base constructor so that the class is initialized.

Table 5-4. Some of the Members Defined by the UserManager<T> Class

Name	Description
Create(user, pass)	Creates a new user with the specified password. I use this method to create the administration user when seeding the database, as shown in Listing 5-16.
Find(user, pass)	Locates the user account with the specific password. This method will return a result only if there is a user account and the provided password matches the one stored in the database. This method is used to perform authentication, and I use it in the "Testing ASP. NET Identity" section.
FindByName(name)	Locates the user with the specified name and returns null if there is no such user.
IsInRole(user, role)	Returns true if the specified user has been assigned to the specified role.
Users	Returns an enumeration of the user objects stored by the Identity system.

The second pattern is to define a static Create class, which will be called by ASP.NET Identity when it requires an instance of the StoreUserManager class. One of the parameters that is passed to the Create method is an IOwinContext object, through which I can obtain instances of the other classes I have defined. I use the strongly typed Get method to get an instance of the StoreIdentityDbContext class, like this:

```
...
StoreIdentityDbContext dbContext = context.Get<StoreIdentityDbContext>();
...
```

This has the effect of instantiating the context class and initializing the database and gives me the instance I require to call the StoreUserManager constructor.

■ **Tip** All of the ASP.NET Identity methods are asynchronous, but there are some synchronous extension methods available that you can use instead. When it comes to working with Web API, which follows a similar pattern, then I prefer using the asynchronous methods, but for initializing databases I find the synchronous methods easier to work with.

I also need to create a class for managing roles. Listing 5-18 shows the contents of the StoreRoleManager.cs file, which I added to the /Infrastructure/Identity folder.

Listing 5-18. The Contents of the StoreRoleManager.cs File

```
using Microsoft.AspNet.Identity;
using Microsoft.AspNet.Identity.EntityFramework;
using Microsoft.AspNet.Identity.Owin;
using Microsoft.Owin;

namespace SportsStore.Infrastructure.Identity {
    public class StoreRoleManager : RoleManager<StoreRole> {

        public StoreRoleManager(RoleStore<StoreRole> store) : base(store) { }
```

```
        public static StoreRoleManager Create(
                IdentityFactoryOptions<StoreRoleManager> options,
                IOwinContext context) {
            return new StoreRoleManager(new
                RoleStore<StoreRole>(context.Get<StoreIdentityDbContext>()));
        }
    }
}
```

I call the base constructor and define a Create method to make sure that the class is instantiated and configured correctly, just as I did for the StoreUserManager class. The base class is RoleManager, which provides methods and properties for operating on the roles defined by the application only, and Table 5-5 shows the ones that I use in this chapter.

Table 5-5. *Some of the Members Defined by the RoleManager<T> Class*

Name	Description
RoleExists(name)	Returns true if the specified role exists
Create(name)	Creates the specified role

I do not require a great deal from the StoreRoleManager class in this chapter because I will be testing that roles are working by applying the MVC framework Authorize attribute, which takes care of checking that users are authenticated and in specific roles. The only use for the StoreRoleManager in this chapter is to see whether the Administrators role exists during database seeding and to create it if it doesn't.

Adding the Configuration Statements

At the start of the chapter, I added the IdentityConfig.cs file to the App_Start folder so that I could start building the application without getting errors from ASP.NET Identity when the application starts. Now that I have created the classes that I need to create and manage user identities, the last step is to register them in the IdentityConfig.cs file and complete the configuration process. Listing 5-19 shows the additions I made to the IdentityConfig.cs file.

Listing 5-19. Adding Configuration Statements to the IdentityConfig.cs File

```
using Owin;
using Microsoft.Owin;
using Microsoft.AspNet.Identity;
using Microsoft.Owin.Security.Cookies;
using SportsStore.Infrastructure.Identity;

[assembly: OwinStartup(typeof(SportsStore.IdentityConfig))]

namespace SportsStore {
    public class IdentityConfig {

        public void Configuration(IAppBuilder app) {
            app.CreatePerOwinContext<StoreIdentityDbContext>(
                StoreIdentityDbContext.Create);
```

```
            app.CreatePerOwinContext<StoreUserManager>(StoreUserManager.Create);
            app.CreatePerOwinContext<StoreRoleManager>(StoreRoleManager.Create);

            app.UseCookieAuthentication(new CookieAuthenticationOptions {
                AuthenticationType = DefaultAuthenticationTypes.ApplicationCookie
            });
        }
    }
}
```

The first three statements register the StoreIdentityDbContext, StoreUserManager, and StoreRoleManager classes so that instances of them can be created as required by ASP.NET Identity. The final statement tells ASP.NET to set a cookie in authentication responses, which the browser will send to identify subsequent requests.

■ **Note**   There is some awkwardness in the way that ASP.NET Identity is set up because Microsoft is in transition between the legacy features in the System.Web assembly and the new world of OWIN and flexible hosting options. I return to OWIN and show you how it relates to Web API in Chapter 26, but until Microsoft completes the transition of ASP.NET, odd-looking configurations will remain.

Testing ASP.NET Identity

I only need to test that ASP.NET Identity is configured and working for this chapter, which means I can take some shortcuts. Listing 5-20 shows the action methods and filters I added to the Prep controller.

Listing 5-20. Adding Action Methods and Filters in the PrepController.cs File

```
using System.Threading.Tasks;
using System.Web.Mvc;
using SportsStore.Models;
using SportsStore.Infrastructure.Identity;
using Microsoft.Owin.Security;
using Microsoft.AspNet.Identity;
using Microsoft.AspNet.Identity.Owin;
using System.Web;
using System.Security.Claims;

namespace SportsStore.Controllers {

    public class PrepController : Controller {
        IRepository repo;

        public PrepController() {
            repo = new ProductRepository();
        }

        public ActionResult Index() {
            return View(repo.Products);
        }
```

```
[Authorize(Roles = "Administrators")]
public async Task<ActionResult> DeleteProduct(int id) {
    await repo.DeleteProductAsync(id);
    return RedirectToAction("Index");
}

[Authorize(Roles = "Administrators")]
public async Task<ActionResult> SaveProduct(Product product) {
    await repo.SaveProductAsync(product);
    return RedirectToAction("Index");
}

public ActionResult Orders() {
    return View(repo.Orders);
}

public async Task<ActionResult> DeleteOrder(int id) {
    await repo.DeleteOrderAsync(id);
    return RedirectToAction("Orders");
}

public async Task<ActionResult> SaveOrder(Order order) {
    await repo.SaveOrderAsync(order);
    return RedirectToAction("Orders");
}

public async Task<ActionResult> SignIn() {
    IAuthenticationManager authMgr = HttpContext.GetOwinContext().Authentication;
    StoreUserManager userMrg = HttpContext.GetOwinContext().GetUserManager<StoreUserManager>();

    StoreUser user = await userMrg.FindAsync("Admin", "secret");
    authMgr.SignIn(await userMrg.CreateIdentityAsync(user,
        DefaultAuthenticationTypes.ApplicationCookie));
    return RedirectToAction("Index");
}

public ActionResult SignOut() {
    HttpContext.GetOwinContext().Authentication.SignOut();
    return RedirectToAction("Index");
}
    }
}
```

I have added a SignIn action that has hard-coded credentials for the administrative user and uses them to authenticate the request with the application and send the client a cookie that can be used to authenticate subsequent requests. I have also defined a SignOut method, which de-activates the cookie and signs the user out.

■ **Tip** I am not going to describe the code in the SignIn action in this chapter. I get into a little more detail about authenticating users in Web API in Chapter 23 and again in Chapter 24, but ASP.NET Identity is a topic in its own right and is not the focus of this book. I get into more detail about ASP.NET Identity, including how to authenticate with Google, Facebook, and other providers, in my *Pro ASP.NET MVC 5 Platform* book, which is published by Apress.

I have applied the Authorize filter to the DeleteProduct and SaveProduct actions in order to restrict access to authenticated users who have been assigned to the Administrators role.

Passing the authorization test means that the client has to be able to invoke the SignIn action, and Listing 5-21 shows the additions I made to the Views/Prep/Index.cshtml file to add buttons that allow sign-in and sign-out.

Listing 5-21. Adding Authentication Controls to the Index.cshtml File

```
@model IEnumerable<SportsStore.Models.Product>

<div class="panel panel-primary ">
    <a href="/prep/signin" class="btn btn-sm btn-primary">Sign In</a>
    <a href="/prep/signout" class="btn btn-sm btn-primary">Sign Out</a>
    User: @(HttpContext.Current.User.Identity.Name)
</div>

<div class="panel panel-primary">
    <div class="panel-heading">Products</div>
    <table class="table table-striped">
        <tr><th>ID</th><th>Name</th><th>Category</th><th>Price</th></tr>
        @foreach (var p in Model) {
            <tr>
                <td>@p.Id</td>
                <td>@p.Name</td>
                <td>@p.Category</td>
                <td>@p.Price</td>
            </tr>
        }
    </table>
</div>

@using (Html.BeginForm("SaveProduct", "Prep")) {
    <input type="hidden" name="Name" value="Zippy Running Shoes" />
    <input type="hidden" name="Category" value="Running" />
    <input type="hidden" name="Description" value="Set a new Record Time" />
    <input type="hidden" name="Price" value="159.99" />

    <button class="btn btn-primary" type="submit">Create</button>
    <a href="/prep/deleteproduct/2" class="btn btn-primary">Delete</a>
}
```

I have added some styled a elements that will invoke the SignIn and SignOut action methods along with the name of the authenticated user, which will be blank when the browser isn't authenticated. (I have hard-coded the URLs that the a elements make, which is poor practice in a real project, but I think this is fine for performing initial configuration testing like this.)

To test Identity, start the application and use the browser to navigate to the /Prep/Index URL. You will see the list of products in the database, along with the additional buttons from Listing 5-21, as illustrated by Figure 5-6.

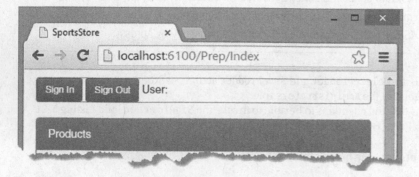

Figure 5-6. *The authentication buttons and username*

■ **Tip** If you receive an error that states that `Microsoft.Owin.Security` or one its dependencies cannot be loaded, then rebuild the application using the Visual Studio Rebuild ➤ Rebuild Solution menu item and try again.

To make sure that the Authorize attributes are working, click the Create or Delete button. The browser hasn't invoked the `SignIn` action method yet, so the request will be sent without an authentication cookie and should be rejected with a 401 (Unauthorized) response, as shown in Figure 5-7.

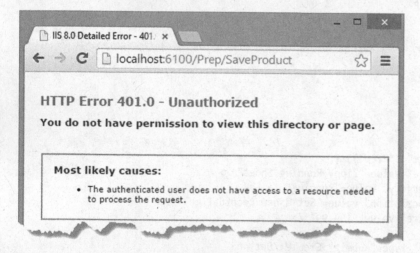

Figure 5-7. *Invoking a restricted action without authentication*

Return to the /Prep/Index URL and click the Sign In button. The browser will send a request that invokes the `SignIn` action method, which adds the authentication cookie to the response and redirects the browser to the /Prep/Index URL. The difference is that now the username will be displayed at the top of the page, indicating that the browser has been authenticated, as shown in Figure 5-8.

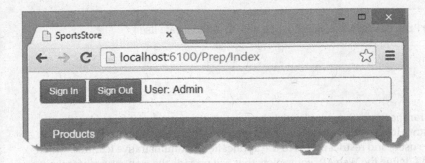

Figure 5-8. *The effect of authenticating the browser*

Now click the Create or Delete button again. This time, the HTTP request that the browser sends will contain an authentication cookie, which will allow the targeted action method to be successful invoked, either adding a product or removing one from the database. If you click the Sign Out button, you will return to making authenticated requests and receiving 401 (Unauthorized) responses.

Removing the Application Cookie

I configured ASP.NET Identity so that it will set a cookie when a request is successfully authenticated, which allows subsequent requests from the same client to be authorized without needing credentials. The cookie is required for round-trip applications, and the authentication test I have used in this chapter will not work without it. I will be using a different approach for the SportsStore application, which is to explicitly set an HTTP header to provide proof that the client has been authenticated. I explain this process in Chapter 6, but my final step in this chapter is to disable the cookie, as shown in Listing 5-22.

Listing 5-22. Disabling the Identity Cookie in the IdentityConfig.cs File

```
using Owin;
using Microsoft.Owin;
using Microsoft.AspNet.Identity;
using Microsoft.Owin.Security.Cookies;
using SportsStore.Infrastructure.Identity;

[assembly: OwinStartup(typeof(SportsStore.IdentityConfig))]

namespace SportsStore {
    public class IdentityConfig {

        public void Configuration(IAppBuilder app) {
            app.CreatePerOwinContext<StoreIdentityDbContext>(
                StoreIdentityDbContext.Create);
            app.CreatePerOwinContext<StoreUserManager>(StoreUserManager.Create);
            app.CreatePerOwinContext<StoreRoleManager>(StoreRoleManager.Create);

            //app.UseCookieAuthentication(new CookieAuthenticationOptions {
            //AuthenticationType = DefaultAuthenticationTypes.ApplicationCookie
            //});
        }
    }
}
```

■ **Caution**   This change means that the `Prep` controller will no longer be able to authenticate itself.

Summary

In this chapter, I created the foundation for the SportsStore application by creating the data model and using the Entity Framework Code First feature to store it persistently in a database. I also installed and configured the ASP.NET Identity system so that I can authenticate users and restrict access to the application's administrative features, which I create in Chapter 6. In the next chapter, I define the Web API controllers that will provide the web services for the SportsStore application.

CHAPTER 6

■ ■ ■

SportsStore: A RESTful Application

In the previous chapter, I laid the foundation for the SportsStore application by creating the Product and Order repository and setting up ASP.NET Identity for user management. In this chapter, I build on that foundation to define the web services that will drive the SportsStore application.

Creating a RESTful Web Service

In Chapter 5, I created the data model and repository and populated the repository with data. I also set up ASP.NET Identity so that I can authenticate and authorize users. These two building blocks create the foundation on which I can build a Web API web service.

When using Web API, it is a simple task to create a RESTful web service. Web API uses controllers, just like the MVC framework, but the action methods return C# data objects rather than Razor views. In fact, getting started with Web API is so simple that you will be forgiven for wondering why I have written such a large book about the topic. The reason is simple: getting started is easy, but creating a truly useful web service requires more effort and a greater understanding of how Web API really works.

To demonstrate how easy it is to get up and running, I right-clicked the Controllers folder, selected Add ➤ Controller from the pop-up menu, selected the Web API 2 Controller – Empty template, and clicked the Add button. I then set the name of the controller to ProductsController and clicked the Add button. Visual Studio has the same approach to templates for Web API controllers as it does for its MVC framework counterparts, and the Empty template contains just the basic controller definition, as shown in Listing 6-1.

■ **Tip** The convention for naming Web API controllers is to prefix the word Controller with the plural form of the model class that the web service will expose. My web service will operate on Product objects, so I have created the ProductsController class.

Listing 6-1. The Contents of the ProductsController.cs File

```
using System;
using System.Collections.Generic;
using System.Linq;
using System.Net;
using System.Net.Http;
using System.Web.Http;
```

```
namespace SportsStore.Controllers {

    public class ProductsController : ApiController {

    }
}
```

There are two important namespaces in Web API development: System.Net.Http and System.Web.Http. Web API relies on an abstract model of HTTP requests and responses that is defined in System.Net.Http. The classes from this namespace that you will work with most often are HttpRequestMessage and HttpResponseMessage, which are used to represent an HTTP request from the client and the response that will be sent in return. I describe these classes in Chapter 9, and you will see them used throughout this book as I dig into the details of how requests are dispatched.

The most important namespace, however, is System.Web.Http, which is where the Web API classes are defined. One of the most important classes in this namespace is ApiController, which is the standard base class for creating Web API controllers and provides support for features such as action methods, model binding, and validation and error handling. I describe all of these features (and the classes contained in the System.Web.Http namespace and its children) in later chapters, but for now I am going to use another ApiController feature: the RESTful action method naming convention. Listing 6-2 shows the changes I made to the Products controller to create a RESTful web service that provides access to the Product model objects in the repository.

Listing 6-2. Adding RESTful Action Methods in the ProductsController.cs File

```
using System;
using System.Collections.Generic;
using System.Linq;
using System.Net;
using System.Net.Http;
using System.Web.Http;
using SportsStore.Models;
using System.Threading.Tasks;

namespace SportsStore.Controllers {

    public class ProductsController : ApiController {

        public ProductsController() {
            Repository = new ProductRepository();
        }

        public IEnumerable<Product> GetProducts() {
            return Repository.Products;
        }

        public Product GetProduct(int id) {
            return Repository.Products.Where(p => p.Id == id).FirstOrDefault();
        }

        public async Task PostProduct(Product product) {
            await Repository.SaveProductAsync(product);
        }
```

```
        public async Task DeleteProduct(int id) {
            await Repository.DeleteProductAsync(id);
        }

        private IRepository Repository { get; set; }
    }
}
```

With just a few lines of code, I am able to define a working RESTful web service that exposes the product repository and its contents over HTTP requests. This is just a starting point, but Web API development is a rewarding experience because you get a solid foundation so quickly.

Testing the Products Web Service

To make sure that the controller is working, start the application by selecting Start Debugging from the Visual Studio Debug menu, and use the browser to request the following URL:

```
http://localhost:6100/api/products/2
```

Enter the URL as though you were requesting a regular web page. I explain the full API that the Products web service supports in the next section, but this simple test will ensure that Web API is receiving requests and dispatching them correctly.

■ **Tip** There will be a short pause between making the first request using Postman after you start the application. This is because I configured the product database so that its contents and schema are regenerated when the application is initialized in Chapter 5. I change this setting to make the data persistent in Chapter 8, but for the moment it is helpful to be able to reset the database so that the results that I show will match the ones that you receive.

If everything is working correctly, then you will see the following response displayed in the browser window:

```
<Product xmlns:i="http://www.w3.org/2001/XMLSchema-instance"
        xmlns="http://schemas.datacontract.org/2004/07/SportsStore.Models">
    <Category>Watersports</Category>
    <Description>Protective and fashionable</Description>
    <Id>2</Id>
    <Name>Lifejacket</Name>
    <Price>48.95</Price>
</Product>
```

The response is an XML document that describes the Lifejacket product from the database, whose Id property corresponds to the one I specified in the URL. XML isn't widely used in modern web applications, and I'll show you how to change the format Chapter 13.

■ **Tip**   The simplest way to test basic GET requests is with the browser, but I will be using the Postman client to create more complex requests as I add features to the SportsStore application. See Chapter 1 for details of getting Postman installed and working.

Putting the Web Service in Context

Table 6-1 describes the web service API that my `Product` controller creates. Knowing the effect of the additions in Listing 6-2 will make it easier to understand how key features work in the sections that follow.

Table 6-1. *The Web Service API Presented by the Products Controller*

Verb	URL	Action Method	Description
GET	/api/products	GetProducts	Returns all the Product objects in the repository
GET	/api/products/1 or /api/products?id=1	GetProduct	Returns a specific Product object
POST	/api/products	PostProduct	Updates or creates a Product object
DELETE	/api/products/1 or /api/products?id=1	DeleteProduct	Removes a Product from the repository

Two things should occur to you when so much functionality appears with so little effort. The first is that there must be a lot of work going on behind the scenes. The second thing is to consider what the catch is.

There *is* a lot going on just out of sight, and the size of this book gives you an indication of just how many features, conventions, and techniques that my simple `Product` controller relies on to deliver the API shown in the table.

You can get a hint of some of the best Web API features by looking at the action methods I added in Listing 6-2. For example, here is the action method that I tested in the previous section:

```
...
public Product GetProduct(int id) {
    return Repository.Products.Where(p => p.Id == id).FirstOrDefault();
}
...
```

Working with Regular C# Objects

The first thing to notice is that I have used regular C# classes throughout the action method. Web API uses a data binding and URL routing processes similar to the MVC framework to extract data values from the request to present as action method parameters. For this action method, URL routing and the binding process are used to extract an `int` value that is used for the `id` parameter.

■ **Tip**   I describe the binding process in Chapters 14 to 17 and Web API routing in Chapters 20 and 21.

The result from the action method is also a regular C# class: the Product class in this case. Within the action method, I use LINQ to query the repository and locate a Product that has the desired Id property value and then return the matching object as the method result. Web API takes care of creating an HTTP response that contains a serialized representation of the result object. You saw this serialization process at work when the browser displayed the XML description of the Lifejacket object.

■ **Tip** Serialization is handled by a feature called *media type formatters*, which I describe in Chapters 12 and 13. Media type formatters are also used to bind data values for action method parameters, as I describe in Chapters 14–17. I change the serialization settings for the SportsStore application in the "Configuring Serialization" section.

The effect of working with regular C# classes is that writing action methods is a simple and natural process, especially when you are exposing the data in a repository and you can map action methods to data operations directly, as I have been able to do in the Products controller.

Using the RESTful Action Method Convention

Web API makes it easy to create RESTful web services by applying a helpful convention when selecting action methods to handle requests: it looks for action methods whose name starts with the request HTTP verb.

I didn't have to specify the name of the action method in the URL when I made a test request. As a reminder, here is the URL I requested:

```
http://localhost:6100/api/products/2
```

The URL *does* specify the name of the controller (/api/**products**/2) but not the action method. Web API selects the action method by looking at the action methods defined by the controllers and filtering out any whose name doesn't begin with the request HTTP verb. In the Products controller, there are two candidate action methods for a GET request.

```
...
public IEnumerable<Product> GetProducts() {
...
```

and

```
...
public Product GetProduct(int id) {
...
```

Web API then looks at the data that has been extracted from the request by the URL routing system and selects the method whose parameters match the data.

■ **Tip** Only the start of the action methods names are used to match requests. The convention is to append the model name to the action method, but that is not required.

The overall effect is that writing action methods is a natural process that doesn't require the developer to think about HTTP verbs, serialization, data binding, or any of the other details that are required to process an HTTP request in order to create a response.

The catch—and, of course, there is one—is that I have created a web service that lacks some important features and is far from useful in a real application.

Web API gives you a big rush of initial functionality right at the start of the project, which I love because it helps compensate for the preparation I had to perform in Chapter 5. But going from the basic web service I created in Listing 6-2 to one that is ready for deployment requires more work—and compromises some aspects of the nice features I described in the previous section. As it stands, the web service that I created in Listing 6-2 doesn't have any security, doesn't validate data, and doesn't handle errors, all of which are serious omissions.

Web API provides features to fill in the gaps, but they are not applied by default. I'll work through the process of completing the web service as I build out the SportsStore application, but it is important to understand that writing the action methods is only the start of the process.

Configuring Serialization

The first thing I am going to change is the way that data model objects are serialized when they are sent to the client. In the previous section, I made a simple GET request with the browser and received a response that contained XML data.

Clients can specify the data formats they are willing to work with in the Accept request header, and Web API will use the formats that are specified to select a serialization format. Web API comes with built-in support for serializing objects to the XML and JSON formats. The reason that I got an XML response is because the Accept header that Google Chrome sends specifies that it will accept *any* data format, but it would rather receive XML.

There are two ways to change the data format: I can alter the Accept header sent by the client, or I can alter the way that Web API responds to it. Since I don't have control over the header that Chrome uses, my only option is to reconfigure Web API.

The serialization of data objects so they can be sent to the client is handled by *media type formatter* classes. Web API comes with some built-in media type formatters and can serialize objects to the XML and JSON data formats by default (although you can add your own data formats, as I explain in Chapter 12).

To disable XML output, I am going to remove the XML media type formatter so that it is no longer used to serialize objects, leaving only the JSON formatter to handle requests.

Listing 6-3 shows the changes that I made to the WebApiConfig.cs file in the App_Start folder to disable XML serialization.

■ **Tip** The WebApiConfig.cs file is used to configure Web API rather than the Global.asax.cs file, and the statements that Visual Studio adds by default configure the URL routes that are used to process requests. (I describe the routing configuration for the SportsStore application in the "Preparing the Routing Configuration" section, and I describe Web API URL routing in detail in Chapters 20 and 21.)

Listing 6-3. Disabling XML Serialization in the WebApiConfig.cs File

```
using System;
using System.Collections.Generic;
using System.Linq;
using System.Web.Http;

namespace SportsStore {
    public static class WebApiConfig {
        public static void Register(HttpConfiguration config) {
```

```
        config.MapHttpAttributeRoutes();

        config.Routes.MapHttpRoute(
            name: "DefaultApi",
            routeTemplate: "api/{controller}/{id}",
            defaults: new { id = RouteParameter.Optional }
        );

        config.Formatters.Remove(config.Formatters.XmlFormatter);
    }
  }
}
```

I have added a statement to the Register method, which is called to configure Web API when the application is started. The Register method accepts an instance of the HttpConfiguration class, which provides properties and methods to configure different aspects of the way that Web API works.

The statement I added uses the Formatters property, which returns the collection of media type formatters in the application. This collection also defines convenience properties that allow me to refer to the important built-in properties directly. The XmlFormatter property returns the object that is used to serialize data objects to XML. I read the XmlFormatter property to get a reference to the XML media type formatter and pass it to the Remove property to remove it from the Formatters collection.

■ **Tip** Although the WebApiConfig.cs file is used to configure Web API, it is the Global.asax.cs file that initiates that process when the application is hosted by IIS, which is required when MVC 5 and Web API 2 are used in the same application. If you look at the Global.asax.cs file, you will see a call to the GlobalConfiguration.Configure method, which is a static method used to configure Web API. The argument passed to the Configure method is an Action that specifies the configuration will be performed by the WebApiConfig.Register method. In Chapter 10, I explain the role of the GlobalConfiguration class and how Web API is configured in detail.

You can see the effect of the statement I added in Listing 6-3 by restarting the application and using the browser to request the http://localhost:6100/api/products/2 URL again. The Accept header that Chrome sends is unchanged, but Web API can no longer use the browser's preferred data format and will produce JSON data instead, as follows:

```
{"Id":2,"Name":"Lifejacket",
 "Description":"Protective and fashionable","Price":48.95,"Category":"Watersports"}
```

This is a representation of the same Product object, but expressed using the JSON format, which has become dominant in the world of HTTP web services.

■ **Tip** There are two reasons to remove a media type formatter. The first is that you are not going to support the format and don't want to have to test the output from your application in, say, JSON *and* XML. The second reason is that Web API *usually* selects the right format for each client, but the process by which this is done, known as *content negotiation*, has some wrinkles that can trap the unwary, resulting in a client receiving data that it doesn't know how to process. I describe how media type formatters work in Chapter 12 and describe the content negotiation process in Chapter 13.

Adding Basic Data Validation

As it stands at the moment, my web service just assumes that the data it is receiving from the client is valid and can be used to manipulate the repository. To see an example of this, request the following URL using the browser:

```
http://localhost:6100/api/products/200
```

This request will invoke the GetProduct method and be interpreted as a request for the Product object in the repository whose Id property is set to 200. There is, unfortunately, no such object, and you can see the result displayed by the browser in Figure 6-1.

Figure 6-1. *The effect of requesting a nonexistent product*

The problem is that Web API has no insight into the purpose and implementation of my action method and so has no way to validate that the value for the int parameter refers to a valid Product object. I need to perform the basic validation myself and report an error to the client when there is no match. Listing 6-4 shows the changes that I made to the GetProduct action method.

■ **Tip** This is only the most basic kind of validation. I describe the support available for binding more complex values, known as *model validation*, in the "Adding Model Validation" section.

Listing 6-4. Handling an Error in the ProductsController.cs File

```
...
public Product GetProduct(int id) {
    Product result = Repository.Products.Where(p => p.Id == id).FirstOrDefault();
    if (result == null) {
        throw new HttpResponseException(HttpStatusCode.BadRequest);
    } else {
        return result;
    }
}
...
```

I have added a simple check to see whether I am able to retrieve a Product object from the repository. If I am, then I return the Product object as the action method result so that it can be serialized and sent to the client as part of the HTTP response. If there is no matching Product, then I create and throw an instance of the HttpResponseException, which is used to specify that an error occurred and to set the HTTP status code that will be used for the response.

In Web API, HTTP status codes are represented using values from the System.Net.HttpStatusCode enumeration. In this example, I have specified the HttpStatusCode.BadRequest value, which means that the status code for the response will be 400 (Bad Request).

■ **Tip** The HttpResponseException class is only one of the ways in which Web API deals with errors. See Chapter 25 for details.

You can see the effect of the exception by restarting the application and using the browser to request the http://localhost:6100/api/products/200 URL. The browser window will be empty, but if you use the browser's F12 tools to examine the network request, you will see that the web service returned the error response, as shown in Figure 6-2.

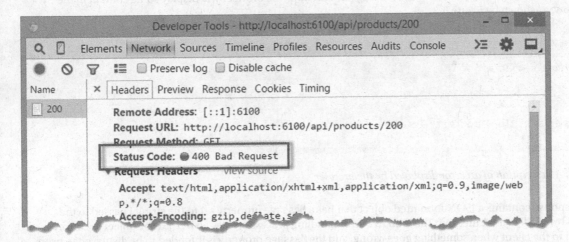

Figure 6-2. The effect of some basic validation

Using Action Results

An alternative approach to using regular C# objects and the HttpResponseException is to use action results, which perform the same function as in the MVC framework and give you greater flexibility in how you structure your action method code. The ApiController class provides a number of convenience methods for creating action results, and I have used two of them in Listing 6-5 to modify the GetProduct action method.

■ **Tip** Web API uses a completely different set of namespaces and classes than the MVC framework. Web API action methods implement the IHttpActionResult interface in the System.Web.Http namespace.

Listing 6-5. Using Action Results in the ProductsController.cs File

```
...
public IHttpActionResult GetProduct(int id) {
    Product result = Repository.Products.Where(p => p.Id == id).FirstOrDefault();
    return  result == null
        ? (IHttpActionResult) BadRequest("No Product Found") : Ok(result);
}
...
```

I have used two of the action result methods that the ApiController class provides. The BadRequest method generates a response with the 400 (Bad Request) status code, and the Ok method generates a 200 (OK) result and serializes its argument.

You can see the effect of the change by starting the application and using the browser to request the http://localhost:6100/api/products/200 URL again. This time, the browser will display some content in the main window, as shown by Figure 6-3.

Figure 6-3. *A description of an error displayed by the browser*

The response contains a JSON-formatted object that has a Message property set to the string I passed to the ApiController.BadRequest method. The Web API error handling process creates an HttpError object to convey information to the client when something goes wrong, and the Message property is intended to be displayed to users. I explain how to use the HttpError class in Chapter 25.

CHOOSING BETWEEN OBJECTS/EXCEPTIONS AND ACTION RESULTS

There is no practical difference in the results generated from action methods that use action methods instead of regular C# objects and the HttpResponseException, and the decision between them is a matter of personal style.

I like the more natural objects and exceptions approach because I like the way it hides the details of the web service and allows me to focus on writing the controller logic, but I generally switch to action results once the web service gets to a certain level of complexity because getting all of the features implemented required embracing, not hiding, the details of HTTP and the requests and responses that a web service details with.

That is just my preference, however, and you are free to develop your own preferences. You can get a long way without needing to even think about action results, so don't feel you have to adopt them if you prefer working with objects and exceptions.

Securing the Product Web Service

By default, there are no restrictions on who can the access action methods defined by a Web API controller, which means that anyone can use the `Products` controller to create, modify, and delete objects in the repository.

To demonstrate the problem, I need to use Postman to generate an HTTP request. Using a browser works for GET requests, but Postman can be used for all types of request.

Enter the `http://localhost:6100/api/products/2` URL into the main part of the Postman window and select the DELETE option from the drop-down list, as shown in Figure 6-4. (Postman has a rather cluttered interface, so I have highlighted the URL and method list.)

Figure 6-4. *Creating an HTTP DELETE request using Postman*

Click the blue Send button, and Postman will send an HTTP DELETE request to the URL, which will invoke the `DeleteProduct` action method. The `Product` object whose `Id` property is 2, which is `Lifejacket`, will be removed from the repository. Postman displays the response from the web service in the area beneath the Send button, as shown in Figure 6-5.

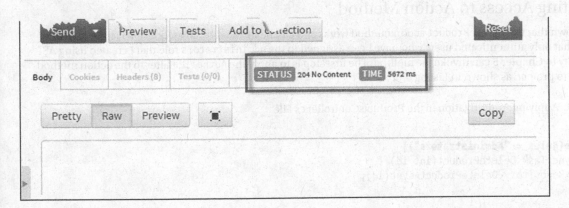

Figure 6-5. *Displaying the results of the DELETE request*

I have highlighted the part of the interface that displays the response status code, which is 204 (No Content) for this request. This response tells the client that the request was successfully processed but that no data was generated, which is a common way for a web service to handle a request to delete a data object. This is the status code used by Web API for asynchronous action methods that return `Task` or `void` synchronous methods. (Another common approach is to return the data object that has been deleted, in which case a 200 [OK] status code would be used.)

■ **Tip** Notice that Postman reports that the request in Figure 6-5 took more than five seconds. This is a combination of the amount of time taken for ASP.NET to initialize the application and for the database to be dropped and re-created. Subsequent requests on my system take 127 milliseconds, but the initial request is slower because of the work required to get the application up and running, which is a process that doesn't start until the first request is received from the client.

You can see the effect of the DELETE request sending a GET request by using Postman to send a GET request to the `http://localhost:6100/api/products` URL or by using the browser to request the `http://localhost:6100/Prep/Index` URL, as shown in Figure 6-6. As expected, the Lifejacket product, which has the `Id` of `2`, is no longer in the list.

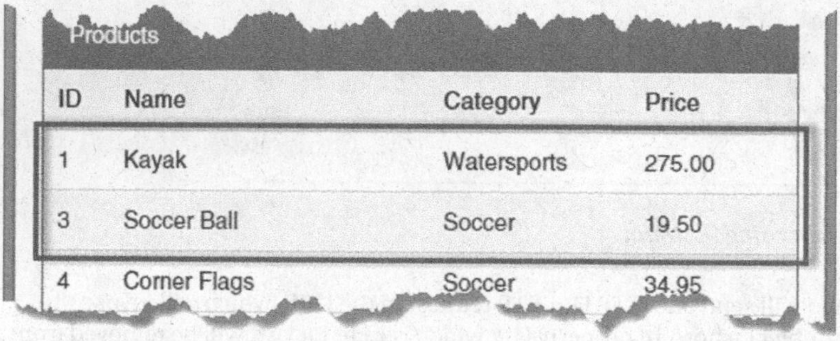

Products

ID	Name	Category	Price
1	Kayak	Watersports	275.00
3	Soccer Ball	Soccer	19.50
4	Corner Flags	Soccer	34.95

Figure 6-6. *The effect of sending a DELETE request*

Restricting Access to Action Method

Having shown that the `DeleteProduct` action method works and can be invoked by any request, it is time to restrict access so that only authenticated users who have been assigned to the `Administrators` role that I created using ASP.NET Identity in Chapter 5 can invoke the method. The first step is to apply the `Authorize` filter to the action method that I want to protect, as shown in Listing 6-6.

Listing 6-6. Applying Authorization in the ProductsController.cs File

```
...
[Authorize(Roles = "Administrators")]
public async Task DeleteProduct(int id) {
    await Repository.DeleteProductAsync(id);
}
...
```

Web API filters have the same effect as their counterparts in the MVC framework, which is to add logic into the request handling process that doesn't belong elsewhere in the components of the MVC pattern, such as logging or security, known as *cross-cutting concerns*. The Authorize filter prevents action methods from being invoked unless the request has been authenticated and the user associated with the request belongs to one or more specified roles. This is the same way that the MVC framework Authorize filter works, but Web API has its own set of interfaces and classes, and the Authorize attribute shown in the listing does not apply the same class as the filter with the same name applied to an MVC framework action method. I describe the Web API filters and explain how they work in Chapters 23 and 24.

■ **Tip** You can also use the Authorize filter to restrict access to individual users, but this is usually a poor strategy because it means you cannot change which users have access without deploying a new version of the application. Using roles means you can assign users in the ASP.NET Identity database and have the changes take effect without needing to write, test, and deploy code.

To see the effect of the Authorize filter, start the application and resend the DELETE request using Postman. (Postman keeps a history of the requests you have made in a list on the left side of the window, which makes it easy to resend requests.) Rather than the 204 (No Content) success method that was returned in the previous section, the web service now returns a 401 (Unauthorized) response, as illustrated in Figure 6-7. If you request the /Prep/Index URL, you will see that the Lifejacket product remains in the repository and has not been deleted.

Figure 6-7. The effect of applying authorization to an action method

Authenticating Requests

Restricting access to authorized users is helpful only if there is also a mechanism for those users to authenticate themselves.

Web API lets you choose your own approach to authenticating requests, and in Chapters 23 and 24, I show you how to create a custom implementation of HTTP *basic authentication*. Basic authentication is a rudimentary system that is safe only over SSL connections and that requires the client to provide the name and password of the user for every request, but it provides a nice demonstration of how you can integrate authentication into a Web API application.

More broadly, authentication for web services is something of a Wild West, with no unified approach for sending credentials to authenticate a user or subsequently identifying authenticated requests. Some web service platforms rely on cookies, others use headers, and some rely on both, but even when two platforms use the same basic approach, there is substantial variation in the implementation detail.

The most common approach to authentication requests in Web API is to use ASP.NET Identity, which I configured in Chapter 5. Authenticating users with ASP.NET Identity requires a specifically formatted request, but once the initial authentication has been performed, subsequent requests are identified as being authenticated by setting the standard HTTP Authorization header or an authentication cookie, using a value that is provided in the initial request. I'll demonstrate the requests that are required—and the responses they produce—as I define the authentication functionality in the sections that follow.

■ **Caution**   The integration of ASP.NET Identity into ASP.NET Web API is something of a mess because Microsoft is trying to make Identity operate in both the old world of the traditional ASP.NET platform and the new world of OWIN and wider hosting options (which I describe in Chapter 26). Getting authentication to work through a web service requires some ugly code, which I show you in the listings that follow but don't explain in depth. My advice is to use the code in the listings— which you can download from Apress.com—verbatim in your own projects and avoid digging to the detail of Identity until it has been more smoothly integrated with Web API.

Defining the Authentication Provider

ASP.NET Identity is an extensible user-management framework that can be used to implement any authentication mechanism. Oddly, however, there is no built-in support for authenticating users against the credentials stored in the database that I created in Chapter 5. This means the first step in setting up authentication is to implement a provider class that will authenticate the user based on the username and password and generate the cookie used to identity subsequent requests from the client. Listing 6-7 shows the contents of the StoreAuthProvider.cs file, which I added to the Infrastructure/Identity folder.

Listing 6-7. The Contents of the StoreAuthProvider.cs File

```
using System.Security.Claims;
using System.Threading.Tasks;
using Microsoft.AspNet.Identity;
using Microsoft.Owin.Security;
using Microsoft.Owin.Security.OAuth;

namespace SportsStore.Infrastructure.Identity {
    public class StoreAuthProvider : OAuthAuthorizationServerProvider {

        public override async Task GrantResourceOwnerCredentials(
                OAuthGrantResourceOwnerCredentialsContext context) {

            StoreUserManager storeUserMgr =
                context.OwinContext.Get<StoreUserManager>("AspNet.Identity.Owin:"
                    + typeof(StoreUserManager).AssemblyQualifiedName);

            StoreUser user = await storeUserMgr.FindAsync(context.UserName,
                context.Password);
            if (user == null) {
                context.SetError("invalid_grant",
                    "The username or password is incorrect");
            } else {
```

```
            ClaimsIdentity ident = await storeUserMgr.CreateIdentityAsync(user,
                    "Custom");
            AuthenticationTicket ticket
                = new AuthenticationTicket(ident, new AuthenticationProperties());
            context.Validated(ticket);
            context.Request.Context.Authentication.SignIn(ident);
        }
    }

    public override Task ValidateClientAuthentication(
            OAuthValidateClientAuthenticationContext context) {
        context.Validated();
        return Task.FromResult<object>(null);
    }
  }
}
```

The authentication provider is derived from the OAuthAuthorizationServerProvider class and overrides the ValidateClientAuthentication and GrantResourceOwnerCredentials methods.

The ValidateClientAuthentication method is called to check whether the client is allowed to perform authentication, which I accept by calling the Validated method on the context object passed as the method parameter. (I allow any client to perform validation because I care only about usernames and passwords in the SportsStore application.)

The GrantResourceOwnerCredentials method is called to authenticate the user, and the context parameter provides access to the username and password provided by the user. I follow the same basic approach that I used for the SignIn method in the Prep controller in Chapter 5 and use the user manager class to check the username and password that I have received and to add a cookie to the response if they are valid.

Configuring Authentication

Using ASP.NET Identity in a web service requires some configuration statements in the IdentityConfig.cs file, in addition to the ones that I needed to perform authentication through an MVC framework controller in Chapter 5. Listing 6-8 shows the statements that I added to configure Identity to use the provider class I created in the previous section and to set up authentication as part of the Web API request handling process.

Listing 6-8. Configuring ASP.NET Identity to Work with Web API in the IdentityConfig.cs File

```
using Owin;
using Microsoft.Owin;
using Microsoft.AspNet.Identity;
using Microsoft.Owin.Security.Cookies;
using SportsStore.Infrastructure.Identity;
using System;
using Microsoft.Owin.Security.OAuth;

[assembly: OwinStartup(typeof(SportsStore.IdentityConfig))]

namespace SportsStore {
    public class IdentityConfig {
```

113

```
public void Configuration(IAppBuilder app) {

    app.CreatePerOwinContext<StoreIdentityDbContext>(
        StoreIdentityDbContext.Create);
    app.CreatePerOwinContext<StoreUserManager>(StoreUserManager.Create);
    app.CreatePerOwinContext<StoreRoleManager>(StoreRoleManager.Create);

    //app.UseCookieAuthentication(new CookieAuthenticationOptions {
    //    AuthenticationType = DefaultAuthenticationTypes.ApplicationCookie
    //});

    app.UseOAuthBearerTokens(new OAuthAuthorizationServerOptions {
        Provider = new StoreAuthProvider(),
        AllowInsecureHttp = true,
        TokenEndpointPath = new PathString("/Authenticate")
    });
    }
  }
}
```

I have set three configuration properties that control the way that requests are authenticated. The `Provider` property specifies the object that will authenticate the user, which is in this case an instance of the `StoreAuthProvider` class that I defined in Listing 6-7.

■ **Tip**   There are many configuration options for authentication—too many for me to describe in this book. See http://msdn.microsoft.com/en-us/library/microsoft.owin.security.oauth.oauthauthorizationserveroptions(v=vs.113).aspx for the full list.

Setting the `AllowInsecureHttp` property to `true` allows authentication to be performed for any HTTP request rather than the default behavior, which is to support only SSL requests.

The final property—`TokenEndpointPath`—specifies a URL that will be used to receive and process authentication requests. I have specified /Authenticate, which means that clients will send their authentication requests to `http://localhost:6100/authenticate`, as I demonstrate in the next section.

Testing Authentication

The process for testing authentication is cumbersome because I am going to create the requests that I need using Postman. I'll write the JavaScript code that will handle authentication in Chapter 7, but I want to focus on just the web service in this chapter. First I am going to show you what happens when authentication is attempted with invalid credentials and then with valid ones.

Set the Postman request URL to `http://localhost:6100/authenticate` and select the POST verb from the drop-down list. When you select POST, a set of buttons will appear that allow the encoding style for the data in the request to be selected; click the `x-www-form-urlencoded` button.

Beneath the buttons are spaces for Key and Value. As you start typing in one of the spaces, a new line will appear beneath so that you can enter multiple values. Enter the key/value data shown in Table 6-2.

Table 6-2. *The Key Value Data Required for an Authentication Request*

Key	Value
grant_type	password
username	Bob
password	secret

The grant_type entry specifies what type of authentication is being requested, and the username and password entries specify the credentials to be validated. I have specified the username Bob, which is invalid because I only created an Admin user in Chapter 5. Figure 6-8 shows how Postman should look before performing the authentication request.

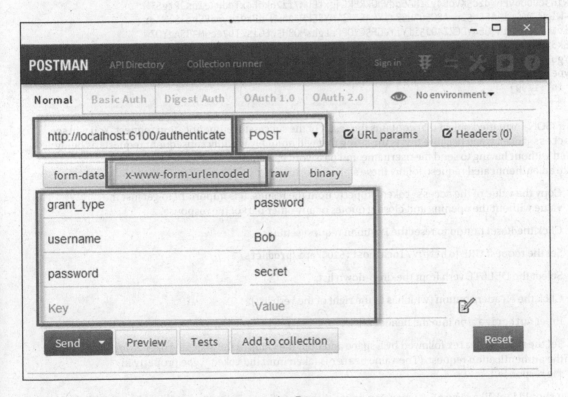

Figure 6-8. *Creating an authentication request using Postman*

Click the Send button when you have configured the request. Postman will show that the response had the 400 (Bad Request) status code and contained the following JSON data:

```
{"error":"invalid_grant","error_description":"The username or password is incorrect"}
```

■ **Tip** A common cause of confusion is the response code for a failed authentication code. Many developers expect to receive a 401 (Unauthorized), but that is sent only when accessing a restricted URL without being authenticated or authorized.

To make a successful authentication request, change the `username` value to `Admin` while leaving all of the other values as they are and click the Send button. This time the credentials are valid, and you will receive a 200 (OK) response. The data returned by the web service will look like this:

```
{"access_token":"vJwc8Aj2r2ntONxtO1uhL7YOc66vMS1fsUfYvvQuZ76X-SQxxRLdaECj1DnuOBpbVi
    ExwX9TEdQQ-4A3d4BSlz8HCOp5nhPaveLifLaflAmj1NGv8KDefOazJBWCgFs2E3IiAGs-qLrXzR
    _9iZyW1W3cdbo6vP6Wdzc5KVoB4y2ihA6qdVbOkREkCjgxtBbH7rz26kbE4xTddPAeIqsJPtgSTM
    XeT4X-WlgW_QAwul3AER_52nmA8UEu7uBBz1YWAEtfl-MYEEkMa2hwN-aPz91mypaYSb4-SlWAqr
    -OY73iv1GTxcEn11hOGE4YDCZZ4DJ5i1YiYeGF5GYQPPnLghWMOBH5nEGlsZTb7ee9M3SSAgYQZw
    k1y8f8k8tDR9DuEniJTSessK2V_8AqTjleDhOkGStzzD5Je_pz3OCP9UZMwsH3yyBpOS-XoXzgO-
    jcyMsYguIfOD_dT9Qp2gBrkuoSaAvlu8_bVAERL1rwZERtoKVkoMCxKxdFgnnKLOaU",
 "token_type":"bearer",
 "expires_in":1199}
```

This is a JSON-formatted object that contains the result of the successful authentication request. You will see a different `access_token` value because this is the string that will uniquely identify subsequent requests as being authenticated without having to send the username and password each time.

To make an authenticated request, follow these steps in Postman:

1. Copy the value of the `access_token` property from the results. It is important to get just the value without the opening and closing quotes or any other part of the response.

2. Click the Reset button to reset the Postman request settings.

3. Set the request URL to `http://localhost:6100/api/products/2`.

4. Select the DELETE verb from the drop-down list.

5. Click the Headers button (which is to the right of the verb list).

6. Enter `Authorization` into the header area.

7. Set the value to `bearer` followed by a space and then the value of the `access_token` from the authentication request. (The value `bearer` is taken from the `token_type` property in the response.)

Postman should look like Figure 6-9 when you have finished configuring the request, and I have highlighted the important changes that have to be made.

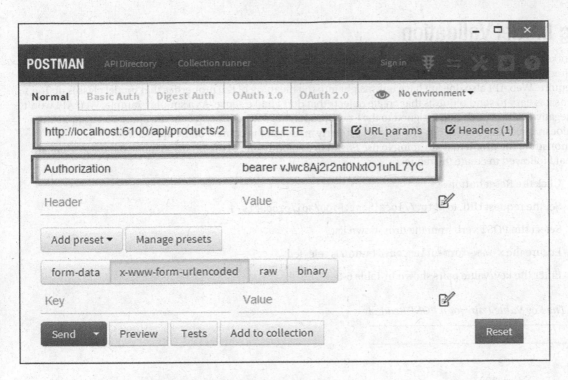

Figure 6-9. Configuring an authenticated DELETE request

Click the Send button, and you should receive a 204 (No Content) response. You can check the contents of the repository by using the browser to request the /Prep/Index URL, and if everything has worked correctly, then there should be no Lifejacket product in the list.

___

■ **Tip** If you don't get the expected result, then the most likely cause is a problem with the access_token value, which is long and difficult to manipulate. Make sure you have not missed any characters or added any extra when copying the value. The access_token value is valid for only 20 minutes by default, so if you are having problems, take care to repeat the authentication request to get a new access_token value every now and again.

___

This is an undeniably awkward process, but it demonstrates the two-stage approach required for web service authentication. The process is somewhat easier to handle when using jQuery to make Ajax requests, as I demonstrate in Chapter 7.

___

■ **Tip** ASP.NET Identity can also be configured to use cookies for authentication, which means you don't need to set the Authorization header. I am using the header approach because it lets me have more control over the authentication process for the SportsStore application, as you will see in Chapter 6, which makes demonstrating the functionality simpler. I disabled the cookie support in Chapter 5, but you can leave it enabled it in your own applications. I also demonstrate the cookie-based approach in *Pro ASP.NET MVC 5 Platform*, which is published by Apress.

___

Adding Model Validation

Web API works on a best-efforts approach when it comes to creating the objects that are passed as arguments to action methods, and it won't complain if there more or less data than is required to create the objects that the action methods require. Web API also doesn't have any insight into the meaning of the properties that model classes define, which means it is easy to send requests that create objects that don't make sense. As a simple example, Web API won't prevent a negative value from being assigned to the Price property of a Product object in the SportsStore application because it doesn't have any knowledge of what that property means in the context of the application.

To demonstrate the problem, I am going to use Postman to modify one of the products in the database. Here are the steps that I followed to create the request:

1. Click the Reset button.

2. Set the request URL to http://localhost:6100/api/products/1.

3. Select the POST verb from the drop-down list.

4. Ensure the x-www-form-urlencoded button is selected.

5. Enter the key/value pairs shown in Table 6-3.

Table 6-3. *The Key Value Pairs for a POST Request*

Key	Value
Id	1
Price	-100

When you have configured the request, Postman should resemble Figure 6-10.

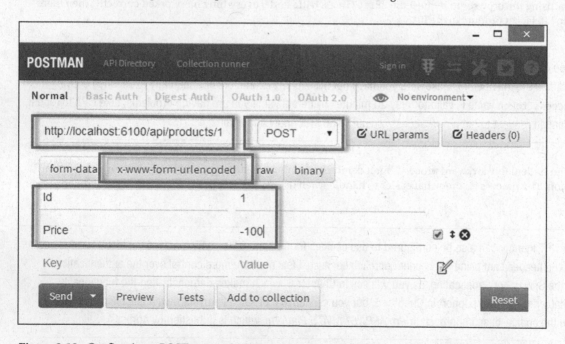

Figure 6-10. *Configuring a POST request in Postman*

Click the Send button to send the request to the web service. The response will be a 204 (No Content) response that indicates success (but does not require the web service to send the client any data), and you can see the changes to the data in the repository by using the browser to display the /Prep/Index URL, as shown in Figure 6-11.

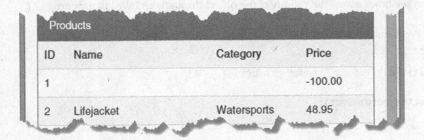

Figure 6-11. *The effect of an unvalidated request*

Applying Validation Attributes

I added some simple validation to the GetProduct method earlier in the chapter, but Web API supports a sophisticated validation feature that shares a lot of common features with the one you will have used in the MVC framework, based on the application of validation attributes to model objects. Listing 6-9 shows the additions I have made to the Product class to prevent poor-quality data from being added to the database.

Listing 6-9. Applying Validation to the Product.cs File

```csharp
using System.ComponentModel.DataAnnotations;

namespace SportsStore.Models {

    public class Product {
        public int Id { get; set; }
        [Required]
        public string Name { get; set; }
        [Required]
        public string Description { get; set; }
        [Required]
        [Range(1, 100000)]
        public decimal Price { get; set; }
        [Required]
        public string Category { get; set; }
    }
}
```

I describe the attributes in detail in Chapter 18, but the ones I have applied to the Product class require the client to provide values for the Name, Description, Price, and Category properties and limit the value of the Price attribute so that it is between 1 and 100,000. This is a pretty simple set of validation attributes, but it is enough to demonstrate the model validation mechanism and to prevent the kind of problem that I demonstrated in the previous section.

Validating the Model

The final step is to check that the model object passed to the action method is valid, which is done through the ModelState property defined by the ApiController class. I describe the model validation process and classes in detail in Chapter 18, but in Listing 6-10 you can see how I assess the validity of the object through the IsValid property.

Listing 6-10. Validating a Model in the ProductsController.cs File

```
...
public async Task<IHttpActionResult> PostProduct(Product product) {
    if (ModelState.IsValid) {
        await Repository.SaveProductAsync(product);
        return Ok();
    } else {
        return BadRequest(ModelState);
    }
}
...
```

I have changed the action method so that it returns an IHttpActionResult (although since this is an async method, the result type is Task<IHttpActionResult>, as I explained in Chapter 3). If the value of the ModelState.IsValid property is true, then I know that the data sent by the client has passed the validation tests defined by the attributes I applied in Listing 6-9 and that I can safely store the object in the repository.

If the IsValue property is false, then I know that there is a problem with the data that the client has sent and that one or more properties have failed to pass its validation test. I call the BadRequest convenience method to generate a 400 (Bad Request) response. I pass the value returned by the ModelState property to the BadRequest method, which has the effect of sending the client details of which properties are problematic and why.

■ **Tip**   I describe the model state in Chapter 18 and the different ways in which errors can be handled in Chapter 25. I list all of the convenience methods defined by the ApiController for creating action method results in Chapter 11.

To see the effect of the validation, start the application and use Postman to resend the POST request I defined at the start of this section. Postman will display the 400 (Bad Request) status code and show the following data, which the web service includes in the response:

```
{"Message":"The request is invalid.",
 "ModelState":{ "product.Name":["The Name field is required."],
    "product.Description":["The Description field is required."],
    "product.Price":["The field Price must be between 1 and 100000."],
    "product.Category":["The Category field is required."]
    }
}
```

The data sent to the client provides information about each property, but, as I explain in Chapter 25, this data doesn't follow any widely accepted standard, and the client has to have prior knowledge that the web service will send this kind of data when there is a validation problem.

Adding Simple Dependency Injection

Dependency injection (DI) is a contentious topic, and either you love the idea and apply it relentlessly to your applications or you hate it entirely and resent the imposition of a pattern that you neither like nor value. (And I really do mean *hate*. You should see some of the e-mails I get on this topic).

If you are reading this book, then you have already made up your mind because you have built applications using the MVC framework. If you are a DI hater, then you can avert your eyes and move on to the next section in which I create another Web API controller (although be warned that I return to the topic of DI again in Chapter 10). If you are interested in DI, then I am going use this section to create a simple custom resolver that will allow me to decouple the `ProductController` class from the `ProductRepository` implementation of the `IRepository` interface.

Recapping the Problem

The problem I am trying to solve is that the constructor of the `Product` controller directly instantiates the `ProductRepository` class so that the action methods in the controller have access to an implementation of the `IRepository` interface.

```
...
public ProductsController() {
    Repository = new ProductRepository();
}
...
```

Tightly coupled components are hard to test because I can't readily separate the behavior of the `ProductController` class from the `ProductRepository` class. A loosely coupled approach would allow the `ProductController` class to obtain an implementation of the `IRepository` interface without needing to specify *which* implementation is used. This allows me to change the `IRepository` implementation without having to also change the `ProductController` class, and that makes testing and maintenance simpler.

Creating the Dependency Resolver

I show you how to use the Ninject package to perform DI in Web API in Chapter 10, but in this chapter I am going to create a custom resolver that will create instances of the `ProductResolver` class to service requests for the `IRepository` interface. This is a small fraction of the functionality that a real DI package like Ninject offers, but it is enough to get the SportsStore application up and running and to demonstrate some useful Web API functionality. I started by adding a class file called `CustomResolver.cs` to the `Infrastructure` folder and using it to define the class shown in Listing 6-11.

Listing 6-11. The Contents of the CustomResolver.cs File

```
using System;
using System.Collections.Generic;
using System.Linq;
using System.Web.Http.Dependencies;
using SportsStore.Models;

namespace SportsStore.Infrastructure {
    public class CustomResolver : IDependencyResolver, IDependencyScope {
```

```
        public object GetService(Type serviceType) {
            return serviceType == typeof(IRepository)
                ? new ProductRepository()
                : null;
        }

        public IEnumerable<object> GetServices(Type serviceType) {
            return Enumerable.Empty<object>();
        }

        public IDependencyScope BeginScope() {
            return this;
        }

        public void Dispose() {
            // do nothing - not required
        }
    }
}
```

Web API uses two interfaces to resolve dependencies: IDependencyResolver and IDependencyScope. I explain the role and purpose of these interfaces in Chapter 10, but for this chapter it is enough to know that the GetService method will be called when Web API needs to get instances of most types, including implementation of the IRepository interface. If this is the type that is required, then I return a new instance of the ProductRepository class. For all other types, I return null, which tells Web API to use its default behavior to create instances of the types it requires. The default behavior is to invoke a public parameterless constructor.

Registering the Dependency Resolver

I have to tell Web API that I want it to use the resolver, which I do in the WebApiConfig.cs file, as shown in Listing 6-12. (I explain more about the Web API configuration options in Chapter 10.)

Listing 6-12. Registering a Dependency Resolver in the WebApiConfig.cs File

```
using System;
using System.Collections.Generic;
using System.Linq;
using System.Web.Http;
using SportsStore.Infrastructure;

namespace SportsStore {
    public static class WebApiConfig {
        public static void Register(HttpConfiguration config) {

            config.MapHttpAttributeRoutes();

            config.Routes.MapHttpRoute(
                name: "DefaultApi",
                routeTemplate: "api/{controller}/{id}",
                defaults: new { id = RouteParameter.Optional }
            );
```

```
        config.Formatters.Remove(config.Formatters.XmlFormatter);
        config.DependencyResolver = new CustomResolver();
        }
    }
}
```

Using the Dependency Resolver in the Controller Class

My dependency resolver is simple and requires the constructor of the Product controller to explicitly request an implementation of the IRepository interface. Real dependency injection packages, such as Ninject (which I demonstrate in Chapter 10), will use reflection to inspect classes and resolve dependencies automatically, which is a more elegant approach. Even so, my simple resolver provides enough functionality for me to decouple the ProductController and ProductRepository classes, as shown in Listing 6-13.

Listing 6-13. Using a Dependency Resolver in the ProductController.cs File

```
using System;
using System.Collections.Generic;
using System.Linq;
using System.Net;
using System.Net.Http;
using System.Web.Http;
using SportsStore.Models;
using System.Threading.Tasks;

namespace SportsStore.Controllers {

    public class ProductsController : ApiController {

        public ProductsController() {
            Repository = (IRepository)GlobalConfiguration.Configuration.
                DependencyResolver.GetService(typeof(IRepository));
        }

        public IEnumerable<Product> GetProducts() {
            return Repository.Products;
        }

        public IHttpActionResult GetProduct(int id) {
            Product result = Repository.Products.Where(p => p.Id == id).FirstOrDefault();
            return  result == null
                ? (IHttpActionResult) BadRequest("No Product Found") : Ok(result);
        }

        public async Task<IHttpActionResult> PostProduct(Product product) {
            if (ModelState.IsValid) {
                await Repository.SaveProductAsync(product);
                return Ok();
            } else {
                return BadRequest(ModelState);
            }
        }
```

```
        [Authorize(Roles = "Administrators")]
        public async Task DeleteProduct(int id) {
            await Repository.DeleteProductAsync(id);
        }

        private IRepository Repository { get; set; }
    }
}
```

This slightly awkward statement accesses the runtime configuration objects to get an implementation of the `IDependencyResolver` interface and uses it to get an implementation of the `IRepository` interface. The result is that the `ProductController` class is not tightly coupled to the `ProductRepository` interface and can be more readily tested and maintained.

Creating a Non-RESTful Web Service

To finish this chapter, I am going to create a Web API controller that will provide access to the `Order` and `OrderLine` objects in the repository. The controller that I created to serve requests for `Product` objects followed the Web API naming convention for a RESTful web service, but that is an optional pattern, and it is perfectly possible—and reasonable—to create non-RESTful web services, and this is what I will do in this section.

Preparing the Routing Configuration

The URL routing system is responsible for matching requests in order to extract data and select the controller that will generate the response for the client. The default Web API configuration doesn't deal with action method names because the assumption is that you will follow the RESTful naming convention, so the first task is to add a new route that will match requests for my non-RESTful controller and extract both the controller and action method names from the URL, as illustrated in Listing 6-14.

■ **Tip**   I describe the Web API URL routing features in detail in Chapters 20 and 21.

Listing 6-14. Defining a New Route in the WebApiConfig.cs File

```
using System;
using System.Collections.Generic;
using System.Linq;
using System.Web.Http;
using SportsStore.Infrastructure;

namespace SportsStore {
    public static class WebApiConfig {
        public static void Register(HttpConfiguration config) {

            config.MapHttpAttributeRoutes();
```

```
config.Routes.MapHttpRoute(
    name: "OrdersRoute",
    routeTemplate: "nonrest/{controller}/{action}/{id}",
    defaults: new { id = RouteParameter.Optional }
);

config.Routes.MapHttpRoute(
    name: "DefaultApi",
    routeTemplate: "api/{controller}/{id}",
    defaults: new { id = RouteParameter.Optional }
);

config.Formatters.Remove(config.Formatters.XmlFormatter);

config.DependencyResolver = new CustomResolver();
        }
    }
}
```

To avoid routes being matched to the wrong kind of controller (RESTful and non-RESTful), I have defined a route with a separate prefix: nonrest. This allows me to continue to send requests to target RESTful controllers using URLs prefixed with api without the route for non-RESTful controllers getting in the way (I explain this problem in detail in Chapter 22).

Preparing the Model Objects

To prepare the Order and OrderLine classes, I have applied attributes for validation, as shown in Listing 6-15.

Listing 6-15. Applying Attributes in the Order.cs File

```
using System.Collections.Generic;
using System.ComponentModel.DataAnnotations;
using System.Web.Http;

namespace SportsStore.Models {
    public class Order {
        [HttpBindNever]
        public int Id { get; set; }
        [Required]
        public string Customer { get; set; }
        [Required]
        [HttpBindNever]
        public decimal TotalCost { get; set; }
        public ICollection<OrderLine> Lines { get; set; }
    }

    public class OrderLine {
        [HttpBindNever]
        public int Id { get; set; }
        [Required]
        [Range(0, 100)]
        public int Count { get; set; }
```

```
    [Required]
    public int ProductId { get; set; }
    [HttpBindNever]
    public int OrderId { get; set; }

    [HttpBindNever]
    public Product Product { get; set; }
    [HttpBindNever]
    public Order Order { get; set; }
    }
}
```

The Required and Range attributes have the same effect as when I applied them to the Product class, ensuring that the request contains a value for a property and limiting the acceptable set of values for that property.

I have also used the HttpBindNever attribute, which prevents Web API from assigning a value to a property from the request. This ensures I don't get unexpected or undesired behavior by accepting request values for properties that I need to set in the application. The best example is the Order.TotalPrice property: I don't want the client to be able to set the total price of the order because it won't take long for an ambitious customer to create an order for all of the SportsStore products in stock and pay only a dollar for them.

Preventing Formatting Loops

There is a circular reference in the relationship between the Order and OrderLine classes: an Order has a collection of OrderLine objects, each of which contains a reference back to the Order. This is a problem for the standard serialization process, which will report an error when it finds such a loop. To prevent this from being a problem, I need to change the behavior of the class responsible for serializing objects into JSON so that it simply ignores circular references, rather than throws an error. Listing 6-16 shows the configuration statement that I added to the WebApiConfig.cs file.

Listing 6-16. Disabling Errors for Circular References in the WebApiConfig.cs File

```
using System;
using System.Collections.Generic;
using System.Linq;
using System.Web.Http;
using SportsStore.Infrastructure;

namespace SportsStore {
    public static class WebApiConfig {
        public static void Register(HttpConfiguration config) {

            config.MapHttpAttributeRoutes();

            config.Routes.MapHttpRoute(
                name: "OrdersRoute",
                routeTemplate: "nonrest/{controller}/{action}/{id}",
                defaults: new { id = RouteParameter.Optional }
            );

            config.Routes.MapHttpRoute(
                name: "DefaultApi",
```

```
        routeTemplate: "api/{controller}/{id}",
        defaults: new { id = RouteParameter.Optional }
    );

    config.Formatters.Remove(config.Formatters.XmlFormatter);
    config.DependencyResolver = new CustomResolver();

    GlobalConfiguration.Configuration.Formatters.JsonFormatter
        .SerializerSettings.ReferenceLoopHandling =
    Newtonsoft.Json.ReferenceLoopHandling.Ignore;
        }
    }
}
```

JSON serialization is handled by the Json.NET package, and this statement that I added to the `WebApiConfig.cs` file sets a configuration property defined by that code. I explain some of the other configuration options that Json.Net provides for serialization in Chapter 13.

Defining the Web API Controller

The final step is to define the controller itself. I added a class file called `OrdersController.cs` to the `Controllers` folder and used it to define the class shown in Listing 6-17.

Listing 6-17. The Contents of the OrdersController.cs File

```
using System.Collections.Generic;
using System.Linq;
using System.Threading.Tasks;
using System.Web.Http;
using SportsStore.Models;

namespace SportsStore.Controllers {
    public class OrdersController : ApiController {

        public OrdersController() {
            Repository = (IRepository)GlobalConfiguration.Configuration
                .DependencyResolver.GetService(typeof(IRepository));
        }

        [HttpGet]
        [Authorize(Roles="Administrators")]
        public IEnumerable<Order> List() {
            return Repository.Orders;
        }

        [HttpPost]
        public async Task<IHttpActionResult> CreateOrder(Order order) {
            if (ModelState.IsValid) {
```

```
            IDictionary<int, Product> products = Repository.Products
                .Where(p => order.Lines.Select(ol => ol.ProductId)
                    .Any(id => id == p.Id)).ToDictionary(p => p.Id);

            order.TotalCost = order.Lines.Sum(ol =>
                ol.Count * products[ol.ProductId].Price);

            await Repository.SaveOrderAsync(order);
            return Ok();
        } else {
            return BadRequest(ModelState);
        }
    }

    [HttpDelete]
    [Authorize(Roles = "Administrators")]
    public async Task DeleteOrder(int id) {
        await Repository.DeleteOrderAsync(id);
    }

    private IRepository Repository { get; set; }
    }
}
```

The Orders controller defines three action methods: List, CreateOrder, and DeleteOrder. These names don't provide Web API with information about which HTTP verbs each will accept, so I have to apply attributes to specify them. In the listing, I have used the HttpGet, HttpPost, and HttpDelete attributes, but Web API provides a wider range of verb attributes, as I describe in Chapter 22.

The only other point of note for this controller is the LINQ that I use to set the Order.TotalPrice property in the CreateOrder action method. I applied the HttpBindNever attribute to this property in Listing 6-15, which means that no value will be taken from the request when the Order parameter for the action method is created. That means I am responsible for determining the value of the order, which I have done using two LINQ statements.

Completing the Product Controller

Before moving on, I need to make a final change to the Product controller, which is to apply the Authorize attribute to the PostProduct action method. I didn't do this earlier because I wanted to demonstrate how to apply model validation without needing to deal with the authentication process. Now that all of the web service features are in place, I can apply the Authorize attribute so that only users assigned to the Administrators role are able to create or modify products, as shown in Listing 6-18.

Listing 6-18. Applying Authorization to the PostProduct Action in the ProductsController.cs File

```
using System;
using System.Collections.Generic;
using System.Linq;
using System.Net;
using System.Net.Http;
using System.Web.Http;
using SportsStore.Models;
using System.Threading.Tasks;
```

```
namespace SportsStore.Controllers {

    public class ProductsController : ApiController {

        public ProductsController() {
            Repository = (IRepository)GlobalConfiguration.Configuration.
                DependencyResolver.GetService(typeof(IRepository));
        }

        public IEnumerable<Product> GetProducts() {
            return Repository.Products;
        }

        public IHttpActionResult GetProduct(int id) {
            Product result = Repository.Products.Where(p => p.Id == id).FirstOrDefault();
            return result == null
                ? (IHttpActionResult)BadRequest("No Product Found") : Ok(result);
        }

        [Authorize(Roles = "Administrators")]
        public async Task<IHttpActionResult> PostProduct(Product product) {
            if (ModelState.IsValid) {
                await Repository.SaveProductAsync(product);
                return Ok();
            } else {
                return BadRequest(ModelState);
            }
        }

        [Authorize(Roles = "Administrators")]
        public async Task DeleteProduct(int id) {
            await Repository.DeleteProductAsync(id);
        }

        private IRepository Repository { get; set; }
    }
}
```

Summary

In this chapter, I created the two Web API controllers that define the HTTP web services for the SportsStore application. I started with a simple RESTful controller that services requests for Product objects and gradually added layers of functionality, such as authentication, data validation, and dependency injection. I finished the chapter by showing you how to create a non-RESTful controller, which I will use to service requests for Order objects. In the next chapter, I create the single-page applications that deliver the SportsStore application to customers and administrators.

■ ■ ■

CHAPTER 7

SportsStore: Creating the Clients

In this chapter, I will create a pair of single-page applications that deliver the functionality of the web services I created in Chapter 6 to clients and to administrators. I will build a common foundation of JavaScript code and then layer on the functionality that is specific to each client.

Client-side development isn't part of the Web API world, but I wanted to show you the end-to-end development process for the SportsStore application. As a consequence, I cover a lot of ground in this chapter and don't explain the implementation of all of the JavaScript functions I define, but I do include enough information for you to see the overall structure and layering I use to target the Web API action methods from Chapter 6.

■ **Tip** There are a lot of files in this chapter. If you don't want to type in all of the code and HTML, you can download the project for this chapter—and all chapters of this book—from Apress.com.

Preparing the Example Project

Before I get into the process of creating the clients, I need to make some general preparations. The first is the addition of an MVC controller that I can use to deliver HTML and JavaScript content to the browser. Listing 7-1 shows the contents of the HomeController.cs class file, which I added to the Controllers folder.

Listing 7-1. The Contents of the HomeController.cs File

```
using System.Web.Mvc;

namespace SportsStore.Controllers {
    public class HomeController : Controller {

        public ActionResult Index() {
            return View();
        }
    }
}
```

For my initial development, I created a placeholder view by creating the Views/Home folder, adding a view file called Index.cshtml, and using it to define the markup shown in Listing 7-2.

Listing 7-2. The Contents of the Index.cshtml File

```
<h2>Client Content Will Go Here</h2>
```

I will use the controller and view to test the lower-level functionality that I begin development with in this chapter and then use them deliver the customer client as the application becomes fully formed.

Setting Up JavaScript IntelliSense

I am going to be writing JavaScript code in this chapter, and I find it easier to do so using Visual Studio IntelliSense, which is the feature responsible for providing autocompletion of class, method, and property names in C# files. IntelliSense will also work with JavaScript, but it needs a little help through the creation of a filed called _references.js in the Scripts folder. I created the _references.js file by right-clicking the Scripts folder and selecting Add ➤ JavaScript File from the pop-up menu. Once Visual Studio created the file, I dragged the JavaScript files I will be depending on from the Solution Explorer and dropped them on the editor window for the _references.js file, producing the result shown in Listing 7-3.

Listing 7-3. The Contents of the _references.js File

```
/// <reference path="jquery-2.1.0.js" />
/// <reference path="bootstrap.js" />
/// <reference path="knockout-3.1.0.js" />
/// <reference path="storeAjax.js" />
/// <reference path="storeCommonController.js" />
/// <reference path="storeOrdersController.js" />
/// <reference path="storeProductsController.js" />
/// <reference path="storeCustomerController.js" />
/// <reference path="storeCustomerModel.js" />
/// <reference path="storeAdminModel.js" />
/// <reference path="storeAdminController.js" />
```

The first three entries are for the JavaScript files from the packages I installed in Chapter 5: jQuery, Bootstrap, and Knockout. The remaining entries—all of which begin with store—are the names of the JavaScript files I will create in this chapter for the SportsStore application.

Updating the Layout

I also need to update the Views/Shared/_Layout.cshtml file so that it contains script elements that reference the JavaScript files that I create in this chapter. Listing 7-4 shows the additions that I made to the layout.

Listing 7-4. Adding script Elements to the _Layout.cshtml File

```
<!DOCTYPE html>
<html>
<head>
    <meta name="viewport" content="width=device-width" />
    <script src="~/Scripts/jquery-2.1.0.min.js"></script>
    <script src="~/Scripts/knockout-3.1.0.js"></script>
    <link href="~/Content/bootstrap.css" rel="stylesheet" />
    <link href="~/Content/bootstrap-theme.css" rel="stylesheet" />
    <script src="~/Scripts/storeAjax.js"></script>
```

```
<script src="~/Scripts/storeModel.js"></script>
<script src="~/Scripts/storeCommonController.js"></script>
<script src="~/Scripts/storeProductsController.js"></script>
<script src="~/Scripts/storeOrdersController.js"></script>
<title>SportsStore</title>
<style>
    body { padding-top: 10px; }
</style>
@RenderSection("Scripts", false)
</head>
<body class="container">
    @RenderBody()
</body>
</html>
```

The order of these `script` elements is important and reflects the order in which they depend upon one another.

■ **Tip**   In a real project, I would generally use fewer files or concatenate the files using the MVC bundles feature, but for this chapter I want to make the structure and nature of the JavaScript code as clear as possible.

Implementing the Common Code

Even though I am creating clients for two different types of user, they will be accessing the same pair of web services that I created in Chapter 6. That means there is a core of common code that I can write once and use for both clients, which will make the SportsStore code base smaller and easier to maintain.

I will loosely follow the same structure in the client as I have done for the Web API part of the application; there will be a model that contains the application data and controllers that update that model based on user interactions. These updates will be performed using Ajax requests sent to the Web API web services. JavaScript doesn't provide the same programming experience as C#, so there will be some differences, but understanding the general shape of what I am writing will help you preserve a sense of context.

Defining the Ajax Layer

I like to start by creating a JavaScript file that contains the code that will make Ajax calls on behalf of other parts of the application so that I don't have to duplicate the code that deals with the web service. I created a JavaScript file called storeAjax.js in the Scripts folder and used it to define the code shown in Listing 7-5.

Listing 7-5. The Contents of the storeAjax.js File

```
var sendRequest = function (url, verb, data, successCallback, errorCallback, options) {

    var requestOptions = options || {};
    requestOptions.type = verb;
    requestOptions.success = successCallback;
    requestOptions.error = errorCallback;
```

```
        if (!url || !verb) {
            errorCallback(401, "URL and HTTP verb required");
        }

        if (data) {
            requestOptions.data = data;
        }
        $.ajax(url, requestOptions);
}

var setDefaultCallbacks = function (successCallback, errorCallback) {
    $.ajaxSetup({
        complete: function (jqXHR, status) {
            if (jqXHR.status >= 200 && jqXHR.status < 300) {
                successCallback(jqXHR.responseJSON);
            } else {
                errorCallback(jqXHR.status, jqXHR.statusText);
            }
        }
    });
}

var setAjaxHeaders = function (requestHeaders) {
    $.ajaxSetup({ headers: requestHeaders });
}
```

The most important function is sendRequest, which the other parts of the client-side application will call to send Ajax requests to the web services I defined in Chapter 6. Table 7-1 lists the parameters defined by the sendRequest function and explains their use.

Table 7-1. *The Parameters for the sendRequest Function*

Name	Description
url	This property specifies the URL that the request will be sent to.
verb	This property specifies the HTTP verb for the request.
data	This property specifies the data for the request, which will be sent to the web service as a query string for GET requests and in the request body for other verbs.
successCallback	This property specifies a callback function that will be invoked if the Ajax request is successful and passed the data from the response.
errorCallback	This property specifies a callback function that will be invoked if the Ajax request is unsuccessful and passed the status code and explanatory text.
options	This property is used to set jQuery options for a single Ajax request.

The only parameters that must be set are url and verb. If either is missing, then the error callback function is invoked to report a problem.

The setAjaxHeaders function sets headers for all subsequent Ajax requests by calling the jQuery $.ajaxSetup method. I'll use this feature to set the header required for authentication.

The setDefaultCallbacks function allows success and error callbacks to be registered so they will be invoked for all requests, which I'll use to control when errors are displayed to the user. This approach allows me to define controller-like functionality that has request-specific callbacks and still update the model, which I define in the next section.

Defining the Model

The next step is to define the client-side model, which I will use to store the product and order data and keep track of the client application state. I created a file called storeModel.js in the Scripts folder and added to it the JavaScript shown in Listing 7-6.

Listing 7-6. The Contents of the storeModel.js File

```
var model = {
    products: ko.observableArray([]),
    orders: ko.observableArray([]),
    authenticated: ko.observable(false),
    username: ko.observable(null),
    password: ko.observable(null),
    error: ko.observable(""),
    gotError: ko.observable(false)
};

$(document).ready(function () {
    ko.applyBindings();
    setDefaultCallbacks(function (data) {
            if (data) {
                console.log("---Begin Success---");
                console.log(JSON.stringify(data));
                console.log("---End Success---");
            } else {
                console.log("Success (no data)");
            }
            model.gotError(false);
        },
        function (statusCode, statusText) {
            console.log("Error: " + statusCode + " (" + statusText + ")");
            model.error(statusCode + " (" + statusText + ")");
            model.gotError(true);
        });
});
```

The model object defines a set of properties, each of which I have described in Table 7-2. I have also defined a handleError function that my client-side controllers will be able to call to handle failed Ajax calls, and I have used the jQuery ready function—which I described in Chapter 2—to set up the Knockout data bindings, which I will start to define in the next section.

Table 7-2. *The Client-Side Model Properties*

Name	Description
products	This property is an observable array that will be used to store the product objects obtained from the server.
orders	This property is an observable array that will be used to store the order objects obtained from the server.
authenticated	This property will be set to true when a successful authentication request has been performed and will be false otherwise.
username	This property will be set to the username entered by the user.
password	This property will be set to the password entered by the user.
error	This property is set to the error string that will be displayed to the user when an Ajax request fails.
gotError	This property is set to true when a request fails and false when a request succeeds. I will use this property to decide when to display error messages to the user.

Defining the Authentication Controller

The first client-side controller that I am going to create will handle authentication. I added a file called storeCommonController.js to the Scripts folder and added the code statements shown in Listing 7-7.

Listing 7-7. The Contents of the storeCommonController.js File

```
var authenticateUrl = "/authenticate"

var authenticate = function (successCallback) {
    sendRequest(authenticateUrl, "POST", {
        "grant_type": "password", username: model.username(), password: model.password()
    }, function (data) {
        model.authenticated(true);
        setAjaxHeaders({
            Authorization: "bearer " + data.access_token
        });
        if (successCallback) {
            successCallback();
        }
    });
};
```

■ **Tip** This isn't really a controller in the Web API or MVC framework sense of that word, but it helps to add structure to the client-side part of the application and ensure that functionality is concentrated in a single place, rather than repeated in different files.

This file defines a function called authenticate, which sends an Ajax request to the /authenticate URL that is maintained by ASP.NET Identity. The function includes the username and password values from the data model, and if the request is successful, it sets the Authorization header for subsequent requests to the access_token value generated by the web service.

Testing Authentication

To test the client-side authentication, I added some JavaScript code and HTML markup to the Index view to display the current authentication status and to send an authentication request, as shown in Listing 7-8.

Listing 7-8. Adding Support for Testing Authentication to the Index.cshtml File

```
<script>
    var testAuth = function () {
        model.username('Admin');
        model.password('secret');
        authenticate();
    }
</script>

<div class="panel panel-primary">
    <div class="panel-heading">Authentication</div>
    <table class="table table-striped">
        <tr><td>Authenticated:</td><td data-bind="text: model.authenticated()"></td></tr>
        <tr><td>User:</td><td data-bind="text: model.username()"></td></tr>
        <tr><td colspan="2"><button
                data-bind="click: testAuth">Authenticate</button></td></tr>
    </table>
</div>
```

The HTML markup is based around a Bootstrap-styled table with rows that contain Knockout data bindings to the authenticated and username model properties. I added an Authenticate button with a binding that calls the testAuth function defined in the script element when it is clicked. The testAuth function sets the model username and password properties to Admin and secret (which are the database seed values that I defined in Chapter 5) and calls the authenticate function that I defined in Listing 7-7.

To test the support for authentication, start the application and use the browser to navigate to the /Home/Index URL. The initial content will show no username and report that the client has not been authenticated. Click the Authenticate button; an Ajax request will be sent to the web service, and the client will be authenticated, causing the layout to be updated through the data bindings, as shown in Figure 7-1.

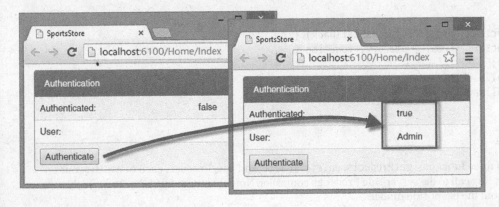

Figure 7-1. *Testing client authentication*

The first authentication request after you start the application will take a couple of seconds because the database will be initialized. This means the username will be displayed immediately because it is set locally in the client but that the Authenticated status will not change to true for a moment. To get a more realistic result, reload the web page in the browser and click the Authenticate button again.

■ **Note**   Reloading the web page in the browser means that the client loses the authentication token required to authorize requests. This is a side effect of using the Authorization header, which makes it easier to build and test client-side code but requires authentication each time the page is loaded.

Defining the Products Controller

The next step is to create the client-side code that will send Ajax requests to get and manipulate products. Listing 7-9 shows the content of the storeProductsController.js file, which I added to the Scripts folder.

Listing 7-9. The Contents of the storeProductsController.js File

```
var productUrl = "/api/products/";

var getProducts = function () {
    sendRequest(productUrl, "GET", null, function (data) {
        model.products.removeAll();
        model.products.push.apply(model.products, data);
    })
};

var deleteProduct = function (id) {
    sendRequest(productUrl + id, "DELETE", null, function () {
        model.products.remove(function (item) {
            return item.Id == id;
        })
    });
}

var saveProduct = function (product, successCallback) {
    sendRequest(productUrl, "POST", product, function () {
        getProducts();
        if (successCallback) {
            successCallback();
        }
    });
}
```

The code consists of three functions, getProducts, deleteProduct, and saveProduct, each of which sends an Ajax call to the corresponding call to the server-side Products controller. Note that these functions exist solely to map server-side data to and from the client-side model.

Testing the Products Controllers

To test the client-side product code, I added some additional HTML and JavaScript to the Index.cshtml file. In addition to adding code that calls the functions defined in Listing 7-9, I have added support for displaying details of the HTTP error message when Ajax requests fail, as shown in Listing 7-10.

Listing 7-10. Adding Markup and JavaScript to the Index.cshtml File

```
<script>

    var testAuth = function () {
        model.username('Admin');
        model.password('secret');
        authenticate();
    }

    var testDeleteProduct = function () {
        deleteProduct(2);
    }

    var testChangeProduct = function () {
        var product = model.products()[2];
        product.Price = product.Price + 10;
        saveProduct(product);
    }

</script>

<div class="alert alert-danger" data-bind="visible: model.gotError(), text: model.error()">
</div>

<div class="panel panel-primary">
    <div class="panel-heading">Authentication</div>
    <table class="table table-striped">
        <tr><td>Authenticated:</td><td data-bind="text: model.authenticated()"></td></tr>
        <tr><td>User:</td><td data-bind="text: model.username()"></td></tr>
        <tr><td colspan="2"><button
                data-bind="click: testAuth">Authenticate</button></td></tr>
    </table>
</div>

<div class="panel panel-primary">
    <div class="panel-heading">Product Controller Functions</div>
    <table class="table table-striped">
        <tr>
            <td><button data-bind="click: getProducts">Get Products</button></td>
            <td><button data-bind="click: testDeleteProduct">Delete Product</button></td>
            <td><button data-bind="click: testChangeProduct">Change Product</button></td>
        </tr>
    </table>
</div>
```

■ **Tip**   You should not show HTTP messages to real users, but since this is a book about web services, I am going to display the low-level messages.

I have added three buttons with Knockout data bindings to the view. The Get Products button invokes the getProducts controller function when it is clicked, but the Delete Product and Change Product buttons call functions defined in the script element so that I can control the arguments passed to the corresponding controller functions.

To test the new functionality, start the application and use the browser to navigate to the /Home/Index URL. The debug output from the JavaScript code will be writing to the JavaScript console, so you will need to open the browser F12 tools to see the messages.

Click the Get Products button, and you will see a JavaScript console message that lists the Product objects contained in the database, formatted as JSON, like this:

```
---Begin Success--- storeModel.js:16
[{"Id":1,"Name":"Kayak","Description":"A boat for one person","Price":275,
    "Category":"Watersports"},
 {"Id":2,"Name":"Lifejacket","Description":"Protective and fashionable",
    "Price":48.95,"Category":"Watersports"},
 {"Id":3,"Name":"Soccer Ball","Description":"FIFA-approved size and weight",
    "Price":19.5,"Category":"Soccer"},
 {"Id":4,"Name":"Corner Flags",
    "Description":"Give your playing field a professional touch",
    "Price":34.95,"Category":"Soccer"},
 {"Id":5,"Name":"Stadium",
    "Description":"Flat-packed 35,000-seat stadium",
    "Price":79500,"Category":"Soccer"},
 {"Id":6,"Name":"Thinking Cap",
    "Description":"Improve your brain efficiency by 75%",
    "Price":16,"Category":"Chess"},
 {"Id":7,"Name":"Unsteady Chair",
    "Description":"Secretly give your opponent a disadvantage",
    "Price":29.95,"Category":"Chess"},
 {"Id":8,"Name":"Human Chess Board",
    "Description":"A fun game for the family",
    "Price":75,"Category":"Chess"},
 {"Id":9,"Name":"Bling-Bling King",
    "Description":"Gold-plated, diamond-studded King",
    "Price":1200,"Category":"Chess"}]
---End Success---
```

This is the same product list you have been seeing since Chapter 5, and the key point to note is that all of the products that I defined in the database seed class are present.

Next, click the Delete Product button. This button sends a request that targets an action method to which the Authorize attribute was applied in Chapter 6. As a consequence, a 401 (Unauthorized) response is returned. This triggers my error handling code and reveals the error element I added to the Index.cshtml file, as shown in Figure 7-2.

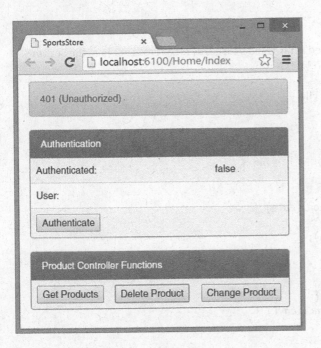

Figure 7-2. *Displaying an HTTP error*

Click the Authenticate button and then, once the Authenticated status is shown as true, click the Delete Product button again. The JavaScript console will show the following message:

```
Success (no data)
```

To see the effect of the operation, click the Get Products button and look at the Id numbers of the objects that are described, as follows:

```
---Begin Success---
[{"Id":1,"Name":"Kayak","Description":"A boat..."},
 {"Id":3,"Name":"Soccer Ball","Description":"FIFA-approved..."},
 {"Id":4,"Name":"Corner Flags","Description":"Give your ..."},
 {"Id":5,"Name":"Stadium","Description":"Flat-packed..."},
 {"Id":6,"Name":"Thinking Cap","Description":"Improve ..."},
 {"Id":7,"Name":"Unsteady Chair","Description":"Secretly..."},
 {"Id":8,"Name":"Human Chess Board","Description":"A fun..."},
 {"Id":9,"Name":"Bling-Bling King","Description":"Gold-plated…"}]
---End Success---
```

As the highlighted statements show, the Product with the Id value of 2 has been removed.

The final test is to click the Change Product button. The client-side controller function reloads the product data when it completes, and you will see that the Price property of the product as index 2 (which will be the Corner Flags if you have followed along and deleted a product) will be incremented by $10.

Defining the Orders Controller

The final controller is to provide access to the orders. I added a file called storeOrdersController.js to the Scripts folder and used it to define the functions shown in Listing 7-11.

Listing 7-11. The Contents of the storeOrdersController.js File

```
var ordersUrl = "/nonrest/orders";
var ordersListUrl = ordersUrl + "/list";
var ordersCreateUrl = ordersUrl + "/createorder/";
var ordersDeleteUrl = ordersUrl + "/deleteorder/";

var getOrders = function () {
    sendRequest(ordersListUrl, "GET", null, function (data) {
        model.orders.removeAll();
        model.orders.push.apply(model.orders, data);
    });
}

var saveOrder = function (order, successCallback) {
    sendRequest(ordersCreateUrl, "POST", order, function () {
        if (successCallback) {
            successCallback();
        }
    });
}

var deleteOrder = function (id) {
    sendRequest(ordersDeleteUrl + id, "DELETE", null, function () {
        model.orders.remove(function (item) {
            return item.Id == id;
        })
    });
}
```

The getOrders, saveOrder, and deleteOrder functions target their server-side counterparts. The server-side Web API controller for Orders objects is non-RESTful, which is why I have had to define URLs for each of the different operations.

Testing the Orders Controller

Following the same approach as for the other client-side controllers, I added some new HTML and JavaScript code to the Index.cshtml file, as shown in Listing 7-12.

Listing 7-12. Adding Support for Testing Orders in the Index.cshtml File

```
<script>

    var testAuth = function () {
        model.username('Admin');
        model.password('secret');
        authenticate();
    }

    var testDeleteProduct = function () {
        deleteProduct(2);
    }

    var testChangeProduct = function () {
        var product = model.products()[2];
        product.Price = product.Price + 10;
        saveProduct(product);
    }

    var testDeleteOrder = function () {
        deleteOrder(1);
    }

    var testSaveOrder = function () {
        var order = model.orders()[0];
        order.TotalPrice = order.TotalPrice + 10;
        saveOrder(order);
    }

</script>
<div class="alert alert-danger"
     data-bind="visible: model.gotError(), text: model.error()">
</div>

<div class="panel panel-primary">
    <div class="panel-heading">Authentication</div>
    <table class="table table-striped">
        <tr><td>Authenticated:</td><td data-bind="text: model.authenticated()"></td></tr>
        <tr><td>User:</td><td data-bind="text: model.username()"></td></tr>
        <tr><td colspan="2"><button
                data-bind="click: testAuth">Authenticate</button></td></tr>
    </table>
</div>

<div class="panel panel-primary">
    <div class="panel-heading">Product Controller Functions</div>
    <table class="table table-striped">
        <tr>
            <td><button data-bind="click: getProducts">Get Products</button></td>
            <td><button data-bind="click: testDeleteProduct">Delete Product</button></td>
            <td><button data-bind="click: testChangeProduct">Change Product</button></td>
        </tr>
    </table>
</div>
```

143

```
<div class="panel panel-primary">
    <div class="panel-heading">Order Controller Functions</div>
    <table class="table table-striped">
        <tr>
            <td><button data-bind="click: getOrders">Get Orders</button></td>
            <td><button data-bind="click: testDeleteOrder">Delete Order</button></td>
            <td><button data-bind="click: testSaveOrder">Save Order</button></td>
        </tr>
    </table>
</div>
```

There are three order-related buttons. The Get Orders button calls the controller getOrders function directly, and the Delete Order and Save Order buttons call functions that I added to the local script element. Figure 7-3 shows the additions.

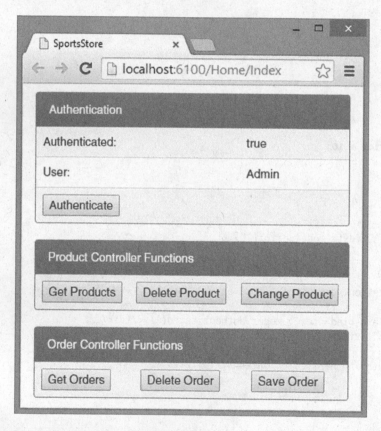

Figure 7-3. Adding order test support

The action methods targeted by the Get Orders and Delete Order buttons require authentication, so click the Authenticate button and wait a moment for the authentication state to change. Click the Get Orders button, and the JavaScript console will display a list of the orders obtained from the web service. Click the Delete Order to remove one of the orders and then click Get Orders again to see the effect. Finally, click Save Order to add a new order to the repository.

Creating the Customer Client

Now that I have a solid foundation of client-side controller and Ajax functions, I can begin to build the client that will present the SportsStore application to clients. In the sections that follow, I will create the JavaScript code and MVC framework views required to allow the user to select and order products.

■ **Note** I am not going to add all the SportsStore features from the version I create in *Pro ASP.NET MVC 5* because I want to demonstrate how to consume the Web API web services that I created in Chapter 6 without spending too much time dealing with the fit-and-finish of the client application. The main features are present, but I have omitted lesser features that are not directly related to web services, such as paginating the list of products, performing client-side validation, and displaying useful error messages—none of which requires interactions with the web service.

Creating the Customer Model

I have created a separate model that contains just the data and state required to manage the customer client, which allows me to keep it separate from the common model that contains the raw product data. Listing 7-13 shows the contents of the storeCustomerModel.js file, which I added to the Scripts folder.

Listing 7-13. The Contents of the storeCustomerModel.js File

```
var customerModel = {
    productCategories: ko.observableArray([]),
    filteredProducts: ko.observableArray([]),
    selectedCategory: ko.observable(null),
    cart: ko.observableArray([]),
    cartTotal: ko.observable(0),
    cartCount: ko.observable(0),
    currentView: ko.observable("list")
}
```

All of the model properties that I define are observable, and you will see that I rely on the automatic updates that Knockout provides to keep the client interface synchronized with the underlying data. To help you keep track of what goes on in the custom client, Table 7-3 describes the purpose of each of the model properties.

Table 7-3. *The Customer Client Model Properties*

Name	Description
productCategories	This property is an array of the product category names, which I use to allow the customer to filter products so that only those in a given category are shown.
filteredProducts	This property contains the set of products that belong to the currently selected category.
selectedCategory	This property specifies the currently selected category and is used to filter the products shown to the customer through the filteredProducts property.
cart	This property represents the customer's shopping cart and contains details of the products they have selected and the quantity of each.
cartTotal	This property specifies the total value of the products in the cart.
cartCount	This property specifies the number of products in the cart.
currentView	This property specifies which view the custom should be shown.

Creating the Customer Controller

I added a file called storeCustomerController.js to the Scripts folder and used it to define the functions that will support the views that present functionality to the customer and operation on the application models—both the common model and the one that is specific to the customer client. Listing 7-14 shows the functions that I defined. This is a lengthy file, and much of the code is responsible for sorting and filtering the common model objects that represent the SportsStore products so they can be presented to the user.

Listing 7-14. The Contents of the storeCustomerController.js File

```
var setCategory = function (category) {
    customerModel.selectedCategory(category);
    filterProductsByCategory();
}

var setView = function (view) {
    customerModel.currentView(view);
}

var addToCart = function (product) {
    var found = false;
    var cart = customerModel.cart();
    for (var i = 0; i < cart.length; i++) {
        if (cart[i].product.Id == product.Id) {
            found = true;
            count = cart[i].count + 1;
            customerModel.cart.splice(i, 1);
            customerModel.cart.push({
                count: count,
                product: product
            });
            break;
        }
    }
```

```
        if (!found) {
            customerModel.cart.push({ count: 1, product: product });
        }

        setView("cart");
    }

    var removeFromCart = function (productSelection) {
        customerModel.cart.remove(productSelection);
    }

    var placeOrder = function () {
        var order = {
            Customer: model.username(),
            Lines: customerModel.cart().map(function (item) {
                return {
                    Count: item.count,
                    ProductId: item.product.Id
                }
            })
        };

        saveOrder(order, function () {
            setView("thankyou");
        });
    }

    model.products.subscribe(function (newProducts) {

        filterProductsByCategory();

        customerModel.productCategories.removeAll();
        customerModel.productCategories.push.apply(customerModel.productCategories,
            model.products().map(function (p) {
                return p.Category;
            })
            .filter(function (value, index, self) {
                return self.indexOf(value) === index;
            }).sort());
    });

    customerModel.cart.subscribe(function (newCart) {

        customerModel.cartTotal(newCart.reduce(
            function (prev, item) {
                return prev + (item.count * item.product.Price);
            }, 0));

        customerModel.cartCount(newCart.reduce(
            function (prev, item) {
                return prev + item.count;
            }, 0));
    });
```

```
var filterProductsByCategory = function () {
    var category = customerModel.selectedCategory();

    customerModel.filteredProducts.removeAll();
    customerModel.filteredProducts.push.apply(customerModel.filteredProducts,
        model.products().filter(function (p) {
            return category == null || p.Category == category;
        }));
}

$(document).ready(function () {
    getProducts();
})
```

Not all of the code is made up of functions for views to call; I have also used the Knockout subscribe function to define functions that are called automatically when there are changes to observable data items, like this:

```
...
model.products.subscribe(function (newProducts) {

    filterProductsByCategory();

    customerModel.productCategories.removeAll();
    customerModel.productCategories.push.apply(customerModel.productCategories,
        model.products().map(function (p) {
            return p.Category;
        })
        .filter(function (value, index, self) {
            return self.indexOf(value) === index;
        }).sort());
});
...
```

This fragment registers a function to be called when the model.products array changes. The function filters the products so that only those in the category that the user is viewing are displayed. It also generates the set of product categories, which is what allows the user to perform the filtering. The effect is that a change in the model.products array automatically updates the customer model, which will, in turn, cause the Knockout data bindings I will apply in the views to update as well.

The controller uses the jQuery ready function, which I described in Chapter 2, to load the product data when the browser has loaded and processed the HTML and JavaScript files, as follows:

```
...
$(document).ready(function () {
    getProducts();
})
...
```

This means that there is no data available until the Ajax request that the getProduct function sends has completed.

Creating the Views

I am at the point where I need to create the views that will consume the data in the models and use the controller functions to respond to user input. This is a departure from the Web API theme of this book, so I am going to describe the contents of the files only briefly. In the sections that follow, I will create a series of MVC framework views that use entirely standard Razor features in order to compose an HTML document that will respond dynamically to user input and data changes.

Creating the Placeholders

I will use a set of MVC framework partial views to break the content into more manageable chunks. I want to be able to demonstrate how the different features fit together as I go, so I have started by creating a set of placeholder view files that I will revise once the structure of the application comes together. Table 7-4 lists the file names, all of which I created in the Views/Home folder, and describes their purpose in the application.

Table 7-4. *The Placeholder View Files for the Customer Client*

Name	Description
ProductList.cshtml	This view is used to present the customer with a list of products that can be filtered by category.
ProductCart.cshtml	This view is used to present the user with a summary of the products they have selected.
Checkout.cshtml	This view is used to present the customer with the (simple) checkout process.
CartWidget.cshtml	This view is used to insert a small summary of the cart in the SportsStore header.
ThankYou.cshtml	This view is displayed to the user when they have completed their order.

Listing 7-15 shows the initial contents of the ProductList.cshtml file.

Listing 7-15. The Contents of the ProductList.cshtml File

```
ProductList View
```

Listing 7-16 shows the initial contents of the ProductCart.cshtml file.

Listing 7-16. The Contents of the ProductCart.cshtml File

```
ProductCart View
```

Listing 7-17 shows the contents of the Checkout.cshtml file.

Listing 7-17. The Contents of the Checkout.cshtml File

```
Checkout View
```

Listing 7-18 shows the contents of the CartWidget.cshtml file. This placeholder requires the application of some Bootstrap styles because it will be displayed in the banner at the top of the page and would not be visible without them.

Listing 7-18. The Contents of the CartWidget.cshtml File

```
<div class="navbar-text navbar-right">
    CartWidget View
</div>
```

The ThankYou.cshtml file is so simple that it doesn't require a placeholder, and Listing 7-19 shows the final content of the file.

Listing 7-19. The Contents of the ThankYou.cshtml File

```
<h2>Thanks!</h2>
Thanks for placing your order. We'll ship your goods as soon as possible.
```

With the exception of the ThankYou.cshtml file, I'll revise the contents and show you the effect as I add each feature.

Creating the Index View

The Views/Home/Index.cshtml file is the top-level view for the customer client. I used this view earlier in the chapter to test the common JavaScript code, but in Listing 7-20 you can see how I have changed the contents to provide the framework in which content will be added so that it can be displayed to the user.

Listing 7-20. The Contents of the Index.cshtml File

```
@section Scripts {
    <script src="~/Scripts/storeCustomerModel.js"></script>
    <script src="~/Scripts/storeCustomerController.js"></script>
}

<div class="navbar navbar-inverse" role="navigation">
    <a class="navbar-brand" href="#">SPORTS STORE</a>
    @Html.Partial("CartWidget");
</div>

<div id="categories" class="col-xs-3">
    <button class="btn btn-block btn-default btn-lg"
            data-bind="click: setCategory.bind(null)">
        Home
    </button>
    <div data-bind="foreach: customerModel.productCategories()">
        <button class="btn btn-block btn-default btn-lg"
                data-bind="click: setCategory.bind($data), text: $data,
                    css: {'btn-primary': $data ==
                        customerModel.selectedCategory()}"></button>
    </div>
</div>

<div class="alert alert-danger col-xs-8"
     data-bind="visible: model.gotError(), text: model.error()">
</div>
```

```
<div class="col-xs-8">
    <div class="row panel" data-bind="visible: customerModel.currentView() == 'list'">
        @Html.Partial("ProductList")
    </div>
    <div class="row panel"
        data-bind="visible: customerModel.currentView() == 'cart'">
        @Html.Partial("ProductCart")
    </div>
    <div class="row panel"
        data-bind="visible: customerModel.currentView() == 'checkout'">
        @Html.Partial("Checkout")
    </div>
    <div class="row panel"
        data-bind="visible: customerModel.currentView() == 'thankyou'">
        @Html.Partial("ThankYou")
    </div>
</div>
```

I have added `script` elements for the customer model and controller files and defined a banner across the page to identify the application. In addition, I have defined a set of category buttons (which is populated based on the categories generated by the customer controller), an alert box to display any errors, and the main content area, which uses Knockout bindings to determine which Razor partial view is displayed to the client.

You can see the initial structure of the layout by starting the application and using the browser to navigate to the /Home/Index URL. As Figure 7-4 shows, there are buttons for each of the categories of product in the repository, and the placeholders for the `CartWidget` and `ProductList` views are visible.

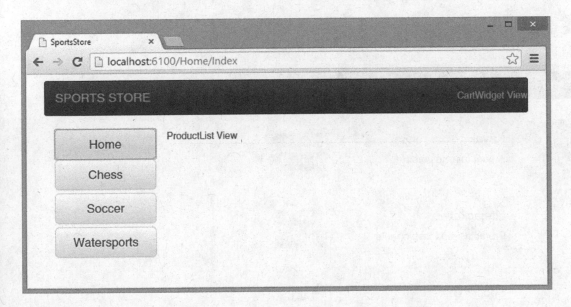

Figure 7-4. The initial structure of the customer client

151

Creating the Product List View

The most important content to present to the customer is a list of the products they can add to their basket, which is the job of the `ProductList` view. Listing 7-21 shows the markup I added to the view to describe each product.

Listing 7-21. Adding Markup to the ProductList.cshtml File

```
<div data-bind="foreach: customerModel.filteredProducts()">
    <div class="well">
        <h3>
            <strong data-bind="text: $data.Name"></strong>
            <span class="pull-right label label-primary"
                    data-bind="text: ('$' + $data.Price.toFixed(2))"></span>
        </h3>
        <span class="lead" data-bind="text: $data.Description"></span>
        <div class="pull-right">
            <button class="btn btn-success"
                    data-bind="click: addToCart">Add to Cart</button>
        </div>
    </div>
</div>
```

I use a Knockout `foreach` binding to generate a `div` element for each of the products in the currently selected category. Each product is displayed with its name, description, and price, as well as an Add to Cart button that calls the `addToCart` function in the customer controller, which adds details of the product to the customer's cart. Figure 7-5 shows the effect of the changes in the listing.

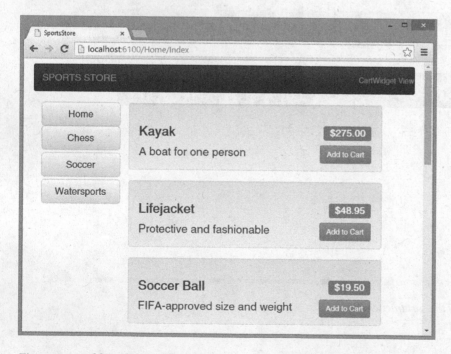

Figure 7-5. *Adding details of the products*

You can filter the products shown in the list by clicking one of the category buttons; you can show all of the products again by clicking the Home button.

Creating the Cart View

When the customer clicks an Add to Cart button, the `ProductCart` view is displayed to summarize the set of chosen products and their cost. Listing 7-22 shows the changes I made to the `ProductCart.cshtml` file to display this information.

Listing 7-22. Displaying Product Selections in the ProductCart.cshtml File

```
<h2>Your Cart</h2>

<div class="panel panel-primary">
    <table class="table">
        <thead>
            <tr>
                <th>Quantity</th><th>Item</th>
                <th>Price</th><th class="text-right">Subtotal</th>
                <td></td>
            </tr>
        </thead>
        <tbody data-bind="foreach: customerModel.cart()">
            <tr>
                <td data-bind="text: $data.count"></td>
                <td data-bind="text: $data.product.Name"></td>
                <td data-bind="text: '$' + $data.product.Price.toFixed(2)"></td>
                <td class="text-right"
                    data-bind="text: '$'
                        + ($data.count * $data.product.Price).toFixed(2)"></td>
                <td><button class="btn btn-xs btn-danger"
                    data-bind="click: removeFromCart.bind($data)">Remove</button></td>
            </tr>
        </tbody>
        <tfoot>
            <tr>
                <td colspan="2"></td><td>Total:</td>
                <th class="text-right"
                    data-bind="text: '$' + customerModel.cartTotal().toFixed(2)"></th>
            </tr>
        </tfoot>
    </table>
</div>

<div class="text-center">
    <button class="btn btn-primary"
            data-bind="click: setView.bind($data, 'list')">Continue Shopping</button>
    <button class="btn btn-primary"
            data-bind="click: setView.bind($data, 'checkout'),
                enable: customerModel.cartCount() > 0">Check Out</button>
</div>
```

The main part of the view is a table that lists the selected products, and there are buttons that use Knockout click bindings to return the customer to the product list and proceed to the checkout stage. Figure 7-6 shows the cart once some products have been selected.

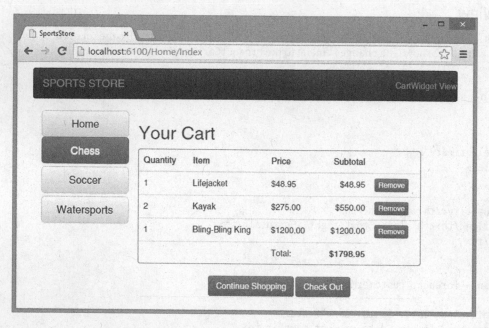

Figure 7-6. *Displaying a summary of the cart*

■ **Tip** I have not included support for varying the quantity of a product in the cart, but you can return to the product list and select a product repeatedly to increase the quantity.

Creating the Cart Widget

The CartWidget view is responsible for displaying a summary of the customer's product selections at the top of the page, along with a button that begins the checkout process. Listing 7-23 shows the changes I made to the CartWidget.cshtml file to define this functionality.

Listing 7-23. Displaying a Summary of the Cart in the CartWidget.cshtml File

```
<div class="navbar-right" style="margin: 0 10px">
    <button class="btn btn-default btn-xs navbar-btn"
            data-bind="click: setView.bind($data, 'checkout'),
                enable: customerModel.cartCount() > 0">
        Checkout
    </button>
</div>
```

```
<div class="navbar-text navbar-right">
    <b>Your cart:</b>
    <span data-bind="text: customerModel.cartCount()"></span> item(s),
    <span data-bind="text: '$' + customerModel.cartTotal().toFixed(2)"></span>
</div>
```

This view displays data values from the model and provides a button that moves to the checkout view. The button is disabled if there are no items in the cart. Figure 7-7 shows the cart widget.

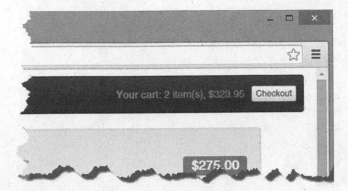

Figure 7-7. *Summarizing the cart*

Creating the Checkout View

The final view to create is the one that lets the client check out and place their order. Listing 7-24 shows the changes that I made to the Checkout.cshtml file.

Listing 7-24. Placing an Order in the Checkout.cshtml File

```
<h2>Your Order</h2>

<div class="form-group">
    <label>Enter your name</label>
    <input class="form-control" data-bind="value: model.username" />
</div>

<div class="panel panel-primary">
    <table class="table">
        <thead>
            <tr>
                <th>Quantity</th>
                <th>Item</th>
                <th>Price</th>
                <th class="text-right">Subtotal</th>
            </tr>
        </thead>
        <tbody data-bind="foreach: customerModel.cart()">
```

155

```
            <tr>
                <td data-bind="text: $data.count"></td>
                <td data-bind="text: $data.product.Name"></td>
                <td data-bind="text: '$' + $data.product.Price.toFixed(2)"></td>
                <td class="text-right"
                    data-bind="text: '$'
                        + ($data.count * $data.product.Price).toFixed(2)">
                </td>
            </tr>
        </tbody>
        <tfoot>
            <tr>
                <td colspan="2"></td>
                <td>Total:</td>
                <th class="text-right"
                    data-bind="text: '$' + customerModel.cartTotal().toFixed(2)"></th>
            </tr>
        </tfoot>
    </table>
</div>

<div class="text-center">
    <button class="btn btn-primary"
            data-bind="click: setView.bind($data, 'list')">Cancel</button>
    <button class="btn btn-danger"
            data-bind="click: placeOrder.bind($data)">Place Order</button>
</div>
```

I need only the customer's name and a list of their products to be able to send an order to the web service because I defined a simple Order model class in Chapter 5. In this view, I show an input element to collect the name and display a summary of the cart, as shown in Figure 7-8.

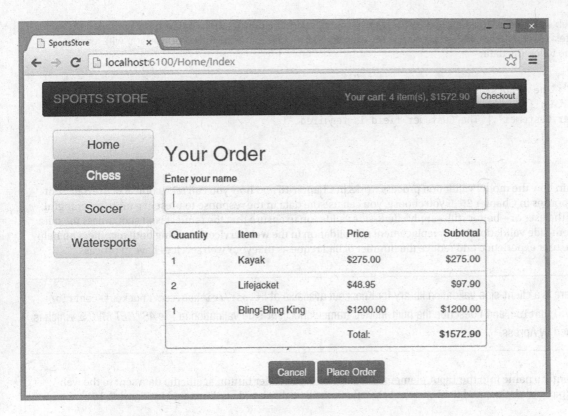

Figure 7-8. *Checking out*

If you click the Place Order button without entering a name, you will see the rudimentary error handling at work, as illustrated by Figure 7-9. This is not a useful message for customers of most applications, but for this book it demonstrates the way in which the web service has responded to a request.

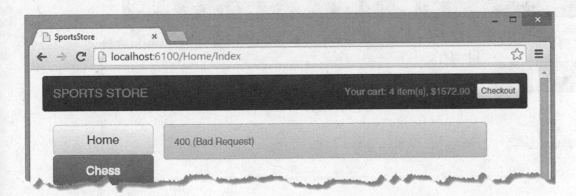

Figure 7-9. *The result of server-side validation error*

The web service sent the 400 (Bad Request) response because the data I sent to the web service failed the validation tests for the Order object. If you use the browser F12 tools to examine the response, you will see that it included the following data:

```
{"Message":"The request is invalid.",
 "ModelState": {
     "order.Customer":["The Customer field is required."]
  }
}
```

I explain how the model validation process works in Chapter 18 and how you can take control of the data sent in error responses in Chapter 25. If you choose, you can use the data in the response to present a more meaningful message to the user or—better still—apply client-side validation to ensure that the request isn't sent unless the data is valid. Client-side validation isn't a replacement for validation in the web service, but using both together can help improve the user experience and reduce the number of bad requests that your web services have to process.

■ **Tip** There is a client-side validation library for Knockout available at `https://github.com/Knockout-Contrib/Knockout-Validation`, and I describe the built-in MVC framework client-side validation in *Pro ASP.NET MVC 5*, which is also published by Apress.

If you enter a name into the input element and click the Place Order button again, the data sent to the web service will pass validation, and the ThankYou.cshtml view will be displayed, as illustrated by Figure 7-10.

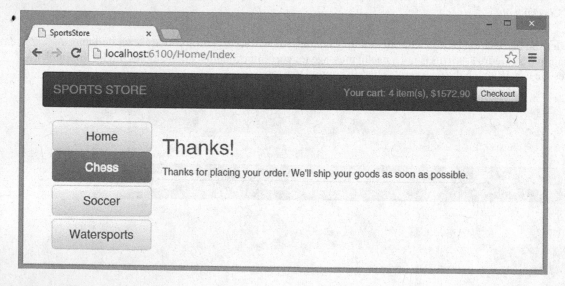

Figure 7-10. Successfully placing an order

Creating the Administration Client

The administration client is simpler than the one required for the customer. I build on the common code I created at the start of the chapter to authenticate the user and provide support for viewing, creating, and deleting products and viewing and deleting orders. In the following sections, I create the model, controller, and views required for the admin client using the same approach I took for the customer client.

■ **Tip**   I am not going to create placeholders for the views for this client, which means that the administration client will not work until you reach the "Testing the Administration Client" section.

Creating the Admin Model

The admin client doesn't need to filter data by category, which means it can work directly with the data in the common model. The result is that the admin client model is small and simple. Listing 7-25 shows the contents of the storeAdminModel.js file, which I added to the Scripts folder.

Listing 7-25. The Contents of the storeAdminModel.js File

```
var adminModel = {
    currentView: ko.observable("signin"),
    listMode: ko.observable("products"),
    newProduct: { name: ""}
}
```

The currentView property is used to control the top-level content displayed to the user, which will switch between a sign-in screen and the administration display. The user can see the products or orders in the repository, and this choice is stored using the listMode property. The newProduct property is where I will gather the details for new products that the user wants to add to the repository.

■ **Tip**   I do not have to define properties for the newProduct object because they will be set by the Knockout bindings that I attach to input elements when I define the views. However, I have added one property—name—so that jQuery will always send request data to the server as part of its POST request, even if the user submits the product without entering any data into the input elements.

Creating the Admin Controller

The admin client requires a few functions to manage its views and to act as intermediaries between the data that will be available to Knockout bindings and the data required by the common controller functions. (For example, the removeProduct function will be passed a complete product object by Knockout, but the underling deleteProduct function operates on the Id property value.) Listing 7-26 shows the contents of the storeAdminController.cs file, which I added to the Scripts folder.

Listing 7-26. The Contents of the storeAdminController.cs File

```
var setView = function (view) {
    adminModel.currentView(view);
}

var setListMode = function (mode) {
    console.log("Mode: " + mode);
    adminModel.listMode(mode);
}

var authenticateUser = function() {
    authenticate(function () {
        setView("productList");
        getProducts();
        getOrders();
    });
}

var createProduct = function () {
    saveProduct(adminModel.newProduct, function () {
        setListMode("products");
    })
}

var removeProduct = function (product) {
    deleteProduct(product.Id);
}

var removeOrder = function (order) {
    deleteOrder(order.Id);
}
```

Creating the Views

The administration client requires only four views: the top-level container, a list of products, a list of orders, and a set of input elements needed to create new products. In the sections that follow, I'll show you how I defined each of them.

Defining the MVC Controller and Top-Level View

I have created a separate MVC framework controller to deliver the administration client. Listing 7-27 shows the contents of the AdminController.cs file, which I added to the Controllers folder.

Listing 7-27. The Contents of the AdminController.cs File

```
using System.Web.Mvc;

namespace SportsStore.Controllers {

    public class AdminController : Controller {
```

```
        public ActionResult Index() {
            return View();
        }
    }
}
```

The controller contains an Index action method that will render the Index.cshtml file I created in the Views/Admin folder. Listing 7-28 shows the content of the view file.

Listing 7-28. The Contents of the Views/Admin/Index.cshtml File

```
@section Scripts {
    <script src="~/Scripts/storeAdminModel.js"></script>
    <script src="~/Scripts/storeAdminController.js"></script>
}

<div class="navbar navbar-inverse" role="navigation">
    <a class="navbar-brand" href="#">SPORTS STORE</a>
</div>

<div class="alert alert-danger text-center"
     data-bind="visible: model.gotError(), text: model.error()">
</div>

<div>
    <div class="text-center" data-bind="visible: adminModel.currentView() == 'signin'">
        <div class="form-group">
            <label>Username</label>
            <input data-bind="value: model.username" />
        </div>
        <div class="form-group">
            <label>Password</label>
            <input type="password" data-bind="value: model.password" />
        </div>
        <button class="btn btn-primary"
            data-bind="click: authenticateUser">Sign In</button>
    </div>

    <div data-bind="visible: adminModel.currentView() == 'productList'">

        <div id="categories" class="col-xs-3">
            <button class="btn btn-block btn-default btn-lg"
                    data-bind="click: setListMode.bind($data, 'products')">
                Products
            </button>
            <button class="btn btn-block btn-default btn-lg"
                    data-bind="click: setListMode.bind($data, 'orders')">
                Orders
            </button>
        </div>
```

```
        <div class="col-xs-8" data-bind="visible: adminModel.listMode() == 'products'">
            @Html.Partial("AdminProductList")
        </div>

        <div class="col-xs-8" data-bind="visible: adminModel.listMode() == 'addProduct'">
            @Html.Partial("AdminProductAdd")
        </div>

        <div class="col-xs-8" data-bind="visible: adminModel.listMode() == 'orders'">
            @Html.Partial("AdminOrderList")
        </div>
    </div>
</div>
```

■ **Tip**   This view relies on the same `_Layout.cshtml` file that I used for the customer client.

This is similar to the structure that I used for the customer client, with the addition of an embedded sign-in view that gathers credentials for the user in order to authenticate the client.

Defining the Product List View

For the administration client, I display a simplified version of the product list but have added buttons to delete individual products and to create new ones. Listing 7-29 shows the contents of the AdminProductList.cshtml file, which I added to the Views/Admin folder.

Listing 7-29. The Contents of the AdminProductList.cshtml File

```
<div class="panel panel-primary">
    <table class="table table-striped">
        <thead>
            <tr><th>ID</th><th>Name</th><th>Category</th><th>Price</th><th></th></tr>
        </thead>
        <tbody data-bind="foreach: model.products()">
            <tr>
                <td data-bind="text: $data.Id"></td>
                <td data-bind="text: $data.Name"></td>
                <td data-bind="text: $data.Category"></td>
                <td data-bind="text: '$' + $data.Price.toFixed(2)"
                    class="text-right"></td>
                <td>
                    <button class="btn btn-xs btn-danger"
                            data-bind="click: removeProduct">Remove</button>
                </td>
            </tr>
        </tbody>
    </table>
</div>
```

```
<div class="text-center">
    <button class="btn btn-primary"
            data-bind="click: setListMode.bind($data, 'addProduct')">
        Add Product
    </button>
</div>
```

Defining the Order List View

To display details of the orders, I have used the same table structure that I created in Chapter 5 when I was writing the web services. The difference is that the elements are generated through Knockout bindings rather than Razor. Listing 7-30 shows the contents of the AdminOrderList.cshtml file, which I added to the /Views/Admin folder.

Listing 7-30. The Contents of the AdminOrderList.cshtml File

```
<div class="panel panel-primary">
    <div class="panel-heading">
        Orders
    </div>
    <table class="table table-striped">
        <thead>
            <tr>
                <th>ID</th>
                <th>Customer</th>
                <th colspan="3"></th>
                <th>Total Cost</th>
                <th></th>
            </tr>
        </thead>
        <tbody data-bind="foreach: model.orders()">
            <tr>
                <td data-bind="text: $data.Id"></td>
                <td data-bind="text: $data.Customer"></td>
                <td colspan="3"></td>
                <td data-bind="text: '$' + $data.TotalCost.toFixed(2)"></td>
                <td>
                    <button class="btn btn-xs btn-danger"
                            data-bind="click: removeOrder">Remove</button>
                </td>
            </tr>
            <tr>
                <th colspan="2"></th>
                <th>Product</th>
                <th>Quantity</th>
                <th>Price</th>
                <th colspan="2"></th>
            </tr>
            <!-- ko foreach: $data.Lines -->
                <tr>
                    <td colspan="2"></td>
                    <td data-bind="text: $data.Product.Name"></td>
```

```
                    <td data-bind="text: $data.Count"></td>
                    <td data-bind="text: '$' + $data.Product.Price.toFixed(2)"></td>
                    <td colspan="2"></td>
                </tr>
            <!-- /ko -->
        </tbody>
    </table>
</div>
```

I have used the Knockout comment feature to generate some of the rows in the table, but otherwise this view contains entirely standard HTML and Knockout data bindings.

Defining the Create Product View

The final view I require allows the user to enter details for a new product. Listing 7-31 shows the contents of the AdminProductAdd.cshtml file, which I added to the View/Admin folder.

Listing 7-31. The Contents of the AdminProductAdd.cshtml File

```
<h2>Add Product</h2>

<div class="form-group">
    <label>Name</label>
    <input class="form-control" data-bind="value: adminModel.newProduct.name" />
</div>

<div class="form-group">
    <label>Description</label>
    <input class="form-control" data-bind="value: adminModel.newProduct.description" />
</div>

<div class="form-group">
    <label>Category</label>
    <input class="form-control" data-bind="value: adminModel.newProduct.category" />
</div>

<div class="form-group">
    <label>Price</label>
    <input class="form-control" data-bind="value: adminModel.newProduct.price" />
</div>

<div class="text-center">
    <button class="btn btn-primary"
            data-bind="click: setListMode.bind($data, 'products')">Cancel</button>
    <button class="btn btn-danger" data-bind="click: createProduct">Create</button>
</div>
```

This is a simple set of input elements that use Knockout bindings to set values on the newProduct object in the data model. There is a Create button that calls the createProduct function to trigger the Ajax request and a Cancel button that returns to the list of products.

As with the customer client, I have not implemented any client-side validation so that all requests are sent to the web service, even when the data they contain won't pass the validation checks.

Testing the Admin Client

All that remains is to test the client, which you can do by starting the application and using the browser to navigate to the /Admin/Index URL. The first view obtains the credentials required for authentication. Enter **Admin** as the username and **secret** as the password, as shown in Figure 7-11.

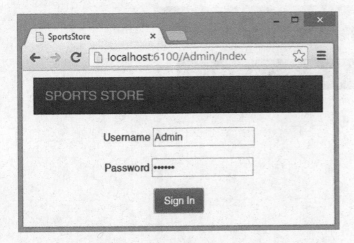

Figure 7-11. *Providing credentials to the admin client*

Click the Sign In button to authenticate the client, and you will be presented with the product list view, as illustrated by Figure 7-12.

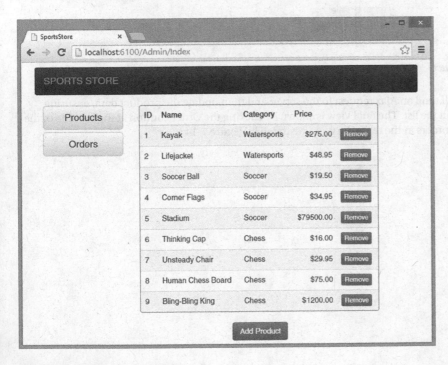

Figure 7-12. *The admin product list*

You can delete products from the repository by clicking the Remove buttons or create a new product by clicking the Add Product button. Clicking Add Product allows you to enter the details of the product you want to create, as shown in Figure 7-13. You can remove individual orders by clicking the Remove buttons or return to the product list by clicking the Products button at the left side of the window.

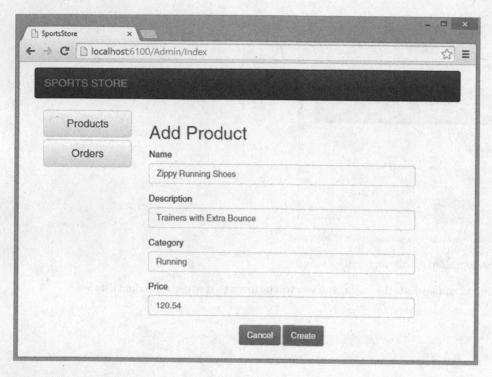

Figure 7-13. *Creating a new product*

Clicking the Create button will send an Ajax request to the server and then update the product data, ensuring that the new product is displayed in the list. The final view is shown by clicking the Orders button at the left side of the window, which shows a list of the orders in the repository, as illustrated by Figure 7-14.

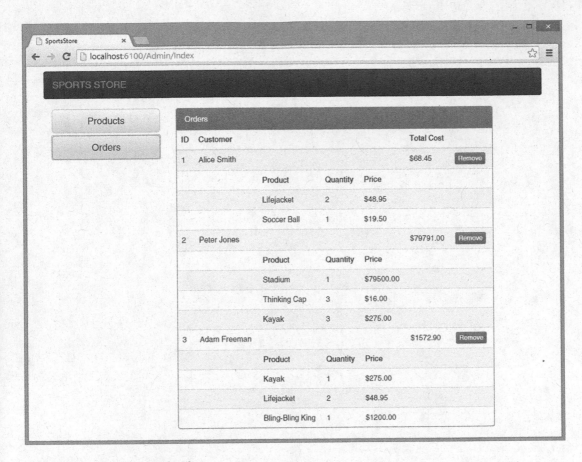

Figure 7-14. *The admin orders list*

Summary

In this chapter, I completed the development of the SportsStore application by creating clients for customers and administrators. I built a common foundation of client code, following the model/controller approach I used on the server side. I used this foundation to build clients that offer different functionality from the pair of Web API web services I created in Chapter 6. I covered a lot of ground without going into too much detail because the client-side development—especially the creation of view—is not directly related to Web API, but you can see how the overall structure of the client shows the use of the single-page application model in practice. In the next chapter, I show you how to deploy the SportsStore application to Microsoft Azure.

CHAPTER 8

■■■

SportsStore: Deployment

The biggest day in the life of any application is the one on which it is deployed and used for the first time. In this chapter, I will show you how to prepare and deploy the SportsStore application to the Microsoft Azure platform.

Web API introduces some new patterns for application deployment through its support for OWIN, which I describe in Chapter 26. However, if you have developed an application that contains MVC and Web API functionality—which is the most common use for Web API currently—then you are limited to deployment to IIS or Azure. I have selected Azure for this chapter because it is universally available and offers free trials, whereas not all developers have access to a Windows Server installation running IIS.

■ **Caution**   Deploying an application can be fraught with problems, and it pays dividends to practice with a test application before doing it for real. It is not that the ASP.NET deployment features are especially dangerous (they are not), but rather, any interaction that involves a running application with real user data deserves careful thought and planning.

Preparing the SportsStore Application

There are a couple of changes I need to make to the project before I can deploy the SportsStore application. I perform the changes—and explain their significance—in the sections that follow.

Preventing the Product Database from Resetting

The first change is to prevent the product database from being dropped and re-created each time that the application is started. That has been a useful feature to ensure that you see the right results in the previous chapters, but it is a dangerous feature to leave in a deployed application. Listing 8-1 shows the changes I made to the database initializer class.

Listing 8-1. Changing the Base Class in the ProductDbInitializer.cs File

```
using System.Collections.Generic;
using System.Data.Entity;

namespace SportsStore.Models {

    public class ProductDbInitializer : CreateDatabaseIfNotExists<ProductDbContext> {

        protected override void Seed(ProductDbContext context) {
```

```csharp
            new List<Product> {
                new Product() { Name = "Kayak", Description = "A boat for one person",
                    Category = "Watersports", Price = 275m },
                new Product() { Name = "Lifejacket",
                    Description = "Protective and fashionable",
                    Category = "Watersports", Price = 48.95m },
                new Product() { Name = "Soccer Ball",
                    Description = "FIFA-approved size and weight",
                    Category = "Soccer", Price = 19.50m },
                new Product() {
                    Name = "Corner Flags",
                    Description = "Give your playing field a professional touch",
                    Category = "Soccer", Price = 34.95m },
                new Product() { Name = "Stadium",
                    Description = "Flat-packed 35,000-seat stadium",
                    Category = "Soccer", Price = 79500m },
                new Product() { Name = "Thinking Cap",
                    Description = "Improve your brain efficiency by 75%",
                    Category = "Chess", Price = 16m },
                new Product() { Name = "Unsteady Chair",
                    Description = "Secretly give your opponent a disadvantage",
                    Category = "Chess", Price = 29.95m },
                new Product() { Name = "Human Chess Board",
                    Description = "A fun game for the family",
                    Category = "Chess", Price = 75m },
                new Product() { Name = "Bling-Bling King",
                    Description = "Gold-plated, diamond-studded King",
                    Category = "Chess", Price = 1200m },
            }.ForEach(product => context.Products.Add(product));

            context.SaveChanges();

            new List<Order> {
                new Order() { Customer = "Alice Smith", TotalCost = 68.45m,
                    Lines = new List<OrderLine> {
                        new OrderLine() { ProductId = 2, Count = 2},
                        new OrderLine() { ProductId = 3, Count = 1},
                    }},
                new Order() { Customer = "Peter Jones", TotalCost = 79791m,
                    Lines = new List<OrderLine> {
                        new OrderLine() { ProductId = 5, Count = 1},
                        new OrderLine() { ProductId = 6, Count = 3},
                        new OrderLine() { ProductId = 1, Count = 3},
                    }}
            }.ForEach(order => context.Orders.Add(order));

            context.SaveChanges();
        }
    }
}
```

I explained the different base classes that can be used in Chapter 5, and applying the `CreateDatabaseIfNotExists` ensures that a new database will be created the first time the application starts but not on subsequent restarts.

Adding Database Connection Strings

The second change I need to make is a little odd. I need to add connection strings to the `Web.config` file so that they can be updated during the publishing process. I have not needed to define connection strings so far because the default behavior for creating databases is to use the LocalDB feature, which is what I wanted. The default behavior will not work within Azure, but the publishing process doesn't work correctly unless there are connection strings for it to modify. Listing 8-2 shows the changes I made to the `Web.config` file.

Listing 8-2. Adding Connection Strings to the Web.config File

```
...
<configuration>
  <configSections>
    <section name="entityFramework"
      type="System.Data.Entity.Internal.ConfigFile.EntityFrameworkSection,
      EntityFramework, Version=6.0.0.0, Culture=neutral, PublicKeyToken=b77a5c561934e089"
        requirePermission="false" />
  </configSections>

  <connectionStrings>
    <add name="SportsStoreDb" providerName="System.Data.SqlClient"
      connectionString="Data Source=(localdb)\v11.0;
        Initial Catalog=SportsStoreDb;Integrated Security=True;
        Connect Timeout=15;Encrypt=False;TrustServerCertificate=False" />
    <add name="SportsStoreIdentityDb" providerName="System.Data.SqlClient"
      connectionString="Data Source=(localdb)\v11.0;
        Initial Catalog=SportsStoreIdentityDb;Integrated Security=True;
        Connect Timeout=15;Encrypt=False;TrustServerCertificate=False" />
  </connectionStrings>

<appSettings>
    <add key="webpages:Version" value="3.0.0.0" />
...
```

■ **Caution** The values for the `connectionString` properties should be on a single line and not wrapped as they are shown in the listing. I had to break up the string to fit it on the page.

These connection strings have no effect, other than to give the publishing process what it needs to replace them with details of the Azure databases I created in the previous section.

Preparing Azure

You have to create an account before you can use Azure, which you can do by going to http://azure.microsoft.com. At the time of writing, Microsoft is offering free trial accounts, and most MSDN packages include Azure services. Once you have created your account, you can manage your Azure services by going to http://manage.windowsazure.com to provide your credentials. When you start, you will see the summary view shown in Figure 8-1.

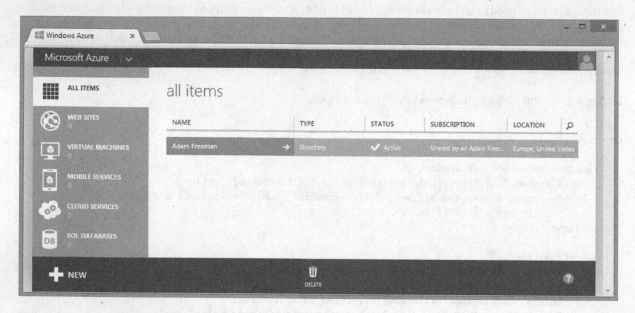

Figure 8-1. *The Azure portal*

Creating the Databases

The first step is to create the databases that will be used to store the product and ASP.NET Identity data. In the sections that follow, I will create the databases and get the information I need to configure the application.

Create the Product Database

Click the large plus (+) sign at the bottom of the window and select Data Services ➤ SQL Database ➤ Quick Create. Populate the input elements using the values in Table 8-1.

Table 8-1. *Creating the Azure Product Database*

Field	Description
Database Name	Enter **SportsStoreDb**.
Subscription	Leave as is.
Server	Leave as New SQL Database Server.
Region	Select the region you want to deploy to. I live in London, so I selected the West Europe region.
Login Name	Enter a memorable account name that will be used by the application to connect to the database. I selected SportsStoreDb.
Password	Select a secure and memorable password. I selected SuperSecurePassword100.

When you have configured the database, the screen should be similar to Figure 8-2.

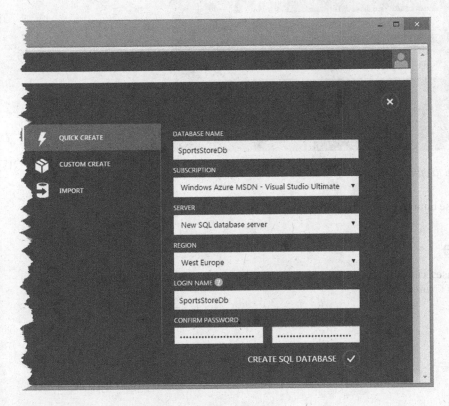

Figure 8-2. *Configuring the Azure product database*

Click the Create SQL Database button to create the database.

Create the Identity Database

Click the plus button again and select Data Services ➤ SQL Database ➤ Quick Create. Populate the input elements using the values in Table 8-2.

Table 8-2. *Creating the Azure Product Database*

Field	Description
Database Name	Enter **SportsStoreIdentityDb**.
Subscription	Leave as is.
Server	Leave as is; the server created for the product server will be selected automatically.

When you have configured the database, the screen should be similar to Figure 8-3.

Figure 8-3. *Configuring the Azure Identity database*

Click the Create SQL Database button to create the database.

Getting the Server Name

Once you have created the databases, click the Servers button and make note of the server name that has been created as part of the process, as shown in Figure 8-4.

Figure 8-4. *Getting the database name*

The server name is a random string. The one that Azure has created for me is called icfw64go15, but your name will differ. You will need the server name when configuring the application for deployment.

Creating the Web Site

I am going to deploy the application using an Azure web site, which is one of the options for deploying ASP.NET applications. Within the Azure management portal, click the plus sign and select Compute ➤ Web Site ➤ Quick Create.

Select a URL for your application and enter it into the URL input element. URLs have to be unique, although you can pay more to use custom URLs. The URL I selected for my deployment is sportsstorews, as shown in Figure 8-5. Click the Create Web Site button to complete the process.

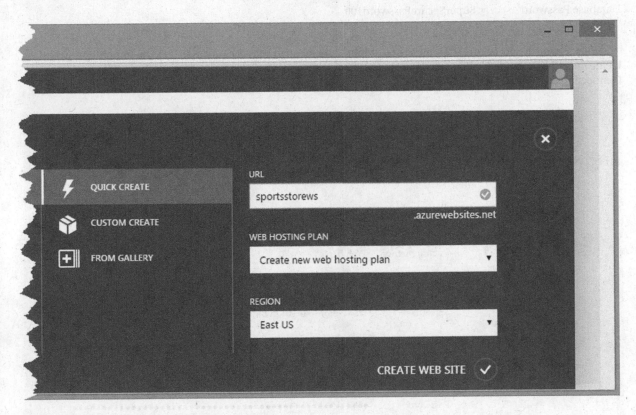

Figure 8-5. *Creating the Azure web site*

Downloading the Publish Profile

Once the web site has been created, you will see an entry under the web sites area with the name you selected in the previous section. Click the name to open the detail page and click the Download the Publish Profile link. This will cause the browser to download a file that contains the configuration details of the web site you created; save this file where you can easily access it.

Deploying the Application

I am now at the stage where I can deploy the application. Table 8-3 shows the pieces of information that are needed for the process.

Table 8-3. *The Information Needed to Deploy the Application*

Item	My Value
Database Server Name	icfw64go15
Database User Name	SportsStoreDb
Database Password	SuperSecurePassword100

Select Publish SportsStore from the Visual Studio Build menu to start the process. Click the Import button and locate the publish profile file that you downloaded after creating the Azure web site. The window will jump to the Connection section, as shown in Figure 8-6.

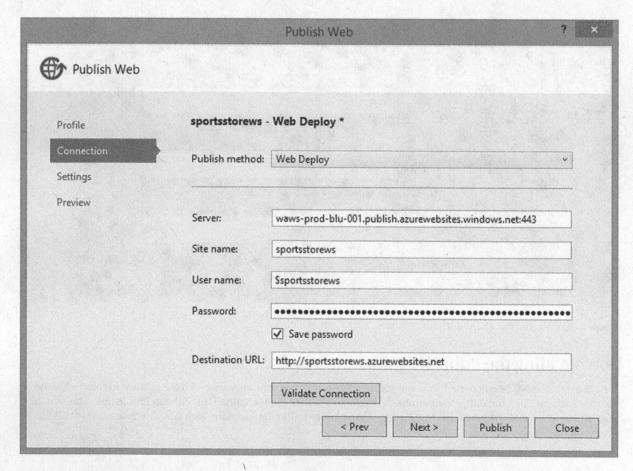

Figure 8-6. *Details of the deployment connection*

There is no need to change any of the values. Click Next to move to the Settings part of the dialog.

Configuring the Databases

This is the part of the deployment process that sets up the database connections. The publishing wizard gets confused at this point and displays more entries than it should. I'll explain how to deal with each of them in turn.

Configuring the ProductDbContext(SportsStoreDb) Entry

Click the ellipsis (...) button to open a dialog that allows a connection string to be composed. Ensure that Microsoft SQL Server is selected as the data source; then enter the name of the database server from the start of this section, followed by .database.windows.net, into the Server Name field. My server is called ijrfbkqxdu, so I entered icfw64go15.database.windows.net. Ensure that the Use SQL Server Authentication option is checked, enter the database username and password into the fields, and check the Save my password option. Enter **SportsStoreDb** into the Select or Enter a Database Name field to specify the database that will be used. Click the OK button to close the database and set the connection string, which will be as follows (although your server name and credentials will differ):

```
Data Source=icfw64go15.database.windows.net;
    Initial Catalog=SportsStoreDb;Persist Security Info=True;
    User ID=SportsStoreDb;Password=SuperSecurePassword100
```

Configuring the SportsStoreIdentityDb Entry

Repeat the same process as in the previous section, but enter **SportsStoreIdentityDb** into the Select or Enter a Database Name field. The connection string will be similar to this, but with a different server name and credentials:

```
Data Source=icfw64go15.database.windows.net;
    Initial Catalog=SportsStoreIdentityDb;Persist Security Info=True;
    User ID=SportsStoreDb;Password=SuperSecurePassword100
```

Configuring the StoreIdentityDbContext Entry

Uncheck the Use this Connection String at Runtime box. This entry isn't required.

Publishing the Application

All that remains is to push the application to Azure, which is done by clicking the Publish button. You can follow the publishing process in the Visual Studio Output window, but it can take a while to publish an application, especially if this is the initial update to the cloud since all of the files have to be uploaded. Only differences are uploaded for future releases.

Once the application has been published, Visual Studio will open a browser window that loads the SportsStore web site URL, which is http://sportsstorews.azurewebsites.net in my case, as shown in Figure 8-7.

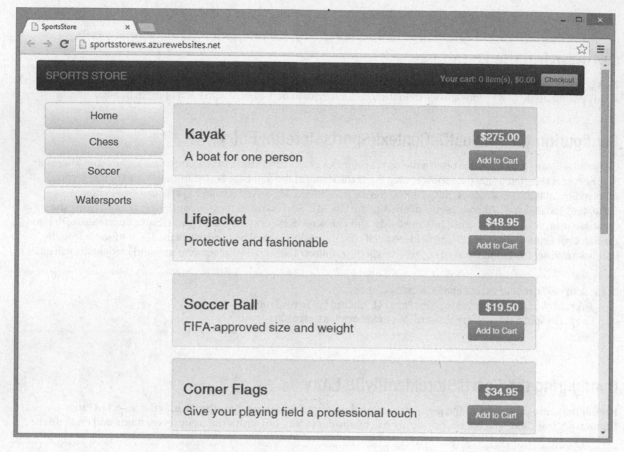

Figure 8-7. Using the published SportsStore application

■ **Tip** My URL won't be in service by the time you read this. I use my Azure web sites to test problems that readers encounter, and I keep these private to avoid generating odd results.

Summary

In this chapter I showed you how to deploy the SportsStore application to Azure, which is one of the platform options for an application that mixes Web API and MVC framework functionality. (The other option is to deploy to IIS running on Windows Server.) Deployment concludes the SportsStore chapters and this part of the book. In Part 2, I start to dig into the details of how Web API works, starting with the results that action methods produce and the parameter values they consume.

PART 2

Results and Parameters

■ ■ ■

CHAPTER 9

The Anatomy of ASP.NET Web API

This chapter isn't meant to be read right away. Instead, it contains a number of tables that you can refer to as you read through the chapters that follow. ASP.NET Web API uses a completely different set of namespaces and types than the ones you are familiar with in the MVC framework, and keeping track of which class or interface is responsible for a feature or behavior can be difficult, especially when you start working on your own Web API projects.

Understanding the Web API Namespaces and Types

Web API and the MVC framework share a common heritage and a common design philosophy, but for every important interface and class that you are familiar with in MVC framework development, there is a completely separate counterpart used by Web API. Table 9-1 provides a loose mapping for the ones that you will encounter most often.

Table 9-1. Commonly Used MVC Framework Classes and Their Web API Counterparts

MVC Class or Interface	Web API Equivalent
System.Web.Mvc.IController	System.Web.Http.Controllers.IHttpController
System.Web.Mvc.Controller	System.Web.Http.ApiController
System.Web.HttpContext	System.Web.Http.Controllers.HttpRequestContext
System.Web.HttpRequest	System.Net.Http.HttpRequestMessage
System.Web.HttpResponse	System.Net.Http.HttpResponseMessage
System.Web.HttpApplication	System.Web.Http.HttpConfiguration

The classes and interfaces are equivalent, but there isn't a one-to-one mapping of methods and properties. In part this is because Web API builds on the System.Net.Http namespace, which was introduced in .NET 4.5 and provides a set of classes that allow any .NET application to support HTTP by providing objects that describe HTTP in a neutral way. Web API uses the types from the System.Net.Http namespace to represent requests and responses (the HttpRequestMessage and HttpResponseMessage classes), HTTP status codes (the HttpStatusCode enum), and HTTP verbs (the HttpMethod class).

Functionality that is specified to Web API is contained in the System.Web.Http namespace and its children, defined as regular interfaces and classes or defined as extension methods that operate on System.Net.Http classes.

Microsoft has avoided the System.Web and System.Web.Mvc namespaces for Web API as part of a gradual effort to rework the ASP.NET platform into something more flexible for web application development and one that can be enhanced independently of the main .NET Framework. At the moment, Web Forms and MVC framework applications get a monolithic block of services through the System.Web assembly, which is shipped as part of the main .NET

Framework. The approach that the ASP.NET team is moving toward allows developers to select just the services they want and to have choices about which implementations are used.

You might, for example, decide to use Microsoft's session state implementation, a third-party logging and tracing implementation, and not to use caching services at all. The engine for this change is a standard called Open Web Interface for .NET (OWIN) that allows more flexibility in how Web API applications are hosted. I describe it in Chapter 26.

For the moment, it is enough to know that Web API doesn't use the System.Web and System.Web.Mvc namespaces that you are familiar with and that even the most venerable ASP.NET classes, such as HttpRequest and HttpResponse, are not used when developing HTTP web services with Web API. As a quick reference, Table 9-2 lists the main namespaces that you will use during Web API development and where in the book I describe them in detail.

Table 9-2. *The Main Web API Namespaces*

Namespace	Description
System.Net.Http	This namespace defines types that represent HTTP requests and responses.
System.Net.Http.Formatting	This namespace contains the *media type formatters*, which are used to serialize data sent to the client and to create model objects from requests. See Chapters 12–17 for details.
System.Web.Http	This is the top-level Web API namespace. The most important class for most projects is ApiController, which is the base for Web API controllers and which I describe in Chapter 22, but there are many other useful classes in this namespace.
System.Web.Http.Controllers	This namespace contains the interface that defines a controller (IHttpController) and all of the support classes that the most common controller base class—ApiController—requires. See Chapter 22 for details of how controllers are used in Web API, and see the chapters in this part of the book for details of the features that ApiController brings conveniently together.
System.Web.Http.Dependencies	This namespace contains the classes that provide dependency injection, which I describe in Chapter 10.
System.Web.Http.Dispatcher	This namespace contains the classes that manage the Web API request dispatch process from receiving a request from the hosting platform through to selecting and executing a controller. I describe the dispatch process in Part 3 of this book.
System.Web.Http.Filters	This namespace contains the filters support, which allows for additional logic to be inserted into the dispatch process. I describe filters in Chapters 23 and 24.
System.Web.Http.Metadata	This namespace contains classes that provide descriptions of model classes. These classes are not used directly but are presented through context objects in the dispatch process (which is the topic of Part 3 of this book) or when data provided by a client is being validated (which I describe in Chapter 18).
System.Web.Http.ModelBinding	This namespace contains classes responsible for creating objects and values from HTTP requests that can be used by action methods. I describe the model binding process in Chapter 14 and explain how the process works in detail in Chapters 15–17.
System.Web.Http.Results	This namespace contains classes that implement the IHttpActionResult interface, which is used by action methods to describe the responses that will be sent to a client. I describe action method results in Chapter 11.

(continued)

Table 9-2. *(continued)*

Namespace	Description
System.Web.Http.Routing	This namespace contains the Web API URL routing classes, which I describe in Chapters 20 and 21.
System.Web.Http.Validation	This namespace contains the classes that are used to validate data sent from a client, a process I describe in Chapter 18.
System.Web.Http.ValueProviders	This namespace contains classes that are used to retrieve values from requests so that they can be used with action methods. I describe this process in Chapters 14–17.

■ **Tip** As the table illustrates, there are a *lot* of Web API namespaces, but many of them contain just a few types, and basic Web API applications can be created with little effort, as I demonstrated in Chapter 2. Even more complicated applications, such as the one I created in Chapters 5–8, can't be created using a small number of classes.

WHY CAN'T I USE THE ASP.NET PLATFORM FEATURES ANYWAY?

It often feels like Microsoft makes changes just for the sake of it, and you may have a familiar sinking feeling as you look over the types and namespaces in Tables 9-1 and 9-2, contemplating another steep learning curve.

At this moment, most experienced ASP.NET developers realize that there is a shortcut: use the static HttpContext.Current property to get access to the familiar set of classes provided by the ASP.NET platform, which are still there behind the scenes as long as you are deploying your application to IIS.

Like most shortcuts, you gain in the near term only to pay a price in the long term. You can ignore the System.Net.Http classes, for example, and focus on the classes you know from the System.Web namespace, such as HttpRequest and HttpResponse. And, at first, you will start to produce Web API HTTP web services more quickly and more easily, which is the near-term gain.

The long-term price is that you can't access advanced Web API features using the old classes and you end up with even more tortured adaptor classes as your Web API needs become more complex. In the end, you'll spend more time trying to avoid the new Web API classes than it takes to learn how they work. Having two separate sets of namespaces in an application is a little awkward, but my advice is to embrace the change and avoid long-term complexity and maintenance problems.

Understanding the Web API Context Objects

Web API provides a set of objects that provide context about the state of the application and the request that is being handled. The main way you will encounter these objects is through properties defined by the ApiController class, from which Web API controller classes are derived. I describe the role of the ApiController class in more detail in Chapter 22, but Table 9-3 describes the properties it defines that return context objects.

Table 9-3. *The Context Properties Defined by the ApiController Class*

Name	Description
Configuration	Returns an HttpConfiguration object, which provides information about the configuration of the application. See Chapter 10.
ControllerContext	Returns the HttpControllerContext object that was passed to the controller's ExecuteAsync method. See Table 9-6.
ModelState	Returns the object used for model binding validation. See Chapter 18.
Request	Returns the HttpRequestMessage that describes the current request. See Table 9-4.
RequestContext	Returns an HttpRequestContext object that provides Web API–specific information about the current request. See Table 9-5.
User	Returns details of the user associated with the current request. See Chapters 5, 23, and 24.

Getting Information About the Request

Requests are represented by the HttpRequestMessage class, which is defined in the System.Net.Http namespace. You are unlikely to need to use the HttpRequestMessage class directly as you start creating simple web services with Web API, but you will begin to use it a lot when you apply some of the more advanced features or begin to customize the way that Web API handles HTTP requests. Table 9-4 describes the properties that the HttpRequestMessage class defines.

Table 9-4. *The Properties Defined by the HttpRequestMessage Class*

Name	Description
Content	Returns an HttpContent object that contains the content of the HTTP request. Request content is generally accessed through the model binding feature, which I describe in Chapter 14.
Headers	Returns an HttpRequestHeaders object that contains the headers sent by the client. I use request headers to demonstrate several features, including data binding (in Chapter 14) and URL routing (in Chapters 20 and 21).
Method	Returns an HttpMethod object that describes the HTTP method/verb for the request.
Properties	Returns a collection that contains objects provided by the hosting environment or by components that need to communicate with one another. Many of the objects that Web API uses to provide context information define a Properties property, but the only one that I use in this book is the one defined by the HttpRequestMessage object in Chapter 23.
RequestUri	Returns the URL requested by the client, expressed as an Uri object.
Version	Returns the version of HTTP that was used to make the request, expressed as a System.Version object.

The HttpRequestMessage class provides a generalized view of an HTTP request, without any detail that is specific to web services. Web API supplements the HttpRequestMessage class with the HttpRequestContext class, the most important properties of which I describe in Table 9-5.

Table 9-5. *The Properties Defined by the HttpRequestContext Class*

Name	Description
Configuration	This property returns the HttpConfiguration object associated with the current request. I describe the HttpConfiguration class in Chapter 10 and explain how to apply custom configurations to individual controllers in Chapter 22.
IncludeErrorDetail	This property is used to control the amount of information sent to the client when an exception is thrown and in an action method or filter and left unhandled. See Chapter 25 for details.
IsLocal	This property returns true if the request originates from the local computer.
Principal	This property returns the IPrincipal implementation object that describes the user associated with the request. I used this property in Chapters 6 and 7 for the SportsStore application, and I demonstrate how to create a custom—albeit simple—authentication mechanism in Chapters 23 and 24.
RouteData	This property returns the routing data associated with the request. See Chapters 20 and 21.

Getting Information About the Controller

The HttpControllerContext class provides access to much of the same context data as the HttpRequestContext class but also describes the controller. The similarity between the properties defined by context classes is a facet of the Web API dispatch process, which I describe in Part 3, which doesn't make assumptions about the controller that will be selected to handle a request—a feature that allows custom controller implementations to be easily created, as I demonstrate in Chapter 22. Some context classes, such as HttpRequestContext, are used more when writing individual web service, and others, such as HttpControllerContext, are more useful when you are customizing the request dispatch process. Table 9-6 lists the properties defined by the HttpControllerContext class.

Table 9-6. *The Properties Defined by the HttpControllerContext Class*

Name	Description
Configuration	Returns a System.Web.Http.HttpConfiguration object, which provides information about the configuration of the application. See Chapter 10.
Controller	Returns the System.Web.Http.Controllers.IHttpController implementation that is handling the request. See Chapter 22.
ControllerDescriptor	Returns a System.Web.Http.Controllers.HttpControllerDescriptor object that provides information about the controller, which can be used to select controllers to handle a request, as described in Chapter 19.
Request	Returns a System.Net.Http.HttpRequestMessage that provides information about the request being handled. See Table 9-4.
RequestContext	Returns a System.Web.Http.Controllers.HttpRequestContext object that provides Web API-specific information about the request, including details of the user identity associated with the request. See Table 9-5 for details.
RouteData	Returns a System.Web.Http.Routing.IHttpRouteData implementation that provides information about how the request was routed. See Chapters 20 and 21 for details of Web API routing.

Getting Information About Everything Else

The Web API namespaces contain other context objects that are of use only for specific—often advanced—tasks. Rather than list all of their properties here, Table 9-7 describes the classes and references the chapter where I describe each of them in more detail.

Table 9-7. *The Web API Context Classes*

Name	Description
ExceptionHandlerContext	This class is used to provide context information to global exception handlers. See Chapter 25.
ExceptionLoggerContext	This class is used to provide context information to global exception loggers. See Chapter 25.
HttpActionContext	This class is used to describe an action method and is employed as part of the data binding process. See Chapter 15.
HttpActionDescriptor	This class is used to describe an action method and is employed as part of the data binding process. See Chapter 15.
HttpActionExecutedContext	This class is used to provide context information to exception filters. See Chapter 24.
HttpAuthenticationChallengeContext	This class is used to provide context information to authentication filters. See Chapter 23.
HttpAuthenticationContext	This class is used to provide context information to authentication filters. See Chapter 23.
HttpControllerContext	This class is used to provide a controller with the information it needs to process a request. See Chapter 19.
HttpControllerDescriptor	This class is used during the selection of a controller to process a request. See Chapter 19.
HttpParameterDescriptor	This class is used to describe an action method parameter during the data binding process. See Chapter 15.
HttpRequestContext	This class is used to provide context information about a request. See Table 9-5.
ModelBindingContext	This class is used to provide context information about a model class during the data binding process. See Chapter 16.

Understanding the Web API Components

The basic approach that Web API follows to handle HTTP requests will be familiar from using the MVC framework, but there are a few wrinkles and some important differences to be aware of. In the sections that follow, I briefly describe the major components in a Web API application and explain how they are applied, along with references to the chapters in this book where you can find more information.

Application Configuration

Web API configuration is performed in the `App_Start/WebApiConfig.cs` file. Add all configuration statements—including those for URL routing—to the `Register` method, including those that set up URL routes. See Chapter 10 for details of configuring a Web API application and remember not to do any configuration in the Global Application Class (the `Global.asax.cs` file) because it isn't supported for all Web API deployment options.

Controllers, Actions, and Results

Web services are defined through controllers. The most common way to create a controller is to derive a class from `ApiController`, which is defined in the `System.Web.Http` namespace. The `ApiController` class provides a number of features that make it simple to create HTTP web services, including action methods, action results, and model binding and validation. I explain how action methods are used to generate results in Chapter 11, how parameters objects and values are created in Chapters 12–17, and how to validate data in Chapter 18.

Although the `ApiController` class is the normal base for controllers, you can also implement your own approach to processing requests by implementing the `IHttpController` interface. I describe this process in Chapter 22 and explain where controllers fit into the wider dispatch process throughout Part 3 of this book.

Services

ASP.NET Web API defines a set of interfaces and classes that are used to process requests, and these are known as *services*. Examples include the interfaces that select controllers and action methods, perform model binding, and validate content. The implementations of these interfaces define the infrastructure of a Web API application.

Services are either *single-instance* or *multiple-instance*. For single-instance services, there is a single implementation of the service interface used across the entire application. An example of a single-instance service interface is `IHttpActionInvoker`, which I describe in Chapter 22 and which is responsible for invoking action methods in Web API controllers. There is a default implementation of this interface included in Web API, and you can choose to replace it with a custom implementation, but only one of them will be used to invoke action methods.

For multiple-instance services, several implementations are available, presenting a choice about which one is used. An example is the `ModelBinderProvider` class, which I describe in Chapter 16 and which provides a model binder for a given type. There are built-in derivations of the `ModelBinderProvider` class included in Web API, and you can define your own—and at runtime, the combined collection is available so that the most appropriate implementation can be selected and used.

Services are set up and accessed through the `HttpConfiguration.Services` property; this property returns an instance of the `ServicesContainer` class, which is defined in the `System.Web.Http.Controllers` namespace. Table 9-8 shows the methods defined by the `ServicesContainer` class that are used to register and obtain services.

Table 9-8. *The Methods Defined by the ServicesContainer Class*

Name	Description
Add(service, impl)	Adds a new implementation of the specified service interface to the collection. There is also an AddRange method that allows multiple implementation objects to be added in a single method call.
AddRange(service, impls)	Adds an enumeration of implementations of the specified interface to the collection.
Clear(service)	Removes all implementations of the specified service interface from the collection.
GetService(service)	Gets an implementation of the specified single-instance service.
GetServices(service)	Gets the implementations of the specified multiple-instance service.
Insert(service, index, impl)	Inserts an implementation of a multiple-instance service into the collection at a specific index. There is also an InsertRange method that allows multiple implementation objects to be inserted in a single method call.
IsSingleService(service)	Returns true if the specified service interface is single-instance and false if it is a multiple-instance service.
Remove(service, impl)	Removes the specified implementation of a service interface from the collection. There are also RemoveAll and RemoveAt methods that allow multiple implementation objects to be removed or an object at a specified index to be removed.
Replace(service, impl)	Replaces the implementation object for the specified service in the collection. This method works for single- and multiple-instance services.

■ **Tip** Implementations of the service interfaces can also be provided through dependency injection, which I describe in Chapter 10.

In addition to the methods described in Table 9-8, Web API provides a set of extension methods that provide strongly typed access to specific services. I describe the most important of these extension methods in Table 9-9, along with details of the service interface they relate to and the chapter of this book where I explain the use of each of them.

Table 9-9. *The Extension Methods Defined for the ServicesContainer Class*

Name	Description
GetActionInvoker	This method returns an implementation of the IHttpActionInvoker interface, which is responsible for executing an action method. See Chapter 22.
GetActionSelector	This method returns an implementation of the IHttpActionSelector interface, which is responsible for selecting an action method. See Chapter 22.
GetActionValueBinder	This method returns an implementation of the IActionValueBinder interface, which is used to bind values for action method parameters. See Chapter 17.
GetAssembliesResolver	This method returns an implementation of the IAssembliesResolver interface, which is used to locate controller classes when the application starts. See Chapter 19.
GetContentNegotiator	This method returns an implementation of the IContentNegotiator interface, which is used to select a media type formatter to serialize the data in a response. See Chapter 11.
GetExceptionHandler	This method returns an implementation of the IExceptionHandler interface, which is used to define the way that unhandled exceptions are processed to create client responses. See Chapter 25.
GetExceptionLoggers	This method returns all of the registered implementations of the IExceptionLogger interface, which are used to record unhandled exceptions. See Chapter 25.
GetHttpControllerActivator	This method returns an implementation of the IHttpControllerActivator interface, which is used to instantiate controller classes. See Chapter 19.
GetHttpControllerSelector	This method returns an implementation of the IHttpControllerSelector interface, which is used to select controllers. See Chapter 19.
GetHttpControllerTypeResolver	This method returns an implementation of the IHttpControllerTypeResolver, which is used to locate controller classes when the application starts. See Chapter 19.
GetModelBinderProviders	This method returns all of the registered classes that are derived from the abstract ModelBinderProvider class, which are used during the model binding process. See Chapter 16.
GetValueProviderFactories	This method returns all of the registered classes that are derived from the abstract ValueProviderFactory class, which are used during the parameter binding process. See Chapter 15.

Dispatchers and Handlers

Web API has a well-defined model for processing requests, which I describe in Part 3 of this book. There are lots of opportunities for customizing or extending this process, including adding message handlers and changing the way that controllers are selected, instantiated, and executed (all of which I describe in Chapter 19). You can also customize the way that errors are handled (Chapter 25) and inject additional logic into the dispatch process through the use of filters (Chapters 23 and 24).

Summary

In this chapter, I described the components that you will encounter in Web API development, briefly explained what they do, and told you which chapters contain more detailed information. A chapter made up of quick-reference tables does not make for exciting reading, but you will find the information that the tables contain useful as you start to create your own Web API projects because there are a bewildering number of new classes and interfaces to understand. In the next chapter, I show you how to create and configure a Web API application.

■■■

CHAPTER 10

Creating and Configuring a Web API Application

In this chapter, I create the example application that I use for all the chapters in this part of the book. I show you how to perform basic configuration and set up dependency injection to create loosely coupled components. In short, this chapter sets the foundation for the more detailed topics that follow so that I don't have to create a new example application in each chapter.

That said, dependency injection for Web API applications is an interesting topic in its own right because it is an example of the kinds of problems that arise when designing applications that have Web API and MVC components that work together. Web API uses a completely different set of namespaces and types, but behind that is an evolution in design that shows up in the way that dependency injection for Web API differs from what you are used to in the MVC framework. Table 10-1 summarizes this chapter.

Table 10-1. *Chapter Summary*

Problem	Solution	Listing
Configure a Web API application.	Add statements that manipulate the properties of the `HttpConfiguration` object in the `Register` method of the `WebApiConfig` class (which can be found in the `App_Start` folder).	1–9
Implement dependency injection for Web API.	Implement the `IDependencyResolver` and `IDependencyScope` interfaces and register the `IDependencyResolver` implementation using the `HttpConfiguration.DependencyResolver` property.	10–16
Implement shared dependency injection for Web API and MVC.	Like for Web API, but add the `System.Web.Mvc.IDependencyResolver` interface to the set implemented by the resolver and call the `DependencyResolver.SetResolver` method.	17–20

Preparing the Example Project

For this chapter, I need to create a new Visual Studio project. Select New Project from the File menu to open the Visual Studio New Project dialog window, select the ASP.NET Web Application project type, and set the name to ExampleApp. Click the OK button to advance through the wizard, selecting the Empty project template and checking the options to add the core references for MVC and Web API, just as I did in Chapter 2. Click the OK button, and Visual Studio will create the new project.

After Visual Studio finishes creating the project, enter the following commands into the Package Manager Console to get the NuGet packages that are required:

```
Update-Package microsoft.aspnet.mvc -version 5.1.1
Update-Package microsoft.aspnet.webapi -version 5.1.1
Update-Package Newtonsoft.json -version 6.0.1
Install-Package jquery -version 2.1.0
Install-Package bootstrap -version 3.1.1
Install-Package knockoutjs -version 3.1.0
```

Creating the Model and Repository

My focus in this part of the book is on components that deliver web application functionality, so I need only a basic model and repository. To keep the example simple, I will create a repository that maintains a collection of data objects in memory. Listing 10-1 shows the contents of the Product.cs file that I added to the Models folder.

Listing 10-1. The Contents of the Product.cs File

```
namespace ExampleApp.Models {
    public class Product {
        public int ProductID { get; set; }
        public string Name { get; set; }
        public decimal Price { get; set; }
    }
}
```

This is a simplified version of the model class that I created for the SportsStore application in Chapter 5. Listing 10-2 shows the contents of the Repository.cs class file that I added to the Models folder.

Listing 10-2. The Contents of the Repository.cs File

```
using System.Collections.Generic;

namespace ExampleApp.Models {
    public class Repository {
        private Dictionary<int, Product> data;
        private static Repository repo;

        static Repository() {
            repo = new Repository();
        }

        public static Repository Current {
            get { return repo; }
        }

        public Repository() {
            Product[] products = new Product[] {
                new Product {ProductID = 1, Name = "Kayak", Price = 275M },
                new Product {ProductID = 2, Name = "Lifejacket", Price = 48.95M },
```

```
            new Product {ProductID = 3, Name = "Soccer Ball", Price = 19.50M },
            new Product {ProductID = 4, Name = "Thinking Cap", Price = 16M },
        };

        data = new Dictionary<int, Product>();

        foreach (Product prod in products) {
            data.Add(prod.ProductID, prod);
        }
    }

    public IEnumerable<Product> Products {
        get { return data.Values; }
    }

    public Product GetProduct(int id) {
        return data[id];
    }

    public Product SaveProduct(Product newProduct) {
        newProduct.ProductID = data.Keys.Count + 1;
        return data[newProduct.ProductID] = newProduct;
    }

    public Product DeleteProduct(int id) {
        Product prod = data[id];
        if (prod != null) {
            data.Remove(id);
        }
        return prod;
    }
    }
}
```

My example repository populates an in-memory collection with Product objects and exposes them through a mix of properties and methods. Storing the data in memory means that the contents of the repository will be reset when the application is restarted. There is a static Current property that returns a shared instance of the Repository class. I use this to get the application up and working and then remove it when I demonstrate how to set up dependency injection.

Creating an HTTP Web Service

I need a Web API controller to provide the HTTP web service for this chapter. I right-clicked the Controllers folder, selected Add ➤ Controller from the pop-up menu, and selected Web API 2 Controller – Empty from the list of controller types. I set the name to ProductsController and edited the Controllers/ProductsController.cs file that Visual Studio created to define the controller shown in Listing 10-3. After editing the file, the controller defines a single action that returns the collection of Product objects contained in the repository.

■ **Tip** By default, the action method is targeted with an HTTP GET request sent to the /api/products URL. I explain how this is handled in Chapter 22.

Listing 10-3. The Contents of the ProductsController.cs File

```
using System.Collections.Generic;
using System.Web.Http;
using ExampleApp.Models;

namespace ExampleApp.Controllers {
    public class ProductsController : ApiController {
        Repository repo;

        public ProductsController() {
            repo = Repository.Current;
        }

        public IEnumerable<Product> GetAll() {
            return repo.Products;
        }
    }
}
```

■ **Note** The Repository object is obtained through the static Current property I added to the Repository class, which means the ProductsController and Repository classes are tightly coupled. This presents the same problems in a Web API application as it does in the MVC framework. I explain how you can use dependency injection to decouple the components later in this chapter.

Creating the Browser Client

I am going to create a simple browser client using the MVC framework. The client will include the initial data available in the repository and provide the user with the means to refresh that data through an Ajax request sent to the web service. I right-clicked the Controllers folder, selected Add ➤ Controller from the pop-up menu, and selected MVC 5 Controller – Empty from the list of controller types. I set the name to HomeController and edited the Controllers/HomeController.cs file that Visual Studio created to define the controller shown in Listing 10-4.

■ **Note** The HomeController class is tightly coupled to the Repository class in the same way that the Web API controller I defined in the previous section is. I explain how to use dependency injection to break the dependency later in the chapter.

Listing 10-4. The Contents of the HomeController.cs File

```
using System.Web.Mvc;
using ExampleApp.Models;

namespace ExampleApp.Controllers {
    public class HomeController : Controller {
        Repository repo;

        public HomeController() {
            repo = Repository.Current;
        }

        public ActionResult Index() {
            return View(repo.Products);
        }
    }
}
```

I created a view for the Index action by right-clicking the method in the code editor and selecting Add View from the pop-up menu. I set the name of the view to Index and checked the option to use a layout page. Listing 10-5 shows the contents of the Views/Index.cshtml file.

Listing 10-5. The Contents of the Index.cshtml File

```
@model IEnumerable<ExampleApp.Models.Product>
@{ ViewBag.Title = "Index";}

@section Scripts {
    <script>
        var products = ko.observableArray(
            @Html.Raw(Newtonsoft.Json.JsonConvert.SerializeObject(Model)));
    </script>
    <script src="~/Scripts/exampleApp.js"></script>
}

<div class="panel panel-primary">
    <div class="panel-heading">RSVPs</div>
    <table id="rsvpTable" class="table table-striped">
        <thead>
            <tr><th>ID</th><th>Name</th><th>Price</th></tr>
        </thead>
        <tbody data-bind="foreach: products">
            <tr>
                <td data-bind="text: ProductID"></td>
                <td data-bind="text: Name"></td>
                <td data-bind="text: Price"></td>
            </tr>
        </tbody>
    </table>
</div>
<button data-bind="click: getProducts" class="btn btn-primary">Refresh</button>
```

This view contains a `table` element, the contents of which I manage using the Knockout techniques that I described in Chapter 3. To that end, I took the view model data and rendered it to a JavaScript array, like this:

```
...
<script>
    var products = ko.observableArray(
        @Html.Raw(Newtonsoft.Json.JsonConvert.SerializeObject(Model)));
</script>
...
```

MVC framework views that process data from HTTP web services need some way of generating HTML content from that data, and the easiest way to approach this is to adopt a single mechanism throughout the view, starting with the view model data that is rendered by Razor.

The view also contains a `script` element that loads the `exampleApp.js` file from the `Scripts` folder. I created this file and added the code that is shown in Listing 10-6, which contains the `getProducts` function that I used in the Knockout click binding on the Refresh button.

■ **Tip** If you are following the examples by typing them in, then see Chapter 7 for details of how to create a `_references.js` file that will enable IntelliSense for JavaScript files. And don't forget that you can download the complete source code for every chapter in this book from `www.apress.com`.

Listing 10-6. The Contents of the exampleApp.js File

```
$(document).ready(function () {
    getProducts = function() {
        $.ajax("/api/products", {
            success: function (data) {
                products.removeAll();
                for (var i = 0; i < data.length; i++) {
                    products.push(data[i]);
                }
            }
        })
    };
    ko.applyBindings();
});
```

The `exampleApp.js` file defines the `getProducts` function, which uses jQuery to make an Ajax GET request to the `/api/products` URL. I have specified a `success` function, as described in Chapter 3, which updates the model that Knockout maintains to update the contents of the `table` element.

The last step is to update the `Views/Shared/_Layout.cshtml` file that Visual Studio created when I added a view for the Index action, as shown in Listing 10-7.

Listing 10-7. The Contents of the _Layout.cshtml File

```
<!DOCTYPE html>
<html>
<head>
    <meta name="viewport" content="width=device-width" />
    <script src="~/Scripts/jquery-2.1.0.min.js"></script>
```

```
<script src="~/Scripts/jquery.validate.js"></script>
<script src="~/Scripts/jquery.validate.unobtrusive.js"></script>
<script src="~/Scripts/knockout-3.1.0.js"></script>
<link href="~/Content/bootstrap.css" rel="stylesheet" />
<link href="~/Content/bootstrap-theme.css" rel="stylesheet" />
<title>@ViewBag.Title</title>
<style>
    body { padding-top: 10px; }
    .validation-summary-errors { font-weight: bold; color: #f00; }
</style>
@RenderSection("Scripts", false)
</head>
<body class="container">
    @RenderBody()
</body>
</html>
```

Visual Studio adds default content that I don't need, so I have replaced the content with a simple document that loads the JavaScript and CSS files I require and renders the Scripts and body sections of views.

Testing the Example Application

I am going to test the web service and web client separately. Start the application and request the /Home/Index URL. If the application is working, then you will see an initial snapshot of the data in the HTML that the MVC controller sends to the browser, as shown in Figure 10-1.

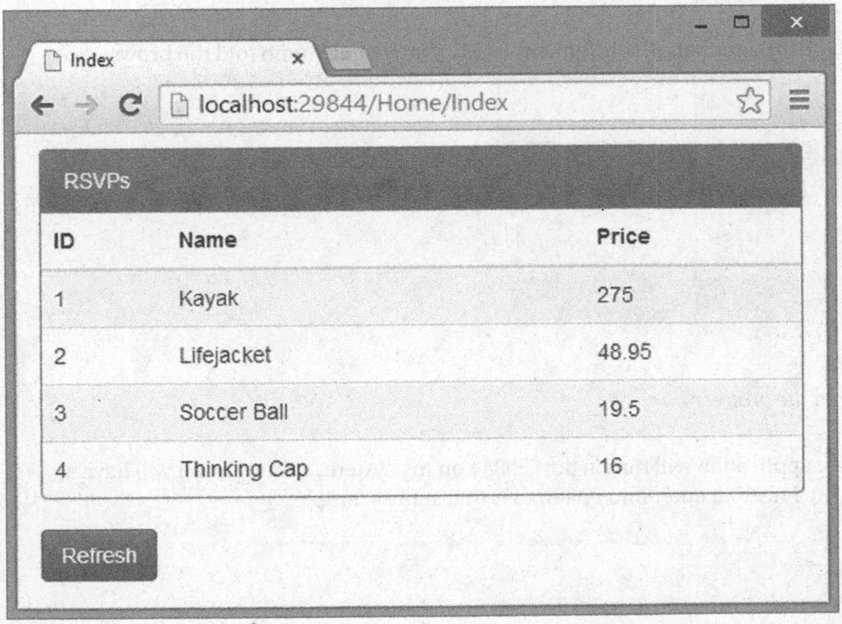

Figure 10-1. *Testing the MVC client for the example application*

■ **Tip** The jQuery code in the `exampleApp.js` file handles the Refresh button click event by requesting the same data from the Web API controller, but you will need to use the F12 tools to monitor the network requests to see what's happening because there is no visible change in the browser window.

I am going to use Postman, which I explained how to set up in Chapter 1, to test the web service. There is only one action method defined by the Web API controller, which is targeted through the /api/products URL.

To test with Postman, I need to know what TCP port the example application will be using to listen for HTTP requests, which there are two ways to determine. The first is to select ExampleApp Properties from the Visual Studio Project menu, select the Web tab, and locate the Project URL field, as shown in Figure 10-2.

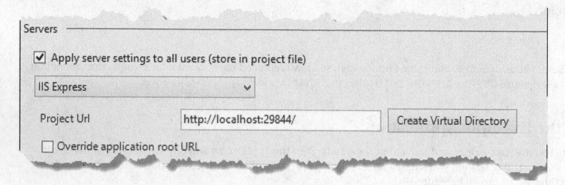

Figure 10-2. *Determining the project URL using Visual Studio*

The other approach is to look at the browser bar, which shows the URL that Visual Studio told the browser to request, as shown in Figure 10-3.

Figure 10-3. *Getting the TCP port from the browser bar*

As both figures show, the example application will run on port 29844 on my system, although you will have a different value. The following is the URL I need to enter into Postman is to test my example:

```
http://localhost:29844/api/products
```

Using Postman to send a GET request to the URL produced the following result:

```
[{"ProductID":1,"Name":"Kayak","Price":275.0},
{"ProductID":2,"Name":"Lifejacket","Price":48.95},
{"ProductID":3,"Name":"Soccer Ball","Price":19.50},
{"ProductID":4,"Name":"Thinking Cap","Price":16.0}]
```

Configuring a Web API Application

It should come as no surprise that Web API applications are configured in a new and different way. In this section, I explain how Web API applications are configured and describe the classes that are used to manage the configuration process. I use these classes later in the chapter when I demonstrate the process for setting up dependency injection and throughout the rest of the book as I describe different Web API features. Table 10-2 puts Web API configuration in context.

Table 10-2. *Putting Web API Configuration in Context*

Question	Answer
What is it?	The configuration system allows the behavior of Web API infrastructure and components to be customized.
When should I use it?	Configuring Web API is required whenever you want to change the default behavior, including defining new routes (see Chapters 20 and 21) or setting up dependency injection (described later in this chapter).
What do I need to know?	Web API doesn't use the standard ASP.NET platform configuration features, such as the Web.config file. Configuration is performed in the App_Start/WebApiConfig.cs file, which is referenced from the global application class when Web API is deployed to IIS.

Configuring Web API Through the ASP.NET Platform

When hosting Web API in IIS, either hosted locally or on Azure, the starting point for the configuration process is the Global Application Class, just as it is for the MVC framework. However, not all Web API deployment options have a global application class, and it is used only to bootstrap the configuration process. Listing 10-8 shows the contents of the Global.asax.cs file, which you can open by double-clicking the Global.asax item in Solution Explorer.

Listing 10-8. The Contents of the Global.asax.cs File

```
using System;
using System.Collections.Generic;
using System.Linq;
using System.Web;
using System.Web.Mvc;
using System.Web.Routing;
using System.Web.Security;
using System.Web.SessionState;
using System.Web.Http;
```

```
namespace ExampleApp {
    public class Global : HttpApplication {
        void Application_Start(object sender, EventArgs e) {
            AreaRegistration.RegisterAllAreas();
            GlobalConfiguration.Configure(WebApiConfig.Register);
            RouteConfig.RegisterRoutes(RouteTable.Routes);
        }
    }
}
```

The important statement is this one, which kicks off the Web API configuration process:

```
...
GlobalConfiguration.Configure(WebApiConfig.Register);
...
```

The System.Web.Http.GlobalConfiguration class provides the entry point for configuring Web API and defines the static members shown in Table 10-3.

Table 10-3. *The Members Defined by the GlobalConfiguration Class*

Name	Description
Configuration	Returns an HttpConfiguration object that represents the Web API configuration. See Table 10-4 for details.
DefaultHandler	Returns the HttpMessageHandler that is used to handle requests by default. See Chapter 19.
Configure(callback)	Registers a callback method that will be invoked to configure the application.

■ **Caution**   Do not add configuration statements for Web API components to the Global Application Class because it won't be available if you deploy your web service outside of IIS or Azure. Use the WebApiConfig.cs file shown in Listing 10-9.

Listing 10-9. The Contents of the WebApiConfig.cs File

```
using System;
using System.Collections.Generic;
using System.Linq;
using System.Web.Http;

namespace ExampleApp {
    public static class WebApiConfig {
        public static void Register(HttpConfiguration config) {

            config.MapHttpAttributeRoutes();
```

```
        config.Routes.MapHttpRoute(
            name: "DefaultApi",
            routeTemplate: "api/{controller}/{id}",
            defaults: new { id = RouteParameter.Optional }
        );
    }
  }
}
```

The Configure method allows a callback method to be specified that will be passed a
System.Web.Http.HttpConfiguration object so that Web API can be configured.

■ **Tip** An instance of the HttpConfiguration class is accessible throughout the application via the static
GlobalConfiguration.Configuration property and through some of the Web API context objects that I described
in Chapter 9.

The call to the GlobalConfiguration.Configure method in the global application class calls the
WebApiConfig.Register method, defined in the App_Start/WebApiConfig.cs file. Listing 10-9 shows the initial
contents of the WebAPiConfig.cs file, as created by Visual Studio.

The default configuration statements in the WebApiConfig.cs file sets up the URL routing, which I describe in
Chapters 20 and 21, but I'll add additional configuration statements that set other HttpConfiguration properties
throughout the book.

■ **Tip** Notice that the routing configuration for Web API is kept separate from the RouteConfig.cs file used to
configure routes for MVC framework and Web Forms applications.

Understanding the Configuration Object

The Web API configuration is managed through an instance of the HttpConfiguration class, which presents a series
of properties that return objects that determine how Web API will handle HTTP requests. Configuring or customizing
Web API means changing the value of these properties in the configuration callback method described in the previous
section. The HttpConfiguration class defines the properties shown in Table 10-4.

Table 10-4. *The Properties Defined by the HttpConfiguration Class*

Name	Description
DependencyResolver	Gets or sets the class used for dependency injection. See the "Configuring Web API Dependency Injection" section of this chapter.
Filters	Gets or sets the request filters, which I describe in Chapters 23 and 24.
Formatters	Gets or sets the media type formatters, which I describe in Chapters 12 and 13.
IncludeErrorDetailPolicy	Gets or sets whether details are included in error messages. See Chapter 25.
MessageHandlers	Gets or sets the message handlers, which I describe in Chapter 19.
ParameterBindingRules	Gets the rules by which parameters are bound, as described in Chapter 14.
Properties	Returns a ConcurrentDictionary<object, object> that can be used as a general property bag to coordinate the behavior of components.
Routes	Gets the set of routes configured for the application. See Chapters 20 and 21.
Services	Returns the Web API services, as described in Chapter 9.

These properties—and the objects they return—define the infrastructure that Web API uses to process HTTP requests, and the table contains references to the parts of the book where I describe of them in depth. I start in the next section, where I show you how to set up an important feature: dependency injection.

■ **Tip**   You can also define configurations for individual controllers. See Chapter 22 for details.

Configuring Web API Dependency Injection

In Chapter 4, I explained the importance of ensuring that web services and their clients are loosely coupled, and this is a theme that carries over to the components within the Web API application.

The controllers and the repository that I created in the example application are tightly coupled: the controllers obtain an instance of the Repository class and use its properties directly to access the data it provides access to. This is a problem for the same reasons that tightly coupled components are avoided in the MVC framework: it makes it harder to test the controller without also implicitly testing the repository, and it means that changing the repository means finding all of the references to the Repository class and replacing them, a process that is time-consuming and error-prone.

Dependency injection (DI) breaks the direct dependency between classes. A dependency injection container is configured with mappings between interfaces and implementation classes and is used by Web API to create instances of the classes it requires to handle HTTP requests. The DI container inspects the classes it has been asked to create and resolves dependencies on the interfaces it has been configured with by creating and injecting the implementation classes. In this way, I can arrange my application so that my controllers depend on the IRepository interface without any direct knowledge of which implementation class they receive in their constructor. DI allows me to change the implementation that I use or to create mock implementations for unit testing without having to make any changes to the controller class.

A WORD ABOUT DEPENDENCY INJECTION

Not everyone likes dependency injection: it can be a mind-bending topic, the tools can be difficult to master, and it is easy to end up creating objects that are disposed of too quickly or kept around too long.

There is no rule that says you *must* use DI in your projects. I am a fan DI, but even I don't use it when prototyping or working on simple applications. If you are a non-DI reader, then skip the rest of this chapter and go to Chapter 11, where I start digging into the detail of Web API.

Although DI plays the same role for Web API as it does in the MVC framework, the approach required is different and a slight improvement, but there are some issues to be aware of, especially when it comes to creating instances of objects for each HTTP request. Table 10-5 puts Web API dependency injection in context.

Table 10-5. Putting Dependency Injection in Context

Question	Answer
What is it?	Dependency injection allows interfaces to be used without direct knowledge of the classes that implement them, creating loosely coupled components.
When should I use it?	You should use dependency injection in any project that you need to unit test or where you expect to make changes following deployment.
What do I need to know?	Web API defines two interfaces to support DI but are some obstacles to implementing per-request object scopes in Web API applications without relying on the ASP.NET platform.

Preparing for Dependency Injection

In this section, I'll add an interface to the example application and use it to break the direct dependency so that the Web API controller can access repository functionality abstractly. I am going to focus on setting up DI for Web API first and then show you how to manage DI in an application that contains both MVC framework and Web API controllers.

I need to define an interface that the Repository class can implement and that the Products controller can depend on. To this end, I created a class file called IRepository.cs in the Models folder and used it to define the interface shown in Listing 10-10.

Listing 10-10. The Contents of the IRepository.cs File

```
using System.Collections.Generic;

namespace ExampleApp.Models {
    public interface IRepository {

        IEnumerable<Product> Products { get; }
        Product GetProduct(int id);
        Product SaveProduct(Product newProduct);
        Product DeleteProduct(int id);
    }
}
```

Having defined the interface, I can update the Repository class to implement it, as shown in Listing 10-11.

Listing 10-11. Implementing the IRepository Interface in the Repository.cs File

```
using System.Collections.Generic;

namespace ExampleApp.Models {
    public class Repository : IRepository {
        private Dictionary<int, Product> data;
        private static Repository repo;

        // ...statements omitted for brevity...
    }
}
```

The final preparatory step is to update the Web API controller so that it declared a dependency on the IRepository interface in its constructor. Listing 10-12 shows the changes I made to the Products controller.

Listing 10-12. Declaring a Dependency in the ProductsController.cs File

```
using System.Collections.Generic;
using System.Web.Http;
using ExampleApp.Models;

namespace ExampleApp.Controllers {
    public class ProductsController : ApiController {
        IRepository repo;

        public ProductsController(IRepository repoImpl) {
            repo = repoImpl;
        }

        public IEnumerable<Product> GetAll() {
            return repo.Products;
        }
    }
}
```

■ **Tip** I am focusing on just the Web API controller for the moment. I'll add DI support for the MVC Home controller in the "Configuring Dependency Injection for Web API and MVC" section.

The controller now declares a dependency on the IRepository interface in its constructor. Ninject supports a range of different ways for classes to declare dependencies, but using the constructor is the one I like to use.

Understanding the Web API Dependency Interfaces

Dependency injection in Web API is handled by the IDependencyResolver and IDependencyScope interfaces, which are defined in the System.Web.Http.Dependencies namespace. Listing 10-13 shows the definition of the IDependencyResolver interface.

Listing 10-13. The Definition of the IDependencyResolver Interface

```
namespace System.Web.Http.Dependencies {
    public interface IDependencyResolver : IDependencyScope {
        IDependencyScope BeginScope();
    }
}
```

Notice that the IDependencyResolver interface is derived from IDependencyScope; I'll explain the effect of this in the "The Relationship Between the Dependency Interfaces" sidebar, but Listing 10-14 shows the definition of the IDependencyScope interface.

Listing 10-14. The Definition of the IDependencyScope Interface

```
using System.Collections.Generic;

namespace System.Web.Http.Dependencies {

    public interface IDependencyScope : IDisposable {

        object GetService(Type serviceType);
        IEnumerable<object> GetServices(Type serviceType);
    }
}
```

This IDependencyScope interface defines GetService and GetServices methods, which perform the same role as in the equivalents in the MVC framework. The GetService method is called when the Web API infrastructure needs a concrete type (such as a controller) or needs to use an interface for which there should be only one implementation (such as the IHttpActionInvoker interface, which I describe in Chapter 22). The GetServices method is used when the Web API infrastructure expects there to be multiple implementations of an interface, all of which are required (such as IFilter, which I describe in Chapter 23).

THE RELATIONSHIP BETWEEN THE DEPENDENCY INTERFACES

The inheritance relationship between the interfaces can be confusing, but it starts to make sense when you understand that the Web API developers were trying to make it easier to deal with the two most common dependency injection scenarios in a web application: creating objects that are used for the life of the application and creating objects that are used for a single request.

When the application starts, a single instance of the IDependencyResolver implementation object is created and kept by Web API for the life of the application, and its GetService and GetServices methods are used whenever an object is required for the Web API infrastructure. In practice, this means it is used to create a lot of objects when the application is started (filters, data formatters, and so on) and then not used again.

There is only ever one instance of the class that implements the IDependencyResolver interface. When Web API needs an object that will be used for a single request, such as a controller or a database context class, then it calls the BeginScope method of the IDependencyResolver object in order to get an implementation of the IDependencyScope interface and uses the GetService and GetServices methods to create the instances it needs. When the request has been handled and the objects that have been created are no longer required, Web API calls the Dispose method on the IDependencyScope object (because it implements IDisposable) so that the objects that have been created can be prepared for destruction.

Most DI containers support *scopes*, which are used to decide when to create a new instance of a class and when to reuse an existing instance. Building the per-request scopes into the dependency interfaces makes it easier to integrate DI containers into the Web API request handling process. Most DI containers rely on the System.Web. HttpContext class to support per-request object life cycles, which can be a problem with Web API because you cannot rely on the System.Web classes. It will be a while before the mainstream dependency injection containers catch up to the new Web API design, and until then, it can be slightly awkward to align container scopes to Web API scopes (as you will see in the "Implementing the Dependency Interfaces" section).

Installing the Dependency Injection Container

Many dependency injection containers are available, and it is worth looking at a few before making a decision. Popular choices include StructureMap, Castle Windsor, and Unity, which comes from Microsoft.

The DI container that I always return to in my projects and my books is Ninject, which I described in *Pro ASP.NET MVC 5*. I like its simple and fluent API, and I have yet to encounter a problem that wasn't easily solved. You don't have to use Ninject in your own projects, of course, and the techniques that I describe in this chapter apply equally to any DI container package.

Ninject, like all of the major DI containers, is available as a NuGet package. To install Ninject, I entered the following commands into the Visual Studio Package Manager Console window:

```
Install-Package Ninject -version 3.0.1.10
Install-Package Ninject.Extensions.ChildKernel -Version 3.0.0.5
```

Implementing the Dependency Interfaces

Ninject makes it easy to support the two Web API resolution interfaces, and although it may seem odd, the easiest way to do so is by creating a single class. I created an Infrastructure folder and added a class file called NinjectResolver.cs to it, the contents of which are shown in Listing 10-15.

Listing 10-15. The Contents of the NinjectResolver.cs File

```
using System;
using System.Collections.Generic;
using System.Web.Http.Dependencies;
using ExampleApp.Models;
using Ninject;
using Ninject.Extensions.ChildKernel;

namespace ExampleApp.Infrastructure {

    public class NinjectResolver : IDependencyResolver {
        private IKernel kernel;

        public NinjectResolver() : this (new StandardKernel()) {}
```

```
    public NinjectResolver(IKernel ninjectKernel, bool scope = false) {
        kernel = ninjectKernel;
        if (!scope) {
            AddBindings(kernel);
        }
    }

    public IDependencyScope BeginScope() {
        return new NinjectResolver(AddRequestBindings(
            new ChildKernel(kernel)), true);
    }

    public object GetService(Type serviceType) {
        return kernel.TryGet(serviceType);
    }

    public IEnumerable<object> GetServices(Type serviceType) {
        return kernel.GetAll(serviceType);
    }

    public void Dispose() {
        // do nothing
    }

    private void AddBindings(IKernel kernel) {
        // singleton and transient bindings go here
    }

    private IKernel AddRequestBindings(IKernel kernel) {
        kernel.Bind<IRepository>().To<Repository>().InSingletonScope();
        return kernel;
    }
}
```

UNDERSTANDING OBJECT SCOPES

When working with dependency injection in web applications, there are three types of objects you need to create: singleton objects, request objects, and transient objects.

Singleton objects are instantiated the first time they are required, and all classes that depend on them share the same instance. As the same suggests, there is a single instance in the application. If my Repository class in the example application were configured as a singleton, then only one instance would be created, and every Products controller object that was created would receive that instance to satisfy its dependency on the IRepository interface. Singleton objects have to be written to deal with their long life and the need to protect their state against multiple concurrent callers.

Transient objects are instantiated every time there is a dependency on them. If my Repository class were configured as a transient, a new instance would be created each time a Products controller was created. Transient objects are not reused by the dependency injection container, and their life is generally tied to the life of the object they are injected into.

Request objects are somewhere in the middle. A new instance is created for each request that the web application receives and is reused to resolve dependencies declared by all of the objects created by the Web API infrastructure to process that request. Or, to put it another way, the objects created to process a single request share a single instance of the request object. The request object is discarded after the request has been handled.

Repository classes are usually configured as request objects, which allows all of the objects that deal with a single request to share a common view of the model, and all see the changes that the request causes. And, since just about every Web API and MVC framework application has a repository, supporting request objects is an important feature.

Each of these object types is configured by creating a *dependency injection scope*. I explain how to create each kind of scope using Ninject later in the chapter.

■ **Caution**   A number of NuGet packages extend Ninject in order to integrate the DI functionality into different environments. As I write this, there are several that are aimed at ASP.NET Web API, but they all assume you will be deploying your application to IIS, and they rely on the ASP.NET platform module feature to manage per-request object life cycles. The class shown in Listing 10-15 supports Web API dependency injection without relying on the ASP.NET platform, so you can deploy your web service freely. See the "Configuring Dependency Injection for Web API and MVC" section for sharing DI between Web API and MVC framework components, where relying on the ASP.NET platform can be an acceptable compromise.

This class acts as the touch point between Web API and Ninject. It implements both of the Web API dependency interfaces (NinjectResolver implements IDependencyResolver, which is derived from IDependencyScope) and responds to the BeginScope method by creating a child kernel, which allows me to use Ninject to create objects scopes for each request. There is only one dependency mapping in the example application, which I set up as follows:

```
...
kernel.Bind<IRepository>().To<Repository>().InSingletonScope();
...
```

I have highlighted the three important parts of the statement. The generic type parameter for the Bind method specifies the interface that I want to configure, which is IRepository in this case. The generic type parameter for the To method specifies the implementation class that Ninject should use to resolve dependencies on the interface, which is the Repository class in this example.

The final part of the mapping statement is a call to the InSingletonScope method, which specifies the scope for the instances of the class that are created to resolve dependencies on the interface.

This is where things get a little confusing because of the way that the NinjectResolver class works: I create a request scope by creating a child kernel for each request and creating a singleton scope on the child kernel, ensuring that there is only one instance of the object created for each request.

■ **Tip**   Don't worry if this doesn't make immediate sense because it is an implementation detail specific to one dependency injection container. You can use the NinjectResolver class as-is in your projects, just as long as you follow the instructions in Table 10-6.

***Table 10-6.** Creating Web API Object Scopes with Ninject*

Scope	Method	Example
Singleton	AddBindings	kernel.Bind<IRepository>().To<Repository>() .InSingletonScope();
Request	AddRequestBindings	kernel.Bind<IRepository>().To<Repository>() .InSingletonScope();
Transient	AddBindings	kernel.Bind<IRepository>().To<Repository>();

This wrinkle means there are two methods in which bindings between interfaces and their implementations are defined: the AddBindings and AddRequestBindings methods. The AddBindings method is used to define singleton and transient scopes, and the AddRequestBindings method is used to define request scopes. Table 10-6 summarizes the three object scopes and gives examples of how to use the methods defined by the NinjectResolver class.

■ **Tip** The singleton and request bindings are both created with the InSingletonScope method, but request scopes are set up in the AddRequestBindings method, which is called on the child Ninject kernels created when the BeginScope method is called.

Configuring Web API

The final step is to configure the Web API to use the NinjectResolver class to resolve dependencies. Listing 10-16 shows the additions I made to the WebApiConfig.cs file to perform the configuration.

***Listing 10-16.** Configuring Dependency Injection in the WebApiConfig.cs File*

```
using System;
using System.Collections.Generic;
using System.Linq;
using System.Web.Http;
using ExampleApp.Infrastructure;

namespace ExampleApp {
    public static class WebApiConfig {
        public static void Register(HttpConfiguration config) {

            config.DependencyResolver = new NinjectResolver();

            config.MapHttpAttributeRoutes();

            config.Routes.MapHttpRoute(
                name: "DefaultApi",
                routeTemplate: "api/{controller}/{id}",
                defaults: new { id = RouteParameter.Optional }
            );
        }
    }
}
```

The `HttpConfiguration.DependencyResolver` is set to a new instance of the `NinjectResolver` class, which means that Web API will use it to instantiate the objects it needs for the application infrastructure and to handle individual requests.

Configuring Dependency Injection for Web API and MVC

Although Web API is using the `NinjectResolver` class to resolve dependency, the MVC Home controller remains tightly coupled to the `Repository` class. In this section, I am going to show you how to set up dependency injection for an application that contains Web API *and* MVC components. This is a simple process because the MVC framework can be hosted only on the ASP.NET platform, which means that the request scope support that DI containers such as Ninject provide can be used, even in the Web API components.

■ **Note**   Using the technique in this section ties your web services the ASP.NET platform because it relies on the `System.Web.HttpContext` class being instantiated and providing access to an `HttpRequest` object that describes the current request. These classes are not part of the Web API namespaces, and using them prevents Web API components from being deployed outside of IIS. For the moment, at least, most Web API applications will be deployed to the ASP.NET platform, but if you decide that you want to separate the Web API and MVC components at a later date, then you will have to revert to the techniques I described earlier in the chapter.

Declaring the Dependency

I am going to start by updating the Home controller so that it no longer uses the `Repository` class directly and instead declares a dependency on the `IRepository` interface, as shown in Listing 10-17.

Listing 10-17. Declaring a Dependency in the HomeController.cs File

```
using System.Web.Mvc;
using ExampleApp.Models;

namespace ExampleApp.Controllers {
    public class HomeController : Controller {
        IRepository repo;

        public HomeController(IRepository repoImpl) {
            repo = repoImpl;
        }

        public ActionResult Index() {
            return View(repo.Products);
        }
    }
}
```

Now that both the Web API and MVC controllers declare dependencies on the `IRepository` interface, I have taken the opportunity to remove the `static` property and constructor from the `Repository` class, which would cause an extra `Repository` object to be created the first time the class was instantiated to resolve a dependency. Listing 10-18 shows the statements that I commented out.

Listing 10-18. Removing the Static Instance from the Repository.cs File

```
using System.Collections.Generic;

namespace ExampleApp.Models {
    public class Repository : IRepository {
        private Dictionary<int, Product> data;
        //private static Repository repo;

        //static Repository() {
        //    repo = new Repository();
        //}

        //public static Repository Current {
        //    get { return repo; }
        //}

        // ...other statements omitted for brevity...
    }
}
```

Installing the Dependency Injection Packages

I need to install two additional Ninject packages, which I do by entering the following commands into the Visual Studio Package Manager Console window:

```
Install-Package Ninject.Web.Common -version 3.0.0.7
Install-Package Ninject.MVC3 -Version 3.0.0.6
```

The Ninject.Web.Common package contains support for integrating dependency injection with the ASP.NET platform so that dependencies on modules and handlers can be resolved. The Ninject.MVC3 package adds additional features required by the MVC framework (don't worry about the reference to MVC3 because the package works happily with MVC 3, 4, and 5). This package adds a NinjectWebCommon.cs file to the App_Start folder that contains code to set up dependency injection for ASP.NET modules and handlers. This file can be ignored or deleted because it has no bearing on Web API.

■ **Tip** See my *Pro ASP.NET MVC 5 Platform* book, published by Apress, if you are not familiar with ASP.NET platform components such as modules and handlers. Even though you should avoid directly relying on the ASP.NET platform when using Web API, there are many features that are useful in MVC framework applications.

Adding MVC Support to the Resolver

MVC framework dependency resolution is handled by the System.Web.Mvc.IDependencyResolver interface, which defines the methods described in Table 10-7.

Table 10-7. *The Methods Defined by the MVC IDependencyResolver Interface*

Name	Description
GetService(type)	Resolves a type for which one implementation is registered
GetServices(type)	Resolves a type for which multiple implementations are registered

These methods match the ones defined by the Web API IDependencyScope interface, which I listed in Listing 10-14. This duplication allows me to extend the NinjectResolver class to support both Web API and the MVC framework, as shown in Listing 10-19.

Listing 10-19. Adding MVC Framework Support to the NinjectResolver.cs File

```
using System;
using System.Collections.Generic;
using System.Web.Http.Dependencies;
using ExampleApp.Models;
using Ninject;
using Ninject.Extensions.ChildKernel;
using Ninject.Web.Common;

namespace ExampleApp.Infrastructure {

    public class NinjectResolver : System.Web.Http.Dependencies.IDependencyResolver,
            System.Web.Mvc.IDependencyResolver {
        private IKernel kernel;

        public NinjectResolver() : this (new StandardKernel()) {}

        public NinjectResolver(IKernel ninjectKernel) {
            kernel = ninjectKernel;
            AddBindings(kernel);
        }

        public IDependencyScope BeginScope() {
            return this;
        }

        public object GetService(Type serviceType) {
            return kernel.TryGet(serviceType);
        }

        public IEnumerable<object> GetServices(Type serviceType) {
            return kernel.GetAll(serviceType);
        }

        public void Dispose() {
            // do nothing
        }
```

```
    private void AddBindings(IKernel kernel) {
        kernel.Bind<IRepository>().To<Repository>().InRequestScope();
    }
  }
}
```

The Web API and MVC framework interfaces have the same name, so I have to use the fully qualified names in the class definition in order to implement both interfaces.

Being able to rely on the ASP.NET platform means that Ninject is able to provide the InRequestScope method, which configures bindings so that the objects they create are scoped to the request. This allows me to support the Web API BeginScope method without using child kernels and, in turn, to consolidate my bindings into a single method. The overall effect is to simplify the dependency resolution class by tying the life of per-request objects to the features provided by the ASP.NET platform.

But this simpler and more elegant approach comes at the cost of depending on the ASP.NET platform, which limits the deployment options for the application, but that is likely to be an acceptable trade-off for most applications if they contain MVC components. Table 10-8 shows how to create the different object scopes using the resolver in Listing 10-19.

Table 10-8. *Creating Web API and MVC Object Scopes with Ninject*

Scope	Method	Example
Singleton	AddBindings	kernel.Bind<IRepository>().To<Repository>().InSingletonScope();
Request	AddBindings	kernel.Bind<IRepository>().To<Repository>().InRequestScope();
Transient	AddBindings	kernel.Bind<IRepository>().To<Repository>();

This is a more natural way of using Ninject and is the same set of methods that you would use if you were working with just the MVC framework on its own.

Configuring the MVC Framework

The final step is to configure the MVC framework so that the NinjectResolver class is used to create objects and resolve dependencies. Listing 10-20 shows the changes that I made to the Global Application Class.

Listing 10-20. Configuring Dependency Injection in the Global.asax.cs File

```
using System;
using System.Collections.Generic;
using System.Linq;
using System.Web;
using System.Web.Mvc;
using System.Web.Routing;
using System.Web.Security;
using System.Web.SessionState;
using System.Web.Http;
```

```
namespace ExampleApp {
    public class Global : HttpApplication {
        void Application_Start(object sender, EventArgs e) {

            AreaRegistration.RegisterAllAreas();
            GlobalConfiguration.Configure(WebApiConfig.Register);
            RouteConfig.RegisterRoutes(RouteTable.Routes);

            System.Web.Mvc.DependencyResolver.SetResolver(
                (System.Web.Mvc.IDependencyResolver)
                GlobalConfiguration.Configuration.DependencyResolver);
        }
    }
}
```

I could have moved the Web API configuration statement from the WebApiConfig.cs file to the Global Application Class, but I wanted to demonstrate the way that the Web API configuration is universally available. The statement I added uses the GlobalConfiguration.Configuration property to obtain an instance of the HttpConfiguration class, reads the DependencyResolver to get the NinjectResolver instance, and uses it as the argument to the DependencyResolver.SetResolver method to configure the MVC framework. The effect is to apply a single instance of the NinjectResolver class as the resolver for the entire application so that the MVC framework and Web API share the same set of singleton objects and have access to the same set of request and transient objects.

Summary

In this chapter, I created and configured the example application that I will use in this part of the book. I explained the most important configuration classes and used them to show you how to set up dependency injection, with and without dependencies on the ASP.NET platform. In the next chapter, I start to dig into the details of ASP.NET Web API, starting with the results that action methods produce. This may not sound like a promising topic, but, as you will see, results define the character of an HTTP web service, and knowing how to produce the results you require is essential for effective Web API development.

CHAPTER 11

∎∎∎

Action Method Results

In this chapter, I start digging into the details of how Web API web services work, starting right at the heart of web services, namely, the different ways that action methods return results and how these are used to generate HTTP responses. As you will learn, Web API has convenient features that use the standard characteristics of C# methods to express results, which makes generating the most common types of results easy. Behind this convenience is a flexible and extensible system of *action results*, which are similar to the ones used by the MVC framework and which allow for complete control over the HTTP response sent to the client. I explain how this system works and demonstrate how you can customize it. Table 11-1 summarizes this chapter.

Table 11-1. *Chapter Summary*

Problem	Solution	Listing
Define an action method that doesn't return any data.	Return void from the method.	1–4
Define an action method that returns a result.	Return an implementation of the IHttpActionResult interface from the action method.	5–10
Select the data format that will be used for serialized data.	Create a content negotiation class.	11, 12
Register a content negotiation class.	Replace the service implementation of the IContentNegotiator interface with the custom class.	13, 14
Specify a result code to be used in a response that contains serialized data.	Create a negotiable action result.	15

Preparing the Example Project

In this chapter, I am going to continue working with the ExampleApp project I created in Chapter 10. There is one change required to prepare for this project, which is to change the dependency injection object life cycle for the Repository class. In Chapter 10, I was focused on showing you how to create objects that are scoped to individual requests because that is what is usually required for real repository objects that are backed by a database, such as the one I used in Chapter 5. My example Repository class, however, keeps its model data in memory, which means I need to create one instance of the Repository class and use it throughout the life of the application; otherwise, each request will be working solely with the default data. Listing 11-1 shows the change I made to the NinjectResolver class to change the scope of the Repository class.

■ **Tip** Remember that you don't have to create the example project yourself. You can download the source code for every chapter for free from Apress.com.

Listing 11-1. Changing an Object Scope in the NinjectResolver.cs File

```
using System;
using System.Collections.Generic;
using System.Web.Http.Dependencies;
using ExampleApp.Models;
using Ninject;
using Ninject.Extensions.ChildKernel;
using Ninject.Web.Common;

namespace ExampleApp.Infrastructure {

    public class NinjectResolver : System.Web.Http.Dependencies.IDependencyResolver,
            System.Web.Mvc.IDependencyResolver {
        private IKernel kernel;

        public NinjectResolver() : this(new StandardKernel()) { }

        public NinjectResolver(IKernel ninjectKernel) {
            kernel = ninjectKernel;
            AddBindings(kernel);
        }

        public IDependencyScope BeginScope() {
            return this;
        }

        public object GetService(Type serviceType) {
            return kernel.TryGet(serviceType);
        }

        public IEnumerable<object> GetServices(Type serviceType) {
            return kernel.GetAll(serviceType);
        }

        public void Dispose() {
            // do nothing
        }

        private void AddBindings(IKernel kernel) {
            kernel.Bind<IRepository>().To<Repository>().InSingletonScope();
        }
    }
}
```

As I explained in Chapter 10, using the InSingletonScope method means that one instance will be created and used to resolve all of the dependencies for the IRequest interface in the application. (As a reminder, this is the version of the resolver that supports applications containing MVC and Web API components.)

Understanding Action Method Results

As I explain in detail in Chapter 22, the goal of a controller is to use an action method to process an HttpRequestMessage object in order to create an HttpResponseMessage object. The HttpRequestMessage describes the request to be handled, and the HttpResponseMessage describes the response to be returned to the client. The hosting environment (which will typically be IIS, but see Chapter 26 for another option) is responsible for creating the HttpResponseMessage object to represent the request and turning the HttpRequestMessage into an HTTP response and sending it to the client. Figure 11-1 shows the basic flow.

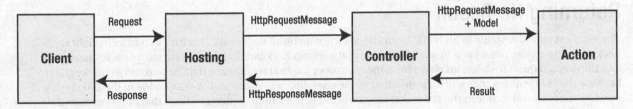

Figure 11-1. *The basic request and result flow*

The controller provides the action method with the data contained in the request using model binding, which I describe in Chapters 14–17, and about the request itself through the HttpRequestMessage object. The HttpRequestMessage object is part of the System.Net.Http namespace and presents a general view of an HTTP request that Web API can operate on using the properties shown in Table 11-2.

Table 11-2. *The Properties Defined by the HttpRequestMessage Class*

Name	Description
Content	Returns an HttpContent object that contains the content of the HTTP request. Request content is accessed through the model binding feature, which I describe in Chapters 14 –17.
Headers	Returns an HttpRequestHeaders object that contains the headers sent by the client.
Method	Returns an HttpMethod object that describes the HTTP method/verb for the request.
Properties	Returns a dictionary that contains objects provided by the hosting environment.
RequestUri	Returns the URL requested by the client, expressed as an Uri object.
Version	Returns the version of HTTP that was used to make the request, expressed as a System.Version object.

Action methods can return C# objects that represent model data or by creating an HttpResponseMessage object directly. Actions can also elect to return a result but still respond to the client to acknowledge that an operation has been successfully completed. I describe the different kinds of results in the sections that follow, and Table 11-3 puts action methods results into context.

Table 11-3. *Putting Action Method Results in Context*

Question	Answer
What is it?	The result from an action method describes the HTTP response that will be sent to the client.
When should you use it?	You need to explicitly specify results when you want control over the HTTP response sent to the client, but all action methods produce results, even when the void keyword is used in the method signature.
What do you need to know?	Web API has some nice features that hide away the details of creating HTTP responses for common outcomes, but you will need to understand the different kinds of results that are available to get full control over the operation of a web service.

Returning No Result

The simplest way to respond to an HTTP request is to return no result data at all. This isn't as odd as it might seem because web services often need to provide actions that perform work but that don't generate a data response. As an example, a request to delete an object from the repository may not require any data to be returned to the client because the HTTP status code will indicate whether the operation was successful. A status code in the 200 range will indicate success, and a code in the 400 or 500 range will indicate a failure. Action methods that don't produce data return void, as shown in Listing 11-2.

Listing 11-2. Adding an Action Method That Returns void in the ProductsController.cs File

```
using System.Collections.Generic;
using System.Web.Http;
using ExampleApp.Models;

namespace ExampleApp.Controllers {
    public class ProductsController : ApiController {
        IRepository repo;

        public ProductsController(IRepository repoImpl) {
            repo = repoImpl;
        }

        public IEnumerable<Product> GetAll() {
            return repo.Products;
        }

        public void Delete(int id) {
            repo.DeleteProduct(id);
        }
    }
}
```

I have added a Delete action method that calls the corresponding method defined by the repository. The method returns void, which means that no data will be returned to the client.

The simplest way to test the action method is with Postman, which will clearly display the HTTP result code returned by the server. Sending an HTTP DELETE request to /api/products/1 will result in status code 204, as shown in Figure 11-2.

Figure 11-2. *Targeting an action method that returns no data*

Status code 204 is the No Data code, which is defined as follows:

The server has fulfilled the request but does not need to return an entity-body.

You can see the full W3C definition of status codes at www.w3.org/Protocols/rfc2616/rfc2616-sec10.html, but this is the result code that is used most commonly for delete operations in web services.

Consuming a No Result Action Method

jQuery treats any HTTP status code in the 200 range as a success, so dealing with action methods that don't return data is a matter of defining a success callback function that updates the client-side data model to reflect the operation that has been performed. Listing 11-3 shows the changes that I made to the Index.cshtml file to add Delete buttons for each product data object.

Listing 11-3. Adding Product Delete Buttons to the Index.cshtml File

```
@model IEnumerable<ExampleApp.Models.Product>
@{ ViewBag.Title = "Index";}

@section Scripts {
    <script>
        var products = ko.observableArray(
            @Html.Raw(Newtonsoft.Json.JsonConvert.SerializeObject(Model)));
    </script>
    <script src="~/Scripts/exampleApp.js"></script>
}

<div class="panel panel-primary">
    <div class="panel-heading">RSVPs</div>
    <table id="rsvpTable" class="table table-striped">
        <thead>
            <tr><th>ID</th><th>Name</th><th>Price</th></tr>
        </thead>
        <tbody data-bind="foreach: products">
            <tr>
                <td data-bind="text: ProductID"></td>
                <td data-bind="text: Name"></td>
                <td data-bind="text: Price"></td>
                <td>
                    <button class="deleteBtn btn btn-danger btn-xs"
                        data-bind="click: deleteProduct">
                        Delete
                    </button>
                </td>
```

```
            </tr>
        </tbody>
    </table>
</div>
<button data-bind="click: getProducts" class="btn btn-primary">Refresh</button>
```

I have added a column to the table, and each td element contains a Deslete button to which I have applied the Knockout click binding to invoke a function called deleteProduct when the button elements are clicked. Listing 11-4 shows the implementation of the deleteProduct function in the exampleApp.js file.

Listing 11-4. Handling Button Events in the exampleApp.js File

```
$(document).ready(function () {

    deleteProduct = function (data) {
        $.ajax("/api/products/" + data.ProductID, {
            type: "DELETE",
            success: function () {
                products.remove(data);
            }
        })
    };

    getProducts = function () {
        $.ajax("/api/products", {
            success: function (data) {
                products.removeAll();
                for (var i = 0; i < data.length; i++) {
                    products.push(data[i]);
                }
            }
        })
    };
    ko.applyBindings();
});
```

As I explained in Chapter 3, Knockout passes the data item associated with the element that triggered the click binding to the callback function, which means I can read the value of the ProductID property to create the URL that I need to target, like this:

```
...
$.ajax("/api/products/" + data.ProductID, {
...
```

I use the type property to tell jQuery to make a DELETE request, and Web API uses the HTTP verb and the URL to target the Delete action method on the Products controller (I explain how this happens in Chapter 22). The action method performs the delete operation on the repository but doesn't return a result because the method was defined with the void keyword.

The 204 status code will cause jQuery to invoke my `success` function, which I defined without arguments because I am not expecting to receive data back from the web service. I remove the data object that Knockout passed to the `deleteProduct` function from the model array, which causes the contents of the `table` element to be updated, as shown in Figure 11-3.

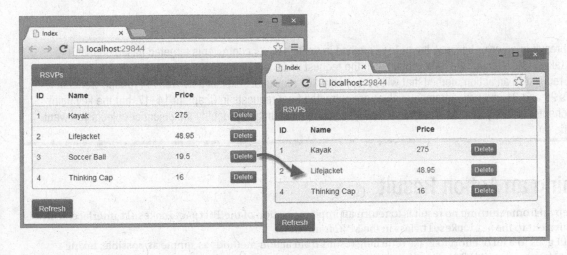

Figure 11-3. *Deleting items from the repository*

AVOIDING THE URL VS. BODY PITFALL

Notice that I constructed the URL for the DELETE request so that it included the `ProductID` property value of the object I wanted to remove from the repository, like this:

```
...
deleteProduct = function (data) {
    $.ajax("/api/products/" + data.ProductID, {
        type: "DELETE",
        success: function () {
            products.remove(data);
        }
    })
};
...
```

If you have experience using jQuery to make Ajax requests, then you might expect to be able to include the value of the `ProductID` property in the request body, like this:

```
...
deleteProduct = function (data) {
    $.ajax("/api/products", {
        type: "DELETE",
        data: {id: data.ProductID},
```

```
        success: function () {
            products.remove(data);
        }
    })
};
...
```

This will result in an error because the Delete method in the Products controller is targeted based on the URL without taking into account the data contained in the request body. The effect of the previous code is to send a DELETE request to an action method that will accept only GET requests. I explain how Web API routing works in Chapters 20 and 21 and how parameter values are extracted from requests in Chapters 14–17, but the key point for this chapter is that you must ensure that the URLs you request uniquely identify the object or objects you want to operate on.

Returning an Action Result

The next step up from returning no result is to return an implementation of the IHttpActionResult interface, which is roughly equivalent to the ActionResult class in the MVC framework.

Web API goes to a lot of effort to make returning results from action methods as simple as possible, taking responsibility for creating HttpResponseMessage objects for you whenever possible. You saw this in the previous section for void action methods, and you'll see it again in the "Returning Model Data" section when I demonstrate how model objects are automatically serialized.

The IHttpActionResult interface allows an action method to specify how HttpResponseMessage objects should be generated as instructions, which are then executed to produce the HttpResponseMessage that is used to respond to the client. In this section of this chapter, I explain how the IHttpActionResult interface fits into Web API and demonstrate the different ways it can be used. Table 11-4 puts action methods that return implementations of the IHttpActionResult interface into context.

Table 11-4. *Putting Action Methods That Return IHttpActionResult into Context*

Question	Answer
What is it?	Action results are implementations of the IHttpActionResult interface that produce an HttpResponseMessage that describes the response that should be sent to the client.
When should you use it?	Action results allow you to take control over the HTTP response that will be returned to the client and, in particular, specify the status code that will be used. Returning void from an action method generates a 204 code, and returning model data (which I describe later in this chapter) generates a 200 code. For all other status codes (or for action methods that need to decide which status code to return dynamically), action results are required.
What do you need to know?	The ApiController class defines a set of convenience methods that create IHttpActionResult implementation objects for most common HTTP status codes. Call these methods to get an object that will generate the response you require and return it as the result from an action method.

Understanding the IHttpActionResult Interface

The IHttpActionResult interface is used to separate an action method from the HttpResponseMessage object that represents its results. This is an example of the *command pattern*, which you can learn about at http://en.wikipedia.org/wiki/Command_pattern and which makes it easier to isolate and test an action method and the action result separately. Listing 11-5 shows the definition of the IHttpActionResult interface, which is defined in the System.Web.Http namespace.

Listing 11-5. The Definition of the IHttpActionResult Interface

```
using System.Net.Http;
using System.Threading;
using System.Threading.Tasks;

namespace System.Web.Http {
    public interface IHttpActionResult {
        Task<HttpResponseMessage> ExecuteAsync(CancellationToken cancellationToken);
    }
}
```

CANCELLING ASYNCHRONOUS TASKS

You will see that many of the interfaces that describe Web API components are asynchronous and return Task objects that produce other Web API or System.Net.Http types. You usually don't have to worry about creating Task objects when you are using the default implementations of these interfaces, but they become important when you start to create custom implementations to change the default behaviors.

Most of the important methods receive a CancellationToken argument, which is used by the caller to signal that the operation has been cancelled, allowing your implementation classes to avoid doing work that will just be discarded when it is complete. You can check to see whether your operation has been cancelled by reading the CancellationToken.IsCancellationRequested property, and it is good practice to do just that in your code. I describe Task cancellation in detail in my *Pro .NET Parallel Programming in C#* book, published by Apress.

The interface defines the ExecuteAsync method, which accepts a CancellationToken object as its argument and returns a Task that produces an HttpResponseMessage object. Table 11-5 shows the properties of the HttpResponseMessage, which gives a sense of the information that is required to generate an HTTP response.

Table 11-5. The Properties Defined by the HttpResponseMessage Class

Name	Description
Content	Gets or sets the content of the response, expressed as an HttpContent object
Headers	Gets the HttpResponseHeaders objects that are used to collect the headers for the response
IsSuccessStatusCode	Returns true if the result of the StatusCode property is between 200 and 299, inclusive
ReasonPhrase	Gets or sets the explanatory phrase associated with the status code, expressed as a string
RequestMessage	Gets or sets the HttpRequestMessage that the HttpResponseMessage is associated with
StatusCode	Gets or sets the status code using the values defined in the HttpStatusCode class
Version	Gets or sets the HTTP version, expressed as a System.Version

Using the ApiController Action Result Methods

The `ApiController` class, which is the default base for Web API controllers, defines a set of convenience methods that make it easy to create a range of `IHttpActionResult` implementation objects, which are suitable for most of the common responses that HTTP web services need. Table 11-6 describes the methods available. These methods instantiate classes defined in the `System.Web.Http.Results` namespace.

Table 11-6. *The ApiController Methods That Return Objects That Implement the IHttpActionResult Interface*

Name	Description
BadRequest()	Creates a `BadRequest` object that uses status code 400.
BadRequest(message)	Creates a `BadRequestErrorMessageResult`, which uses a status code of 400 and contains the specified message in the response body.
BadRequest(modelstate)	Creates an `InvalidModelStateResult` that uses status code 400 and includes validation information in the response body. See Chapter 18 for details of Web API data validation.
Conflict()	Creates a `ConflictResult`, which uses status code 409. This status code is used when the request contravenes the internal rules defined by the web service. The standard example is trying to upload an older version of a file than is already stored by the web service, but this is a rarely used result.
Content(status, data)	See the "Bypassing Content Negotiation" section of this chapter for details.
Created(url, data)	See the "Creating Negotiable Action Results" section of this chapter for details.
CreatedAtRoute(name, vals, data)	See the "Creating Negotiable Action Results" section of this chapter for details.
InternalServerError()	Creates an `InternalServerError`, which uses status code 500.
InternelServerError(exception)	Creates an `ExceptionResult`, which uses status code 500 and which details of the specified exception in the response body.
NotFound()	Creates a `NotFoundResult`, which uses status code 404.
Ok()	Creates an `OkResult`, which uses status code 200.
Ok(data)	See the "Creating Negotiable Action Results" section of this chapter for details.
Redirect(target)	Creates a `RedirectResult`, which uses status code 302 to redirect the client to the URL, which can be specified as a string or a `Uri`.
RedirectToRoute(name, props)	Creates a `RedirectToRouteResult`, which generates a URL from the routing configuration and uses it to send a 302 response to the client. See Chapters 20 and 21 for details of Web API routing.

(continued)

Table 11-6. (continued)

Name	Description
ResponseMessage(message)	Creates a ResponseMessageResult, which is a wrapper around an existing HttpResponseMessage object. See the "Creating an HttpResponseMessage Object" section.
StatusCode(code)	Creates a StatusCodeResult, which uses the specified status code, expressed as a value from the HttpStatusCode class. See the "Creating an HttpResponseMessage Object" section.
Unauthorized(headers)	Creates a UnauthorizedResult, which uses the 401 status code. See Chapters 23 and 24 for the details of authentication.

The methods that return objects that include information in the response body, such as BadRequest(message) and InternalServerError(exception), rely on the *media formatting* and *content negotiation* features to format the response content so that it can be processed by the client. I explain these features in the "Understanding Content Negotiation" section.

The methods shown in Table 11-6 create the IHttpActionResult objects, which you then return as the result from an action method, just as with ActionResult objects in the MVC framework. Listing 11-6 shows the addition of an action method to the Products controller that just returns a result code to the client without doing any work.

Listing 11-6. Adding an Action Method in the ProductsController.cs File

```
using System.Collections.Generic;
using System.Web.Http;
using ExampleApp.Models;

namespace ExampleApp.Controllers {
    public class ProductsController : ApiController {
        IRepository repo;

        public ProductsController(IRepository repoImpl) {
            repo = repoImpl;
        }

        public IEnumerable<Product> GetAll() {
            return repo.Products;
        }

        public void Delete(int id) {
            repo.DeleteProduct(id);
        }

        [HttpGet]
        [Route("api/products/noop")]
        public IHttpActionResult NoOp() {
            return Ok();
        }
    }
}
```

The NoOp action method calls the Ok method to create an OkResult object and then returns it as the result of the action. You can test the action method by starting the application and using Postman to send a GET request to /api/products/noop.

■ **Tip**   I had to apply the Route attributes to prevent the default Web API routes for RESTful web services from directing the request to the GetAll method, which I explain in Chapter 22. The HttpGet attribute enables the action method to receive HTTP GET requests, as described in Chapter 14.

For quick reference, Table 11-7 lists the action result methods ordered by the status codes they produce, which is usually what you need to know in the middle of a project.

Table 11-7. *ApiController Action Result Methods by HTTP Status Code*

Status Code	Meaning	Method
200	Operation successful	Ok() Ok(data)
302	Temporary redirection	Redirect(target) RedirectToRoute(name, props)
400	Bad request	BadRequest() BadRequest(message) BadRequest(model)
404	Not found	NotFound()
409	Conflict	Conflict()
500	Internal server error	InternalServerError() InternalServerError(exception)

Returning Other Status Codes

There are predefined IHttpActionResult implementations for the most widely used HTTP result codes, but Web API makes it easy to return other codes using the IHttpActionResult mechanism, which I'll demonstrate by returning a result from the Delete method, which currently relies on the controller to detect the void keyword and send the 204 response.

Creating a StatusCodeResult Object

The simplest approach is to use the StatusCode method, which returns a StatusCodeResult object whose ExecuteAsync method yields an HttpResponseMessage with an arbitrary HTTP status code, as shown in Listing 11-7.

Listing 11-7. Using a StatusCodeResult in the ProductsController.cs File

```
using System.Collections.Generic;
using System.Web.Http;
using ExampleApp.Models;
using System.Net;

namespace ExampleApp.Controllers {
    public class ProductsController : ApiController {
        IRepository repo;

        public ProductsController(IRepository repoImpl) {
            repo = repoImpl;
        }

        public IEnumerable<Product> GetAll() {
            return repo.Products;
        }

        public IHttpActionResult Delete(int id) {
            repo.DeleteProduct(id);
            return StatusCode(HttpStatusCode.NoContent);
        }

        [HttpGet]
        [Route("api/products/noop")]
        public IHttpActionResult NoOp() {
            return Ok();
        }
    }
}
```

A lot of different HTTP status codes are available, and this technique is useful if you find yourself needing one of them that isn't covered by the other controller convenience methods. The set of status codes that you can use is defined by the System.Net.HttpStatusCode class, which has properties for each code.

To be clear, there is little need to explicitly return code 204 (No Data) in a real application because using the void keyword is more elegant and natural, although it can be a useful technique when performing data validation, which I describe in Chapter 18.

Creating an HttpResponseMessage Object

You can use the ResponseMessage method as an IHttpActionResult wrapper around an HttpResponseMessage that you have already created or obtained. This isn't something you will need to do for most web services, but it can be useful when modifying the Web API request dispatch process, which I describe in Part 3. Listing 11-8 shows the changes I made in the Delete method in the Products controller to create an HttpResponseMessage object and pass it to the ResponseMessage method.

Listing 11-8. Using the ResponseMessage Method in the ProductsController.cs File

```
using System.Collections.Generic;
using System.Web.Http;
using ExampleApp.Models;
using System.Net;
using System.Net.Http;

namespace ExampleApp.Controllers {
    public class ProductsController : ApiController {
        IRepository repo;

        public ProductsController(IRepository repoImpl) {
            repo = repoImpl;
        }

        public IEnumerable<Product> GetAll() {
            return repo.Products;
        }

        public IHttpActionResult Delete(int id) {
            repo.DeleteProduct(id);
            return ResponseMessage(new HttpResponseMessage(HttpStatusCode.NoContent));
        }

        [HttpGet]
        [Route("api/products/noop")]
        public IHttpActionResult NoOp() {
            return Ok();
        }
    }
}
```

The `HttpResponseMessage` class has a constructor that takes a value from the `HttpStatusCode` class to specify the status code. I didn't need to set the other properties of the `HttpResponseMethod` because I was not trying to send any content back to the client. This technique produces the same effect as using the `StatusCode` method or defining the action method with the `void` keyword.

Creating a Custom Action Result

If you frequently need to return a result for which there is no controller convenience method, then you can define a custom implementation of the `IHttpActionResult` interface that yields the response you need. I created a `NoContentResult.cs` class file in the `Infrastructure` folder and used it to define the action result shown in Listing 11-9.

Listing 11-9. The Contents of the NoContentResult.cs File

```
using System.Net;
using System.Net.Http;
using System.Threading;
using System.Threading.Tasks;
using System.Web.Http;
```

```
namespace ExampleApp.Infrastructure {
    public class NoContentResult : IHttpActionResult {

        public Task<HttpResponseMessage> ExecuteAsync(CancellationToken
                cancellationToken) {
            return Task.FromResult(new HttpResponseMessage(HttpStatusCode.NoContent));
        }
    }
}
```

The convenience methods defined by the ApiController class are protected, which means they can't be built on in custom action results. Instead, my NoContentResult class creates a new HttpResponseMessage object, using the constructor argument to specify the 204 status code.

■ **Tip** Notice that I used the static Task.FromResult method to create a Task that yields the HttpResponseMessage object as the result from the ExecuteAsync method. Almost all Web API operations are asynchronous, but the overhead of creating a new Task and performing work asynchronously isn't always worthwhile when the work you have to do is simple. In these cases, the Task.FromResult method allows you to create a Task wrapper that yields the object you provide as the argument.

I can now use my custom implementation of the IHttpActionResult interface as the result in an action method, as shown in Listing 11-10.

Listing 11-10. Using a Custom Action Method in the ProductsController.cs File

```
using System.Collections.Generic;
using System.Web.Http;
using ExampleApp.Models;
using System.Net;
using System.Net.Http;
using ExampleApp.Infrastructure;

namespace ExampleApp.Controllers {
    public class ProductsController : ApiController {
        IRepository repo;

        public ProductsController(IRepository repoImpl) {
            repo = repoImpl;
        }

        public IEnumerable<Product> GetAll() {
            return repo.Products;
        }

        public IHttpActionResult Delete(int id) {
            repo.DeleteProduct(id);
            return new NoContentResult();
        }
```

```
    [HttpGet]
    [Route("api/products/noop")]
    public IHttpActionResult NoOp() {
        return Ok();
    }
  }
}
```

Returning Model Data

One of the headline features of Web API is the ability to return model data objects and have them serialized and sent the client automatically. In this section, I demonstrate this feature, explain one of the two components responsible for the process, and show you how to customize it. (The other component, *the media formatter*, is described in Chapters 12 and 13.) Table 11-8 puts returning model data into context.

Table 11-8. Putting Returning Model Data in Context

Question	Answer
What is it?	To make creating web services simple, Web API allows you to return one or more model objects from action methods, which are then serialized into a format that can be processed by the client.
When should you use it?	You should use this feature whenever you need to return data to a client with a 200 status code. See the "Returning Negotiable Action Results" section if you need to send data with another status code.
What do you need to know?	The data format used to serialize the data is selected based on a process called *content negotiation*, which relies on the client sending an HTTP Accept header. This means different clients can receive the same data in different formats, so make sure you test thoroughly or limit the formats that your application supports (which I describe in the "Implementing a Custom Negotiator" section in this chapter and in Chapter 13).

Understanding the Default Behavior

Understanding the default behavior means making a couple of requests to the Web API web service and studying the results. First start the application and use Postman to send a GET request to the /api/products URL. You will see that the following data is returned:

```
[{"ProductID":1,"Name":"Kayak","Price":275.0},
 {"ProductID":2,"Name":"Lifejacket","Price":48.95},
 {"ProductID":3,"Name":"Soccer Ball","Price":19.50},
 {"ProductID":4,"Name":"Thinking Cap","Price":16.0}]
```

This request targets the `GetAll` action method defined by the `Products` controller, which is defined like this:

```
...
public IEnumerable<Product> GetAll() {
    return repo.Products;
}
...
```

The action method returns an enumeration of `Product` objects, which Web API has serialized as a JSON array. That's useful, but there is something else that is happening behind the scenes that requires a second request to understand. If you request the `/api/products` URL using Google Chrome, you will see the following data displayed in the browser tab:

```
<ArrayOfProduct xmlns:i="http://www.w3.org/2001/XMLSchema-
        instance"xmlns="http://schemas.datacontract.org/2004/07/ExampleApp.Models">
    <Product>
        <Name>Kayak</Name><Price>275</Price><ProductID>1</ProductID>
    </Product>
    <Product>
        <Name>Lifejacket</Name><Price>48.95</Price><ProductID>2</ProductID>
    </Product>
    <Product>
        <Name>Soccer-Ball</Name><Price>19.50</Price><ProductID>3</ProductID>
    </Product>
    <Product>
        <Name>Thinking Cap</Name><Price>16</Price><ProductID>4</ProductID>
    </Product>
</ArrayOfProduct>
```

This time, the enumeration of `Product` objects has produced XML data, which happens because Google Chrome sent headers as part of the HTTP request that expressed a preference for XML.

There are two important Web API features at work here. The first is *content negotiation*, where Web API inspects the request and uses the information it contains to figure out what data formats the client can process. The second feature is *media formatting*, where Web API serializes the data into the format that has been identified—JSON and XML in these examples—so that it can be sent to the client. I describe basic content negotiation in this chapter and media formatters and advanced negotiation in Chapters 12 and 13.

Understanding the Content Negotiation Process

Content negotiation is the process by which an appropriate format is selected for serializing the data format. The word *negotiation* is misleading because it conjures up a back-and-forth exchange between the client and the web service, rather like haggling in a back room. The reality is much simpler: the client includes an `Accept` header in the HTTP request that describes the data formats that it can handle, expressed as MIME types with information about the order of preference. The web service works its way down the preference list until it finds a format that it can produce and then uses that format to serialize the data. (There are other headers that clients use to express preferences—`Accept-Charset`, `Accept-Encoding` and `Accept-Language`—but I focus on the `Accept` header in this chapter. See Chapter 12 for details of how Web API supports the `Accept-Charset` header and how you can use *any* header for negotiation.)

Here is the `Accept` header that Google Chrome sent in the previous section, which I obtained using the Network panel of the F12 tools (I added some spaces to make it easier to read):

```
Accept: text/html, application/xhtml+xml, application/xml;q=0.9, image/webp, */*;q=0.8
```

Each content type has a q value, which is a measure of preference, and greater q values indicate more preferable formats. A value of `1.0`—the maximum value—is implied when a q value isn't expressed. This header is interpreted as follows:

- Chrome prefers the `text/html` (HTML), `application/xhtml+xml` (XHTML), and `image/webp` formats above all others.

- If HTML, XHTML, and `image/webp` are not available, then XML is the next most preferred format.

- If none of the preferred formats is available, then Chrome will accept any format (expressed as */*).

Web API has built-in support for JSON, BSON, and XML. (JSON and XML are widely used and understood. BSON is Binary JSON, which isn't supported by browser-based clients.)

The content negotiation process compares the Chrome preferences with the Web API formats and determines that Chrome would prefer to receive the model data formatted as XML. If there is no `Accept` header in the request, then the web service is allowed to assume that the client will accept any data format. Postman sets the `Accept` header to */* by default, so it receives the default Web API data format, which is JSON. The `Accept` header for jQuery Ajax requests is controlled through the `accept` setting (as described in Chapter 3) and is also set to */* by default. This is why clicking the Refresh button rendered by the `Index.cshtml` view obtains JSON data, even though requesting the same URL directly through Chrome produces XML data.

■ **Tip** The `image/webp` MIME type refers to an image format called WebP that Google has developed. By giving the format a preference of `1.0`, Chrome is expressing a preference to receive images in this format over all others. WebP doesn't have any bearing on HTTP web services, but you can learn more about it here: `http://en.wikipedia.org/wiki/WebP`.

Implementing a Custom Content Negotiator

The *content negotiator* is the class responsible for examining requests and identifying the format that best suits the client. The content negotiator is not responsible for formatting the data; that's the job of the media formatter, which I describe in Chapters 12 and 13. Content negotiators implement the `IContentNegotiator` interface, which is defined in the `System.Net.Http.Formatting` namespace. Listing 11-11 shows the definition of the interface.

Listing 11-11. The IContentNegotiator Interface

```
using System.Collections.Generic;
using System.Net.Http.Headers;

namespace System.Net.Http.Formatting {
```

```
public interface IContentNegotiator {
    ContentNegotiationResult Negotiate(Type type, HttpRequestMessage request,
        IEnumerable<MediaTypeFormatter> formatters);
    }
}
```

The Negotiate method is called to examine a request and is passed the Type of the data to be serialized, the HttpRequestMessage that represents the HTTP request from the client, and an enumeration of the available media formatters, which are responsible for serializing content and are derived from the MediaTypeFormatter class (which I describe in Chapter 12).

The result from the Negotiate method is an instance of the ContentNegotiationResult class, which defines the properties shown in Table 11-9.

Table 11-9. *The Properties Defined by the ContentNegotiationResult*

Name	Description
Formatter	Returns the instance of the MediaTypeFormatter that will be used to serialize the data. I describe media formatters in Chapter 12.
MediaType	Returns an instance of the MediaTypeHeaderValue class, which details the headers that will be added to the response to describe the selected format.

■ **Tip** Returning null from the Negotiate method in a custom negotiator returns a 406 (Unacceptable) response to the client, indicating that there is no overlap between the data formats that the web service can produce and that the client can process. However, the default content negotiator class doesn't return a 406 response by default even where there is no suitable content type available; see Chapter 13 for details.

The MediaType property returns an instance of the MediaTypeHeaderValue class, which contains the details required to set the Content-Type header for the HTTP response. The MediaTypeHeaderValue class defines the members shown in Table 11-10.

Table 11-10. *The Members Defined by the MediaTypeHeaderValue*

Name	Description
CharSet	Gets or sets the character set component of the Content-Type header.
MediaType	Gets or sets the MIME type that will be used in the Content-Type header.
Parameters	Returns a collection that can be used to add properties to the Content-Type header.
Parse(header)	A static method that parses a header string and returns a MediaTypeHeaderValue object. This method is used by the model binding feature, which I described in Chapters 14–17.
TryParse(header, output)	A static method that attempts to parse the header string and populates the output argument, which is a MediaTypeHeaderValue parameter decorated with the out keyword. This method is used by the model binding feature, which I described in Chapters 14–17.

233

Web API includes a default content negotiator class, called DefaultContentNegotiator, that inspects the Accept header and selects a media formatter based on the preferences expressed by the client. Content negotiation can take into account any aspect of the request, and I am going to create a custom negotiator that builds on the default behavior but ensures that requests from Chrome receive JSON responses rather than XML. I added a class file called CustomNegotiator.cs to the Infrastructure folder and used it to define the class shown in Listing 11-12.

Listing 11-12. The Contents of the CustomNegotiator.cs File

```
using System;
using System.Collections.Generic;
using System.Linq;
using System.Net.Http;
using System.Net.Http.Formatting;
using System.Net.Http.Headers;

namespace ExampleApp.Infrastructure {
    public class CustomNegotiator : DefaultContentNegotiator {

        public override ContentNegotiationResult Negotiate(Type type,
                HttpRequestMessage request, IEnumerable<MediaTypeFormatter> formatters) {

            if (request.Headers.UserAgent.Where(x => x.Product != null
                && x.Product.Name.ToLower().Equals("chrome")).Count() > 0) {

                return new ContentNegotiationResult(new JsonMediaTypeFormatter(),
                    new MediaTypeHeaderValue("application/json")
                );

            } else {
                return base.Negotiate(type, request, formatters);
            }
        }
    }
}
```

Rather than implement my custom negotiator directly from the IContentNegotiator interface, I have derived my CustomNegotiator from the DefaultContentNegotiator class so that I can benefit from the built-in support for dealing with the Accept header for those requests that don't come from Chrome. I have overridden the Negotiate method to inspect the User-Agent header and look for requests that have been made from Chrome; see the "Working with Request Headers" sidebar for details.

When I identify a Chrome request, I return a new ContentNegotiationResult that specifies one of the built-in media formatters, JsonMediaTypeFormatter, and the application/json MIME type. I explain how media formatters work in Chapter 12 (and hard-coding a dependency on a specific class is far from ideal), but it is enough to demonstrate the role that the content negotiator plays in Web API.

WORKING WITH REQUEST HEADERS

The headers sent by a client in an HTTP request are available through the `HttpRequestMessage.Headers` property, which returns an instance of the `System.Net.Http.Headers.HttpRequestHeaders` class. The `HttpRequestHeaders` class defines properties for each of the headers defined by the HTTP standard, such as `Accept` and `UserAgent`, as well as `Contains` and `GetValues` methods that let you check to see whether a header is present and get the value of an arbitrary header.

The header values are processed to make them easier to work with. In the case of the `User-Agent` header, for example, the `HttpRequestHeaders.UserAgent` property returns an `HttpHeaderValueCollection<ProductInfoValueHeader>`, which is essentially an enumeration of `ProductInfoValueHeader` objects, each of which represents part of the `User-Agent` header. The `ProductInfoValueHeader` class defines `Comment` and `Product` properties. The `Comment` property returns a string, and the `Product` property returns a `ProductValueHeader` object, which in turn defines `Name` and `Version` properties.

It may seem confusing, but the effect is that headers are parsed into their constituent parts, which makes them easy to work with. As an example, Google Chrome sends a `User-Agent` string like this:

```
User-Agent: Mozilla/5.0 (Windows NT 6.3; WOW64) AppleWebKit/537.36
    (KHTML, like Gecko) Chrome/35.0.1901.0 Safari/537.36
```

The header string is broken into its individual components, which are separated by spaces, and each component is represented by the `ProductInfoValueHeader`. The components that contains the / character are represented by a `ProductValueHeader` object. For example, the Mozilla/5.0 component is represented by a `ProductValueHeader` whose `Name` is Mozilla and `Version` is 5.0. The components in parentheses are available through the `Comment` property of the `ProductInfoValueHeader` that represents them.

This may seem like a mass of confusing types, but it comes together when you use LINQ to process the headers. In my custom content negotiator, I am looking for requests that come from Chrome, which means that I need to locate a `ProductInfoValueHeader` object whose `Product` property returns a `ProductValueHeader` whose `Name` property is set to `Chrome`, which I can do like this:

```
...
request.Headers.UserAgent.Where(x => x.Product != null
    && x.Product.Name.ToLower().Equals("chrome")).Count() > 0
...
```

The advantage of this approach is it reduces the scope for errors because there is no chance of my matching on a `User-Agent` header that has `Chrome` as part of a comment or part of another browser name. By contrast, here is how I matched the `User-Agent` header in one of the examples for my *Pro ASP.NET MVC 5* book in order to demonstrate the URL routing feature:

```
...
httpContext.Request.UserAgent.Contains(requiredUserAgent)
...
```

Far fewer classes are involved, but there's a higher chance of misidentifying the client. The way that headers are processed by the `System.Net.Http` classes may seem awkward at first but is more flexible and useful than parsing them manually, especially when combined with LINQ.

Configuring the Content Negotiator

I need to tell Web API that I want to use my custom content negotiator. Listing 11-13 shows the changes I made to the WebApiConfig.cs file to register my CustomNegotiator class.

Listing 11-13. Registering a Custom Content Negotiator in the WebApiConfig.cs File

```
using System;
using System.Collections.Generic;
using System.Linq;
using System.Web.Http;
using ExampleApp.Infrastructure;
using System.Net.Http.Formatting;

namespace ExampleApp {
    public static class WebApiConfig {
        public static void Register(HttpConfiguration config) {

            config.DependencyResolver = new NinjectResolver();

            config.Services.Replace(typeof(IContentNegotiator), new CustomNegotiator());

            config.MapHttpAttributeRoutes();

            config.Routes.MapHttpRoute(
                name: "DefaultApi",
                routeTemplate: "api/{controller}/{id}",
                defaults: new { id = RouteParameter.Optional }
            );
        }
    }
}
```

I have called the HttpConfig.Services.Replace method to replace the default implementation of the IContentNegotiator with an instance of my CustomNegotiator class. Web API offers extensibility in different ways, and this is the approach you should use if you have not set up dependency injection in your application. If you have set up DI, as I have for the example project, then you can set up the mapping in the DI container because Web API calls the IDependencyResolver.GetService method before creating the default service classes. Listing 11-14 shows the mapping I added to the NinjectResolver class.

■ **Note** You need to register the custom negotiator using only one of these techniques, so I commented out the statement in Listing 11-13.

Listing 11-14. Registering a Custom Content Negotiator in the NinjectResolver.cs File

```
using System;
using System.Collections.Generic;
using System.Web.Http.Dependencies;
using ExampleApp.Models;
using Ninject;
```

```
using Ninject.Extensions.ChildKernel;
using Ninject.Web.Common;
using System.Net.Http.Formatting;

namespace ExampleApp.Infrastructure {

    public class NinjectResolver : System.Web.Http.Dependencies.IDependencyResolver,
            System.Web.Mvc.IDependencyResolver {
        private IKernel kernel;

        public NinjectResolver() : this(new StandardKernel()) { }

        public NinjectResolver(IKernel ninjectKernel) {
            kernel = ninjectKernel;
            AddBindings(kernel);
        }

        public IDependencyScope BeginScope() {
            return this;
        }

        public object GetService(Type serviceType) {
            return kernel.TryGet(serviceType);
        }

        public IEnumerable<object> GetServices(Type serviceType) {
            return kernel.GetAll(serviceType);
        }

        public void Dispose() {
            // do nothing
        }

        private void AddBindings(IKernel kernel) {
            kernel.Bind<IRepository>().To<Repository>().InSingletonScope();
            kernel.Bind<IContentNegotiator>().To<CustomNegotiator>();
        }
    }
}
```

Notice that I have not set a scope on the mapping between the IContentNegotiator interface and the CustomNegotiator class, as described in Chapter 10. Web API will make only one request to the resolver for each of its service classes, which means I don't have to worry about dealing with the life cycle of multiple instances.

Testing the Content Negotiator

To test the custom content negotiator, start the application and request the /api/products URL. JSON data will be displayed instead of the XML response you received earlier, as shown in Figure 11-4.

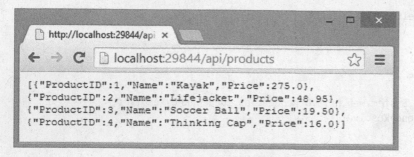

Figure 11-4. *The data sent by a custom content negotiator*

■ **Caution**   Care is required with custom content negotiators that don't use the standard HTTP negotiation headers. They result in web services that may ignore the preferences of the client and send a data format that can't be processed. As a general rule, most clients will process JSON these days, but you can't rely on this always being true, especially if you are supporting legacy clients. Test content negotiators thoroughly and stop to check that ignoring the Accept header is the best solution to the problem you are trying to solve.

Bypassing Content Negotiation

The ApiController class defines a group of methods that allow action methods to override the regular content negotiation process and specify the data format that should be used, as described in Table 11-11.

Table 11-11. *The ApiController Methods That Bypass Content Negotiation*

Name	Description
Json(data)	Returns a JsonResult, which serializes the data as JSON, irrespective of the preferences expressed by the client.
Content(status, data, formatter)	Returns a FormattedContentResult, which bypasses the content negotiation process and uses the specified formatter to serialize the data. The specified status code is used in the response. The formatter is responsible for setting the value of the Content-Type header.
Content(status, data, formatter, mimeType)	Like the previous method but uses the specified MIME type, expressed as a MediaTypeHeaderValue object, for the Content-Type header in the response.
Content(status, data, formatter, mimeString)	Like the previous method but uses the specified MIME type, expressed as a string, for the Content-Type header in the response.

Implementing a custom content negotiator allows you to select a data format based on the characteristic of the request from the client. The methods shown in Table 11-11 allow you to select a data format based on all the context information that is available to an action method. This includes the request, of course, but also the data that is going to be returned in the response.

Bypassing the content negotiation process is not a decision to make lightly because it exists to ensure that clients get content they can process, based on the preferences they express. If you need to force the data format your application uses, then you can change the configuration of the media formatters, which I describe in Chapter 12, or implement a custom content negotiator that gives precedence to a particular formatter (as I demonstrated in the "Implementing a Custom Content Negotiator" section earlier in this chapter). Not only do these approaches better respect the separation of concerns between Web API components, but they also consolidate the decision-making logic in one place, making it easier to change the formats that are used and to perform unit testing.

Returning Negotiable Action Results

Being able to return model objects and let Web API figure out what to do with them is, without a doubt, a helpful and elegant feature, but it does assume that you will return the data to the client with a 200 (OK) status code in the response. A negotiable action result is one that allows you to produce a different HTTP status code but still take advantage of the content negotiation and data formatting features. Table 11-12 puts negotiable action results in context.

Table 11-12. *Putting Negotiable Action Results in Context*

Question	Answer
What is it?	A negotiable action result allows you more control over the HttpResponseMessage that is sent to the client while still benefitting from the content negotiation and data formatting features.
When should you use it?	Use a negotiable action result whenever you need to send data to the client with a status code other than 200.
What do you need to know?	Most web clients will expect to receive data with a 200 status code, and breaking this convention—even to increase adherence to the HTTP standard as I describe next—creates the risk of making the client misbehave, especially when the client predates the web service or is written by programmers who have a different interpretation of REST.

Creating Negotiable Action Results

The ApiController class defines a set of methods that return implementations of the IHttpActionResult interface that let you take more control over the response, providing the benefits of the negotiation and formatting processes while allowing you to select the status code that will be used. Table 11-13 describes these methods.

Table 11-13. *The ApiController Methods That Return Negotiable Action Results*

Name	Description
Ok(data)	This method returns an OkNegotiatedContentResult object, which sets the result status code to 200 and is equivalent to returning the model objects as the result of the action method.
Created(url, data)	This method returns a CreatedNegotiatedContentResult object, which sets the response status code to 201, indicating that a new resource has been created as a consequence of the request. The url argument is used to specify the URL that can be used to request the new object.
CreatedAtRoute(name, values, data)	This method returns a CreatedAtRouteNegotiatedContentResult object, which uses a 201 status code and generates the URL that refers to the new object using the named route and route values. See Chapters 20 and 21 for details of Web API routing.
Content(staus, data)	This method creates a NegotiatedContentResult object, which allows an arbitrary status code to be set for the HTTP response.

You will rarely need to use these methods, and so far, the only time I have found them useful is when replacing a legacy web service that made unusual—and entirely nonstandard—use of HTTP status codes to signal service status to its equally nonstandard clients. That said, make sure you read the "Returning 200 or 201 Results from POST Requests" sidebar to learn about why the Created and CreatedAtRoute methods are sometimes used. Listing 11-15 shows the use of the Ok method applied to the GetAll action to re-create the same effect achieved by returning model objects as the method result.

Listing 11-15. Using the Ok Method in the ProductsController.cs File

```
using System.Collections.Generic;
using System.Web.Http;
using ExampleApp.Models;
using System.Net;
using System.Net.Http;
using ExampleApp.Infrastructure;

namespace ExampleApp.Controllers {
    public class ProductsController : ApiController {
        IRepository repo;

        public ProductsController(IRepository repoImpl) {
            repo = repoImpl;
        }

        public IHttpActionResult GetAll() {
            return Ok(repo.Products);
        }

        public IHttpActionResult Delete(int id) {
            repo.DeleteProduct(id);
            return new NoContentResult();
        }
```

```
    [HttpGet]
    [Route("api/products/noop")]
    public IHttpActionResult NoOp() {
        return Ok();
    }
  }
}
```

RETURNING 200 OR 201 RESULTS FROM POST REQUESTS

The Created and CreatedAtRoute methods are interesting because they touch on a design decision about how a RESTful web service responds to POST requests. Most web services will return a 200 status code and include the new data object in the response to the client. The new object will, at least, contain the unique key that can be used to refer to the object and a set of HATEOAS links if that pattern is being followed.

This is the most common approach, but it doesn't follow the HTTP specification that states that the web service should return a 201 response that contains a Location header with a URL that can be requested to get the newly created resource. The client can then request this URL to retrieve the new data item.

The reason that most web services return a 200 response that includes the newly created object is because most clients will display newly created data items to the user, and including the data in the response preempts the obvious next task for the client, avoiding an additional request.

Adhering to the HTTP specification is generally a good thing, but returning a 201 response that requires another request to be made immediately is needless pattern purity for most web services, especially since using a 200 response has become the accepted convention. Unless you have a compelling need to the contrary, avoid the complexity (and the additional bandwidth) required for the 201 response and use the 200 status code to response to POST messages with the data that the client is likely to need.

Summary

In this chapter, I showed you the different kinds of results that an action method can return and how these affect the responses sent to the client. I started by demonstrating how void methods produce responses with the 204 status code and how action methods can return IHttpActionResult objects to further control the response. One of the headline features of Web API is the automatic serialization of model data objects, and I explained the first part of this process: content negotiation. I explained how the client sends the Accept header to detail the data formats that it is willing to receive and how the IContentNegotiator is used to select a media formatter to serialize the data based on those preferences. In the next chapter, I explain how media formatters work and show you how to create a custom one.

CHAPTER 12

■■■

Creating Media Type Formatters

Media type formatters are the component responsible for serializing model data so that it can be sent to the client. In this chapter, I explain how media type formatters work by creating a custom data format and using it to explain the different ways in which a formatter can be applied. Table 12-1 summarizes this chapter.

Table 12-1. *Chapter Summary*

Problem	Solution	Listing
Create a media type formatter.	Derive from the MediaTypeFormatter class and implement the CanReadType, CanWriteType, and WriteToStreamAsync methods.	1–3
Register a media type formatter.	Add an instance of the custom class to the formatter collection during Web API configuration.	4
Consume a media type formatter in the client.	Use the dataType and accepts settings to configure the Ajax request.	5
Add support for content encoding.	Use the SupportedEncodings collection to define character encodings.	6
Set headers on the responses generated by the media type formatters.	Override the SetDefaultContentHeaders method.	7
Allow a media type formatter to participate in the content negotiation process.	Create media type mappings or use the media type mapping extension methods.	8–9, 11
Add headers to client HTTP requests.	Use the headers setting to configure the Ajax request.	10
Create a new instance of the media type formatter class for each request.	Override the GetPerRequestFormatterInstance method.	12

■ **Note** Web API includes built-in media type formatters that generate JSON and XML data; I explain how these work and how they can be configured in Chapter 13. Media type formatters are also used to deserialize data as part of the model binding process, which I explain in Chapter 14.

Preparing the Example Project

I am going to continue working with the ExampleApp project I created in Chapter 10 and added to in Chapter 11. In preparation for this chapter, I am going to tidy up the code in the Product controller to use the conventional mechanism for producing results. Listing 12-1 shows the revised controller, from which I have removed the NoOp action method and changed the results of the GetAll and Delete methods.

Listing 12-1. Changes to the ProductsController.cs File

```
using System.Collections.Generic;
using System.Web.Http;
using ExampleApp.Models;

namespace ExampleApp.Controllers {
    public class ProductsController : ApiController {
        IRepository repo;

        public ProductsController(IRepository repoImpl) {
            repo = repoImpl;
        }

        public IEnumerable<Product> GetAll() {
            return repo.Products;
        }

        public void Delete(int id) {
            repo.DeleteProduct(id);
        }
    }
}
```

■ **Tip**   Remember that you don't have to create the example project yourself. You can download the source code for every chapter for free from Apress.com.

I want to disable the custom content negotiator class I created in Chapter 11 so that I can demonstrate the interaction between the default implementation and the media type formatter classes. Listing 12-2 shows the change I made to the AddBindings method of the NinjectResolver class.

Listing 12-2. Disabling a Mapping in the NinjectResolver.cs File

```
...
private void AddBindings(IKernel kernel) {
    kernel.Bind<IRepository>().To<Repository>().InSingletonScope();
    // kernel.Bind<IContentNegotiator>().To<CustomNegotiator>();
}
...
```

To make sure that the default content negotiator is being used, start the application and use the browser to request the /api/products URL. The default negotiator will return XML content. If you see JSON, then you have forgotten to comment out the statement in the WebApiConfig.cs file, as described in Chapter 11.

Creating a Media Type Formatter

The best way to understand how media type formatters work is to create one, which is done by deriving from the abstract MediaTypeFormatter class defined in the System.Net.Http.Formatting namespace. In the sections that follow, I describe different aspects of implementing a media type formatter that supports a custom data format. My formatter will serialize Product objects and will do so by generating a set of comma-separated values for the properties defined by the Product class in the following order: ProductID, Name, Price. The effect will mean that while a JSON representation of the data in the repository looks like this:

```
[{"ProductID":1,"Name":"Kayak","Price":275.0},
 {"ProductID":2,"Name":"Lifejacket","Price":48.95},
 {"ProductID":3,"Name":"Soccer Ball","Price":19.50},
 {"ProductID":4,"Name":"Thinking Cap","Price":16.0}]
```

My custom format will serialize the same data like this:

```
1,Kayak,275.0,2,Lifejacket,48.95,3,Soccer Ball,19.50,4,Thinking Cap,16.0
```

My custom data format is can be used only to represent Product objects, which allows me to demonstrate some important characteristics of media type formatting. I need to pick a MIME type so that I can set the Accept request header and Content-Type response header. I will use the following:

```
application/x.product
```

This MIME type will allow the content negotiator to select my custom media type formatter, as I explained in Chapter 11.

■ **Tip**   MIME types are expressed in the form *<type>*/*<subtype>*, and prefixing the subtype with x. indicates a private content type. The MIME type specification—RFC 6838—discourages the use of private content types, but they remain useful for custom data formats and are still widely used. Older versions of the standard allowed a x- prefix, which is no longer supported. See http://tools.ietf.org/html/rfc6838#section-3.4 for details.

Table 12-2 puts custom media type formatters into context.

Table 12-2. *Putting Custom Media Type Formatters in Context*

Question	Answer
What are they	Media type formatters are responsible for serializing model data so that it can be sent to the client (and reversing the process as part of the model binding process that I describe in Chapter 14).
When should you use them?	There are built-in formatters for the JSON and XML formats, which I describe in Chapter 13. Custom formatters are required for other data formats.
What do you need to know?	Media type formatters can alter the way that content is serialized based on different aspects of the request, including request headers and character encodings. Media type formatters can also take an active role in content negotiation, as described in the "Participating in the Negotiation Process" section.

Implementing a Basic Media Type Formatter

To demonstrate how to create a custom media type formatter, I added a class file called `ProductFormatter.cs` to the `Infrastructure` folder of the example project and used it to define the class shown in Listing 12-3.

Listing 12-3. The Contents of the ProductFormatter.cs File

```
using System;
using System.Collections.Generic;
using System.IO;
using System.Net;
using System.Net.Http;
using System.Net.Http.Formatting;
using System.Net.Http.Headers;
using System.Threading.Tasks;
using ExampleApp.Models;

namespace ExampleApp.Infrastructure {
    public class ProductFormatter : MediaTypeFormatter {

        public ProductFormatter() {
            SupportedMediaTypes.Add(new MediaTypeHeaderValue("application/x.product"));
        }

        public override bool CanReadType(Type type) {
            return false;
        }

        public override bool CanWriteType(Type type) {
            return type == typeof(Product) || type == typeof(IEnumerable<Product>);
        }
```

```
    public override async Task WriteToStreamAsync(Type type, object value,
            Stream writeStream, HttpContent content,
            TransportContext transportContext) {

        List<string> productStrings = new List<string>();
        IEnumerable<Product> products = value is Product
            ? new Product[] { (Product)value } : (IEnumerable<Product>)value;

        foreach (Product product in products) {
            productStrings.Add(string.Format("{0},{1},{2}",
                product.ProductID, product.Name, product.Price));
        }

        StreamWriter writer = new StreamWriter(writeStream);
        await writer.WriteAsync(string.Join(",", productStrings));
        writer.Flush();
    }
}
```

The MediaTypeFormatter class defines a SupportedMediaTypes collection, which is used by the content negotiator to match MIME types in the client Accept header to a formatter. When creating a custom formatter, you add instances of the MediaTypeHeaderValue class to the SupportedMediaTypes collection to list the content types that the formatter can serialize, like this:

```
...
public ProductFormatter() {
    SupportedMediaTypes.Add(new MediaTypeHeaderValue("application/x.product"));
}
...
```

The constructor argument for the MediaTypeHeaderValue class is a MIME type, and I have specified the private content type I will be using.

Indicating Type Support

There are only two methods that custom media type formatters must implement because they are marked as abstract by the base class: CanReadType and CanWriteType. Media type formatters can use these methods to restrict the range of data types that they operate on, which makes it easy to create narrowly focused formatters that have explicit knowledge of the classes they will serialize.

The CanReadType method is used as part of the model binding process, which I describe in Chapter 14. The CanWriteType method is called by the content negotiator to see whether the formatter is able to serialize a specific type. It is important that you return true from the CanWriteType for all permutations of data object you want to serialize. The Web API Product controller in the example application has an action method that returns IEnumerable<Product>, and I have added support for the Product type on its own (not in an array or enumeration) so I can support action methods that return a single Product object, as follows:

```
...
public override bool CanWriteType(Type type) {
    return type == typeof(Product) || type == typeof(IEnumerable<Product>);
}
...
```

247

Serializing Model Data

Setting the supported MIME types and implementing the CanWriteType method provide the content negotiator with the information it needs to determine whether the formatter is able to deal with a request. The WriteToStreamAsync method is where the real work happens and is called when the content negotiator has selected the formatter for serializing the model objects returned by the action method. The WriteToStreamAsync method accepts the argument types described in Table 12-3.

Table 12-3. *The Argument Types Accepted by the WriteToStreamAsync Method*

Argument Type	Description
Type	The type of the model data as returned by the action method.
object	The data to serialize.
Stream	The stream to which the serialized data should be written. You must not close the stream.
HttpContent	A context object that provides access to the response headers. You must not modify this object.
TransportContext	A context object that provides information about the network transport, which can be null.

The WriteToStreamAsync method is asynchronous, and it returns a Task that will serialize the data objects to the stream, optionally using the HttpContent object to get information about the response that will be sent. The HttpContent object provides access to the headers for the response through a Headers property, which I use in the "Supporting Content Encodings" section later in the chapter.

One of the benefits of creating narrowly focused formatters that deal with just a small number of types is that they are simple to implement. The WriteToStreamAsync method in the ProductFormatter class returns a Task that creates a string for each Product object it receives, joins them together with commas, and writes the combined result to the stream.

```
...
public override async Task WriteToStreamAsync(Type type, object value,
        Stream writeStream, HttpContent content,
        TransportContext transportContext) {

    List<string> productStrings = new List<string>();
    IEnumerable<Product> products = value is Product
        ? new Product[] { (Product)value } : (IEnumerable<Product>)value;

    foreach (Product product in products) {
        productStrings.Add(string.Format("{0},{1},{2}",
            product.ProductID, product.Name, product.Price));
    }

    StreamWriter writer = new StreamWriter(writeStream);
    await writer.WriteAsync(string.Join(",", productStrings));
    writer.Flush();
}
...
```

■ **Note** Although the `WriteToStreamAsync` method is asynchronous, there is an alternative base class, `BufferedMediaTypeFormatter`, which you can use if you prefer to work synchronously and are willing to accept that request handling threads may block while the formatter performs its serialization. I recommend you take the time to write asynchronous implementations because the `BufferedMediaTypeFormatter` class just provides a synchronous wrapper around the asynchronous methods defined by the `MediaTypeFormatter` class anyway.

Registering the Media Type Formatter

The set of media type formatter classes is accessed through the `HttpConfiguration.Formatters` property, which returns an instance of the `System.Net.Http.MediaTypeFormatterCollection` class. The `MediaTypeFormatterCollection` class defines the methods I have listed in Table 12-4 for manipulating the collection of formatters, as well as some convenience properties for working with the built-in formatters that I describe in Chapter 11.

Table 12-4. *The Methods Defined by the MediaTypeFormattingCollection for Manipulating the Collection*

Name	Description
Add(formatter)	Adds a new formatter to the collection
Insert(index, formatter)	Inserts a formatter at the specified index
Remove(formatter)	Removes the specified formatter
RemoveAt(index)	Removes the formatter at the specified index

Listing 12-4 shows how I have used the Add method to register my `ProductFormatter` class with Web API in the `WebApiConfig.cs` file.

Listing 12-4. Registering a Media Type Formatter in the WebApiConfig.cs File

```
using System.Web.Http;
using ExampleApp.Infrastructure;

namespace ExampleApp {
    public static class WebApiConfig {
        public static void Register(HttpConfiguration config) {

            config.DependencyResolver = new NinjectResolver();

            //config.Services.Replace(typeof(IContentNegotiator),
            //  new CustomNegotiator());

            config.MapHttpAttributeRoutes();
```

```
        config.Routes.MapHttpRoute(
            name: "DefaultApi",
            routeTemplate: "api/{controller}/{id}",
            defaults: new { id = RouteParameter.Optional }
        );

        config.Formatters.Add(new ProductFormatter());
    }
  }
}
```

Using the Custom Formatter

Testing the custom formatter is easy with Postman. Click the Headers button and add an Accept header with a value of application/x.product. (Postman provides a helpful list of HTTP headers to aid your selection.) Set the verb to GET and set the URL so that it targets the /api/products URL on your local machine, using the port that Visual Studio assigned to the example project. Start the application and then click the Postman Send button. The content negotiator will use the Accept header in the request and the type of the object returned by the action method to select the ProductFormatter media type formatter, producing the result shown in Figure 12-1.

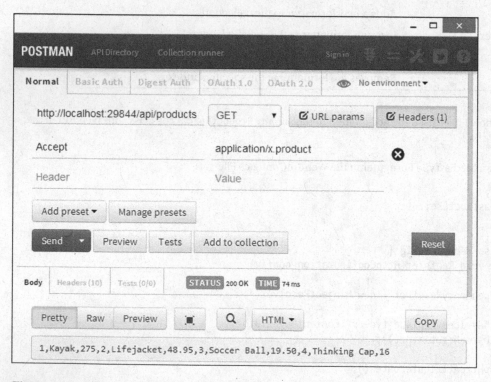

Figure 12-1. *Testing the custom formatter with Postman*

As the figure shows, the result from the request matches my target output, shown here:

```
1,Kayak,275.0,2,Lifejacket,48.95,3,Soccer Ball,19.50,4,Thinking Cap,16.0
```

Consuming the Formatted Data with jQuery

jQuery makes it easy to target custom formatters by setting the Accept header in Ajax requests, although using a custom data format means that the data returned by the web service won't be automatically converted into JavaScript objects like it is for JSON. Listing 12-5 shows the changes I made to the exampleApp.js file to specify the application/x.product MIME type and process the data that the formatter generates.

Listing 12-5. Consuming a Custom Data Format in the exampleApp.js File

```javascript
$(document).ready(function () {

    deleteProduct = function (data) {
        $.ajax("/api/products/" + data.ProductID, {
            type: "DELETE",
            success: function () {
                products.remove(data);
            }
        })
    };

    getProducts = function() {
        $.ajax("/api/products", {
            dataType: "text",
            accepts: {
                text: "application/x.product"
            },
            success: function (data) {
                products.removeAll();
                var arr = data.split(",");
                for (var i = 0; i < arr.length; i += 3) {
                    products.push({
                    ProductID: arr[i],
                        Name: arr[i + 1],
                        Price: arr[i + 2]
                    });
                }
            }
        })
    };
    ko.applyBindings();
});
```

Two jQuery Ajax settings are required to configure the Accept heading. The dataType setting tells jQuery how to process the data that will be received from the web service. The value of text means that plain text is expected and should not be processed by jQuery the way that other formats such as JSON are. The accepts (note the plural: accepts and *not* accept) setting tells jQuery which MIME type should be used for the data format specified by the dataType setting. It is a convoluted technique, but it works and has the effect of setting the Accept header in the HTTP request to application/x.product.

When I receive the data in the success callback function, I use the split method to break up the string into an array and then process the array items to create JavaScript objects that I add to the Knockout observable array. You can test the changes by starting the application and clicking the Refresh button, using the browser F12 tools to inspect the resulting HTTP request and response.

Refining the Custom Formatter

Now that I have the basic functionality in place, I can use some of the more advanced formatter features to refine the way that the formatter is matched to requests and the serialized data produced by the formatter.

Supporting Content Encodings

The Accept header is the main mechanism by which formatters are selected to serialize data, but clients can express a preference about the character encodings they want to receive by using the Accept-Charset request header.

■ **Tip** If you are not familiar with text encoding, then see the useful Wikipedia article at http://en.wikipedia.org/wiki/Character_encoding for an introduction.

Testing the Accept-Charset header can be difficult because the standard that describes how Ajax requests are made prohibits some headers from being set explicitly, including the Accept-Charset header, and this means there is no way to set this header using jQuery.

In fact, the only reliable way to test the effect of different values for the Accept-Charset header is through the Interceptor add-on for Postman, which overrides the default behavior enforced by the browser and allows all headers to be set. I explained how to install Interceptor in Chapter 1, and you will need to follow these instructions before testing the code in this section.

The MediaTypeFormatter class defines a SupportedEncodings property, which returns a Collection<System.Text.Encoding> object that custom formatters can populate with details of the encodings they support. By default, formatters are assumed to support all encodings, but in Listing 12-6, I have added a statement to the constructor of the ProductFormatter class that restricts the formatter to specific encodings.

Listing 12-6. Supporting a Specific Encoding in the ProductFormatter.cs File

```
using System;
using System.Collections.Generic;
using System.IO;
using System.Net;
using System.Net.Http;
using System.Net.Http.Formatting;
using System.Net.Http.Headers;
using System.Threading.Tasks;
using ExampleApp.Models;
using System.Text;
```

```
namespace ExampleApp.Infrastructure {
    public class ProductFormatter : MediaTypeFormatter {

        public ProductFormatter() {
            SupportedMediaTypes.Add(new MediaTypeHeaderValue("application/x.product"));
            SupportedEncodings.Add(Encoding.Unicode);
            SupportedEncodings.Add(Encoding.UTF8);
        }

        public override bool CanReadType(Type type) {
            return false;
        }

        public override bool CanWriteType(Type type) {
            return type == typeof(Product) || type == typeof(IEnumerable<Product>);
        }

        public override async Task WriteToStreamAsync(Type type, object value,
                Stream writeStream, HttpContent content,
                TransportContext transportContext) {

            List<string> productStrings = new List<string>();
            IEnumerable<Product> products = value is Product
                ? new Product[] { (Product)value } : (IEnumerable<Product>)value;

            foreach (Product product in products) {
                productStrings.Add(string.Format("{0},{1},{2}",
                    product.ProductID, product.Name, product.Price));
            }

            Encoding enc = SelectCharacterEncoding(content.Headers);
            StreamWriter writer = new StreamWriter(writeStream, enc ?? Encoding.Unicode);
            await writer.WriteAsync(string.Join(",", productStrings));
            writer.Flush();
        }
    }
}
```

The System.Text.Encoding class defines static properties for widely used encodings, and the additions I made to the constructor add the UTF-16 (accessed through the Unicode property) and UTF-8 encodings to the SupportedEncodings collection.

■ **Tip**   The HTML5 specification recommends using the UTF-8 encoding for all web content. See https://www.w3.org/International/questions/qa-choosing-encodings for more details.

In the WriteToStreamAsync method, I call the SelectCharacterEncoding methods defined by the base class, pass in the value of the HttpContent.Headers property, and receive the Encoding that should be used for the content—or null if there is no content encoding that matches the client preferences. The final step is to set the encoding on the StreamWriter object that I create to serialize the data.

```
...
StreamWriter writer = new StreamWriter(writeStream, enc ?? Encoding.Unicode);
...
```

■ **Tip**   The way that the content encoding is selected is a little odd. The `Accept` and `Accept-Charset` request headings are used to create the `Content-Type` response header before the formatter is asked to render the content. If there is a match between the encodings requested by the client and those supported by the formatter, the `Content-Type` header will include the encoding, like this: `application/x.product; charset=utf-16`. The `SelectCharacterEncoding` method then parses the `Content-Type` header to figure out which encoding should be used. This is awkward—and it has the feel of trying to shoehorn a feature into the formatter without having access to the request context object.

Testing the character encoding support requires the following steps in Postman:

1.   Set the URL so that it targets `/api/products` on your local machine.

2.   Set the verb to GET.

3.   Click the Interceptor button on the menu bar (the one that looks like a stoplight) so that it turns green. (If you can't find the Interceptor button, it is likely that you forgot to install the extension. See Chapter 1 for instructions.) Click the Header button and add an `Accept` header with a value of `application/x.product` and an `Accept-Charset` header with a value of `utf-16`.

4.   Click the Send button.

Click the Headers tab below the Send button once the request has completed to see the response headers. The model data in the example application doesn't contain any characters that require a specific encoding, but you can see the effect of the changes I made by looking at the `Content-Length` and `Content-Type` headers, which are as follows:

```
Content-Length: 138
Content-Type: application/x.product; charset=utf-16
```

The `Content-Length` headers reports that the response is 138 bytes, and the `Content-Type` header reports that the data the response contains is of the `application/x.product` type, encoded with `utf-16`.

Next, change the value of the `Accept-Charset` request header to `utf-8` and click the Send button again. You will see the following headers in the response:

```
Content-Length: 71
Content-Type: application/x.product; charset=utf-8
```

The size of the response is smaller because the UTF-8 encoding uses fewer bits to encode each character. Finally, set the `Accept-Charset` request header to `utf-32`, and click the Send button again to produce the following response headers:

```
Content-Length: 138
Content-Type: application/x.product; charset=utf-16
```

The specification for the Accept-Charset header allows two outcomes when there is no overlap between the encodings requested by the client and those supported by the web service. The first option is to send a 406 (Not Acceptable) response. The second option—which is the one that Web API uses—is to use *any* encoding and hope that the client can make some sense of it. The encoding that is used is the first one in the SupportedEncodings collection, which is utf-16 for the ProductFormatter class.

Setting the HTTP Response Headers

Web API sets the HTTP response headers based on the media type and character encoding that have been selected. You can change the headers that are added to the response by overriding the SetDefaultContentHeaders method and either set different headers or supplement the ones defined by the base class. Listing 12-7 shows how I have added a new header to the HTTP responses for which the ProductFormatter class serializes data.

Listing 12-7. Setting the HTTP Response Headers in the ProductFormatter.cs File

```
using System;
using System.Collections.Generic;
using System.IO;
using System.Net;
using System.Net.Http;
using System.Net.Http.Formatting;
using System.Net.Http.Headers;
using System.Threading.Tasks;
using ExampleApp.Models;
using System.Text;

namespace ExampleApp.Infrastructure {
    public class ProductFormatter : MediaTypeFormatter {

        public ProductFormatter() {
            SupportedMediaTypes.Add(new MediaTypeHeaderValue("application/x.product"));
            SupportedEncodings.Add(Encoding.Unicode);
            SupportedEncodings.Add(Encoding.UTF8);
        }

        public override bool CanReadType(Type type) {
            return false;
        }

        public override bool CanWriteType(Type type) {
            return type == typeof(Product) || type == typeof(IEnumerable<Product>);
        }

        public override void SetDefaultContentHeaders(Type type,
            HttpContentHeaders headers, MediaTypeHeaderValue mediaType) {
            base.SetDefaultContentHeaders(type, headers, mediaType);
            headers.Add("X-ModelType",
                type == typeof(IEnumerable<Product>)
                    ? "IEnumerable<Product>" : "Product");
            headers.Add("X-MediaType", mediaType.MediaType);
        }
```

```
    public override async Task WriteToStreamAsync(Type type, object value,
            Stream writeStream, HttpContent content,
            TransportContext transportContext) {

        List<string> productStrings = new List<string>();
        IEnumerable<Product> products = value is Product
            ? new Product[] { (Product)value } : (IEnumerable<Product>)value;

        foreach (Product product in products) {
            productStrings.Add(string.Format("{0},{1},{2}",
                product.ProductID, product.Name, product.Price));
        }

        Encoding enc = SelectCharacterEncoding(content.Headers);
        StreamWriter writer = new StreamWriter(writeStream, enc ?? Encoding.Unicode);
        await writer.WriteAsync(string.Join(",", productStrings));
        writer.Flush();
    }
}
```

The SetDefaultContentHeaders method is passed the type that will be serialized, an HttpContentHeaders object that is used to create new headers, and a MediaTypeHeaderValue object that contains details of the MIME type and character encoding that have been selected by the content negotiator.

I have called the base implementation of the method to set the Content-Type header and used the method arguments to add two nonstandard headers to the response (headers whose names start with X- are nonstandard). The HttpContentHeaders class defines methods that allow headers to be defined, as described in Table 12-5.

Table 12-5. *The Methods Defined by the HttpContentHeaders Class*

Name	Description
Add(header, value)	Adds a new header to the response with the specified value
Remove(header)	Removes a header from the response

■ **Tip** The HttpContentHeaders class also defines a number of convenience properties that get common header values. I have not listed them in the table because they are not used by media type formatters, which are focused on setting, rather than reading, header values.

I call the Add method to define the X-ModelType header, which I set to a human-readable representation of the model type that the formatter will serialize, as follows:

```
...
headers.Add("X-ModelType", type == typeof(IEnumerable<Product>)
    ? "IEnumerable<Product>" : "Product");
...
```

The other header I added relies on the `MediaTypeHeaderValue` object, which provides details of the media type and encoding that the negotiator selected through the properties shown in Table 12-6. (This is the same `MediaTypeHeaderValue` class that I used to express the MIME types that the formatter supports in Listing 12-3.)

Table 12-6. *The Methods Defined by the MediaTypeHeaderValue Class*

Name	Description
CharSet	Gets or sets the character encoding, expressed as a string
MediaType	Gets or sets the MIME type, expressed as a string

I used the `MediaType` property to set the value of the `X-MediaType` header, as follows:

```
...
headers.Add("X-MediaType", mediaType.MediaType);
...
```

These nonstandard response headers don't affect the way that the client processed the data, but they can be useful for debugging. To test the changes that I made in Listing 12-7, start the application and use Postman to send a GET request to the `/api/products` URL with an `Accept` header of `application/x.product`. The headers shown by Postman will include the `X-ModelType` and `X-MediaType` headers, like this:

```
Cache-Control: no-cache
Content-Length: 138
Content-Type: application/x.product; charset=utf-16
Date: Thu, 27 Mar 2014 17:41:15 GMT
Expires: -1
Pragma: no-cache
Server: Microsoft-IIS/8.0
X-AspNet-Version: 4.0.30319
X-MediaType: application/x.product
X-ModelType: IEnumerable<Product>
X-Powered-By: ASP.NET
X-SourceFiles=?UTF-8?B?QzpcVXNlcNlcnN...
```

Notice that my nonstandard headers are not the only ones in the response: ASP.NET adds several headers for diagnostics purposes.

Participating in the Negotiation Process

The basic negotiation process I described in Chapter 11 relies on the content negotiator doing all of the work, examining the `Accept` header sent by the client and matching it to one of the MIME types that the formatters have declared support for.

Formatters can take a more active role in the negotiation process by defining one or more implementations of the abstract `MediaTypeMapping` class, which is used to decide how the MIME types supported by the formatter fit into the client preferences for each request. Table 12-7 puts media type mappings into context.

Table 12-7. *Putting Media Type Mappings in Context*

Question	Answer
What is it?	Media type formatters can participate in the content negotiation process by inspecting the request and overriding the Accept header sent by the client.
When should you use it?	Use this feature to extend the negotiation process beyond the Accept header, which can be useful when working with widely used but badly implementing clients (such as legacy browsers).
What do you need to know?	Use this feature sparingly so that you don't send a format to the client that it can't understand.

Creating a Media Type Mapping

As a demonstration, I added a class file called `ProductMediaMapping.cs` to the `Infrastructure` folder and used it to define the class shown in Listing 12-8.

Listing 12-8. The Contents of the ProductMediaMapping.cs File

```
using System.Collections.Generic;
using System.Linq;
using System.Net.Http;
using System.Net.Http.Formatting;

namespace ExampleApp.Infrastructure {

    public class ProductMediaMapping : MediaTypeMapping {

        public ProductMediaMapping()
            : base("application/x.product") {
        }

        public override double TryMatchMediaType(HttpRequestMessage request) {
            IEnumerable<string> values;
            return request.Headers.TryGetValues("X-UseProductFormat", out values)
                && values.Where(x => x == "true").Count() > 0 ? 1 : 0;
        }
    }
}
```

The `MediaTypeMapping` class defines a constructor that accepts the MIME type that the mapping relates to. The `TryMatchMediaType` method is passed the `HttpRequestMessage` object that represents the current request and is responsible for returning a `double` value that indicates the client preference for the specified MIME type.

The `double` has the same effect as the q values in the `Accept` header sent by the client. The `MediaTypeMapping` class provides a mechanism by which formatters can override the preferences expressed by the client and promote or demote their formats in the list of matches. There are no constraints on which details of the request are used to make the decision. My example looks for an `X-UseProductFormat` header in the request. If the header is `true`, then I return a value of 1, indicating that the client has a strong preference for the `application/x.product` format. If the header isn't included in the request or isn't set to `true`, then I return 0 to indicate that the client does not want to accept the data format. Listing 12-9 shows how I have applied the `ProductMediaMapping` to the constructor of the custom formatter.

Listing 12-9. Using a MediaTypeMapping in the ProductFormatter.cs File

```
...
public ProductFormatter() {
    //SupportedMediaTypes.Add(new MediaTypeHeaderValue("application/x.product"));
    SupportedEncodings.Add(Encoding.Unicode);
    SupportedEncodings.Add(Encoding.UTF8);
    MediaTypeMappings.Add(new ProductMediaMapping());
}
...
```

■ **Caution**   Use this feature sparingly. Clients expect their format preferences to be managed through the Accept header, and you can create problems by overriding this behavior.

I have commented out the call to the SupportedMediaTypes.Add method to prevent the formatter from participating passively in the negotiation process and added a call to the MediaTypeMappings.Add method to register an instance of the ProductMediaMapping class. The MediaTypeMappings property returns a collection of MediaTypeMapping objects, and a formatter can register as many mappings as it requires.

Testing the Negotiation Process

The best way to test the effect of the mapping is with Postman because it makes it easy to control the headers. Send a GET request to the /api/products URL with the headers and values shown in Table 12-8.

Table 12-8. *The Request Headers and Values Required to Test the MediaTypeMapping Implementation*

Header	Value
Accept	application/json;q=0.9
X-UseProductFormat	true

The Accept header is set so that the client expresses a 0.9 preference for the application/json format, which will be overridden by the 1.0 preference that the ProductMediaMapping class will report for the application/x.product format because the request contains the X-UseProductFormat header, as shown in Figure 12-2. If you remove the X-UseProductFormat header and send another request, the web service will honor the Accept header and send JSON data.

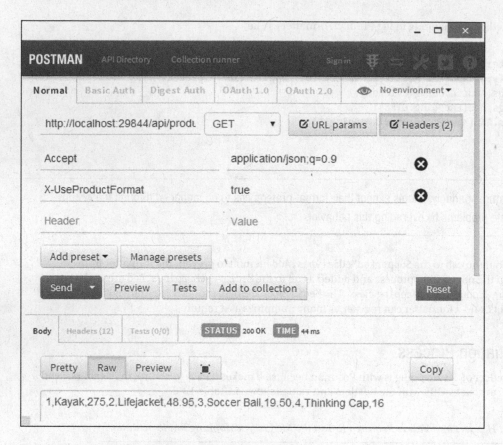

Figure 12-2. *Overriding client format preferences*

Adding Headers to jQuery Ajax Requests

Adding headers to jQuery Ajax requests is simple, as shown in Listing 12-10.

Listing 12-10. Adding a Nonstandard Request Header in the exampleApp.js File

```
$(document).ready(function () {

    deleteProduct = function (data) {
        $.ajax("/api/products/" + data.ProductID, {
            type: "DELETE",
            success: function () {
                products.remove(data);
            }
        })
    };
```

```
getProducts = function() {
    $.ajax("/api/products", {
        headers: { "X-UseProductFormat": "true" },
        dataType: "text",
        accepts: {
            text: "application/x.product"
        },
        success: function (data) {
            products.removeAll();
            var arr = data.split(",");
            for (var i = 0; i < arr.length; i += 3) {
                products.push({
                    ProductID: arr[i],
                    Name: arr[i + 1],
                    Price: arr[i + 2]
                });
            }
        }
    })
};
ko.applyBindings();
});
```

■ **Caution**   The code in the listing assumes that you live in a locale that doesn't use commas to represent fractional amounts.

The headers setting is set to an object whose properties correspond to the headers that will be added to the request. This change allows the client to continue to receive the application/x.product format, even though there is no longer a static mapping for the media type formatter.

Using the Mapping Extension Methods

Deriving from the MediaTypeMapping class allows you to dig right into the details of the request as part of the negotiation process, but Web API also provides some convenient extension methods that make it easy to set up the most common mappings. Table 12-9 describes the extension methods, all of which are applied to MediaTypeFormatter objects.

Table 12-9. *The Extension Methods for Mapping Media Types to Requests*

Method	Description
AddQueryStringMapping(name, value, mimeType)	Selects the specified mimeType when the request query string contains the name property with the specified value.
AddRequestHeaderMapping(name, value, comparison, substring, mimeType)	Selects the specified mimeType when the request contains a name header with the specified value. The comparison argument is a System.StringComparison value used to compare the request value, which will accept substrings is the substring argument is true.
AddUriPathExtensionMapping(extension, mimeType)	Selects the specified mimeType if the request URL has the specified extension.

261

These extension methods can be used during the registration of a media type formatter, as shown in Listing 12-11.

Listing 12-11. Using Media Type Formatter Mapping Methods in the WebApiConfig.cs File

```
using System.Web.Http;
using ExampleApp.Infrastructure;
using System.Net.Http.Formatting;
using System;

namespace ExampleApp {
    public static class WebApiConfig {
        public static void Register(HttpConfiguration config) {

            config.DependencyResolver = new NinjectResolver();

            //config.Services.Replace(typeof(IContentNegotiator),
            //  new CustomNegotiator());

            config.MapHttpAttributeRoutes();

            config.Routes.MapHttpRoute(
                name: "Api with extension",
                routeTemplate: "api/{controller}.{ext}/{id}",
                defaults: new { id = RouteParameter.Optional,
                    ext = RouteParameter.Optional }
            );

            config.Routes.MapHttpRoute(
                name: "DefaultApi",
                routeTemplate: "api/{controller}/{id}",
                defaults: new { id = RouteParameter.Optional }
            );

            MediaTypeFormatter prodFormatter = new ProductFormatter();
            prodFormatter.AddQueryStringMapping("format", "product",
                "application/x.product");
            prodFormatter.AddRequestHeaderMapping("X-UseProductFormat", "true",
                StringComparison.InvariantCultureIgnoreCase, false,
                "application/x.product");
            prodFormatter.AddUriPathExtensionMapping("custom", "application/x.product");
            config.Formatters.Add(prodFormatter);
        }
    }
}
```

The AddQueryStringMapping extension method gives preference to a media type formatter when a query string contains a specific property and value. I used this method in the listing so that the ProductFormatter class will be selected when the request contains a query string property called format that is set to product, like this:

```
...
prodFormatter.AddQueryStringMapping("format", "product", "application/x.product");
...
```

You can test the effect by using Postman to send a GET request to the /api/products?format=product URL. A URL that doesn't include the format property or that has a different value won't be affected.

I used the AddRequestHeaderMapping extension method to achieve the same effect I created with the ProductMediaMapping class (although defining your own mapping classes provides a wider range of customization options).

```
...
prodFormatter.AddRequestHeaderMapping("X-UseProductFormat", "true",
    StringComparison.InvariantCultureIgnoreCase, false, "application/x.product");
...
```

Requests that contain the X-UseProductFormat header with a case-insensitive value of true will select the ProductFormatter class. This statement is redundant in the example because the ProductFormatter class is already configured to support this header.

The AddUriPathExtensionMapping method is a little more complex than the others and requires a URL route to be defined. This method registers a mapping that looks for a routing segment variable called ext, which is the convention for capturing file extensions but which can be used to match any URL segment. I explain how Web API routes work in Chapters 20 and 21, but here is the route that I defined that captures the ext segment:

```
...
config.Routes.MapHttpRoute(
    name: "Api with extension",
    routeTemplate: "api/{controller}.{ext}/{id}",
    defaults: new { id = RouteParameter.Optional, ext = RouteParameter.Optional }
);
...
```

I used the AddUriPathExtensionMapping method so that the ProductFormatter class will be selected when the value of the ext segment variable is custom. You can test this mapping by using Postman to send a GET request to /api/products.custom.

Creating Per-Request Media Type Formatters

A single instance of a media type formatter class is usually used to serialize data for multiple requests, but an alternative approach is to override the GetPerRequestFormatterInstance method defined by the MediaTypeFormatter class. Table 12-10 puts per-request media type formatters into context.

Table 12-10. Putting Per-Request Media Type Formatters in Context

Question	Answer
What is it?	Per-request formatters allow the nature of individual requests to be used to influence the way that data is serialized and allow code that it not thread-safe to be integrated into Web API.
When should you use it?	You don't often have to tailor serialized data based on the request, and this feature is most often used to integrate legacy serialization code into Web API so that the application can support clients from older applications.
What do you need to know?	This feature is simple to use, but remember that a new instance of the formatter class is created for each request for which the formatter is selected by the negotiation process.

263

Creating the Formatter Instance

The GetPerRequestFormatterInstance method is passed the Type of the data that is to be serialized, the HttpRequestMessage that represents the current request, and a MediaTypeHeaderValue that provides details of the required MIME type and character set encoding. The result of the GetPerRequestFormatterInstance method is a MediaTypeFormatter object that will be used for a single request. This feature is useful when you need to adapt the data serialization based on the individual requests or when dealing with code that is not thread-safe and that cannot afford to have its WriteToStreamAsync method called concurrently. Listing 12-12 shows how I have overridden the GetPerRequestFormatterInstance method in the ProductFormatter class to include details from the request in the serialized data.

Listing 12-12. Creating Per-Request Media Type Formatters in the ProductFormatter.cs File

```
using System;
using System.Collections.Generic;
using System.IO;
using System.Net;
using System.Net.Http;
using System.Net.Http.Formatting;
using System.Net.Http.Headers;
using System.Threading.Tasks;
using ExampleApp.Models;
using System.Text;

namespace ExampleApp.Infrastructure {
    public class ProductFormatter : MediaTypeFormatter {
        private string controllerName;

        public ProductFormatter() {
            //SupportedMediaTypes.Add(new MediaTypeHeaderValue("application/x.product"));s
            SupportedEncodings.Add(Encoding.Unicode);
            SupportedEncodings.Add(Encoding.UTF8);
            MediaTypeMappings.Add(new ProductMediaMapping());
        }

        public ProductFormatter(string controllerArg) : this() {
            controllerName = controllerArg;
        }

        public override bool CanReadType(Type type) {
            return false;
        }

        public override bool CanWriteType(Type type) {
            return type == typeof(Product) || type == typeof(IEnumerable<Product>);
        }

        public override void SetDefaultContentHeaders(Type type,
            HttpContentHeaders headers, MediaTypeHeaderValue mediaType) {
            base.SetDefaultContentHeaders(type, headers, mediaType);
            headers.Add("X-ModelType",
                type == typeof(IEnumerable<Product>)
                    ? "IEnumerable<Product>" : "Product");
            headers.Add("X-MediaType", mediaType.MediaType);
        }
```

```
public override MediaTypeFormatter GetPerRequestFormatterInstance(Type type,
        HttpRequestMessage request, MediaTypeHeaderValue mediaType) {
    return new ProductFormatter(
        request.GetRouteData().Values["controller"].ToString());
}

public override async Task WriteToStreamAsync(Type type, object value,
        Stream writeStream, HttpContent content,
        TransportContext transportContext) {

    List<string> productStrings = new List<string>();
    IEnumerable<Product> products = value is Product
        ? new Product[] { (Product)value } : (IEnumerable<Product>)value;

    foreach (Product product in products) {
        productStrings.Add(string.Format("{0},{1},{2}",
            product.ProductID,
            controllerName == null ? product.Name :
            string.Format("{0} ({1})", product.Name, controllerName),
            product.Price));
    }

    Encoding enc = SelectCharacterEncoding(content.Headers);
    StreamWriter writer = new StreamWriter(writeStream, enc ?? Encoding.Unicode);
    await writer.WriteAsync(string.Join(",", productStrings));
    writer.Flush();
    }
  }
}
```

I have modified the ProductFormatter class so that it includes the name of the controller to which the routing system has matched the request. I explain how Web API routing works in Chapters 20 and 21, but the key point for this chapter is that each request may be handled by a different controller, so I need to use the GetPerRequestFormatterInstance method so that I have access to the HttpRequestMessage object to get the information about the request that I need.

Testing the Per-Request Formatter

To test the changes, start the application and click the Refresh button in the browser window that Visual Studio opens. The jQuery client code sends the nonstandard request header required to match the request to the ProductFormatter class, which adds products to the name of the serialized data since that is the name of the controller that handles the request (and, of course, the only Web API controller in the application, but you get the idea). Figure 12-3 shows the effect.

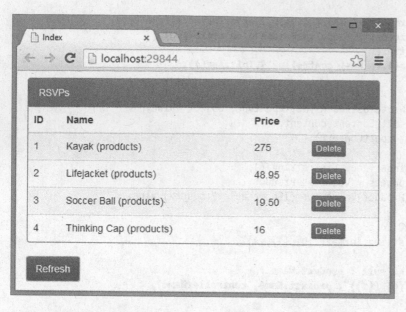

Figure 12-3. *Including per-request information in serialized data*

■ **Tip** If you don't get the expected result, then right-click the Chrome Refresh button and select Empty Cache and Hard Reload from the pop-up window. This option is available only when the F12 developer tools window is opened, and it ensures that Chrome requests the most recent version of the JavaScript file from the server.

Summary

In this chapter, I showed you how to create and use media type formatters to serialize model data so that it can be sent to the web service client. I explained how formatters fit within Web API, demonstrated how to support different media types and character encodings, and demonstrated how to create formatters that are able to participate in the content negotiation process. In the next chapter, I show you how to work with the built-in media type formatters, which are responsible for producing JSON and XML data.

■ ■ ■

CHAPTER 13

Using the Built-in Media Formatters

In this chapter, I focus on the built-in media type formatter classes, which are used to serialize data model objects into JSON and XML. I start by showing you how to control the way that the default media type formatters are used when there is no match between the formats they support and the request Accept header and then show you how to manage the serialized data that the formatters produce.

My emphasis in this chapter is on the JSON format, rather than XML. JSON has become the dominant data format for HTTP web services because it is relatively concise, easy to work with (especially in JavaScript code), and supported by all the major programming languages and web application development platforms. As you will learn, JSON serialization is performed by the latest versions of a popular and well-maintained open source .NET package, while XML serialization is performed using classes that have been around since .NET 1.1 and .NET 3.0. Table 13-1 summarizes this chapter.

Table 13-1. *Chapter Summary*

Problem	Solution	Listing
List the built-in type formatters.	Enumerate the collection returned by the HttpConfiguration. Formatters property.	1–4
Change the order in which formatters are queried to serialize a type by the match-on-type feature.	Manipulate the collection returned by the HttpConfiguration. Formatters property.	5
Enable or disable the match-on-type feature.	Use the bool constructor argument defined by the DefaultContentNegotiator class.	6–9
Indent JSON data.	Set the JsonMediaTypeFormatter.Indent property to true.	10
Select a format for date values.	Set the SerializerSettings.DateFormatHandling property.	11–16
Escape dangerous characters in serialized JSON data.	Set the SerializerSettings.StringEscapeHandling property.	17
Include or exclude null and default values in serialized JSON data.	Set the SerializerSettings.DefaultValueHandling property.	18, 19
Process XML at the client.	Use jQuery to locate elements contained in an XMLDocument object.	20, 21

Preparing the Example Project

I am going to continue working with the ExampleApp project from the previous chapter, but I need to disable the custom media formatter that I created so I can focus on the built-in ones instead. Listing 13-1 shows the simplified WebApiConfig.cs file.

Listing 13-1. Disabling a Custom Media Formatter in the WebApiConfig.cs File

```
using System.Web.Http;
using ExampleApp.Infrastructure;
using System.Net.Http.Formatting;
using System;

namespace ExampleApp {
    public static class WebApiConfig {
        public static void Register(HttpConfiguration config) {

            config.DependencyResolver = new NinjectResolver();

            //config.Services.Replace(typeof(IContentNegotiator),
            //  new CustomNegotiator());

            config.MapHttpAttributeRoutes();

            config.Routes.MapHttpRoute(
                name: "Api with extension",
                routeTemplate: "api/{controller}.{ext}/{id}",
                defaults: new {
                    id = RouteParameter.Optional,
                    ext = RouteParameter.Optional
                }
            );

            config.Routes.MapHttpRoute(
                name: "DefaultApi",
                routeTemplate: "api/{controller}/{id}",
                defaults: new { id = RouteParameter.Optional }
            );

            //MediaTypeFormatter prodFormatter = new ProductFormatter();
            //prodFormatter.AddQueryStringMapping("format", "product",
            //    "application/x.product");
            //prodFormatter.AddRequestHeaderMapping("X-UseProductFormat", "true",
            //    StringComparison.InvariantCultureIgnoreCase, false,
            //    "application/x.product");
            //prodFormatter.AddUriPathExtensionMapping("custom",
            // "application/x.product");
            //config.Formatters.Add(prodFormatter);
        }
    }
}
```

■ **Tip** Remember that you don't have to create the example project yourself. You can download the source code for every chapter for free from Apress.com.

I have commented out the statements that configure and register the ProductFormatter media formatter class, which means that only the built-in formatters will be used.

Working with the Built-in Media Type Formatters

Web API includes a set of four built-in media formatters. All of the built-in media type formatters participate in the model binding process I describe in Chapters 14–17, but there are two that are interesting in this chapter because they are used to serialize object to generate JSON or XML data so it can be sent to the client. In the sections that follow, I show you how to manage and configure the built-in formatters. Table 13-2 puts the built-in formatters in context.

Table 13-2. Putting the Built-in Media Type Formatters in Context

Question	Answer
What are they?	The built-in media type formatters are responsible for serializing data into the JSON and XML formats.
When should you use them?	These media type formatters are configured for use by default and will be selected by the content negotiation process, which I explained in Chapter 12, to produce data in a format that can be consumed by the client.
What do you need to know?	The default content negotiator class will select the first media type formatter that is able to serialize the data model type if there is no match between the Accept header sent by the client and the formats available through the media type formatter classes. See the "Dealing with Type Matching During Negotiation" section for details.

Listing the Built-in Media Type Formatters

As I explained in Chapter 12, Web API maintains a collection of media type formatters that is accessed through the HttpConfiguration.Formatters property. In addition to the Add, Insert, Remove, and RemoveAt methods that I described in Chapter 12, the MediaTypeFormatterCollection class that is returned by the Formatters property defines convenience properties that provide direct access to three of the four built-in media type formatters, as described in Table 13-3.

Table 13-3. The Convenience Properties Defined by the MediaTypeFormattingCollection Class

Name	Description
FormUrlEncodedFormatter	Returns an instance of the FormUrlEncodedMediaTypeFormatter class, which is used to parse form data in the model binding process
JsonFormatter	Returns an instance of the JsonMediaTypeFormatter class, which serializes data into the JSON format
XmlFormatter	Returns an instance of the XmlMediaTypeFormatter class, which serializes data into the XML format

The `MediaTypeFormattingCollection` class is enumerable, which makes it easy to list the available formatters and establish their relative order in the collection. As you'll learn, ordering the formatters can change the data format that is used to serialize data for a response.

I am going to display details of the built-in media type using the MVC framework, which allows me to demonstrate the technique required to render Razor views that use classes from the `System.Net.Http` namespace. I started by adding a class file called `FormattersController.cs` to the `Controllers` folder and using it to define the MVC framework controller shown in Listing 13-2.

Listing 13-2. The Contents of the FormattersController.cs File

```
using System.Web.Http;
using System.Web.Mvc;

namespace ExampleApp.Controllers {
    public class FormattersController : Controller {

        public ActionResult Index() {
            return View(GlobalConfiguration.Configuration.Formatters);
        }
    }
}
```

This is an MVC framework controller with an `Index` action method that renders the default view, passing in the collection of media type formatters obtained through the static `GlobalConfiguration.Configuration` property. To create the view, I right-clicked the `Index` method in the code editor, selected Add View, and accepted the default settings. Visual Studio created the `Views/Formatters/Index.cshtml` file, which I used to define the view shown in Listing 13-3.

Listing 13-3. The Contents of the Index.cshtml File in the Views/Formatters Folder

```
@model IEnumerable<System.Net.Http.Formatting.MediaTypeFormatter>
@{ ViewBag.Title = "Formatters";}

<div class="panel panel-primary">
    <div class="panel-heading">Media Type Formatters</div>
    <table class="table table-striped">
        <thead>
            <tr><th>Name</th><th>MIME Types</th></tr>
        </thead>
        <tbody>
            @foreach (var formatter in Model) {
                <tr>
                    <td>@formatter.GetType().Name</td>
                    <td>
                        @((string)string.Join(", ",
                            formatter.SupportedMediaTypes.Select(x => x.MediaType)))
                    </td>
                </tr>
            }
        </tbody>
    </table>
</div>
```

The view contains a table element that I populate using Razor and the view model data to display the name of each media type formatter and the MIME types it supports. If you start the application and request the /formatters URL, you will see an error message like this:

Compiler Error Message: CS0012: The type 'System.Net.Http.Headers.MediaTypeHeaderValue' is defined in an assembly that is not referenced. You must add a reference to assembly 'System.Net.Http, Version=4.0.0.0, Culture=neutral, PublicKeyToken=b03f5f7f11d50a3a'.

This problem is caused because Razor doesn't automatically pick up the reference to the System.Net.Http assembly, which is obtained from the global assembly cache and not from one of the NuGet packages I installed in Chapter 10. To resolve this problem, I need to add an assembly reference in to the compilation configuration section in the Web.config file (the one in the root of the folder, not the one in the Views folder), as shown in Listing 13-4.

Listing 13-4. Adding a Reference to the System.Net.Http Assembly in the Web.config File

```
...
<system.web>
  <compilation debug="true" targetFramework="4.5.1">
    <assemblies>
      <add assembly="System.Net.Http, Version=4.0.0.0, Culture=neutral,
          PublicKeyToken=b03f5f7f11d50a3a"/>
    </assemblies>
  </compilation>
  <httpRuntime targetFramework="4.5.1" />
  <pages>
    <namespaces>
      <add namespace="System.Web.Helpers" />
      <add namespace="System.Web.Mvc" />
      <add namespace="System.Web.Mvc.Ajax" />
      <add namespace="System.Web.Mvc.Html" />
      <add namespace="System.Web.Routing" />
      <add namespace="System.Web.WebPages" />
    </namespaces>
  </pages>
</system.web>
<system.webServer>
...
```

I have changed the compilation element so that it contains the assemblies element, which is used to manage the collection of explicit references to runtime assemblies. I define a new reference using an add element to create a reference to the System.Net.Http assembly, using the version and public key from the error message.

■ **Tip** Remember that Web API doesn't use the Web.config file and that the changes I made in the listing are required only by the MVC framework. See my *Pro ASP.NET MVC 5 Platform* book for details of the ASP.NET configuration system, how it works, and how it can be customized.

This change allows you to access the Web API configuration information—and other components—from MVC controllers and views. Start the application and request the /formatters URL to see the contents of the media type formatters collection, as shown in Figure 13-1.

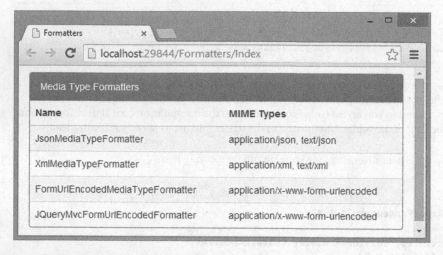

Figure 13-1. *The collection of Web API media type formatters*

WHAT ABOUT BSON?

BSON is *binary JSON* and is, as its name suggests, a binary variation on the JSON specification. BSON is used most widely by the MongoDB database but has been proposed as a more efficient and expressive alternative to JSON—a proposal that has not been universally welcomed, and, as I write this, there are active and heated discussions about the efficiency benefits. You can learn more about the BSON specification at http://bsonspec.org.

BSON may find a wider role in the future, but the limiting factor at the moment is that there is little support for BSON in clients, and no JavaScript implementations are available for clients running in browsers. This means that it is not possible to receive BSON data and have it automatically parsed to JavaScript objects the way that JSON data is.

Web API includes a BSON media formatter (the BsonMediaTypeFormatter class in the System. Net.Http.Formatting namespace), but it is disabled by default. I don't describe BSON or cover the BsonMediaTypeFormatter in this book because the BSON specification is not usable in clients developed using the MVC framework.

Dealing with Type Matching During Negotiation

I showed you the contents of the media type formatter collection because there is a confusing quirk in the content negotiation process that relies on the order in which the formatters appear in the list shown in Figure 13-1.

Most of the time, the order of the formatters doesn't matter because clients will send an Accept header that specifies a format that Web API can support. You saw this in Chapter 12 when I used Chrome to send a GET request to the /api/products URL. Chrome sends an Accept header that gives preference to XML, and that's the format that was sent back. You can see in Figure 13-1 that the XmlMediaTypeFormatter class is the formatter responsible for the application/xml and text/xml MIME types, and this is the formatter that is selected for the Chrome request. In this situation, the order of the formatters does not have any impact on the format of the data sent to the client.

You can test this process explicitly by using Postman to send a GET request to the /api/products URL with the following Accept header:

```
application/x.product;q=1.0, application/xml;q=0.9, application/json;q=0.5
```

The Accept header specifies a first preference for the application/x.product format that I created in Chapter 12. I disabled the media type formatter for the custom MIME type in Listing 13-1, so the content negotiator won't be able to find a formatter to produce this format, even though it is the one that the client would prefer to receive.

The next most preferred format is application/xml, which has a higher q value than the only other format that the client is willing to accept, which is application/json. The content negotiator selects the XmlMediaTypeFormatter class to serialize the data returned by the GetAll action method in the Products controller, even though it is second in the collection of media type formatters illustrated in Figure 13-1. Figure 13-2 shows the XML data that is returned by the web service.

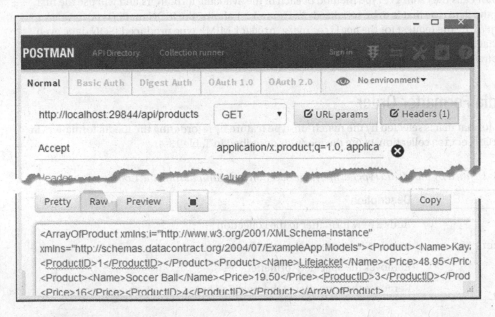

Figure 13-2. *Selecting a data format during normal negotiation*

This is the behavior that I described in Chapter 11, but it bears repetition for two reasons. The first is that it is how the data format for most requests will be selected for web browser clients, because both the browser and jQuery will sent an Accept header that specifies either XML or JSON directly.

The other reason I have emphasized the default behavior is because the default content negotiator does something odd when there is no match between the data formats that the web service can use to serialize data and the formats that the client is willing to accept. To see what happens, change the value of the Postman Accept header to the following:

```
application/x.product;q=1.0
```

This header specifies that the client will accept only the application/x.product format, for which there is no media type formatter available in the application. When you send the request, Web API responds with the following data:

```
[{"ProductID":1,"Name":"Kayak","Price":275.0},
 {"ProductID":2,"Name":"Lifejacket","Price":48.95},
 {"ProductID":3,"Name":"Soccer Ball","Price":19.50},
 {"ProductID":4,"Name":"Thinking Cap","Price":16.0}]
```

The default content negotiator class has responded with JSON data, which is unexpected since the client has indicated that it can't process JSON data.

The DefaultContentNegotiator class, which I described in Chapter 11, has a feature called *match-on-type* that is enabled by default and is used to select a formatter when there the Accept header doesn't specify a format that Web API can work with.

The content negotiator calls the CanWriteType method of each of the available formatters and will use the first one that returns true for the data type that is to be serialized. As Figure 13-1 shows, the JSON media type formatter is first on the list, and that's why the request for the application/x.product MIME type produced JSON data, even though it isn't a format that the client would accept. In the following sections, I'll describe how you can take control of this process and demonstrate how to disable it entirely.

Changing the Media Formatter Order

You can change the data format that is selected by the match-on-type feature by re-ordering the media formatters in the MediaTypeFormatterCollection collection, using the methods described in Table 13-4.

Table 13-4. *The Methods Defined by the MediaTypeFormattingCollection for Manipulating the Collection*

Name	Description
Add(formatter)	Adds a new formatter to the collection
Insert(index, formatter)	Inserts a formatter at the specified index
Remove(formatter)	Removes the specified formatter
RemoveAt(index)	Removes the formatter at the specified index

The easiest way to change the order is to use the convenience properties I described in Table 13-3 to obtain a reference to the formatter object that you want to move and use it as an argument to the methods in Table 13-4. Listing 13-5 shows how I have promoted the XML formatter in the collection using the WebApiConfig.cs file. (I have removed the commented out statements from previous examples.)

Listing 13-5. Changing the Order of the Media Type Formatters in the WebApiConfig.cs File

```
using System.Web.Http;
using ExampleApp.Infrastructure;
using System.Net.Http.Formatting;
using System;
```

```
namespace ExampleApp {
    public static class WebApiConfig {
        public static void Register(HttpConfiguration config) {

            config.DependencyResolver = new NinjectResolver();

            config.MapHttpAttributeRoutes();

            config.Routes.MapHttpRoute(
                name: "DefaultApi",
                routeTemplate: "api/{controller}/{id}",
                defaults: new { id = RouteParameter.Optional }
            );

            MediaTypeFormatter xmlFormatter = config.Formatters.XmlFormatter;
            config.Formatters.Remove(xmlFormatter);
            config.Formatters.Insert(0, xmlFormatter);
        }
    }
}
```

I removed the XML formatter from the collection and inserted it back at position 0, making it the first formatter that will be asked whether it can serialize the data type when there are no matching formats from the Accept header.

■ **Tip** Working with the MediaTypeFormatterCollection object is awkward. The convenience properties return the instances of the formatters that are created automatically during the Web API configuration process. If you remove or replace a formatter, the corresponding convenience property will return null.

Start the application and use the browser to request the /formatters URL; you will see that the XmlMediaTypeFormatter class appears first in the collection. If you use Postman to send a GET request to the /api/products URL with an Accept header that specifies just the application/x.product format, you will receive XML data rather than JSON.

Disabling the Match-on-Type Feature

Changing the order of the formatters doesn't address the underlying problem with the match-on-type feature, which is sending a format to the client that it may not be able to process. The best outcome will be that the client misstated its Accept preferences and is able to process the format after all—but isn't a solid foundation for making data format choices. A more common outcome is that the client will assume that it is dealing with the format it asked for, which either generates an error or almost—but not quite—works.

You can see an example of a data format almost working by starting the application and using the browser to request the /Home/Index URL. Click the Refresh link to send an Ajax request that targets the /api/products URL with a GET request whose Accept header contains only the application/x.product MIME type (because the request is being created by the jQuery code that I set up in Chapter 12 to process the custom data format).

The custom format negotiator uses the match-on-type feature to select the XML formatter, which has the effect shown in Figure 13-3.

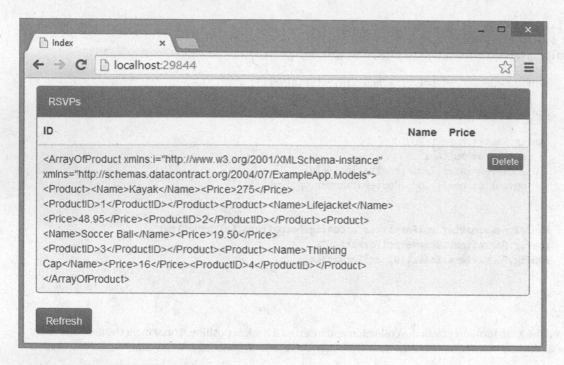

Figure 13-3. *The effect of sending a client an unknown format*

Few web service clients check to see whether the format they received is the one that they asked for. In this case, the jQuery code I wrote in Chapter 12 assumes that it has received the expected format and tries to break it up for processing but does so using separators that are not present in the XML data. The result is a single row in the table that contains the complete XML data response in the first column.

One of the reasons that web services don't check the received data format is that the match-on-type feature doesn't follow the HTTP specification, which states that the web service should send the client a 406 (Not Acceptable) response if there is no match between the data formats in the Accept header and the ones supported by the application. This is a much better outcome because it doesn't assume that the client is mistaken about the data formats that it is able to process.

The DefaultContentNegotiator class defines a constructor argument that disables the match-on-type feature. Listing 13-6 shows how to set this option when using the NinjectResolver class that I created in Chapter 10 for dependency injection.

Listing 13-6. Disabling the Match-on-Type Feature in the NinjectResolver.cs File

```
...
private void AddBindings(IKernel kernel) {
    kernel.Bind<IRepository>().To<Repository>().InSingletonScope();
    kernel.Bind<IContentNegotiator>().To<DefaultContentNegotiator>()
        .WithConstructorArgument("excludeMatchOnTypeOnly", true);
}
...
```

I have defined a mapping between the IContentNegotiator interface and the DefaultContentNegotiator class and used the Ninject WithConstructorArgument method to set a value for the excludeMatchOnTypeOnly constructor argument. When Web API asks Ninject to provide an implementation of the IContentNegotiator interface, an instance of the DefaultContentNegotiator class will be created with the constructor argument of true, equivalent to calling this:

```
new DefaultContentNegotiator(true)
```

A true value for the constructor argument disables the match-on-type feature and causes the web service to send a 406 (Not Acceptable) message to the client, as shown in Figure 13-4.

Figure 13-4. *Getting a 406 (Not Acceptable) response from the web service*

> ■ **Tip** If you don't receive a 406 (Not Acceptable) response, you may have forgotten to add the Accept header to the request. You must specify the application/x.product MIME type so that no media type formatter can be selected based on content type.

You will need to take a more direct approach if you are not using dependency injection in your application. Listing 13-7 shows how to disable match-on-type in the WebApiConfig.cs file.

Listing 13-7. Disabling the Match-on-Type Feature in the WebApiConfig.cs File

```
using System.Web.Http;
using ExampleApp.Infrastructure;
using System.Net.Http.Formatting;
using System;

namespace ExampleApp {
    public static class WebApiConfig {
        public static void Register(HttpConfiguration config) {

            config.DependencyResolver = new NinjectResolver();

            config.MapHttpAttributeRoutes();

            config.Routes.MapHttpRoute(
                name: "DefaultApi",
                routeTemplate: "api/{controller}/{id}",
                defaults: new { id = RouteParameter.Optional }
            );
```

```
        MediaTypeFormatter xmlFormatter = config.Formatters.XmlFormatter;
        config.Formatters.Remove(xmlFormatter);
        config.Formatters.Insert(0, xmlFormatter);

        config.Services.Replace(typeof(IContentNegotiator),
            new DefaultContentNegotiator(true));
    }
  }
}
```

I use the `HttpConfiguration.Services` property to get the `ServicesContainer` object that contains the Web API service objects. I create a new instance of the `DefaultContentNegotiator` class, using the constructor argument to disable the match-on-type feature, and tell Web API to use this class as the implementation of the `IContentNegotiator` interface with the `Replace` method.

Handling a Not Acceptable Response in the Client

To deal with 406 (Not Acceptable) responses, I need to add support for displaying errors to the user. First, I have defined a Knockout observable array that will contain the errors that are to be displayed along with some HTML elements that will present the errors to the user. Listing 13-8 shows the changes I made to the `Index.cshtml` file in the Views/Home folder.

Listing 13-8. Preparing to Display Errors in the Views/Home/Index.cshtml File

```
@model IEnumerable<ExampleApp.Models.Product>
@{ ViewBag.Title = "Index";}

@section Scripts {
    <script>
        var products = ko.observableArray(
            @Html.Raw(Newtonsoft.Json.JsonConvert.SerializeObject(Model)));
        var errors = ko.observableArray();
    </script>
    <script src="~/Scripts/exampleApp.js"></script>
}

<div class="alert alert-danger" data-bind="visible: errors().length">
    <p><strong>Something has gone wrong:</strong></p>
    <ul data-bind="foreach: errors">
        <li data-bind="text: $data"></li>
    </ul>
</div>

<div class="panel panel-primary">
    <div class="panel-heading">RSVPs</div>
    <table id="rsvpTable" class="table table-striped">
        <thead>
            <tr><th>ID</th><th>Name</th><th>Price</th></tr>
        </thead>
```

```
<tbody data-bind="foreach: products">
    <tr>
        <td data-bind="text: ProductID"></td>
        <td data-bind="text: Name"></td>
        <td data-bind="text: Price"></td>
        <td>
            <button class="deleteBtn btn btn-danger btn-xs"
                    data-bind="click: deleteProduct">
                Delete
            </button>
        </td>
    </tr>
</tbody>
</table>
</div>
<button data-bind="click: getProducts" class="btn btn-primary">Refresh</button>
```

The new observable array is called errors, and the HTML elements I have added are displayed when the observable array contains one or more items. I have styled the new elements using the Bootstrap alert style, and I enumerate the contents of the errors array to generate an li element for each of them using the Knockout foreach binding. Listing 13-9 shows the changes that I have made to the exampleApp.js file in the Scripts folder to respond to the 406 (Not Accepted) status code using the errors observable array.

Listing 13-9. Responding to a Not Acceptable Response in the exampleApp.js File

```
$(document).ready(function () {

    deleteProduct = function (data) {
        $.ajax("/api/products/" + data.ProductID, {
            type: "DELETE",
            success: function () {
                products.remove(data);
            }
        })
    };

    getProducts = function () {
        errors.removeAll();
        $.ajax("/api/products", {
            headers: { "X-UseProductFormat": "true" },
            //dataType: "text",
            accepts: {
                "*": "application/x.product"
            },
            success: function (data) {
                products.removeAll();
                var arr = data.split(",");
```

```
                    for (var i = 0; i < arr.length; i += 3) {
                        products.push({
                            ProductID: arr[i],
                            Name: arr[i + 1],
                            Price: arr[i + 2]
                        });
                    }
                },
            error: function (jqXHR) {
                switch (jqXHR.status) {
                    case 406:
                        errors.push("Request not accepted by server");
                        break;
                    }
                }
            })
    };
    ko.applyBindings();
});
```

To handle the response from the server, I have used the error setting to specify a callback function. The argument passed to the callback function is a jqXHR object, and I check to see kind of error I am dealing with by checking the status property. For the 406 (Not Acceptable) status code, I add a new item to the errors observable array. (I remove any items in the errors array when the getProducts function is invoked so that errors don't accumulate through several attempts.)

In addition to the callback function, I have changed the way I use the dataType and accepts settings. By default, jQuery adds */* to the Accept header for Ajax requests, which indicates that any data type is acceptable—and that's not what I require for this example. To disable the default header, I have commented out the statement that sets the dataType setting and change the accepts setting to override the default value that jQuery adds to all requests, which is associated with a property called "*", like this:

```
...
accepts: {
    "*": "application/x.product"
},
...
```

This isn't a technique that you will need to use in many situations, other than when including */* in the Accept header results in a data format that you can't process—and this rarely happens since JSON has become the de facto standard for web services.

To test the changes, start the application, navigate to the /Home/Index URL, and click the Refresh button. jQuery will make an Ajax request to the Web API web service that contains the following Accept header:

```
Accept: application/x.product
```

The web service is unable to produce serialized data in that format and sends back the 406 status code, which results in the error display shown in Figure 13-5.

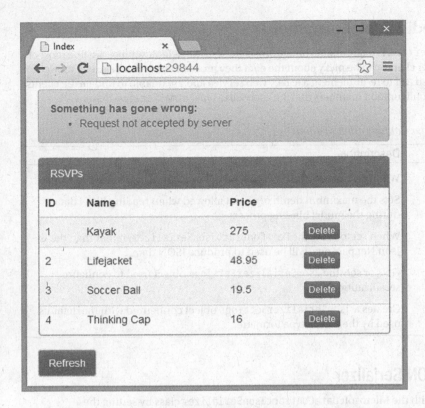

Figure 13-5. *Displaying an error to the user*

Working with the JSON Media Type Formatter

The `JsonMediaTypeFormatter` class is responsible for producing JSON data. Behind the scenes, the JSON data is generated by the Json.Net package, which is an open source library that has become the most popular JSON package for .NET applications. Table 13-5 puts the `JsonMediaTypeFormatter` in context.

Table 13-5. *Putting the JsonMediaTypeFormatter in Context*

Question	Answer
What is it?	The JSON media type formatter is responsible for serializing objects into the JSON data format.
When should you use it?	The formatter will be selected automatically during the content negotiation process.
What do you need to know?	The serialization work is done by an open source library called Json.Net. There are a number of options that can be specified to control the JSON that the Json. Net package produces, which can be useful for ensuring compatibility with clients that expect JSON to be structured in a specific way. See the "Configuring Json.Net" section for details.

Configuring the JSON Media Type Formatter

Configuring the JsonMediaTypeFormatter class is really about configuring Json.Net. The default settings are fine most of the time, but you will find that some older clients can be picky about the data they process, and it can be useful to tweak the output, especially if you are using Web API to re-implement a legacy web service and are unable to update the clients at the same time. Table 13-6 shows the configuration members that the JsonMediaTypeFormatter class defines.

Table 13-6. *The JsonMediaTypeFormatter Configuration Methods*

Name	Description
Indent	When set to true, the JSON will be indented, making it easier to read.
MaxDepth	Sets the maximum depth of object allowed when reading JSON data during the model binding process.
UseDataContractJsonSerializer	When set to true, the DataContractJsonSerializer, rather than the Json.Net package, will be used to produce JSON data.
SerializerSettings	Gets or sets the JsonSerializerSettings object used to configure serialization.
CreateDefaultSerializerSettings()	Creates a JsonSerializerSettings object configured with the defaults used by the media type formatter.

Changing the Underlying JSON Serializer

You can replace the Json.Net package with the Microsoft DataContractJsonSerializer class by setting the UseDataContractJsonSerializer property to true. The DataContractJsonSerializer class is slower and less fully featured than Json.Net, but it can be useful if you are re-implementing a legacy web service that used the DataContractJsonSerializer class and you want to preserve the quirks of its JSON formatting so that you don't have to make changes in the clients. For all other situations, the Json.Net package should be used—it is faster, is more flexible, and produces JSON that is easily consumed by clients.

Indenting the JSON Data

The easiest way to configure the JSONMediaTypeFormatter is through the convenience property defined by the MediaTypeFormatterCollection class. Listing 13-10 shows how I have used this property to set the value of the Indent property in the WebApiConfig.cs file.

Listing 13-10. Configuring the JSON Media Type Formatter in the WebApiConfig.cs File

```
using System.Web.Http;
using ExampleApp.Infrastructure;
using System.Net.Http.Formatting;
using System;

namespace ExampleApp {
    public static class WebApiConfig {
        public static void Register(HttpConfiguration config) {
```

```
        config.DependencyResolver = new NinjectResolver();

        config.MapHttpAttributeRoutes();

        config.Routes.MapHttpRoute(
            name: "DefaultApi",
            routeTemplate: "api/{controller}/{id}",
            defaults: new { id = RouteParameter.Optional }
        );

        MediaTypeFormatter xmlFormatter = config.Formatters.XmlFormatter;
        config.Formatters.Remove(xmlFormatter);
        config.Formatters.Insert(0, xmlFormatter);

        config.Services.Replace(typeof(IContentNegotiator),
            new DefaultContentNegotiator(true));

        JsonMediaTypeFormatter jsonFormatter = config.Formatters.JsonFormatter;
        jsonFormatter.Indent = true;
    }
  }
}
```

Setting the Indent property causes the JsonMediaTypeFormatter class to indent the JSON so that each object and property is defined on its own line, indented so that it is easier to read. Start the application and use Postman to send a GET request to /api/products with an Accept header of application/json; you will receive data like this:

```
[
  {
    "ProductID": 1,
    "Name": "Kayak",
    "Price": 275.0
  },
  {
    "ProductID": 2,
    "Name": "Lifejacket",
    "Price": 48.95
  },
...
```

I have shown only the first two Product objects because the indented JSON takes up a lot of space. Setting the Indent property to true makes it easier to read the JSON that the media type formatter produces, but it creates larger HTTP responses, and the extra characters added to indent the data can cause problems with poorly written client JSON parsers.

283

Configuring Json.Net

The design of the `JsonMediaTypeFormatter` class doesn't hide the fact that it usually depends on the Json.Net package. In fact, the `SerializerSettings` property and the `CreateDefaultSerializerSettings` method operate directly on the `Json.Net.JsonSerializerSettings` class, which is part of the Json.Net package and not part of Web API at all. The Json.Net classes are defined in the `Newtonsoft.Json` namespace.

The `CreateDefaultSerializerSettings` method creates a new instance of the `JsonSerializerSettings` class with the default settings used by Web API. The `SerializerSettings` property is used to get or set the `JsonSerializerSettings` object that is used to configure Json.Net when the `JsonMediaTypeFormatter` class reads and writes JSON data. (I explain how JSON is read in Chapter 17 when I describe the model binding process.)

In Table 13-7, I have listed the properties defined by the `JsonSerializerSettings` class that you may want to change in a Web API project and the default values that `JsonMediaTypeFormatter` uses. They largely relate to data types for which the JSON specification doesn't contain a definition and some kind of agreement between the client and the web service about how they are expressed.

Table 13-7. *The Most Useful SerializerSettings Properties*

Name	Description
DateFormatHandling	Specifies how dates are written in JSON, expressed as a value from the `DateFormatHandling` enumeration. The values are `IsoDateFormat` (the default), which writes dates as `2015-01-20T09:20Z`, and `MicrosoftDateFormat`, which preserves compatibility with earlier Microsoft web services. See the "Handling JSON Dates" section for details.
DateFormatString	Overrides the `DateFormatHandling` property and sets a custom format for dates. The value used when `DateFormatHandling` is `IsoDateFormat` is `yyyy'-'MM'-'dd'T'HH':'mm':'ss.FFFFFFFK`.
DefaultValueHandling	Specifies how default values are handled, expressed using the `DefaultValueHandling` enumeration. The default value is `Include`, but see the "Handling Default Values" section for further details.
NullValueHandling	Specifies whether properties that are `null` are included in JSON data, using a value from the `NullValueHandling` enumeration. The default value is `Include`, meaning that the properties are included. The other value available is `Ignore`, which omits such properties from the JSON data.
StringEscapeHandling	Specifies how string values are escaped in the JSON data, using a value from the `StringEscapeHandling` enumeration. The default value is `Default`, but see the "Handling String Escaping" section for more details.

■ **Tip** See `http://james.newtonking.com/json/help/index.html` for full details of the properties defined by the `JsonSerializerSettings` class, including the ones that I have not included in this chapter.

Creating the Example Controller and Client

Some of the JSON serializer options are worth further explanation. I get into the details in the sections that follow, but first I need to enhance the example project so that I can demonstrate the formatting features. First I added a class file called `FormatsController.cs` to the `Controllers` and used it to define the controller shown in Listing 13-11.

Listing 13-11. The Contents of the FormatsController.cs File

```
using System;
using System.Web.Http;

namespace ExampleApp.Controllers {
    public class FormatsController : ApiController {

        public object GetData() {
            return new {
                Time = DateTime.Now,
                Text = "Joe <b>Smith</b>",
                Count = 0
            };
        }
    }
}
```

The Web API controller defines a single action method that returns a dynamic object containing Time, Text, and Count properties. I'll use these properties to demonstrate different formatting options shortly.

I need to have some way to target the Web API controller, so I added an action method to the MVC Home controller, as shown in Listing 13-12.

Listing 13-12. Adding an Action Method in the HomeController.cs File

```
using System.Web.Mvc;
using ExampleApp.Models;

namespace ExampleApp.Controllers {
    public class HomeController : Controller {
        IRepository repo;

        public HomeController(IRepository repoImpl) {
            repo = repoImpl;
        }

        public ActionResult Index() {
            return View(repo.Products);
        }

        public ActionResult Formats() {
            return View();
        }
    }
}
```

The new action method, Formats, calls the View method to render the default view. There is no view model data required because I use Ajax to send an HTTP request to the web service. Listing 13-13 shows the contents of the Views/Home/Formats.cshtml file, which I created to be rendered by the Formats action method.

Listing 13-13. The Contents of the Formats.cshtml File

```
@{ ViewBag.Title = "Formats"; }

@section Scripts {
    <script>
        $(document).ready(function () {
            $.ajax("/api/formats", {
                success: function (data) {
                    dataObject = ko.observable(data);
                    ko.applyBindings();
                }
            });
        });
    </script>
}

<div class="panel panel-primary">
    <div class="panel-heading">RSVPs</div>
    <table id="rsvpTable" class="table table-striped">
        <thead><tr><th>Property</th><th>Value</th></tr></thead>
        <tbody>
            <tr><td>Time</td><td data-bind="text: dataObject().Time"></td></tr>
            <tr><td>Text</td><td data-bind="text: dataObject().Text"></td></tr>
            <tr><td>Count</td><td data-bind="text: dataObject().Count"></td>
            </tr>
        </tbody>
    </table>
</div>
```

The JavaScript code in this view uses jQuery to make an Ajax request as soon as the document is ready. The success callback for the Ajax request assigns the JavaScript object that has been parsed from the JSON data to a variable called dataObject and calls the Knockout applyBindings method so that the properties of the data object are displayed in the HTML table element via the Knockout text bindings I added to the td elements. To see the effect of these additions, start the application and request the /Home/Formats URL. The result is shown in Figure 13-6.

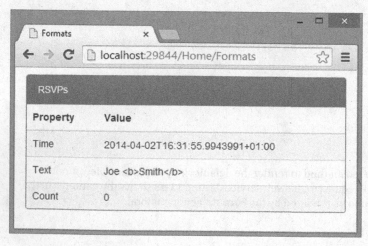

Figure 13-6. *Displaying JSON data*

The three properties sent in the JSON from the web service as displayed just as they are received. In the following sections, I'll show you how to control the JSON output produced by the web service to get different effects.

Handling JSON Dates

Dates are a source of difficulty in any environment because of the multitude of ways that they can be expressed and the endless permutations of regional calendars and time zones. The situation is made worse only when using JSON because the format acts as a neutral interchange between two different programming languages and has no definitive definition for how dates should be expressed.

The best approach—and the one most widely used in web services—is to express dates so they are easily processed in JavaScript. This is the default option used by the Json.Net package, so no changes are required within Web API. In Listing 13-14, you can see the changes that I made to the `script` element in the `Formats.cshtml` file to process the date value in JavaScript.

Listing 13-14. Processing a Date Value in the Formats.cshtml File

```
...
<script>
    $(document).ready(function () {
        $.ajax("/api/formats", {
            success: function (data) {
                dataObject = ko.observable(data);
                var date = new Date(data.Time);
                dataObject().Time = date.toLocaleTimeString();
                ko.applyBindings();
            }
        });
    });
</script>
...
```

JavaScript has a built-in `Date` type, and instances are created by calling new `Date` and using the string generated by the `JsonMediaTypeFormatter` as the constructor argument. Once you have a `Date` object, there are a range of methods you can use to get information about the date and time specified. I used the `toLocateTimeString` method to obtain a time string, as shown in Figure 13-7.

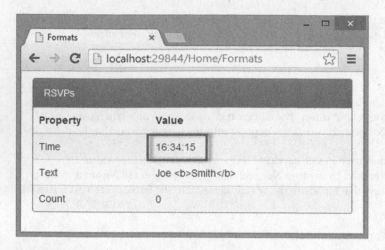

Figure 13-7. *Processing a date value*

The SerializerSettings.DateFormatHandling setting can be set to the DateFormatHandling.MicrosoftDateFormat value if you need to generate dates for compatibility with clients that rely on an older format that Microsoft used to promote, where dates are expressed like this:

```
{ "Time": "\/Date(1396385762063+0100)\/", "Text": "Joe <b>Smith</b>", "Count": 0}
```

Listing 13-15 shows how I have enabled the Microsoft date format in the WebApiConfig.cs file.

Listing 13-15. Enabling the Microsoft Date Format in the WebApiConfig.cs File

```csharp
using System.Web.Http;
using ExampleApp.Infrastructure;
using System.Net.Http.Formatting;
using System;
using Newtonsoft.Json;

namespace ExampleApp {
    public static class WebApiConfig {
        public static void Register(HttpConfiguration config) {

            config.DependencyResolver = new NinjectResolver();

            config.MapHttpAttributeRoutes();

            config.Routes.MapHttpRoute(
                name: "DefaultApi",
                routeTemplate: "api/{controller}/{id}",
                defaults: new { id = RouteParameter.Optional }
            );
```

```
        MediaTypeFormatter xmlFormatter = config.Formatters.XmlFormatter;
        config.Formatters.Remove(xmlFormatter);
        config.Formatters.Insert(0, xmlFormatter);

        config.Services.Replace(typeof(IContentNegotiator),
            new DefaultContentNegotiator(true));

        JsonMediaTypeFormatter jsonFormatter = config.Formatters.JsonFormatter;
        jsonFormatter.Indent = true;
        jsonFormatter.SerializerSettings.DateFormatHandling
            = DateFormatHandling.MicrosoftDateFormat;
        }
    }
}
```

The JavaScript Date object can't process this kind of format, so some additional manipulation is required. Listing 13-16 shows the changes I made to the script element in the Formats.cshtml view to process the Microsoft date format. This incantation extracts the numerical value from the date string and uses it to create a Date object and can be used verbatim when you are working with the legacy format.

Listing 13-16. Processing a Microsoft Date Value in the Formats.cshtml File

```
...
<script>
    $(document).ready(function () {
        $.ajax("/api/formats", {
            success: function (data) {
                dataObject = ko.observable(data);
                var date = new Date(parseInt(data.Time.replace("/Date(", "")
                    .replace(")/", ""), 10));
                dataObject().Time = date.toLocaleTimeString();
                ko.applyBindings();
            }
        });
    });
</script>
...
```

Handling String Escaping

By default, only control characters are escaped in string values when generating JSON data. The StringEscapeHandling setting allows you to change this behavior by specifying a value from the StringEscapeHandling enumeration, which defines the values shown in Table 13-8.

Table 13-8. *The Values Defined by the StringEscapeHandling Enumeration*

Value	Description
Default	Only control characters are escaped.
EscapeNonAscii	Control characters and non-ASCII characters are escaped.
EscapeHtml	HTML characters and control characters are escaped.

In any web application, it is important to guard against interpreting text as HTML if it has not been escaped. This prevents script injection, where data values are crafted to include `script` elements that contain JavaScript that attacks the application or the user. The data that I return from the web service contains some benign HTML, as follows:

```
{ "Time": "\/Date(1396385762063+0100)\/", "Text": "Joe <b>Smith</b>", "Count": 0}
```

I have used the b element to add emphasis to part of the value for the Text property. The Knockout text binding automatically escapes dangerous HTML characters, which is why the word Smith isn't shown in bold in Figure 13-7.

Relying on the client to escape dangerous HTML characters isn't enough when working with web services. You should also escape dangerous characters in the web service itself because the set of clients—or the developers who write the client—may change, presenting the risk that your web service may be used as an attack vector to undermine them. Listing 13-17 shows how I have enabled the EscapeHtml option from Table 13-8 in the WebApiConfig.cs file.

Listing 13-17. Enabling HTML Character Escaping in the WebApiConfig.cs File

```
using System.Web.Http;
using ExampleApp.Infrastructure;
using System.Net.Http.Formatting;
using System;
using Newtonsoft.Json;

namespace ExampleApp {
    public static class WebApiConfig {
        public static void Register(HttpConfiguration config) {

            // ...other statements omitted for brevity...

            JsonMediaTypeFormatter jsonFormatter = config.Formatters.JsonFormatter;
            jsonFormatter.Indent = true;
            jsonFormatter.SerializerSettings.DateFormatHandling
                = DateFormatHandling.MicrosoftDateFormat;
            jsonFormatter.SerializerSettings.StringEscapeHandling
                = StringEscapeHandling.EscapeHtml;
        }
    }
}
```

There is no change in the content rendered by the MVC controller, but if you use Postman to send a GET request to the /api/formats URL with an Accept header of application/json, you will see that the dangerous HTML characters have been escaped, like this:

```
{ "Time": "\/Date(1396421325274+0100)\/",
    "Text": "Joe \u003cb\u003eSmith\u003c/b\u003e", "Count": 0 }
```

■ **Tip** Postman formats HTML content in the Pretty view of the result data. Be sure to select the Raw view to see the characters sent by the web service.

Handling Default Values

The DefaultValueHandling setting specifies how default values for properties are handled in Json data. Default values are null for object and nullable properties, zero for numeric properties, and false for bool properties. The DefaultValueHandling setting is defined using a value from the DefaultValueHandling enumeration, which defines the values shown in Table 13-9.

Table 13-9. *The Values Defined by the DefaultValueHandling Enumeration*

Value	Description
Include	This is the default value, and it includes properties with default values in the JSON data.
Ignore	This setting excludes properties with default values from the JSON data.
Populate	This setting is used when deserializing JSON data. It sets the default value for properties in C# objects when there is no corresponding property in the JSON data. Deserialization is part of the model binding process, which I describe in Chapter 14.
IgnoreAndPopulate	This setting combines the Ignore and Populate values.

■ **Tip** There is also a NullValueHandling setting that applies only to null values.

The Include value is the default, which means that the Count property in my example data object is included in the JSON that the web service generates, even though its value is zero.

```
{ "Time": "\/Date(1396421325274+0100)\/",
    "Text": "Joe \u003cb\u003eSmith\u003c/b\u003e", "Count": 0 }
```

Listing 13-18 shows how I have set DefaultValueHandling to exclude any property that has the default value in the WebApiConfig.cs file.

Listing 13-18. Ignoring Default Values in the WebApiConfig.cs File

```
using System.Web.Http;
using ExampleApp.Infrastructure;
using System.Net.Http.Formatting;
using System;
using Newtonsoft.Json;

namespace ExampleApp {
    public static class WebApiConfig {
        public static void Register(HttpConfiguration config) {

            // ...other statements omitted for brevity...

            JsonMediaTypeFormatter jsonFormatter = config.Formatters.JsonFormatter;
            jsonFormatter.Indent = true;
```

```
            jsonFormatter.SerializerSettings.DateFormatHandling
                = DateFormatHandling.MicrosoftDateFormat;
            jsonFormatter.SerializerSettings.StringEscapeHandling
                = StringEscapeHandling.EscapeHtml;
            jsonFormatter.SerializerSettings.DefaultValueHandling
                = DefaultValueHandling.Ignore;
        }
    }
}
```

The effect is that the Count property is omitted from the JSON data:

```
{ "Time": "\/Date(1396421578038+0100)\/",
    "Text": "Joe \u003cb\u003eSmith\u003c/b\u003e"}
```

Omitting properties with default values means that the client has to be able to work without the missing properties or be able to reconstruct them with default values. Listing 13-19 shows how I updated the JavaScript code in the Formats.cshtml file to add the Count property if it is missing.

Listing 13-19. Re-creating Missing Properties in the Formats.cshtml File

```
...
<script>
    $(document).ready(function () {
        $.ajax("/api/formats", {
            success: function (data) {
                if (!("Count" in data)) {
                    data.Count = 0;
                }
                dataObject = ko.observable(data);
                var date =
                    new Date(parseInt(data.Time.replace("/Date(", "")
                    .replace(")/", ""), 10));
                dataObject().Time = date.toLocaleTimeString();
                ko.applyBindings();
            }
        });
    });
</script>
...
```

■ **Tip** I prefer to include properties that have default values because it means that the client always works on a consistent representation of the data objects and doesn't require any prior knowledge about properties that may be missing.

Using the XML Media Type Formatter

The XmlMediaTypeFormatter class is responsible for serializing model objects into XML data, and like the JSON media type formatter, it relies on other classes to generate the serialized data. In this case, the System.Runtime.DataContractSerializer class is used by default. XML used to be the predominant data format for web services but has been all but replaced by JSON, which is compact and easier to work with. There are JSON libraries available for just about every combination of platform and programming language, so the only reason to use XML is for compatibility with legacy clients. Table 13-10 puts the XmlMediaTypeFormatter class into context.

Table 13-10. Putting the XmlMediaTypeFormatter Class in Context

Question	Answer
What is it?	The XML media type formatter is responsible for serializing objects into the XML data format.
When should you use it?	The formatter will be selected automatically during the content negotiation process.
What do you need to know?	The classes that are used to produce XML data are old, slow, and inflexible. They don't support recent .NET and C# features, such as dynamic objects. XML support in Web API is largely so that web services can support clients originally developed to consume web services created with legacy Microsoft web service tools.

■ **Tip**   In real projects, I use the HttpConfiguration.Configuration.Formatters.Remove method to take the XmlMediaTypeFormatter out of the media type formatter collection for applications that don't need to support legacy clients. Not only is JSON widely supported and easier to work with, but supporting only one data format reduces the amount of unit and integration testing required for the project.

WHAT HAPPENED TO XML WEB SERVICES?

The term *XML web services* was used in the early 2000s to describe heavily structured web services that were carefully described by different XML documents and standards, including the Simple Object Access Protocol (SOAP) and the Web Service Description Language (WSDL). These standards were used to create loosely coupled clients and services but required complex XML documents that were difficult to work with. These days, those web services that still use XML use the format only to describe fragments of data without the overhead of precise type and service descriptions—rather like the JSON strings that you have seen in other examples but expressed using XML elements and attributes instead of JavaScript-style objects and properties.

Configuring the XML Media Type Formatter

Table 13-11 shows the configuration members defined by the XmlMediaTypeFormatter class.

Table 13-11. *The XmlMediaTypeFormatter Configuration Methods*

Name	Description
Indent	When set to true, the XML will be indented, making it easier to read (but more verbose).
MaxDepth	Sets the maximum depth of object allowed when reading XML data during the model binding process.
UseXmlSerializer	When set to true, the XmlSerializer class will be used to produce XML data.
WriterSettings	Gets the XmlWriterSettings object used to configure serialization.

I am not going to go into any detail about configuring the XmlMediaTypeFormatter class because XML is the lesser data format in Web API applications and because the default configuration works fine for most applications.

The DataContractSerializer class was introduced in .NET 3.0 and is the default serializer used by the XmlMediaTypeFormatter class to create XML. You can configure the serializer by changing the property values of the XmlWriterSettings object returned by the WriterSettings property—although most of the properties have little impact beyond basic formatting. You can find a complete list of the properties defined by the XmlWriterSettings class at http://goo.gl/iMDEFZ.

If you set the WriterSettings property to true, the XmlMediaTypeFormatter will use the XmlSerializer class, which has been around since .NET 1.1. Both classes are rather poor, and it is a measure of how little XML is used in web services that the choice available is a class from 2006 or a class from 2003 and that no non-Microsoft alternative package has entered the mainstream as a replacement. The only reason to use XML in Web API applications is to preserve compatibility with legacy clients, and you should use JSON for projects where this is not a requirement. There is an old, but still useful, comparison of the two XML serializer classes at http://goo.gl/gzOlyH that can help you understand the strengths and (many) weaknesses of each class.

Getting the Xml Media Type Formatter Working

The first task is to get the XmlMediaTypeFormatter class working because at the moment it isn't able to serialize the data returned by the GetData action method in the Formats controller and the client-side code doesn't support XML at the moment.

Updating the Web API Controller

The problem with the Web API controller is that you can't return dynamic objects from action methods. This means you need to create the equivalent of view model classes in the MVC framework to return results from action methods. The only time I find this frustrating is when I can't return an enumeration of dynamically created objects from a LINQ select clause. Listing 13-20 shows how I have replaced the dynamic object I used for the JSON formatter with a simple class that defines the same properties.

Listing 13-20. Defining a Model Object in the FormatsController.cs File

```
using System;
using System.Web.Http;

namespace ExampleApp.Controllers {
    public class FormatsController : ApiController {
```

```
        public DataObject GetData() {
            return new DataObject {
                Time = DateTime.Now,
                Text = "Joe <b>Smith</b>",
                Count = 0
            };
        }
    }

    public class DataObject {
        public DateTime Time { get; set; }
        public string Text { get; set; }
        public int Count { get; set; }
    }
}
```

The DataObject class defines the DateTime, string, and int properties that I need to represent the data. To test the XML serialization, start the application and use Postman to send a GET request to the /api/formats API. (There is no need to specify an Accept header because the WebApiConfig.cs file sets up the XmlMediaTypeFormatter class as the first in the formatter collection and Postman sends an Accept header of */* if one isn't explicitly specified.) You will receive the following output:

```
<DataObject xmlns:i="http://www.w3.org/2001/XMLSchema-instance"
    xmlns="http://schemas.datacontract.org/2004/07/ExampleApp.Controllers">
<Count>0</Count>
<Text>Joe <b>Smith</b></Text>
<Time>2014-04-02T19:27:30.8006076+01:00</Time>
</DataObject>
```

Updating the Client JavaScript Code

jQuery automatically parses XML data received from Ajax to create an XMLDocument object, which—as the name suggests—is a representation of an XML document, provided by the browser. The API for XMLDocument is awkward to work with, and the simplest way to create JavaScript objects from XML data is to use jQuery methods that are usually used to handle HTML. Listing 13-21 shows how I have updated the script element in the Formats.cshtml file to process the XML data that is returned by the Web API controller.

Listing 13-21. Processing XML Data in the Formats.cshtml File

```
...
<script>
  $(document).ready(function () {
    $.ajax("/api/formats", {
      dataType: "xml",
      success: function (data) {
        var props = ["Time", "Text", "Count"];
        var jsObject = {};
        for (var i = 0; i < props.length; i++) {
          jsObject[props[i]] = $(data).find(props[i]).text();
        }
```

```
        dataObject = ko.observable(jsObject);
        ko.applyBindings();
    }
  });
});
</script>
...
```

Setting `dataType` to `xml` when making the Ajax requests tells jQuery to treat the data as XML and pass the `XMLDocument` object to the `success` callback function. Within the callback, I created an array of the properties that I need to extract from the XML and use jQuery to get values for each of them.

```
...
jsObject[props[i]] = $(data).find(props[i]).text();
...
```

There are three parts to the jQuery statement. The `$(data)` part creates a jQuery wrapper around the `XMLDocument` object, which means that the jQuery methods can be used. The `find` method locates all of the elements of a specific type, and the `text` method returns the combined text content of the matching elements. The effect of this JavaScript and jQuery code is that I create an object with the properties for which I have defined Knockout bindings, populated with the values from the XML data.

Summary

In this chapter, I explained how to work with the built-in media type formatters. I explained how the default content negotiator matches media type formatters based on data types and how you can override this behavior to create a response that is more in keeping with the HTTP standard. I described how to work with the JSON media type formatter, showing you the configuration options defined by the media type formatter itself and the JSON serializer that it depends on. I finished the chapter by showing you how to work with the XML media type formatter and explained that XML has taken a back seat to JSON in web services and that the classes that the media type formatter can use to generate XML are old and mostly available for backward compatibility with legacy clients. In the next chapter, I describe the parameter and model binding features in which media type formatters play a part.

CHAPTER 14

■ ■ ■

Understanding Parameter and Model Binding

In the MVC framework, *model binding* is the process used to extract values from the HTTP request to provide values for the arguments needed to invoke action methods. In Web API, there are two processes that do this work: *parameter binding* and *model binding*. They work in loosely the same way model binding in the MVC framework works, but they are optimized to improve the performance of request handling for web services—and this means there are some important differences to the approach you are used to using.

In any complex Web API project, you will spend a lot of time dealing with the parameter and model binding processes. There is a lot of detail in how these work, and this is the first in a set of chapters that dig into that detail, explain how everything fits together, and demonstrate how to address common binding problems.

In this chapter, I explain the difference between the parameter and model binding processes and demonstrate how they work by default. In Chapter 15, I dig into the detail of how simple types—such as `int` and `string` values—are handled. In Chapter 16 and Chapter 17, I do the same for complex types. Along the way, I describe the different ways in which you can customize the parameter and model binding processes, and at the end of Chapter 17, I demonstrate how you can completely replace them with ones of your own design (although, as I explain, there is little reason to do so). Table 14-1 summarizes this chapter.

Table 14-1. *Chapter Summary*

Problem	Solution	Listing
Use parameter or model binding to find data values in the request.	Define an action method with simple or complex type arguments.	1–5, 8–13
Find values for simple data types in POST requests.	Ensure that the client includes the values for the parameters in the URL, either in the URL so that the values are accessible through the query string or in routing data.	6–7
Read a complex type value from the request URL.	Apply the `FromUri` attribute to the parameter.	14, 15
Read a simple type value from the request body.	Apply the `FromBody` attribute to the parameter.	16–17
Apply the effect of the `FromUri` or `FromBody` attribute for all parameters of a given type.	Create a parameter binding rule with the `BindWithAttribute` extension method.	18–20
Obtain data values directly from the HTTP request without using the parameter and model binding features.	Use the properties and extension methods to access the URL and request body.	21–25

Preparing the Example Project

I am going to continue working with the ExampleApp project I have been developing in previous chapters. I am using the project to get the benefit from some of the existing functionality I defined, such as the shared Razor layout that references all of the JavaScript and CSS files I need, but I won't be working with the part of the application that deals with the Product model and the Web API Products controller for a while.

Creating the Controller

I need to define a new web service that doesn't follow the RESTful convention so that I can separate the parameter and model binding processes from other Web API features. I added a class file called BindingsController.cs to the Controllers folder and used it to define the Web API controller shown in Listing 14-1.

Listing 14-1. The Contents of the BindingsController.cs File

```
using System.Web.Http;
using ExampleApp.Models;

namespace ExampleApp.Controllers {
    public class BindingsController : ApiController {
        private IRepository repo;

        public BindingsController(IRepository repoArg) {
            repo = repoArg;
        }

        [HttpGet]
        [HttpPost]
        public int SumNumbers(int first, int second) {
            return first + second;
        }
    }
}
```

The Bindings controller defines an action method called SumNumbers, which takes two int arguments, which are added together to create the result. Since this is a simple—rather than RESTful—web service, I have to apply the HttpGet and HttpPost attributes so that the action method can be targeted by HTTP GET and POST requests. (I explain how these attributes work in Web API and why RESTful web services don't need to use the attributes in Chapter 22.)

Creating the Client

I need a client to consume the new web service. I started by adding an action method to the Home controller, as shown in Listing 14-2.

Listing 14-2. Adding an Action Method in the HomeController.cs File

```
using System.Web.Mvc;
using ExampleApp.Models;

namespace ExampleApp.Controllers {
    public class HomeController : Controller {
        IRepository repo;

        public HomeController(IRepository repoImpl) {
            repo = repoImpl;
        }

        // ...other action methods omitted for brevity...

        public ActionResult Bindings() {
            return View();
        }
    }
}
```

The Bindings action method renders the default Razor view. Listing 14-3 shows the contents of the Bindings.cshtml view file that I created in the Views/Home folder.

Listing 14-3. The Contents of the Bindings.cshtml File in the Views/Home Folder

```
@{ ViewBag.Title = "Bindings"; }

@section Scripts { <script src="~/Scripts/bindings.js"></script> }

<div class="alert alert-success" data-bind="css: { 'alert-danger': gotError }">
    <span data-bind="text: response()"></span>
</div>
<div class="form-group">
    <label>First Number</label>
    <input class="form-control" data-bind="value: viewModel().first" />
</div>
<div class="form-group">
    <label>Second Number</label>
    <input class="form-control" data-bind="value: viewModel().second" />
</div>
<button class="btn btn-primary" data-bind="click: sendRequest">Send Request</button>
```

The view contains HTML form elements that collect the values to be sent to the web service and a button that triggers a function called sendRequest through a Knockout click binding.

I have included a div element styled with the Bootstrap alert class that will display the results from the request, using a Knockout css binding to change color when an error occurs. I defined the bindings (and the view model they apply to) in the bindings.js JavaScript file, which I added to the Scripts folder. Listing 14-4 shows the contents of the JavaScript file.

Listing 14-4. The Contents of the bindings.js File in the Scripts Folder

```javascript
var viewModel = ko.observable({ first: 2, second: 5 });
var response = ko.observable("Ready");
var gotError = ko.observable(false);

var sendRequest = function () {
    $.ajax("/api/bindings/sumnumbers", {
        type: "GET",
        data: viewModel(),
        success: function (data) {
            gotError(false);
            response("Total: " + data);
        },
        error: function (jqXHR) {
            gotError(true);
            response(jqXHR.status + " (" + jqXHR.statusText + ")");
        }
    });
};

$(document).ready(function () {
    ko.applyBindings();
});
```

■ **Tip**   For variety, I have included only the call to the Knockout `applyBindings` method in the jQuery `ready` function. I usually put all jQuery code inside the `ready` function out of habit, but when working with Knockout, only the `applyBindings` method cannot be called until the browser has finished processing the HTML document.

The JavaScript file defines the observable items needed for the Knockout bindings shown in Listing 14-3, along with the `sendRequest` function that will be invoked by the `click` binding on the `button` element.

■ **Tip**   I have to specify the action method as part of the URL, since I did not follow the RESTful convention in the `Bindings` controller. I explain how this convention is managed through the Web API routing system in Chapters 20 and 21, but for the purposes of this chapter, it is enough to know that I have to use `/api/bindings/sumnumbers` as the URL for the Ajax request.

Adding a New Route

For some of the examples in this chapter, I need to define a new URL route that will let me target the SumNumbers action method in the `Bindings` controller with a URL like this one:

```
http://localhost:29844/api/bindings/sumnumbers/10/12
```

To enable this, I have added a new route to the `WebApiConfig.cs` file, as shown in Listing 14-5. I explain how Web API URL routing works in Chapters 20 and 21, but for now you can see from the listing that capturing values from segment variables works just as it does in the MVC framework. In addition to defining the new URL route, I have removed the code from the previous chapter that configured the media type formatters.

Listing 14-5. Tidying Up the WebApiConfig.cs File and Defining a New URL Route

```
using System.Web.Http;
using ExampleApp.Infrastructure;

namespace ExampleApp {
    public static class WebApiConfig {
        public static void Register(HttpConfiguration config) {

            config.DependencyResolver = new NinjectResolver();

            config.MapHttpAttributeRoutes();

            config.Routes.MapHttpRoute(
                name: "Api with extension",
                routeTemplate: "api/{controller}.{ext}/{id}",
                defaults: new {
                    id = RouteParameter.Optional,
                    ext = RouteParameter.Optional
                }
            );

            config.Routes.MapHttpRoute(
                name: "Binding Example Route",
                routeTemplate: "api/{controller}/{action}/{first}/{second}"
            );

            config.Routes.MapHttpRoute(
                name: "DefaultApi",
                routeTemplate: "api/{controller}/{id}",
                defaults: new { id = RouteParameter.Optional }
            );
        }
    }
}
```

Testing the Example Application

To test the new web service, start the application and navigate to the /Home/Bindings URL. Enter two numbers into the input elements and click the Send Request button. jQuery will send an Ajax request that targets the SumNumbers action method in the Bindings controller and will display the result when it arrives, as shown in Figure 14-1.

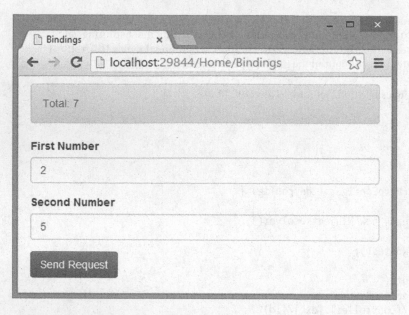

Figure 14-1. *Testing the example application*

Understanding the Default Binding Behavior

Parameter binding and model binding both extract data from the request so that it can be used as arguments to invoke action methods. The result is that you can define action methods that accept .NET types as parameters and let Web API worry about how to get values for them behind the scenes.

Using parameter and model binding ensures that values for action method parameters are extracted from requests consistently, using code that can be applied throughout an application, but Web API doesn't make you use either kind of binding in your web services. The alternative is to get the data values you need directly from the HttpRequestMessage object, but this can be awkward, duplicative, and error-prone and prevents you from benefitting from features such as model validation, which I describe in Chapter 18. I show you how to get data values from the request without using binding in the "Manually Obtaining Request Values" section later in this chapter.

■ **Note**   Strictly speaking, the term *parameter* describes the definition of a variable that a method or function accepts, and an *argument* is the value of that variable when the method or function is invoked. In practice, these terms are used interchangeably.

In the sections that follow, I describe the default behavior for parameter and model binding. I explain the relationship between the two binding processes, explain when each is used, and show you the most common cause of binding problems. Table 14-2 puts the default binding behavior in context.

Table 14-2. *Putting the Default Binding Behavior in Context*

Question	Answer
What is it?	Parameter and model binding locates values for action method parameters from requests, simplifying the process of working with the data sent by a client.
When should you use it?	Bindings are used automatically when you define an action method that has parameters.
What do you need to know?	Parameter binding is used to locate values for simple .NET types but will do so only using the request URL. Model binding is used to create complex .NET types but will do so only using the request body. This is the default behavior—see the "Performing Binding Customizations" section for details of how to change the source of data used for binding.

■ **Note** I explain the default binding behavior in some detail, and I focus on the two most common pitfalls that you will encounter. My focus on the common problems may give you the impression that parameter and model binding are of limited use, but that's not the case. In fact, you can control and customize the way that both processes work to address almost any situation, but doing that effectively requires a solid understanding of how the binding processes work by default and the traps that changing the behavior helps to avoid. I dig into the details of how both processes work in Chapters 15, 16, and 17.

Understanding Parameter Binding

Parameter binding is used when an parameter is a *simple* type, which means it is a TimeSpan, DateTime, or Guid object or one of the .NET primitive types: string, char, bool, int, uint, byte, sbyte, short, ushort, long, ulong, float, double, and decimal.

By default, parameter binding obtains values only from the request URL, which means there are two sources of data values: the routing segments in the URL that has been requested and the query string. Consider the SumNumbers method in the BindingsController class.

```
...
[HttpGet]
public int SumNumbers(int first, int second) {
    return first + second;
}
...
```

The two parameters for the action method are both int values, so Web API will use parameter binding to extract values from the response. There are two different styles of URL that can be used to target the SumNumbers method and specify a value for the first and second arguments, as shown in Table 14-3.

Table 14-3. *The URLs That Will Target the Action Method*

URL	Description
/api/bindings/sumnumbers/10/12	The values for the arguments are obtained from the URL routing information (which I describe in Chapters 20 and 21).
/api/bindings/sumnumbers?first=10&second=12	The values for the arguments are obtained from the query string.

The first URL in Table 14-3 requires the URL route I defined in Listing 14-5, and the easiest way to test it is to use Postman. Send a GET request to the /api/bindings/sumnumbers/10/12 URL, and the parameter binding process will assign 10 and 12 as the values for the action method arguments, returning a result of 22.

JSON AND XML FORMATTING OF SIMPLE VALUES

If you use Postman to send a GET request to the /api/bindings/sumnumbers/10/12 URL, you will see that the result returned by the web service is just 22. This result has been through the standard media type formatting process that I described in Chapter 13 and been formatted as JSON. It just looks like the unaltered result from the action method because JSON expresses simple values concisely, with no additional packaging required.

If you request the same URL using Google Chrome, the XML media type formatter will be used because Chrome prefers to receive XML over JSON. Here is the result that you will receive:

```
<int xmlns="http://schemas.microsoft.com/2003/10/Serialization/">
    22
</int>
```

The more you work with JSON, you more you will come to see why it has displaced the more verbose XML for web applications: JSON is simpler, more concise, and easier to work with.

The first URL is the format you will be familiar with from MVC applications, where it is good practice to create a URL schema that is easy for users to understand and manipulate directly. Not all users want to enter URLs directly, but those that do can start with a URL like this one:

/api/bindings/sumnumbers/10/12

---

and with a little experimentation work out that changing the last two URL segments allows calculations to be performed directly.

Supporting simple and editable URLs is important in Web API, too, because it allows users to work directly with the web service, but when you are implementing a browser-based client, it is usually the second kind of URL from Table 14-3 that you will rely on because jQuery makes it simple to translate JavaScript objects and Knockout observables into query strings. Consider the sendRequest method that I defined in the bindings.js file.

```
...
var sendRequest = function () {
    $.ajax("/api/bindings/sumnumbers", {
        type: "GET",
        data: viewModel(),
```

```
        success: function (data) {
            gotError(false);
            response("Total: " + data);
        },
        error: function (jqXHR) {
            gotError(true);
            response(jqXHR.status + " (" + jqXHR.statusText + ")");
        }
    });
};
...
```

jQuery takes the object assigned to the data setting property and generates a string that contains the name and value of each property it defines. The viewModel object I used in the bindings.js file is a Knockout observable. To get an object that jQuery can process through the data setting, I call the observable name with parentheses: viewModel(). This returns an object with first and second properties, which is then encoded by jQuery to produce a string like this:

```
first=10&second=20
```

jQuery uses the HTTP verb being used in the request to decide how to use the encoded string. For GET requests, the encoded string is used as the URL query string, creating a request URL like this:

```
/api/bindings/sumnumbers?first=10&second=20
```

Understanding the Parameter Binding Pitfall

By default, parameter binding will *only* extract values from the URL, which leads to the most common binding problem: trying to bind simple types from the request body. This problem usually occurs because jQuery adapts the way it uses the string generated from the data setting based on the HTTP verb. For GET requests, the string is appended to the URL as the query string, which matches the way that parameter binding works. For other HTTP verbs, jQuery puts the data string in the request body. To demonstrate the problem, I have changed the HTTP verb used by the client in the sendRequest function, as shown in Listing 14-6.

Listing 14-6. Using a Different HTTP Verb in the bindings.js File

```
...
var sendRequest = function () {
    $.ajax("/api/bindings/sumnumbers", {
        type: "POST",
        data: viewModel(),
        success: function (data) {
            gotError(false);
            response("Total: " + data);
        },
```

```
        error: function (jqXHR) {
            gotError(true);
            response(jqXHR.status + " (" + jqXHR.statusText + ")");
        }
    });
};
...
```

When you submit a request using the code shown in the listing, jQuery sends the request to the /api/bindings/sumnumbers URL without any query string and includes the encoded string in the request body. Here is a snapshot of the request that jQuery sends:

```
POST http://localhost:29844/api/bindings/sumnumbers HTTP/1.1
Host: localhost:29844
Connection: keep-alive
Content-Length: 16
Accept: */*
Origin: http://localhost:29844
X-Requested-With: XMLHttpRequest
User-Agent: Mozilla/5.0 (Windows NT 6.3; WOW64) ...(truncated)...
Content-Type: application/x-www-form-urlencoded; charset=UTF-8
Referer: http://localhost:29844/Home/Bindings
Accept-Encoding: gzip,deflate,sdch
Accept-Language: en-GB,en-US;q=0.8,en;q=0.6
Cookie: __RequestVerificationToken=XuxQqvAa36- ...(truncated)...
```

first=2&second=5

I have highlighted the data string, which is in the same format used for the query string. But, since parameter binding works only on data contained in the URL, values for the first and second arguments required by the SumNumbers action method won't be located, producing the response shown in Figure 14-2.

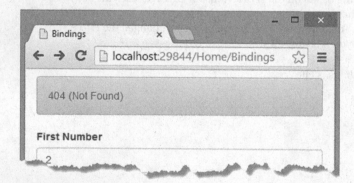

Figure 14-2. Parameter binding works only on the request URL

■ **Tip**   I captured the details of the request using Fiddler, which is an excellent web debugging proxy, available free from www.telerik.com/fiddler. The Google Chrome F12 tools provide details of the request but won't let you see the raw content.

The web service returns a 404 (Not Found) response because the sole action method defined by the `Bindings` controller has a signature that can't be matched to the request. I touch on the process of Web API action method selection in Chapter 19 and describe it in depth in Chapter 22, but for this chapter it is enough to know that the request won't target the action method if the data required by the parameter binding process is in the request body.

This problem comes up at some point in most complex Web API projects, either because you need to change the verb used for a particular kind of request or because you want to make a POST or DELETE request that targets an action method that receives simple data types. There are two ways to solve this problem. The first is to explicitly add values that correspond to simple data type action method parameters to the query string, rather than allowing jQuery to handle the data for you. Listing 14-7 shows the changes required to use this technique in the `sendRequest` function.

Listing 14-7.   Explicitly Setting the Query String in the bindings.js File

```
...
var sendRequest = function () {
    $.ajax("/api/bindings/sumnumbers?" + $.param(viewModel()), {
        type: "POST",
        //data: viewModel(),
        success: function (data) {
            gotError(false);
            response("Total: " + data);
        },
        error: function (jqXHR) {
            gotError(true);
            response(jqXHR.status + " (" + jqXHR.statusText + ")");
        }
    });
};
...
```

I have commented out the data setting and changed the URL to which the request will be sent to include a question mark and the encoded string. I have to encode the string explicitly using the jQuery `$.param` method, which takes an object as its argument and returns a string suitable for use in the query string (this is the same method that jQuery uses for the `data` setting).

The second technique is to let jQuery put the data in the body and use model binding to extract the values for the action method arguments, overriding the default behavior. I describe how this works in the "Performing Binding Customizations" section.

Understanding Model Binding

Model binding is the counterpart to parameter binding and is used for complex types—which means it is used for any type not in the list I gave in the previous section. Whereas parameter binding works only on the URL by default, model binding works only on the request body.

Since model binding works only on complex types, I need to add a model class to the example application. Listing 14-8 shows the contents of the BindingModels.cs class file that I added to the Models folder.

Listing 14-8. The Contents of the BindingModels.cs File

```
namespace ExampleApp.Models {

    public class Numbers {
        public int First { get; set; }
        public int Second { get; set; }
    }
}
```

The Numbers class I defined has First and Second properties that correspond to the simple type parameters from the previous section. Listing 14-9 shows how I updated the SumNumbers action method to use the Numbers class.

Listing 14-9. Using a Model Class in the BindingsController.cs File

```
using System.Web.Http;
using ExampleApp.Models;

namespace ExampleApp.Controllers {
    public class BindingsController : ApiController {
        private IRepository repo;

        public BindingsController(IRepository repoArg) {
            repo = repoArg;
        }

        [HttpGet]
        [HttpPost]
        public int SumNumbers(Numbers calc) {
            return calc.First + calc.Second;
        }
    }
}
```

I also updated the sendRequest method in the bindings.js file so that the client sends a request that can be processed by model binding, as shown in Listing 14-10.

Listing 14-10. Sending a Complex Type in the bindings.js File

```
...
var sendRequest = function () {
    $.ajax("/api/bindings/sumnumbers", {
        type: "POST",
        data: viewModel(),
        success: function (data) {
            gotError(false);
            response("Total: " + data);
        },
```

```
        error: function (jqXHR) {
            gotError(true);
            response(jqXHR.status + " (" + jqXHR.statusText + ")");
        }
    });
};
...
```

■ **Tip**   Notice that this is the same request configuration that caused problems for parameter binding in Listing 14-6, and if you look at the request that jQuery sends to the web service, you will see that it is identical to the one I showed you in the previous section. There are a few basic patterns of HTTP request that you will see throughout web service development.

Model binding doesn't require the client to have any knowledge about the data type that the action method requires. Instead, all of the work to create an object of the type required by the action method is performed at the web service. In this case, the client sends a request that contains values for first and second properties, like this:

```
first=2&second=5
```

Web API looks at the URL routing information and determines that the request is intended to target the SumNumbers action method, which requires a Numbers object. Since Numbers is a complex type, the model binding process is applied to transform the first and second values into a Numbers instance. For such a simple object, the transformation process is simple. You create a new instance of the Numbers class and assign values to the properties it defines, but the model binding process can be used to deal with more complex situations, as I describe in Chapter 16 and 17.

Understanding the Model Binding Pitfall

The obvious pitfall with model binding is that it can create objects only from data in the request body, which is the mirror of the most common *parameter* binding problem. This means that, by default, you can't use a complex type parameter to receive data from a GET request, but I'll show you how to resolve this in the "Performing Binding Customizations" section, albeit with some limitations.

The second pitfall is that model binding can extract only one object from the request body. In the MVC framework, the entire request body is processed and stored in memory before request processing starts. The data in the request is available as a collection of name-value pairs that can be used to create as many objects as you need, even to the extent that different objects can be created from the same data items.

The body of Web API requests isn't read into memory before the model binding process. Instead, the data is available as a stream, and once a model binder has read the data from the stream, it is no longer available for further use. I show you many different ways of customizing and controlling the model binding process in this chapter and the ones that follow, but there is no neat way to step around the one-object-per-request limit.

This problem usually appears when you need to extend the functionality of an action method. To demonstrate, I have defined a new model class in the BindingModels.cs file, as shown in Listing 14-11.

Listing 14-11. Adding a New Class to the BindingModels.cs File

```
namespace ExampleApp.Models {

    public class Numbers {
        public int First { get; set; }
        public int Second { get; set; }
    }

    public class Operation {
        public bool Add { get; set; }
        public bool Double { get; set; }
    }
}
```

In Listing 14-12, I have used the new Operation class to extend the SumNumbers action method.

Listing 14-12. Adding an Action Method Parameter in the BindingsController.cs File

```
using System.Web.Http;
using ExampleApp.Models;

namespace ExampleApp.Controllers {
    public class BindingsController : ApiController {
        private IRepository repo;

        public BindingsController(IRepository repoArg) {
            repo = repoArg;
        }

        [HttpGet]
        [HttpPost]
        public int SumNumbers(Numbers calc, Operation op) {
            int result = op.Add ? calc.First + calc.Second :
                calc.First - calc.Second;
            return op.Double ? result * 2 : result;
        }
    }
}
```

I have defined a new Operation class and changed the signature of the SumNumbers action method so that it defines Numbers and Operation parameters. I use the Operation class properties to perform different calculations within the action method, but the important part of this change is that calling the action method now requires *two* complex type arguments.

In Listing 14-13, you can see the corresponding changes that I made to the bindings.js file. The values for the Operation properties don't affect the model binding process, so I have assigned values to the Knockout observable object without giving the user any way to change those values.

Listing 14-13. Adding Data in the bindings.js File

```javascript
var viewModel = ko.observable({ first: 2, second: 5, add: true, double: false });
var response = ko.observable("Ready");
var gotError = ko.observable(false);

var sendRequest = function () {
    $.ajax("/api/bindings/sumnumbers", {
        type: "POST",
        data: viewModel(),
        success: function (data) {
            gotError(false);
            response("Total: " + data);
        },
        error: function (jqXHR) {
            gotError(true);
            response(jqXHR.status + " (" + jqXHR.statusText + ")");
        }
    });
};

$(document).ready(function () {
    ko.applyBindings();
});
```

Although the client will now send all of the data values required to create a Numbers object and an Operation object, the limitation of one object per request body will stop that from happening. Start the application, navigate to the /Home/Bindings URL, and click the Send Request button; you will see the response illustrated by Figure 14-3.

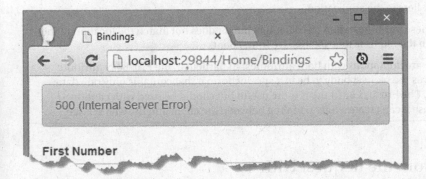

Figure 14-3. Sending a request to an action method with two complex type arguments

The values that I added for the Operation object don't matter because Web API will throw an exception before the SumNumbers method is invoked. I explain how exceptions are handled by Web API in Chapter 25, but if you use the Chrome F12 tools to look at the response sent back by the web service, you will see the following message:

```
Can't bind multiple parameters ('calc' and 'op') to the request's content.
```

The only way to resolve this problem with the default binding behavior is to create a single complex type that contains all the data values that the action method requires—in this case, a combination of the numeric values and details of the operation that should be performed on them. This is an awful solution because it undermines the benefit of being able to work with complex types in action methods by adopting classes that are just buckets of the name-value pairs; you might as well work directly from the `HttpRequestMessage` object.

That said, most Web API action methods don't take multiple complex type arguments, and the more RESTful the web service, the more likely it is to require a single complex argument. The argument is the data object to be created or modified and all of the other information required to process the request—such as the user's identity, for example—is handled through request headers that are exposed through different parts of Web API and not received as an action method argument. (I explain how user authentication and authorization are performed in Chapters 23 and 24.)

Performing Binding Customizations

Now that you have seen how parameter and model binding work, I can show you how to customize the binding processes and work around the limitations that I described in the previous section. Binding data values to action method parameters in Web API is flexible and fully featured, but it requires more work than the MVC framework to get control of the process. In the sections that follow, I show you the day-to-day customizations that you use to alter the way that parameter and model binding work. These are the simple customizations that tweak the existing behavior. In Chapters 16 and 17, I show you how to perform advanced customizations that alter the binding processes in more profound ways. Table 14-4 puts the simple binding customizations in context.

Table 14-4. Putting the Simple Binding Customizations in Context

Question	Answer
What are they?	The `FromUri` and `FromBody` attributes can be used to override the default parameter and model binding behavior and specify a location for the binding data. A binding rule can be used to create the same effect for all Web API controllers in the application.
When should you use them?	Use these attributes when the default behavior does not match the location of the data in the requests that you receive from clients.
What do you need to know?	There are limitations with both attributes. In particular, the `FromBody` attribute requires the request body to be in a specific format that contains only one data value. The `FromUri` attribute is more useful but should be used with caution because it can create a tight coupling between the client and the web service.

Binding Complex Types from the Request URL

The first kind of customization is to override the default behavior for model binding so that values are taken from the request URL rather than the body. This customization is performed by applying the `FromUri` attribute, defined in the `System.Web.Http` namespace, to the parameters you created from the data in the URL. Listing 14-14 shows how I have applied the `FromUri` attribute to the parameters defined by the `SumNumbers` action method in the `Bindings` controller.

Listing 14-14. Getting Values for a Complex Type from the Request URL in the BindingsController.cs File

```
...
[HttpGet]
[HttpPost]
public int SumNumbers([FromUri] Numbers calc, [FromUri] Operation op) {
    int result = op.Add ? calc.First + calc.Second :
        calc.First - calc.Second;
    return op.Double ? result * 2 : result;
}
...
```

I have applied the FromUri attribute to both parameters, which means that the data extracted from the URL segments by the routing configuration or from the query string will be used to set the properties of the Numbers *and* Operation objects that will be passed to the SumNumbers method. Listing 14-15 shows the client-side code that includes the data in the query string for a POST request.

Listing 14-15. Making a POST Request with Query String Data in the bindings.js File

```
var viewModel = ko.observable({ first: 2, second: 5, add: true, double: false });
var response = ko.observable("Ready");
var gotError = ko.observable(false);

var sendRequest = function () {
    $.ajax("/api/bindings/sumnumbers", {
        type: "GET",
        data: viewModel(),
        success: function (data) {
            gotError(false);
            response("Total: " + data);
        },
        error: function (jqXHR) {
            gotError(true);
            response(jqXHR.status + " (" + jqXHR.statusText + ")");
        }
    });
};

$(document).ready(function () {
    ko.applyBindings();
});
```

■ **Tip** You may notice that Microsoft uses the term *URI* in the name of the FromUri attribute but that I use *URL*. All URLs are URIs, as defined by RFC 3986, and both terms are correct when talking about web applications and web services, but URL is more widely used and understood. Microsoft is being a little pedantic by sticking with the more general term.

You don't have to use the FromUri attribute on all of the complex type parameters defined by an action method, but it is usually a sign of a problem if you are mixing and matching the locations for the data used for different parameters. See the "Using the FromUri Attribute" sidebar for details.

USING THE FROMURI ATTRIBUTE

For GET requests, the FromUri attribute should be applied to all of the complex data type parameters because the client expects to put its data into the query string, and, as you have seen, this is what jQuery will do automatically.

For other HTTP verbs, the FromUri attribute should not be used at all. The client will put its data into the request body by default, and applying the FromUri attribute to some parameters and not others means that the client has to know where the web service is going to look for different pieces of information, which causes the tight-coupling problem I described in Chapter 4.

One common reason for using the FromUri attribute for non-GET requests is to create objects from the URL that can be validated using the model binding process, which I describe in Chapter 18. The problem with this approach is that the client is then required to differentiate between model errors that relate to the data item contained in the body and model errors that relate to some opaque aspect of the URL.

I see this most frequently for PUT requests, where the modified object is contained in the body but a complex type is pulled from the URL routing data and used to validate the format of the URL and to make sure that the request relates to a data object that exists. The end result is a client that requires detailed knowledge of the web service implementation or that displays validation errors to the user about the structure of the URL, which is just confusing.

Use URL routing (as described in Chapters 20 and 21) to enforce URL structure and use standard HTTP status codes to tell the client when a request can't be processed (as described in Chapter 11).

Binding Simple Types from the Request Body

The FromBody attribute allows simple types to be obtained from the request body, rather than the URL. The FromBody attribute doesn't work around the one-object-per-request limit, which means you can get one simple type or one complex type from the request body—and that means you can apply the attribute only to a single action method parameter. If you apply the FromBody attribute more than once or use the attribute in method that also has a complex type parameters, then you will receive a Can't bind multiple parameters error.

The FromBody attribute is almost useless for reading simple types because it is so limited in the way that it reads values from the request body. The body must contain only a single value, and it must be encoded in a particular way. The attribute is more useful when used for complex types, as I describe in Chapter 16 and Chapter 17. In Listing 14-16, you can see that I have revised the SumNumbers action method so that it defines one simple type parameter, decorated with the FromBody attribute.

Listing 14-16. Using the FromBody Attribute in the BindingsController.cs File

```
...
[HttpGet]
[HttpPost]
public int SumNumbers([FromBody] int number) {
    return number * 2;
}
...
```

The SumNumbers method has an int parameter called number that is decorated with the FromBody attribute. Listing 14-17 shows the changes I have made to the sendRequest function in the bindings.js file to create a request that will target the new version of the SumNumbers method.

Listing 14-17. Targetting an Action Method with the FromBody Attribute in the bindings.js File

```
...
var sendRequest = function () {
    $.ajax("/api/bindings/sumnumbers", {
        type: "POST",
        data: {'': viewModel().first },
        success: function (data) {
            gotError(false);
            response("Total: " + data);
        },
        error: function (jqXHR) {
            gotError(true);
            response(jqXHR.status + " (" + jqXHR.statusText + ")");
        }
    });
};
...
```

I use the data setting to encode an object that has a single property and value. I set the name of the property to the empty string (' '), and the value is obtained from the first property of the view model (I am going to ignore the other view model properties for this example).

This awkward hack causes jQuery to create a request body like this, assuming that the first property has a value of 50:

```
=50
```

This is the format that the FromBody attribute requires. There can be only one value, it cannot be assigned a name, and it must be prefixed with the equal sign (=). To test the use of the attribute, start the application and navigate to /Home/Bindings in the browser. Enter **50**—or any other numeric value that you like—and click the SendRequest button.

When the SumNumbers action method is invoked, the FromBody attribute will have caused the value for the number attribute to be obtained from the body, producing the result shown in Figure 14-4.

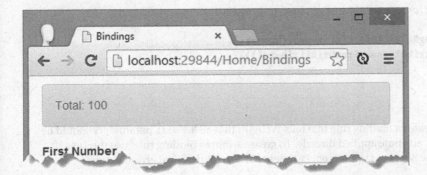

Figure 14-4. Using the FromBody attribute to get a simple type value from a request body

The FromBody attribute isn't quite as useless as it appears. The problem is that the default Web API classes that support the attribute are not adept at dealing with this kind of request. I'll show you how to increase the flexibility of the FromBody attribute in Chapter 17.

Defining a Binding Rule

The `FromUri` and `FromBody` attributes let you specify the source of the data for a binding, but they need to be applied to every action method parameter, which is just the sort of thing you can easily forget to do consistently across an application. An alternative is to define a *binding rule*, which tells Web API how to bind parameters of a specific type throughout an application.

The binding rule system allows for a lot of configuration, and in this chapter I will describe two simple rules that you can create that have the same effect as using the `FromUri` and `FromBody` attributes but apply to all of the parameters of a specific type throughout the Web API controllers in an application.

The `HttpConfiguration.ParameterBindingRules` property returns a collection of parameter binding rules. Binding rules are added to the collection during the configuration stage and then used to figure out how values for parameters are going to be obtained. (I am simplifying this process; I explain it in more detail in Chapter 15.)

When you define a new rule, you need to define a method that receives a description of an action method parameter and returns an object that will be able to bind a value for it. The description is provided by an `HttpParameterDescriptor` object, and the binding is performed by an `HttpParameterBinding` object. I describe `HttpParameterDescriptor` and `HttpParameterBinding` in detail in Chapter 16, but for the simple rules you can use an extension method defined in the `System.Web.Http.Controllers` namespace, which operates on an instance of the `HttpParameterDescriptor` class and creates an `HttpParameterBinding` object that applies either the `FromUri` or `FromBody` attribute throughout the application.

Listing 14-18 shows the use of the extension method to define the binding rule in the `WebApiConfig.cs` file.

Listing 14-18. Defining a Binding Rule in the WebApiConfig.cs File

```
using System.Web.Http;
using ExampleApp.Infrastructure;
using System.Web.Http.Controllers;
using ExampleApp.Models;

namespace ExampleApp {
    public static class WebApiConfig {
        public static void Register(HttpConfiguration config) {

            config.DependencyResolver = new NinjectResolver();

            // ...other configuration statements omitted for brevity...

            config.ParameterBindingRules.Insert(0, typeof(Numbers),
                x => x.BindWithAttribute(new FromUriAttribute()));
        }
    }
}
```

The new statement in the listing creates a binding rule that tells Web API that all `Numbers` parameters should be treated as though they have the `FromUri` attribute applied directly. To create a simple binding rule, use the `Insert` method on the collection returned by the `HtppConfiguration.ParameterBindingRules` property, like this:

```
...
config.ParameterBindingRules.Insert(0, typeof(Numbers),
    x => x.BindWithAttribute(new FromUriAttribute()));
...
```

The rules in the collection are evaluated in order, and using the `Insert` method allows control over how binding is performed. Complex binding rules can match parameters using fine-grained detail about the action method and controller that contain them, but for simple rules it is best to insert them at position zero to be sure that no other rules take precedence.

The `Insert` method takes three arguments: the position in the collection into which the new rule should be inserted, the type to which the rule will apply (`Numbers` in this case), and a function that takes an `HttpParameterDescriptor` object and returns an `HttpParameterBinding` object. The `BindWithAttribute` extension method sidesteps the need to write the function. It takes an instance of the attribute that you want to apply in the rule and uses it to create an `HttpParameterBinding` object for you.

```
...
config.ParameterBindingRules.Insert(0, typeof(Numbers),
    x => x.BindWithAttribute(new FromUriAttribute()));
...
```

In this example, I have used an instance of the `FromUriAttribute` class. The convention in C# is that attributes are implemented by classes whose names combine the name of the attribute and `Attribute` so that the `FromUri` attribute is implemented by the `FromUriAttribute` class and the `FromBody` attribute is implemented by the `FromBodyAttribute` class.

Updating the Controller and Client

Having defined a binding rule, I no longer need to apply an attribute directly to the parameter defined by the SumNumbers action method, as shown in Listing 14-19.

Listing 14-19. Removing the Binding Attribute in the BindingsController.cs File

```
using System.Web.Http;
using ExampleApp.Models;

namespace ExampleApp.Controllers {
    public class BindingsController : ApiController {
        private IRepository repo;

        public BindingsController(IRepository repoArg) {
            repo = repoArg;
        }

        [HttpGet]
        [HttpPost]
        public int SumNumbers(Numbers calc) {
            return calc.First + calc.Second;
        }
    }
}
```

___

■ **Tip** Applying the `FromUri` or `FromBody` attribute to a parameter overrides the binding rules. You can use a binding rule to define a default behavior and then change it for specific parameters.

___

Since my binding rule uses the `FromUri` attribute, I have updated the `sendRequest` function in the `bindings.js` file to make a GET request so that jQuery will use the data object values to create a query string, as shown in Listing 14-20. I have also change the `data` property so that all of the properties of the `viewModel` object are included, rather than just the single value I sent in the previous section to satisfy the `FromBody` attribute.

Listing 14-20. Using a GET Request in the bindings.js File

```
...
var sendRequest = function () {
    $.ajax("/api/bindings/sumnumbers", {
        type: "GET",
        data: viewModel(),
        success: function (data) {
            gotError(false);
            response("Total: " + data);
        },
        error: function (jqXHR) {
            gotError(true);
            response(jqXHR.status + " (" + jqXHR.statusText + ")");
        }
    });
};
...
```

The result is that the `Numbers` parameter defined by the `SumNumbers` action method—and any other `Numbers` parameter defined by an action method in a Web API controller—will be obtained from the URL, either from the query string or from the routing data.

Manually Obtaining Request Values

Now that you have seen how the basic parameter and mode binding features work, I am going to finish this chapter by demonstrating how you can bypass both processes and get the data you need directly from the request data.

My advice is to use the binding features wherever you can, but working directly with the request can be useful if you have multiple generations of clients targeting the same action method with different data—and, potentially, different expectations of what the web service will do with that data.

This isn't something you should need to do often, not least because it is easy to create a web service that doesn't get the data it requires or that breaks when some aspect of the request changes. But I want to demonstrate that binding values to parameters is entirely optional and is intended only to make web service development simpler and more natural. If you find yourself getting bogged down by the quirks and oddities of the binding features, it can be helpful to know that there is an alternative approach available.

To prepare for this example, I am going to modify the client I have been using in this chapter so that it sends different requests to the same action method so that I can demonstrate how to work directly with the request data in the Web API action method to work out what kind of request has been received and deal with it appropriately.

In Listing 14-21, you can see the changes that I have made to the `Bindings.cshtml` file in the `Views/Home` folder.

Listing 14-21. Extending the Client in the Bindings.cshtm File

```
@{ ViewBag.Title = "Bindings"; }

@section Scripts { <script src="~/Scripts/bindings.js"></script> }

<div class="alert alert-success" data-bind="css: { 'alert-danger': gotError }">
    <span data-bind="text: response()"></span>
</div>

<button class="btn btn-primary" data-bind="click: sendRequest.bind($data, 'sum')">
    Send Sum Request
</button>
<button class="btn btn-primary" data-bind="click: sendRequest.bind($data, 'difference')">
    Send Difference Request
</button>
```

I removed the input elements that allow the user to change the view model values and defined two buttons
that call the sendRequest method with an argument indicating the kind of request that is required, either sum or
difference. You can see how I use the argument to alter the data sent in the request in Listing 14-22, which shows the
changes I made to the bindings.js file.

Listing 14-22. Sending Different Request Data in the bindings.js File

```
var viewModel = ko.observable({ first: 2, second: 5});
var response = ko.observable("Ready");
var gotError = ko.observable(false);

var sendRequest = function (requestType) {
    $.ajax("/api/bindings/sumnumbers", {
        type: "GET",
        data: requestType == "sum"
            ? viewModel() : {value1: viewModel().first, value2: viewModel().second },
        success: function (data) {
            gotError(false);
            response("Total: " + data);
        },
        error: function (jqXHR) {
            gotError(true);
            response(jqXHR.status + " (" + jqXHR.statusText + ")");
        }
    });
};

$(document).ready(function () {
    ko.applyBindings();
});
```

If the argument received by the sendRequest function is sum, then I send a request that contains properties called first and second. Otherwise, I send a request that contains value1 and value2 properties. The values assigned to these properties are not important—just the fact that different data properties will be sent. In Listing 14-23, you can see how I have updated the SumNumbers action method to receive these requests.

Listing 14-23. Getting Request Data Directly in the BindingsController.cs File

```
using System.Web.Http;
using ExampleApp.Models;
using System.Linq;
using System.Net.Http;
using System.Collections.Generic;
using System.Net;

namespace ExampleApp.Controllers {
    public class BindingsController : ApiController {
        private IRepository repo;

        public BindingsController(IRepository repoArg) {
            repo = repoArg;
        }

        [HttpGet]
        [HttpPost]
        public IHttpActionResult SumNumbers() {
            Dictionary<string, string> jqData
                = Request.GetQueryNameValuePairs().ToDictionary(x => x.Key,
                    x => x.Value);
            int firstValue, secondValue;
            if (TryGetValues(jqData, "first", "second", out firstValue,
                out secondValue)) {
                    return Ok(firstValue + secondValue);
            } else if (TryGetValues(jqData, "value1", "value2", out firstValue,
                out secondValue)) {
                    return Ok(firstValue - secondValue);
            } else {
                return StatusCode(HttpStatusCode.BadRequest);
            }
        }

        private bool TryGetValues(Dictionary<string, string> data, string key1,
                string key2, out int val1, out int val2) {
            val1 = val2 = 0;
            return data.ContainsKey(key1) && data.ContainsKey(key2)
                && int.TryParse(data[key1], out val1) && int.TryParse(data[key2],
                    out val2);
        }
    }
}
```

In this example, I am dealing with a GET request that contains the data I require in the query string (I show you how to deal with a POST request in the next section). The easiest way to get the query string data is to use one of the extension methods that Web API adds to the System.Net namespace that operate on the HttpRequestMessage object that represents the request, like this:

```
...
Dictionary<string, string> jqData
    = Request.GetQueryNameValuePairs().ToDictionary(x => x.Key, x => x.Value);
...
```

The Request property is defined by the ApiController class and returns the HttpRequestMessage object. The GetQueryNameValuePairs method is an extension that returns a IEnumerable<KeyValuePair<string, string>> object, which is an entirely useless way to present the data unless you want to enumerate it with a foreach loop. I use the LINQ ToDictionary method to process the data and create a Dictionary<string, string>, which maps the query string properties to their values. This gives me a more useful data collection to work with.

■ **Tip** You might be concerned that the query string is *supposed* to be enumerated for performance reasons, rather like the request body (which I demonstrate in the next section). In fact, the use of IEnumerable is just poor design because the data objects have already been read into memory and stored in an array in the GetQueryNameValuePairs method anyway.

When dealing with the request data directly, you take responsibility for ensuring that the values you require are part of the request and can be parsed into the required data type. I defined the TryGetValues method to check that pairs of properties are contained in the request and can be parsed into int values. (This relies on the use of the out keyword, which I always regard as an indicator of gnarly, twisted code in web services and keep an eye out for when taking over a project.)

Within the SumNumbers method itself, I try to get the pairs of data properties that define the different requests and perform operations on them. I have changed the result to IHttpActionResult, which I described in Chapter 11 and which allows me to use the Ok method to return data to the client for successful requests and use the StatusCode method to return 400 (Bad Request) responses when the request doesn't contain the data I am expecting.

To test the changes, start the application, navigate the browser to /Home/Bindings, and click each button in turn. As shown in Figure 14-5, clicking the Send Sum Request button will generate a response of 7 (having added 2 and 5 together), while clicking the Send Difference Request button will generate a request of -3 (having subtracted 5 from 2).

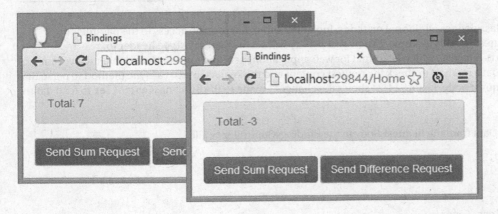

Figure 14-5. *Obtaining data directly from the request*

Handling POST Requests

The key to working with the request body is the HttpContent class, which is defined in the System.Net.Http namespace. An instance of the HttpContent class is returned by the HttpRequestMessage.Content property and can be used to determine the nature of the content and access it. The methods and properties of the HttpContent class are supplemented by Web API extension methods that make it easier to work with different types of request. Table 14-5 describes the property and methods that provide information about the content represented an instance of the HttpContent class. (I have not differentiated between extension methods and those defined directly by HttpContent because there is no reason not to use the extension methods when writing a Web API application.)

Table 14-5. *The Descriptive Members Defined by HttpContent*

Name	Description
Headers	Returns an HttpContentHeaders object that contains the headers in the request
IsFormData()	Returns true if the Content-Type header is application/x-www-form-urlencoded
IsMimeMultipartContent()	Returns true if the Content-Type header indicates that MIME multipart encoding has been used for the request body

The methods described in Table 14-5 operate on the request headers. The request body isn't read until it is required—which is why there is a limit of one value when using the binding features. Table 14-6 lists the most useful methods for reading the message body.

Table 14-6. *The Methods Defined by HttpContent for Reading the Request Body*

Name	Description
ReadAsStreamAsync()	Returns a Stream that can be used to read the raw contents of the request body
ReadAsStringAsync()	Returns the contents of the request body as a string
ReadAsFormDataAsync()	Returns a NameValueCollection containing name-value pairs parsed from x-www-form-urlencoded data
ReadAsMultipartAsync()	Returns a MultipartMemoryStreamProvider that parses the contents of a MIME multipart encoded body

The HttpContent class defines additional methods, including some that provide access to the parameter and model binding features. For this example, I know that jQuery will set the Content-Type header to application/x-www-form-encoded, which is normal for web applications sending form data, and that means I am interested in the IsFormData method to check the request content and the ReadAsFormDataAsync method to parse the data contained in the request body. Listing 14-24 shows the changes I made to the BindingsController to read data from the request body.

Listing 14-24. Reading Data from the Request Body in the BindingsController.cs File

```
using System.Web.Http;
using ExampleApp.Models;
using System.Linq;
using System.Net.Http;
using System.Collections.Generic;
using System.Net;
```

```
using System.Collections.Specialized;
using System.Threading.Tasks;

namespace ExampleApp.Controllers {
    public class BindingsController : ApiController {
        private IRepository repo;

        public BindingsController(IRepository repoArg) {
            repo = repoArg;
        }

        [HttpGet]
        [HttpPost]
        public async Task<IHttpActionResult> SumNumbers() {
            if (Request.Content.IsFormData()) {
                NameValueCollection jqData = await Request.Content.ReadAsFormDataAsync();
                int firstValue, secondValue;
                if (TryGetValues(jqData, "first", "second", out firstValue,
                        out secondValue)) {
                    return Ok(firstValue + secondValue);
                } else if (TryGetValues(jqData, "value1", "value2", out firstValue,
                        out secondValue)) {
                    return Ok(firstValue - secondValue);
                }
            }
            return StatusCode(HttpStatusCode.BadRequest);
        }


        private bool TryGetValues(NameValueCollection data, string key1,
                string key2, out int val1, out int val2) {
            string val1string, val2string;
            val1 = val2 = 0;
            return (val1string = data[key1]) != null
                && int.TryParse(val1string, out val1)
                && (val2string = data[key2]) != null
                && int.TryParse(val2string, out val2);
        }
    }
}
```

Most of the changes relate to getting values from the collection that holds the parsed request data. The
ReadAsFormDataAsync method returns an instance of the System.Collections.Specialized.NameValueCollection
class, which presents a different API than the Dictionary I used in the previous example.

■ **Tip**   Notice that the methods that read the request body are asynchronous. I used the async keyword on the
SumNumbers method and changed the result to Task<IHttpActionResult>. Within the method body I used the await
keyword when calling the ReadAsFormDataAsync method.

I need to change the client-side code to send a POST request with the data in the request body to test the new implementation of the SumNumbers method. Listing 14-25 shows the changes that I made to the bindings.js file.

Listing 14-25. Sending a POST Request in the bindings.js File

```
...
var sendRequest = function (requestType) {
    $.ajax("/api/bindings/sumnumbers", {
        type: "POST",
        data: requestType == "sum"
            ? viewModel() : {value1: viewModel().first, value2: viewModel().second },
        success: function (data) {
            gotError(false);
            response("Total: " + data);
        },
        error: function (jqXHR) {
            gotError(true);
            response(jqXHR.status + " (" + jqXHR.statusText + ")");
        }
    });
};
...
```

There is no visible change to the way that the client works, but you can use the browser F12 tools to check that a POST request is being sent and processed by the web service. This example demonstrates that it is possible to get data directly from the request, but at the cost of having to check that the required values exist and can be parsed into the required types.

Summary

In this chapter, I introduced you to the Web API parameter and model binding features and explained how they work by default. I demonstrated how you can change the behavior by using the FromUri and FromBody attributes and how you can define a simple binding rule that has the same effect throughout a Web API application. I finished this chapter by showing you how to sidestep the parameter and model binding processes and work directly with the HttpRequestMessage object. There are occasions when this can be useful, but you should use the binding features whenever possible because it frees you from the tedious and error-prone tasks of finding and parsing data values. In Chapter 15, I dig into the details of parameter binding and explain what happens behind the scenes—and how you can take control of the process.

CHAPTER 15

∎∎∎

Binding Simple Data Types

In this chapter, I describe the parameter binding system in depth, showing you different ways to obtain values for simple type parameters and explaining how Web API uses a range of different components to get the data values needed to invoke an action method. The features I describe in this chapter are also used to bind complex types using data from the URL, which I explain in Chapter 16. Table 15-1 summarizes this chapter.

Table 15-1. *Chapter Summary*

Problem	Solution	Listing
Add a new source of data for binding simple action method parameter types.	Implement a custom value provider and value provider factory.	1–9
Apply a value provider to a single action method argument.	Use the ValueProvider attribute or derive a new attribute from the ModelBindingAttribute or ParameterBindingAttribute class.	10–15
Integrate a custom value provider into the default Web API behavior so that it is used without the need for attributes.	Register the value provider factory with the services collection. Ensure that the custom factory implements the IUriValueProviderFactory interface and that the action method parameter is optional.	16–19
Integrate a custom value provider so that it is used based on the name of the action method parameter.	Define a parameter binding rule.	20
Integrate a custom value provider so that it is used only if there are no values from other providers.	Define a parameter binding that queries all of the value providers that have been registered.	21–24

Preparing the Example Project

I am going to continue working with the ExampleApp project from earlier chapters, but I am going to clean it up from the previous chapter to remove the code that manually obtains data from the HttpRequestMessage object. Listing 15-1 shows the revised BindingsController class.

Listing 15-1. Tidying Up the Code in the BindingsController.cs File

```
using System.Web.Http;
using ExampleApp.Models;

namespace ExampleApp.Controllers {
    public class BindingsController : ApiController {
        private IRepository repo;

        public BindingsController(IRepository repoArg) {
            repo = repoArg;
        }

        [HttpGet]
        [HttpPost]
        public int SumNumbers(Numbers numbers) {
            return numbers.First + numbers.Second;
        }
    }
}
```

■ **Tip**   Remember that you don't have to create the example project yourself. You can download the source code for every chapter for free from Apress.com.

I have returned to using the Numbers model class as the parameter of the SumNumbers action method. Listing 15-2 shows the corresponding changes to the Bindings.cshtml file that allow the user to change the data values that are used to target the action method.

Listing 15-2. Resetting the Contents of the Bindings.cshtml File

```
@{ ViewBag.Title = "Bindings"; }

@section Scripts { <script src="~/Scripts/bindings.js"></script> }

<div class="alert alert-success" data-bind="css: { 'alert-danger': gotError }">
    <span data-bind="text: response()"></span>
</div>
<div class="form-group">
    <label>First Number</label>
    <input class="form-control" data-bind="value: viewModel().first" />
</div>
<div class="form-group">
    <label>Second Number</label>
    <input class="form-control" data-bind="value: viewModel().second" />
</div>
<button class="btn btn-primary" data-bind="click: sendRequest">Send Request</button>
```

Listing 15-3 shows the contents of the bindings.js file, in which I have returned to using a POST request that includes the properties defined by the client-side view model.

Listing 15-3. *Resetting the Contents of the bindings.js File*

```
var viewModel = ko.observable({ first: 2, second: 5 });
var response = ko.observable("Ready");
var gotError = ko.observable(false);

var sendRequest = function (requestType) {
    $.ajax("/api/bindings/sumnumbers", {
        type: "POST",
        data: viewModel(),
        success: function (data) {
            gotError(false);
            response("Total: " + data);
        },
        error: function (jqXHR) {
            gotError(true);
            response(jqXHR.status + " (" + jqXHR.statusText + ")");
        }
    });
};

$(document).ready(function () {
    ko.applyBindings();
});
```

The final preparatory change is to remove the binding rule from the WebApiConfig.cs file, as shown in Listing 15-4, and tidy up the routing configuration statements to remove the ones I no longer require.

Listing 15-4. *Resetting the Contents of the WebApiConfig.cs File*

```
using System.Web.Http;
using ExampleApp.Infrastructure;

namespace ExampleApp {
    public static class WebApiConfig {
        public static void Register(HttpConfiguration config) {

            config.DependencyResolver = new NinjectResolver();

            config.MapHttpAttributeRoutes();

            config.Routes.MapHttpRoute(
                name: "Binding Example Route",
                routeTemplate: "api/{controller}/{action}/{first}/{second}"
            );

            config.Routes.MapHttpRoute(
                name: "DefaultApi",
                routeTemplate: "api/{controller}/{id}",
                defaults: new { id = RouteParameter.Optional }
            );
        }
    }
}
```

Preparing the Common Code

For the first part of this chapter, I focus on customizing the way that simple data types are bound through the parameter binding process. Web API comes with a complete set of classes that can bind the built-in simple types so that a string or int parameter is matched to a value in the request URL or body, as I demonstrated in Chapter 14.

Rather than duplicate this functionality, I am going to show you how to bind parameters to request headers. This isn't something that is overwhelmingly useful in a real project, but it provides a suitable foundation for demonstrating the customization techniques available.

I am going to show you how to bind headers in different ways in the sections that follow, and to reduce duplication, I have put the code that processes the headers into its own class file. Listing 15-5 shows the contents of the HeadersMap.cs class file that I added to the Infrastructure folder.

Listing 15-5. The Contents of the HeadersMap.cs File

```
using System.Collections.Generic;
using System.Linq;
using System.Net.Http.Headers;

namespace ExampleApp.Infrastructure {
    public class HeadersMap {
        private Dictionary<string, string> headersCollection;

        public HeadersMap(HttpHeaders headers) {
            headersCollection = headers.ToDictionary(
                x => x.Key.ToLower().Replace("-", string.Empty),
                x => string.Join(",", x.Value));
        }

        public string this[string header] {
            get {
                string key = header.ToLower();
                return headersCollection.ContainsKey(key) ?
                    headersCollection[key] : null;
            }
        }

        public bool ContainsHeader(string header) {
            return this[header] != null;
        }
    }
}
```

The HeadersMap class maintains a dictionary that is populated with header names and values from an HttpHeaders object. To make it easier to use header names as action method parameters, I remove hyphens and convert the names to lowercase so that User-Agent is stored as useragent.

The HttpHeaders class is defined in the System.Net.Http namespace, and I will be obtaining instances through the HttpRequestMessage.Headers property when I start to build the binding code. The HttpHeader class is a collection, and for each header in the request, it maps a string containing the header name to an IEnumerable<string> containing one or more values. The individual headers can be accessed through the methods described in Table 15-2.

Table 15-2. The Methods Defined by the HttpHeaders Class

Name	Description
Add(header, IEnumerable<value>)	Adds the specified header with the enumeration of values to the collection
Add(header, value)	Adds the specified header and value to the collection
Clear()	Removes all the headers from the collection
Contains(header)	Returns true if there is a header with the specified name in the collection
GetValues(header)	Returns an IEnumerable<string> containing the values for the specified header
Remove(header)	Removes the specified header from the collection

■ **Note** Some of the methods in Table 15-2 can be used to modify the headers because the HttpHeader class is also used by HttpResponseMessage to define the headers that will be sent in an HTTP response.

I can't work directly with the HttpHeaders object because I want to allow a parameter such as userAgent to match the User-Agent header, which means I need to extract the header data and process it so that it becomes easier to work with. The HttpHeader class implements the IEnumerable<KeyValuePair<string, IEnumerable<string>>> interface, which can be used to enumerate all of the collected headers. This is the same interface I encountered in Chapter 14 when working with the query string parameters, and I deal with it same way: using the LINQ ToDictionary method to create a data structure that it easier to work with, like this:

```
...
headersCollection = headers.ToDictionary(
    x => x.Key.ToLower().Replace("-", string.Empty), x => string.Join(",", x.Value));
...
```

I process each header name so that it will match the format I will use for parameter names and use the string.Join method to concatenate multiple header values into a single string.

■ **Tip** I have omitted some detail in this section. In fact, there are two subclasses of the HttpHeaders class—HttpRequestHeaders and HttpResponseHeaders—that provide additional members that make it easy to get and set the set of headers that the HTTP specification allows in request and response messages. I use the HttpRequestHeaders class in the "Creating a Parameter Binding Rule" section later in this chapter, but I prefer to work with the HttpHeaders class directly.

Working with Value Providers and Value Provider Factories

Value providers are responsible for getting a single simple data value. Value providers are given the name of the data item that is required and return its value. The value usually comes from the request, but any source of data can be used including the data model. The name of the data item depends on the context in which the value provider is being used. For parameter binding it will be the name of the action method parameter, and for model binding it will be the name of a property from the class that is being instantiated.

Value provider factories are responsible for creating instances of value providers based on the description of an action method parameter. It is the factory that tends to do most of the work in processing a request to prepare a source of multiple data values—like the headers of a request—and the value provider then returns a single value when a request arrives. Table 15-3 puts value providers and their factories in context.

Table 15-3. Putting Value Providers and Value Provider Factories in Context

Question	Answer
What are they?	Value providers are responsible for providing a value for a single parameter before an action method is processed. A value provider factory is responsible for deciding whether the value provider is able to provide a value and provide an instance of it to Web API.
When should you use it?	Use value providers and value provider factories when you want to bind parameter values from parts of the request other than the URL or the body or from some other data source entirely.
What do you need to know?	Value providers and value provider factories are also used in the model binding process. See Chapters 16 and 17 for details.

Understanding Value Providers and Value Provider Factories

Value providers implement the `IValueProvider` interface, which is defined in the `System.Web.Http.ValueProviders` namespace. Listing 15-6 shows the definition of the `IValueProvider` interface.

Listing 15-6. The IValueProvider Interface

```
namespace System.Web.Http.ValueProviders {

    public interface IValueProvider {

        bool ContainsPrefix(string prefix);

        ValueProviderResult GetValue(string key);
    }
}
```

I describe the role of the `ContainsPrefix` method in Chapters 16 and 17, but for the moment it is the `GetValue` method that is of interest. This method is called when a value is needed, and the result is expressed using an instance of the `ValueProviderResult` class, which defines the properties and method shown in Table 15-4.

Table 15-4. The Properties and Method Defined by the ValueProviderResult Class

Name	Description
RawValue	This property is used to store the value obtained by the value provider from the request.
AttemptedValue	This property is initially set to be the same as RawValue but will be used to contain an error message if there is a model validation error. See Chapter 18 for details of Web API model validation.
Culture	Gets the culture for the value. This is used when converting the object returned by the RawValue property and should be set to CultureInfo.InvariantCulture if there are no cultural considerations for a value.
ConvertTo(T)	Attempts to convert the value to the specified type. See Chapter 16 for details.

The RawValue and AttemptedValue properties cause confusion, but you simply set both properties to the value extracted from the request and let Web API change the AttempedValue if there are model validation problems. You can't set the properties in Table 15-4 directly, but the ValueProviderResult class provides a constructor that accepts arguments for all three properties, which you can see used in Listing 15-8.

Notice that the methods defined by the IValueProvider interface do not provide access to details of the request. This is because instances of IValueProvider are created by ValueProviderFactory classes, which are responsible for giving a value provider access to the context information it requires. Listing 15-7 shows the definition of the abstract ValueProviderFactory class.

Listing 15-7. The Abstract ValueProviderFactory Class

```
using System.Web.Http.Controllers;

namespace System.Web.Http.ValueProviders {

    public abstract class ValueProviderFactory {
        public abstract IValueProvider GetValueProvider(HttpActionContext context);
    }
}
```

■ **Caution**   Don't be tempted to use value providers used to perform data operations. As an example, for the SumNumbers action method in the BindingsController, a value provider might locate the first and second values in the request and add them together to provide a sum argument to the action method. This breaks the separation of concerns that helps make applications easy to understand and maintain. Use value providers only to—as their name suggests—provide data values and leave the operations where they belong.

The ValueProviderFactory class defines a single abstract method called GetValueProvider, which is called when a value is required for an action method parameter. An HttpActionContext object is passed to the GetValueProvider, which allows classes derived from ValueProviderFactory to inspect the request and decide whether the IValueProvider implementations for which they are responsible for may be able to provide values for the request. (Don't worry if this doesn't make immediate sense; I show you how to create a custom factory and provider shortly.) Table 15-5 describes the properties defined by the HttpActionContext class.

Table 15-5. *The Properties Defined by the HttpActionContext Class*

Name	Description
ActionArguments	Returns a `Dictionary<string, object>` that maps the names of the action method arguments to their types.
ActionDescriptor	Returns an `HttpActionDescriptor` object that describes the action method that is going to be invoked. See Chapter 22.
ControllerContext	Returns an `HttpControllerContext` object that describes the controller in which the action method is defined. See Chapter 19 for details of this class.
ModelState	Returns a `ModelStateDictionary` object used in the model validation process, which I describe in Chapter 18.
Request	Returns the `HttpRequestMessage` object that describes the current request.
RequestContext	Returns the `HttpRequestContext` object that provides supplementary information about the request.
Response	Returns the `HttpResponseMessage` object that will be used to produce the response to the client.

The `HttpActionContext` class provides a lot of context information, but most `ValueProviderFactory` implementations will either always create and return a value provider or do so based on some aspect of the `HttpRequestMessage` object, such as the HTTP verb that has been used for the request.

Creating a Custom Value Provider and Factory

The `GetValue` method defined by a value provider can be called multiple times to obtain values for different parameters, and this means it is sensible to perform any parsing of request data in the value provider constructor inside the `GetValueProvider` method of the factory class. To demonstrate, I added a class file called `HeaderValueProvider.cs` to the `Infrastructure` folder and used it to define the value provider shown in Listing 15-8.

Listing 15-8. The Contents of the HeaderValueProvider.cs File

```
using System.Globalization;
using System.Web.Http.ValueProviders;

namespace ExampleApp.Infrastructure {
    public class HeaderValueProvider : IValueProvider {
        private HeadersMap headers;

        public HeaderValueProvider(HeadersMap map) {
            headers = map;
        }

        public ValueProviderResult GetValue(string key) {
            string value = headers[key];
            return value == null
                ? null
                : new ValueProviderResult(value, value, CultureInfo.InvariantCulture);
        }
```

```
        public bool ContainsPrefix(string prefix) {
            return false;
        }
    }
}
```

The `HeaderValueProvider` class defines a constructor that receives an instance of the `HeadersMap` class, and the `GetValue` method checks to see whether the `HeadersMap` contains a header that matches the name of the property. If it has, it creates and returns an instance of the `ValueProviderResult` class that contains the header value.

The `GetValue` method is not required to return a value, and I return `null` if there is no corresponding header, indicating that the data that the value provider represents can't be used to bind to the parameter. Web API will generally use multiple value provider factories and value providers when trying to perform parameter binding, and when one value provider returns null, Web API moves on to the next one and tries again.

To define the value provider factory, I added a class file called `HeaderValueProviderFactory.cs` to the `Infrastructure` folder and used it to define the class shown in Listing 15-9.

Listing 15-9. The Contents of the HeaderValueProviderFactory.cs File

```
using System.Net.Http;
using System.Web.Http.Controllers;
using System.Web.Http.ValueProviders;

namespace ExampleApp.Infrastructure {

    public class HeaderValueProviderFactory : ValueProviderFactory {
        public override IValueProvider GetValueProvider(HttpActionContext context) {
            if (context.Request.Method == HttpMethod.Post) {
                return new HeaderValueProvider(new HeadersMap(context.Request.Headers));
            } else {
                return null;
            }
        }
    }
}
```

When you start working with value providers, it is easy to believe that the factory is a passive participant in the binding process, but that isn't the case. The job of the factory is to examine the `HttpActionContext` object and decide whether the value provider it is responsible for can be used to bind values for the current request.

That doesn't mean the factory has to figure out whether the value provider will be able to produce a value for a specific parameter—just whether this is a request that the provider will be able to work with at all. This allows a value provider factory to return different value providers to cope with a range of request types or to decide not to create a value provider at all.

To demonstrate how this works, I made the GetValueProvider method a little more complex than it needed to be in the HeaderValueProviderFactory class. I use the Request.Method property defined by the HttpActionContext class to determine whether the request has been made using the POST verb. If it has, then I create and return an instance of the HeaderValueProvider. If not, I return null, indicating that the factory is unwilling to contribute a value provider to bind parameters for this request. When this happens, Web API will try to bind through another value provider factory or, if none are available, generate a binding error.

Applying a Custom Value Provider and Factory

Creating a custom value provider and factory is only part of the process; you must also apply it so that Web API uses it to obtain parameter values. There are several different ways of configuring the way that the value provider and its factory are used, which I describe in the following sections. Some of the techniques I describe are less useful and convenient than others, but they allow me to demonstrate how some of the most important Web API components fit together and how you can customize or replace their behavior.

Understanding How Web API Looks for Values

When Web API needs a value for a simple type parameter, it tries to find one in three different ways. In the sections that follow, I'll show you each of them and demonstrate how they can be used to set up the value provider factory so that values for parameters are obtained from the value provider.

First, Web API checks to see whether a model binding attribute has been applied directly to the attribute. You saw an example of this in Chapter 14 when I used the FromBody attribute to direct Web API to find a value in the request body.

If there is no such attribute, Web API looks for a parameter binding rule. I demonstrated these in Chapter 14 as well when I showed you how to apply an attribute across the application. That was a basic rule; as you will learn, the binding rules system can do a lot more.

Finally, if there is no directly applied attribute and no parameter binding rule, then Web API acts as though the parameter has been decorated with the FromUri attribute. This is the default behavior and means values are obtained from the request routing or query string if an alternative source for values hasn't been specified.

The source of a value for a specific parameter can be worked out statically during the configuration stage of the application. Web API can look at the parameter to see whether there is an attribute, check the set of parameter binding rules to see whether there is one for a specific parameter, or decide to use the default behavior, all before the application starts processing requests.

Working out how specific parameters will be bound during the configuration stage allows values to be obtained faster when processing requests because the analysis has already been performed and the results cached, avoiding the need to perform reflection on action methods every time one is invoked.

Caching binding information requires Web API to define a class that describes what the source of a value will be for each parameter, and that is the job of the HttpParameterBinding class, which is defined in the System.Web.Http.Controllers namespace and which defines the properties and methods described in Table 15-6.

Table 15-6. *The Properties and Method Defined by the HttpParameterBinding Class*

Name	Description
Descriptor	Returns the HttpParameterDescriptor object associated with this binding (and which is passed to the constructor).
ErrorMessage	Returns a string that is used as an error message if the binding fails. If not overridden, this property will return null.
IsValid	Returns true if the binding was successful. If not overridden, this property returns true if the ErrorMessage property returns null.
WillReadBody	Returns true if the value for the parameter will be read from the request body. This property is used to detect when more than one parameter value is going to be read from the body so that an error can be reported (as demonstrated in Chapter 14).
ExecuteBindingAsync(metadata, context, cancelToken)	This method is called to perform the binding and get a value for the parameter. See the following text for details.
SetValue(context, value)	This protected method is used to set the parameter value. The arguments are the HttpActionContext object passed to the ExecuteBindingAsyncMethod and the parameter value.

The HttpParameterBinding class is abstract and is derived to provide binding implementation classes that override the ExecuteBindingAsync method to provide values from different data sources, including the request URL and body.

Don't worry too much about the HttpParameterBinding class at the moment, other than to keep in mind that each of the techniques that I show you in the sections that follow produces an instance of the HttpParameterBinding class that Web API will cache and then use when it needs a value for a parameter. I show you how to create a custom HttpParameterBinding implementation in the "Creating a Custom Attribute Based on the ParameterBindingAttribute Class" section.

Applying a Value Provider Factory with an Attribute

The first place that Web API looks when it needs a value is at the attributes that have been applied to the parameter in the action method. In particular, Web API looks for attributes that are derived from the abstract ParameterBindingAttribute class, which is defined in the System.Web.Http.Controllers namespace. Listing 15-10 shows the definition of the ParameterBindingAttribute class.

Listing 15-10. The Definition of the ParameterBindingAttribute Class

```
using System.Web.Http.Controllers;

namespace System.Web.Http

    [AttributeUsage(AttributeTargets.Class | AttributeTargets.Parameter,
        Inherited = true, AllowMultiple = false)]
    public abstract class ParameterBindingAttribute : Attribute {

        public abstract HttpParameterBinding GetBinding(HttpParameterDescriptor
            parameter);
    }
}
```

335

The definition of the attribute is simple once you know that Web API is trying to find an HttpParameterBinding object for each parameter. The ParameterBindingAttribute defines an abstract GetBinding method, which takes an HttpParameterDescriptor object and returns an HttpParameterBinding that can be cached and then used when Web API handles a request that targets the action method that defines the parameter.

The HttpParameterDescriptor class is used to describe the parameter for which Web API is looking for a binding. It defines the properties shown in Table 15-7. Some of these properties are used only when binding and validating complex types, which I describe in Chapter 18.

Table 15-7. *The Properties Defined by the HttpParameterDescriptor Class*

Name	Description
ActionName	Returns the name of the action method.
Configuration	Returns the HttpConfiguration object.
DefaultValue	Returns the default value for the parameter type.
IsOptional	Returns true if the parameter is optional. (See the "Extending the Default Behavior" section for an interesting aspect of using optional parameters.)
ParameterBindingAttribute	Returns the attribute, if any, applied to the parameter to control binding.
ParameterName	Returns the name of the parameter.
ParameterType	Returns the type of the parameter.
Prefix	Returns the prefix of the parameter. I explain prefixes in Chapters 16 and 17.

The job of the ParameterBindingAttribute.GetBinding method is to process an HttpParameterDescriptor object that describes a parameter and produce an HttpParameterBinding object that will be able to produce a value for that parameter at runtime. This pattern—producing an HttpParameterBinding in exchange for an HttpParameterDescriptor—recurs through this part of the chapter because it is the fundamental mechanism that Web API uses to handle parameter binding.

Using the Built-in Parameter Binding Attribute

Web API includes a ValueProvider attribute that can be applied to attributes so that values are obtained through a value provider factory. In Listing 15-11, you can see how I have updated the SumNumbers action method in the Bindings controller to define a new parameter and used the ValueProvider attribute to tell Web API that the value should be obtained from the value provider factory that I defined in the previous section.

Listing 15-11. Adding a Parameter Bound by a Value Provider Factory in the BindingsController.cs File

```
using System.Web.Http;
using ExampleApp.Models;
using System.Web.Http.ValueProviders;
using ExampleApp.Infrastructure;

namespace ExampleApp.Controllers {
    public class BindingsController : ApiController {
        private IRepository repo;
```

```
    public BindingsController(IRepository repoArg) {
        repo = repoArg;
    }

    [HttpGet]
    [HttpPost]
    public string SumNumbers(Numbers numbers,
            [ValueProvider(typeof(HeaderValueProviderFactory))] string accept) {
        return string.Format("{0} (Accept: {1})",
            numbers.First + numbers.Second, accept);
    }
    }
}
```

I have defined a new parameter called `accept`, to which I have applied the `ValueProvider` attribute. In addition to defining the new parameter and applying the attribute, I have changed the return type of the method to `string` so that I can include the value of the `accept` parameter in the response sent to the client.

The `accept` parameter is a simple type for which the default behavior would not be able to find a value without the `ValueProvider` attribute. (Without the attribute, the default behavior would be to act as though the `FromUri` attribute had been applied and try to find a value for `accept` in the routing data or query string.)

To override the default behavior, I have used the `ValueProvider` attribute, which takes an argument that specifies the type of the value provider factory that should be used to get a value for the parameter, like this:

```
...
[ValueProvider(typeof(HeaderValueProviderFactory))] string accept
...
```

To test the parameter binding attribute, start the application, navigate to `/Home/Bindings` using the browser, and click the Send Request button. The data that is displayed includes the Accept header. For jQuery, the Accept header defaults to `*/*`, as shown in Figure 15-1.

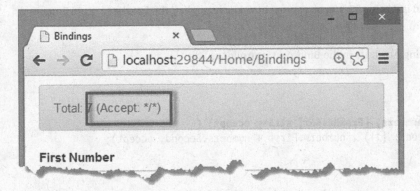

Figure 15-1. *Displaying a value obtained from a request header via parameter binding*

Creating a Custom Attribute Based on the ModelBindingAttribute Class

Using the ValueProvider attribute works, but including the name of the value provider factory alongside every parameter leads to code that is hard to read. Fortunately, it is a simple matter to create a custom attribute class that is tailored to a specific value provider factory by deriving from the ModelBinderAttribute class. (It isn't possible to derive from the ValueProviderAttribute class because it is sealed.)

The ModelBindingAttribute class is derived from ParameterBindingAttribute, and it is used to specify the means by which a complex type parameter is created—a process that I describe in detail in Chapter 16. For the purposes of this chapter, the ModelBindingAttribute class is interesting because it defines a GetValueProviderFactories method that can be overridden to return an enumeration of ValueProviderFactory classes that should be used to obtain a value for a simple type parameter.

Listing 15-12 shows the contents of the FromHeaderAttribute.cs class file that I added to the Infrastructure folder and used to define a custom attribute from the ModelBindingAttribute class.

Listing 15-12. The Contents of the FromHeaderAttribute.cs File

```
using System.Collections.Generic;
using System.Web.Http;
using System.Web.Http.ModelBinding;
using System.Web.Http.ValueProviders;

namespace ExampleApp.Infrastructure {
    public class FromHeaderAttribute : ModelBinderAttribute {

        public override IEnumerable<ValueProviderFactory>
            GetValueProviderFactories(HttpConfiguration configuration) {
              return new ValueProviderFactory[] { new HeaderValueProviderFactory() };
        }
    }
}
```

I have overridden the GetValueProviderFactories method so that it returns an instance of the HeaderValueProviderFactory class, and in Listing 15-13 you can see how I have applied the FromHeader attribute to the Bindings controller.

Listing 15-13. Applying a Custom Binding Attribute in the BindingsController.cs File

```
...
[HttpGet]
[HttpPost]
public string SumNumbers(Numbers numbers, [FromHeader] string accept) {
    return string.Format("{0} (Accept: {1})", numbers.First + numbers.Second, accept);
}
...
```

My custom attribute allows me to bind parameters to header values without having to specify the type of the value provider factory in the action method signature.

Creating a Custom Attribute Based on the ParameterBindingAttribute Class

Creating a custom attribute using the ModelBindingAttribute is the simplest technique, but I am also going to demonstrate how to create an attribute based on the ParameterBindingAttribute class, without the use of any intermediary classes that have other roles within Web API.

The first step is to derive from the `HttpParameterBinding` class to create an implementation whose `ExecuteBindingAsync` method gets its values via my custom value provider factory. Listing 15-14 shows the contents of the `HeaderValueParameterBinding.cs` class file that I added to the `Infrastructure` folder.

Listing 15-14. The Contents of the HeaderValueParameterBinding.cs File

```
using System.Threading;
using System.Threading.Tasks;
using System.Web.Http.Controllers;
using System.Web.Http.Metadata;
using System.Web.Http.ValueProviders;

namespace ExampleApp.Infrastructure {
    public class HeaderValueParameterBinding : HttpParameterBinding {
        private HeaderValueProviderFactory factory;

        public HeaderValueParameterBinding(HttpParameterDescriptor descriptor)
            : base(descriptor) {
            factory = new HeaderValueProviderFactory();
        }

        public override Task ExecuteBindingAsync(ModelMetadataProvider metadataProvider,
                HttpActionContext context, CancellationToken cancellationToken) {

            IValueProvider valueProvider = factory.GetValueProvider(context);
            if (valueProvider != null) {
                ValueProviderResult result
                    = valueProvider.GetValue(Descriptor.ParameterName);
                if (result != null) {
                    SetValue(context, result.RawValue);
                }
            }
            return Task.FromResult<object>(null);
        }
    }
}
```

Remember that the goal of a parameter binding is to call the `SetValue` method to provide the value that will be used for the parameter when its action method is invoked. The `ExecuteBindingAsync` method is asynchronous, but all of the classes that I rely on are synchronous, so I satisfy the return type of the method by using the `Task.FromResult` method, which returns a `Task` that completes immediately, like this:

```
...
return Task.FromResult<object>(null);
...
```

This technique is perfectly acceptable for short, simple methods where the cost of creating and starting a `Task` is likely to require more work and time than performing the work synchronously.

Now that I have a custom derivation of the `HttpParameterBinding` class, I can update the custom binding attribute, as shown in Listing 15-15.

Listing 15-15. Deriving from the ParameterBindingAttribute Class in the FromHeaderAttribute.cs File

```
using System.Collections.Generic;
using System.Web.Http;
using System.Web.Http.ModelBinding;
using System.Web.Http.ValueProviders;
using System.Web.Http.Controllers;

namespace ExampleApp.Infrastructure {
    public class FromHeaderAttribute : ParameterBindingAttribute {
        public override HttpParameterBinding GetBinding(HttpParameterDescriptor param) {
            return new HeaderValueParameterBinding(param);
        }
    }
}
```

The FromHeaderAttribute class directly follows the pattern I described earlier: processing an HttpParameterDescriptor object in order to create an HttpParameterBinding object that Web API will cache and use to get values for a parameter when requests target its action method.

Extending the Default Behavior

I am going to jump ahead to the third place that Web API looks for a value during parameter binding. If there is no directly applied parameter binding attribute and no binding rule (which I describe in the "Creating a Parameter Binding Rule" section), then binding proceeds as though the parameter had been decorated with the FromUri attribute, even if it has not.

■ **Tip** This applies only to simple type parameters. The default behavior for complex type parameters is to proceed as though the FromBody attribute has been applied. I explain how this works in Chapters 16 and 17.

Listing 15-16 shows the definition of the FromUriAttribute class, tidied up and with some error handling statements removed. You can see that this attribute is derived from ModelBinderAttribute and overrides the GetValueProviderFactories method to produce an enumeration of value provider factories.

Listing 15-16. The Definition of the FromUriAttribute Class

```
using System.Collections.Generic;
using System.Web.Http.ModelBinding;
using System.Web.Http.ValueProviders;

namespace System.Web.Http {

    [AttributeUsage(AttributeTargets.Class | AttributeTargets.Parameter,
        Inherited = true, AllowMultiple = false)]
    public sealed class FromUriAttribute : ModelBinderAttribute {
```

```
        public override IEnumerable<ValueProviderFactory>
            GetValueProviderFactories(HttpConfiguration configuration) {

        foreach (ValueProviderFactory f
                in base.GetValueProviderFactories(configuration)) {
            if (f is IUriValueProviderFactory) {
                yield return f;
            }
        }
    }
  }
}
```

The attribute class is simple, but there are two aspects of it that bear explanation, one of which is a trap for the unwary. First, notice that the FromUriAttribute.GetValueProviderFactories implementation gets its data from the base class implementation of the same method.

```
...
foreach (ValueProviderFactory f in base.GetValueProviderFactories(configuration)) {
...
```

This is important because I want to add my value provider factory to the set used by the FromUri attribute so that it becomes part of the default behavior. Here is the implementation of the GetValueProviderFactories method in the ModelBinderAttribute class:

```
...
public virtual IEnumerable<ValueProviderFactory>
        GetValueProviderFactories(HttpConfiguration configuration) {
    return configuration.Services.GetValueProviderFactories();
}
...
```

The value provider factories used by the FromUri attribute are obtained from the configuration services collection, which I described in Chapter 9.

The second aspect of the way that the FromUri attribute works is the one to watch out for. Not all of the value provider factory classes are used to locate values.

```
...
foreach (ValueProviderFactory f in base.GetValueProviderFactories(configuration)) {
    if (f is IUriValueProviderFactory) {
        yield return f;
    }
}
...
```

Only those value provider factory classes that implement the IUriValueProviderFactory interface are returned from the FromUriAttribute.GetValueProviderFactories method. The IUriValueProviderFactory interface defines no methods, and no error will be reported if you don't declare the interface in a custom factory class; it just won't be used to get simple type values as part of the default behavior.

Registering the Value Provider Factory

Knowing how the FromUri attribute works allows me to easily integrate header values into my application. First I have to update the HeaderValueProviderFactory class to implement the IUriValueProviderFactory interface, as shown in Listing 15-17.

Listing 15-17. Implementing IUriValueProviderFactory in the HeaderValueProviderFactory.cs File

```
using System.Net.Http;
using System.Web.Http.Controllers;
using System.Web.Http.ValueProviders;

namespace ExampleApp.Infrastructure {

    public class HeaderValueProviderFactory : ValueProviderFactory,
            IUriValueProviderFactory {
        public override IValueProvider GetValueProvider(HttpActionContext context) {
            if (context.Request.Method == HttpMethod.Post) {
                return new HeaderValueProvider(new HeadersMap(context.Request.Headers));
            } else {
                return null;
            }
        }
    }
}
```

Now I can register my value provider factory as part of the services collection, either through the dependency injection system or directly during application configuration. Listing 15-18 shows the changes I made to the WebApiConfig.cs file to register the provider factory.

Listing 15-18. Registering a Value Provider Factory in the WebApiConfig.cs File

```
using System.Web.Http;
using ExampleApp.Infrastructure;
using System.Web.Http.ValueProviders;

namespace ExampleApp {
    public static class WebApiConfig {
        public static void Register(HttpConfiguration config) {

            config.DependencyResolver = new NinjectResolver();

            config.MapHttpAttributeRoutes();

            config.Routes.MapHttpRoute(
                name: "Binding Example Route",
                routeTemplate: "api/{controller}/{action}/{first}/{second}"
            );
```

```
        config.Routes.MapHttpRoute(
            name: "DefaultApi",
            routeTemplate: "api/{controller}/{id}",
            defaults: new { id = RouteParameter.Optional }
        );

        config.Services.Add(typeof(ValueProviderFactory),
            new HeaderValueProviderFactory());
    }
  }
}
```

I have used the Add method that I described in Chapter 9 to register an instance of the HeaderValueProviderFactory class.

REGISTERING A FACTORY USING DEPENDENCY INJECTION

You can also register value provider factories through the dependency resolver class, which is asked for instances of the ValueProviderFactory class during application startup. Here is the change that would be required to the NinjectResolver.cs file:

```
...
private void AddBindings(IKernel kernel) {
    kernel.Bind<IRepository>().To<Repository>().InSingletonScope();
    kernel.Bind<ValueProviderFactory>().To<HeaderValueProviderFactory>();
}
...
```

You need register the value provider factory only once, either directly as in Listing 15-18 or in the resolver.

Updating the Controller

The final step in extending the default behavior is to update the parameter in the action method signature. There are two required changes: removing the FromHeader attribute that I added in Listing 15-12 and making the parameter optional by assigning a default value, as shown in Listing 15-19.

Listing 15-19. Updating the Action Method Parameter in the BindingsController.cs File

```
using System.Web.Http;
using ExampleApp.Models;
using System.Web.Http.ValueProviders;
using ExampleApp.Infrastructure;

namespace ExampleApp.Controllers {
    public class BindingsController : ApiController {
        private IRepository repo;
```

```
    public BindingsController(IRepository repoArg) {
        repo = repoArg;
    }


    [HttpGet]
    [HttpPost]
    public string SumNumbers(Numbers numbers, string accept = null) {
        return string.Format("{0} (Accept: {1})",
            numbers.First + numbers.Second, accept);
    }
}
}
```

I need to remove the attribute so that Web API will fall back to using the default behavior, as explained at the start of this section. The need to make the parameter optional is a little more complicated, and it arises because I am doing something that runs counter to an optimization in the way that Web API selection action methods handle requests.

For each request that it receives, Web API needs to select an action method. I describe the selection process in Chapter 22, but for the purposes of this chapter, the important part is an optimization that Web API uses to reduce the pool of possible candidates. For action methods that have one or more parameters, Web API checks to see that there is a mapping between each parameter name and a value in the combined set of properties obtained from the routing data and query string. Knowing that there are different sources of data—including the request body, which has yet to be read—the optimization checks only the parameters that are the following:

- Not optional (a default value is not assigned in the parameter definition)

- Is one of the simple types I listed in Chapter 14

- Has a binding that will obtain a value from provider factory that implements the IUriValueProviderFactory interface

There are other checks that happen as part of the selection process, but if a parameter meets all three of these conditions, Web API assumes that there must be a value in the query string or routing data in order for the action method to be able to receive the request. This is a problem for my accept header, which meets all three of the conditions but doesn't get its value from the URL. The effect is that the request sent by the client no longer selects the SumNumbers action method and generates a 404 (Not Found) response.

To get around this problem, I must ensure that my accept parameter *doesn't* meet all three conditions. I can't remove the implementation of the IUriValueProviderFactory interface from the value provider factory because the FromUriAttribute class would ignore the factory as a potential source of parameter values.

I could change the parameter so that it isn't a simple type, but that would take me into the model binding process, which I describe in Chapters 16 and 17. I want to remain focused on simple type parameters in this chapter.

That leaves the first condition that is checked: whether the parameter is optional. By assigning a default value to the accept parameter, I allow Web API to match the action method to requests that don't have a routing or query string property called accept, solving the problem.

Creating a Parameter Binding Rule

Parameter binding rules are functions that receive an HttpParameterDescriptor object and return an HttpParameterBinding object if the binding they represent will be able to provide a value for the parameter.

These functions are called while Web API is being configured and before any requests are processed, which means that the decisions the functions make are based on the definition of the parameter without any request context.

In Chapter 14, I showed you how to create a parameter binding rule that had the effect of applying the `FromUri` or `FromBody` attribute for a specific type throughout the application. Here is the statement that I added to the `WebApiConfig.cs` file to create the rule:

```
...
config.ParameterBindingRules.Insert(0, typeof(Numbers),
    x => x.BindWithAttribute(new FromUriAttribute()));
...
```

I used an extension method, `BindWithAttribute`, as shorthand to create an `HttpParameterBinding` object whose `ExecuteBindingAsync` method gets its values from the `FromUriAttribute` class for parameters whose type is `Numbers`.

Most parameter binding rules are for a specific type, which works nicely for complex type parameters where the effect of a rule will be limited and contained. I can't use a type-specific rule for my header values because the rule would apply to all `string` parameters, even those whose values should come from somewhere else. I need to be more specific about the parameters that my rule applies to or ensure that I can provide values for all simple-type parameters. I'll show you both approaches in the sections that follow.

Relying on the Parameter Name

To identify a parameter that will correspond to a header value, I need to use the properties defined by the `HttpParameterDescriptor` class, as described in Table 15-7. This is the only source of information that my rule function has and means I need some way of detecting the parameters I am interested in based on their name, type, optionality, or the action method in which they are defined.

The obvious choice is to use the parameter name and compare it to a list of request headers. This is not ideal because it creates a special class of reserved names that can't be used for action method parameters that are not going to be bound from the headers, but it is an interesting technique that lets me demonstrate how the parameter binding rule system works.

At the start of the chapter, I explained that request headers are represented by the `HttpHeaders` class and accessed through the `HttpRequestMessage.Headers` property. In fact, the `Headers` property returns an `HttpRequestHeaders` object, which is derived from `HttpHeaders` and defines convenience properties for the headers that the HTTP specification allows in requests. I find the convenience properties rather frustrating to work with because they return objects that parse the header values, rather than let me work directly with the string values, so I prefer to work with the members defined by the `HttpHeaders` class directly. However, the `HttpRequestHeaders` convenience properties are useful to me here because I can treat them as an authoritative list of parameter names for which values should be obtained from the request headers.

In Listing 15-20, you can see the binding parameter rule that I added to the `WebApiConfig.cs` file. The rule tells Web API to use the `HeaderValueParameterBinding` class I defined in Listing 15-14 when a property name corresponds to a value HTTP header name.

Listing 15-20. Adding a Parameter Binding Rule to the WebApiConfig.cs File

```
using System.Web.Http;
using ExampleApp.Infrastructure;
using System.Web.Http.ValueProviders;
using System.Net.Http.Headers;

namespace ExampleApp {
    public static class WebApiConfig {
        public static void Register(HttpConfiguration config) {
```

```
        config.DependencyResolver = new NinjectResolver();

        config.MapHttpAttributeRoutes();

        config.Routes.MapHttpRoute(
            name: "Binding Example Route",
            routeTemplate: "api/{controller}/{action}/{first}/{second}"
        );

        config.Routes.MapHttpRoute(
            name: "DefaultApi",
            routeTemplate: "api/{controller}/{id}",
            defaults: new { id = RouteParameter.Optional }
        );

        config.Services.Add(typeof(ValueProviderFactory),
            new HeaderValueProviderFactory());

        config.ParameterBindingRules.Add(x =>
            typeof(HttpRequestHeaders).GetProperty(x.ParameterName) != null
                ? new HeaderValueParameterBinding(x)
                : null);
    }
  }
}
```

I have expressed the parameter binding rule as a lambda expression. I use standard .NET reflection to see whether the HttpRequestHeaders class has a property that matches the parameter name; if it does, I return an instance of the HeaderValueParameterBinding class.

If there is no matching HTTP header, then I return null, which tells Web API that this binding rule is unable to provide a value for the parameter. The search will continue through any other parameter binding rules that have been defined, and the default behavior described in the previous section will be used if none of the rules provides an HttpParameterBinding object.

■ **Tip** Parameters bound using the rule shown in Listing 15-21 must still be optional. I have changed the way that values are located for the parameter, but that has no effect on the optimization I described in the action method selection process.

Handling All Simple Type Values

The problem with the technique in the previous section is that it creates a list of reserved parameter names. It isn't a huge problem because you can apply the FromUri attribute to parameters that need to get values from the URL that are also header names, but it can cause confusion for the unwary.

I need some way to tell which parameters should have values bound from a request header, allowing me to focus on the HeaderValueParameterBinding class as narrowly as possible.

An alternative approach is to provide values for a wider range of parameters but take responsibility for finding values for them even when there is no corresponding header. The simplest way to do this is to build on the built-in functionality and follow the approach taken by the FromUriAttribute by using all of the value provider factories in the service collection.

To demonstrate how this can be done, I added a `MultiFactoryParameterBinding.cs` file to the `Infrastructure` folder and used it to define the class shown in Listing 15-21.

Listing 15-21. The Contents of the MultiFactoryParameterBinding.cs File

```
using System.Threading;
using System.Threading.Tasks;
using System.Web.Http;
using System.Web.Http.Controllers;
using System.Web.Http.Metadata;
using System.Web.Http.ValueProviders;

namespace ExampleApp.Infrastructure {
    public class MultiFactoryParameterBinding : HttpParameterBinding {

        public MultiFactoryParameterBinding(HttpParameterDescriptor descriptor)
            : base(descriptor) {
                // do nothing
        }

        public override Task ExecuteBindingAsync(ModelMetadataProvider metadataProvider,
                HttpActionContext actionContext, CancellationToken cancellationToken) {

            foreach (ValueProviderFactory factory in
                GlobalConfiguration.Configuration.Services.GetValueProviderFactories()) {

                if (factory is HeaderValueProviderFactory
                        || factory is IUriValueProviderFactory) {
                    IValueProvider provider = factory.GetValueProvider(actionContext);
                    ValueProviderResult result = null;
                    if (provider != null && (result =
                            provider.GetValue(Descriptor.ParameterName)) != null) {
                        SetValue(actionContext, result.RawValue);
                        break;
                    }
                }
            }
            return Task.FromResult<object>(null);
        }
    }
}
```

■ **Tip** This class relies on the order in which the value providers are registered in the services collection. This allows you to control the source of data values, but you must ensure that the built-in factories appear before custom ones if you want to give preference to locating data from the request URL. The built-in factories are registered before custom ones, so you should use the Add method when registering your factory. If you want your factory to have precedence over the built-in classes, then use the Insert method instead.

The ExecuteBindingAsync method gets the set of ValueProviderFactory objects in the services collection and uses a foreach loop to call the GetValueProvider method on each of them to try to get an IValueProvider object and, in turn, get a value for the parameter. This continues until a value is provided, at which point I call the SetValue method and break out of the loop.

■ **Tip** The ExecuteBindingAsync method is asynchronous, which is useful if you need to look up a data value from a database or perform a complex calculation. It is, however, overkill if you are simply obtaining a value from the request. Rather than create a Task to get the data value, I perform the work synchronously and call Task.FromResult<object>(null) to create a completed Task that has no result.

This is the same approach taken by the default behavior I described in the previous section, except that I have added explicit support for the HeaderValueProviderFactory class as well as factories that implement the IUriValueProviderFactory interface. By default, there are three value provider factories that may be able to provide a value—my custom factory and the two built-in factories described in Table 15-8.

Table 15-8. *The Built-in Value Provider Factory Classes*

Name	Description
QueryStringValueProviderFactory	Provides values from the query string.
RouteDataValueProviderFactory	Provides values from the routing data. See Chapters 20 and 21 for details of Web API routing.

The reason that I have added explicit support for the HeaderValueProviderFactory class is so that I can work around the action method selection optimization I described earlier. I had to implement the IUriValueProviderFactory interface in the HeaderValueProviderFactory when I was relying on the default behavior and then make the accept parameter optional so that the action method would match the request—but with explicit support in the parameter binding, I can remove the IUriValueProviderFactory interface, and the accept parameter no longer needs to be optional. Listing 15-22 shows how I revised the HeaderValueProviderFactory class to remove the IUriValueProviderFactory interface.

Listing 15-22. Removing an Interface in the HeaderValueProviderFactory.cs File

```
using System.Net.Http;
using System.Web.Http.Controllers;
using System.Web.Http.ValueProviders;

namespace ExampleApp.Infrastructure {

    public class HeaderValueProviderFactory : ValueProviderFactory {
        public override IValueProvider GetValueProvider(HttpActionContext context) {
            if (context.Request.Method == HttpMethod.Post) {
                return new HeaderValueProvider(new HeadersMap(context.Request.Headers));
            } else {
                return null;
            }
        }
    }
}
```

Listing 15-23 shows the change I made to the Bindings controller so the accept parameter defined by the SumNumbers action method is not optional.

Listing 15-23. Changing a Parameter Definition in the BindingsController.cs File

```
...
[HttpGet]
[HttpPost]
public string SumNumbers(Numbers numbers, string accept) {
    return string.Format("{0} (Accept: {1})", numbers.First + numbers.Second, accept);
}
...
```

The final step is to create the parameter binding rule in the WebApiConfig.cs file, as shown in Listing 15-24.

Listing 15-24. Defining a Parameter Binding Rule in the WebApiConfig.cs File

```
using System.Web.Http;
using ExampleApp.Infrastructure;
using System.Web.Http.ValueProviders;
using System.Net.Http.Headers;

namespace ExampleApp {
    public static class WebApiConfig {
        public static void Register(HttpConfiguration config) {

            config.DependencyResolver = new NinjectResolver();

            // ...routing statements omitted for brevity...

            config.Services.Add(typeof(ValueProviderFactory),
                new HeaderValueProviderFactory());

            config.ParameterBindingRules.Add(x => {
                return x.ParameterType.IsPrimitive || x.ParameterType == typeof(string)
                    ? new MultiFactoryParameterBinding(x) :
                    null;
            });
        }
    }
}
```

I created the parameter binding rule using the version of the Add method that takes a Func<HttpParameterDescriptor, HttpParameterBinding> argument. When using a lambda expression, this means that the HttpParameterDescriptor goes to an HttpParameterBinding instance, but only if the parameter is one that the rule wants to support. I use the HttpParameterDescriptor.ParameterType property to see whether the property is a primitive type or a string and, if so, return an instance of the MultiFactoryParameterBinding class. If the parameter isn't a type I want to work with, I return null to signal that I don't want to provide a binding and that Web API should continue checking other rules.

Summary

In this chapter, I showed you how value providers and value provider factories work and how they are used by ASP. NET Web API. I explained the sequence that Web API uses to locate parameter bindings during the application startup process and how the results are used to obtain values for action method parameters when requests arrive, allowing custom value providers and factories to supplement the standard sources of data. In Chapter 16, I explain how value providers form the foundation of the model binding feature, which allows complex types to be bound from data obtained by value providers.

CHAPTER 16

■ ■ ■

Binding Complex Data Types Part I

In Chapter 15, I showed you how to bind simple data types from the request URL using value providers. In this chapter, I describe *model binders*, which build on the foundation of value providers to allow binding of complex types. I describe the built-in model binders, which bind a comprehensive range of types, in this chapter. I also explain how to create and apply a custom model binder for dealing with types that the built-in binders cannot deal with.

Model binders work only with value providers, meaning that data values are obtained from the URL. It is media type formatters that are responsible for create complex types from the data in the request body. I introduced media type formatters in Chapter 12 when I showed you how data objects are serialized from action method results. In Chapter 17, I explain how media type formatters are used to deserialize data and create model objects for action method parameters. Table 16-1 summarizes this chapter.

Table 16-1. *Chapter Summary*

Problem	Solution	Listing
Bind an object from the URL.	Format the URL or query string so that the properties it contains correspond to the properties of the model class.	1–8
Broaden the source of values for model binding.	Use the ModelBinder interface to include value providers that implement the IUriValueProviderFactory interface.	9–12
Bind arrays of simple types.	Format the data so that the routing or query string properties have the same name.	13–17
Bind key-value pairs.	Format the data to use array-style indexers.	18–19
Create a custom model binder.	Implement the IModelBinder interface.	20–24
Apply a custom model binder.	Use the ModelBinder attribute and, optionally, add the binder to the services collection. You can also create a parameter binding rule to apply the model binder.	25–31
Instantiate a model class using data expressed in a single routing or query string property.	Create a type converter and apply it with the TypeConverter attribute.	32–35

Preparing the Example Project

I am going to continue working with the ExampleApp project I have been using throughout this part of the book. To prepare for this chapter, I have removed the statement in the WebApiConfig.cs file that I used in Chapter 17 to create a parameter binding rule. Listing 16-1 shows WebApiConfig.cs after I removed the statements.

Listing 16-1. The WebApiConfig.cs File

```
using System.Web.Http;
using ExampleApp.Infrastructure;
using System.Web.Http.ValueProviders;
using System.Net.Http.Headers;

namespace ExampleApp {
    public static class WebApiConfig {
        public static void Register(HttpConfiguration config) {

            config.DependencyResolver = new NinjectResolver();

            config.MapHttpAttributeRoutes();

            config.Routes.MapHttpRoute(
                name: "Binding Example Route",
                routeTemplate: "api/{controller}/{action}/{first}/{second}"
            );

            config.Routes.MapHttpRoute(
                name: "DefaultApi",
                routeTemplate: "api/{controller}/{id}",
                defaults: new { id = RouteParameter.Optional }
            );

            config.Services.Add(typeof(ValueProviderFactory),
                new HeaderValueProviderFactory());
        }
    }
}
```

■ **Tip** Remember that you don't have to create the example project yourself. You can download the source code for every chapter for free from Apress.com.

Without the binding rule, Web API won't be able to find a value for the accept parameter on the SumNumbers action method of the Binding controller. I will be focused on binding classes in this chapter, so I removed the parameter, as shown in Listing 16-2.

Listing 16-2. Removing an Action Method Parameter in the BindingsController.cs File

```
using System.Web.Http;
using ExampleApp.Models;
using System.Web.Http.ValueProviders;
using ExampleApp.Infrastructure;

namespace ExampleApp.Controllers {
    public class BindingsController : ApiController {
        private IRepository repo;
```

```
    public BindingsController(IRepository repoArg) {
        repo = repoArg;
    }

    [HttpGet]
    [HttpPost]
    public string SumNumbers([FromUri]Numbers numbers) {
        return string.Format("{0}", numbers.First + numbers.Second);
    }
  }
}
```

Notice that I have applied the FromUri attribute to the numbers parameter. I start this chapter by showing you how to bind complex type arguments from the URL, so I need to specify that the data values for the Numbers object should not be obtained from the request body.

The final preparation I need to make for this chapter is to change the Ajax request made in the bindings.js file so that it uses the GET verb and includes the model data in the query string, as shown in Listing 16-3.

Listing 16-3. Changing the Ajax Request Verb in the bindings.js File

```
var viewModel = ko.observable({ first: 2, second: 5 });
var response = ko.observable("Ready");
var gotError = ko.observable(false);

var sendRequest = function (requestType) {
    $.ajax("/api/bindings/sumnumbers", {
        type: "GET",
        data: viewModel(),
        success: function (data) {
            gotError(false);
            response("Total: " + data);
        },
        error: function (jqXHR) {
            gotError(true);
            response(jqXHR.status + " (" + jqXHR.statusText + ")");
        }
    });
};

$(document).ready(function () {
    ko.applyBindings();
});
```

To test the changes before proceeding to the rest of the chapter, start the application and use the browser to navigate to the /Home/Bindings URL. Click the Send Request button; the values in the input elements will be sent to the web services, and the results will be displayed at the top of the browser window, as illustrated in Figure 16-1.

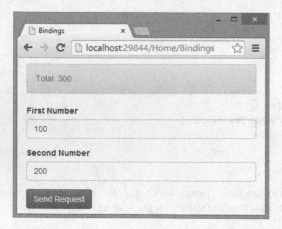

Figure 16-1. *Preparing the example application*

Using the Built-in Model Binders

In Chapter 15, I showed you how value providers are able to obtain data values from the URL to bind simple type parameters. Model binders build on the foundation of value providers to combine data values from the request into instances of complex types.

■ **Tip**   As a reminder, the simple types are TimeSpan, DateTime, Guid, string, char, bool, int, uint, byte, sbyte, short, ushort, long, ulong, float, double, and decimal. Any other type is a complex type, including arrays and collections of simple types.

Web API comes with a set of built-in model binders that can bind objects in the most common situations. The built-in binders are comprehensive enough that most applications don't need customizations at all. In this section, I explain how the built-in model binders work and how you can adapt their behavior if you need customized binding support.

Table 16-2 lists the built-in binder classes that you will encounter most often. You don't need to work directly with these classes, but they can be useful as a foundation when creating custom binders, as I describe in the "Working with Custom Model Binders" section later in this chapter. The classes listed in Table 16-2 are defined in the System.Web.Http.ModelBinding.Binders namespace.

Table 16-2. *The Built-in Model Binder Classes*

Name	Description
ArrayModelBinder	Binds an array of objects. See the "Binding Collections and Arrays" section for details.
CollectionModelBinder	Binds a strongly typed List or Enumerable. See the "Binding Collections and Arrays" section for details.
DictionaryModelBinder	Binds key-value pairs to a strongly typed Dictionary. See the "Binding Key-Value Pairs" section for details.
MutableObjectModelBinder	Binds objects. See the "Binding Objects" section for details.
TypeConverterModelBinder	Binds objects using a type converter, which I describe in the "Using Type Converters" section.

Later in this chapter, I explain how the overall model binding feature works and show you how to create and apply a custom model binder. Table 16-3 puts the default model binders in context.

Table 16-3. *Putting the Default Model Binders in Context*

Question	Answer
What are they?	The built-in model binders are used by Web API to instantiate classes, arrays, and collections using request data values obtained from value providers.
When should you use them?	The built-in model binders are used when the FromUri or ModelBinder attribute is used. See the "Broadening the Source of Binding Values" section for details of the difference between these two attributes.
What do you need to know?	Web API includes default model binders that can deal with instantiating and populating most classes. You should need to create a custom binder only when a class requires special care to instantiate.

Binding Objects

I am going to start by describing how Web API binds a single instance of a class to a parameter, not least because this is what is already happening when the SumNumbers action method is invoked in the example application.

I used the FromUri attribute in Chapter 15 to enable the binding of simple type parameters using value type providers. As I explained in the previous section, model binders build on value providers to get multiple values to create an object, and the FromUri attribute can enable this feature for complex type arguments, which is why I applied it to the numbers parameter.

```
...
public string SumNumbers([FromUri]Numbers numbers) {
...
```

The FromUri attribute *isn't* a model binder, which is a class that is responsible for creating a specific type of object. Instead, FromUri is a *model binding attribute*, which tells Web API to use the model binder classes to create an instance of the parameter type, which is Numbers in this case.

A model binder is a class responsible for using one or more values from the value providers to create an instance of the *model type*, which is used as an argument when invoking the action method. The built-in model binder that deals with objects works in two steps:

1. Use the parameterless constructor to create a new instance of the model type.

2. Set each property defined by the model type using a value from the value providers.

These two steps are the reason why most model types are just a collection of automatically implemented properties: there is no point in defining a constructor with parameters because it will prevent the model binder from creating an instance and because methods and get-only properties will be ignored by the model binder. The Numbers class is a good, although simple, example.

```
...
public class Numbers {
    public int First { get; set; }
    public int Second { get; set; }
}
...
```

■ **Note**   Throughout this chapter, I will make changes to the bindings.js file to send different kinds of requests to the web service, but I don't change the corresponding HTML in the Razor view because it is the format of the request that is important, not the ability of the user to change the data values used in the request. To test the changes, start the application, navigate to the /Home/Bindings URL, and click the Send Request button.

Binding Multiple Objects

By default, the object model binder tries to use the name of the parameter as a prefix when asking the value providers for values for each of the properties. In the case of my example, the parameter is called numbers, which means that the model binder will try to obtain values for numbers.first and numbers.second in the request.

If the value provides can't obtain values for the prefixed names, then the model binder will ask for values without the prefix: first and second. This is the behavior I have been relying on in my examples.

Prefixes are useful because they allow a client to send data for multiple objects of the same type in the same URL. Listing 16-4 shows how I have changed the bindings.js file so that values for two Numbers objects are sent in the request query string.

Listing 16-4. Changing the Request Query String in the bindings.js File

```
var viewModel = ko.observable({ first: 2, second: 5, third: 10, fourth: 100 });
var response = ko.observable("Ready");
var gotError = ko.observable(false);

var sendRequest = function (requestType) {
    $.ajax("/api/bindings/sumnumbers", {
        type: "GET",
        data: {
            "numbers1.first": viewModel().first,
            "numbers1.second": viewModel().second,
            "numbers2.first": viewModel().third,
            "numbers2.second": viewModel().fourth
        },
```

```
        success: function (data) {
            gotError(false);
            response("Total: " + data);
        },
        error: function (jqXHR) {
            gotError(true);
            response(jqXHR.status + " (" + jqXHR.statusText + ")");
        }
    });
};

$(document).ready(function () {
    ko.applyBindings();
});
```

■ **Tip**   Notice that I have quoted the property names in the `data` settings object. The dot notation required to express a prefix can't be used as a literal property name, but JavaScript is flexible enough to be able to define properties as quoted strings.

I have added two properties to the view model and used them to create an object for the `data` setting that groups them into two prefixed sets. The changes in Listing 16-4 will send a request with the following URL:

```
/api/bindings/sumnumbers?numbers1.first=2&numbers1.second=5&numbers2.first=10
    &numbers2.second=100
```

■ **Tip**   If you test the changes now, you will see that everything seems to work but that the result returned from the web service is zero. The problem is that the model binder has created an instance of the `Numbers` class, which has initialized the two `int` properties to zero, which is their default value. The binder then tries to find `numbers.first` and `numbers.second` values, which are not in the request. The binder drops the prefix and looks for `first` and `second` values, which are not in the request either. At this point, the binder gives up, and the action method is invoked with a `Numbers` object whose properties are set to zero. The binder makes a best-effort attempt to get values, and it assumes that it isn't a problem when they don't exist. You must use the model validation feature if you want to ensure that the request contains certain values. See Chapter 18 for details.

I need to update the action method so that it has two `Numbers` parameters whose names correspond to the prefixed included in the request URL, as shown in Listing 16-5.

Listing 16-5. Changing the Action Method Parameters in the BindingsController.cs File

```
...
[HttpGet]
[HttpPost]
public string SumNumbers([FromUri] Numbers numbers1, [FromUri] Numbers numbers2) {
    return string.Format("{0}", numbers1.First + numbers1.Second
        + numbers2.First + numbers2.Second);
}
...
```

■ **Tip**   I have used parameter names numbers1 and numbers2, but that isn't required. You can use any parameter names you like and they will be used as prefixes when the binder is looking for property values.

Binding Nested Objects

Prefixes can also be used to define the structure of more complex objects. To demonstrate how this works, I have added a property to the Numbers class that is a complex type—in this case, an Operation object that is the other class defined in the BindingModels.cs file, as shown in Listing 16-6.

Listing 16-6. Adding a Property to the Numbers Class in the BindingModels.cs File

```
namespace ExampleApp.Models {

    public class Numbers {
        public int First { get; set; }
        public int Second { get; set; }
        public Operation Op { get; set; }
    }

    public class Operation {
        public bool Add { get; set; }
        public bool Double { get; set; }
    }
}
```

In Listing 16-7, you can see how I have modified the jQuery request so that it contains the prefixed values needed to create an instance of the modified Numbers class.

Listing 16-7. Changing the Request Query String in the bindings.js File

```
var viewModel = ko.observable({ first: 2, second: 5, add: true, double: true });
var response = ko.observable("Ready");
var gotError = ko.observable(false);

var sendRequest = function (requestType) {
    $.ajax("/api/bindings/sumnumbers", {
        type: "GET",
```

```
    data: {
        "numbers.first": viewModel().first,
        "numbers.second": viewModel().second,
        "numbers.op.add": viewModel().add,
        "numbers.op.double": viewModel().double
    },
    success: function (data) {
        gotError(false);
        response("Total: " + data);
    },
    error: function (jqXHR) {
        gotError(true);
        response(jqXHR.status + " (" + jqXHR.statusText + ")");
    }
    });
};


$(document).ready(function () {
    ko.applyBindings();
});
```

These changes create a request like this:

```
api/bindings/sumnumbers?numbers.first=2&numbers.second=5&numbers.op.add=true
    &numbers.op.double=true
```

Listing 16-8 shows the changes that I made to the action method to receive the data values from the query string via the model binder.

Listing 16-8. Changing the Action Method Parameters in the BindingsController.cs File

```
...
[HttpGet]
[HttpPost]
public string SumNumbers([FromUri] Numbers numbers) {
    var result = numbers.Op.Add ? numbers.First + numbers.Second
        : numbers.First - numbers.Second;
    return string.Format("{0}", numbers.Op.Double ? result * 2: result);
}
...
```

I don't need to take any special steps to ensure that the model binder populates the properties of the nested Operations object because the model binder tries to locate values for it automatically.

Broadening the Source of Binding Values

A model binding attribute is a broker between a set of value provider factories and the model binding classes that can create different types. In using the FromUri attribute, I activated the model binding process, but I did so with a subset of the available value providers. As I explained in Chapter 15, the FromUri attribute filters out any value provider factory that doesn't implement the IUriValueProviderFactory interface. I worked around this in Chapter 15 by implementing the interface in my custom value provider factory so that I could bind simple type parameters from request headers, but there is an alternative approach: you can use the ModelBinder attribute, from which the FromUri attribute is derived.

The only difference between the ModelBinder and FromUri attributes is that ModelBinder uses all of the available value provider factories. In this section, I demonstrate how to use the ModelBinder attribute so that values from individual model type properties can come from a broader range of value provider factories.

The first change is to add a new property to the model class that will correspond to a request header. Listing 16-9 shows the addition of an Accept property to the Numbers class. (Ignore that there is no good reason to mix headers with the int values in the Numbers class—it is the technique that is important in this example.)

Listing 16-9. Adding a Property to a Model Class in the BindingModels.cs File

```
...
public class Numbers {
    public int First { get; set; }
    public int Second { get; set; }
    public Operation Op { get; set; }
    public string Accept { get; set; }
}
...
```

I removed the IUriValueProviderFactory interface from the HeaderValueProviderFactory at the end of Chapter 15, but I still need to make some changes to the class. When I created the HeaderValueProviderFactory class, I implemented the GetValueProvider method so that it would return an instance of the HeaderValueProvider class only for POST requests. I am working with GET requests in this chapter, so I have removed statements from the GetValueProvider method so that the request verb isn't checked, as shown in Listing 16-10.

Listing 16-10. Removing the HTTP Method Restriction in the HeaderValueProviderFactory.cs File

```
using System.Net.Http;
using System.Web.Http.Controllers;
using System.Web.Http.ValueProviders;

namespace ExampleApp.Infrastructure {

    public class HeaderValueProviderFactory : ValueProviderFactory {
        public override IValueProvider GetValueProvider(HttpActionContext context) {
            //if (context.Request.Method == HttpMethod.Post) {
                return new HeaderValueProvider(new HeadersMap(context.Request.Headers));
            //} else {
            //    return null;
            //}
        }
    }
}
```

I also need to modify the HeaderValueProvider class so that is able to cope with prefixes. Listing 16-11 shows the changes.

Listing 16-11. Adding Prefix Support in the HeaderValueProvider.cs File

```
using System.Globalization;
using System.Web.Http.ValueProviders;
using System.Linq;

namespace ExampleApp.Infrastructure {
    public class HeaderValueProvider : IValueProvider {
        private HeadersMap headers;

        public HeaderValueProvider(HeadersMap map) {
            headers = map;
        }

        public ValueProviderResult GetValue(string key) {
            string value = headers[key.Split('.').Last()];
            return value == null
                ? null
                : new ValueProviderResult(value, value, CultureInfo.InvariantCulture);
        }

        public bool ContainsPrefix(string prefix) {
            return false;
        }
    }
}
```

The binder starts by calling the GetPrefix method of the value providers to see whether any of them can process requests with the prefix numbers. Since the request data contains this prefix, the value provider responsible for managing the query string returns true, and the binder requests values for the numbers.first and numbers.second. The binder then repeats the process for the numbers.Op prefix. Finally, the binder tries to get a value for numbers.Accept.

As you can see in Listing 16-11, I used the Add method to register the HeaderValueProvider class with the services collection, and that means the built-in value providers are queried before my custom class. The effect of this is that the ContainsPrefix method isn't called because the query string value provider is asked first and is able to provide all of the values that the binder needs, with the exception of numbers.Accept. The change I made to the GetValue method splits up the request property name and extracts the last component so that I can match it to a header, providing the header with the information it needs.

■ **Tip** You might wonder why my GetValue method is asked for numbers.Accept when the ContainsPrefix method always returns false. This happens because the model binder is given access to only a single value provider, so Microsoft has defined a composite provider that consolidates the results from all of the registered value providers. The model binder is told by the consolidated provider that it can produce values with the numbers prefix because the query string value provider says it can—and that affirmation is therefore applied to all of the value providers.

The final step is to modify the controller so that it uses the ModelBinder attribute, and the result it returns to the client includes the value of the Accept request header, as shown in Listing 16-12.

Listing 16-12. Updating the Action Method in the BindingsController.cs File

```csharp
using System.Web.Http;
using ExampleApp.Models;
using System.Web.Http.ValueProviders;
using ExampleApp.Infrastructure;
using System.Web.Http.ModelBinding;

namespace ExampleApp.Controllers {
    public class BindingsController : ApiController {
        private IRepository repo;

        public BindingsController(IRepository repoArg) {
            repo = repoArg;
        }

        [HttpGet]
        [HttpPost]
        public string SumNumbers([ModelBinder] Numbers numbers) {
            var result = numbers.Op.Add
                ? numbers.First + numbers.Second
                : numbers.First - numbers.Second;

            return string.Format("{0} (Accept:{1})",
                numbers.Op.Double ? result * 2 : result, numbers.Accept);
        }
    }
}
```

The use of the ModelBinder attribute means that all of the value provider factories are used to obtain sources of data, including the custom provider that provides access to the request headers.

▪ **Tip** The name of the action method parameter is used as the prefix by default, but you can use the Name property when applying the ModelBinder attribute to specify another prefix. See the "Applying a Custom Model Binder" section for more information on using the ModelBinder attribute.

Binding Collections and Arrays

The built-in model binders are able to bind multiple related values to create collections and arrays. In Listing 16-13, you can see that I have changed the query string data sent by the client so that it includes a sequence of numeric values.

Listing 16-13. Changing the Request Data in the bindings.js File

```javascript
var viewModel = ko.observable({ first: 2, second: 5, third: 100});
var response = ko.observable("Ready");
var gotError = ko.observable(false);
```

```javascript
var sendRequest = function (requestType) {
    $.ajax("/api/bindings/sumnumbers", {
        type: "GET",
        data: {
            numbers: [viewModel().first, viewModel().second, viewModel().third]
        },
        success: function (data) {
            gotError(false);
            response("Total: " + data);
        },
        error: function (jqXHR) {
            gotError(true);
            response(jqXHR.status + " (" + jqXHR.statusText + ")");
        }
    });
};

$(document).ready(function () {
    ko.applyBindings();
});
```

These changes produce a request that targets the following URL:

```
/api/bindings/sumnumbers?numbers[]=2&numbers[]=5&numbers[]=100
```

■ **Tip** The [and] characters are escaped when the request is sent in this format and replaced with the %5B and %5D sequences.

You can omit the square brackets by setting the jQuery traditional Ajax setting to true, which will send the request in this format (both are accepted by Web API).

```
/api/bindings/sumnumbers?numbers=2&numbers=5&numbers=100
```

I have changed the SumNumbers action method to receive the array of data values, as shown in Listing 16-14.

Listing 16-14. Binding Request Data As an Array in the BindingsController.cs File

```csharp
using System.Web.Http;
using ExampleApp.Models;
using System.Web.Http.ValueProviders;
using ExampleApp.Infrastructure;
using System.Web.Http.ModelBinding;
using System.Linq;
```

```
namespace ExampleApp.Controllers {
    public class BindingsController : ApiController {
        private IRepository repo;

        public BindingsController(IRepository repoArg) {
            repo = repoArg;
        }

        [HttpGet]
        [HttpPost]
        public string SumNumbers([ModelBinder] int[] numbers) {
            return numbers.Sum().ToString();
        }
    }
}
```

The process of creating and populating the array is handled by the model binder and passed to the action method. You can elect to receive the same data as a strongly typed List, as shown in Listing 16-15.

Listing 16-15. Binding Request Data As a Strongly Typed Collection in the BindingsController.cs File

```
using System.Web.Http;
using ExampleApp.Models;
using System.Web.Http.ValueProviders;
using ExampleApp.Infrastructure;
using System.Web.Http.ModelBinding;
using System.Linq;
using System.Collections.Generic;

namespace ExampleApp.Controllers {
    public class BindingsController : ApiController {
        private IRepository repo;

        public BindingsController(IRepository repoArg) {
            repo = repoArg;
        }

        [HttpGet]
        [HttpPost]
        public string SumNumbers([ModelBinder] List<int> numbers) {
            return numbers.Sum().ToString();
        }
    }
}
```

■ **Tip** You can also bind to a strongly typed Enumerable, such as Enumerable<T>, by changing the type of the action method parameter.

Binding Arrays and Lists of Complex Types

The approach I used in the previous section can be combined with the use of prefixes to bind arrays of complex types. Listing 16-16 shows the changes I made to the bindings.js file so that jQuery sends properties that will correspond to an array of Numbers objects.

Listing 16-16. Changing the Request Data in the bindings.js File

```javascript
var viewModel = ko.observable({ first: 2, second: 5, third: 100, fourth: 200});
var response = ko.observable("Ready");
var gotError = ko.observable(false);

var sendRequest = function (requestType) {
    $.ajax("/api/bindings/sumnumbers", {
        type: "GET",
        data: {
            "numbers": [{ first: viewModel().first, second: viewModel().second },
                        { first: viewModel().third, second: viewModel().fourth }],
        },
        success: function (data) {
            gotError(false);
            response("Total: " + data);
        },
        error: function (jqXHR) {
            gotError(true);
            response(jqXHR.status + " (" + jqXHR.statusText + ")");
        }
    });
};

$(document).ready(function () {
    ko.applyBindings();
});
```

I have set the data property to an object that has a property called numbers, which in turn is set to an array of objects with first and second properties. The result is a request in this format:

```
/api/bindings/sumnumbers?numbers[0][first]=22&numbers[0][second]=5
    &numbers[1][first]=100&numbers[1][second]=200
```

The built-in binders work out the relationships between the different data items and use them to create an array of objects. Listing 16-17 shows the corresponding changes to the action method to receive an array of Numbers objects.

Listing 16-17. Receiving an Array of Complex Objects in the BindingsController.cs File

```csharp
using System.Web.Http;
using ExampleApp.Models;
using System.Web.Http.ValueProviders;
using ExampleApp.Infrastructure;
using System.Web.Http.ModelBinding;
using System.Linq;
using System.Collections.Generic;
```

```
namespace ExampleApp.Controllers {
    public class BindingsController : ApiController {
        private IRepository repo;

        public BindingsController(IRepository repoArg) {
            repo = repoArg;
        }

        [HttpGet]
        [HttpPost]
        public string SumNumbers([ModelBinder] Numbers[] numbers) {
            return numbers.Select(x => x.First + x.Second).Sum().ToString();
        }
    }
}
```

■ **Caution**   You must ensure that there are no gaps in the index values for array items. The binder stops looking for data when it fails to get a value for a specific index. If your data jumps from numbers[1] to numbers[3], for example, then the binder will fail to get a value for numbers[2] and never ask for numbers[3] or any subsequent item.

Binding Key-Value Pairs

The built-in binders are able to create a strongly typed Dictionary that contains key-value pairs. Listing 16-18 shows the changes that I made to the binders.js file to send a request with data in the format that the Dictionary binder looks for.

Listing 16-18. Sending Key-Value Request Data in the bindings.js File

```
var viewModel = ko.observable({ first: 2, second: 5, third: 100, fourth: 200 });
var response = ko.observable("Ready");
var gotError = ko.observable(false);

var sendRequest = function (requestType) {
    $.ajax("/api/bindings/sumnumbers", {
        type: "GET",
        data: { numbers: [{ key: "one", value: { first: viewModel().first,
                                second: viewModel().second }},
                        { key: "two", value: { first: viewModel().third,
                                second: viewModel().fourth }}]},
        success: function (data) {
            gotError(false);
            response("Total: " + data);
        },
        error: function (jqXHR) {
            gotError(true);
            response(jqXHR.status + " (" + jqXHR.statusText + ")");
        }
    });
};
```

```
$(document).ready(function () {
    ko.applyBindings();
});
```

The format of the object used for the data setting contains a number property (named so that the binder will match it to the action method parameter) that is set to an array of objects that has key and value properties. For this example, I am going to bind this data to a Dictionary<string, Numbers> object, and you can see that I have set the key and value properties accordingly. The key will be left as a string (although I could have used data that could be bound to any type), and the value is set to an object that has first and second properties so that it can be bound to a Numbers object. The changes in Listing 16-18 create a request with this format URL.

```
/api/bindings/sumnumbers?numbers[0][key]=one&numbers[0][value][first]=2
    &numbers[0][value][second]=52&numbers[1][key]=two&numbers[1][value][first]=100
    &numbers[1][value][second]=200
```

In Listing 16-19, you can see how I receive the dictionary in the action method.

Listing 16-19. Receiving Key-Value Pairs in the BindingsController.cs File

```
using System.Web.Http;
using ExampleApp.Models;
using System.Web.Http.ValueProviders;
using ExampleApp.Infrastructure;
using System.Web.Http.ModelBinding;
using System.Linq;
using System.Collections.Generic;

namespace ExampleApp.Controllers {
    public class BindingsController : ApiController {
        private IRepository repo;

        public BindingsController(IRepository repoArg) {
            repo = repoArg;
        }

        [HttpGet]
        [HttpPost]
        public string SumNumbers([ModelBinder] Dictionary<string, Numbers> numbers) {
            return numbers.Select(x => x.Value.First + x.Value.Second).Sum().ToString();
        }
    }
}
```

You can mix and match the techniques in this part of the chapter, and the binders will usually be able to figure it out. You can, for example, send a collection of key-value pairs where the value is an array of complex types that has a property that is an array of key-value pairs and so on.

Working with Custom Model Binders

As I demonstrated in the previous section, the built-in model binders are capable of dealing with a good range of bindings. But not every scenario is catered for; the main limitation is that classes can be instantiated only if they have a parameterless constructor, and data values can be set only through properties, for example. In the sections that follow, I explain how model binders work and show you how custom model binders can be used to address situations that the default binders are unable to deal with. Table 16-4 puts custom model binders in context.

Table 16-4. *Putting Custom Model Binders in Context*

Question	Answer
What are they?	Custom model binders allow classes that require special handling to be included in the model binding process.
When should you use them?	Use custom model binders for classes that don't have parameterless constructors or require any kind of special handling.
What do you need to know?	Custom model binders are reasonably straightforward, but be careful when handling prefixes.

Preparing the Application

The main reason to create a custom binder is to instantiate a class that the built-in binders cannot handle. This is most often the case when there is no parameterless constructor or when a particular initialization process must be performed. I see this most often with some object-relational mapping (ORM) systems that need to create the objects they operate on so they can track changes to data values. I am going to create a model binder for the Numbers class. I want to make the example more realistic, and I made some changes to the class, as shown in Listing 16-20.

Listing 16-20. Changing the Numbers Classin the BindingModels.cs File

```
namespace ExampleApp.Models {

    public class Numbers {
        private int first, second;

        public Numbers(int firstVal, int secondVal) {
            first = firstVal; second = secondVal;
        }

        public int First {
            get { return first; }
        }

        public int Second {
            get { return second; }
        }

        public Operation Op { get; set; }
        public string Accept { get; set; }
    }
```

```
    public class Operation {
        public bool Add { get; set; }
        public bool Double { get; set; }
    }
}
```

I have added a constructor that requires parameters and changed two of the properties that are read-only. These changes will prevent the default model binder from being able to create instances of the application, as I will demonstrate shortly. In Listing 16-21, you can see how I revised the action method in the Bindings controller so that it receives a Numbers object as a parameter.

Listing 16-21. Changing the Action Method Parameters in the BindingsController.cs File

```
using System.Web.Http;
using System.Web.Http.ModelBinding;
using ExampleApp.Models;

namespace ExampleApp.Controllers {
    public class BindingsController : ApiController {
        private IRepository repo;

        public BindingsController(IRepository repoArg) {
            repo = repoArg;
        }

        [HttpGet]
        [HttpPost]
        public string SumNumbers([ModelBinder] Numbers numbers) {
            var result = numbers.Op.Add ? numbers.First + numbers.Second
                : numbers.First - numbers.Second;
            return string.Format("{0}", numbers.Op.Double ? result * 2 : result);
        }
    }
}
```

The final preparatory change I need to make is to change the data sent by jQuery in the Ajax request. Listing 16-22 shows how I have returned to sending first and second properties, both of which are prefixed with numbers, matching the name of the action method parameter. I have also included the numbers.op.sum and numbers.op.double properties so I can populate the nested Operation object.

Listing 16-22. Changing the Ajax Request Data in the bindings.js File

```
var viewModel = ko.observable({ first: 2, second: 5});
var response = ko.observable("Ready");
var gotError = ko.observable(false);

var sendRequest = function (requestType) {
    $.ajax("/api/bindings/sumnumbers", {
        type: "GET",
```

```
        data: {
            "numbers.first": viewModel().first,
            "numbers.second": viewModel().second,
            "numbers.op.add": true,
            "numbers.op.double": true
        },
        success: function (data) {
            gotError(false);
            response("Total: " + data);
        },
        error: function (jqXHR) {
            gotError(true);
            response(jqXHR.status + " (" + jqXHR.statusText + ")");
        }
    });
};


$(document).ready(function () {
    ko.applyBindings();
});
```

Testing the Preparations

These changes have created a binding situation that the built-in model binders can't deal with: the SumNumbers action method has a Numbers parameter, but the Numbers class doesn't follow the default pattern to be instantiated. You can see the effect by starting the application, navigating to /Home/Bindings in the browser, and clicking the Send Request button.

The response from the web service will be reported in the browser as a 500 (Internal Server Error), and if you look at the response in the browser F12 tools, you will see that the following problem has been reported:

```
No parameterless constructor defined for this object
```

I show you how to deal with errors in Chapter 25, but for the moment it is enough to have confirmed that the built-in model binders can't instantiate the modified Numbers class.

Understanding Model Binders

Model binders implement the IModelBinder interface, which is defined in the System.Web.Http.ModelBinding namespace. Listing 16-23 shows the definition of the IModelBinder interface.

Listing 16-23. The IModelBinder Interface

```
using System.Web.Http.Controllers;

namespace System.Web.Http.ModelBinding {

    public interface IModelBinder {
        bool BindModel(HttpActionContext actionContext,
            ModelBindingContext bindingContext);
    }
}
```

The IModelBinder interface defines a single method called BindModel. The way this model works is a little convoluted. The result and the first argument are entirely standard: the bool result is used to indicate whether the model binder was able to create an instance of the require type, and the HttpActionContext object. describes the action method that defines the parameter that is to be bound. Table 16-5 shows the properties and methods that are defined by the HttpActionDescriptor class. that are useful in model binding; there are additional method and properties, but they are used when selecting and executing an action method, which I describe in Chapter 22.

Table 16-5. *Selected Members Defined by the HttpActionDescriptor Class*

Name	Description
ActionName	Returns the name of the action method
ReturnType	Returns the Type that the action method returns
SupportedHttpMethods	Returns a collection of HttpMethod objects that represent the HTTP verbs that can be used to target the action method
GetParameters()	Returns a collection of HttpParameterDescription objects that represent the action method parameters

The ModelBindingContext argument is different: it describes the parameter for which a value is required, but it *also* provides the means by which the value for the parameter is given to Web API and through which any errors are expressed. This will make more sense as I demonstrate the process of creating a custom model binder, but just bear in mind that the ModelBindingContext class provides information to the model binder *and* provides the parameter value to Web API so that the action method can be invoked. The ModelBindingContext class defines the properties shown in Table 16-6.

Table 16-6. *Selected Properties Defined by the ModelBindingContext Class*

Name	Description
FallbackToEmptyPrefix	Returns true if the model binder can ignore the binding prefix.
Model	Set by the model binder when it is able to create an instance of the model class.
ModelMetadata	Returns a ModelMetadata object that describes the type of the parameter that is to be bound.
ModelName	Returns the name of the parameter that is to be bound.
ModelState	Returns a ModelStateDictionary object that is used to perform validation. See Chapter 18 for details.
ModelType	Returns the type of the parameter that is bound.
PropertyMetadata	Provides a dictionary of ModelMetadata objects that describe each property defined by the model type, indexed by name.
ValidationNode	Returns a ModelValidationNode object used to perform validation. See Chapter 18 for details.
ValueProvider	Returns an IValueProvider that can be used to obtain individual data values from the request. The IValueProvider that is returned by default consolidates access to all the individual value providers that have been registered in the services container or via dependency injection.

The role of the model binder is to examine the action method and the parameter using the `HttpActionDescriptor` and `ModelBindingContext` and, if suitable data is available, create an instance of the class—the model—specified by the `ModelBindingContext.Type` property. The model is provided to Web API by setting the `ModelBindingContext.Model` property and returning `true` as the result from the `BindModel` method.

Tip If suitable data isn't available, then the `ModelBinding.ModelState` property is used to report errors. I explain how models are validated and how errors are handled in Chapter 18.

Creating a Custom Model Binder

There are two categories of model binders. The first is *loosely coupled* binders., which use the metadata in the `HttpActionDescriptor` and `ModelBindingContext` objects passed to the `BindModel` method to instantiate classes of which they have no prior knowledge. The built-in model binders are loosely coupled because they will try to bind any complex action method parameter, but the limitation of this approach is that they can't deal with classes that have constructor parameters or require special configuration.

The other category is *tightly coupled* binders, which are written to handle a specific class. Tightly coupled binders have prior knowledge of the steps required to create and configure a particular class and usually don't need to use the metadata in order to do so. The problem with tightly coupled classes is that they break when the class they operate on changes, but this is usually an acceptable trade-off in order to be able to use model binding for difficult classes. It is tightly coupled binders that most applications require and that I demonstrate in this section.

Caution Loosely coupled classes are difficult to write and require thorough testing because they will be used to bind all sorts of odd classes that have characteristics that have not been foreseen. You should rely on the built-in binders unless you have expert-level understanding of .NET reflection and metadata and you are willing to set aside a substantial amount of time for making your binders work.

My tightly coupled binder will create instances of the `Numbers` class, which means I need to extract several values from the request and use them to create and populate a `Numbers` object, as described in Table 16-7.

Table 16-7. The Request Properties Required by a Numbers Model Binder

Name	Description
`numbers.first`	Required to set the `First` property defined by the `Numbers` class, set via the constructor
`numbers.second`	Required to set the `Second` property defined by the `Numbers` class, set via the constructor
`numbers.op.sum`	Required to set the `Sum` property of the `Operation` class, set via the `Op` property
`numbers.op.double`	Required to set the `Double` property of the `Operation` class, set via the `Op` property
`numbers.accept`	Required to set the `Accept` property defined by the `Numbers` class

I added a class file called NumbersBinder.cs to the Infrastructure folder and used it to define the model binder shown in Listing 16-24.

Listing 16-24. The Contents of the NumbersBinder.cs File

```csharp
using System.Collections.Generic;
using System.Linq;
using System.Web.Http.Controllers;
using System.Web.Http.ModelBinding;
using System.Web.Http.ValueProviders;
using ExampleApp.Models;

namespace ExampleApp.Infrastructure {

    public class NumbersBinder : IModelBinder {

        public bool BindModel(HttpActionContext actionContext,
                ModelBindingContext bindingContext) {

            string modelName = bindingContext.ModelName;

            Dictionary<string, ValueProviderResult> data
                = new Dictionary<string, ValueProviderResult>();

            data.Add("first", GetValue(bindingContext, modelName, "first"));
            data.Add("second", GetValue(bindingContext, modelName, "second"));
            data.Add("add", GetValue(bindingContext, modelName, "op", "add"));
            data.Add("double", GetValue(bindingContext, modelName, "op", "double"));
            data.Add("accept", GetValue(bindingContext, modelName, "accept"));

            if (data.All(x => x.Value != null)) {
                bindingContext.Model = CreateInstance(data);
                return true;
            }
            return false;
        }

        private ValueProviderResult GetValue (ModelBindingContext context,
                params string[] names) {

            for (int i = 0; i < names.Length -1; i++) {
                string prefix = string.Join(".",
                    names.Skip(i).Take(names.Length - (i + 1)));
                if (context.ValueProvider.ContainsPrefix(prefix)) {
                    return context.ValueProvider.GetValue(prefix + "." + names.Last());
                }
            }
            return context.ValueProvider.GetValue(names.Last());
        }
    }
```

```
        private Numbers CreateInstance(Dictionary<string, ValueProviderResult> data) {
            return new Numbers(Convert<int>(data["first"]),
                    Convert<int>(data["second"])) {
                Op = new Operation {
                    Add = Convert<bool>(data["add"]),
                    Double = Convert<bool>(data["double"])
                },
                Accept = Convert<string>(data["accept"])
            };
        }

        private T Convert<T>(ValueProviderResult result) {
            try {
                return (T)result.ConvertTo(typeof(T));
            } catch {
                return default(T);
            }
        }
    }
}
```

■ **Caution**   Model binders can be used to service multiple requests. Don't use instance variables when writing a model binder, but ensure that you write thread-safe code and reset the shared state after if you can't avoid instance variables.

This binder is a little more complex than it needs to because I have structured the code to break up the steps a binder has to follow. In the sections that follow, I use that structure to explain each step.

Getting Model Property Values from the Value Provider

The first step that my binder takes is to try to locate values for each of the properties that it needs to create an instance of the Numbers class and that I listed in Table 16-7. I defined the GetValue method in the binder, which receives the ModelBindingContext and an array of strings as its arguments.

```
...
private ValueProviderResult GetValue (ModelBindingContext context,
        params string[] names) {

    for (int i = 0; i < names.Length -1; i++) {
        string prefix = string.Join(".",
            names.Skip(i).Take(names.Length - (i + 1)));
        if (context.ValueProvider.ContainsPrefix(prefix)) {
            return context.ValueProvider.GetValue(prefix + "." + names.Last());
        }
    }
    return context.ValueProvider.GetValue(names.Last());
}
...
```

In Chapter 15, I explained that value providers will return a ValueProviderResult object if they are able to provide a value and null if not. My first job is to try to gather the set of ValueProviderResult results that contains the values I need, and I need to do this in a way that deals with the prefixes that the client sends.

I have taken a different approach to dealing with prefixes than Microsoft has used in the built-in binders. Instead of checking each prefix just once, I handle each property independently and try to locate a value for multiple levels of prefix. So, for example, if I want the numbers.op.add property, I request the following:

1. numbers.op.add

2. op.add

3. add

I receive the prefixes and name using a params argument, which makes it easy for me to use LINQ to generate the property name permutations I look for. I check these values with the value providers through the ModelBindingContext.ValueProvider property, which returns an IValueProvider that queries all of the value providers registered in the service collection. I terminate the search as soon as I get a ValueProviderResult object for one of the prefix/name permutations and return it as the result.

I call the GetValue method from the GetBinding method to create a dictionary of ValueProviderResult objects that are indexed by property name, like this:

```
...
data.Add("first", GetValue(bindingContext, modelName, "first"));
data.Add("second", GetValue(bindingContext, modelName, "second"));
data.Add("add", GetValue(bindingContext, modelName, "op", "add"));
data.Add("double", GetValue(bindingContext, modelName, "op", "double"));
data.Add("accept", GetValue(bindingContext, modelName, "accept"));
...
```

Checking Values

Once I have asked the value providers for each of the properties, I have a collection of responses that can be either ValueProviderResult objects (indicating that the provider located a value) or null (indicating that the provider could not locate a value). This is the point at which I have to decide whether I am able to bind the model and so I perform a basic check to ensure that I have not received any null responses, like this:

```
...
if (data.All(x => x.Value != null)) {
    bindingContext.Model = CreateInstance(data);
    return true;
}
return false;
...
```

I use LINQ to check for null values, and I return false if there are. A false result from the BindModel method tells Web API that the binder can't create an instance of the model object.

■ **Note** Web API provides a model validation mechanism that allows errors to be usefully reported to the user. I am focused solely on the binding process in this chapter, but I describe model validation and validation errors in Chapter 18.

Creating the Model Object

I use a method called `CreateInstance` if there are no `null` responses from the value providers. As its name suggests, the `CreateInstance` method is responsible for creating an instance of the `Numbers` class and populating it with data.

An important task when creating an instance of the model object is to convert the values from the `ValueProviderResult` objects into the types required for the constructor, methods, and properties. In the custom binder, I have separated this step into a strongly typed method called `Convert`, as follows:

```
...
private Numbers CreateInstance(Dictionary<string, ValueProviderResult> data) {
    return new Numbers(Convert<int>(data["first"]), Convert<int>(data["second"])) {
        Op = new Operation {
            Add = Convert<bool>(data["add"]),
            Double = Convert<bool>(data["double"])
        },
        Accept = Convert<string>(data["accept"])
    };
}
...
```

The `CreateInstance` method creates the `Numbers` object, but it gets its values by calling the `Convert` method and specifying the required type using a generic type parameter and the `ValueProviderResult`. The `Convert` method uses the `ValueProviderResult.ConvertTo` method to perform the type conversion.

```
...
private T Convert<T>(ValueProviderResult result) {
    try {
        return (T)result.ConvertTo(typeof(T));
    } catch {
        return default(T);
    }
}
...
```

The `ConvertTo` method will throw an exception if the value cannot be converted. Handling the conversion in a strongly typed method lets me use the `default` keyword to provide the caller with a default value for the required type. In Chapter 18, I show you how to report binding problems as part of the model validation process.

Applying a Custom Model Binder

Having created a custom model binder, I need to tell Web API to use it to bind `Numbers` action method parameters. There are several ways to apply a binder, depending on how widely you want to apply the binding process. Web API looks in three different places for a model binding instruction before using the built-in binders, in order:

1. The `ModelBinder` attribute applied to the action method parameter

2. The `ModelBinder` attribute applied to the model class

3. A parameter binding rule

In the sections that follow, I explain each of the options and demonstrate their use.

Applying a Custom Binder Directly to the Parameter

The most direct way to apply a model binder is to specify the binder type to the action method parameter using the ModelBinder attribute.., which defines the configuration properties described in Table 16-8.

Table 16-8. *The Properties Defined by the ModelBinder Attribute*

Name	Description
BinderType	This property specifies the model binder class that will be used for the parameter.
Name	This property specifies the name that will be used as the top-level prefix, overriding the name of the parameter, which is used by default.

■ **Tip** There is an additional property—SuppressPrefixCheck—defined by the ModelBinder attribute, but its value is not checked by the other model binding classes.

Listing 16-25 shows how I applied the ModelBinder attribute and set the BinderType property to specify the NumbersBinder class for the action method parameter.

Listing 16-25. Applying a Custom Model Binder in the BindingsController.cs File

```
using System.Web.Http;
using System.Web.Http.ModelBinding;
using ExampleApp.Models;
using ExampleApp.Infrastructure;

namespace ExampleApp.Controllers {
    public class BindingsController : ApiController {
        private IRepository repo;

        public BindingsController(IRepository repoArg) {
            repo = repoArg;
        }

        [HttpGet]
        [HttpPost]
        public string SumNumbers([ModelBinder(BinderType=typeof(NumbersBinder))]
                Numbers numbers) {
            var result = numbers.Op.Add ? numbers.First + numbers.Second
                : numbers.First - numbers.Second;
            return string.Format("{0}", numbers.Op.Double ? result * 2 : result);
        }
    }
}
```

I have not set the Name property, so the metadata passed to the binder will specify that the name of the action method parameter will be used as a prefix. To test the custom model binder, start the application, use the browser to navigate to the /Home/Bindings URL, and click the Send Request button. The ModelBinder.BinderType property will override the use of the built-in binders and use my custom binder to instantiate the Numbers class, avoiding the problems with the constructor parameters and read-only properties.

Registering the Model Binder with the Services Collection

If you don't want to use the `BinderType` property every time you apply the `ModelBinder` attribute, you can register the binder with the services collection. Listing 16-26 shows the change I made to the `WebApiConfig.cs` file to register the binder.

Listing 16-26. Registering a Model Binder in the WebApiConfig.cs File

```
using System.Web.Http;
using ExampleApp.Infrastructure;
using System.Web.Http.ValueProviders;
using System.Net.Http.Headers;
using System.Web.Http.ModelBinding;
using System.Web.Http.ModelBinding.Binders;
using ExampleApp.Models;

namespace ExampleApp {
    public static class WebApiConfig {
        public static void Register(HttpConfiguration config) {

            config.DependencyResolver = new NinjectResolver();

            config.MapHttpAttributeRoutes();

            config.Routes.MapHttpRoute(
                name: "Binding Example Route",
                routeTemplate: "api/{controller}/{action}/{first}/{second}"
            );

            config.Routes.MapHttpRoute(
                name: "DefaultApi",
                routeTemplate: "api/{controller}/{id}",
                defaults: new { id = RouteParameter.Optional }
            );

            config.Services.Add(typeof(ValueProviderFactory),
                new HeaderValueProviderFactory());

            config.Services.Insert(typeof(ModelBinderProvider), 0,
                new SimpleModelBinderProvider(typeof(Numbers), new NumbersBinder()));
        }
    }
}
```

A subclass of the abstract `ModelBinderProvider` class. is required to register a model binder, but it is easier to use the `SimpleModelBinderProvider` class, defined in the `System.Web.Http.ModelBinding.Providers` namespace, when you want a binder to be used for all parameters of a specific type. The arguments to the `SimpleModelBinderProvider` constructor are the type the binder instantiates and an instance of the model binder class.

■ **Tip** I have used the Insert method to register the custom model binder so that it is used in preference to the built-in binders, which will not be able to instantiate the Numbers class.

Having registered the binder, I am able to remove the type from the attribute applied to the action method parameter, as shown in Listing 16-27.

Listing 16-27. Removing the Model Binder Type in the BindingsController.cs File

```
...
[HttpGet]
[HttpPost]
public string SumNumbers([ModelBinder] Numbers numbers) {
    var result = numbers.Op.Add ? numbers.First + numbers.Second
        : numbers.First - numbers.Second;
    return string.Format("{0}", numbers.Op.Double ? result * 2 : result);
}
...
```

Applying a Binder to the Model Class

The ModelBinder attribute can also be applied to the model class, which has the effect of applying the model binder to every action method parameter of that type. Listing 16-28 shows the application of the ModelBinder attribute to the Numbers model class, with the BinderType property used to specify the custom model binder.

Listing 16-28. Using the ModelBinder Attribute in the BindingModels.cs File

```
using System.Web.Http.ModelBinding;
using ExampleApp.Infrastructure;

namespace ExampleApp.Models {

    [ModelBinder(BinderType = typeof(NumbersBinder))]
    public class Numbers {
        private int first, second;

        public Numbers(int firstVal, int secondVal) {
            first = firstVal; second = secondVal;
        }

        public int First {
            get { return first; }
        }

        public int Second {
            get { return second; }
        }
```

```
        public Operation Op { get; set; }
        public string Accept { get; set; }
    }

    public class Operation {
        public bool Add { get; set; }
        public bool Double { get; set; }
    }
}
```

■ **Tip**   I have shown the attribute with the `BinderType` property because I like to make it obvious which binder will be used. However, registering the binder with the services collection affects the `ModelBinder` attribute wherever it is used, and you can omit the `BinderType` property if you prefer.

There is no need to apply the attribute to the action method when the `ModelBinder` attribute is applied to the model class. Listing 16-29 shows how I removed the attribute from the controller.

Listing 16-29. Removing the ModelBinding Attribute in the BindingsController.cs File

```
...
[HttpGet]
[HttpPost]
public string SumNumbers(Numbers numbers) {
    var result = numbers.Op.Add ? numbers.First + numbers.Second
        : numbers.First - numbers.Second;
    return string.Format("{0}", numbers.Op.Double ? result * 2 : result);
}
...
```

Creating a Parameter Binding Rule

Applying the `ModelBinder` attribute to the model class affects all the action method parameters of that type, and that can be overreaching if you need to apply a custom binder only for some action method parameters. You can get more control over when the model binder is used by defining a parameter binding rule. However, the main benefit of a parameter binding rule for a model binder is to restrict the set of value providers that are used to obtain data values, which can be useful when you want to make sure that, say, routing data isn't used in the model binding process.

Before I define a binding rule, I need to remove the `ModelBinder` attribute from the `Numbers` class, as shown in Listing 16-30. With the attribute in place, the binding process will not look for a parameter binding rule.

Listing 16-30. Removing the ModelBinder Attribute in the BinderModels.cs File

```
...
//[ModelBinder(BinderType = typeof(NumbersBinder))]
public class Numbers {
        private int first, second;
...
```

Listing 16-31 shows a parameter binding rule that I added to the `WebApiConfig.cs` file, which restricts the sources of data to the query string and request headers.

Listing 16-31. Defining a Parameter Model Binding in the WebApiConfig.cs File

```
using System.Web.Http;
using ExampleApp.Infrastructure;
using System.Web.Http.ValueProviders;
using System.Net.Http.Headers;
using System.Web.Http.ModelBinding;
using System.Web.Http.ModelBinding.Binders;
using ExampleApp.Models;
using System.Web.Http.ValueProviders.Providers;

namespace ExampleApp {
    public static class WebApiConfig {
        public static void Register(HttpConfiguration config) {

            config.DependencyResolver = new NinjectResolver();

            config.MapHttpAttributeRoutes();

            config.Routes.MapHttpRoute(
                name: "Binding Example Route",
                routeTemplate: "api/{controller}/{action}/{first}/{second}"
            );

            config.Routes.MapHttpRoute(
                name: "DefaultApi",
                routeTemplate: "api/{controller}/{id}",
                defaults: new { id = RouteParameter.Optional }
            );

            config.Services.Add(typeof(ValueProviderFactory),
                new HeaderValueProviderFactory());

            config.Services.Insert(typeof(ModelBinderProvider), 0,
                new SimpleModelBinderProvider(typeof(Numbers), new NumbersBinder()));

            config.ParameterBindingRules.Add(x => {
                return x.ParameterType == typeof(Numbers)
                    ? new ModelBinderParameterBinding(x, new NumbersBinder(),
                        new ValueProviderFactory[] {
                        new QueryStringValueProviderFactory(),
                        new HeaderValueProviderFactory()})
                    : null;
            });
        }
    }
}
```

■ **Tip** I described the built-in value providers in Chapter 15.

The ModelBinderParameterBinding class is derived from HttpParameterBinding and defines a constructor that receives an HttpParameterDescriptor object, an IModelBinder implementation, and an enumeration of ValueProviderFactory classes. In the listing, I created a rule that specifies the NumbersBinder binder class but limits the source of values to the query string and request headers.

■ **Note** I described the HttpParameterBinding and HttpParameterDescriptor classes in Chapter 15.

Using Type Converters

Type converters are an oddity. They allow a complex type parameter to be created from the query string, using a mechanism that has been part of .NET since version 1.1. I have included them in this chapter for completeness, but the URL format they require isn't especially useful in most web services. Table 16-9 puts type converters in context.

Table 16-9. Putting Type Converters in Context

Question	Answer
What are they?	Type converters integrate the .NET type conversion features into the Web API model binding process.
When should you use them?	Use type converters when all of the data required to instantiate a class is contained in a single query string property or routing segment variable.
What do you need to know?	Type converters don't really fit into the rest of the model binding system, and I have yet to find them useful in a real project.

Understanding Type Converters

Type converters are responsible for creating an object from the URL, from a single query string property or routing segment. Type converters are derived from the System.ComponentModel.TypeConverter class and associated with action method parameters with the TypeConverter attribute.

The problem with type converters is that they require all the information necessary to create an instance of a model object to be expressed in a single query string parameter or routing segment. I need four values to create an instance of the Numbers model class; doing so using a type converter means sending a query string like this one:

```
api/bindings/sumnumbers?numbers=2,54,true,true
```

In fact, you can encode the data in any way that suits you, but to keep things simple, I have expressed the data values so they are separated by a comma.

> ■ **Caution** Separating values with a single character is common when using a type converter, but be careful when using characters like + as separators. The string taken from the URL is assumed to be URL encoded, which means that the + character is replaced with a space.

Creating a Type Converter

The TypeConverter class—and, in fact, the entire System.ComponentModel namespace—is a general-purpose mechanism for managing and converting types, and most of its features have no role in Web API.

Creating a Web API type converter is relatively simple, especially since you can ignore all but the type and value parameters defined by the methods in Table 16-10, which are the only ones required to use a type converter in a Web API application.

Table 16-10. The Methods Required to Create a Web API Type Converter

Name	Description
CanConvertFrom(context, type)	Called to check whether the type converter is able to create an instance of its model object from a specified type. In Web API, implementations of this method should return true for strings and return false for all other types.
ConvertFrom(context, culture, value)	Called to create an instance of the model object from a request value, which will be a string. This method should return null if the data cannot be converted into a model object.

To demonstrate how to create a type converter, I added a class file called NumbersTypeConverter.cs to the Infrastructure folder and used it to define the class shown in Listing 16-32.

Listing 16-32. The Contents of the NumbersTypeConverter.cs File

```
using System;
using System.ComponentModel;
using System.Globalization;
using ExampleApp.Models;

namespace ExampleApp.Infrastructure {
    public class NumbersTypeConverter : TypeConverter {

        public override bool CanConvertFrom(ITypeDescriptorContext context,
                Type sourceType) {
            return sourceType == typeof(string);
        }

        public override object ConvertFrom(ITypeDescriptorContext context,
                CultureInfo culture, object value) {

            string valueToParse = value as string;
            string[] elements = null;
```

```
            if (valueToParse != null
                    && (elements = valueToParse.Split(',')).Length == 4) {

                int firstVal, secondVal; bool addVal, doubleVal;
                if (int.TryParse(elements[0], out firstVal)
                        && int.TryParse(elements[1], out secondVal)
                        && bool.TryParse(elements[2], out addVal)
                        && bool.TryParse(elements[3], out doubleVal)) {

                    return new Numbers(firstVal, secondVal) {
                        Op = new Operation {
                            Add = addVal,
                            Double = doubleVal
                        }
                    };
                }
            }
            return null;
        }
    }
}
```

The work of creating an object for an action method happens in the ConvertFrom method, which is passed the data from the request and must convert it into an instance of the model class. In the listing, I split the string I receive into an array and use the int.TryParse and bool.TryParse methods to convert individual values to the types I need to create an instance of the Numbers class. If I don't receive data in the format that I expect, then I return null to indicate that I cannot create an instance of the model class.

Applying a Type Converter

Type converters are applied to the model class, rather than the action method parameter. The TypeConverter attribute, defined in the System.ComponentModel namespace, specifies the type converter class that is used to create instances of the model. Listing 16-33 shows how I have applied the attribute to the Numbers class.

Listing 16-33. Applying a Type Converter in the BindingModels.cs File

```
using System.Web.Http.ModelBinding;
using ExampleApp.Infrastructure;
using System.ComponentModel;

namespace ExampleApp.Models {

    //[ModelBinder(BinderType = typeof(NumbersBinder))]
    [TypeConverter(typeof(NumbersTypeConverter))]
    public class Numbers {
        private int first, second;

        public Numbers(int firstVal, int secondVal) {
            first = firstVal; second = secondVal;
        }
```

```
        public int First {
            get { return first; }
        }

        public int Second {
            get { return second; }
        }

        public Operation Op { get; set; }
        public string Accept { get; set; }
    }

    public class Operation {
        public bool Add { get; set; }
        public bool Double { get; set; }
    }
}
```

Type converters only read their data from the URL, which means I need to configure the client to send a GET request in the format I described in the previous section. Listing 16-34 shows the changes that I made to the bindings.js file to configure the jQuery Ajax request.

Listing 16-34. Configuring the Ajax Request in the bindings.js File

```
var viewModel = ko.observable({ first: 2, second: 5});
var response = ko.observable("Ready");
var gotError = ko.observable(false);

var sendRequest = function (requestType) {
    $.ajax("/api/bindings/sumnumbers", {
        type: "GET",
        data: "numbers=" + viewModel().first + ","
            + viewModel().second + "," + "true" + "," + true,
        success: function (data) {
            gotError(false);
            response("Total: " + data);
        },
        error: function (jqXHR) {
            gotError(true);
            response(jqXHR.status + " (" + jqXHR.statusText + ")");
        }
    });
};

$(document).ready(function () {
    ko.applyBindings();
});
```

I format the query string that the Ajax request will be sent to so that it uses the format that the type converter can process. The final step is to disable the parameter binding rule in the WebApiConfig.cs file, which preempts the TypeConverter attribute. Listing 16-35 shows the changes.

Listing 16-35. Disabling the Parameter Binding Rule in the WebConfig.cs File

```
using System.Web.Http;
using ExampleApp.Infrastructure;
using System.Web.Http.ValueProviders;
using System.Net.Http.Headers;
using System.Web.Http.ModelBinding;
using System.Web.Http.ModelBinding.Binders;
using ExampleApp.Models;
using System.Web.Http.ValueProviders.Providers;

namespace ExampleApp {
    public static class WebApiConfig {
        public static void Register(HttpConfiguration config) {

            config.DependencyResolver = new NinjectResolver();

            config.MapHttpAttributeRoutes();

            config.Routes.MapHttpRoute(
                name: "Binding Example Route",
                routeTemplate: "api/{controller}/{action}/{first}/{second}"
            );

            config.Routes.MapHttpRoute(
                name: "DefaultApi",
                routeTemplate: "api/{controller}/{id}",
                defaults: new { id = RouteParameter.Optional }
            );

            config.Services.Add(typeof(ValueProviderFactory),
                new HeaderValueProviderFactory());

            config.Services.Insert(typeof(ModelBinderProvider), 0,
                new SimpleModelBinderProvider(typeof(Numbers), new NumbersBinder()));

            //config.ParameterBindingRules.Add(x => {
            //    return x.ParameterType == typeof(Numbers)
            //        ? new ModelBinderParameterBinding(x, new NumbersBinder(),
            //            new ValueProviderFactory[] {
            //            new QueryStringValueProviderFactory(),
            //            new HeaderValueProviderFactory()})
            //        : null;
            //});
        }
    }
}
```

To test the type converter, start the application and navigate to the /Home/Bindings URL. When you click the Send Request button, jQuery will send an Ajax request that contains a query string that contains all of the values in a single property, which will then be parsed by the type converter and passed as an argument to the action method. The result is shown in Figure 16-2.

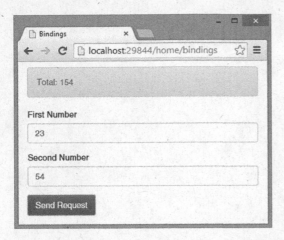

Figure 16-2. *Using a type converter*

Summary

In this chapter, I showed you how you can use Web API to bind complex types from data contained in the request URL using model binders. I demonstrated how to use the built-in model providers to bind objects, arrays, and collections and how to create and apply a custom model binder, which is useful when working with classes that require special handling. I focused on the query string, but the same techniques apply to routing data, which I detail in Chapters 20 and 21. I finished this chapter by explaining type converters, which are an odd adaptation of an old .NET feature into the Web API class framework. In the next chapter, I show you how media type formatters—which I introduced in Chapter 12 to serialize action method results—can be used to deserialize objects from the request body. I also show you how to completely replace the default parameter binding system with one of your own creation.

CHAPTER 17

■ ■ ■

Binding Complex Data Types Part II

In this chapter, I conclude the coverage of the parameter and model binding processes by explaining how media type formatters can be used to deserialize complex types from the request body. I show you how to perform deserialization with a custom media type formatter and then detail how the built-in formatters work, including how to send data in the required format from the client. I finish this chapter by showing you how to replace the class that is responsible for integrating the behavior I have been describing since Chapter 15 with a custom implementation. Table 17-1 summarizes this chapter.

Table 17-1. *Chapter Summary*

Problem	Solution	Listing
Deserialize a custom data format.	Create a media type formatter and override the ReadFromStreamAsync method.	1–6
Register a custom media type formatter.	Add or insert an instance of the formatter class to the HttpConfiguration.Formatters collection.	7
Process URL-encoded data.	Target the FormUrlEncodedMediaTypeFormatter or JQueryMvcFormUrlEncodedFormatter media type formatters.	8–11
Instantiate difficult types from URL-encoded data.	Derive a custom class from the FormUrlEncodedMediaTypeFormatter class and override the ReadFromStreamAsync method to read the data and bind the object.	12–15
Process JSON-encoded data.	Target the JsonMediaTypeFormatter media type formatter.	16
Instantiate difficult types from JSON-encoded data.	Derive a custom class from the MediaTypeFormatter class and use the Json.Net library directly.	17–18
Process XML-encoded data.	Apply the DataContract and DataMember attributes to the model class and target the XmlMediaTypeFormatter media type formatter.	19–20
Instantiate difficult types from XML-encoded data.	Derive a custom class from the MediaTypeFormatter class and use LINQ to XML to process the data.	21–22
Change the entire parameter and model binding processes.	Create a custom implementation of the IActionValueBinder interface, either by implementing the interface directly or by deriving from the DefaultActionValueBinder class.	23–26

Preparing the Example Project

I am going to continue using the ExampleApp project I have been working with throughout this part of the book, but I need to make some preparatory changes for this chapter. First I need to simplify the Numbers class so that it has a parameterless constructor and settable properties—changes that are required so that I can demonstrate the default behavior. Listing 17-1 shows the changes I made, which include removing the ModelBinder and TypeConverter attributes that I applied in Chapter 16. I have left the constructor with parameters in place so that I can demonstrate dealing with objects that require special handling.

Listing 17-1. Simplifying the Class in the BindingModels.cs File

```
namespace ExampleApp.Models {

    public class Numbers {

        public Numbers() { /* do nothing */ }

        public Numbers(int first, int second) {
            First = first; Second = second;
        }

        public int First { get; set; }
        public int Second { get; set; }
        public Operation Op { get; set; }
        public string Accept { get; set; }
    }

    public class Operation {
        public bool Add { get; set; }
        public bool Double { get; set; }
    }
}
```

■ **Tip** Remember that you don't have to create the example project yourself. You can download the source code for every chapter for free from Apress.com.

I need to remove the model binding configuration from the WebApiConfig.cs file. The features that I will describe in this chapter do not use value providers or model binders. Listing 17-2 shows the revised configuration file.

Listing 17-2. Simplifying the WebApiConfig.cs File

```
using System.Web.Http;
using System.Web.Http.ModelBinding;
using System.Web.Http.ModelBinding.Binders;
using System.Web.Http.ValueProviders;
using ExampleApp.Infrastructure;
using ExampleApp.Models;
```

```
namespace ExampleApp {
    public static class WebApiConfig {
        public static void Register(HttpConfiguration config) {

            config.DependencyResolver = new NinjectResolver();

            config.MapHttpAttributeRoutes();

            config.Routes.MapHttpRoute(
                name: "Binding Example Route",
                routeTemplate: "api/{controller}/{action}/{first}/{second}"
            );

            config.Routes.MapHttpRoute(
                name: "DefaultApi",
                routeTemplate: "api/{controller}/{id}",
                defaults: new { id = RouteParameter.Optional }
            );

            config.Services.Add(typeof(ValueProviderFactory),
                new HeaderValueProviderFactory());

            config.Services.Insert(typeof(ModelBinderProvider), 0,
                new SimpleModelBinderProvider(typeof(Numbers), new NumbersBinder()));
        }
    }
}
```

The final change is to the bindings.js file so that the jQuery Ajax request uses standard data encoding and uses the POST verb. Listing 17-3 shows the changes.

Listing 17-3. Changing the Request Verb and Data Format in the bindings.js File

```
var viewModel = ko.observable({
    first: 2, second: 5, "op.add": true, "op.double": true
});
var response = ko.observable("Ready");
var gotError = ko.observable(false);

var sendRequest = function (requestType) {
    $.ajax("/api/bindings/sumnumbers", {
        type: "POST",
        data: viewModel(),
        success: function (data) {
            gotError(false);
            response("Total: " + data);
        },
        error: function (jqXHR) {
            gotError(true);
            response(jqXHR.status + " (" + jqXHR.statusText + ")");
        }
    });
};
```

```
$(document).ready(function () {
    ko.applyBindings();
});
```

I also want to change the SumNumbers action method in the Bindings controller so that it returns an int result. I changed the result to a string so that I could include the value of the Accept header, but I only need to report the result of the calculation performed by the SumNumbers action method in this chapter. Listing 17-4 shows the change to the action method.

Listing 17-4. Changing the Action Method Result in the BindingsController.cs File

```
using System.Web.Http;
using System.Web.Http.ModelBinding;
using ExampleApp.Models;
using ExampleApp.Infrastructure;

namespace ExampleApp.Controllers {
    public class BindingsController : ApiController {
        private IRepository repo;

        public BindingsController(IRepository repoArg) {
            repo = repoArg;
        }

        [HttpGet]
        [HttpPost]
        public int SumNumbers(Numbers numbers) {
            var result = numbers.Op.Add ? numbers.First + numbers.Second
                : numbers.First - numbers.Second;
            return numbers.Op.Double ? result * 2 : result;
        }
    }
}
```

Testing the Application

To test the changes, start the application and use the browser to navigate to the /Home/Bindings URL. When you click the Send Request button, the client will display the result, which will be twice the sum of the values in the input elements, as shown in Figure 17-1.

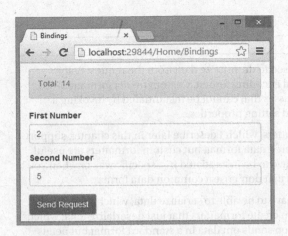

Figure 17-1. *Testing the application preparation*

Creating a Custom Media Type Formatter

By default, Web API assumes that any complex type parameter will be obtained from the request body and uses a media type formatter to try to get and bind a value. I introduced media type formatters in Chapter 12 and described the built-in JSON and XML media type formatters in Chapter 13, but my focus in both chapters was on using them to serialize data from action method results so that it could be sent to the client. Media type formatters are also able to deserialize data and use it to create instances of the classes required to invoke an action method.

■ **Tip** As a reminder, the simple types are the TimeSpan, DateTime, or Guid object or any one of the .NET primitive types: string, char, bool, int, uint, byte, sbyte, short, ushort, long, ulong, float, double, and decimal. Any other type—and that includes arrays and collections of simple types—is a complex type.

In Chapter 12, I created the ProductFormatter class, which was responsible for formatting a Product object into a string like this:

1,Kayak,275.0

The three comma-separated values represented the ProductId, Name, and Price properties defined by the Product model object. In this section, I am going to return to this data format and create a media type formatter that can deserialize it to create Numbers objects. Table 17-2 puts creating a custom media type formatter to deserialize data into context.

Table 17-2. *Putting Custom Media Type Formatters in Context*

Question	Answer
What are they?	Custom media types can be used to deserialize data from the request body that is in a bespoke or unusual encoding format. Custom media formatters are also useful for dealing with classes that cannot be instantiated by invoking a parameterless constructor and setting properties.
When should you use them?	The built-in media type formatters, which I describe later in this chapter, support the most commonly encountered data format, but custom formatters are useful for dealing with classes that have to be instantiated in a specific way or when you need to support legacy clients that don't use a common data format.
What do you need to know?	Media type formatters don't have to be able to serialize data, which I described in Chapter 12. Instead, you can create formatters that just deserialize data, which is helpful when your application sends out data in a standard format but needs to work around poor encoding sent by clients.

Preparing the Client

The first change I need to make is to change the Ajax request that jQuery sends so that the data is in the expected format and that the Content-Type header is correctly set, as shown in Listing 17-5.

Listing 17-5. *Changing the Ajax Request in the bindings.js File*

```
var viewModel = ko.observable({
    first: 2, second: 5, add: true, double: true
});
var response = ko.observable("Ready");
var gotError = ko.observable(false);

var sendRequest = function (requestType) {
    $.ajax("/api/bindings/sumnumbers", {
        type: "POST",
        contentType: "application/x.product",
        data: [viewModel().first, viewModel().second, viewModel().add,
               viewModel().double].join(),
        success: function (data) {
            gotError(false);
            response("Total: " + data);
        },
        error: function (jqXHR) {
            gotError(true);
            response(jqXHR.status + " (" + jqXHR.statusText + ")");
        }
    });
};

$(document).ready(function () {
    ko.applyBindings();
});
```

I have used the contentType setting to specify that the content is in my custom application/x.product encoding (the MIME type I used in Chapter 12) and created a formatted string for the data setting by creating an array with the values from the view model and by calling the join method, which combines the values with a comma separator. If you start the application and send a request, you will see the following URL in the F12 tools:

```
/api/bindings/sumnumbers
```

It has a payload of the following:

```
2,5,true,true
```

The web service will report an error because I have not implemented the deserialization support.

Creating the Media Type Formatter

Now that I have a request I can process, it is time to create the custom media type formatter. I added a class file called XNumbersFormatter.cs to the Infrastructure folder and used it to create the media type formatter shown in Listing 17-6.

Listing 17-6. The Contents of the XNumbersFormatter.cs File

```csharp
using System;
using System.IO;
using System.Linq;
using System.Net.Http;
using System.Net.Http.Formatting;
using System.Net.Http.Headers;
using System.Text;
using System.Threading.Tasks;
using ExampleApp.Models;

namespace ExampleApp.Infrastructure {
    public class XNumbersFormatter : MediaTypeFormatter {
        long bufferSize = 256;

        public XNumbersFormatter() {
            SupportedMediaTypes.Add(new MediaTypeHeaderValue("application/x.product"));
        }

        public override bool CanWriteType(Type type) {
            return false;
        }

        public override bool CanReadType(Type type) {
            return type == typeof(Numbers);
        }
```

```
public async override Task<object> ReadFromStreamAsync(Type type,
    Stream readStream, HttpContent content, IFormatterLogger formatterLogger) {

    byte[] buffer = new byte[Math.Min(content.Headers.ContentLength.Value,
        bufferSize)];
    string[] items = Encoding.Default.GetString(buffer, 0,
        await readStream.ReadAsync(buffer, 0, buffer.Length)).Split(',', '=');

    if (items.Length == 4) {
        return new Numbers(
            GetValue<int>("First", items[0], formatterLogger),
            GetValue<int>("Second", items[1], formatterLogger)) {

            Op = new Operation {
                Add = GetValue<bool>("Add", items[2], formatterLogger),
                Double = GetValue<bool>("Double", items[3], formatterLogger)
            }
        };
    } else {
        formatterLogger.LogError("", "Wrong Number of Items");
        return null;
    }
}

private T GetValue<T>(string name, string value, IFormatterLogger logger) {
    T result = default(T);
    try {
        result = (T)System.Convert.ChangeType(value, typeof(T));
    } catch {
        logger.LogError(name, "Cannot Parse Value");
    }
    return result;
}
}
}
```

■ **Note** I am not going to build on the `ProductFormatter` class I created in Chapter 12 because it is specific to the `Product` model class and because I made all sorts of additions to demonstrate different features, ending up with an overly complicated class. I want to focus on just deserializing data in this chapter, so I have created a new class to keep the example simple.

This formatter binds instances of the Numbers class for requests whose Content-Type header is application/x. product. In the sections that follow, I'll break down each part of the class and explain how it works.

Defining the Formatter Structure

The MediaTypeFormatter class is abstract and requires only the CanWriteType and CanReadType methods to be implemented—but there are two other steps required to create a working media type formatter. First you need to add the MIME type that you want to support to the SupportedMediaTypes collection in the class constructor, as follows:

```
...
public XNumbersFormatter() {
    SupportedMediaTypes.Add(new MediaTypeHeaderValue("application/x.product"));
}
...
```

For my implementations of the CanWriteType and CanReadType methods, I want to tell Web API that I am not willing to serialize any data and that I can deserialize only Numbers objects.

```
...
public override bool CanWriteType(Type type) {
    return false;
}

public override bool CanReadType(Type type) {
    return type == typeof(Numbers);
}
...
```

Getting the Request Data

Media type formatters that deserialize data override the ReadFromStreamAsync method, and that is where the bulk of the work is done in the XNumbersFormatter class. The ReadFromStreamAsync method is passed arguments of the types described in Table 17-3 and is responsible for using them to instantiate an object.

Table 17-3. *The Parameter Types of the MediaTypeFormatter.ReadFromStreamAsync Method*

Type	Description
Type	The type that the formatter is required to instantiate. This is useful if the implementation of the CanReadType method responds with true to multiple types.
Stream	A System.IO.Stream object from which the request body can be read. This must be used cautiously; see the warnings and examples that follow this table.
HttpContent	A System.Net.Http.HttpContent object that describes the request content and provides access to it. This object is used to gain access to an HttpContentHeaders object through its Headers property. See Table 17-4 for details of the headers that are available.
IFormatterLogger	An implementation of the System.Net.Http.Formatting.IFormatterLogger interface that can be used to report problems processing the data. See the "Creating the Model Object" section.

Table 17-4. *The Request Header Convenience Properties Defined by the HttpContentHeaders Class*

Name	Description
ContentEncoding	Returns the value of the Content-Encoding header, which is used to indicate when additional encodings have been applied to the content in addition to the one specified by the Content-Type header.
ContentLength	Returns the value of the Content-Length header, which reports the size of the request body in bytes. When using the value of the Content-Length header, be sure to apply an upper limit to how much data you read from the request body; see the following text for details.
ContentMD5	Returns the value of the Content-MD5 header, which contains a hash code to ensure the integrity of the data.
ContentType	Returns the value of the Content-Type header, which specifies the primary encoding of the request body. Additional encodings can be specified with the Content-Encoding header.

The HttpContent class provides information about the request and provides methods that can be used to read the request body, but the ReadFromStreamAsync method is required to read data from the Stream object it receives as an argument. This means the value of the HttpContent object is its Headers property, which returns an instance of the HttpContentHeaders class. The HttpContentHeaders class is derived from HttpHeaders and adds convenience properties for content-related headers, as described in Table 17-4. (The HttpContentHeaders class contains properties that are used in responses and requests. I have included the request headers only in the table.)

■ **Tip** See www.w3.org/Protocols/rfc2616/rfc2616-sec14.html for the detailed specification and use of HTTP headers.

For my purposes, it is the ContentLength property that is most useful because it tells me how much data I need to read from the Stream argument to the ReadFromStreamAsync method. Here is the code that reads the body of the request and converts it into an array of strings:

```
...
byte[] buffer = new byte[Math.Min(content.Headers.ContentLength.Value, bufferSize)];
string[] items = Encoding.Default.GetString(buffer, 0,
    await readStream.ReadAsync(buffer, 0, buffer.Length)).Split(',', '=');
...
```

These statements follow three important rules that you should follow when writing a custom media type formatter:

- Don't use the convenience methods to read basic types.

- Limit the amount of data you read.

- Read data asynchronously.

A simple but effective denial-of-service attack is for a client to send an HTTP server misleading information in the Content-Length header, either to cause an error or to try to get the server to exhaust its memory by reading enormous amounts of data. A custom media type formatter requires care because the content is read and processed by your code, rather than that of the ASP.NET Framework as is the case in an MVC application.

The first precaution you should take is to avoid using the convenience methods provided by the stream and reader classes in the System.IO namespace. Using a ReadLine or ReadString method would allow me to simplify my media type formatter, but these methods just keep reading data from the underlying stream until they get the data they expect. Instead, you should read the content into a byte[] buffer directly from the stream.

The second precaution you should take is to limit the amount of data you read from the stream. In Listing 17-6, I defined a maximum buffer size of 256 bytes, which is enough to represent my Numbers class. When I create the byte array, I set the size of the array using the Content-Length header only if it is smaller than 256 (and I ignore negative Content-Length headers, which are sent to generate an error, although this is largely habit).

```
...
byte[] buffer = new byte[Math.Min(content.Headers.ContentLength.Value, bufferSize)];
...
```

■ **Tip**   You don't have to guard against negative Content-Length header values, which used to be a popular attack. Basic validation is performed on the headers when the request is processed and requests with illegal headers are rejected by ASP.NET.

The final rule you should follow is to read data asynchronously from the Stream to maximize the request throughput of the web service. I used the Stream.ReadAsync method to read the request body.

```
...
string[] items = Encoding.Default.GetString(buffer, 0,
    await readStream.ReadAsync(buffer, 0, buffer.Length)).Split(',', '=');
...
```

I have used the await keyword for my read operation, and that is why I have added the async keyword to the ReadFromStreamAsync method.

Creating the Model Object

Once I have the data from the request body, I can use it to create an instance of the Numbers class, which is handled by this statement:

```
...
return new Numbers(
    GetValue<int>("First", items[0], formatterLogger),
    GetValue<int>("Second", items[1], formatterLogger)) {

    Op = new Operation {
        Add = GetValue<bool>("Add", items[2], formatterLogger),
        Double = GetValue<bool>("Double", items[3], formatterLogger)
    }
};
...
```

I have used the Numbers constructor that takes parameters, just to show that you can instantiate objects in any way you need when writing a custom media type formatter. I get the values I require for the constructor parameters and the Operation properties through a method called GetValue, which I defined to let me take advantage of C# generic types so that I can easily convert string values to different types.

```
...
private T GetValue<T>(string name, string value, IFormatterLogger logger) {
    T result = default(T);
    try {
        result = (T)System.Convert.ChangeType(value, typeof(T));
    } catch {
        logger.LogError(name, "Cannot Parse Value");
    }
    return result;
}
...
```

The caller specifies the type that is required using the generic type parameter T, and I use the System.Convert.ChangeType method to perform the conversion. The important part of the GetValue method is the use of the IFormatterLogger parameter object, which is used to record any problems processing the request data to create the model object. The default implementation of the IFormatterLogger interface adds errors to the model state, which is part of the model validation process I describe in Chapter 18. The IFormatterLogger interface defines the methods I have listed in Table 17-5.

Table 17-5. *The Methods Defined by the IFormatterLogger Interface*

Method	Description
LogError(property, message)	Records an error for the specified property. The error is described by a string message.
LogError(property, exception)	Records an error for the specified property. The error is described by an Exception.

In the listing, I note any problems parsing values, but I still return the default value for the required type. This will make more sense once I describe the model validation process in Chapter 18.

Registering and Testing the Media Type Formatter

Having created the custom media type formatter (and explained how it works), I can tell Web API to start using it to deserialize Numbers objects for requests that use my application/x.product format. Listing 17-7 shows the change I made to the WebApiConfig.cs file to register the XNumbersFormatter class.

Listing 17-7. Registering a Media Type Formatter in the WebApiConfig.cs File

```
using System.Web.Http;
using System.Web.Http.ModelBinding;
using System.Web.Http.ModelBinding.Binders;
using System.Web.Http.ValueProviders;
using ExampleApp.Infrastructure;
using ExampleApp.Models;

namespace ExampleApp {
    public static class WebApiConfig {
        public static void Register(HttpConfiguration config) {

            config.DependencyResolver = new NinjectResolver();
```

```
        // ...routing statements omitted for brevity...

    config.Services.Add(typeof(ValueProviderFactory),
        new HeaderValueProviderFactory());

    config.Services.Insert(typeof(ModelBinderProvider), 0,
        new SimpleModelBinderProvider(typeof(Numbers), new NumbersBinder()));

    config.Formatters.Add(new XNumbersFormatter());
        }
    }
}
```

For variety, I am going to test the custom formatter with Postman. Set the URL to
`http://localhost:29844/api/bindings/sumnumbers` (replacing 29844 with your application's port number), the
request type to POST, and the Content-Type header to `application/x.product`.

Click the Raw button to specify a request body that won't be formatted by Postman and enter the following into
the text box:

```
100,150,true,false
```

Click the Send button, and Postman will send the request to the web service, which will return the following
result (the previous values specified that the web service should add 100 and 150 but not double the result):

```
250
```

Using the Built-in Media Type Formatters

The default behavior for a complex type parameter is to act as though the FromBody attribute has been applied. I
introduced the FromBody attribute in Chapter 14 when I showed you how to use it to force Web API to look in the
request body for a value that it would otherwise try to obtain it from the URL. Behind the scenes, the FromBody
attribute is used to select a media type formatter that can process the body of a request based on the MIME type. Web
API comes with four built-in media type formatters enabled by default, which I have listed in Table 17-6.

Table 17-6. The Built-in Media Type Formatters

MIME Types	Media Type Formatter
application/json, text/json	JsonMediaTypeFormatter
application/xml, text/json	XmlMediaTypeFormatter
application/x-www-form-urlencoded	FormUrlEncodedMediaTypeFormatter
application/x-www-form-urlencoded	JQueryMvcFormUrlEncodedFormatter

---

■ **Tip**   There is an additional media type formatter for the BSON data format, which is disabled by default and which I am not describing in this book because BSON isn't widely used.

When a request arrives, the MIME type in the `Content-Type` header selects the media type formatter that can handle that type. In the sections that follow, I explain how each formatter works and show you how to format the client request data to target them. Table 17-7 puts binding complex types with the built-in media type formatters in context.

Table 17-7. *Putting Binding Complex Types with the Built-in Media Type Formatters in Context*

Question	Answer
What are they?	The built-in formatters support the three most commonly used data formats for a web service. They are used by default but can be supplemented or replaced by custom media type formatters.
When should you use them?	The built-in media type formatters are used by default and are suitable for dealing with requests that lead to the instantiation of classes with parameterless constructors and settable properties.
What do you need to know?	It is usually a simple matter to create a custom media type formatter that deals with inconsistent or incorrectly formatted data sent by a client—or to deal with classes that must be instantiated carefully.

Handling URL-Encoded Data

If you use jQuery to write your application client, then you will usually end up dealing with form-encoded data because it is the default format that jQuery uses when sending an Ajax request. As Table 17-7 shows, two media type formatters can handle the `application/x-www-form-urlencoded` MIME type: `FormUrlEncodedMediaTypeFormatter` and `JQueryMvcFormUrlEncodedFormatter`. I explain the relationship between them and how each of them works in the sections that follow.

SELECTING OTHER DATA FORMATS

I have covered the media type formatter that deals with URL-encoded data first because it is the format that you are most likely to encounter as an MVC framework developer and you are in a position to write your own web service clients. It is the default encoding used by jQuery, and it is well-understood and supported.

The other data formats are important if you need to support clients that you have not written yourself or that are not browser-based. Just about every web-connected platform can create and process JSON or XML data, and by supporting these formats, you broaden the kinds of clients that can consume your web service.

I recommend making a deliberate decision about the data formats you support. Each additional format requires testing and maintenance and adds to the burden of building and running the web service. I recommend starting with URL-encoded and JSON data and enabling XML only if you can't deliver your web service without it. See Chapter 13 for details of how to disable media type formatters.

Handling URL-Encoded Requests

The `FormUrlEncodedMediaTypeFormatter` class can bind only to an instance of the `FormDataCollection` class, which is defined in the `System.Net.Http.Formatting` namespace and which presents form-encoded data as a collection of name-value pairs.

The real value of the `FormUrlEncodedMediaTypeFormatter` class is that it provides a foundation for creating formatters that handle more useful types, such as the `JQueryMvcFormUrlEncodedFormatter` class that I describe in the next section.

I need to change the data format for the Ajax request that jQuery makes in order to target the `FormUrlEncodedMediaTypeFormatter` class, as shown in Listing 17-8.

Listing 17-8. Changing the Request Format in the bindings.js File

```
var viewModel = ko.observable({
    first: 2, second: 5, add: true, double: true
});
var response = ko.observable("Ready");
var gotError = ko.observable(false);

var sendRequest = function (requestType) {
    $.ajax("/api/bindings/sumnumbers", {
        type: "POST",
        data: viewModel(),
        success: function (data) {
            gotError(false);
            response("Total: " + data);
        },
        error: function (jqXHR) {
            gotError(true);
            response(jqXHR.status + " (" + jqXHR.statusText + ")");
        }
    });
};

$(document).ready(function () {
    ko.applyBindings();
});
```

The changes to the client-side code are minor because jQuery sends URL-encoded data by default. Listing 17-9 shows the change I made to the action method to receive that data using a `FormDataCollection` object.

Listing 17-9. Receiving Request Data in the BindingsController.cs File

```
using System.Web.Http;
using System.Web.Http.ModelBinding;
using ExampleApp.Models;
using ExampleApp.Infrastructure;
using System.Net.Http.Formatting;

namespace ExampleApp.Controllers {
    public class BindingsController : ApiController {
        private IRepository repo;
```

```
    public BindingsController(IRepository repoArg) {
        repo = repoArg;
    }

    [HttpGet]
    [HttpPost]
    public IHttpActionResult SumNumbers(FormDataCollection numbers) {

        int first, second;
        bool add, doubleVal;

        if (int.TryParse(numbers["first"], out first)
            && int.TryParse(numbers["second"], out second)
            && bool.TryParse(numbers["add"], out add)
            && bool.TryParse(numbers["double"], out doubleVal)) {

            int result = add ? first + second : first - second;
            return Ok(string.Format("{0}", doubleVal ? result * 2 : result));

        } else {
            return BadRequest();
        }
    }
}
```

I have to take responsibility for converting the form data values into the types I require to do the work in the action method, which in this case means using the `int.TryParse` and `bool.TryParse` methods to convert form data values (which are expressed as `string` values) to `int` and `bool` types. If I receive all of the data values I need—and I can convert them to the types I need—then I perform the calculation and return the result using the `Ok` method, which I introduced in Chapter 11. If I don't get the values I need, then I use the `BadRequest` method to send the client a 400 (Bad Request) response.

■ **Note**   You won't often rely on the `FormUrlEncodedMediaTypeFormatter` class directly because the other built-in media type formatters can bind to .NET classes, but I have included the details for completeness and because I use this formatter when showing you how to customize the binding process.

Creating Complex Types from URL-Encoded Requests

The `JQueryMvcFormUrlEncodedFormatter` class is derived from `FormUrlEncodedMediaTypeFormatter` and adds support for binding values to complex types, which is a lot more useful than working with the `FormDataCollection` class.

Behind the scenes, the `JQueryMvcFormUrlEncodedFormatter` class uses extension methods defined in the `System.Web.Http.ModelBinding.FormDataCollectionExtensions` class to create objects using the model binding feature that I described in Chapter 16. Unfortunately, the `FormDataCollectionExtensions` extension methods are written to use only the built-in media formatters and value providers, preventing the use of custom classes and limiting the range of types that can be bound from `application/x-www-form-urlencoded` data to classes with parameterless constructors and settable properties, arrays, lists, and key-value pairs.

■ **Tip**   The name of the `JQueryMvcFormUrlEncodedFormatter` class reflects the fact that the property names are converted from the jQuery default to that used by the MVC framework.

Using model binders also means that the data sent by the client needs to be structured with prefixes in order to be properly processed. Listing 17-10 shows the changes I made to the view model in the `bindings.js` file.

Listing 17-10. Adding Prefixes to the View Model in the bindings.js File

```
...
var viewModel = ko.observable({
    first: 2, second: 5,
    "op.add": true, "op.double": true
});
...
```

If I had not prefixed add and double with op, then the media type formatter would not have assigned values to the Op and Add properties of the Numbers object it creates. Listing 17-11 shows the changes I made to the action method in the Bindings controller to use the `JQueryMvcFormUrlEncodedFormatter` formatter.

Listing 17-11. Changing the Action Method Parameter in the BindingsController.cs File

```
using System.Web.Http;
using System.Web.Http.ModelBinding;
using ExampleApp.Models;
using ExampleApp.Infrastructure;
using System.Net.Http.Formatting;

namespace ExampleApp.Controllers {
    public class BindingsController : ApiController {
        private IRepository repo;

        public BindingsController(IRepository repoArg) {
            repo = repoArg;
        }

        [HttpGet]
        [HttpPost]
        public int SumNumbers(Numbers numbers) {
            var result = numbers.Op.Add ? numbers.First + numbers.Second
                : numbers.First - numbers.Second;
            return numbers.Op.Double ? result * 2 : result;
        }
    }
}
```

It is this change—specifying a parameter that is a complex type but not the `FormDataCollection` class—that causes Web API to select the `JQueryMvcFormUrlEncodedFormatter` class instead of the `FormUrlEncodedMediaTypeFormatter` class.

■ **Tip** You might be wondering how the `JQueryMvcFormUrlEncodedFormatter` class is able to use the model binding system when the built-in value providers read values from the URL. The answer is that the `NameValuePairsValueProvider` class is used behind the scenes. This class takes an arbitrary set of key-value pairs and presents them through the `IValueProvider` interface. The `NameValuePairsValueProvider` class is the superclass of the `QueryStringValueProvider` and `RouteDataValueProvider` classes, which get their key-value pairs from the query string and routing data, respectively. The `JQueryMvcFormUrlEncodedFormatter` works directly with the `NameValuePairsValueProvider` class and gets its key-value pairs from the `FormUrlEncodedMediaTypeFormatter` class, which decodes the URL-encoded request body.

Instantiating Difficult Types Using URL-Encoded Data

Although the `JQueryMvcFormUrlEncodedFormatter` doesn't allow the use of custom model binders, I can use the `FormUrlEncodedMediaTypeFormatter` class to create a custom media type formatter that does—and that means I can instantiate classes that require special handling, such as those with constructor parameters. Listing 17-12 shows the contents of a class file called `UrlNumbersFormatter.cs` that I added to the `Infrastructure` folder and used to create a media type formatter that can instantiate the `Numbers` class using the constructor with parameters.

Listing 17-12. The Contents of the UrlNumbersFormatter.cs File

```
using System;
using System.Globalization;
using System.IO;
using System.Net.Http;
using System.Net.Http.Formatting;
using System.Threading.Tasks;
using System.Web.Http;
using System.Web.Http.Controllers;
using System.Web.Http.Metadata;
using System.Web.Http.ModelBinding;
using System.Web.Http.ValueProviders.Providers;
using ExampleApp.Models;

namespace ExampleApp.Infrastructure {
    public class UrlNumbersFormatter : FormUrlEncodedMediaTypeFormatter {

        public override bool CanWriteType(Type type) {
            return false;
        }

        public override bool CanReadType(Type type) {
            return type == typeof(Numbers);
        }

        public override async Task<object> ReadFromStreamAsync(Type type,
            Stream readStream, HttpContent content, IFormatterLogger formatterLogger) {

            FormDataCollection fd = (FormDataCollection)
                await base.ReadFromStreamAsync(typeof(FormDataCollection),
                    readStream, content, formatterLogger);
```

```
            HttpActionContext actionContext = new HttpActionContext { };

            ModelMetadata md = GlobalConfiguration.Configuration
                .Services.GetModelMetadataProvider().GetMetadataForType(null, type);

            ModelBindingContext bindingContext = new ModelBindingContext {
                ModelMetadata = md,
                ValueProvider = new NameValuePairsValueProvider(fd,
                    CultureInfo.InvariantCulture)
            };

            if (new NumbersBinder().BindModel(actionContext, bindingContext)) {
                return bindingContext.Model;
            }
            return null;
        }
    }
}
```

The ReadFromStreamAsync method calls the base implementation to create a FormDataCollection object, which I then pass to an instance of the NameValuePairsValueProvider class. The NameValuePairsValueProvider class implements the IValueProvider interface and allows me to take values from the body and feed them into the custom model binder I created in Chapter 16.

Many of the rest of the statements in the ReadFromStreamAsync method prepare the context objects that I need in order to use the model binder. I need HttpActionContext and ModelBindingContext objects to call the BindModel method of an IModelBinder implementation, but I need to provide only the context that the binder relies on. For my NumbersBinder class, that means I can instantiate an HttpActionContext object without needing to set any properties. For the ModelBindingContext, I assign the NameValuePairsValueProvider object to the ValueProvider property. I also have to set the ModelMetadata property because it is checked by the ModelBindingContext class when the Model property is set by the model binder class. I describe the ModelMetadata class in Chapter 18, but for the moment it is enough to know that I get the ModelMetadata instance from the services collection.

Once I have creating the context objects, I can instantiate the model binder class and call the BindModel method. The BindModel method returns true when it is able to bind an object, and when I get that result, I return the value of the BindingContext.Model property.

The reason that the built-in JQueryMvcFormUrlEncodedFormatter media type formatter doesn't allow custom binders and value providers is because the problems that feeding data from the body to model binders can cause. For my custom model binder, there are two problems that I need to resolve, and you can see the changes that I made to the NumbersBinder class in Listing 17-13.

Listing 17-13. Adapting a Model Binder in the NumbersBinder.cs File

```
using System.Collections.Generic;
using System.Linq;
using System.Web.Http.Controllers;
using System.Web.Http.ModelBinding;
using System.Web.Http.ValueProviders;
using ExampleApp.Models;

namespace ExampleApp.Infrastructure {

    public class NumbersBinder : IModelBinder {
```

```csharp
public bool BindModel(HttpActionContext actionContext,
        ModelBindingContext bindingContext) {

    string modelName = bindingContext.ModelName;

    Dictionary<string, ValueProviderResult> data
        = new Dictionary<string, ValueProviderResult>();

    data.Add("first", GetValue(bindingContext, modelName, "first"));
    data.Add("second", GetValue(bindingContext, modelName, "second"));
    data.Add("add", GetValue(bindingContext, modelName, "op", "add"));
    data.Add("double", GetValue(bindingContext, modelName, "op", "double"));
    data.Add("accept", GetValue(bindingContext, modelName, "accept"));

    if (data.All(x => x.Key == "accept" || x.Value != null)) {
        bindingContext.Model = CreateInstance(data);
        return true;
    }
    return false;
}

private ValueProviderResult GetValue(ModelBindingContext context,
        params string[] names) {

    for (int i = 0; i < names.Length - 1; i++) {
        string prefix = string.Join(".",
            names.Skip(i).Take(names.Length - (i + 1)));
        if (prefix != string.Empty &&
                context.ValueProvider.ContainsPrefix(prefix)) {
            return context.ValueProvider.GetValue(prefix + "." + names.Last());
        }
    }
    return context.ValueProvider.GetValue(names.Last());
}

private Numbers CreateInstance(Dictionary<string, ValueProviderResult> data) {
    // ...statements omitted for brevity...
}

private T Convert<T>(ValueProviderResult result) {
    // ...statements omitted for brevity...
}
}
}
```

I need to fix two problems. The first is in the BindModel method, when I check to see whether I have been able to obtain values for all the properties and constructor parameters I need to set. The Numbers class defines the Accept property, which I have been setting using data from the request header. Media type formatters don't have access to the request, and there is no global property that provides access to it, unlike in the MVC framework. To get the model binder working with the media type formatter, I have to relax the check that I perform to exclude the value for the Accept value.

```
...
if (data.All(x => x.Key == "accept" || x.Value != null)) {
    bindingContext.Model = CreateInstance(data);
    return true;
}
...
```

The second problem is that binders use the parameter name, which is available through the
ModelBindingContext.ModelName property. Media type formatters don't have access to details about which
parameter they are being used to bind and can't provide the model binder with the name. To make my custom model
binder work in this situation, I have added support for working with an empty string as the model name, which is the
value that the binder is presented with from the ModelBindingContext that I created in the UrlNumbersFormatter
class.

```
...
if (prefix != string.Empty && context.ValueProvider.ContainsPrefix(prefix)) {
...
```

Now that the model binder can be used by the media type formatter, all that remains is to register the
UrlNumbersFormatter class with Web API, as shown in Listing 17-14.

Listing 17-14. Registering a Media Type Formatter in the WebApiConfig.cs File

```
using System.Web.Http;
using System.Web.Http.ModelBinding;
using System.Web.Http.ModelBinding.Binders;
using System.Web.Http.ValueProviders;
using ExampleApp.Infrastructure;
using ExampleApp.Models;

namespace ExampleApp {
    public static class WebApiConfig {
        public static void Register(HttpConfiguration config) {

            config.DependencyResolver = new NinjectResolver();

            config.MapHttpAttributeRoutes();

            // ...routing statements omitted for brevity...

            config.Services.Add(typeof(ValueProviderFactory),
                new HeaderValueProviderFactory());

            config.Services.Insert(typeof(ModelBinderProvider), 0,
                new SimpleModelBinderProvider(typeof(Numbers), new NumbersBinder()));

            config.Formatters.Add(new XNumbersFormatter());
            config.Formatters.Insert(0, new UrlNumbersFormatter());
        }
    }
}
```

Notice that I have used the Insert method to register the UrlNumbersFormatter class. Media type formatters are queried in the order in which they are placed in the HttpConfiguration.Formatters collection, and this means I must ensure that my custom formatter appears before the JQueryMvcFormUrlEncodedFormatter class if I want it to deserialize the request data.

Simplifying the Custom Media Type Formatter

The media type formatter that I created in the previous section demonstrated how you can use model binders, which is helpful if you have already invested time and effort in the code that can instantiate difficult classes. If you don't have a model binder that you want to use, then you can read the data values directly from the FormDataCollection object. Listing 17-15 shows how I simplified the UrlNumbersFormatter class so that it gets the data values and instantiates the Numbers class directly.

Listing 17-15. Simplifying the Media Type Formatter in the UrlNumbersFormatter.cs File

```
using System;
using System.IO;
using System.Net.Http;
using System.Net.Http.Formatting;
using System.Threading.Tasks;
using ExampleApp.Models;

namespace ExampleApp.Infrastructure {
    public class UrlNumbersFormatter : FormUrlEncodedMediaTypeFormatter {

        public override bool CanWriteType(Type type) {
            return false;
        }

        public override bool CanReadType(Type type) {
            return type == typeof(Numbers);
        }

        public override async Task<object> ReadFromStreamAsync(Type type,
            Stream readStream, HttpContent content, IFormatterLogger formatterLogger) {

            FormDataCollection fd = (FormDataCollection)
                await base.ReadFromStreamAsync(typeof(FormDataCollection),
                    readStream, content, formatterLogger);

            return new Numbers(
                GetValue<int>("First", fd, formatterLogger),
                GetValue<int>("Second", fd, formatterLogger)) {
                Op = new Operation {
                    Add = GetValue<bool>("Add", fd, formatterLogger),
                    Double = GetValue<bool>("Double", fd, formatterLogger)
                }
            };
        }
```

```
        private T GetValue<T>(string name, FormDataCollection fd,
                IFormatterLogger logger) {
            T result = default(T);
            try {
                result = (T)System.Convert.ChangeType(fd[name], typeof(T));
            } catch {
                logger.LogError(name, "Cannot Parse Value");
            }
            return result;
        }

    }
}
```

This class uses the same techniques I employed in the "Creating a Custom Media Type Formatter" section, except that I use the base class to read and parse the data from the request body.

Handling JSON Requests

The `JsonMediaTypeFormatter` class is responsible for deserializing content in requests that are encoded with `application/json` or `text/json` MIME types (which are equivalent—both MIME types are JSON). It relies on the excellent Json.Net package to handle the JSON data. One of the reasons that I like the Json.Net package so much is that I have found it will decode even the sloppiest JSON data, which makes it well-suited for web services that have to deal with a wide range of clients, including those written by third parties with a less than complete understanding of the JSON format. Listing 17-16 shows how I have changed the Ajax request sent by jQuery so that the data is encoded via JSON.

Listing 17-16. Changing the jQuery Request Encoding to JSON in the bindings.js File

```
var viewModel = ko.observable({
    first: 2, second: 5, op: { add: true, double: true }
});
var response = ko.observable("Ready");
var gotError = ko.observable(false);

var sendRequest = function (requestType) {
    $.ajax("/api/bindings/sumnumbers", {
        type: "POST",
        data: JSON.stringify(viewModel()),
        contentType: "application/json",
        success: function (data) {
            gotError(false);
            response("Total: " + data);
        },
        error: function (jqXHR) {
            gotError(true);
            response(jqXHR.status + " (" + jqXHR.statusText + ")");
        }
    });
};
```

```
$(document).ready(function () {
    ko.applyBindings();
});
```

I have altered the structure of the view model so that there is an op property that is set to an object with add and double properties. I have also used the contentType property to specify that the request contains JSON data and used the JSON.stringify method to serialize the view model object into a JSON string like this:

```
{"first":2,"second":5,"op":{"add":true,"double":true}}
```

Notice how closely the JSON representation matches the definition of the view model in the JavaScript code. The JsonMediaTypeFormatter class will be matched to the request based on the MIME type and will create an instance of the Numbers class.

UNDERSTANDING THE JSON.STRINGIFY METHOD

The JSON.stringify method takes an object and serializes it into the JSON format. The JSON object that defines the stringify method—and its counterpart, JSON.parse—isn't part of jQuery. Instead, it is provided by the browser as part of a set of global JavaScript objects that provide commonly used functionality.

All modern browsers have a built-in implementation of JSON.stringify, but if you find yourself having to support older browsers, then you can get an implementation from https://github.com/douglascrockford/JSON-js that you can include in your application. The file is small, especially if you use the minified version. You can see which browsers have built-in support for JSON.stringify at http://caniuse.com/json.

Creating Complex Types

The Json.Net package that JsonMediaTypeFormatter relies on can instantiate classes with parameterless constructors and settable properties, in just the same way as the media type handler for URL-encoded data.

Json.Net provides many options for customizing the instantiation process based on the JSON data, including attributes that can be applied to the model class to help instantiation. You can get full details of both approaches—and the rest of the Json.Net features—at http://james.newtonking.com.

In this section, I am going to demonstrate how to use a different Json.Net feature: *LINQ to JSON*. I like working with LINQ and find it endlessly useful for wrangling different formats into usable data. Listing 17-17 shows the contents of the JsonNumbersFormatter.cs file that I added to the Infrastructure folder.

Listing 17-17. The Contents of the JsonNumbersFormatter.cs File

```
using System;
using System.Collections.Generic;
using System.IO;
using System.Net.Http;
using System.Net.Http.Formatting;
using System.Net.Http.Headers;
using System.Text;
using System.Threading.Tasks;
using ExampleApp.Models;
using Newtonsoft.Json.Linq;
```

```csharp
namespace ExampleApp.Infrastructure {
    public class JsonNumbersFormatter : MediaTypeFormatter {
        long bufferSize = 256;

        public JsonNumbersFormatter() {
            SupportedMediaTypes.Add(new MediaTypeHeaderValue("application/json"));
            SupportedMediaTypes.Add(new MediaTypeHeaderValue("text/json"));
        }

        public override bool CanWriteType(Type type) {
            return false;
        }

        public override bool CanReadType(Type type) {
            return type == typeof(Numbers);
        }

        public async override Task<object> ReadFromStreamAsync(Type type,
            Stream readStream, HttpContent content, IFormatterLogger formatterLogger) {

            byte[] buffer = new byte[Math.Min(content.Headers.ContentLength.Value,
                bufferSize)];
            string jsonString = Encoding.Default.GetString(buffer, 0,
                await readStream.ReadAsync(buffer, 0, buffer.Length));

            JObject jData = JObject.Parse(jsonString);
            return new Numbers((int)jData["first"], (int)jData["second"]) {
                Op = new Operation {
                    Add = (bool)jData["op"]["add"],
                    Double = (bool)jData["op"]["double"]
                }
            };
        }
    }
}
```

I access the LINQ to JSON feature through this statement:

```
...
JObject jData = JObject.Parse(jsonString);
...
```

The result is an implementation of the IEnumerable<KeyValuePair<string, JToken>>, where the JToken class describes one property from the JSON string I read from the request body. You can use the standard LINQ query syntax or extension methods to process the JSON data, which is useful if you are processing an array of data.

It is more helpful to be able to access all of the JSON properties when instantiating a single object, and JSON to LINQ helpfully presents the data values through array-style indexers. In the listing, I used the indexers to get the four data values I require to create an instance of the Numbers class. Listing 17-18 shows the statement I added to the WebApiConfig.cs file to register the media type formatter.

Listing 17-18. Registering a Media Type Formatter in the WebApiConfig.cs File

```
using System.Web.Http;
using System.Web.Http.ModelBinding;
using System.Web.Http.ModelBinding.Binders;
using System.Web.Http.ValueProviders;
using ExampleApp.Infrastructure;
using ExampleApp.Models;

namespace ExampleApp {
    public static class WebApiConfig {
        public static void Register(HttpConfiguration config) {

            config.DependencyResolver = new NinjectResolver();

            // ...routing statements omitted for brevity...

            config.Services.Add(typeof(ValueProviderFactory),
                new HeaderValueProviderFactory());

            config.Services.Insert(typeof(ModelBinderProvider), 0,
                new SimpleModelBinderProvider(typeof(Numbers), new NumbersBinder()));

            config.Formatters.Add(new XNumbersFormatter());
            config.Formatters.Insert(0, new UrlNumbersFormatter());
            config.Formatters.Insert(0, new JsonNumbersFormatter());
        }
    }
}
```

Handling XML Requests

Dealing with XML data can be tricky because there are so many ways in which the same data can be expressed. If you have control over the clients that will consume your web service, then you should use one of the other data formats I described in this chapter. The most common need to support XML arises in a web service that has to support legacy clients, under which circumstances you will have to adapt to process whatever format—or formats—you are sent. Using the built-in XML media type serializer involves carefully formatting the data sent by the client and preparing the model class for use by the web service.

jQuery doesn't have built-in support for generating XML data from a JavaScript object, but in Listing 17-19 you can see how I have manually formatted the data I will process in the web service.

Listing 17-19. Using jQuery to Send XML Data in the bindings.js File

```
var viewModel = ko.observable({
    first: 2, second: 5, op: { add: true, double: true }
});
var response = ko.observable("Ready");
var gotError = ko.observable(false);

var sendRequest = function (requestType) {
    $.ajax("/api/bindings/sumnumbers", {
        type: "POST",
```

```
        data: "<Numbers>"
            + "<First>" + viewModel().first + "</First>"
            + "<Op>"
                + "<Add>" + viewModel().op.add + "</Add>"
                + "<Double>" + viewModel().op.double + "</Double>"
            + "</Op>"
            + "<Second>" + viewModel().second + "</Second>"
            + "</Numbers>",
        contentType: "application/xml",
        success: function (data) {
            gotError(false);
            response("Total: " + data);
        },
        error: function (jqXHR) {
            gotError(true);
            response(jqXHR.status + " (" + jqXHR.statusText + ")");
        }
    });
};

$(document).ready(function () {
    ko.applyBindings();
});
```

■ **Note**   This code is messy because jQuery lacks built-in support for XML. Clients that send XML will generally have a better mechanism for creating the data they will send to the web service.

The result of the changes in Listing 17-19 is that the body of the HTTP request will contain the following XML fragment:

```
<Numbers>
    <First>2</First>
    <Op>
        <Add>true</Add>
        <Double>true</Double>
    </Op>
    <Second>5</Second>
</Numbers>
```

I find using the built-in media type formatter to be awkward because there are some important constraints on the way that XML data has to be structured. These can be worked around by changing the way the model class is configured—which I explain shortly—but these changes just create a different rigid data structure.

The first constraint is that the name and capitalization of each attribute name much exactly match the class or property name that it corresponds to. That means the top-level element must be Numbers, for example, and not numbers, and certainly not something like myNumbersXML.

The second constraint—and the one that I find the most problematic—is that the attributes must be organized in alphabetical order. This is the reason the Second attribute follows the Op attribute—because, of course, the letter O appears before S in the alphabet. I explain how to change the order of the attributes shortly, but it is possible only to create a different enforced order and not to create a more flexible approach (for that you need a custom media type formatter such as the one I describe in the next section).

The XML serializer that the built-in media type formatter uses will instantiate only the objects that have been annotated with the DataContract attribute and will set only the properties that have been decorated with the DataMember attribute. Both attributes are defined in the System.Runtime.Serialization namespace, and you can see how I have applied them to the Numbers and Operation classes in Listing 17-20.

Listing 17-20. Applying the Data Contract Attributes in the BindingModels.cs File

```
using System.Runtime.Serialization;

namespace ExampleApp.Models {

    [DataContract(Namespace="")]
    public class Numbers {

        public Numbers() { /* do nothing */ }

        public Numbers(int first, int second) {
            First = first; Second = second;
        }

        [DataMember]
        public int First { get; set; }
        [DataMember]
        public int Second { get; set; }
        [DataMember]
        public Operation Op { get; set; }
        public string Accept { get; set; }
    }

    [DataContract(Namespace="")]
    public class Operation {
        [DataMember]
        public bool Add { get; set; }
        [DataMember]
        public bool Double { get; set; }
    }
}
```

I have set the Namespace property of the DataContract attributes to the empty string ("") so that the serializer won't expect an xmlns attribute on the top-level element of the data that is received from the client.

The DataContract and DataMember attributes are defined in an assembly that is not added to Web API projects by default. Select Add Reference from the Visual Studio Project menu, click the Framework section, and locate and check the option for the System.Runtime.Serialization assembly, as shown in Figure 17-2.

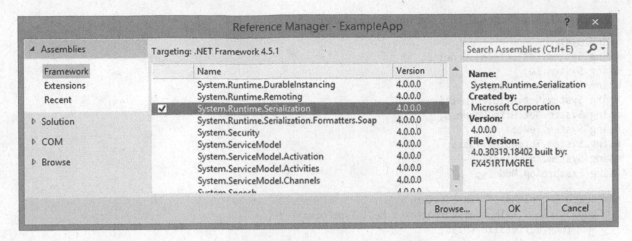

Figure 17-2. Adding the System.Runtime.Serialization assembly

The DataMember attribute defines properties that can be used to change the way that the XML data is processed, as described in Table 17-8. The problem with these properties, however, is that they just create a different kind of rigid data structure that the client has to adhere to, and the media type formatter won't deserialize the request if there is a mismatch between the data from the client and the format implied by the attributes.

Table 17-8. The Properties Defined by the DataMember Attribute

Name	Description
IsRequired	When true, the serializer will not deserialize the data if it does not contain a value for the property to which the attribute has been applied. Missing data feeds an error into the model state, which is used for validation. I describe model state and validation in Chapter 18. The default value is false.
Name	Set the name of the XML element from which the value for the property will be read. The default behavior is to use the name of the property.
Order	When set, this specifies the position of the element in the XML data that will be used to read a value for the property. This overrides the alphabetic order that is the default behavior.

Creating Complex Types from XML Data

When trying to instantiate classes using XML, I avoid treating the elements and attributes as a document with namespaces and schemas. Instead, I use LINQ to mine the XML data for key-value pairs. This approach has its limitations—not least that it incurs the overhead of XML without getting any of the benefits that structured data offers—but in most web services the use of XML is a legacy holdover, and the task at hand is to support XML clients with the minimum of effort. To that end, I created a class file called XmlNumbersFormatter.cs in the Infrastructure folder and used it to create the media type formatter shown in Listing 17-21.

Listing 17-21. The Contents of the XmlNumbersFormatter.cs File

```
using System;
using System.Collections.Generic;
using System.IO;
using System.Net.Http;
using System.Net.Http.Formatting;
using System.Net.Http.Headers;
using System.Text;
using System.Threading.Tasks;
using System.Xml.Linq;
using ExampleApp.Models;

namespace ExampleApp.Infrastructure {
    public class XmlNumbersFormatter : MediaTypeFormatter {
        long bufferSize = 256;

        public XmlNumbersFormatter() {
            SupportedMediaTypes.Add(new MediaTypeHeaderValue("application/xml"));
            SupportedMediaTypes.Add(new MediaTypeHeaderValue("text/xml"));
        }

        public override bool CanWriteType(Type type) {
            return false;
        }

        public override bool CanReadType(Type type) {
            return type == typeof(Numbers);
        }

        public async override Task<object> ReadFromStreamAsync(Type type,
            Stream readStream, HttpContent content, IFormatterLogger formatterLogger) {

            byte[] buffer = new byte[Math.Min(content.Headers.ContentLength.Value,
                bufferSize)];
            XElement xmlData = XElement.Parse(Encoding.Default.GetString(buffer, 0,
                await readStream.ReadAsync(buffer, 0, buffer.Length)));

            Dictionary<string, string> items = new Dictionary<string, string>();
            GetKvps(xmlData, items);

            if (items.Count == 4) {
                return new Numbers(
                    GetValue<int>(items["first"], formatterLogger),
                    GetValue<int>(items["second"], formatterLogger)) {
                        Op = new Operation {
                            Add = GetValue<bool>(items["add"], formatterLogger),
                            Double = GetValue<bool>(items["double"], formatterLogger)
                        }
                    };
            } else {
                formatterLogger.LogError("", "Wrong Number of Items");
                return null;
            }
        }
```

```
        private void GetKvps(XElement elem, Dictionary<string, string> dict) {
            if (elem.HasElements) {
                foreach (XElement innerElem in elem.Elements()) {
                    GetKvps(innerElem, dict);
                }
            } else {
                dict.Add(elem.Name.LocalName.ToLower(), elem.Value);
            }
        }

        private T GetValue<T>(string value, IFormatterLogger logger) {
            T result = default(T);
            try {
                result = (T)System.Convert.ChangeType(value, typeof(T));
            } catch {
                logger.LogError("", "Cannot Parse Value");
            }
            return result;
        }
    }
}
```

You will recognize some of the code and techniques from earlier custom media type formatters in this chapter. In this case, I read the body of the request and use the XElement.Parse method to enter the world of XML to LINQ. I enumerate the XML elements and create a dictionary of key-value pairs, which I then use to instantiate the Numbers class (using the constructor that defines parameters) and set its properties. This is less elegant than treating the XML data as a stream that is handled only once, but it has the benefit of not enforcing a rigid order in which the XML elements must appear. Listing 17-22 shows how I registered the media type formatter in the WebApiConfig.cs file.

Listing 17-22. Registering the Custom Media Type Formatter in the WebApiConfig.cs File

```
using System.IO;
using System.Text;
using System.Web.Http;
using System.Web.Http.ModelBinding;
using System.Web.Http.ModelBinding.Binders;
using System.Web.Http.ValueProviders;
using ExampleApp.Infrastructure;
using ExampleApp.Models;

namespace ExampleApp {
    public static class WebApiConfig {
        public static void Register(HttpConfiguration config) {

            config.DependencyResolver = new NinjectResolver();

            // ...routing statements omitted for brevity...

            config.Services.Add(typeof(ValueProviderFactory),
                new HeaderValueProviderFactory());
```

```
        config.Services.Insert(typeof(ModelBinderProvider), 0,
            new SimpleModelBinderProvider(typeof(Numbers), new NumbersBinder()));

        config.Formatters.Add(new XNumbersFormatter());
        config.Formatters.Insert(0, new UrlNumbersFormatter());
        config.Formatters.Insert(0, new JsonNumbersFormatter());
        config.Formatters.Insert(0, new XmlNumbersFormatter());
    }
  }
}
```

I have used the Insert method once again because I need to ensure that Web API uses my custom media type formatter before the built-in ones.

Customizing the Model Binding Process

Web API delegates the entire process of binding values for parameters to an implementation of the IActionValueBinder interface, which is defined in the System.Web.Http.Controllers namespace. Listing 17-23 shows the definition of the interface.

Listing 17-23. The IActionValueBinder Interface

```
namespace System.Web.Http.Controllers {
    public interface IActionValueBinder {
        HttpActionBinding GetBinding(HttpActionDescriptor actionDescriptor);
    }
}
```

The interface defines a GetBinding method. The important thing to note about the IActionValueBinder interface is that the GetBinding method operates on action methods and is being asked to find bindings for all of the parameters defined by an action—not just a single parameter.

You can see this in the classes that the IActionValueBinder interface uses. The GetBinding method is passed an instance of the HttpActionDescriptor class, which I introduced in Chapter 9 and where I listed the four most important members, which I have repeated in Table 17-9. There are other members, but they are not useful for the purposes of parameter bindings.

Table 17-9. Selected Members Defined by the HttpActionDescriptor Class

Name	Description
ActionName	Returns the name of the action method
ReturnType	Returns the Type that the action method returns
SupportedHttpMethods	Returns a collection of HttpMethod objects that represent the HTTP verbs that can be used to target the action method
GetParameters()	Returns a collection of HttpParameterDescription objects that represent the action method parameters

The `HttpActionBinding` class, which is returned by the `GetBinding` method, is a wrapper around the `HttpActionDescriptor` and an array of `HttpParameterBinding` objects that are used to get values for the parameters defined by an action method. The `HttpActionBinding` class defines a constructor with the following signature:

```
...
public HttpActionBinding(HttpActionDescriptor actionDescriptor,
    HttpParameterBinding[] bindings) {
...
```

The members defined by the `HttpActionBinding` class are not important in this chapter—it is enough to know that the purpose of an implementation of the `IActionValueBinder` interface is to be able to create an `HttpActionBinding` object using this constructor. In the sections that follow, I'll show you how to change the behavior of the default `IActionValueBinder` implementation and how to create a custom one. Table 17-10 puts changing the action value binder in context.

Table 17-10. Putting Changing the Action Value Binder in Context

Question	Answer
What is it?	A custom action value binder allows you to change the way that Web API locates values for action method parameters.
When should you use it?	Use this feature with caution because it takes a lot of effort to create a complete binding system and a lot of testing to make sure it works.
What do you need to know?	You can override the `GetParameterBinding` method of the `DefaultActionValueBinder` class if you want to change the default behavior but still take advantage of features such as value providers, model binders, and media type formatters.

Changing the Behavior of the Default Action Value Binder

All of the functionality that I have described since Chapter 14—value providers, model binders, and media type formatters—is provided by the `DefaultActionValueBinder` class, which is the Web API default implementation of the `IActionValueBinder` interface.

There are no configuration options for changing the behavior of the `DefaultActionValueBinder` class, but it is possible to create a subclass and override the method that defines the default policy for how values are sought for parameters. As a reminder, here is the default sequence that yields an `HttpParameterBinding` object for a single parameter:

1. If the parameter has been decorated with a subclass of the `ParameterBindingAttribute`, then call the attribute's `GetBinding` method.

2. Try to obtain an `HttpParameterBinding` object from the parameter binding rules collection.

3. For simple types, proceed as though the `FromUri` attribute has been applied to the parameter.

4. For complex types, proceed as though the `FromBody` attribute has been applied to the parameter.

This sequence is implemented in the GetParameterBinding method of the DefaultActionValueBinder class. To demonstrate how to change the sequence, I created a file called CustomActionValueBinder.cs in the Infrastructure folder and used it to define the class shown in Listing 17-24.

Listing 17-24. The Contents of the CustomActionValueBinder.cs File

```
using System.Web.Http;
using System.Web.Http.Controllers;
using System.Web.Http.ModelBinding;

namespace ExampleApp.Infrastructure {
    public class CustomActionValueBinder : DefaultActionValueBinder {

        protected override HttpParameterBinding GetParameterBinding(
            HttpParameterDescriptor parameter) {

            if (parameter.ParameterBinderAttribute != null) {
                return parameter.ParameterBinderAttribute.GetBinding(parameter);
            }

            HttpParameterBinding binding =
                parameter.Configuration.ParameterBindingRules.LookupBinding(parameter);
            if (binding != null) {
                return binding;
            }

            if (parameter.ParameterType.IsPrimitive
                    || parameter.ParameterType == typeof(string)) {
                return parameter.BindWithAttribute(new ModelBinderAttribute());
            }

            return new FromBodyAttribute().GetBinding(parameter);

        }

    }
}
```

■ **Note** Although the IActionValueBinder interface deals with an entire action method in one go, the GetParameterBinding method in the DefaultActionValueBinder class deals with one parameter at a time. The DefaultActionValueBinder implementation of the GetBinding method calls the GetParameterBinding method for each parameter defined by the action method described by the HttpActionDescriptor class.

This class follows the same sequence of the DefaultActionValueBinder class but with one important difference: for simple types, I act as though the ModelBinder attribute has been applied, rather than the FromUri attribute. The FromUri attribute excludes any value provider factory class that does not implement the IUriValueProviderFactory interface. By using the ModelBinder attribute—which I described in Chapter 15—I allow all value provider factories to participate in the binding process.

■ **Tip** There is a second difference between `CustomActionValueBinder` and `DefaultActionValueBinder`: I check only for primitive types and strings, rather than the full set of simple types. If you override the `GetParameterBinding` method in a real project, take care to consider how you draw the line between types you will obtain from the URL and those you will obtain from the body.

Listing 17-25 shows how I registered the `CustomActionValueBinder` class as the implementation of the `IActionValueBinder` interface that Web API should use.

Listing 17-25. Registering an Action Value Binder in the WebApiConfig.cs File

```
using System.IO;
using System.Text;
using System.Web.Http;
using System.Web.Http.ModelBinding;
using System.Web.Http.ModelBinding.Binders;
using System.Web.Http.ValueProviders;
using ExampleApp.Infrastructure;
using ExampleApp.Models;
using System.Web.Http.Controllers;

namespace ExampleApp {
    public static class WebApiConfig {
        public static void Register(HttpConfiguration config) {

            config.DependencyResolver = new NinjectResolver();

            // ...routing statements omitted for brevity...

            config.Services.Add(typeof(ValueProviderFactory),
                new HeaderValueProviderFactory());

            config.Services.Insert(typeof(ModelBinderProvider), 0,
                new SimpleModelBinderProvider(typeof(Numbers), new NumbersBinder()));

            config.Formatters.Add(new XNumbersFormatter());
            config.Formatters.Insert(0, new UrlNumbersFormatter());
            config.Formatters.Insert(0, new JsonNumbersFormatter());
            config.Formatters.Insert(0, new XmlNumbersFormatter());

            config.Services.Replace(typeof(IActionValueBinder),
                new CustomActionValueBinder());
        }
    }
}
```

I used the `HttpConfiguration.Services.Replace` method to replace the `DefaultActionValueBinder` with a `CustomActionValueBinder` object.

Creating a Custom Action Value Binder

You can completely replace the process used to bind parameter values by directly implementing the IActionValueBinder interface. There is little reason to do this because there is a lot of flexibility in how the DefaultActionValueBinder can be used. But, if you have a compelling need to completely change the way that binding works, then this is the technique to use. As a demonstration, Listing 17-26 shows how I updated the CustomActionValueBinder class to implement the IActionValueBinder interface, rather than derive from DefaultActionValueBinder.

Listing 17-26. Implementing the IActionValueBinder Interface in the CustomActionValueBinder.cs File

```
using System.Web.Http;
using System.Web.Http.Controllers;
using System.Web.Http.ModelBinding;
using System.Linq;

namespace ExampleApp.Infrastructure {
    public class CustomActionValueBinder : IActionValueBinder {

        public HttpActionBinding GetBinding(HttpActionDescriptor actionDescriptor) {
            return new HttpActionBinding(
                actionDescriptor,
                actionDescriptor.GetParameters()
                    .Select(p => GetParameterBinding(p)).ToArray()
            );
        }

        protected HttpParameterBinding GetParameterBinding(
                HttpParameterDescriptor parameter) {

            if (parameter.ParameterBinderAttribute != null) {
                return parameter.ParameterBinderAttribute.GetBinding(parameter);
            }

            HttpParameterBinding binding =
                parameter.Configuration.ParameterBindingRules.LookupBinding(parameter);
            if (binding != null) {
                return binding;
            }

            if (parameter.ParameterType.IsPrimitive
                    || parameter.ParameterType == typeof(string)) {
                return parameter.BindWithAttribute(new ModelBinderAttribute());
            }

            return new FromBodyAttribute().GetBinding(parameter);
        }
    }
}
```

The changes are simple because I am reproducing the behavior of the default class, and all of the complexity of the model binding process is contained in the value providers, model binders, and media type formatters that Web API includes.

■ **Tip**   You can elect to use as many or as few of the existing binding classes as you require, but before you embark on a project to replace the model binding process, I recommend taking a moment to consider the problem you are trying to solve. The default binding process is flexible and customizable, and smaller changes made within the default process are easier to test and maintain than a completely new process.

Summary

In this chapter, I explained how media type formatters can be used to bind complex types from the body of a request. I showed you how deserialization works by creating and using a custom media type formatter and by using the built-in media type formatters. I explained the limitations on the classes that the built-in formatters will instantiate and demonstrated how to override this behavior to deserialize classes that require special handling. I finished this chapter by demonstrating how to replace the class that drives the parameter and model binding processes with a custom implementation. In the next chapter, I show you the features that Web API provides to ensure that the data you bind from requests is what you expected.

CHAPTER 18

■ ■ ■

Model Validation

The way that Web API binds complex types is useful and flexible, but Web API is a little too trusting and tries to carry on to the point where the action method can be executed, even if the data that has been sent to the client can't be used to bind to the parameters that the action method requires or if the data cannot be used within the application.

Three main problems arise when processing client data: *under-posting*, *over-posting*, and *unusable data*. In this chapter, I describe each in turn and explain why it presents a problem in web service development before showing you the Web API features you can use to guard against them. Table 18-1 summarizes this chapter.

Table 18-1. *Chapter Summary*

Problem	Solution	Listing
Check the validity of a model object passed as a parameter to an action method.	Read the IsValid property of the ModelStateDictionary class to get the overall validity and enumerate the Keys and Values collections to get details of specific validation errors.	1–9
Protect against under- and over-posting.	Use the binding control attributes.	10, 11
Protect against bad data.	Use the validation attributes or create a self-validating model object.	12–14
Validate data as the model object is created.	Use the IFormatterLogger object in a custom media type formatter.	15–17

Preparing the Example Project

I am going to continue working with the ExampleApp project I created in Chapter 10 and have been using for examples since. For this chapter, I am going to add a simple form that sends data to the web service using an Ajax POST request so that I can demonstrate how model validation works. My first change is to add a new action method to the Home controller so that I can render an MVC Razor view to produce the HTML form, as shown in Listing 18-1.

Listing 18-1. Adding an Action Method to the HomeController.cs File

```
using System.Web.Mvc;
using ExampleApp.Models;

namespace ExampleApp.Controllers {
    public class HomeController : Controller {
        IRepository repo;
```

```
        public HomeController(IRepository repoImpl) {
            repo = repoImpl;
        }

        public ActionResult Index() {
            return View(repo.Products);
        }

        public ActionResult Formats() {
            return View();
        }

        public ActionResult Bindings() {
            return View();
        }

        public ActionResult Validation() {
            return View();
        }
    }
}
```

Listing 18-2 shows the contents of the Validation.cshtml view file that I created in the Views/Home directory. This is the view file that will be rendered when the Validation action method in the MVC Home controller is invoked.

Listing 18-2. The Contents of the Views/Home/Validation.cshtml File

```
@{ ViewBag.Title = "Model Validation"; }

@section Scripts {
    <script src="~/Scripts/validation.js"></script>
}

<div class="alert alert-success" data-bind="css: { 'alert-danger': gotError }">
    <span data-bind="text: response()"></span>
</div>
<div class="form-group">
    <label>ProductID</label>
    <input class="form-control" data-bind="value: viewModel().productID" />
</div>
<div class="form-group">
    <label>Name</label>
    <input class="form-control" data-bind="value: viewModel().name" />
</div>
<div class="form-group">
    <label>Price</label>
    <input class="form-control" data-bind="value: viewModel().price" />
</div>
<button class="btn btn-primary" data-bind="click: sendRequest">Send Request</button>
```

This view contains a set of input elements that update a Knockout observable object and a `script` element that imports the `validation.js` file from the `Scripts` folder. This is the file that contains the JavaScript code that sends the Ajax request to the web service, as shown in Listing 18-3.

Listing 18-3. The Contents of the Scripts/validation.js File

```javascript
var viewModel = ko.observable({
    productID: 1,
    name: "Emergency Flare",
    price: 12.99
});

var response = ko.observable("Ready");
var gotError = ko.observable(false);

var sendRequest = function (requestType) {
    $.ajax("/api/products", {
        type: "POST",
        data: viewModel(),
        success: function (data) {
            gotError(false);
            response("Success");
        },
        error: function (jqXHR) {
            gotError(true);
            response(jqXHR.status + " (" + jqXHR.statusText + ")");
        }
    });
};

$(document).ready(function () {
    ko.applyBindings();
});
```

The JavaScript code sends a POST request to the /api/products URL and updates the HTML content based on the response. The final step is to create the action method on the `Products` controller that will be invoked when the Ajax request is received by the web service, as shown in Listing 18-4.

Listing 18-4. Defining an Action Method in the ProductsController.cs File

```csharp
using System.Collections.Generic;
using System.Web.Http;
using ExampleApp.Models;

namespace ExampleApp.Controllers {
    public class ProductsController : ApiController {
        IRepository repo;

        public ProductsController(IRepository repoImpl) {
            repo = repoImpl;
        }
```

429

```
        public IEnumerable<Product> GetAll() {
            return repo.Products;
        }

        public void Delete(int id) {
            repo.DeleteProduct(id);
        }

        public void Post(Product product) {
            repo.SaveProduct(product);
        }
    }
}
```

The Products method is a RESTful Web API controller, which means that the Post method will be invoked when Web API receives an HTTP POST request that targets the /api/products URL. I explain how RESTful controllers work—and how Web API URLs are defined—in Part 3 of this book.

Testing the Changes

To test the changes, start the application and navigate to the /Home/Validation URL. The Validation.cshtml view will be rendered to generate the HTML form shown in Figure 18-1, with the input elements populated with the defaults that I defined in the validation.js file.

Figure 18-1. *The HTML form rendered by the Validation.cshtml view*

Clicking the Send Request button will send an Ajax request that targets the new `Post` method in the `Products` controller. This will trigger the model binding process so that the `Post` method can be passed a `Product` object, which is then added to the model via the repository.

You can check to see whether the product has been created by using the browser to navigate to the `/Home/Index` URL, which displays the contents of the repository, as illustrated by Figure 18-2.

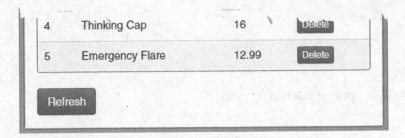

Figure 18-2. *Adding a new product to the repository*

Understanding Common Data Problems

You will face three main problems when dealing with data in a web service: too little data (*under-posting*), too much data (*over-posting*), and bad data (as good a term as any). I describe and demonstrate each kind of problem in the sections that follow before showing you the Web API features that can be used to handle them.

Understanding Under-Posting

Under-posting occurs when the request doesn't contain values for all of the properties defined by a model object. This usually occurs because the client doesn't validate the data provided by the user, but it can also be a deliberate attack that aims to take advantage of ill-chosen default values.

The underlying problem is that the model binding process has no inherent understanding of the way in which model objects are used. An instance of the model class required for a parameter is created, and values for all of the properties it defines are sought from the request. No error is reported if there are properties for which the request doesn't provide a value and if the default value for the property type will be used. To demonstrate under-posting, I have changed the data that the client sends to the web service so that the `Price` property isn't provided. Listing 18-5 shows the changes to the `validation.js` file.

Listing 18-5. Under-Posting in the validation.js File

```
var viewModel = ko.observable({
    productID: 1,
    name: "Emergency Flare",
    price: 12.99
});
```

■ **Tip** Don't forget to clear the browser cache when you make changes to the `validation.js` file; otherwise, the changes may not take effect, and you won't get the expected results.

```
var response = ko.observable("Ready");
var gotError = ko.observable(false);

var sendRequest = function (requestType) {
    $.ajax("/api/products", {
        type: "POST",
        data: { productID: viewModel().productID, name: viewModel().name },
        success: function (data) {
            gotError(false);
            response("Success");
        },
        error: function (jqXHR) {
            gotError(true);
            response(jqXHR.status + " (" + jqXHR.statusText + ")");
        }
    });
};

$(document).ready(function () {
    ko.applyBindings();
});
```

To test the effect of the omission, start the application and use the browser to navigate to the /Home/Validate URL. Click the Send Request button to trigger the Ajax request, which will cause the model binding feature to create an instance of the Product object and seek values from the request for the Product properties. Since there is no value for the Price property, the default value for the Price property type that was assigned when the instance was created will be left unchanged when the action method is invoked. The default value for decimal values is zero, and you can see the result by using the browser to navigate to the /Home/Index URL, which will display the list of Product objects in the repository, as illustrated in Figure 18-3.

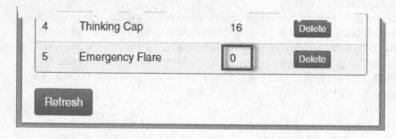

Figure 18-3. *The effect of under-posting on the repository*

The impact of under-posting depends on the type of the properties that are affected and the way that the model object is used. For a storefront application, allowing a product to be added to the catalog with a zero price is a quick way to lose money on profitless sales. The most troublesome problems arise when default values infer some kind of special status on a request, such as an IsAdminUser property that defaults to true.

Understanding Over-Posting

Over-posting occurs when the request contains values for model properties that the developer expected to come from elsewhere. This typically occurs when the model object contains a property that confers special status on the request, such as the IsAdminUser property I described for under-posting. The default binding process will look for request values for all the objects in a model object, even if you expected the values to be set elsewhere in the application. As a demonstration, Listing 18-6 shows the addition of a property that I added to the Product class that indicates the discount rate for the price.

Listing 18-6. Adding a Property in the Product.cs File

```
namespace ExampleApp.Models {
    public class Product {
        public int ProductID { get; set; }
        public string Name { get; set; }
        public decimal Price { get; set; }
        public bool IncludeInSale { get; set; }
    }
}
```

My application may expect to set the IncludeInSale property entirely separately from the process of populating the repository, but the Web API binding process has no way to know that and will set the property if there is a corresponding value in the request. Listing 18-7 shows the change I made to the client-side code to include a value for the new property.

Listing 18-7. Over-Posting Data in the validation.js File

```
var viewModel = ko.observable({
    productID: 1,
    name: "Emergency Flare",
    price: 12.99
});

var response = ko.observable("Ready");
var gotError = ko.observable(false);

var sendRequest = function (requestType) {

    var requestData = viewModel();
    requestData.IncludeInSale = true;

    $.ajax("/api/products", {
        type: "POST",
        data: requestData,
        success: function (data) {
            gotError(false);
            response("Success");
        },
```

```
        error: function (jqXHR) {
            gotError(true);
            response(jqXHR.status + " (" + jqXHR.statusText + ")");
        }
    });
};

$(document).ready(function () {
    ko.applyBindings();
});
```

Over-posting isn't always malicious and can occur when clients send values for all the properties defined by a model object even when the user hasn't directly provided a value. The impact can vary from inconsistent data—products that are on sale when there is no sale, for example—to security breaches, where accounts or request are given elevated access to the application.

■ **Tip** Although I show you how to deal with over-posting using the Web API validation features, the best solution is to avoid defining model properties that cause problems, which prevents requests from being able to cause unwanted effects. If you can't separate out the safe and unsafe properties in your model classes, then consider using a *data transfer object* (DTO), which is a class used solely as an action method parameter and contains only the safe properties. The binding process will set the DTO properties, which you can then copy to an instance of the model class within the action method.

Understanding Bad Data

The final category of problem is bad data, where the client sends data values that cannot be used, either because the values cannot be parsed to the types required by the data model or because the values do not make sense. Most bad data arises because the user has made a mistake, but it can also represent a deliberate attempt to get the web service to act in unexpected or unpredictable ways.

To see the effect of a value that cannot be parsed into a model property, start the application, use the browser to navigate to the /Home/Validation URL, and change the value of the Price property so that it isn't a numeric value. Click the Send Request button and navigate to the /Home/Index URL to see the effect, which is illustrated by Figure 18-4.

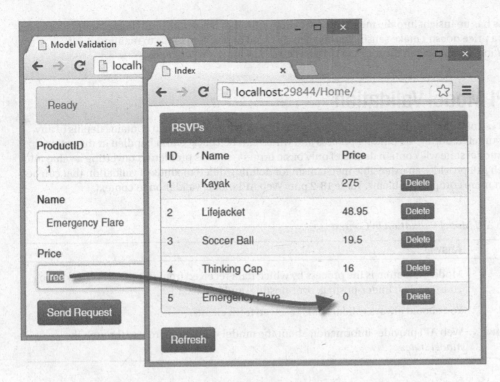

Figure 18-4. *The effect of a data value that cannot be parsed to a model property value*

The Web API binding process doesn't throw an exception when it tries to use the value in the request (free in this example) to set the Price property of the Product object. Instead, it just fails quietly, and the default value for the property type is used (zero in this case since the Price property is a double).

The other kind of bad data problem arises when the request contains a value that can be parsed into the right type but doesn't make sense. To see the effect of this kind of problem, repeat the process to create a new product, but set the Price field to -1, as shown in Figure 18-5.

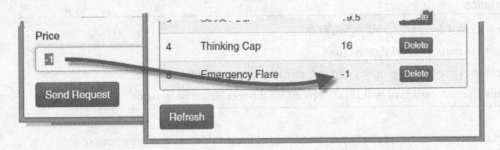

Figure 18-5. *The effect of a data value that can be parsed but is still invalid*

The binding process has no insight into the meaning of the properties that it is setting and has no understanding that a negative value for a price doesn't make sense. The effect of this kind of problem tends to manifest itself elsewhere in the application, such as when the total cost of a basket of products is calculated.

Using Web API Model Validation

To help manage the process of validating data, Web API keeps track of the *model state*, which contains details of any problems that were encountered during the binding process and which can be checked and handled in the action method. By default, the model state will contain details of only basic errors—such as problems converting a value into a property type—but Web API provides an extensible mechanism for defining different kinds of validation that can be used to detect and report more complex problems. Table 18-2 puts Web API model validation in context.

Table 18-2. *Putting Web API Model Validation in Context*

Question	Answer
What is it?	Model validation is the process by which data received from the client is checked to guard against under-posting, over-posting, and bad data.
When should you use it?	You should always validate data received from clients.
What do you need to know?	Web API provides information about the model validation process through the *model state.*

Understanding Model State

The model state for a request is described with an instance of the `ModelStateDictionary` class, which is defined in the `System.Web.Http.ModelBinding` namespace. There are two distinct parts to the life of a `ModelStateDictionary` object. When you are writing action methods, you will use the `ModelStateDictionary` object to check the overall state of the validation process and to get details about individual errors. For these tasks, the `ModelStateDictionary` class defines the properties described in Table 18-3.

Table 18-3. *The Properties Defined by the ModelStateDictionary Class Used to Check Validation*

Name	Description
`IsValid`	Returns `true` if there are no validation errors
`Count`	Returns the number of validation errors
`Keys`	Returns the collection of property names for which there are validation errors
`Values`	Returns an enumeration of `ModelState` objects for the specific property name

The `ModelStateDictionary` also provides an array-style indexer, which provides an alternative way of accessing the `ModelState` objects that are used to represent validation errors. This is the most common way to obtain validation errors that arise when processing a request.

Listing 18-8 shows how I have changed the `Post` action method in the `Products` controller so that I check for model state errors, enumerate them, and vary the response for requests that contain invalid data.

Listing 18-8. Using Model State in the ProductsController.cs File

```
using System.Collections.Generic;
using System.Web.Http;
using ExampleApp.Models;
using System.Diagnostics;
using System.Web.Http.ModelBinding;

namespace ExampleApp.Controllers {
    public class ProductsController : ApiController {
        IRepository repo;

        public ProductsController(IRepository repoImpl) {
            repo = repoImpl;
        }

        public IEnumerable<Product> GetAll() {
            return repo.Products;
        }

        public void Delete(int id) {
            repo.DeleteProduct(id);
        }

        public IHttpActionResult Post(Product product) {
            if (ModelState.IsValid) {
                repo.SaveProduct(product);
                return Ok();
            } else {
                foreach (string property in ModelState.Keys) {
                    ModelState mState = ModelState[property];
                    IEnumerable<ModelError> mErrors = mState.Errors;
                    foreach (ModelError error in mErrors) {
                        Debug.WriteLine("Property: {0}, Error: {1}",
                            property, error.ErrorMessage);
                    }
                }
                return BadRequest(ModelState);
            }
        }
    }
}
```

I have made the Post action method more complex than it would be in a real application so that I can describe all of the types involved in the model state; I'll show you a more typical usage in the "Removing the Debug Output Code" section.

The ApiController class is the default base class for Web API controllers, and the ModelStateDictionary object is exposed through its ModelState property. Within the Post action method, I check the ModelState.IsValid property to see whether there have been any validation errors when the request was processed. If there are no validation errors, I add the new Product object to the repository and call the Ok method to generate the result from the method.

■ **Tip** When working with model validation, you need to return an `IHttpActionResult` from the action method even if you don't want to return data to the client. This allows the action method to differentiate between requests that were processed correctly and those for which there were validation errors.

If there are validation errors, indicated when the `IsValid` property returns `false`, then I use the `ModelStateDictionary.Keys` property to get an enumeration of the property names for which there were problems.

Each property is represented by a `ModelState` object. The `ModelState` class is separate from the `ModelState` property that the `ApiController` class defines, but the fact that the same name is used twice leads to this confusing statement:

```
...
ModelState mState = ModelState[property];
...
```

The `ModelState` property returns the `ModelStateDictionary` object, which defines the array-style indexer that returns instances of the `ModelState` class. The `ModelState` class defines the properties shown in Table 18-4.

Table 18-4. *The Properties Defined by the ModelState Class*

Name	Description
Errors	Returns a collection of `ModelError` objects representing the validation errors for a property
Value	Returns the `ValueProviderResult` associated with the property

Individual validation errors are represented by instances of the `ModelError` class, which defines the properties shown in Table 18-5.

Table 18-5. *The Properties Defined by the ModelError Class*

Name	Description
ErrorMessage	Returns an error message that describes the validation problem
Exception	Returns an exception associated with the validation problem

I use the `ModelState` and `ModelError` classes in the `Post` action method to enumerate any validation errors that were encountered during the binding process and write a description of each of them to the Visual Studio Output window.

Testing the Model State

To test the model state, start the application and use the browser to navigate to the `/Home/Validation` URL. Change the value of the `Price` field to `free` and click the Send Request button.

The model binding process will try to use free as a value for the Product.Price property and fail, since free cannot be converted to a double. There is little built-in validation in Web API, but problems converting values are reported by default, and the ModelState.IsValid property will return true, triggering my validation problem handling code. In the Visual Studio Output window, you will see the following output:

```
Property: product.Price, Error: The value 'free' is not valid for Price.
```

The response sent back to the client will contain the 400 (Bad Request) status code. If you use the browser F12 tools to examine the HTTP response, you will see that it contains a JSON object that contains the same error information that I wrote to the Output window.

```
{"Message":"The request is invalid.",
 "ModelState": { "product.Price":["The value 'free' is not valid for Price."]·}}
```

There is no standard format for expressing data validation errors in HTTP responses, but clients that are written specifically for a Web API web service can parse the JSON object and display appropriate error messages to the user.

■ **Tip** The JSON object that is included in the response is part of the broader Web API error-handling functionality, which I describe in detail in Chapter 25.

Removing the Debug Output Code

I included the code to write out details of the validation errors in the Post action method so that I could explain how the ModelState and ModelError classes are used. In Listing 18-9, you can see how I have removed this code from the action method, leaving a much simpler and easier-to-read action method.

Listing 18-9. Removing the Debug Code from the ProductsController.cs File

```
...
public IHttpActionResult Post(Product product) {
    if (ModelState.IsValid) {
        repo.SaveProduct(product);
        return Ok();
    } else {
        return BadRequest(ModelState);
    }
}
...
```

This is the typical pattern for dealing with validation errors: check the ModelState.IsValid property and respond by performing the operation and returning a 200 (OK) response or by reporting an error to the client with a 400 (Bad Request) response.

Using the Binding Control Attributes

The simplest way to guard against under- and over-posting is to use one of the attributes that Web API provides to control the binding process. The attributes are defined in the System.Web.Http namespace and are described in Table 18-6.

Table 18-6. *The Binding Control Attributes*

Name	Description
HttpBindNever	This attribute tells the built-in model binder to ignore any request values for the property to which it has been applied to.
HttpBindRequired	This attribute reports a validation error if the request does not contain a value for the property to which it has been applied.

Listing 18-10 shows how I applied these attributes to the Product model class to prevent under-posting for the Price property and over-posting for the IncludeInSale property.

Listing 18-10. Applying the Binding Control Attributes in the Product.cs File

```
using System.Web.Http;

namespace ExampleApp.Models {

    public class Product {

        public int ProductID { get; set; }
        public string Name { get; set; }

        [HttpBindRequired]
        public decimal Price { get; set; }

        [HttpBindNever]
        public bool IncludeInSale { get; set; }
    }
}
```

To test the attributes, I changed the data that the client-side code sends in the Ajax request, as shown in Listing 18-11.

Listing 18-11. Changing the Request Data in the validation.js File

```
...
var sendRequest = function (requestType) {

    $.ajax("/api/products", {
        type: "POST",
        data: { Name: viewModel().name, IncludeInSale: true },
        success: function (data) {
            gotError(false);
            response("Success");
        },
        error: function (jqXHR) {
            gotError(true);
            response(jqXHR.status + " (" + jqXHR.statusText + ")");
        }
    });
};
...
```

The request contains no value for the `Price` property, which will trigger a validation error, and the `IncludeInSale` property, which will be ignored.

Performing Validation with Validation Attributes

The binding control attributes are an effective way of dealing with under- and over-posting, but they don't address the bad data problem. The simplest way to increase the amount of validation that is performed is to apply the attributes defined in the `System.ComponentModel.DataAnnotations` namespace, which work exactly as they do in the MVC framework. The attributes are applied to the model class to restrict the range of acceptable values, and the results of the validation can then be checked within the action method. Table 18-7 puts data validation attributes in context.

Table 18-7. *Putting Data Validation Attributes in Context*

Question	Answer
What is it?	The data validation attributes allow you to guard against bad data in requests.
When should you use it?	You should use the validation attributes whenever the application is unable to process the complete range of values for a property type.
What do you need to know?	The validation attributes will not report a validation error if there is no value in the request for the property to which it has been applied.

Using the Built-in Validation Attributes

There is a set of built-in validation attributes that can be used to perform common validation tasks, as described in Table 18-8. Some of the built-in attributes can be configured when they are applied, so I have included a usage example for each of them.

Table 18-8. *The Built-in Validation Attributes*

Name	Example	Description
Compare	[Compare("OtherProperty")]	This attribute reports a validation error if the property it is applied to does not have the same value as the property whose name is specified as the configuration string: OtherProperty in this case. This attribute is useful for e-mail addresses and passwords.
CreditCard	[CreditCard]	This attribute reports a validation error if the value for the property to which it has been applied is not a credit card number. This attribute just checks the format of the number and not whether the card itself is valid.
Email	[Email]	This attribute reports a validation error if the value for the property to which it has been applied is not a valid e-mail address. Only the format is checked and not whether the address exists and can accept e-mail.

(continued)

Table 18-8. *(continued)*

Name	Example	Description
Enum	[Enum(typeof(MyEnum))]	This attribute reports a validation error if the value for the property to which it has been applied cannot be parsed into a value for the specified enum.
MaxLength	[MaxLength(10)]	This attribute is applied to string properties and reports a validation error if the value exceeds the specific number of characters (10 in the example).
MinLength	[MinLength(2)]	This attribute is applied to string properties and reports a validation error if the number of characters in the value is less than the specific value (2 in the example).
Range	[Range(10, 20)]	This attribute is applied to numeric properties and reports a validation error if the value falls outside the specified limits.
RegularExpression	[RegularExpression ("blue|green")]	This attribute reports a validation error if the value doesn't match the specific regular expression.
Required	[Required]	This attribute reports a validation error if no value has been supplied for the property to which it has been applied. This is functionally equivalent to the HttpBindRequired attribute.
StringLength	[StringLength(10)]	This attribute is applied to string properties and reports a validation error if the value contains more than the specific number of characters.

The HttpBindRequired binding control attribute ensures that the request contains a value for a model property, but it doesn't place any limits on what the value is. To guard against bad data, some of the other validation attributes must be used. In Listing 18-12, you can see how I applied the Range attribute to constrain the set of acceptable values for the Price property defined by the Product class.

Listing 18-12. Limiting the Range of Valid Values in the Product.cs File

```
using System.Web.Http;
using System.ComponentModel.DataAnnotations;

namespace ExampleApp.Models {
    public class Product {
        public int ProductID { get; set; }
        public string Name { get; set; }

        [HttpBindRequired]
        [Range(1, 20000)]
        public decimal Price { get; set; }

        [HttpBindNever]
        public bool IncludeInSale { get; set; }
    }
}
```

I applied the Range attribute to limit the acceptable range of values from 1 to 20,000 (these are inclusive so that 1 and 20,000 are both valid). To test the change, I need to change the client-side JavaScript code so that it sends a value for the Price property, as shown in Listing 18-13.

Listing 18-13. Restoring the Price Property in the validation.js File

```
...
var sendRequest = function (requestType) {

    $.ajax("/api/products", {
        type: "POST",
        data: viewModel(),
        success: function (data) {
            gotError(false);
            response("Success");
        },
        error: function (jqXHR) {
            gotError(true);
            response(jqXHR.status + " (" + jqXHR.statusText + ")");
        }
    });
};
...
```

To test the combined attributes, start the application, use the browser to navigate to the /Home/Validation URL, enter a value for the Price field, and click the Send Request button. The model will be valid if the value falls between 1 and 20,000 and the request will succeed, but a 400 (Bad Request) response will be sent for values outside of that range.

■ **Caution** Always take care to combine attributes from Table 18-8 with the HttpBindRequired or Required attribute. The other attributes perform validation only if there is a value in the request for the property to which they are applied, which means that under-posting doesn't cause a validation error to be added to the ModelStateDictionary unless the HttpBindRequred or Required attribute is used as well.

Creating a Self-validating Model Class

An alternative to using attributes is to put the validation logic into the model class and implement the IValidatableObject interface, which is defined in the System.ComponentModel.DataAnnotations namespace. The IValidatableObject interface defines the Validate method, which receives a ValidationContext object and returns an enumeration of the validation errors, expressed as ValidationResult objects.

The ValidatonContext and ValidatonResult objects don't provide any functionality that is specific to Web API validation, but implementing the Validate method provides an opportunity to inject validation logic that is specific to the model class. In Listing 18-14, you can see how I have removed the validation attributes from the Product class and implemented the IValidatableObject interface.

Listing 18-14. Applying the IValidatableObject Interface in the Product.cs File

```
using System.ComponentModel.DataAnnotations;
using ExampleApp.Infrastructure;
using System.Collections.Generic;
```

```
namespace ExampleApp.Models {

    public class Product : IValidatableObject {

        public int ProductID { get; set; }
        public string Name { get; set; }
        public decimal Price { get; set; }
        public bool IncludeInSale { get; set; }

        public IEnumerable<ValidationResult> Validate(ValidationContext
                validationContext) {

            List<ValidationResult> errors = new List<ValidationResult>();

            if (Name == null || Name == string.Empty) {
                errors.Add(new ValidationResult(
                    "A value is required for the Name property"));
            }

            if (Price == 0) {
                errors.Add(new ValidationResult(
                    "A value is required for the Price property"));
            } else if (Price < 1 || Price > 2000) {
                errors.Add(new ValidationResult("The Price value is out of range"));
            }

            if (IncludeInSale) {
                errors.Add(new ValidationResult(
                    "Request cannot contain values for IncludeInSale"));
            }
            return errors;
        }
    }
}
```

This technique works best when the validation logic is unlikely to be used on other model objects. If the validation logic is reusable, then I recommend creating custom validation attributes instead.

Performing Validation in a Media Type Formatter

In Chapter 17, I showed you how to create a custom media type formatter that reads model objects from requests. The base class for media type formatters, MediaTypeFormatter, provides its subclasses with access to the model validation feature, which means you can perform validation as the model object is being created. Table 18-9 puts performing validation in a custom media type formatter in context.

Table 18-9. *Putting Media Type Formatter Validation Context*

Question	Answer
What is it?	The media type formatter base class provides support for reporting validation errors when creating a model object.
When should you use it?	You should perform basic validation for each model property that you set in a custom media type formatter.
What do you need to know?	The binding control attributes are implemented by the default complex model formatter and are not automatically applied in custom classes.

Creating a Validating Media Type Formatter

Listing 18-15 shows the contents of the ValidatingProductFormatter.cs file that I added to the Infrastructure folder and used to create a custom media formatter that reports validation errors.

Listing 18-15. The Contents of the ValidatingProductFormatter.cs File

```
using System;
using System.IO;
using System.Linq;
using System.Net.Http;
using System.Net.Http.Formatting;
using System.Net.Http.Headers;
using System.Text;
using System.Threading.Tasks;
using ExampleApp.Models;
using Newtonsoft.Json.Linq;

namespace ExampleApp.Infrastructure {
    public class ValidatingProductFormatter : MediaTypeFormatter {
        long bufferSize = 256;

        public ValidatingProductFormatter() {
            SupportedMediaTypes.Add(new MediaTypeHeaderValue("application/json"));
            SupportedMediaTypes.Add(new MediaTypeHeaderValue("text/json"));
        }

        public override bool CanReadType(Type type) {
            return type == typeof(Product);
        }

        public override bool CanWriteType(Type type) {
            return false;
        }

        public async override Task<object> ReadFromStreamAsync(Type type,
            Stream readStream, HttpContent content,
                IFormatterLogger formatterLogger) {

            byte[] buffer = new byte[Math.Min(content.Headers.ContentLength.Value,
                bufferSize)];
```

445

```
        string jsonString = Encoding.Default.GetString(buffer, 0,
            await readStream.ReadAsync(buffer, 0, buffer.Length));

        JObject jData = JObject.Parse(jsonString);

        if (jData.Properties().Any(p =>
                string.Compare(p.Name, "includeinsale", true) == 0)) {
            formatterLogger.LogError("IncludeInSale",
                "Request Must Not Contain IncludeInSale Value");
        }

        return new Product {
            Name = (string)jData["name"],
            Price = (decimal)jData["price"]
        };
    }
  }
}
```

The ReadFromStreamAsync method is called to parse data from the request and is passed an IFormatterLogger parameter. The IFormatterLogger interface is defined in the System.Net.Http.Formatting namespace and defines the methods shown in Table 18-10.

Table 18-10. *The Methods Defined by the IFormatterLogger*

Name	Description
LogError(name, message)	Registers a validation error for the specified property name and message
LogError(name, exception)	Registers a validation error for the specified property name and exception

In the listing, I use the IFormatterLogger parameter to register a validation error if the request contains a value for the IncludeInSale property. (This isn't something I recommend you do in real projects—see the "Rewarding Bad Behavior with Error Messages" sidebar).

REWARDING BAD BEHAVIOR WITH ERROR MESSAGES

In Listing 18-15, I reject requests that contain a value for the IncludeInSale property and report a descriptive error. This is a different approach to using the HttpBindNever attribute, which quietly ignores values for the properties to which it is applied.

There is a difficult balance to be struck when it comes to validation messages. On one hand, you want to provide meaningful messages so that users and third-party developers can figure out what is going wrong. On the other hand, you don't want to reveal anything about the internal structure of your application to deliberate over-posters.

There is no absolutely right answer, but my advice is to report errors when it comes to validating the properties that you have publically described and quietly ignore attempts to over-post by using the HttpBindNever attribute. That said, silence is not a proper defense against a determined attack, and you should also consider using professional penetration testers to ensure that your application is not susceptible to obvious security weaknesses.

Registering and Using the Custom Media Type Formatter

I need to register the media type formatter before I can test it. Listing 18-16 shows the change I made to the WebApiConfig.cs file.

Listing 18-16. Registering a Media Type Formatter in the WebApiConfig.cs File

```
using System.Web.Http;
using System.Web.Http.ModelBinding;
using System.Web.Http.ModelBinding.Binders;
using System.Web.Http.ValueProviders;
using ExampleApp.Infrastructure;
using ExampleApp.Models;
using System.Web.Http.Controllers;

namespace ExampleApp {
    public static class WebApiConfig {
        public static void Register(HttpConfiguration config) {

            config.DependencyResolver = new NinjectResolver();

            config.MapHttpAttributeRoutes();

            config.Routes.MapHttpRoute(
                name: "Binding Example Route",
                routeTemplate: "api/{controller}/{action}/{first}/{second}"
            );

            config.Routes.MapHttpRoute(
                name: "DefaultApi",
                routeTemplate: "api/{controller}/{id}",
                defaults: new { id = RouteParameter.Optional }
            );

            config.Services.Add(typeof(ValueProviderFactory),
                new HeaderValueProviderFactory());

            config.Services.Insert(typeof(ModelBinderProvider), 0,
                new SimpleModelBinderProvider(typeof(Numbers), new NumbersBinder()));

            config.Formatters.Add(new XNumbersFormatter());
            config.Formatters.Insert(0, new UrlNumbersFormatter());
            config.Formatters.Insert(0, new JsonNumbersFormatter());
            config.Formatters.Insert(0, new XmlNumbersFormatter());
            config.Formatters.Insert(0, new ValidatingProductFormatter());

            config.Services.Replace(typeof(IActionValueBinder),
                new CustomActionValueBinder());
        }
    }
}
```

447

I also need to change the format of the data that the client sends in the Ajax request so that my validating media type formatter will be used to bind the model object. Listing 18-17 shows the changes that I made so that the data is formatted as JSON.

Listing 18-17. Sending JSON Data in the validation.js File

```
var viewModel = ko.observable({
    productID: 1,
    name: "Emergency Flare",
    price: 12.99
});

var response = ko.observable("Ready");
var gotError = ko.observable(false);

var sendRequest = function (requestType) {

    $.ajax("/api/products", {
        type: "POST",
        data: JSON.stringify(viewModel()),
        contentType: "application/json",
        success: function (data) {
            gotError(false);
            response("Success");
        },
        error: function (jqXHR) {
            gotError(true);
            response(jqXHR.status + " (" + jqXHR.statusText + ")");
        }
    });
};

$(document).ready(function () {
    ko.applyBindings();
});
```

When you test the changes, validation will be performed by the media type formatter and by the attributes applied to the Product class. Being able to mix and match validation techniques allows you to create flexible validation polices that mix the generic (such as an acceptable range of values) with the specific (such that a request doesn't attempt to set a property value).

Summary

In this chapter, I described the different ways in which you can perform validation to protect your model objects from the three most common web service data problems: under-posting, over-posting, and bad data. In Part 3 of this book, I describe the Web API request dispatch process and provide the context in which the features I have described so far exist.

PART 3

Dispatching Requests

■ ■ ■

CHAPTER 19

Dispatching Requests

In this part of the book, I describe the process by which Web API *dispatches requests*, which is the sequence of steps by which an incoming HttpRequestMessage object is processed to produce an HttpResponseMessage that can be sent to the client.

You have already seen some of the steps in Part 2, in which I described how parameter binding and model binding are used to provide an action method with the values it needs to handle a request and how the action method can produce a response. In this chapter, I explain how Web API selects and invokes an action method. I detail the interfaces that describe different areas of functionality and explain how the default implementation of those interfaces work together to create the default dispatching process. In the chapters that follow, I dig into the details and show you how to can take control of request dispatching to tailor the process to your own needs. Table 19-1 summarizes this chapter.

Table 19-1. *Chapter Summary*

Problem	Solution	Listing
Prevent requests from being processed.	Create a custom message handler that generates an HttpResponseMessage object without invoking the handler chain.	1–7
Add support for a custom header.	Create a custom message handler that modifies the HttpRequestMessage before passing it on to the next handler in the chain.	8–9
Use a message handler as a diagnostic tool.	Create a custom message handler that calls the Debugger.Break method.	10
Change the suffix used to identify controller classes.	Create custom implementations of the IHttpControllerTypeResolver and IHttpControllerSelector interfaces or use reflection to modify the default implementation classes.	11–15

Preparing the Example Project

The ExampleApp project I have been using since Chapter 10 is now overcrowded with classes, so I created a new project for this chapter. I selected the ASP.NET Web Application project type and set the name to Dispatch. I clicked the OK button to advance through the New Project Wizard, selected the Empty project template, and checked the options to add the core references for MVC and Web API, just as I did in Chapter 2. I clicked the OK button, and Visual Studio created the new project.

After Visual Studio created the project, I entered the following commands into the Package Manager Console to get the NuGet packages I require:

```
Update-Package microsoft.aspnet.mvc -version 5.1.1
Update-Package microsoft.aspnet.webapi -version 5.1.1
Update-Package Newtonsoft.json -version 6.0.1
Install-Package jquery -version 2.1.0
Install-Package bootstrap -version 3.1.1
Install-Package knockoutjs -version 3.1.0
```

This is the standard set of NuGet packages that I use for Web API applications that includes an MVC framework component.

Creating the Model Class

I require only a simple model class for this chapter, and I don't need any means to store instances persistently. I added a class file called Product.cs to the Models folder and used it to define the class shown in Listing 19-1.

Listing 19-1. The Contents of the Product.cs File

```csharp
namespace Dispatch.Models {

    public class Product {
        public int ProductID { get; set; }
        public string Name { get; set; }
        public decimal Price { get; set; }
    }
}
```

Creating the Web API Web Service

For this chapter, I need a simple web service controller that defines some basic action methods. I added a class file called ProductsController.cs to the Controllers folder and used it to define the controller shown in Listing 19-2.

Listing 19-2. The Contents of the ProductsController.cs File

```csharp
using System.Collections.Generic;
using System.Linq;
using System.Web.Http;
using Dispatch.Models;

namespace Dispatch.Controllers {
    public class ProductsController : ApiController {
        private static List<Product> products = new List<Product> {
                new Product {ProductID = 1, Name = "Kayak", Price = 275M },
                new Product {ProductID = 2, Name = "Lifejacket", Price = 48.95M },
                new Product {ProductID = 3, Name = "Soccer Ball", Price = 19.50M },
                new Product {ProductID = 4, Name = "Thinking Cap", Price = 16M },
            };
```

```
    public IEnumerable<Product> Get() {
        return products;
    }

    public Product Get(int id) {
        return products.Where(x => x.ProductID == id).FirstOrDefault();
    }

    public Product Post(Product product) {
        product.ProductID = products.Count + 1;
        products.Add(product);
        return product;
    }
}
}
```

This is a RESTful controller that defines Get and Post methods that will be targeted by the GET and POST HTTP verbs. (I explain how the verbs are mapped to the action methods in Chapter 22.)

■ **Caution**   I have included a static List of Product objects so that I can respond to requests without having to define and implement a repository. This is suitable for a simple example, but for real projects, follow the repository pattern that I used for the SportsStore application in Chapter 5.

The Get action method return either a Product object or all of the Products objects, which will be serialized and sent to the client using one of the media type formatters I described in Chapter 17. The Post method receives a Product object as an argument, which I add to the static List.

Creating the MVC Controller and View

As with my previous examples, I am going use the MVC framework to deliver HTML and JavaScript code to the client, which will then use Ajax requests to talk to a Web API web service. I created a HomeController.cs class file in the Controllers folder and used it to define the controller shown in Listing 19-3.

Listing 19-3. The Contents of the HomeController.cs File

```
using System.Web.Mvc;

namespace Dispatch.Controllers {

    public class HomeController : Controller {

        public ActionResult Index() {
            return View();
        }
    }
}
```

The Home controller exists solely to deliver the contents of a view to the client. Listing 19-4 shows the contents of the Index.cshtml file, which I added to the Views/Home folder.

Listing 19-4. The Contents of the Index.cshtml File

```
@{ Layout = null;}
<!DOCTYPE html>
<html>
<head>
    <meta name="viewport" content="width=device-width" />
    <title>Index</title>
    <link href="~/Content/bootstrap.min.css" rel="stylesheet" />
    <link href="~/Content/bootstrap-theme.min.css" rel="stylesheet" />
    <script src="~/Scripts/jquery-2.1.0.min.js"></script>
    <script src="~/Scripts/knockout-3.1.0.js"></script>
    <script src="~/Scripts/dispatch.js"></script>
    <style>
        body { padding-top: 10px; }
    </style>
</head>
<body class="container">
    <div class="alert alert-success" data-bind="css: { 'alert-danger': gotError }">
        <span data-bind="text: response()"></span>
    </div>

    <div class="panel panel-primary">
        <div class="panel-heading">Products</div>
        <table class="table table-striped">
            <thead>
                <tr><th>ID</th><th>Name</th><th>Price</th></tr>
            </thead>
            <tbody data-bind="foreach: products">
                <tr>
                    <td data-bind="text: ProductID"></td>
                    <td data-bind="text: Name"></td>
                    <td data-bind="text: Price"></td>
                </tr>
            </tbody>
        </table>
    </div>

    <button class="btn btn-primary" data-bind="click: getAll">Get All</button>
    <button class="btn btn-primary" data-bind="click: getOne">Get One</button>
    <button class="btn btn-primary" data-bind="click: postOne">Post</button>
</body>
</html>
```

I am not using a layout in this project, so the view contains all of the HTML that will be sent to the client. The body element contains a div element that I styled as an alert using Bootstrap and a button that relies on Knockout to call a function called sendRequest.

There is also a table element whose rows are populated by Knockout foreach binding and three button elements, all of which use Knockout to invoke functions when they are clicked.

The last script element in the Index.cshtml file references a file called dispatch.js in the Scripts folder. I created this file to keep the JavaScript code separate from the view. As Listing 19-5 shows, this file defines the data used in the Index.cshtml Knockout bindings and defines the functions that the button elements invoke.

Listing 19-5. The Contents of the dispatch.js File

```javascript
var viewModel = ko.observable({
    productId: 100, name: "Bananas", price: 12.34
});

var products = ko.observableArray();
var response = ko.observable("Ready");
var gotError = ko.observable(false);

var getAll = function () {
    sendRequest("GET");
}

var getOne = function () {
    sendRequest("GET", 2);
}

var postOne= function () {
    sendRequest("POST");
}

var sendRequest = function (verb, id) {

    var url = "/api/products/" + (id || "");

    var config = {
        type: verb || "GET",
        data: verb == "POST" ? viewModel() : null,
        success: function (data) {
            gotError(false);
            response("Success");
            products.removeAll();
            if (Array.isArray(data)) {
                data.forEach(function (product) {
                    products.push(product);
                });
            } else {
                products.push(data);
            }
        },
        error: function (jqXHR) {
            gotError(true);
            products.removeAll();
            response(jqXHR.status + " (" + jqXHR.statusText + ")");
        }
    }

    $.ajax(url, config);
};
```

```
$(document).ready(function () {
    ko.applyBindings();
});
```

The three functions that the button elements invoke—getAll, getOne, and postOne—all rely on the sendRequest function to send an Ajax request to the web service. Within the sendRequest method, I create the URL and the configuration object based on the function arguments, which allows me to send the three different types of request I need using the same code.

■ **Note** There are no input elements to allow the user to change the values in the view model. I will change the view model in the code when I want to send different data to the web service.

Testing the Example Application

To test the web service, start the application. Navigate to the /Home URL with the browser and click the Get One button. jQuery will send a GET request to the server, receive a serialized representation of a Product object, and use its property values to update the alert div element, as shown in Figure 19-1.

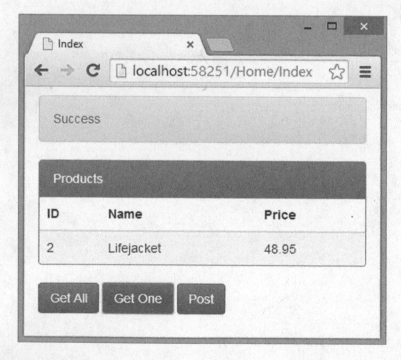

Figure 19-1. *Testing the example application*

Understanding Request Dispatching

Three classes coordinate the way that Web API handles HTTP requests, known collectively as the *message handlers*. The term *message handler* arises because all three classes are derived from the abstract HttpMessageHandler class in the System.Web.Http namespace. The HttpMessageHandler class defines one important method, which derived classes are required to implement.

```
...
protected internal override Task<HttpResponseMessage> SendAsync(
    HttpRequestMessage request,
    CancellationToken cancellationToken
)
...
```

The method is called SendAsync, and it receives an HttpRequestMessage object and returns a Task that produces an HttpResponseMessage object when it completes. The use of the Task result and the CancellationToken parameter indicate that the method should execute asynchronously.

Processing HttpRequestMessage objects to produce HttpResponseMessage objects is the task of any web application framework that uses the System.Net.Http classes. The three MessageHandler classes that I describe in this chapter are the gatekeepers to the world of Web API.

Message handlers are organized into a chain, and each handler processes the request in turn, which gives handlers the chance to modify or enhance the HttpRequestMessage object. The last message handler in the chain creates the HttpResponseMessage, which then passes back along the list, allowing each message handler to modify the response before it is sent to the client. You can see the overall effect in Figure 19-2.

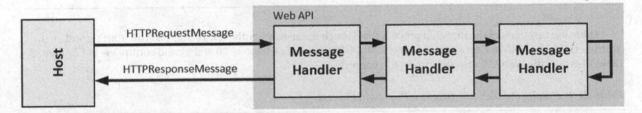

Figure 19-2. *The chain of message handlers*

The host will usually be IIS, especially if you are also using the MVC framework, but there are other options, as I explain in Chapter 26.

From the moment that the host passes on an HttpRequestMessage object, its progress through the request handling pipeline is always under the supervision of a message handler, right until the point where the HttpResponseMessage object is given to the host so a response can be sent to the client.

Web API defines a number of interfaces that are used by the message handlers to hand off important tasks. The use of interfaces means that the dispatch process can be customized, as I describe in the

"Customizing the Dispatch Process" section. It can be hard to keep track of the message handlers, interfaces, and implementation classes involved in the dispatch process, so I have summarized them in Table 19-2. I explain the purpose and role of each of them in the sections that follow.

Table 19-2. *The Dispatcher Interfaces and Default Implementation Classes*

Name	Description
HttpServer	The first message handler to receive new HttpRequestMessage objects.
HttpRoutingDispatcher	The second message handler, which creates routing data for the request.
HttpControllerDispatcher	The third and final message handler, which selects, activates, and executes a controller to create an HttpResponseMessage object.
IHttpControllerSelector	The interface that the HttpControllerDispatcher class uses to delegate controller selection. The default implementation is the DefaultHttpControllerSelector class.
IHttpControllerTypeResolver	The interface used by the DefaultHttpControllerSelector class to locate the controller classes in the application. The default implementation is the DefaultHttpControllerTypeResolver.
IAssembliesResolver	The interface used to locate the assemblies in the application so that the IHttpControllerTypeResolver implementation can search them for controllers. The default implementation is the DefaultAssembliesResolver class.
IHttpControllerActivator	The interface used by the HttpControllerDispatcher class to delegate creating an instance of the selected controller. The default implementation is the DefaultHttpControllerActivator class.
IHttpController	The interface used to denote a controller. I describe controllers fully in Chapter 22, but most controllers are derived from the ApiController class, which implements the IHttpController interface.

There are two parts of the dispatch process that I touch upon only lightly in this chapter: URL routing and controllers. I cover both in later chapters, specifically, URL routing in Chapters 20 and 21 and controllers in Chapter 22. Table 19-3 puts the Web API dispatch process in context.

Table 19-3. *Putting the Web API Dispatch Process in Context*

Question	Answer
What is it?	Web API uses the dispatch process to receive an HttpRequestMessage object representing an HTTP request and to produce a corresponding HttpResponseMessage object that will be used to generate the response sent to the client.
When should you use it?	The dispatch process is automatically applied to all incoming HTTP requests in a Web API application and requires no explicit action.
What do you need to know?	The dispatch process is managed by three message handler classes. The HttpServer class receives requests from the hosting environment, the HttpRoutingDispatcher integrates URL routing, and the HttpControllerDispatcher selects a controller to handle the request. I explain the details of the URL routing system in Chapters 20 and 21 and of controllers in Chapter 22.

Understanding the HttpServer Class

The first message handler in the chain is an instance of the HttpServer class, which acts as the contact point between the hosting environment and Web API.

The HttpServer class has a simple job: it receives an HttpRequestMessage object, prepares it for use in a Web API application, and passes it on to the next message handler in the chain. The preparation involves associating a security principal with the request, creating the HttpRequestContext object, and setting up the classes that will deal with any errors when the HttpResponeMessage comes back along the chain.

■ **Tip** I describe web service security in Chapters 23 and 24, I described the HttpRequestContext class in Chapter 9, and I show you how Web API deals with errors in Chapter 25.

The HttpServer class is instantiated by the GlobalConfiguration class during the configuration phase of the application life cycle. The GlobalConfiguration class also specifies the next message handler in the list, and you can access both classes through the GlobalConfiguration properties shown in Table 19-4.

Table 19-4. *The GlobalConfiguration Properties That Relate to the HttpServer Class*

Name	Description
DefaultHandler	Returns the HttpMessageHandler implementation that the HttpServer class should pass the HttpRequestMessage object to when it has finished its preparations. By default, this is the HttpRoutingDispatcher class, which I describe in the next section. You can add custom message handlers to the chain, which I describe in the "Customizing the Dispatch Process" section.
DefaultServer	Returns the HttpMessageHandler implementation that is the entry point into Web API, which is the HttpServer class.

You can't change the values returned by the DefaultHandler and DefaultServer properties, and the HttpServer class cannot be replaced as the entry point into Web API. But you can add custom message handler classes to change the way requests are processed; see Chapters 23 and 24 for details and examples. Knowing that the HttpServer class is the first message handler in the chain allows me to revise my pipeline diagram, as shown in Figure 19-3.

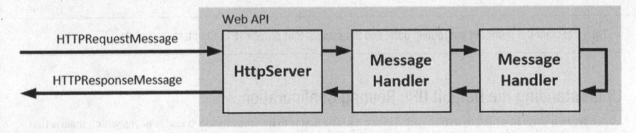

Figure 19-3. *Revising the pipeline diagram to include the HttpServer class*

Understanding the HttpRoutingDispatcher Class

The second message handler in the chain is an instance of the `HttpRoutingDispatcher` class, which integrates *URL routing* into the Web API request handling pipeline. The `HttpRoutingDispatcher` class is defined in the `System.Web.Http.Dispatcher` namespace.

The URL routing system has one purpose: to inspect the request in order to produce data that other components will need to process further along the message handler chain. The data that the routing system produces is called *routing data* or *route data*. Consolidating the functionality that inspects requests to extract the routing data means that a request can be inspected just once by the routing system, even though the routing data that is generated will be used repeatedly by other components.

Routing data is expressed as a collection of name-value pairs. To generate the routing data, the URL routing system tries to match a request against a *routing pattern*, which usually means examining the URL that the client has requested, but it can also incorporate other aspects of the request such as header values. The instructions for matching a request and for generating the routing data are collectively known as a *route*.

Routing data is typically used to extract three types of data from a request:

- The name of a controller

- The name of an action method

- Values that can be used for parameter binding

I say that URL routing *typically* extracts this data because there is a lot of variability in how routing can be configured and how much information each request can provide. Requests won't always contain parameter binding values or an action method name, for example, and even when they do, the components that consume the routing data may choose to ignore the values and use some other source of information to do their work.

Even though it may be used to extract controller and action method names, the URL routing system doesn't do anything with those names. It doesn't select the controller or action method, and it doesn't generate the `HttpResponseMessage` that will be sent to the client. The routing system doesn't assign any meaning to the data it retrieves; it just extracts the data and does nothing more.

In fact, the routing system doesn't have any knowledge of what controllers and action methods are, which is why URL routing works as well in a Web Forms application as it does in Web API and the MVC framework. Routing data is also used for parameter binding, but the routing system doesn't do that binding itself; instead, there is a built-in value provider that gets its data from the routing data associated with a request.

The purpose of the `HttpRoutingDispatcher` class uses the routing system to inspect the `HttpRequestMessage` object and produce routing data, which is then associated with the `HttpRequestContext` object associated with the request and made accessible through the `HttpRequestContext.RouteData` property.

■ **Tip** I explain the format of the routing data, and the classes that provide it, in Chapters 20 and 21.

Understanding the Default URL Routing Configuration

There are two ways in which to define Web API routes. The first is to use *convention-based routing*, which means that routes are configured in a single location and are written to match as many requests as possible. This is the traditional use of URL routing, and it originates from the MVC framework where a uniform and standardized URL schema makes it easier for users to interact with the application.

The other way to define routes is *direct routing* or *attribute-based routing*. There are some common RESTful URL formats that are hard to implement easily with convention-based routing but that are more easily expressed by applying routing information directly to the controllers and action methods that support a specific URL pattern. I am not a fan of direct routing for MVC framework applications, but it can be extremely useful in Web API applications.

There are no default direct routes defined in a Web API application, but I describe the feature in detail in Chapters 20 and 21. Web API routing is set up in the `WebApiConfig.cs` file, as follows:

```
using System;
using System.Collections.Generic;
using System.Linq;
using System.Web.Http;

namespace Actions {
    public static class WebApiConfig {
        public static void Register(HttpConfiguration config) {

            config.MapHttpAttributeRoutes();

            config.Routes.MapHttpRoute(
                name: "DefaultApi",
                routeTemplate: "api/{controller}/{id}",
                defaults: new { id = RouteParameter.Optional }
            );
        }
    }
}
```

The two highlighted statements set up the default URL routing configuration. The `MapHttpAttributesRoutes` method sets up direct routing (which I describe in Chapter 21).

■ **Tip** Web API and MVC framework URL routing work in similar ways but do not share a common class hierarchy or configuration files. Applications that use both frameworks have two separate routing configurations. MVC framework routing is configured in the `App_Start/RouteConfig.cs` file using classes in the `System.Web.Routing` namespace. Web API routing is configured in the `App_Start/WebApiConfig.cs` file using classes from the `System.Web.Http` namespace. Be careful when creating your routing configuration, especially when using Visual Studio to resolve namespaces, because it is easy to end up with a class that mixes classes with the same names from different namespaces and so won't compile.

The other statement calls the `Routes.MapHttpRoute` method on the `HttpConfiguration` argument passed to the `Register` method. The `MapHttpRoute` method sets up a new route called `DefaultApi` that generates two pieces of routing data, `controller` and `id`, both of which are extracted from the request URL. This is an example of convention-based routing, which I describe in detail in Chapter 20.

The `controller` value is used to select the controller that will handle the request, and the `id` value is for parameter binding. You can see how the `controller` and `id` values are extracted from the URL by looking at the `routeTemplate` property used to create the route.

```
...
routeTemplate: "api/{controller}/{id}",
...
```

For this URL:

/api/products

---

the DefaultApi route would produce routing data that contains only the products value for controller because there is no value for the id key. I explain how route templates are defined and applied in Chapters 20 and 21.

For this URL: .

/api/products/1

---

the routing data produced by the DefaultApi route would contain products as the value for controller and 1 as the value for id. Table 19-5 summarizes the routing data for the /api/products/1 URL, which I will use as the exemplar request for the rest of this section.

Table 19-5. *The Routing Data Generated by the Default Route for the Exemplar URL*

Key	Value
controller	products
id	1

■ **Tip**   Notice that the DefaultApi route doesn't generate a routing data value for an action method name. I explain why in Chapter 22.

Figure 19-4 shows my pipeline diagram, updated to show the HttpRoutingDispatcher class, the routing system, and the routing data.

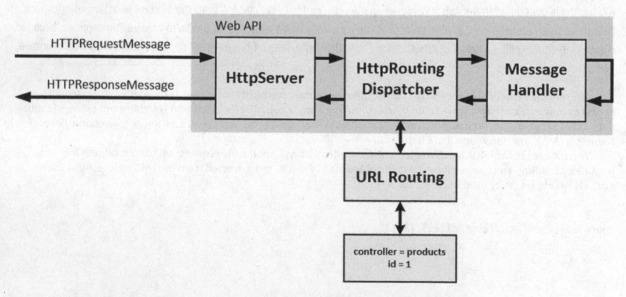

Figure 19-4. *Revising the pipeline diagram to include the HttpRoutingDispatcher class*

Understanding the HttpControllerDispatcher Class

The third and final built-in message handler class is HttpControllerDispatcher, and it is responsible for locating a controller class, creating an instance of it, and asking it to process the request to produce the HttpResponseMessage that will be passed back to the hosting environment via the other message handlers in the chain. The HttpControllerDispatcher class relies on several components to achieve its goal. In the sections that follow, I describe how controllers are located and instantiated.

Selecting the Controller

The HttpControllerDispatcher class delegates the selection of the controller class to an implementation of the IHttpControllerSelector interface, which is defined in the System.Web.Http.Dispatcher namespace. Here is the definition of the IHttpControllerSelector interface:

```
using System.Collections.Generic;
using System.Diagnostics.CodeAnalysis;
using System.Net.Http;
using System.Web.Http.Controllers;

namespace System.Web.Http.Dispatcher {

    public interface IHttpControllerSelector {

        IDictionary<string, HttpControllerDescriptor> GetControllerMapping();

        HttpControllerDescriptor SelectController(HttpRequestMessage request);
    }
}
```

The GetControllerMapping method returns a collection of all the controllers that are available in the application. I explain the purpose of this method in the "Customizing Other Dispatch Components" section later in the chapter, but it is not of interest at the moment.

Instead, it is the SelectController method that is important, and it is called by the HttpControllerDispatcher to obtain an HttpControllerDescriptor object that describes the controller that can handle the request. The HttpControllerDescriptor class is defined in the System.Web.Http.Controllers namespace and provides the properties and methods shown in Table 19-6.

Table 19-6. *The Members Defined by the HttpControllerDescriptor Class*

Name	Description
Configuration	Returns the HttpConfiguration object associated with the controller. Controllers can have their own configurations, as I explain in Chapter 22.
ControllerName	Returns the name of the controller.
ControllerType	Returns the Type of the controller.
CreateController(request)	Creates an instance of the controller that will handle the specified HttpRequestMessage object.
GetCustomAttributes<T>()	Returns the collection of attributes of type T that have been applied to the controller class.
GetFilters()	Returns the filters that have been applied to the class. I describe Web API filters in Chapters 23 and 24.

The default implementation of the IHttpControllerSelector interface is the DefaultHttpControllerSelector class, which is defined in the System.Web.Http.Dispatcher namespace. To select a controller, the DefaultHttpControllerSelector class needs to do the following tasks: identify all of the controllers in the application, select the controller to handle the current request, and then, finally, create an instance of that controller. I describe how each task is completed in the following sections.

During application startup, the DefaultHttpControllerSelector builds a list of all the controller classes in the application, which is later used as the basis for selecting a controller to handle each request. It delegates the identification of controllers to the IHttpControllerTypeResolver interface, as follows:

```
using System.Collections.Generic;
using System.Diagnostics.CodeAnalysis;

namespace System.Web.Http.Dispatcher {

    public interface IHttpControllerTypeResolver {

        ICollection<Type> GetControllerTypes(IAssembliesResolver assembliesResolver);
    }
}
```

The IHttpControllerTypeResolver interface defines the GetControllerTypes method, which is required to return a collection of all the controller types in the application. The GetControllerTypes method is passed an implementation of the IAssembliesResolver interface. This interface defines the GetAssemblies method, which is responsible for returning a collection of all the assemblies in the application, as follows:

```
using System.Collections.Generic;
using System.Diagnostics.CodeAnalysis;
using System.Reflection;

namespace System.Web.Http.Dispatcher {

    public interface IAssembliesResolver {
        ICollection<Assembly> GetAssemblies();
    }
}
```

The default implementations of these interfaces are simple. The DefaultAssembliesResolver class implements the IAssembliesResolver interface and returns all the assemblies in the application domain. A custom implementation could filter the assembly collection to include just those that are known to contain controllers, but the benefit would be a marginally quicker startup process at the cost of an application that won't work properly if the assembly structure is changed.

The default implementation of the IHttpControllerTypeResolver interface is the DefaultHttpControllerTypeResolver class, and it inspects the classes in the assemblies returned by the IAssembliesResolver interface and identifies those that are controllers. Controllers are identified by three characteristics:

1. They are classes that implement the IHttpController interface.

2. The name of the class has the Controller suffix (for example, ProductsController).

3. The class is public and is not abstract.

The DefaultHttpControllerSelector class creates a cache of HttpControllerDescriptor objects for each controller class that the IHttpControllerTypeResolver implementation identifies.

When the HttpControllerDispatcher class asks for a controller by calling the SelectController method, the DefaultHttpControllerSelector class looks through its cache of HttpControllerDescriptor objects until it finds one with a ControllerName value that matches the controller value from the routing data created by the HttpRoutingDispatcher class.

Activating the Controller

At this point, the HttpControllerDispatcher class has obtained an HttpControllerDescriptor object that describes the controller that will handle the request. The next step is to instantiate the controller class, a process known as *activation*.

Activation is performed by calling the CreateController method of the HttpControllerDescriptor class, which in turn delegates the process to an implementation of the IControllerActivator interface.

```
using System.Net.Http;
using System.Web.Http.Controllers;

namespace System.Web.Http.Dispatcher {

    public interface IHttpControllerActivator {
        IHttpController Create(HttpRequestMessage request,
            HttpControllerDescriptor controllerDescriptor, Type controllerType);
    }
}
```

The Create method is called to create an IHttpController object and is provided with the HttpRequestMessage that describes the current request, the HttpControllerDescriptor that describes the controller, and the controller Type.

The default IHttpControllerActivator implementation is the DefaultHttpControllerActivator class, which is defined in the System.Web.Http.Dispatcher namespace. The process that the DefaultHttpControllerActivator class follows is simple:

1. Try to get an instance of the controller type from the dependency resolver.

2. Create an instance of the controller by invoking a parameterless constructor.

This approach supports the dependency injection model I described in Chapter 10 but falls back to instantiating classes directly if there is no resolver in the application. It also means that if you need to define controllers without parameterless constructors, you must either create a custom implementation of the IHttpControllerActivator interface or configure a dependency resolver that knows how to instantiate them (as I did in the SportsStore application for controllers that defined a repository constructor argument).

Executing the Controller

The HttpControllerDispatcher has almost completed its task: it has selected a controller and created an instance of it, and all that remains is to ask it to process the result so that the HttpResponseMessage can be returned along the chain of message handlers and, ultimately, sent to the client. As I mentioned in the previous section, one of the identifying characteristics of a controller is that it implements the IHttpController interface.

```
using System.Net.Http;
using System.Threading;
using System.Threading.Tasks;

namespace System.Web.Http.Controllers {

    public interface IHttpController {
        Task<HttpResponseMessage> ExecuteAsync(HttpControllerContext controllerContext,
            CancellationToken cancellationToken);
    }
}
```

The IHttpController interface defines the ExecuteAsync method, which is passed an HttpControllerContext and a CancellationToken. The purpose of the method is to asynchronously process the request using the information provided by the HttpControllerContext and return a Task that produces an HttpResponseMessage object when it completes.

The HttpControllerContext object is created by the HttpControllerDispatcher class in order to provide the controller with all the details it needs to do its work. The HttpControllerContext class defines the properties shown in Table 19-7.

Table 19-7. *The Properties Defined by the HttpControllerContext Class*

Name	Description
Configuration	Returns the HttpConfiguration object that should be used to service the request. As I explain in Chapter 22, controllers can be given their own configuration to work with.
Controller	Returns the IHttpController instance. This is not entirely useful when the HttpControllerContext is being passed an argument to the controller but is more useful when used for other tasks such as action method selection (which I describe in Chapter 22).
ControllerDescriptor	Returns the HttpControllerDescriptor that led to the controller being instantiated.
Request	Returns the HttpRequestMessage that describes the current request.
RequestContext	Returns the HttpRequestContext that provides additional information about the request.
RouteData	Returns the IHttpRouteData object that contains the routing data for the request. See Chapters 20 and 21 for details.

The details of how the IHttpController implementation processes the HttpControllerContext into an HttpResponseMessage are entirely opaque to the message handlers, but I explain how the default controller class, ApiController, works in Chapter 22. You won't be surprised that it relies on delegating work to implementations of interfaces that you can replace or customize.

Now that I have explained how the HttpControllerDispatcher works, I can update my diagram to reflect the end-to-end flow of a request and its response through the Web API dispatch process, as illustrated in Figure 19-5.

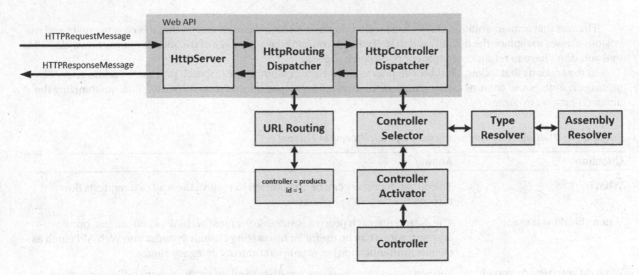

Figure 19-5. *The end-to-end Web API dispatch process*

There are two areas that I have only lightly touched on as I described the dispatch process: URL routing and controllers. In both cases, this is because they are big enough features to warrant their own chapters. I describe URL routing in Chapters 20 and 21 and explain how controllers work in Chapter 22.

Customizing the Dispatch Process

The reason that there are so many interfaces involved in the dispatch process is so that the way requests are handled can be customized. Although I described the default implementation classes in the previous section, implementations of the dispatch interfaces are obtained from the services collection, using the extension methods listed in Table 19-8.

Table 19-8. *The Extension Methods That Obtain Dispatcher Objects from the Services Collection*

Name	Description
GetAssembliesResolver()	Returns an implementation of the IAssembliesResolver interface
GetHttpControllerActivator()	Returns an implementation of the IHttpControllerActivator interface
GetHttpControllerSelector()	Returns an implementation of the IHttpControllerSelector interface
GetHttpControllerTypeResolver()	Returns an implementation of the IHttpControllerTypeResolver interface

These extension methods are defined in the System.Web.Http namespace and operate on the ServicesContainer class. That means you can obtain a reference to instances of the default classes by calling one of these methods on the HttpConfiguration.Services property, like this:

```
...
GlobalConfiguration.Configuration.Services.GetHttpControllerSelector()
...
```

The fact that implementation classes are located via the services collection means that it is easy to create and use custom classes to replace the defaults and that, if you do, you can take advantage of the services in your own classes so that you don't have to reimplement the entire dispatch process.

In the sections that follow, I'll show you how to extend and customize the dispatch process, by adding new message handlers and creating custom implementations of the dispatch interfaces. Table 19-9 puts customizing the dispatch process in context.

Table 19-9. *Putting the Customizing the Dispatch Process in Context*

Question	Answer
What is it?	The dispatch process can be customized to control the way that requests flow through the Web API application.
When should you use it?	The default dispatch process is suitable for most Web API applications, but customizations can be useful for integrating custom systems into Web API (such as custom authentication) or to support unusual or legacy clients.
What do you need to know?	You can use custom message handlers to adapt requests from difficult clients to the standard Web API model or to stop requests from being processed. Finer-grained customizations are possible by reimplementing the interfaces that are used to locate and select controller classes.

Creating Custom Message Handlers

Web API allows custom message handlers to be added to the chain between the HttpServer and HttpRoutingDispatch classes. Custom message handlers are similar to traditional ASP.NET modules and can be used to prepare an HttpRequestMessage for process or modify an HttpResponseMessage before it is used to produce a response to the client.

Custom message handlers are derived from the DelegatingHandler class, which is derived from MessageHandler, but adds support for an *inner handler*, which is the next handler in the chain. A custom handler can call the inner handler to advance the request to the next stage in the dispatch pipeline or generate a response itself to terminate the request handing process. As a demonstration, I created a folder called Infrastructure and added to it a class file called CustomMessageHandler.cs. Listing 19-6 shows the custom message handle that I created.

Listing 19-6. The Contents of the CustomMessageHandler.cs File

```
using System.Net;
using System.Net.Http;
using System.Threading;
using System.Threading.Tasks;
```

```
namespace Dispatch.Infrastructure {
    public class CustomMessageHandler : DelegatingHandler {

        protected async override Task<HttpResponseMessage> SendAsync(HttpRequestMessage
            request, CancellationToken cancellationToken) {

            if (request.Method == HttpMethod.Post) {

                return request.CreateErrorResponse(HttpStatusCode.MethodNotAllowed,
                    "POST Not Supported");
            } else {
                return await base.SendAsync(request, cancellationToken);
            }
        }
    }
}
```

This class demonstrates how a message handler can intercept requests and create a result directly. Within the SendAsync method, I look for POST requests by checking the `HttpRequestMessage.Method` property. When the method is POST, I create an `HttpResponseMessage` with the 405 (Method Not Allowed) status code, like this:

```
...
return request.CreateErrorResponse(HttpStatusCode.MethodNotAllowed,
    "POST Not Supported");
...
```

CreateErrorResponse is one of the extension methods that can be applied to `HttpRequestMessage` objects to create `HttpResponseMessage` objects. These methods conveniently populate the `HttpResponseMessage` fields from their parameter values and details of the request. There are methods available to create successful and error responses, all of which are defined by the `HttpRequestMessageExtensions` class. I have shown the most useful methods for creating `HttpResponseMessage` objects in Table 19-10. (I have omitted a few versions that specify a particular media type formatter to encode data objects or provide additional detail about an error.)

Table 19-10. *The Methods for Creating HttpResponseMessage Objects from an HttpRequestMessage*

Method	Description
CreateResponse()	Creates a basic `HttpResponseMessage` with the 200 (OK) status code and no content.
CreateResponse(status)	Creates an `HttpResponseMessage` with the specified status code, which is expressed as an `HttpStatusCode` value.
CreateResponse(data)	Creates an `HttpResponseMessage` with the 200 (OK) status code and the specified data object as the content. The data object is encoded using the content negotiation process that I described in Part 2.
CreateResponse(status, data)	Creates an `HttpResponseMessage` with the specified status code and data object. The status code is expressed as an `HttpStatusCode`, and the data object is encoded using the content negotiation process I described in Part 2.

(continued)

Table 19-10. (*continued*)

Method	Description
CreateResponse(status, data, mime)	Creates an HttpResponseMessage with the specified status code and data object. The status code is expressed as an HttpStatusCode, and the data object is encoded using the specified MIME type using the media type formatter process I described in Part 2.
CreateErrorResponse(status, message)	Creates an HttpResponseMessage with the specified status code and error message. The status code is expressed using HttpStatusCode, and the message is a string. I describe Web API error handling in Part 2.
CreateErrorResponse(status, error)	Creates an HttpResponseMessage with the specified status code and error. The status code is expressed using HttpStatusCode, and the error is an HttpError. I describe Web API error handling in Chapter 25.

A message handle that returns an HttpResponseMessage from its SendAsync method terminates the normal process of the HttpRequestMessage through the chain of message handlers. For my example message handler, this means that POST requests are rejected, and both requests with other verbs are allowed to processed.

If a handler wants to pass on a request to the next handler in the chain, then it calls the SendAsync method of the base class and returns the result, like this:

```
...
return await base.SendAsync(request, cancellationToken);
...
```

Each message handler is automatically configured with details of the next message handler so that you don't have to manage details of the handler chain inside your custom class.

Message handlers are registered through the HttpConfiguration.MessageHandlers property, as shown in Listing 19-7.

Listing 19-7. Registering a Custom Message Handler in the WebApiConfig.cs File

```
using System;
using System.Collections.Generic;
using System.Linq;
using System.Web.Http;
using Dispatch.Infrastructure;

namespace Dispatch {
    public static class WebApiConfig {
        public static void Register(HttpConfiguration config) {

            config.MapHttpAttributeRoutes();

            config.Routes.MapHttpRoute(
                name: "DefaultApi",
                routeTemplate: "api/{controller}/{id}",
                defaults: new { id = RouteParameter.Optional }
            );
```

```
        config.MessageHandlers.Add(new CustomMessageHandler());
    }
  }
}
```

The MessageHandlers collection contains only custom message handlers, which are always placed after HttpServer and before HttpRoutingDispatcher in the message handler chain. To test the new message handler, start the application and click the Post button—the handler will intercept the request and return the error response shown in Figure 19-6.

Figure 19-6. *Testing the custom message handler*

■ **Caution**   A single instance of the message handler class is created and used to service all of the requests that the Web API application receives. This means your code must be thread-safe and must be able to deal with concurrent execution of the SendAsync method.

Modifying Requests or Responses in a Message Handler

Although you can use a message handler to stop or allow requests through the application—as I did in the previous section—a more common use for a message handler is to modify the HttpRequestMessage or HttpResponseMessage object to add new features to your web service.

The problem is that Web API already has every feature that a web service needs, and while it is useful that you can intercept and modify the request and response, there is little need to do so.

The standard demonstration for message handlers is to add support for the X-HTTP-Method-Override header, which isn't supported by Web API by default. It isn't an example that I like (for the reasons I set out in the "Understanding the X-HTTP-Method-Override Header" sidebar), but it is a simple and self-contained demonstration of how a message handler can be used, so I have included it in this chapter. Listing 19-8 shows how I have revised the CustomMessageHandler class so that it supports the X-HTTP-Method-Override header.

Listing 19-8. Supporting a Nonstandard Header in the CustomMessageHandler.cs File

```
using System.Net;
using System.Net.Http;
using System.Threading;
using System.Threading.Tasks;
using System.Linq;

namespace Dispatch.Infrastructure {
    public class CustomMessageHandler : DelegatingHandler {

        protected async override Task<HttpResponseMessage> SendAsync(HttpRequestMessage
            request, CancellationToken cancellationToken) {

            if (request.Method == HttpMethod.Post
                && request.Headers.Contains("X-HTTP-Method-Override")) {

                HttpMethod requestedMethod = new HttpMethod(
                    request.Headers.GetValues("X-HTTP-Method-Override").First());

                if (requestedMethod == HttpMethod.Put
                        || requestedMethod == HttpMethod.Delete) {
                    request.Method = requestedMethod;
                } else {
                    return request.CreateErrorResponse(HttpStatusCode.MethodNotAllowed,
                        "Only PUT and DELETE can be overridden");
                }
            }
            return await base.SendAsync(request, cancellationToken);
        }
    }
}
```

UNDERSTANDING THE X-HTTP-METHOD-OVERRIDE HEADER

The X-HTTP-Method-Override header allows clients to tell the web service that the request should be handled as though it has a different HTTP verb. For example, if the server receives an HTTP POST request with the X-HTTP-Method-Override set to PUT, then the request should be handled as though the PUT verb had been used.

The X-HTTP-Method-Override arose to work around limitations in some clients that could send only GET or POST requests or to work around firewalls that blocked any verb except GET or POST. Using the X-HTTP-Method-Override allows clients to work around these limitations and take full advantage of a RESTful web service.

As helpful as the X-HTTP-Method-Override header can be, it requires coordination between the client and the server: the client needs to know that the server is looking for the header and will honor it. If the client and server are not coordinated, then the header will be ignored, and POST requests will always be taken as POST requests, even if the X-HTTP-Method-Override header specifies a different verb. In addition, clients have no way of knowing whether there are verbs that cannot be used; there is no way of detecting the policy of a corporate firewall, for example. In short, the X-HTTP-Method-Override has some issues, and I recommend avoiding it if at all possible. It is no accident that neither Web API nor the MVC framework supports the header.

I look for POST requests that contain the X-HTTP-Method-Override header, which I apply only to the PUT and DELETE verbs (although if you are supporting this header in a real project, you should take care to allow all of the verbs that your web service requires). For requests that meet my criteria, I set the value of the HttpRequestMethod.Method property, which has the effect of causing the rest of the Web API message handlers to treat the request as though it was made using the verb specified by the X-HTTP-Method-Override header.

The example web service supports only POST and GET, but Listing 19-9 shows the changes that are required to the dispatch.js file to support the X-HTTP-Method-Override header.

Listing 19-9. Adding Support for the X-HTTP-Method-Override Header in the dispatch.js File

```
...
var sendRequest = function (verb, id) {

    var url = "/api/products/" + (id || "");

    var config = {
        type: verb || "GET",
        data: verb == "POST" ? viewModel() : null,
        success: function (data) {
            gotError(false);
            response("Success");
            products.removeAll();
            if (Array.isArray(data)) {
                data.forEach(function (product) {
                    products.push(product);
                });
            } else {
                products.push(data);
            }
        },
        error: function (jqXHR) {
            gotError(true);
            products.removeAll();
            response(jqXHR.status + " (" + jqXHR.statusText + ")");
        }
    }

    if (verb != "GET" && verb != "POST") {
        config.type = "POST";
        config.headers = {
            "X-HTTP-Method-Override": verb
        };
    }

    $.ajax(url, config);
};
...
```

Using Message Handlers as Diagnostic Tools

I find message handlers most useful as a diagnostic tool for when I can't figure out the cause of a problem and I start to lose trust in my tools. Sometimes this is a consequence of desperation—a growing conviction that I am missing something fundamental—but most often I use message handlers so I can break the Visual Studio debugger right at the start of the dispatch process and follow a request all the way through the application and follow the response all the way back out again. This is especially useful when using the debugger to display the Web API source code, which allows all of the objects and variables to be inspected and makes it easy (or at least easier) to find out what is causing a problem.

You can manually apply breakpoints to your application code, but a request handler can break the debugger while the request has just entered the world of Web API. Listing 19-10 shows how I have changed the CustomMessageHandler class so that it breaks the debugger.

Listing 19-10. Creating a Diagnostic Tool in the CustomMessageHandler.cs File

```
using System.Net;
using System.Net.Http;
using System.Threading;
using System.Threading.Tasks;
using System.Linq;

namespace Dispatch.Infrastructure {
    public class CustomMessageHandler : DelegatingHandler {

        protected async override Task<HttpResponseMessage> SendAsync(HttpRequestMessage
            request, CancellationToken cancellationToken) {

            if (request.Method == HttpMethod.Post) {
                System.Diagnostics.Debugger.Break();
            }
            return await base.SendAsync(request, cancellationToken);

        }
    }
}
```

The System.Diagnostics.Debugger class controls the debugger, and the Break method stops execution of the application and hands it control. With this message handler installed, every POST request causes the debugger to break so that you can step through the dispatch process. To see the effect, start the application and click the Post button in the browser. The Break method will be called and execution of the application will be stopped so that you can control it through the standard Visual Studio debugger.

Customizing Other Dispatch Components

You can create custom implementations of all the interfaces that I described in this chapter, but there is little point in doing so because the Web API default implementations are serviceable for most applications. That said, it is always useful to know that you can replace the standard components if you need to, and in the sections that follow, I show the process for changing the suffix used to identify controller classes, which is Controller by default.

Implementing the Interfaces

An implementation of the IHttpControllerTypeResolver interface is responsible for identifying the controller classes in the application. The default implementation of the interface is the DefaultHttpControllerTypeResolver class, and it defines a method called IsControllerType that is called for each type in the application to see whether it is a controller, as follows:

```
...
internal static bool IsControllerType(Type t) {
    return
        t != null &&
        t.IsClass &&
        t.IsVisible &&
        !t.IsAbstract &&
        typeof(IHttpController).IsAssignableFrom(t) &&
        HasValidControllerName(t);
}
...
```

This method is exactly what you would expect to see; it looks for classes that are public, not abstract, and that are derived from IHttpController. The final test is the one that is interesting for this example: only classes for which the HasValidControllerName method returns true are selected. Here is the definition of the HasValidControllerName method:

```
...
internal static bool HasValidControllerName(Type controllerType) {
    string controllerSuffix = DefaultHttpControllerSelector.ControllerSuffix;
    return controllerType.Name.Length > controllerSuffix.Length
        && controllerType.Name.EndsWith(controllerSuffix,
            StringComparison.OrdinalIgnoreCase);
}
...
```

The DefaultHttpControllerSelector.ControllerSuffix property is set to Controller, and the HasValidControllerName method checks to see that the class name contains the suffix (and isn't *just* the suffix so that a class called Controller won't be identified as a controller).

Ideally, I could change the suffix used to identify controllers by deriving from the DefaultHttpControllerTypeResolver class and overriding either the IsControllerType or HasValidControllerName method; these are both marked as internal. An alternative would be to change the value of the DefaultHttpControllerSelector.ControllerSuffix property, but that isn't possible because it has been marked as readonly.

```
...
public static readonly string ControllerSuffix = "Controller";
...
```

The implementation of the DefaultHttpControllerSelector and DefaultHttpControllerTypeResolver classes means that I need to create my own implementation of the IHttpControllerTypeResolver interface in order to change the controller suffix. I added a class file called CustomControllerTypeResolver.cs to the Infrastructure folder and used it to define the class shown in Listing 19-11.

Listing 19-11. The Contents of the CustomControllerTypeResolver.cs Class

```
using System;
using System.Collections.Generic;
using System.Linq;
using System.Web.Http.Controllers;
using System.Web.Http.Dispatcher;

namespace Dispatch.Infrastructure {
    public class CustomControllerTypeResolver : IHttpControllerTypeResolver {

        public string Suffix { get; set; }

        public ICollection<Type> GetControllerTypes(IAssembliesResolver
            assembliesResolver) {

            return assembliesResolver.GetAssemblies()
                .Select(assembly => assembly.GetTypes())
                .SelectMany(t => t)
                .Where(t => t != null
                    && t.IsClass
                    && t.IsVisible
                    && !t.IsAbstract
                    && typeof(IHttpController).IsAssignableFrom(t)
                    && HasValidControllerName(t)).ToList();
        }

        private bool HasValidControllerName(Type t) {
            return t.Name.Length > Suffix.Length
                && t.Name.EndsWith(Suffix, StringComparison.OrdinalIgnoreCase);
        }
    }
}
```

My custom implementation has a Suffix property that is used to locate controller classes in the assemblies provided by the IAssembliesResolver implementation object that is passed to the GetControllerTypes method.

Unfortunately, the class shown in Listing 19-11 doesn't have the effect you might expect, which is because the DefaultHttpControllerSelector class uses a cache to speed up controller selection, and the class that handles the caching (the HttpControllerTypeCache class) has a hard-coded dependency on the DefaultHttpControllerSelector.ControllerSuffix property that it uses to retrieve cached classes. This means that if I want to change the suffix used by controllers, it isn't enough to create a new implementation of the IHttpControllerTypeResolver class—I also have to create a new implementation of the IHttpControllerSelector interface as well. Listing 19-12 shows the contents of the CustomControllerSelector.cs file that I added to the Infrastructure folder.

Listing 19-12. The Contents of the CustomControllerSelector.cs File

```
using System;
using System.Collections.Generic;
using System.Linq;
using System.Net;
using System.Net.Http;
```

```
using System.Web.Http;
using System.Web.Http.Controllers;
using System.Web.Http.Dispatcher;

namespace Dispatch.Infrastructure {

    public class CustomControllerSelector : IHttpControllerSelector {
        private IDictionary<string, HttpControllerDescriptor> dictionary;
        private ILookup<string, HttpControllerDescriptor> mappings;

        public CustomControllerSelector(string suffix) {

            Suffix = suffix;
            HttpConfiguration config = GlobalConfiguration.Configuration;

            IHttpControllerTypeResolver typeFinder =
                config.Services.GetHttpControllerTypeResolver();
            IAssembliesResolver assemblyFinder = config.Services.GetAssembliesResolver();

            IEnumerable<HttpControllerDescriptor> descriptors
                = typeFinder.GetControllerTypes(assemblyFinder)
                .Select(type => new HttpControllerDescriptor {
                    Configuration = GlobalConfiguration.Configuration,
                    ControllerName = type.Name.Substring(0,
                        type.Name.Length - Suffix.Length),
                    ControllerType = type});

            mappings = descriptors.ToLookup(descriptor =>
                    descriptor.ControllerName, StringComparer.OrdinalIgnoreCase);

            dictionary = descriptors.ToDictionary(d => d.ControllerName, d => d);
        }

        private string Suffix { get; set; }

        public IDictionary<string, HttpControllerDescriptor> GetControllerMapping() {
            return dictionary;
        }

        public HttpControllerDescriptor SelectController(HttpRequestMessage request) {
            string key
                = request.GetRequestContext().RouteData.Values["controller"] as string;
            IEnumerable<HttpControllerDescriptor> matches = mappings[key];
            switch (matches.Count()) {
                case 1:
                    return matches.First();
                case 0:
                    throw new HttpResponseException(HttpStatusCode.NotFound);
```

```
                default:
                    throw new HttpResponseException(HttpStatusCode.InternalServerError);
            }
        }
    }
}
```

The IHttpControllerSelector interface requires two methods to be implemented. The GetControllerMapping method is used by the attribute routing feature to configure itself during application startup and requires a Dictionary that maps controller names to HttpControllerDescriptor objects. I use LINQ to create an enumeration of HttpControllerDescriptor object in the CustomControllerSelector constructor and then use the always-convenient LINQ ToDictionary method to create the collection that the GetControllerMapping mapping demands.

I have taken a different approach for the SelectController method and used the LINQ ToLookup method. This little-used method groups together objects based on a key, which is useful because a Web API application can contain multiple controller classes with the same name but defined in different namespaces. I follow the default behavior and throw an exception if more than one controller matches the value of the controller routing data value.

Registering the Interface Implementations

Listing 19-13 shows how I replaced the default implementations of the IHttpControllerTypeResolver and IHttpControllerSelector interfaces with my custom classes in the WebApiConfig.cs file.

Listing 19-13. Registering Custom Classes in the WebApiConfig.cs File

```
using System;
using System.Collections.Generic;
using System.Linq;
using System.Web.Http;
using Dispatch.Infrastructure;
using System.Web.Http.Dispatcher;

namespace Dispatch {
    public static class WebApiConfig {
        public static void Register(HttpConfiguration config) {

            config.MapHttpAttributeRoutes();

            config.Routes.MapHttpRoute(
                name: "DefaultApi",
                routeTemplate: "api/{controller}/{id}",
                defaults: new { id = RouteParameter.Optional }
            );

            config.MessageHandlers.Add(new CustomMessageHandler());

            config.Services.Replace(typeof(IHttpControllerTypeResolver),
                new CustomControllerTypeResolver { Suffix = "Service" });
            config.Services.Replace(typeof(IHttpControllerSelector),
                new CustomControllerSelector("Service"));
        }
    }
}
```

■ **Tip** Notice that I set the suffix when I create instances of both classes. The `CustomControllerTypeResolver` class needs to know the suffix so that it can select classes from the application assemblies that are controllers. The `CustomControllerSelector` class needs to know the suffix because it needs to remove it from the class names to create the controller name for the `HttpControllerDescriptor` objects. It is this dual use of the suffix that has led Microsoft to define a field in the `DefaultHttpControllerSelector` class that is then used in other classes. A better approach would be to define an `IHttpControllerNameSelector` interface that would consolidate the naming policy in a single place, but I have chosen to take the more direct—if less ideal—path of just repeating the suffix as a string literal when instantiating the classes that require it.

Creating a Controller with the New Suffix

The final step is to create a controller class that has the new suffix and will be selected by the custom classes. Listing 19-14 shows the contents of the `ProductsService.cs` file that I added to the `Controllers` folder and used to define a simple Web API controller.

Listing 19-14. The Contents of the ProductsService.cs File

```
using System.Net;
using System.Web.Http;
using Dispatch.Models;

namespace Dispatch.Controllers {
    public class ProductsService : ApiController {

        public IHttpActionResult Get() {
            return StatusCode(HttpStatusCode.ServiceUnavailable);
        }

        public IHttpActionResult Get(int id) {
            return StatusCode(HttpStatusCode.ServiceUnavailable);
        }

        public IHttpActionResult Post(Product product) {
            return StatusCode(HttpStatusCode.ServiceUnavailable);
        }
    }
}
```

I want it to be obvious that this is the controller that the application is using to respond to requests from the client, so I have defined the same actions methods as in the `ProductsController.cs` file but modified them so that they return the 503 (Service Unavailable) status code. To test the custom implementation classes, start the application and click the Get All or Get One button. The classes I defined in this section will be used to match the request to a controller; the `ProductsService` class will be selected, the appropriate action methods executed, and the status code displayed in the browser window, as shown in Figure 19-7.

Figure 19-7. Changing the controller class suffix

■ **Tip**   You can also click the Post button, but the custom message handler that I defined earlier will break the debugger, so you will have to click the Visual Studio Continue button to see the result.

Taking the Simpler Path

Creating two new interface implementations is a lot of work just to change the controller class suffix, but it provided a nice demonstration of how you can create custom implementations of the dispatcher interfaces and use them to customize the dispatch process.

In a real project, I would take a much more direct route, albeit an ugly one. All of the work in this section was required because Microsoft defines the suffix in a field like this:

```
...
public static readonly string ControllerSuffix = "Controller";
...
```

I can't change the value of the field because it is readonly—but it is also marked as static, and that means it is possible to use reflection to change the value of the field and bypass the readonly constraint. Listing 19-15 shows the changes required to the WebApiConfig.cs file.

Listing 19-15. Using Reflection to Change the Controller Class Suffix in the WebApiConfig.cs File

```
using System;
using System.Collections.Generic;
using System.Linq;
using System.Web.Http;
using Dispatch.Infrastructure;
using System.Web.Http.Dispatcher;
using System.Reflection;
```

```
namespace Dispatch {
    public static class WebApiConfig {
        public static void Register(HttpConfiguration config) {

            config.MapHttpAttributeRoutes();

            config.Routes.MapHttpRoute(
                name: "DefaultApi",
                routeTemplate: "api/{controller}/{id}",
                defaults: new { id = RouteParameter.Optional }
            );

            config.MessageHandlers.Add(new CustomMessageHandler());

            //config.Services.Replace(typeof(IHttpControllerTypeResolver),
            //    new CustomControllerTypeResolver { Suffix = "Service" });
            //config.Services.Replace(typeof(IHttpControllerSelector),
            //    new CustomControllerSelector("Service"));

            FieldInfo field = typeof(DefaultHttpControllerSelector)
                .GetField("ControllerSuffix", BindingFlags.Static | BindingFlags.Public);
            if (field != null) {
                field.SetValue(null, "Service");
            }
        }
    }
}
```

■ **Caution** This is a terrible, terrible example of the worst kind of behavior that all programmers should avoid at all times. It circumvents the restrictions placed on the ControllerSuffix field by the original developers, it creates a hard-coded dependency on a private implementation of an interface, and it will almost certainly break when a future version of Web API takes a more helpful approach to defining the suffix. That said, I use this technique in a real projects because I think it is a reasonable trade-off against reimplementing two low-level interfaces with the testing and maintenance requirements that implies. But just because I think it is a good trade-off doesn't mean that it will be appropriate for your projects.

Summary

In this chapter, I explained how Web API dispatches requests, which is the process of receiving an HttpRequestMethod object and using it to produce an HttpResponseMessage that will be used to generate a response to the client. I explained the role of the message handler classes and the different dispatch interfaces that control the flow of a request through a Web API application. I also demonstrated how to customize the dispatch process by creating custom message handlers and by reimplementing some of the dispatch interfaces. In the next chapter, I start to describe the URL routing feature, which is the first step for requests in the dispatch process.

CHAPTER 20

∎∎∎

URL Routing: Part I

In Chapter 19, I explained that URL routing is integrated into the Web API dispatch process by one of the built-in message handlers. In this chapter, I explain how URL routing works in a Web API application and demonstrate how to create convention-based routes, where routes are defined in a single place and used to match requests to controllers and actions throughout the application, known as *convention-based* routing. In Chapter 21, I continue on the topic of URL routing and show you a different approach that defines routes through attributes applied to controller classes and action methods, known as *direct* or *attribute-based* routing. Table 20-1 summarizes this chapter.

Table 20-1. *Chapter Summary*

Problem	Solution	Listing
Specify the HTTP verb that an action method can receive.	Apply the one of the verb attributes, such as HttpGet.	1–7
Obtain the action method from the request URL.	Define a variable segment called action in the route template.	8
Restrict the URLs that a route will match.	Increase the use of fixed segments or apply constraints.	9, 13–15
Broaden the URLs that a route will match.	Use default segment values and optional segments.	10–12

Preparing the Example Project

I am going to continue working with the Dispatch project I created in Chapter 19, but there are some changes I need to make. Listing 20-1 shows the WebApiConfig.cs file after I deleted the statements that changed the controller class suffix and the statement that registers the message handler that causes the debugger to break for POST requests.

Listing 20-1. The Contents of the WebApiConfig.cs File

```
using System.Web.Http;

namespace Dispatch {
    public static class WebApiConfig {
        public static void Register(HttpConfiguration config) {

            config.MapHttpAttributeRoutes();
```

```
        config.Routes.MapHttpRoute(
            name: "DefaultApi",
            routeTemplate: "api/{controller}/{id}",
            defaults: new { id = RouteParameter.Optional }
        );
    }
  }
}
```

I also need to add a new Web API controller so that I can define routes that target it later in the chapter. Listing 20-2 shows the contents of the TodayController.cs file that I added to the Controllers folder.

Listing 20-2. The Content of the TodayController.cs File

```
using System;
using System.Web.Http;

namespace Dispatch.Controllers {

    public class TodayController : ApiController {

        public string DayOfWeek() {
            return DateTime.Now.ToString("dddd");
        }
    }
}
```

This is a controller with a single action method that returns the name of the current day as a string. Getting the current day doesn't make for an interesting web service, but it is enough functionality for me to demonstrate how the Web API URL routing system works.

I need to create a client that will target the controller, and in Listing 20-3 you can see the action method I added to the HomeController.cs file.

Listing 20-3. Adding an Action in the HomeController.cs File

```
using System.Web.Mvc;

namespace Dispatch.Controllers {

    public class HomeController : Controller {

        public ActionResult Index() {
            return View();
        }

        public ActionResult Today() {
            return View();
        }
    }
}
```

The new action renders the default view associated. You can see that view in Listing 20-4, which shows the content of the Today.cshtml file I created in the /Views/Home folder.

Listing 20-4. The Contents of the Today.cshtml file

```
@{ Layout = null;}
<!DOCTYPE html>
<html>
<head>
    <meta name="viewport" content="width=device-width" />
    <title>Today</title>
    <link href="~/Content/bootstrap.min.css" rel="stylesheet" />
    <link href="~/Content/bootstrap-theme.min.css" rel="stylesheet" />
    <script src="~/Scripts/jquery-2.1.0.min.js"></script>
    <script src="~/Scripts/knockout-3.1.0.js"></script>
    <script src="~/Scripts/today.js"></script>
    <style>
        body { padding-top: 10px; }
    </style>
</head>
<body class="container">
    <div class="alert alert-success" data-bind="css: { 'alert-danger': gotError }">
        <span data-bind="text: response()"></span>
    </div>
    <button class="btn btn-primary" data-bind="click: sendRequest">Get Day</button>
</body>
</html>
```

This is the same basic approach I have been using for many of the MVC views in this book. There is a Bootstrap-styled div element that provides information about the outcome of the Ajax requests that the client makes and a button element that uses Knockout to invoke a JavaScript function. The JavaScript function that the button invokes is called sendRequest, and I defined it in the today.js file, which I added to the Scripts folder and which is shown in Listing 20-5.

Listing 20-5. The Contents of the today.js File

```
var response = ko.observable("Ready");
var gotError = ko.observable(false);

var sendRequest = function () {
    $.ajax("/api/today/dayofweek", {
        type: "GET",
        success: function (data) {
            gotError(false);
            response(data);
        },
        error: function (jqXHR) {
            gotError(true);
            response(jqXHR.status + " (" + jqXHR.statusText + ")");
        }
    });
};

$(document).ready(function () {
    ko.applyBindings();
});
```

Testing the Application Changes

To test the changes for this chapter, start the application and use the browser to navigate to the /Home/Today URL. This will cause the MVC framework to render the Today.cshtml view for the browser. Click the Get Day button, and you will see a 405 (Method Not Allowed) error message displayed in the alert div element at the top of the window, as illustrated by Figure 20-1.

Figure 20-1. *Testing the new controller*

The default routing configuration of the application doesn't match the Ajax request sent by the client to the DayOfWeek action method defined by the new Today web service controller. I explain why this is—and how it can be resolved—in the sections that follow.

Understanding URL Routing

The purpose of URL routing is to match HTTP requests to *routes*, which contain instructions for producing *routing data* that is consumed by other components.

The HttpRoutingDispatcher message handler is responsible for processing HttpRequestMessage objects in order to produce routing data and assign it to the HttpRequestContext.RouteData property. Figure 20-2 shows the dispatch process with the details I described in Chapter 19.

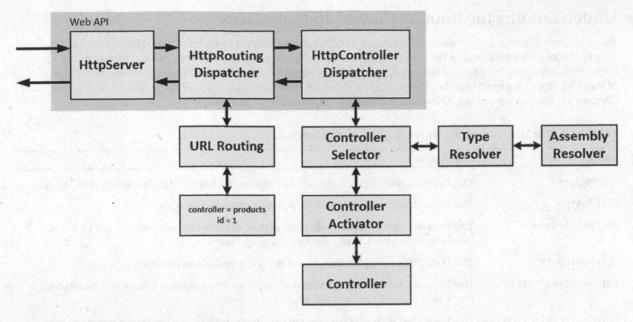

Figure 20-2. The Web API dispatch process

This chapter is all about the URL routing part of the diagram, which represents the process by which the routing system processes requests so that a URL such as this will produce the routing data values products and 1 for the controller and id properties.

```
/api/products/1
```

Table 20-2 puts URL routing in context.

Table 20-2. Putting URL Routing in Context

Question	Answer
What is it?	URL routing processes requests in order to extract data that is used by other components in the dispatch process, such as the classes that select controllers and action methods.
When should you use it?	URL routing is applied to all requests automatically.
What do you need to know?	The default route defined in the WebApiConfig.cs file is suitable for simple RESTful web services, but most complex applications will need some form of customization.

■ **Note** Remember that the URL routing system just generates routing data; it doesn't use that data to modify the request (other than to set the HttpRequest.RouteData property) or generate the response. Those tasks are handled by the HttpControllerDispatcher and its interfaces, which I described in Chapter 21 and return to again in Chapter 21.

Understanding the Routing Classes and Interfaces

There are four important types within URL routing: the IHttpRoute and IHttpRouteData interfaces and the HttpRouteCollection class. The IHttpRoute interface describes a route, and Web API provides a default implementation—the HttpRoute class—that is used in most applications. In the sections that follow, I describe each of these types and the members they define, and I'll show you how they work together throughout this chapter and in Chapter 21. For quick reference, I have summarized the important types in Table 20-3.

Table 20-3. *The Most Important URL Routing Classes and Interfaces*

Name	Description
IHttpRoute	This interface describes a route. See the "Understanding the IHttpRoute Interface" section.
HttpRoute	This is the default implementation of the IHttpRoute interface.
IHttpRouteData	This interface describes the collection of data values extracted from a request. See the "Understanding the IHttpRouteData Interface" section.
HttpRouteData	This is the default implementation of the IHttpRouteData interface.
IHttpRouteConstraint	This interface defines a restriction that limits the requests that a route will match. See the "Using Routing Constraints" section.
HttpRouteCollection	This is the class with which routes are registered and which receives requests from the HttpRoutingDispatcher. See the "Understanding the HttpRouteCollection Class" section.
HttpRoutingDispatcher	This message handler class integrates routing into the dispatch process. See Chapter 19.
RouteAttribute	This class defines the Route attribute used to create direct routes on controller classes and action methods. See Chapter 21.
RouteFactoryAttribute	This class allows custom attributes to be defined that customize the generation of direct routes. See Chapter 21.
RoutePrefix	This attribute is used to define a route template prefix that applies to all of the direct routes defined on a controller. See Chapter 21.

Using the classes I have described in the table, I can update my diagram of the dispatch process, as shown in Figure 20-3. I explain how the different interfaces and classes operate in the sections that follow and in Chapter 19.

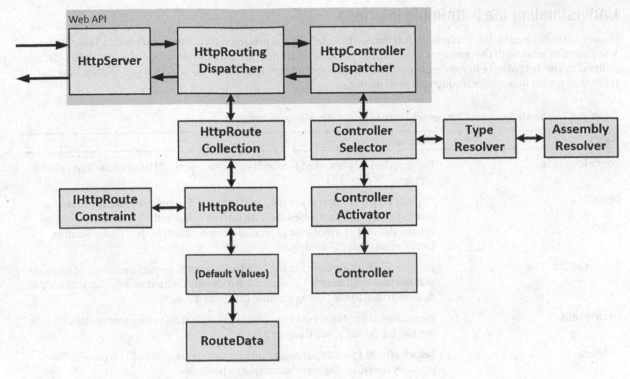

Figure 20-3. *Updating the dispatch diagram*

Understanding the IHttpRouteData Interface

The IHttpRouteData interface describes the collection of data values that are extracted from a request when it is processed. The interface defines the properties shown in Table 20-4.

Table 20-4. *The Properties Defined by the IHttpRouteData Interface*

Name	Description
Route	Returns the IHttpRoute object that generated the route data
Values	Returns an IDictionary<string, object> that contains the routing data

An implementation of the IHttpRouteData interface is the result of the URL routing process and the means by which the routing system provides data about the request for other components to consume.

The Values property is used to access the routing data that has been extracted from a request. Most routing data is expressed as string values, but routes can produce any kind of data that other components may find helpful, which is why the Values property returns a dictionary that maps keys to objects, rather than just strings. The default implementation of the IHttpRouteData interface is the HttpRouteData class.

Understanding the IHttpRoute Interface

Routes are described by the IHttpRoute interface, which defines the properties and methods listed in Table 20-5. You generally work with route objects indirectly, as I explain in the next section, but the properties and methods defined by the IHttpRoute interface are useful in understanding how URL routing works, and you will see how the types they return fit together throughout this chapter.

Table 20-5. *The Methods and Properties Defined by the IHttpRoute Interface*

Name	Description
RouteTemplate	Returns the template used to match requests. See the "Using Route Templates" section.
Defaults	Returns an IDictionary<string, object> used to provide default values for routing data properties when they are not included in the request. Defaults are usually defined as a dynamic object, as demonstrated in the "Using Routing Data Default Values" section.
Constraints	Returns an IDictionary<string, object> used to restrict the range of requests that the route will match. Constraints are usually defined as a dynamic object, as demonstrated in the "Using Routing Constraints" section.
DataTokens	Returns an IDictionary<string, object> with data values that are available to the routing handler. See Chapter 21.
Handler	Returns the HttpMessageHandler onto which the request will be passed. This property overrides the standard dispatch process.
GetRouteData(path, request)	Called by the routing system to generate the routing data for the request.

Understanding the HttpRouteCollection Class

The HttpRouteCollection class orchestrates the entire routing process, and as a consequence, it plays several different roles.

First, the HttpRouteCollection provides the CreateRoute method that creates new routes using the HttpRoute class, which is the default implementation of the IHttpRoute interface. There are several versions of the CreateRoute method, as described in Table 20-6. This is the *convention-based* style of routing that I described in Chapter 19 and is used to define routes in the WebApiConfig.cs file.

Table 20-6. *The HttpRouteCollection Methods for Creating New Routes*

Name	Description
CreateRoute(template, defaults, constraints)	Returns an IHttpRoute implementation object that has been configured with the specified template, defaults, and constraints
CreateRoute(template, defaults, constraints, tokens)	Returns an IHttpRoute implementation object that has been configured with the specified template, defaults, constraints, and tokens
CreateRoute(template, defaults, constraints, tokens, handler)	Returns an IHttpRoute implementation object that has been configured with the specified template, defaults, constraints, tokens, and message handler

The different versions of the CreateRoute method all take parameters that correspond directly to the properties defined by the IHttpRoute method. Using the CreateRoute method allows you to obtain implementations of the IHttpRoute interface without tightly coupling your code to a specific implementation class, although there is nothing to stop you from creating your own implementation of the interface or simply instantiating the HttpRoute class directly.

The CreateRoute method creates the route, but it doesn't register it so that it will be used to match requests. The second role that the HttpRouteCollection class plays is to provide a collection that is used to register routes for use with an application. Table 20-7 lists the methods that provide the collection feature.

Table 20-7. *The Collection Members Defined by the HttpRouteCollection Class*

Name	Description
Count	This returns the number of routes in the collection.
Add(name, route)	This adds a new route to the collection.
Clear()	This removes all the routes from the collection.
Contains(route)	This returns true if the collection contains the specified route.
ContainsKey(name)	This returns true if the collection contains a route with the specified name.
Insert(index, name, route)	This inserts a route with the specified name at the specified index.
Remove(name)	This removes the route with the specified name from the collection.
TryGetValue(name, out route)	This attempts to retrieve a route with the specified name from the collection. If there is a route with that name, the method returns true and assigns the route to the out parameter.
this[int]	The HttpRouteCollection class defines an array-style indexer that retrieves routes by their position in the collection.
this[name]	The HttpRouteCollection class defines an array-style indexer that retrieves routes by their name.

■ **Note** As you will learn, routes are tested to see whether they can match a request, which means that the order in which the routes are added to the collection is important. Just as with the MVC framework, you should add the most specific routes first so that they are able to match requests before more general routes.

If you use the HttpRouteCollection class methods, then setting up a new route requires two steps: a call to the CreateRoute method to create a new IHttpRoute object and a call to the Add or Insert method to add the route to the collection.

A more common approach is to use the extension methods that are defined on the HttpRouteCollection class, which allow routes to be set up in a single step. Table 20-8 shows the available extension methods.

Table 20-8. *The HttpRouteCollection Extension Methods*

Name	Description
IgnoreRoute(name, template)	Creates and registers a route with the specified name and template that prevents a request from being handled by Web API
IgnoreRoute(name, template, constraints)	Creates and registers a route with the specified name, template, and constraints that prevents a request from being handled by Web API
MapHttpBatchRoute(name, template handler)	Creates and registers a route for the batch handling of HTTP requests
MapHttpRoute(name, template)	Creates and registers a route with the specified name and template
MapHttpRoute(name, template, defaults)	Creates and registers a route with the specified name, template, and defaults
MapHttpRoute(name, template, defaults, constraints)	Creates and registers a route with the specified name, template, defaults, and constraints
MapHttpRoute(name, template, defaults, constraints, handler)	Creates and registers a route with the specified name, template, defaults, constraints, and message handler

Understanding the Route Attributes

The Route attribute—defined as the RouteAttribute class in the System.Web.Http.Routing namespace—is applied directly to classes and methods. This is the *direct* or *attribute* style of routing, where the routes are more specific than those in the WebConfig.cs file and are defined alongside the code that will handle the request.

■ **Note**   Microsoft hasn't settled on clear terminology for routes that are created using attributes applied to controller classes or action methods. They switch between the terms *attribute-based routes* and *direct routes*, with the latter term being emphasized in the names of classes and interfaces in the System.Web.Http.Routing namespace. It doesn't matter which term you use, but I have tried to be consistent in this chapter and use *direct routes*.

Working with Convention-Based Routing

In this section, I am going to use the WebApiConfig.cs file to define a series of convention-based routes that will demonstrate the different ways in which you can match requests and generate routing data. Many of the techniques apply equally to direct routes, which I describe in Chapter 21. Table 20-9 puts convention-based routing in context.

Table 20-9. *Putting Convention-Based Routing in Context*

Question	Answer
What is it?	Convention-based routing defines URL routes in a single location—the WebApiConfig.cs file—for the entire application. The alternative is to define routes by applying attributes to classes and methods, which I describe in Chapter 19.
When should you use it?	The choice between convention-based routing and defining routes with attributes is largely a matter of personal preference, as I explain in Chapter 21.
What do you need to know?	The default routing configuration relies on matching action methods based on the HTTP verb. Define a custom route with an action variable segment if you want to specify an action method in the URL. See the "Routing to the New Controller" section for details.

Using Route Templates

Templates are at the heart of the routing system and are the start point for matching requests and extracting information from the URL. Web API route templates work in the same way as those in the MVC framework, and you can see an example of a Web API route template in the WebApiConfig.cs file, where Visual Studio has set up the default convention-based route for web services.

```
using System.Web.Http;

namespace Dispatch {
    public static class WebApiConfig {
        public static void Register(HttpConfiguration config) {

            config.MapHttpAttributeRoutes();

            config.Routes.MapHttpRoute(
                name: "DefaultApi",
                routeTemplate: "api/{controller}/{id}",
                defaults: new { id = RouteParameter.Optional }
            );
        }
    }
}
```

The routing system treats URLs as a series of *segments* separated by the / character. The URL http://myhost.com/api/products/1 has three segments: api, products, and 1. (The protocol, port, and hostname are all ignored.)

■ **Tip** The terminology here gets a bit muddled because there are segments in the request URL and in the routing template. Don't worry if it doesn't make immediate sense—it will all start to fall into place through examples.

Routing templates match requests based on the segments in the URL that has been asked for using a system of fixed (or static) and variable segments. Fixed segments will match URLs only if they have the same text in the corresponding segment. As an example, the routing template for the default route has one fixed segment: api. This means the route will match only URLs whose first segment is the string api. URLs that have different first segments will not be matched by the route template.

■ **Tip** Route templates are defined without a leading / character. If you do put in a leading /, then an exception will be thrown when the application is started.

The template variable segments will match any URL that has a corresponding segment, irrespective of what the value of the segment is. Variable segments are denoted with the { and } characters, and the value of the URL segment is assigned to a variable of the specified name in the routing data, known—confusingly—as *segment variables*.

The default route template contains two variable segments, as follows:

```
...
routeTemplate: "api/{controller}/{id}",
...
```

The template will match any URL that contains three segments where the first segment is api. The contents of the second and third segments will be assigned to route data variables called controller and id.

■ **Tip** You can vary the set of URLs that a route template will match by using constraints and defaults, which I explain in the "Controlling Route Matching" section.

Routing to the New Controller

Two segment variables have special importance in Web API: controller and action. The controller variable is used to match the controller that will be used to handle the request, as I explained in Chapter 19. The action variable can be used to specify the action method defined by the controller, just as in the MVC framework, but there isn't a segment to capture this variable in the default route.

This is because Web API uses the HTTP verb from the request to select an action method by default. I explain the action method selection process in detail in Chapter 22, but as part of the drive toward RESTful web services, Web API takes notice of the type of HTTP request.

The reason that the client code that I added at the start of the chapter can't reach the new controller is because the action method it contains doesn't provide the selection process with the information it requires to perform the default action method selection.

The URL that the client requests is as follows:

```
/api/today/dayofweek
```

The api prefix matches the fixed segment at the start of the route template. The variable segments extract a value of today for the controller variable and dayofweek for the id property. This doesn't provide the selection mechanism with enough information to match the request to an action method, which is why an error is reported. There are two ways to get Web API to route requests to the new controller.

Mapping Request Verbs to Action Methods

One way to give the action method selection mechanism the information it requires is to specify which HTTP verbs an action method can handle. For my example controller, I need to specify that the DayOfWeek action method should be used for GET requests, which is the request type that the jQuery client is sending. You can see how I did this in Listing 20-6.

Listing 20-6. Associating an HTTP Verb with an Action Method in the TodayController.cs File

```
using System;
using System.Web.Http;

namespace Dispatch.Controllers {

    public class TodayController : ApiController {

        [HttpGet]
        public string DayOfWeek() {
            return DateTime.Now.ToString("dddd");
        }
    }
}
```

The HttpGet attribute is one of a set that Web API provides so that you can specify which HTTP methods an action method can receive. There are attributes for different HTTP verbs: HttpGet, HttpPost, HttpPut, and so on.

You don't need to use these attributes if the action methods in your controller follow the Web API RESTful pattern, which is why I have not had to apply attributes to the action methods in the Products controller. I explain the pattern that Web API looks for to match verbs to action methods in Chapter 22, but for this chapter it is enough to know that you can provide the verb information needed to select the action method using one of the verb attributes.

However, caution is required because it is easy to create an unwanted effect. Using a verb attribute allows the default route to direct requests to the DayOfWeek action method, but it does so using only part of the URL that has been requested. As a reminder, here is the default route template:

```
...
routeTemplate: "api/{controller}/{id}"
...
```

And here is the URL from the today.js file that jQuery uses to make the HTTP request:

```
...
$.ajax("/api/today/dayofweek", {
...
```

The problem is that the part of the requested URL intended to specify the action method is being assigned to the id route variable, which is then ignored when the action method is selected. By default, only the value of the controller variable and the verb attribute are considered when an action method is selected. To demonstrate the effect this causes, I have added a new action method to the Today controller, as shown in Listing 20-7.

Listing 20-7. Adding a New Action Method to the TodayController.cs File

```
using System;
using System.Web.Http;

namespace Dispatch.Controllers {

    public class TodayController : ApiController {

        [HttpGet]
        public string DayOfWeek() {
            return DateTime.Now.ToString("dddd");
        }
```

```
        [HttpGet]
        public int DayNumber() {
            return DateTime.Now.Day;
        }
    }
}
```

If you start the application and click the Get Day button, you will see a 500 (Internal Server Error) message reported. The F12 developer tools will allow you to look at the HTTP response sent by the web service, which includes this message:

```
Multiple actions were found that match the request
```

The response from the web service also contains a stack trace, so you may have to dig around to see the error message. The error arises because Web API can't work out which of the action methods the request is intended for. It is impossible to differentiate between the action methods when only the `controller` routing variable and the verb specified by the attributes are available with which to make a decision.

■ **Tip** I explain how to deal with errors properly in Chapter 25.

Creating a Custom Route Template

The `HttpGet` attribute—and the other verb attributes—is useful when the action methods in a controller are distinctive enough that the selection process can tell them apart, but a better solution to this problem is to define a custom route that has a template that uses all of the information in the URL sent by the client. Listing 20-8 shows the route I defined in the `WebApiConfig.cs` file.

Listing 20-8. Defining a Custom Route in the WebApiConfig.cs File

```
using System.Web.Http;

namespace Dispatch {
    public static class WebApiConfig {
        public static void Register(HttpConfiguration config) {

            config.MapHttpAttributeRoutes();

            config.Routes.MapHttpRoute(
                name: "IncludeAction",
                routeTemplate: "api/{controller}/{action}"
            );

            config.Routes.MapHttpRoute(
                name: "DefaultApi",
                routeTemplate: "api/{controller}/{id}",
                defaults: new { id = RouteParameter.Optional }
            );

        }
    }
}
```

■ **Caution** The route that I have added in Listing 20-8 contains a common problem that prevents requests to the Products controller from working correctly. I explain what the problem is and how to avoid it in Chapter 22.

I have used the simplest version of the MapHttpRoute extension method, which requires only a name and a routing template. My new route defines a template that matches all of the segments in the URL sent by the client and captures the last segment as a route variable called action. This is one of the special variables—along with controller—that are used in the action method selection process, and it is assumed to contain the name of the action method that will receive the request. If the route data contains an action value, then it is used in preference to the HTTP verb to select the action method.

■ **Tip** Route template segments usually match exactly one URL segment, but you can make the last segment in a template match multiple URL segments by prefixing it with an asterisk, such as {*catchall}. This feature isn't often needed in web services because the request URL generally contains the segments needed to target the controller (and, optionally, the action method) and the data required for parameter binding (as described in Part 2).

The URL routing system evaluates routes in the order in which they are defined in the HttpRouteCollection, and the evaluation process stops as soon as a route is found that matches the current request. The MapHttpRoute method appends new routes to the end of the collection, which means that I must define my new route before the default one to ensure it is asked to route the requests from the client.

SPECIFYING ROUTE PARAMETER NAMES

You will notice that I used the C# named parameter feature in Listing 20-8 to denote which argument was the route name and which is the template, like this:

```
...
config.Routes.MapHttpRoute(
    name: "IncludeAction",
    routeTemplate: "api/{controller}/{action}"
);
...
```

This is just a convention, and I could have achieved the same effect by calling the MapHttpRoute method with normal parameters, like this:

```
...
config.Routes.MapHttpRoute("IncludeAction", "api/{controller}/{action}");
...
```

Using named parameters is helpful because some of the arguments required to define complex routes look similar, and making it clear which arguments are which makes the purpose of the route more obvious to someone reading your code. Ensuring routes work properly can be a troublesome process in large projects, and it is a good idea to make routes as clear as possible—specifying parameter names can help make the purpose and function of a route more obvious.

You can see the effect of the new route by starting the application, using the browser to navigate to the /Home/Today URL, and clicking the Get Day button. The client will send a request to the /api/today/dayofweek URL, which will be matched by the route I defined in Listing 20-8. The route template will create route data variables called controller and action—corresponding to the variable segments—with the values today and dayofweek. The action method selection process will invoke the DayOfWeek action method defined by the Today controller, which results in Figure 20-4.

Figure 20-4. *The effect of defining a custom route*

UNDERSTANDING THE URL PREFIX

The convention is to prefix Web API URLs with /api, which is why the route templates I define in this chapter begin with a fixed /api segment. You don't have to follow this convention, but you need to understand why it exists and what the impact of ignoring it will be.

The URL routing feature is available across all the technologies in the ASP.NET family and is implemented as part of the ASP.NET platform as a module. (For details of modules and how they work, see my *Pro ASP.NET MVC Platform* book, published by Apress.)

Web API has its own implementation of the routing system, but when the application is hosted by IIS—which is required when using the MVC framework as well—then the Web API routes are consolidated with the MVC routes into a single collection.

The order in which the Web API and MVC framework routes are arranged depends on the Application_Start method defined in the Global.asax file. The default is that the Web API routes are set up first, as follows:

```
...
void Application_Start(object sender, EventArgs e) {
    AreaRegistration.RegisterAllAreas();
    GlobalConfiguration.Configure(WebApiConfig.Register);
    RouteConfig.RegisterRoutes(RouteTable.Routes);
}
...
```

You can change the order so that the MVC routes are defined first if you prefer. Whichever way the routes are set up, you must ensure that requests are routed to the right part of the application—and that is where the /api prefix helps, by defining a fixed segment that clearly denotes web service requests and allows them to be captured by the Web API routes.

If you stop using a prefix, then you must ensure that your routes are specific enough to capture the requests intended for the Web API controllers without matching requests intended for the MVC controllers. That requires careful route planning and lots of testing.

If you just want to deliver a web service without prefixes, then reverse the order of the routing configuration statements in the Global.asax file and use an /mvc prefix for requests that are intended for MVC controllers.

Controlling Route Matching

Defining a custom route has fixed the problem with my new client code, but it has done so by causing another kind of problem. To see what has happened, start the application, using the browser to navigate to /Home/Index and clicking the Get One button. You will see a 404 (Not Found) message displayed, as shown in Figure 20-5.

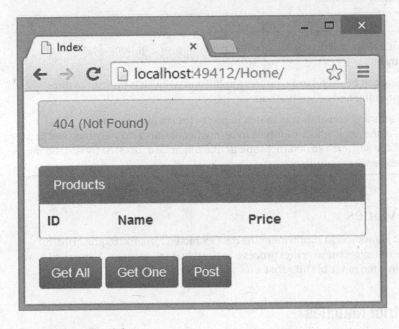

Figure 20-5. Receiving an error

Clicking the Get One button causes the client to request the following URL:

```
/api/products/2
```

This URL is matched by the route template of the route defined in Listing 20-8.

```
...
routeTemplate: "api/{controller}/{action}"
...
```

The route matches the request and generates route data that contains `controller` and `action` variables whose values are `products` and `2`, respectively. The `controller` variable is fine—it contains the name of the Web API controller that the request was intended for. The problem is with the `action` variable, which is given special meaning and causes the action method selection process to look for an action method called 2. Since there is no such method, Web API produces a 404 (Not Found) response.

The URL routing system doesn't know about the significance of individual segments or segment variables (it doesn't even know that the action method selection process gives special meaning to the `controller` and `action` variables), so it diligently locates a route whose route template matches the request and uses it to produce routing data.

In the sections that follow, I'll show you different techniques for controlling the way that routes match requests, allowing for both greater specificity (matching fewer requests) and greater generality (matching more requests). Table 20-10 puts controlling route matching in context.

Table 20-10. *Putting Controlling Route Matching in Context*

Question	Answer
What is it?	The range of requests that a route will match can be changed by applying optional segments, default values, and constraints.
When should you use it?	Controlling route matching can be useful in a complex application where it is difficult to direct requests to the correct controller and action method.
What do you need to know?	If you rely heavily on defaults and constraints to match requests, then it may be worth reconsidering the design of the application. Complex route configurations are rarely required in a Web API application and can suggest a structural problem that might be addressed by simplifying and consolidating the web service controllers.

Using Routing Data Default Values

Route data defaults are a flexible feature that allows you to supplement the data extracted from the request URL in order to control the route matching and controller/action selection process. In the following sections, I show you how to use default values to restrict—and broaden—the range of URLs that a route will match.

Using Segment Defaults to Restrict Matches

The most direct way to limit the set of URLs that a route will match is to increase the number of fixed segments. For my example route, I can stop it matching requests for other controllers by including the name of the controller in a static segment, as shown in Listing 20-9.

Listing 20-9. Fixing the Controller Segment in the Custom Route in the WebApiConfig.cs File

```
using System.Web.Http;

namespace Dispatch {
    public static class WebApiConfig {
        public static void Register(HttpConfiguration config) {

            config.MapHttpAttributeRoutes();

            config.Routes.MapHttpRoute(
                name: "IncludeAction",
                routeTemplate: "api/today/{action}",
                defaults: new { controller = "today" }
            );

            config.Routes.MapHttpRoute(
                name: "DefaultApi",
                routeTemplate: "api/{controller}/{id}",
                defaults: new { id = RouteParameter.Optional }
            );
        }
    }
}
```

I removed the controller variable segment and replaced it with a fixed segment that means the route template will match only URLs that start with /api/today. The controller selection process—which I described in Chapter 19—still requires a value for the controller routing variable, so I have used the defaults parameter to define a set of values that should be used for routing data if there is no value in the URL.

```
...
defaults: new { controller = "today" }
...
```

Defaults are specified with a dynamic object with properties that correspond to variables to be added to the routing data. In this case, there is only one property—controller—and it is set to today so that the selection process will route matching requests to the Today controller class.

Using Optional Segments to Widen Matches

Default values can also be used to widen the set of URLs that a route will match by denoting *optional segments*. This allows a route template to match URLs that don't contain a corresponding segment, as shown in Listing 20-10.

Listing 20-10. Using Optional Segments in the WebApiConfig.cs File

```
...
config.Routes.MapHttpRoute(
    name: "IncludeAction",
    routeTemplate: "api/today/{action}/{day}",
```

```
    defaults: new {
        controller = "today",
        day = RouteParameter.Optional
    }
);
...
```

I have defined a new variable segment that will define a routing variable called day, and I have defined a corresponding default property that is set to the RouteParameter.Optional value.

This allows my custom route to match URLs such as /api/today/dayofweek/1 (which contains a day segment) and /api/today/dayofweek (which contains no day segment).

Simply broadening the range of URLs that are matched isn't useful in its own right, but the presence of route data variables is taken into account when selecting an action method. In Listing 20-11, you can see a new action method I defined on the Today controller.

Listing 20-11. Defining a New Action Method in the TodayController.cs File

```
using System;
using System.Web.Http;

namespace Dispatch.Controllers {

    public class TodayController : ApiController {

        [HttpGet]
        public string DayOfWeek() {
            return DateTime.Now.ToString("dddd");
        }

        [HttpGet]
        public string DayOfWeek(int day) {
            return Enum.GetValues(typeof(DayOfWeek)).GetValue(day).ToString();
        }

        [HttpGet]
        public int DayNumber() {
            return DateTime.Now.Day;
        }
    }
}
```

■ **Tip** Notice that I still have to apply the HttpGet attribute. The action route data variable helps the action method selection process, but Web API still checks for the attribute that corresponds to the HTTP verb as a precaution before executing the method. I explain this process in detail in Chapter 22.

The new action method is also called DayOfWeek, but it defines a day parameter that corresponds to the optional segment in the custom route. When the action method is selected, the presence of a day variable in the route data will determine the version of the method chosen. If there is no day value, then the parameterless DayOfWeek method will be chosen. If there is a day value, then it will be used in the parameter binding process that I described in Part 2, and the other version of the DayOfWeek method will be used.

CHAPTER 20 ■ URL ROUTING: PART I

The simplest way to test the new action method is with Postman. If you send GET requests to /api/today/dayofweek and /api/today/dayofweek/4, you will see different days returned in the response (unless you do this on Thursday, in which case both methods will return the same value). For testing on a Thursday, request /api/today/dayofweek/5 instead.

Using Default Segment Values to Widen Matches

I used default values in the previous section to create an optional segment, which allowed a broader range of URLs to be matched to action methods. The standard use of default values is to allow a range of URLs to be mapped to a *single* action method by providing a value for the routing data that is used when a segment isn't defined in the request URL. Listing 20-12 shows how I have changed the definition of the day property in the defaults object for the custom route.

Listing 20-12. Setting a Default Value for a Custom Route in the WebApiConfig.cs File

```
...
config.Routes.MapHttpRoute(
    name: "IncludeAction",
    routeTemplate: "api/today/{action}/{day}",
    defaults: new {
        controller = "today",
        day = 6
    }
);
...
```

I have specified a default value of 6. The default value is used only when the route matches a URL that doesn't contain a day segment. The URL sent from the jQuery client I created at the start of the chapter is /api/today/dayofweek, and since there is no day segment, the default value is applied—and this has the effect of treating the request as though the URL was actually /api/today/dayofweek/6. The default value is *not* used when the URL contains a day segment, so the overall effect is to direct all requests whose URLs start with /api/today/dayofweek to the DayOfWeek action method that takes a parameter (the one I defined in Listing 20-11).

To test the default value, start the application, use the browser to navigate to /Home/Today, and click the Get Day button. The URL sent by the client will not contain a day segment, so the default value will be used, which means that the response from the action method will always be the name of the sixth day of the week, as shown in Figure 20-6. (As far as .NET is concerned, the week starts with Sunday, which is day zero. You may get different results depending on your calendar and locale settings.)

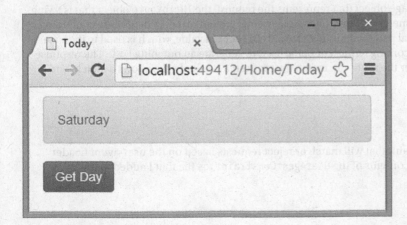

Figure 20-6. *The effect of a default value*

Using Routing Constraints

Routing constraints allow you to narrow the range of requests that a route will match by adding additional checks beyond matching the routing template. In the sections that follow, I'll show you the different ways in which constraints can be applied.

■ **Caution**　Use constraints only to control route matching and not to perform validation of the data values that will be used as action method parameters or by the parameter binding process I described in Part 2. Validating the data that is passed to action methods is the job of the model validation process, which I describe in Chapter 18. Using routing constraints to perform validation will cause the client to receive a 404 (Not Found) response for requests that contain bad data, which is confusing to the user because their client will have targeted a valid URL but will have done so with unsuitable data. Model validation allows you to reject requests and provide information about what the problems with the data are.

Understanding Constraints

Constraints are expressed using implementations of the IHttpRouteConstraint interface, which is defined in the System.Web.Http.Routing namespace. Here is the definition of the interface:

```
using System.Collections.Generic;
using System.Net.Http;

namespace System.Web.Http.Routing {

    public interface IHttpRouteConstraint {

        bool Match(HttpRequestMessage request, IHttpRoute route, string parameterName,
            IDictionary<string, object> values, HttpRouteDirection routeDirection);
    }
}
```

The IHttpRouteConstraint interface defines the Match method, which is passed arguments required to constrain the match: the HttpRequestMessage object that represents the request, the IHttpRoute object that is trying to match the request, the name of the parameter that the constraint is being applied to, and a dictionary containing the data matched from the request. The final parameter is an HttpRouteDirection value, which is used to indicate whether the route is being applied to an incoming request or being used to generate an outgoing URL. The response from the Match method determines whether the route can match the request; a result of true allows a match, and a result of false prevents matching.

Creating a Custom Constraint

My goal in this section is to create a constraint that will match or reject requests based on the user-agent header sent by the client. Listing 20-13 shows the contents of the UserAgentConstraint.cs file that I added to the Infrastructure folder.

Listing 20-13. The Contents of the UserAgentConstraint.cs File

```
using System.Collections.Generic;
using System.Linq;
using System.Net.Http;
using System.Web.Http.Routing;

namespace Dispatch.Infrastructure {

    public class UserAgentConstraint : IHttpRouteConstraint {
        private string requiredUA;

        public UserAgentConstraint(string agentParam) {
            requiredUA = agentParam.ToLowerInvariant();
        }

        public bool Match(HttpRequestMessage request, IHttpRoute route,
            string parameterName, IDictionary<string, object> values,
                HttpRouteDirection routeDirection) {

            return request.Headers.UserAgent
                .Where(x =>
                    x.Product != null && x.Product.Name != null &&
                    x.Product.Name.ToLowerInvariant().Contains(requiredUA))
                .Count() > 0;
        }
    }
}
```

This constraint receives a constructor argument that is used to match user-agent strings. When the Match method is called, I get the value of the User-Agent header through the HttpRequestMessage object and check to see whether it contains the target string.

■ **Tip**   You can see an example of a constraint that operates on a segment variable in Chapter 21.

To demonstrate the use of the constraint, I have defined two routes in the WebApiConfig.cs file, as shown in Listing 20-14.

Listing 20-14. Defining Routes in the WebApiConfig.cs File

```
using System.Web.Http;
using Dispatch.Infrastructure;

namespace Dispatch {
    public static class WebApiConfig {
        public static void Register(HttpConfiguration config) {

            config.MapHttpAttributeRoutes();
```

```
        config.Routes.MapHttpRoute(
            name: "ChromeRoute",
            routeTemplate: "api/today/DayOfWeek",
            defaults: new { controller = "today", action = "dayofweek"},
            constraints: new { useragent = new UserAgentConstraint("Chrome") }
        );

        config.Routes.MapHttpRoute(
            name: "NotChromeRoute",
            routeTemplate: "api/today/DayOfWeek",
            defaults: new { controller = "today", action = "daynumber" }
        );

        config.Routes.MapHttpRoute(
            name: "DefaultApi",
            routeTemplate: "api/{controller}/{id}",
            defaults: new { id = RouteParameter.Optional }
        );
    }
  }
}
```

As I noted at the start of this section, constraints should be used only to control whether a request matches a route—and not to perform validation of data that is going to be passed to the action method. Constraints work best when you use them to select between related routes, such as the ones in Listing 20-14. All requests to the /api/today/dayofweek URL are routed to the Today controller, but requests made from the Chrome browser are directed to the DayOfWeek action method, while all other clients are directed to the DayNumber action method.

You can see the effect by starting the application and using two browsers (one of which must be Chrome and one of which must not be Chrome) to navigate to the /Home/Today URL; then click the Get Day button. The response sent by the web service will be different for each browser, as shown by Figure 20-7, which illustrates Chrome and Internet Explorer.

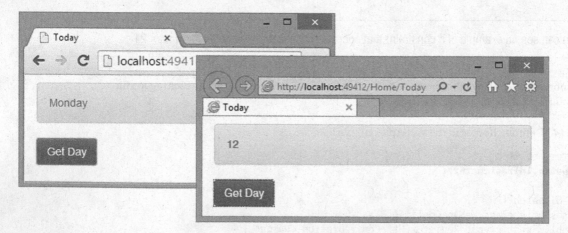

Figure 20-7. *Using a custom constraint*

Using the Built-in Constraints

The `System.Web.Http.Routing.Constraints` namespace contains classes that provide a range of built-in constraints. Table 20-11 lists the constraint classes.

Table 20-11. *The Built-in Route Constraint Classes*

Name	Description
AlphaRouteConstraint	Matches a route when the segment variable contains only alphabetic characters.
BoolRouteConstraint	Matches a route when the segment variable contains only `true` or `false`.
DateTimeRouteConstraint	Matches a route when the segment variable can be parsed as a `DateTime` object.
DecimalRouteConstraint DoubleRouteConstraint FloatRouteConstraint IntRouteConstraint LongRouteConstraint	Matches a route when the segment variable can be parsed as a `decimal`, `double`, `float`, `int`, or `long` value.
HttpMethodConstraint	Matches a route when the request has been made with a specific verb. (This class is defined in the `System.Web.Http.Routing` namespace.)
MaxLengthRouteConstraint MinLengthRouteConstraint	Matches a route when the segment variable is a `string` with a maximum or minimum length.
MaxRouteConstraint MinRouteConstraint	Matches a route when the segment variable is an `int` with a maximum or minimum value.
RangeRouteConstraint	Matches a route when the segment variable is an `int` within a range of values.
RegexRouteConstraint	Matches a route when the segment variable matches a regular expression.

■ **Caution**   I don't want to endlessly labor the point, but these constraint classes make it easy to validate data in the wrong place, generating 404 (Not Found) errors that will confuse the client application and the user. See Chapter 18 for details of the model validation process, which can be used to return meaningful errors when the data sent by the client cannot be used.

In Listing 20-15, you can see how I have used the `RegExpRouteConstraint` class to allow the route to match a limited range of controller names.

Listing 20-15. Using a Built-in Constraint in the WebApiConfig.cs File

```
using System.Web.Http;
using Dispatch.Infrastructure;
using System.Web.Http.Routing.Constraints;

namespace Dispatch {
    public static class WebApiConfig {
        public static void Register(HttpConfiguration config) {

            config.MapHttpAttributeRoutes();
```

```
        config.Routes.MapHttpRoute(
            name: "ChromeRoute",
            routeTemplate: "api/today/{action}",
            defaults: new { controller = "today" },
            constraints: new {
                useragent = new UserAgentConstraint("Chrome"),
                action = new RegexRouteConstraint("daynumber|othermethod")
            }
        );

        config.Routes.MapHttpRoute(
            name: "NotChromeRoute",
            routeTemplate: "api/today/DayOfWeek",
            defaults: new { controller = "today", action = "daynumber" }
        );

        config.Routes.MapHttpRoute(
            name: "DefaultApi",
            routeTemplate: "api/{controller}/{id}",
            defaults: new { id = RouteParameter.Optional }
        );
    }
  }
}
```

I have added an action variable segment to the route template and used the RegexRouteConstraint class to limit the range of values that will match the route to daynumber and othermethod.

■ **Tip** There is no othermethod action defined by the Today controller. As I explained earlier, the routing system has no insight into the data it extracts from the request, and this extends to constraints and default values. The URL system doesn't know that special attention is paid to the action route variable by the action method selection process and so has no means—or interest—in ensuring that the constrained values are useful.

Notice that I have assigned the RegexRouteConstraint object to a property called action in the dynamic object used to set the constraints property. This is how you tell the routing system which route data variable the constraint applies to.

The effect of my constraint is to prevent the route matching the request sent by the client I created at the start of the chapter if Chrome is used—that's because there is no combination of user-agent and URL that the client can produce that will match the combined constraints. As a consequence, all requests made from the client in Chrome to the Today controller will be matched by the NotChromeRoute and directed to the DayNumber action, as shown in Figure 20-8.

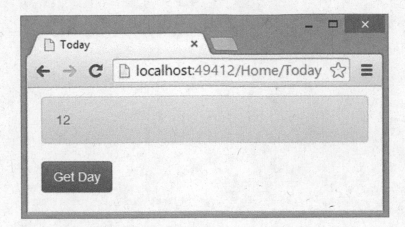

Figure 20-8. *The effect of a route constraint*

Summary

In this chapter, I explained how URL routing fits into the dispatch process and showed you how to create convention-based routes to match requests. I showed you how basic matching is configured with a routing template and changed through default values and constraints. In the next chapter, I describe how to create direct routes, where the route is specified by applying attributes to controllers or action methods.

■ ■ ■

CHAPTER 21

URL Routing: Part II

In this chapter, I continue describing the Web API URL routing feature, focusing on *direct routes*, which are defined by applying attributes to controllers and action methods. I also show you different ways in which you can customize the routing process. Table 21-1 summarizes this chapter.

Table 21-1. *Chapter Summary*

Problem	Solution	Listing
Define a direct route.	Apply the Route attribute to one or more action methods or to the controller itself.	1, 2, 10, 11
Define a common prefix that will be used in all of the direct routes in a controller.	Apply the RoutePrefix attribute to the controller class.	3
Define an optional segment in a direct route.	Add a question mark to the segment name and define a default parameter name.	4, 5
Define a default segment in a direct route.	Assign a value to the segment in the route template.	6
Constrain a direct route.	Add a constraint shorthand to the segment in the route template.	7, 8, 16–20
Change the precedence of direct routes.	Set the Order property of the Route attribute.	9
Handle a request matched by a contention-based route without a controller.	Create a custom route handler.	12, 13
Pass information from the route to other components.	Use data tokens.	14, 15

Preparing the Example Project

I am going to carry on using the Dispatch project, but I am going to remove the custom routes that I added in Chapter 20 so that the application has only the default routing configuration defined in the WebApiConfig.cs file, as shown in Listing 21-1.

Listing 21-1. The Contents of the WebApiConfig.cs File

```
using System.Web.Http;

namespace Dispatch {
    public static class WebApiConfig {
        public static void Register(HttpConfiguration config) {

            config.MapHttpAttributeRoutes();

            config.Routes.MapHttpRoute(
                name: "DefaultApi",
                routeTemplate: "api/{controller}/{id}",
                defaults: new { id = RouteParameter.Optional }
            );
        }
    }
}
```

Removing the custom routes means that the client I added in Chapter 20 is unable to target the action methods in the Today controller because the default convention-based route doesn't capture an action value and there are multiple actions that have been decorated with the HttpGet attribute. To see the effect of removing the custom routes, start the application and navigate to the /Home/Today URL using the browser. Clicking the Get Day button will produce a 500 (Internal Server Error) message, as shown in Figure 21-1.

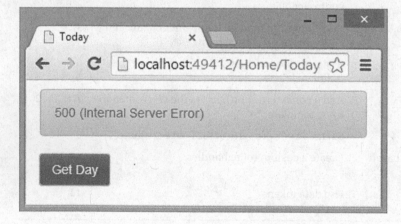

Figure 21-1. The effect of removing custom routes from the example application

Understanding Direct Routing

Direct routes are applied using attributes to the controller class and action methods, rather than in the WebApiConfig.cs file. Direct routing supports all of the same features as convention-based routing—including route templates, fixed and variable segments, defaults, and constraints—but they are applied directly to the controller class. In the sections that follow, I show you how to create direct routes and demonstrate how they work. Table 21-2 puts direct routing in context.

Table 21-2. *Putting Direct Routing in Context*

Question	Answer
What is it?	Direct routing allows routes to be defined by applying attributes to action methods or controller classes.
When should you use it?	See the "Selecting Convention-Based or Direct Routing" sidebar.
What do you need to know?	Features such as optional segments, default segment values, and segment constraints are all applied to the route template.

SELECTING CONVENTION-BASED OR DIRECT ROUTING

The difference between the two styles of routing is how individual routes are defined. As you saw in Chapter 20, convention-based routing puts all of the routes in the WebApiConfig.cs file. By contrast, direct routing defines routes through the use of attributes.

There is no technical difference in the routes that are created or the way that they are evaluated, and when it comes to choosing a style of routing, you should pick whichever one feels right to you. For me, this is convention-based routing because I like to keep the different parts of the application separate, but for many others, the attraction of direct routing is that you can see how routes relate to action methods by looking at the controller classes.

There are programmers who firmly believe that one approach to routing is superior to the other, but they are mistaking their preferences for a perceived benefit that doesn't exist, regardless of which routing style they advocate. You can match any pattern of URLs using either technique, and you can safely ignore anyone who argues otherwise.

Don't worry if you don't have a preference for one style of routing. Web API allows convention-based and direct routing to coexist in an application, and you can easily experiment to see what works best for you. If you don't know where to start, then I recommend you start with convention-based routing. If you find yourself staring blankly at the routes you end up with in the WebApiConfig.cs file trying to remember what you were aiming for, then give direct routing a try. Or, if you try direct routing but you are forever surprised by the way requests are matched because you have forgotten where you applied the attributes, then convention-based routing is worth a go.

The bottom line is that both techniques work the same behind the scenes and produce the same result: one or more routes that are used to match requests. The path you follow to generate those routes is entirely up to you, and you should take the time to experiment until you find an approach that you feel comfortable with.

Creating a Direct Route

At the heart of the direct routing feature is the Route attribute, which is defined by the RouteAttribute class in the System.Web.Http namespace. The Route attribute defines the properties shown in Table 21-3.

Table 21-3. *The Properties Defined by the Route Attribute*

Name	Description
Name	Specifies the name of the route. Route names are used when generating outgoing URLs.
Template	Specifies the route template that will be used to match requests. See the next section for details.
Order	Specifies the order in which routes are applied; see the "Ordering Direct Routes in a Controller" section.

There are only three properties, but as you will learn, direct routing manages to pack a lot of functionality into them, especially the routing template.

Applying the Route Attribute

To create a direct route, simply apply the Route attribute to an action method and define a route template that will match the URLs you are interested in. Multiple instances of the Route attribute can be applied to an action method, and you can apply the attribute to as many action methods as you require. Listing 21-2 shows the addition of the Route attribute to the action methods in the Today controller.

Listing 21-2. Defining Direct Routes in the TodayController.cs File

```
using System;
using System.Web.Http;

namespace Dispatch.Controllers {

    public class TodayController : ApiController {

        [HttpGet]
        [Route("api/today/dayofweek")]
        public string DayOfWeek() {
            return DateTime.Now.ToString("dddd");
        }

        [HttpGet]
        [Route("api/today/dayofweek/{day}")]
        public string DayOfWeek(int day) {
            return Enum.GetValues(typeof(DayOfWeek)).GetValue(day).ToString();
        }

        [HttpGet]
        [Route("getdaynumber")]
        public int DayNumber() {
            return DateTime.Now.Day;
        }
    }
}
```

I have applied the Route attribute to all three action methods in the controller. I have used the simplest form of the attribute, which takes a route template as its argument. The first two route templates I have defined (for the two versions of the DayOfWeek method) match the kind of URL pattern that I demonstrated in Chapter 20: there is an api prefix, followed by fixed and variable segments.

The third use of the Route attribute—on the DayNumber method—follows a different pattern, just to demonstrate that you can define route templates that match any kind of URL, even if the route template pattern is not consistent with the others defined by the controller.

Notice that I don't have to specify the controller or action route data values. The configuration process that locates the Route attribute and sets up the direct routes uses the context in which the attribute has been applied to generate the information required for the controller and action method selection processes.

■ **Note** Behind the scenes, Web API doesn't actually set the controller and action route data values for direct routes. Direct routes use the *data tokens* feature, which allows data to be passed from a route to other components in the system outside of the standard route data. A data token is defined that contains a reference to the action method that the route applies to, which means the method doesn't have to be located from the route data values. This is an optimization because the direct route system has to locate the action methods to find the Route attribute instances, and using route data would mean rendering this information to controller and action values, which would later be used to locate the action method once again. The drawback of this approach is that the meaning of the data tokens is hard-coded into the default classes that select controllers and action methods, which means you have to replicate the behavior in custom implementations.

To test the new route, start the application and use the browser to navigate to the /Home/Today URL. When you click the Get Day button, the URL requested by the client will be matched against one of the routes generated from the Route attribute, and the corresponding action method will be used to handle the request, as illustrated by Figure 21-2.

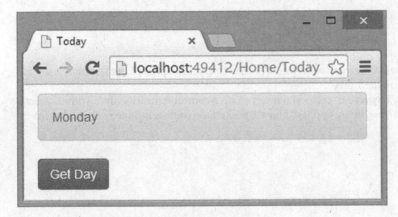

Figure 21-2. *The effect of creating direct routes*

Defining a Common Prefix

The RoutePrefix attribute can be applied to a controller to define a common prefix for routes defined with the Route attribute, which can help simplify the use of the attribute. In Listing 21-3, you can see how I have added the RoutePrefix attribute to the Today controller.

Listing 21-3. Applying a Common Prefix in the TodayController.cs File

```
using System;
using System.Web.Http;

namespace Dispatch.Controllers {

    [RoutePrefix("api/today")]
    public class TodayController : ApiController {

        [HttpGet]
        [Route("dayofweek")]
        public string DayOfWeek() {
            return DateTime.Now.ToString("dddd");
        }

        [HttpGet]
        [Route("dayofweek/{day}")]
        public string DayOfWeek(int day) {
            return Enum.GetValues(typeof(DayOfWeek)).GetValue(day).ToString();
        }

        [HttpGet]
        [Route("~/getdaynumber")]
        public int DayNumber() {
            return DateTime.Now.Day;
        }
    }
}
```

I have used the RoutePrefix attribute to define a common prefix of api/today and updated the template used for the Route attributes I applied to the DayOfWeek methods.

The route template that I defined for the DayNumber method doesn't share a common prefix with the other direct routes in the controller. To prevent the prefix from being applied, I have updated the route template so that it begins with ~/, like this:

```
...
[Route("~/getdaynumber")]
...
```

Defining Optional Segments

Direct routes support optional segments directly in the route template, which provides a more natural syntax than is available in convention-based routing. In Listing 21-4, you can see how I have made the id segment optional in a route and used this to collapse together two action methods.

Listing 21-4. Defining an Optional Segment in the TodayController.cs File

```
using System;
using System.Web.Http;

namespace Dispatch.Controllers {

    [RoutePrefix("api/today")]
    public class TodayController : ApiController {

        //[HttpGet]
        //[Route("dayofweek")]
        //public string DayOfWeek() {
        //    return DateTime.Now.ToString("dddd");
        //}

        [HttpGet]
        [Route("dayofweek/{day?}")]
        public string DayOfWeek(int day = -1) {
            if (day != -1) {
                return Enum.GetValues(typeof(DayOfWeek)).GetValue(day).ToString();
            } else {
                return DateTime.Now.ToString("dddd");
            }
        }

        [HttpGet]
        [Route("~/getdaynumber")]
        public int DayNumber() {
            return DateTime.Now.Day;
        }
    }
}
```

The overall effect of an optional segment is the same in a direct route, but there are some important implementation differences. First, the segment is marked as optional by appending a ? character after the variable name so that the day segment becomes the day? segment, like this:

```
...
 [Route("dayofweek/{day?}")]
...
```

I also have to set a default value on the action method parameter, as follows:

```
...
public string DayOfWeek(int day = -1) {
...
```

The route that the Route attribute generates will match URLs with a day segment (such as /api/today/dayofweek/2) and without (such as /api/today/dayofweek). For URLs that do not contain a day segment, the route data will not contain a day value, and the default parameter value will be used instead.

■ **Caution**   The route won't match URLs properly if you define an optional route template segment but forget to set a default parameter value.

In the listing, I have assigned a default parameter value of -1 to the day parameter, and I check for this value to see whether I should return today's name or the name of a specific day of the week.

There is, however, a problem with this approach, which is that I can't tell whether I have received a value of -1 because the client requested a URL without a day segment or because the day segment was provided, but with a value of -1. This may seem like a subtle distinction, but a URL with a day segment of -1 (meaning /api.today/dayofweek/-1) is something that I should deal with using an error since there is no corresponding day of the week. (I explain how to handle this kind of error using the model validation feature in Chapter 18.) The action method shown in the listing handles badly formed requests by ignoring the problem and pretending that a different URL has been sent, which is likely to lead to confusion. Listing 21-5 shows how I have revised the action method to take better advantage of the direct routing optional segment.

Listing 21-5. Handling an Optional Segment in the TodayController.cs File

```
...
[HttpGet]
[Route("dayofweek/{day?}")]
public IHttpActionResult DayOfWeek(int day = -1) {
    if (RequestContext.RouteData.Values.ContainsKey("day")) {
        return day != -1
            ? Ok(Enum.GetValues(typeof(DayOfWeek)).GetValue(day).ToString())
            : (IHttpActionResult)BadRequest("Value Out of Range");
    } else {
        return Ok(DateTime.Now.ToString("dddd"));
    }
}
...
```

In this implementation of the action method, I obtain the IHttpRouteData object via the RequestContext.RouteData property and check to see whether there is a day routing variable. (The RequestContext property is defined by the ApiController class, which is the base for the Today controller and which I describe in Chapter 22.)

I have changed the return type of the action method to IHttpActionResult, which allows me to send an error response when the request URL includes a day segment that is -1 and a success response otherwise.

■ **Tip**   I am showing you only how to differentiate between a default parameter value and a value provided by the client in this example. See Chapter 18 for details of how to validate data properly.

Defining a Default Segment Value

Direct routes also define default segment values within the route template. Listing 21-6 shows how I have changed the optional segment defined in the Today controller to one that has a default value.

Listing 21-6. Defining a Default Segment Value in the TodayController.cs File

```
...
[HttpGet]
[Route("dayofweek/{day=-1}")]
public string DayOfWeek(int day) {
    if (day != -1) {
        return Enum.GetValues(typeof(DayOfWeek)).GetValue(day).ToString();
    } else {
        return DateTime.Now.ToString("dddd");
    }
}
...
```

The default value is defined by using the equal sign after the segment name followed by the default value, expressed literally, like this:

```
...
[Route("dayofweek/{day=-1}")]
...
```

Defining a default value means that I don't need to define a default parameter value, but it also means that I can't tell whether the request contained a matching segment (which is the same behavior that default segment values the convention-based routes provide), so I have returned to the simpler implementation of the action method.

■ **Tip**   There is one important difference between a default segment value defined in a route and a default parameter value used for an optional segment: the default segment value is processed through the parameter/model binding processes that I described in Part 2. This can be useful if you are using bindings to validate data, but it also means there is no compile-time checking of the default value. Take care to test that your default values are valid, regardless of whether they are defined in direct or convention-based routes.

Applying a Constraint to a Direct Route

In addition to default and optional segments, direct route templates are also used to apply constraints. As I explained in Chapter 20, the System.Web.Http.Routing.Constraints namespace contains classes that can be used to constrain the range of URLs that a route will match. Listing 21-7 shows how I have applied one of the constraints to the day segment variable in the direct route I defined in the Today controller.

Listing 21-7. Constraining a Route in the TodayController.cs File

```
...
[HttpGet]
[Route("dayofweek/{day:int=-1}")]
public string DayOfWeek(int day) {
    if (day != -1) {
        return Enum.GetValues(typeof(DayOfWeek)).GetValue(day).ToString();
```

```
    } else {
        return DateTime.Now.ToString("dddd");
    }
}
...
```

■ **Caution** As I explained in Chapter 20, constraints should be used only to manage the set of URLs that a route will match and not to validate the data that the client sends. See Chapter 18 for details of the model validation feature, which is how data should be validated.

The constraint is applied by using a colon (the : character) after the segment name, followed by a shorthand reference for the constraint that is required. Each of the constraint classes has a shorthand name, and int, which I used in the listing, applies the IntRouteConstraint class, which has the effect of matching only the URLs where the day segment can be parsed to an int value.

```
...
[Route("dayofweek/{day:int=-1}")]
...
```

I applied the constraint alongside the default value in this example, but this is not required, and default values and constraints are independent of one another. Table 21-4 lists the shorthand values and the classes they represent.

Table 21-4. *The Shorthand References for Constraint Classes Used in Direct Route Templates*

Short Hand	Class	Description
alpha	AlphaRouteConstraint	Matches a route when the segment variable contains only alphabetic characters
bool	BoolRouteConstraint	Matches a route when the segment variable contains only true or false
datetime	DateTimeRouteConstraint	Matches a route when the segment variable can be parsed as a DateTime object
decimal double float int long	DecimalRouteConstraint DoubleRouteConstraint FloatRouteConstraint IntRouteConstraint LongRouteConstraint	Matches a route when the segment variable can be parsed as a decimal, double, float, int, or long value
maxlength minlength	MaxLengthRouteConstraint MinLengthRouteConstraint	Matches a route when the segment variable is a string with a maximum or minimum length
max min	MaxRouteConstraint MinRouteConstraint	Matches a route when the segment variable is an int with a maximum or minimum value
range	RangeRouteConstraint	Matches a route when the segment variable is an int within a range of values
regex	RegexRouteConstraint	Matches a route when the segment variable matches a regular expression

Parameters to configure constraints are defined literally within the route template. In Listing 21-8, you can see how I have applied the range constraint to limit the range of values that the day segment will match.

Listing 21-8. Using a Direct Route Constraint with Parameters in the TodayController.cs File

```
using System;
using System.Web.Http;

namespace Dispatch.Controllers {

    [RoutePrefix("api/today")]
    public class TodayController : ApiController {

        [HttpGet]
        [Route("dayofweek")]
        public string DayOfWeek() {
            return DateTime.Now.ToString("dddd");
        }

        [HttpGet]
        [Route("dayofweek/{day:range(0, 6)}")]
        public string DayOfWeek(int day) {
            return Enum.GetValues(typeof(DayOfWeek)).GetValue(day).ToString();
        }

        [HttpGet]
        [Route("~/getdaynumber")]
        public int DayNumber() {
            return DateTime.Now.Day;
        }
    }
}
```

I have used the range shorthand to apply the RangeRouteConstraint class to the day segment, and the parameters I have specified will allow the route to match a URL if the segment value is an int between 0 and 6. Constraining the route means I can't use an optional segment (the two are counter functional), so I have restored the version of the DayOfWeek method that takes no parameters.

Ordering Direct Routes in a Controller

As I explained in Chapter 20, the URL routing system enumerates the routes in the application until it finds one that can match the current request. No effort is made to find the best match—just the first one, after which all of the untested routes are ignored. When using convention-based routing, the order in which the routes are added to the HttpRouteCollection class is used to specify the order in which routes are tested against requests.

For direct routing, the routes defined by the Route attribute are automatically sorted so that the most specific routes are registered first, irrespective of the order in which the action methods are defined in the controller class.

To work out the order in which direct routes in a controller are applied, the URL routing feature calculates the precedence of each segment in the route template of each direct route. The precedence is a decimal value, which is then used to sort the routes so that the lowest values match first. For each segment, a score is awarded based on the segment type, as described in Table 21-5.

Table 21-5. The Scores Assigned to Direct Route Segment Types

Segment Type	Score
Fixed segment	1
Variable segment with a constraint	2
Variable segment without a constraint	3
Catchall segment with a constraint	4
Catchall segment without a constraint	5

The scores are concatenated (not summed) to form a single decimal value. To explain how this works, Table 21-6 shows the segments from one of the direct routes in the Today controller, along with the segment types and scores. (Notice that the segments defined by the `RoutePrefix` attribute are included.)

Table 21-6. The Scores for an Example Direct Route

Segment	Segment Type	Score
api	Fixed segment	1
today	Fixed segment	1
dayofweek	Fixed segment	1
day:range(0, 6)	Variable segment with a constraint	2

The individual scores are concatenated to form the precedence value `1.112` (the first score is always expressed as a whole number and subsequent scores as decimal fractions). Table 21-7 shows all of the routes defined in the Today controller and their precedence values.

Table 21-7. The Precedence Values for the Direct Routes in the Today Controller

Route	Precedence
api/today/dayofweek	1.11
api/today/dayofweek/{day:range(0, 6)}	1.112
getdaynumber	1.0

The lowest-precedence routes are used to match requests first, which produces the following route order:

1. /getdaynumber (precedence 1.0)

2. /api/today/dayofweek (precedence 1.11)

3. /api/today/dayofweek/{day} (precedence 1.112)

The precedence system usually creates a useful ordering of routes, but you can get odd results if a controller defines two routes that have the same precedence because Web API compares the route templates as alphabetic strings.

Using the alphabet to resolve route ordering isn't especially helpful, but you can use the `Order` property defined by the `Route` attribute to take control of the order in which routes are checked, as demonstrated in Listing 21-9.

Listing 21-9. Applying the Order Property to the Route Attribute in the TodayController.cs File

```csharp
using System;
using System.Web.Http;

namespace Dispatch.Controllers {

    [RoutePrefix("api/today")]
    public class TodayController : ApiController {

        [HttpGet]
        [Route("dayofweek")]
        public string DayOfWeek() {
            return DateTime.Now.ToString("dddd");
        }

        [HttpGet]
        [Route("dayofweek/{day:range(0, 6)}")]
        public string DayOfWeek(int day) {
            return Enum.GetValues(typeof(DayOfWeek)).GetValue(day).ToString();
        }

        [HttpGet]
        [Route("~/getdaynumber", Order=1)]
        public int DayNumber() {
            return DateTime.Now.Day;
        }
    }
}
```

Routes are assigned an Order value of 0 by default, and the routes with the lowest Order values are checked first. By setting the Order property to 1, I have demoted the route defined for the DayNumber method, producing the following route order:

1. /api/today/dayofweek (order 0, precedence 1.11)

2. /api/today/dayofweek/{day} (order 0, precedence 1.112)

3. /getdaynumber (order 1, precedence 1.0)

■ **Note** The Order value is checked first, but if there are routes with the same Order value, then the precedence score is taken into account.

Creating a Controller-wide Direct Route

In the previous section, I applied the Route attribute to individual action methods to create direct routes, but you can also apply the attribute to the controller class to create a direct route that applies to any action method for which a direct route has not already been defined. Listing 21-10 shows how I applied the Route attribute to the Today controller.

Listing 21-10. Applying the Route Attribute to the Controller in the TodayController.cs File

```
using System;
using System.Web.Http;

namespace Dispatch.Controllers {

    [RoutePrefix("api/today")]
    [Route("{action=DayOfWeek}")]
    public class TodayController : ApiController {

        [HttpGet]
        //[Route("dayofweek")]
        public string DayOfWeek() {
            return DateTime.Now.ToString("dddd");
        }

        [HttpGet]
        [Route("dayofweek/{day:range(0, 6)}")]
        public string DayOfWeek(int day) {
            return Enum.GetValues(typeof(DayOfWeek)).GetValue(day).ToString();
        }

        [HttpGet]
        //[Route("~/getdaynumber", Order=1)]
        public int DayNumber() {
            return DateTime.Now.Day;
        }
    }
}
```

I have applied the Route attribute to the class with a template of {action=DayOfWeek}, which is combined with the RoutePrefix template to create this template:

```
api/today/{action=DayOfWeek}
```

By providing a default value for the action variable, I have created a route that will match URLs that specify action methods (such as /api/today/daynumber and /api/today/dayofweek). The route template will also match a URL that doesn't specify an action method (/api/today) and will use the DayOfWeek method by default.

I have left the Route attribute applied to the DayOfWeek method that takes a parameter, which means that it will not be covered by the controller-wide Route attribute. However, if I apply the Route attribute to a controller, I generally prefer to define all the routes at that level because I end up forgetting that there are method-specific routes defined as well. Listing 21-11 shows how I consolidated all of the direct routes in the Today controller.

Listing 21-11. Consolidating the Direct Routes in the TodayController.cs File

```
using System;
using System.Web.Http;

namespace Dispatch.Controllers {

    [RoutePrefix("api/today")]
    [Route("{action=DayOfWeek}")]
    [Route("{action=DayOfWeek}/{day:range(0, 6)}")]
    public class TodayController : ApiController {

        [HttpGet]
        public string DayOfWeek() {
            return DateTime.Now.ToString("dddd");
        }

        [HttpGet]
        public string DayOfWeek(int day) {
            return Enum.GetValues(typeof(DayOfWeek)).GetValue(day).ToString();
        }

        [HttpGet]
        public int DayNumber() {
            return DateTime.Now.Day;
        }
    }
}
```

■ **Tip** This is my personal practice, and I suspect it arises because I am trying to re-create the centralization of convention-based routing while using the Route attribute. You need not adopt this convention if you are comfortable with defining direct routes throughout the application.

Customizing URL Routing

As you have learned, the default behavior of the routing system provides a lot of flexibility to manage the API that web services present to their clients. That said, if you find you are unable to create the behavior that you want, there are several ways in which you can customize the routing process, as I describe in the following section.

Using a Route-Specific Message Handler

If you are using convention-based routing, you can specify a message handler that will be used to process a request when it is matched by the route, allowing a request to be dealt with outside of the standard dispatch handler chain. (This feature is not available for direct routing.) Listing 21-12 shows the contents of the CustomRouteHandler.cs file, which I added to the Infrastructure folder.

Listing 21-12. The Contents of the CustomRouteHandler.cs File

```
using System.Net;
using System.Net.Http;
using System.Threading;
using System.Threading.Tasks;

namespace Dispatch.Infrastructure {
    public class CustomRouteHandler : HttpMessageHandler {

        protected override Task<HttpResponseMessage> SendAsync(
            HttpRequestMessage request, CancellationToken cancellationToken) {

            return Task.FromResult<HttpResponseMessage>(
                request.CreateResponse(HttpStatusCode.OK, "Today"));
        }
    }
}
```

■ **Tip** I find route-specific message handlers useful when I need to support a legacy API that doesn't quite fit into the Web API model, where it can be useful to redirect the client to other URLs or return fixed responses for certain requests. Otherwise, I use technique sparingly because it changes the normal flow of requests through the application and creates a special category of requests that will need to be tested thoroughly for every new release.

When I showed you how to add a message handler to the dispatch chain in Chapter 19, I derived my custom class from the DelegatingHandler class so that Web API could provide a reference to the next handler in the chain.

There is no chain when you set a handler for a route, so I have derived the CustomRouteHandler class directly from HttpMessageHandler. I have implemented the SendAsync method so that I create and return an HttpResponseMessage with the 200 (OK) status code and the string Today as the result.

Registering the Route and Handler

When defining a route, a custom handler can be specified using a version of the MapHttpRoute extension method, as shown in Listing 21-13.

Listing 21-13. Creating a Route with a Custom Handler in the WebApiConfig.cs File

```
using System.Web.Http;
using Dispatch.Infrastructure;

namespace Dispatch {
    public static class WebApiConfig {
        public static void Register(HttpConfiguration config) {

            config.Routes.MapHttpRoute(
                name: "CustomHandler",
                routeTemplate: "api/{controller}/{action}",
```

```
        defaults: null,
        constraints: null,
        handler: new CustomRouteHandler());

config.MapHttpAttributeRoutes();

config.Routes.MapHttpRoute(
    name: "DefaultApi",
    routeTemplate: "api/{controller}/{id}",
    defaults: new { id = RouteParameter.Optional }
);
    }
  }
}
```

I have defined a routing template that will match all three-segment URLs that start with /api. The null values tell the routing system that I don't want to use default values or constraints. The final argument is the handler that should be used to process the request when the route matches, which is an instance of the CustomRouteHandler class that I defined in the previous section.

To test the custom handler, start the application and use the browser to navigate to the /Home/Today URL. When you click the Get Day button, the client will send an Ajax request to the /api/today/dayofweek URL. The URL will be matched by the new route, and the CustomRouteHandler class will be used to send the Today response to the client, as illustrated by Figure 21-3.

Figure 21-3. *Using a custom message handler in a route*

Using Data Tokens

Routes can be defined with *data tokens*, which are expressed as a Dictionary<string, object> and are used to provide additional information to objects that will process the request. I am not a fan of using data tokens—for reasons I explain in the sidebar "The Problem with Data Tokens"—and I recommend you approach them with caution.

Listing 21-14 shows how I have redefined the route with a custom message handler in the WebApiConfig.cs file so that it defines data tokens. There is no version of the MapHttpRoute extension method that allows data tokens to be specified, so I have to use the CreateRoute and Add methods defined by the HttpRouteCollection object, as described in Chapter 20.

Listing 21-14. Defining a Route with Data Tokens in the WebApiConfig.cs File

```
using System.Web.Http;
using Dispatch.Infrastructure;
using System.Collections.Generic;

namespace Dispatch {
    public static class WebApiConfig {
        public static void Register(HttpConfiguration config) {

            config.Routes.Add(
                "CustomHandler",
                config.Routes.CreateRoute(
                    routeTemplate: "api/{controller}/{action}",
                    defaults: null,
                    constraints: null,
                    dataTokens: new Dictionary<string, object> {
                        { "response", "Tomorrow" }
                    },
                    handler: new CustomRouteHandler()));

            config.MapHttpAttributeRoutes();

            config.Routes.MapHttpRoute(
                name: "DefaultApi",
                routeTemplate: "api/{controller}/{id}",
                defaults: new { id = RouteParameter.Optional }
            );
        }
    }
}
```

The `Dictionary` that I used to set the `dataToken` parameter of the `CreateRoute` method contains a single key, response. Listing 21-15 shows how I use this key in the `CustomRouteHandler` class to set the data in the response to the client.

Listing 21-15. Consuming Data Tokens in the CustomRouteHandler.cs File

```
using System.Net;
using System.Net.Http;
using System.Threading;
using System.Threading.Tasks;

namespace Dispatch.Infrastructure {
    public class CustomRouteHandler : HttpMessageHandler {

        protected override Task<HttpResponseMessage> SendAsync(HttpRequestMessage
            request, CancellationToken cancellationToken) {

            string responseString
                = (string)request.GetRequestContext()
                    .RouteData.Route.DataTokens["response"];
```

```
        return Task.FromResult<HttpResponseMessage>(
            request.CreateResponse(HttpStatusCode.OK, responseString));
    }
  }
}
```

Data tokens are defined for the route, rather than for each request that the route matches, and they are accessed through the DataTokens property defined by the IHttpRoute interface, which I described in Chapter 20. To get the IHttpRoute implementation object that matched the request, I call the GetRequestContext extension method on the HttpRequestMessage object to get an instance of the HttpRequestContext class and then read the Route property.

THE PROBLEM WITH DATA TOKENS

The built-in handlers and routing classes use data tokens to communicate with one another. One example is precedence information for direct routes, which I described earlier in this chapter. The problem with data tokens is that they creating a coupling between a route handler and other components, generally, the classes that select the controller and action method that will handle the request. This coupling makes it harder to create custom implementations of Web API interfaces without understanding the purpose and meaning of the data tokens, which are undocumented. In the case of direct route precedence, you either need to spend some time with the debugger and the source code to figure out how they work, which is what I did for this chapter, or re-create the feature from scratch, which requires more work and testing. My advice is to avoid data tokens in your own code and check for their use carefully when you are creating a custom implementation of a Web API interface.

You can see the effect of the data token by starting the application and navigating to the /Home/Today URL with the browser. When you click the Get Day button, the client will send a request that will be matched by the route defined in Listing 21-14, and the custom handler will read the token value to produce the result, as illustrated by Figure 21-4.

Figure 21-4. *Using a data token*

Applying Custom Constraints to Direct Routes

In Chapter 20, I showed you how to apply a custom constraint to a convention-based route, but direct routes apply constraints in the route template, which is a problem because there are no built-in shorthand names for custom classes.

Fortunately, it is a simple matter to define a new shorthand name. To demonstrate how this works, I have defined a new constraint by adding the `SpecificValueConstraint.cs` file to the `Infrastructure` folder and using it to define the class shown in Listing 21-16.

Listing 21-16. The Contents of the SpecificValueConstraint.cs File

```
using System.Collections.Generic;
using System.Net.Http;
using System.Web.Http.Routing;

namespace Dispatch.Infrastructure {

    public class SpecificValueConstraint : IHttpRouteConstraint {
        private int targetValue;

        public SpecificValueConstraint(int value) {
            targetValue = value;
        }

        public bool Match(HttpRequestMessage request, IHttpRoute route,
            string parameterName, IDictionary<string, object> values,
                HttpRouteDirection routeDirection) {

            int candidateValue;

            return (values.ContainsKey(parameterName))
                && int.TryParse(values[parameterName].ToString(), out candidateValue)
                && targetValue == candidateValue;
        }
    }
}
```

This constraint checks that a segment variable is a specified `int` value and will prevent the route from matching the request unless it is.

Registering and Using the Constraint Shorthand Name

In Listing 21-17, you can see how I have created a shorthand name for the constraint in the `WebApiConfig.cs` file.

Listing 21-17. Registering a Shorthand Constraint Name in the WebApiConfig.cs File

```
using System.Web.Http;
using Dispatch.Infrastructure;
using System.Collections.Generic;
using System.Web.Http.Routing;

namespace Dispatch {
    public static class WebApiConfig {
        public static void Register(HttpConfiguration config) {

            //config.Routes.Add(
            //    "CustomHandler",
```

```
//     config.Routes.CreateRoute(
//         routeTemplate: "api/{controller}/{action}",
//         defaults: null,
//         constraints: null,
//         dataTokens: new Dictionary<string, object> {
//             { "response", "Tomorrow" }
//         },
//         handler: new CustomRouteHandler()));

    DefaultInlineConstraintResolver resolver
        = new DefaultInlineConstraintResolver();
    resolver.ConstraintMap.Add("specval", typeof(SpecificValueConstraint));
    config.MapHttpAttributeRoutes(resolver);

    config.Routes.MapHttpRoute(
        name: "DefaultApi",
        routeTemplate: "api/{controller}/{id}",
        defaults: new { id = RouteParameter.Optional }
    );
        }
    }
}
```

■ **Tip**   Notice that I have commented out the convention-based route that uses a custom handler so that it doesn't preempt the direct routes defined on the Today controller.

The DefaultInlineConstraintResolver class is used to resolve shorthand constrain names and defines a property called ConstraintMap that returns a dictionary used to map shorthand names to constraint types.

In the listing, I create a new instance of the DefaultInlineConstraintResolver class and use the ConstraintMap.Add method to define a new shorthand name, specval, to represent the SpecificValueConstraint class. I then call the MapHttpAttributeRoutes method to set up the direct routes, passing in the DefaultInlineConstraintResolver object as the argument. The final step is to apply the constraint to a direct route using the shorthand name I defined in Listing 21-17. In Listing 21-18, you can see how I update the direct routes in the Today class.

Listing 21-18. Using a Custom Constraint in the TodayController.cs File

```
using System;
using System.Web.Http;

namespace Dispatch.Controllers {

    [RoutePrefix("api/today")]
    [Route("{action=DayOfWeek}")]
    [Route("{action=DayOfWeek}/{day:specval(2)}")]
    public class TodayController : ApiController {

        // ...action methods omitted for brevity...
    }
}
```

With this change, the custom constraint will prevent the highlighted route from matching unless the day segment variable is 2.

Applying a Route-wide Custom Constraint

The custom constraint in the previous section operates on a single variable segment, which fits into the direct route model of applying constraints within the route template. It doesn't work, however, for constraints that are not specific to a segment, such as the UserAgentConstraint class that I defined in Chapter 20. This constraint applies to the entire route, which means I can't use it in the route template.

The Web API URL system includes the abstract RouteFactoryAttribute class, which can be used to create routes that don't fit into the standard direct routing system. The RouteFactoryAttribute class defines the virtual properties shown in Table 21-8, which can be overridden in derived classes.

Table 21-8. *The Virtual Properties Defined by the RouteFactoryAttribute Class*

Name	Description
Constraints	Returns the set of constraints applied to the route
DataTokens	Returns the data token for the route
Order	Returns the Order value that will be used to sort the routes

To apply the UserAgentConstraint to a direct route, I added a class file called UserAgentConstraintRouteAttribute.cs to the Infrastructure folder and used it to define the class shown in Listing 21-19.

Listing 21-19. The Contents of the UserAgentConstraintRouteAttribute.cs File

```
using System.Collections.Generic;
using System.Web.Http.Routing;

namespace Dispatch.Infrastructure {
    public class UserAgentConstraintRouteAttribute : RouteFactoryAttribute {

        public UserAgentConstraintRouteAttribute(string template)
            : base(template) {
        }

        public override IDictionary<string, object> Constraints {
            get {
                IDictionary<string, object> constraints
                    = base.Constraints ?? new Dictionary<string, object>();
                constraints.Add("useragent", new UserAgentConstraint("Chrome"));
                return constraints;
            }
        }
    }
}
```

The UserAgentConstraintRouteAttribute class derives from RouteFactoryAttribute and overrides the Constraints property to return the set of constraints defined by the base class (or creates a new dictionary if required). I added a new instance of the UserAgentConstraint class to the collection, like this:

```
...
constraints.Add("useragent", new UserAgentConstraint("Chrome"));
...
```

You can use any key to register the constraint object as long as it doesn't correspond to a variable segment name in the route template. Listing 21-20 shows how I replaced the Route attribute with UserAgentConstraintRoute in the Today controller.

Listing 21-20. Using a Custom Route Attribute in the TodayController.cs File

```
using System;
using System.Web.Http;
using Dispatch.Infrastructure;

namespace Dispatch.Controllers {

    [RoutePrefix("api/today")]
    [Route("{action=DayOfWeek}")]
    [UserAgentConstraintRoute("{action=DayOfWeek}/{day:specval(2)}")]
    public class TodayController : ApiController {

        // ...action methods omitted for brevity...
    }
}
```

The effect is to apply the UserAgentConstraint to the route, in addition to the per-segment constraints defined in the route template.

Summary

In this chapter, I described how Web API direct routes works, allowing you to define routes on action methods or controllers, rather than in the WebApiConfig.cs file. I explained how the Route attribute is used to create direct routes, how to define optional segments, how to define segments with default values, and how constraints can be applied. I finished this chapter by showing you how to customize the routing process. In the next chapter, I continue describing the dispatch process and explain how controllers and action methods are used to handle requests.

CHAPTER 22

■ ■ ■

Controllers and Actions

In this chapter, I continue describing the Web API dispatch process and focus on controllers and action methods. I explain how controllers work in Web API and describe the dispatch process implemented by the default controller class, ApiController. Along the way, I show you how to resolve a common routing problem, explain how requests are mapped to action methods in RESTful Web API controllers, and show you how to customize request dispatching. Table 22-1 summarizes this chapter.

Table 22-1. *Chapter Summary*

Problem	Solution	Listing
Create a controller.	Define a class that implements the IHttpController interface and use the services collection to access Web API features such as parameter and model binding.	1-5
Create a controller that follows the action method model without having to handle the request directly.	Define a class that is derived from ApiController.	6
Specify the HTTP verbs that an action can handle.	Use the RESTful naming convention or apply an HTTP verb attribute.	7
Avoid routing conflicts between controllers that follow the RESTful naming convention and those that do not.	Use direct routing or restrict convention-based routes (either with a constraint or with a different prefix).	8-10
Customize the way that action methods are invoked.	Create an implementation of the IHttpActionInvoker interface.	11
Customize the way that action methods are selected.	Create an implementation of the IHttpActionSelector interface.	12
Apply a custom configuration to a controller.	Create an implementation of the IControllerConfiguration interface.	13-14

Preparing the Example Project

I will continue working with the Dispatch project from the previous chapter, but to prepare for this chapter, I am going to tidy up the URL routes I defined. Listing 22-1 shows the Today controller, from which I have removed the direct routes.

Listing 22-1. Removing the Direct Routes from the TodayController.cs File

```
using System;
using System.Web.Http;

namespace Dispatch.Controllers {

    public class TodayController : ApiController {

        [HttpGet]
        public string DayOfWeek() {
            return DateTime.Now.ToString("dddd");
        }

        [HttpGet]
        public string DayOfWeek(int day) {
            return Enum.GetValues(typeof(DayOfWeek)).GetValue(day).ToString();
        }

        [HttpGet]
        public int DayNumber() {
            return DateTime.Now.Day;
        }
    }
}
```

Instead of direct routes, I have defined a convention-based route in the WebApiConfig.cs file that allows the action methods in the Today controller to be reached, and I have removed the custom constraints and other additions from Chapter 21, as shown in Listing 22-2.

Listing 22-2. Revising the URL Routing Configuration in the WebApiConfig.cs File

```
using System.Web.Http;

namespace Dispatch {
    public static class WebApiConfig {
        public static void Register(HttpConfiguration config) {

            config.Routes.MapHttpRoute(
                name: "ActionMethods",
                routeTemplate: "api/{controller}/{action}/{day}",
                defaults: new { day = RouteParameter.Optional }
            );

            config.Routes.MapHttpRoute(
                name: "DefaultApi",
                routeTemplate: "api/{controller}/{id}",
                defaults: new { id = RouteParameter.Optional }
            );
        }
    }
}
```

Understanding Controllers

Controllers are the classes where the world of Web API delivers `HttpRequestMessages` into your custom application logic so that you can transform them into `HttpResponseMessages`. This transformation will usually involve interactions with the *model*, which is another of the big components in the *Model View Controller* pattern. As I explained in Chapter 4, web services don't have views because they deliver data back to the client, rather than components for a user interface (although some people regard the media type formatters to be the equivalent of a view because they transform the data in a way that can be consumed by the client).

Figure 22-1 shows the dispatch process as I left it in Chapter 20, and in this chapter I dig into the details of how an `HttpRequestMessage` object is processed, starting with the definition of a Web API controller and then turning to the default implementation classes that are used in most Web API applications.

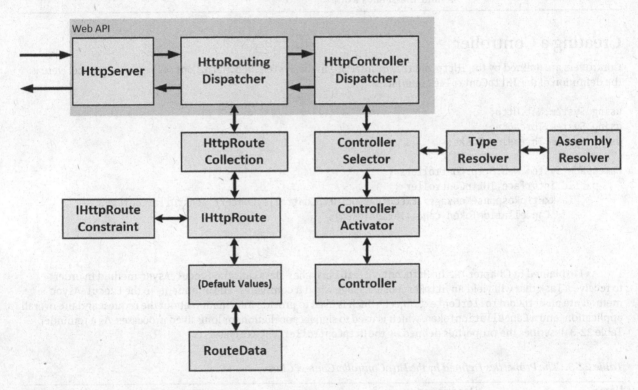

Figure 22-1. *The Web API dispatch process*

Table 22-2 puts controllers into context.

537

Table 22-2. *Putting Controllers into Context*

Question	Answer
What is it?	Controllers contain the logic required to handle a request and are the point at which the HttpResponseMessage object is created so it can be relayed back along the dispatcher chain and used to create a response for the client.
When should you use it?	Controllers are used by the HttpControllerDispatcher class and fully integrated into the request pipeline. No specific action is required to use controllers.
What do you need to know?	Controllers are defined by the IHttpController interface, but most applications are better served by deriving from the ApiController class, which takes care of a lot of behind-the-scenes work.

Creating a Controller

Controllers are defined by the IHttpController interface in the System.Web.Http.Controllers namespace. Here is the definition of the IHttpController interface:

```
using System.Net.Http;
using System.Threading;
using System.Threading.Tasks;

namespace System.Web.Http.Controllers {
    public interface IHttpController {
        Task<HttpResponseMessage> ExecuteAsync(HttpControllerContext controllerContext,
            CancellationToken cancellationToken);
    }
}
```

As I explained in Chapter 19, the HttpControllerDispatcher class calls the ExecuteAsync method in order to receive a Task that will yield an HttpResponseMessage when it completes. The arguments to the ExecuteAsync method are an HttpControllerContext object, which is used to provide information about the request and the overall application, and a CancellationToken, which is used to signal cancellation for long-lived processes. As a reminder, Table 22-3 describes the properties defined by the HttpControllerContext class.

Table 22-3. *The Properties Defined by the HttpControllerContext Class*

Name	Description
Configuration	Returns the HttpConfiguration object that should be used to service the request. As I explain in Chapter 22, controllers can be given their own configuration to work with.
Controller	Returns the IHttpController instance. This is not entirely useful when the HttpControllerContext is being passed an argument to the controller.
ControllerDescriptor	Returns the HttpControllerDescriptor that led to the controller being instantiated.
Request	Returns the HttpRequestMessage that describes the current request.
RequestContext	Returns the HttpRequestContext that provides additional information about the request.
RouteData	Returns the IHttpRouteData object that contains the routing data for the request. See Chapters 20 and 21 for details.

Most projects will use the default implementation of the IHttpController interface—the ApiController class—to create web services because there are lots of useful built-in features. But it is easy enough to create a custom implementation, and it helps put the role of the controller in context within the dispatch process. Listing 22-3 shows the contents of the CustomController.cs file, which I added to the Controllers folder.

Listing 22-3. The Contents of the CustomController.cs File

```
using System;
using System.Net;
using System.Net.Http;
using System.Threading;
using System.Threading.Tasks;
using System.Web.Http.Controllers;
using System.Web.Http.Routing;

namespace Dispatch.Controllers {
    public class CustomController : IHttpController {

        public Task<System.Net.Http.HttpResponseMessage> ExecuteAsync(
            HttpControllerContext context, CancellationToken cancellationToken) {

            return Task<HttpResponseMessage>.Factory.StartNew(() => {

                IHttpRouteData rd = context.RouteData;
                object result = null;
                if (rd.Values.ContainsKey("action")) {

                    switch (rd.Values["action"].ToString().ToLowerInvariant()) {
                        case "dayofweek":
                            if (rd.Values.ContainsKey("day")) {
                                int dayValue;
                                if (int.TryParse((string)rd.Values["day"],
                                        out dayValue)) {
                                    result = DayOfWeek(dayValue);
                                } else {
                                    return context.Request.CreateErrorResponse(
                                        HttpStatusCode.BadRequest, "Cannot parse data");
                                }
                            } else {
                                result = DayOfWeek();
                            }
                            break;
                        case "daynumber":
                            result = DayNumber();
                            break;
                        default:
                            return context.Request.CreateErrorResponse(
                                HttpStatusCode.NotFound, "Cannot parse data");
                    }
                }
```

```
            return result == null
                ? context.Request.CreateResponse(HttpStatusCode.OK)
                : context.Request.CreateResponse(HttpStatusCode.OK, result);
        });
    }

    ////////////////////////////////
    // Action Methods Start Here //
    ////////////////////////////////

    public string DayOfWeek() {
        return DateTime.Now.ToString("dddd");
    }

    public string DayOfWeek(int day) {
        return Enum.GetValues(typeof(DayOfWeek)).GetValue(day).ToString();
    }

    public int DayNumber() {
        return DateTime.Now.Day;
    }
}
}
```

This class implements the same action methods as the Today controller that I added to the project. The difference is that my new controller has to take responsibility for implementing the ExecuteAsync method, selecting and invoking the action method, and generating an HttpResponseMessage that can be returned to the client.

To test the new controller, I need to change the URL that the client requests, as shown in Listing 22-4.

Listing 22-4. Changing the Request URL in the today.js File

```
var response = ko.observable("Ready");
var gotError = ko.observable(false);

var sendRequest = function () {
  $.ajax("/api/custom/dayofweek/1", {
        type: "GET",
        success: function (data) {
            gotError(false);
            response(data);
        },
        error: function (jqXHR) {
            gotError(true);
            response(jqXHR.status + " (" + jqXHR.statusText + ")");
        }
    });
};

$(document).ready(function () {
    ko.applyBindings();
});
```

Notice that I have changed the segment that will match the name of the controller and added a segment that will be mapped to the day variable by the route I added in Listing 22-3. I have done this so I can demonstrate how my manual parameter binding works—and how this can be improved upon in later examples.

To test the new controller, start the application and use the browser to navigate to the /Home/Today URL. Click the Get Day button, and the client will send a request, which will be matched by the route I defined at the start of the chapter; this leads to the ExecuteAsync method of my custom controller class being invoked. The result is created and sent back to the client, as shown in Figure 22-2. Since the client always specifies the same day, the result will always be Monday.

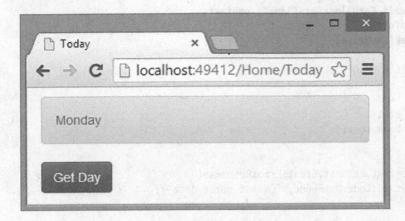

Figure 22-2. *Sending a request to a custom implementation of the IHttpController interface*

Using Built-in Services and Features

When you implement a controller directly from the IHttpController interface, you lose the built-in features provided by the ApiController class (which I describe in the next section), but you can still use the core Web API services and features, such as model binding. This means you don't have to reinvent important features, although there can be a lot of work to get to the point where a feature can be used. In Listing 22-5, I have modified the Custom controller class to use the model binding feature to get the argument value required to call the DayOfWeek action method.

Listing 22-5. Using the Built-in Parameter Binding Feature in the CustomController.cs File

```
using System;
using System.Net;
using System.Net.Http;
using System.Threading;
using System.Threading.Tasks;
using System.Web.Http.Controllers;
using System.Web.Http.ModelBinding;
using System.Web.Http.Routing;
using System.Web.Http;
using System.Reflection;

namespace Dispatch.Controllers {
    public class CustomController : IHttpController {

        public Task<System.Net.Http.HttpResponseMessage> ExecuteAsync(
            HttpControllerContext context, CancellationToken cancellationToken) {
```

541

```
            return Task.Run<HttpResponseMessage>(async () => {

                IHttpRouteData rd = context.RouteData;
                object result = null;
                if (rd.Values.ContainsKey("action")) {

                    switch (rd.Values["action"].ToString().ToLowerInvariant()) {
                        case "dayofweek":
                            if (rd.Values.ContainsKey("day")) {
                                int dayValue = await GetValue<int>("day", context,
                                    cancellationToken);
                                result = DayOfWeek(dayValue);
                            } else {
                                result = DayOfWeek();
                            }
                            break;
                        case "daynumber":
                            result = DayNumber();
                            break;
                        default:
                            return context.Request.CreateErrorResponse(
                                HttpStatusCode.NotFound, "Cannot parse data");
                    }
                }

                return result == null
                    ? context.Request.CreateResponse(HttpStatusCode.OK)
                    : context.Request.CreateResponse(HttpStatusCode.OK, result);
            });
    }

    private async Task<T> GetValue<T>(string name, HttpControllerContext ctx,
            CancellationToken token) {

        HttpControllerDescriptor ctrlDescriptor = new HttpControllerDescriptor(
            ctx.Configuration, "Custom", this.GetType());
        MethodInfo methodInfo
            = GetType().GetMethod("DayOfWeek", new Type[] { typeof(int)});

        IActionValueBinder binder
            = ctx.Configuration.Services.GetActionValueBinder();
        HttpActionBinding binding = binder.GetBinding(
            new ReflectedHttpActionDescriptor(ctrlDescriptor, methodInfo));
        HttpActionContext actionCtx = new HttpActionContext(ctx, new
            ReflectedHttpActionDescriptor(ctrlDescriptor, methodInfo));

        await binding.ExecuteBindingAsync(actionCtx, token);

        return actionCtx.ActionArguments.ContainsKey(name)
            ? (T)Convert.ChangeType(actionCtx.ActionArguments[name], typeof(T))
            : default(T);
    }
```

```
////////////////////////////
// Action Methods Start Here //
////////////////////////////

public string DayOfWeek() {
    return DateTime.Now.ToString("dddd");
}

public string DayOfWeek(int day) {
    return Enum.GetValues(typeof(DayOfWeek)).GetValue(day).ToString();
}

public int DayNumber() {
    return DateTime.Now.Day;
}
    }
}
```

The GetValue method I added to the controller uses parameter binding to get the int value required to call the DayOfWeek method. To get the value, I have to create a number of classes to provide the context needed to process the request. These classes are created behind the scenes when you use the ApiController, but the advantage of this approach is that it can be applied to all method parameters, rather than needing to hard-code knowledge of the action methods in the ExecuteAsync method. I am not going to go into detail about the implementation of the GetValue method because—as I explain in the next section—there is little reason to implement this functionality in a real project.

IMPLEMENTING NEW KINDS OF CONTROLLER

The Custom controller I defined in Listing 22-3 and Listing 22-5 show you how you can create a custom implementation of the IHttpController interface and still benefit from Web API features such as parameter and model binding. That said, the controller follows the model provided by the ApiController class that I have been using as the base class for all of my web service controllers so far in this book: a request is matched to action methods—some of which require arguments—that produce data or HttpResponseMessage objects that can be returned to the client.

Re-creating this model in a custom implementation of the IHttpController interface isn't a good idea when there is a fully featured and well-tested alternative in the ApiController class, which I describe in the next section. The only time it makes sense to implement the IHttpController interface directly is when you require a completely different approach for transforming HttpRequestMessage objects into HttpResponseMessage objects. I occasionally have to create a custom implementation as a wrapper around legacy code that can't readily be exposed through action methods, but this is a rare occurrence. For most applications, the ApiController class should be used as the base for controllers.

Understanding the ApiController Dispatch Process

The ApiController class, defined in the System.Web.Http namespace, is the base class used for most Web API controllers. The ApiController class implements the IHttpController interface and provides two important areas of functionality: dispatching requests to action methods and helping developers to keep action methods as simple as possible.

Action methods are the basic unit of logic used to process a request to create a result, expressed as a standard C# method. The `ApiController` class makes it possible to use C# methods as actions through its implementation of the `IHttpController.ExecuteAsync` method, which takes care of locating an action method for the request, using parameter and model binding to get the method arguments, and processing the method result to create an `HttpResponseMessage` object that can be returned through the message handler chain and, ultimately, sent to the client. It is this process that I describe in the sections that follow. Table 22-4 puts the `ApiController` dispatch process in context.

Table 22-4. *Putting the ApiController Dispatch Process in Context*

Question	Answer
What is it?	The `ApiController` class is the built-in implementation of the `IHttpController` interface and adds support for important convenience features such as action methods, action results, and filters.
When should you use it?	You should use the `ApiController` class as the base for all of your controllers. Implement the `IHttpController` interface directly only if you need to create a completely different approach to handling requests.
What do you need to know?	The `ApiController` class relies on implementations of the `IHttpActionSelector` and `IHttpActionInvoker` interfaces to select and invoke action methods. You can change the way that the `ApiController` class behaves by creating custom implementations, which I demonstrate in the "Customizing the Controller Dispatch Process" section.

As you may expect, there are a number of key dispatch tasks that the `ApiController` delegates to implementations of interfaces that are obtained from the services collection. I describe each interface in turn in the sections that follow and describe the customization opportunities in the "Customizing the Controller Dispatch Process" section. To provide an overview of the dispatch process, Figure 22-3 shows a revised diagram of the overall request dispatch process.

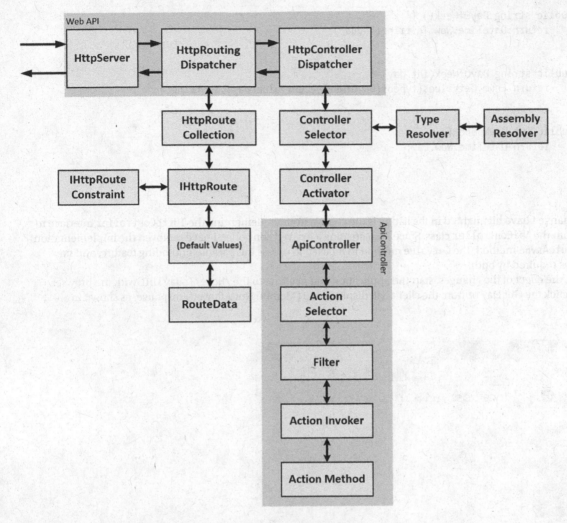

Figure 22-3. *Adding ApiController to the request dispatch process*

Preparing the Example Controller

To describe the dispatch process, I need a controller that is derived from the ApiController class. Listing 22-6 shows how I have changed the Custom controller so that it is derived from ApiController, rather than implementing the IHttpController interface directly.

Listing 22-6. Deriving from the ApiController Class in the CustomController.cs File

```
using System;
using System.Web.Http;

namespace Dispatch.Controllers {
    public class CustomController : ApiController {
```

```
        public string DayOfWeek() {
            return DateTime.Now.ToString("dddd");
        }

        public string DayOfWeek(int day) {
            return Enum.GetValues(typeof(DayOfWeek)).GetValue(day).ToString();
        }

        public int DayNumber() {
            return DateTime.Now.Day;
        }
    }
}
```

The change I have highlighted in the listing is the change from implementing the IHttpController interface to deriving from the ApiController class. Since I am creating a derived controller, I have removed the implementation of the ExecuteAsync method, the GetValue method that I used to access the parameter binding feature, and the namespaces required by both.

To test the effect of the changes, start the application and navigate to the /Home/Today URL with the browser. When you click the Get Day button, the client will display a 405 (Method Not Allowed) response, as shown in Figure 22-4.

Figure 22-4. *The effect of deriving from the ApiController class*

As I explained briefly in Chapter 19, the ApiController class selects action methods using a specific sequence. In the sections that follow, I describe the sequence that is used and explain why it doesn't match the request from the client to the action methods defined by the Custom controller.

Understanding the Action Selection Process

The `ApiController` class delegates the selection of the action method for a request to an implementation of the `IHttpActionSelector` interface, which is defined in the `System.Web.Http.Controllers` namespace. Here is the definition of the `IHttpActionSelector` interface:

```
using System.Linq;

namespace System.Web.Http.Controllers {
    public interface IHttpActionSelector {

        HttpActionDescriptor SelectAction(HttpControllerContext controllerContext);

        ILookup<string, HttpActionDescriptor> GetActionMapping(HttpControllerDescriptor
            controllerDescriptor);
    }
}
```

The `SelectAction` method is called when the controller needs to identify the action method that will be used to process the request. The parameter to the `SelectAction` method is an `HttpControllerContext` object, which describes the controller that is handling the request. (I described the `HttpControllerDescriptor` class in Chapter 19, but Table 22-5 recaps the properties that it defines.)

Table 22-5. *The Properties Defined by the HttpControllerContext Class*

Name	Description
Configuration	Returns the `HttpConfiguration` object that should be used to service the request. As I explain in the "Creating a Controller-Specific Configuration" section, controllers can be given their own configuration to work with.
Controller	Returns the `IHttpController` instance that is handling the request.
ControllerDescriptor	Returns the `HttpControllerDescriptor` that led to the controller being instantiated. See Chapter 22 for details.
Request	Returns the `HttpRequestMessage` that describes the current request.
RequestContext	Returns the `HttpRequestContext` that provides additional information about the request.
RouteData	Returns the `IHttpRouteData` object that contains the routing data for the request. See Chapters 20 and 21 for details.

■ **Tip** The `GetActionMapping` method returns information about the set of action methods that can be selected from the specified controller. This method is used by the direct routing system—which I described in Chapter 21—so that each action method can be inspected for `Route` attributes. It is also useful when creating a custom `IHttpActionSelector` implementation, which I described in the "Creating a Custom IHttpActionSelector Implementation" section.

The result from the `SelectAction` method is an `HttpActionDescriptor` object, which defines the properties and methods described in Table 22-6.

Table 22-6. *The Properties and Methods Defined by the HttpActionDescriptor Class*

Name	Description
ActionBinding	Returns an HttpActionBinding that describes how the parameters defined by the action method will be bound to values from the request.
ActionName	Returns the name of the action method.
Configuration	Returns the HttpConfiguration object for the action method. See the "Creating a Controller-Specific Configuration" section for details about how to create controller-specific configurations.
ControllerDescriptor	Returns the HttpControllerDescriptor object that describes the controller that contains the action method. See Chapter 19.
ExecuteAsync(controller, arguments, cancelToken)	Executes the action method. The arguments are an HttpControllerContext object; an IDictionary<string, object> that contains the arguments for the action method, indexed by name; and a CancellationToken that can be monitored for cancellation in action methods that take time to complete.
GetCustomAttributes<T>()	Returns a collection of attributes of type T.
GetFilterPipeline()	Returns a collection of FilterInfo objects that describe the filters that have been applied to the action method. See Chapters 23 and 24 for details of filters.
GetFilters()	Returns a collection of IFilter implementation objects that represent the filters applied to the action method. See Chapters 23 and 24 for details.
GetParameters()	Returns a collection of HttpParameterDescriptor objects that describe the parameters defined by the action method.
ResultConverter	Returns an implementation of the IActionResultConverter interface that will convert the response from the action method into an HttpResponseMessage object.
ReturnType	Returns the Type produced by the action method when it is executed.
SupportedHttpMethods	Returns a collection of HttpMethod values that specify which HTTP methods the action method can support.

Understanding the Default Action Method Selection Process

The default implementation of the IHttpActionSelector interface is the ApiControllerActionSelector class, which is defined in the System.Web.Http.Controllers namespace. The process that the ApiControllerActionSelector class follows to select an action method is described in Table 22-7. I have taken some liberties in describing the process to make it easier to follow.

Table 22-7. *The Selection Process Used by the ApiControllerActionSelector Class*

Step	Description
1	Reflection is used to identify candidate action methods. For a method to be selected at this stage, it must be a normal method (not a constructor, for example), must be defined in a class that is derived from ApiController, and must not be annotated with the NonAction attribute.
2	The candidate action methods are inspected for the Route attribute to see whether the request can be mapped directly. If direct routing has been used, action methods whose direct route does not match the request are discarded.
3	The route data is inspected to see whether an action value has been extracted from the request. If so, the set of candidate action methods is checked to see whether there are matches for the name. Candidates that do not match the name are discarded if an action value is provided.
4	The names of the candidate action methods are checked to see whether they follow the Web API RESTful convention. I describe this convention in the "Understanding the RESTful Naming Convention" section, but the simple version is that the method name is checked to see whether it contains an HTTP verb. For example, a method called GetProducts is assumed to be able to handle GET requests. The naming convention is used to discard candidate action methods that do not support the request HTTP verb.
5	Where the naming convention is not used, the HTTP verb attributes, such as HttpGet and HttpPost, are used to discard any candidate actions that do not support the requested HTTP verb.
6	The number and type of parameters are used to discard any candidate action methods that cannot be matched to the routing data, as described in Chapters 20 and 21.

The process starts with all of the potential action methods defined by the controller and eliminates the ones that can't handle the request at each stage. At the end of the final selection step, there should be exactly one action method remaining, which the ApiControllerActionSelector class describes using an HttpActionDescriptor object.

■ **Tip** If there are no suitable action methods, then the selector hasn't been able to match the request to one of the methods defined by the controller. If there is more than one method left, then the selector has been unable to differentiate between the action methods and doesn't know which method should be used. Both outcomes are a problem, and both will result in an error message being sent to the client. I describe Web API error handling in Chapter 25.

Understanding the RESTful Naming Convention

One of the most important aspects of the selection process is the way that the name of the action method is used to figure out which HTTP methods the method can handle. This is the basis of how Web API makes creating a RESTful web service simple. When I created the example project in Chapter 19, I defined the Products controller, as follows:

```
using System.Collections.Generic;
using System.Linq;
using System.Web.Http;
using Dispatch.Models;

namespace Dispatch.Controllers {
    public class ProductsController : ApiController {
        private static List<Product> products = new List<Product> {
                new Product {ProductID = 1, Name = "Kayak", Price = 275M },
```

549

```
            new Product {ProductID = 2, Name = "Lifejacket", Price = 48.95M },
            new Product {ProductID = 3, Name = "Soccer Ball", Price = 19.50M },
            new Product {ProductID = 4, Name = "Thinking Cap", Price = 16M },
        };

    public IEnumerable<Product> Get() {
        return products;
    }

    public Product Get(int id) {
        return products.Where(x => x.ProductID == id).FirstOrDefault();
    }

    public Product Post(Product product) {
        product.ProductID = products.Count + 1;
        products.Add(product);
        return product;
    }
    }
}
```

I have used the simplest possible naming scheme and have used HTTP verbs as the action method names. The selection process looks at the names to figure out which method should be targeted for the request HTTP verb. Methods that have the same name—such as the Get methods in the Products controller—are disambiguated by the parameters they define, which are mapped against values in the routing data, as described in Chapters 20 and 21. The Products controller is relatively simple, but when combined with the default route defined in the WebApiConfig.cs file, it produces the RESTful web service API described in Table 22-8.

Table 22-8. *The RESTful Web Service Defined by the Product Controller*

HTTP Verb	URL	Action Method
GET	/api/products	Get()
GET	/api/products/2	Get(int)
POST	/api/products	Post(product)

■ **Tip**   The RESTful naming convention works only for the GET, POST, PUT, and DELETE verbs. You will need to apply an HTTP verb attribute for other request types. See the "Explicitly Specifying HTTP Verbs" section for details.

I like to keep the names I use in RESTful controllers as simple as possible, which is why I used just the HTTP verb names in the Products controller. You can use more friendly names if you prefer, and the ApiControllerActionSelector class will still select your action methods as long as their name begins with one of the verbs. A common alternative is to include the name of the model class in the method name, such that Get() would be replaced with GetProducts(), Get(id) with GetProduct(id) or GetProductById(id), and so on. The ApiControllerActionSelector class does not take into account any part of the action method name other than the HTTP verb, which means you are free to adopt any naming scheme that you find easy to work with.

Explicitly Specifying HTTP Verbs

As part of the selection process, the ApiControllerActionSelector class checks to see which HTTP verbs candidate action methods can support. For controllers that follow the RESTful naming convention, the HTTP verb is taken from the method name: an action method called Get or GetProducts is assumed to be able to handle HTTP get requests.

For non-RESTful controllers, details of which HTTP verbs are supported must be explicitly specified, and it is for this reason that sending a request to the Custom controller results in a 405 (Method Not Allowed) response, as shown in Figure 22-4. (Remember that HTTP verbs are also known as *HTTP methods*.)

Support for HTTP verbs is specified by applying attributes that implement the IActionHttpMethodProvider interface, which is defined in the System.Web.Http.Controllers namespace. Here is the definition of the interface:

```
using System.Collections.ObjectModel;
using System.Net.Http;

namespace System.Web.Http.Controllers {

    public interface IActionHttpMethodProvider {

        Collection<HttpMethod> HttpMethods { get; }
    }
}
```

The interface defines the HttpMethods get-only property, which returns a collection of HttpMethod values that specify the verbs that an action method supports. Web API includes a set of attributes in the System.Web.Http namespace that implement the IActionHttpMethodProvider interface and use the HttpMethods property to return the HttpMethod values that represent most commonly used HTTP verbs, as listed in Table 22-9.

Table 22-9. The Web API Attributes That Implement the IActionHttpMethodProvider Interface

Name	Description
AcceptVerbs	Declares that the action method supports one or more HTTP verbs (see the text following the table)
HttpGet	Declares that the action method supports the GET verb
HttpPost	Declares that the action method supports the POST verb
HttpDelete	Declares that the action method supports the DELETE verb
HttpPut	Declares that the action method supports the PUT verb
HttpPatch	Declares that the action method supports the PATCH verb
HttpOptions	Declares that the action method supports the OPTIONS verb
HttpHead	Declares that the action method supports the HEAD verb

The attributes whose name starts with Http declare support for a single HTTP verb and are defined for the most commonly used verbs. Use the AcceptVerbs attribute if you want to declare support for less commonly used verbs or multiple verbs. In Listing 22-7, you can see how I have applied attributes to the Custom controller.

■ **Note** The HEAD verb is a little odd because it asks the web service to process the request as it would normally but send back only the headers. Supporting the HEAD verb in a web service controller is unusual, and I have done so only to demonstrate how verb attributes are used.

Listing 22-7. Specifying HTTP Verbs in the CustomController.cs File

```
using System;
using System.Web.Http;

namespace Dispatch.Controllers {

    public class CustomController : ApiController {

        [AcceptVerbs("GET", "HEAD")]
        public string DayOfWeek() {
            return DateTime.Now.ToString("dddd");
        }

        [HttpGet]
        [HttpHead]
        public string DayOfWeek(int day) {
            return Enum.GetValues(typeof(DayOfWeek)).GetValue(day).ToString();
        }

        [HttpGet]
        public int DayNumber() {
            return DateTime.Now.Day;
        }
    }
}
```

I have used the AcceptVerbs attribute to specify that the parameterless DayOfWeek method can handle GET and HEAD requests. When using the AcceptVerbs attribute, the verbs are specified as strings. The AcceptVerbs method is the simplest way to declare that an action method supports one of the verbs for which is there no predefined attribute.

■ **Caution**   Most web services require only a small number of verbs (usually GET, POST, PUT, and DELETE), and using other verbs—especially less well-known ones like PATCH or PURGE—is likely to cause problems, especially if you are delivering a web service for which third-party developers will write clients. I recommend careful consideration if you find yourself needing to support a verb for which there is no built-in attribute.

I have also specified that the DayOfWeek method that takes an int parameter supports the GET and HEAD verbs, but I have done so by applying two of the built-in verbs. I recommend you try to avoid creating action methods that support multiple verbs that have different meanings, but this technique can be useful if you want to treat POST and PUT the same way, which is a common web service convention (as described in Chapter 4).

■ **Tip**   If you apply verb attributes to action methods that follow the RESTful naming convention, then the name of the method will not be taken into account during the action method selection process. Or, put another way, the verbs specified by the attributes take precedence over the verb specified by the method name. I recommend relying on just the method name, since a mismatch between the method name and the supported HTTP verb causes confusion.

For the DayNumber method, I have used the HttpGet attribute to specify support for GET requests. This is the usual approach to using the verb attributes, such that one attribute is applied to each action method.

USING COMMON SENSE TO RESOLVE CLASHES IN PHILOSOPHY

Some developers have a mild obsession about the Don't Repeat Yourself (DRY) principle, which aims to reduce duplication by ensuring that every operation is written just once (see http://en.wikipedia.org/wiki/Don't_repeat_yourself). This is an excellent principle—and one I follow myself—but it can be taken too far, and I often encounter controllers that contain a single action method to which all the verb attributes have been applied. When I ask why this has been done, the answer is always "because we follow DRY."

When taken to an extreme, DRY starts to interfere with the principles of the Web API model, which encourages distinct action methods for each operation that the web service provides, unless those operations are essentially indistinguishable. That means there will always be a degree of duplication since most action methods will need to access the model repository, validate user data, and handle errors. Duplication can be reduced by defining nonaction methods that contain common code, but collapsing action methods together in the name of deduplication causes long-term maintenance problems as the web service evolves because all of the request handling code is squashed together, making changes difficult to apply and test.

DRY is a good principle to follow, but it would be better expressed as Don't Repeat Yourself Unless Doing So Prevents Long-Term Problems. If you find that your controllers look like the direct implementation of the IHttpController interface that I created at the start of the chapter, then dial back on the deduplication and use common sense to strike a balance between the principles and patterns that you follow.

Now that I have specified the HTTP verbs that the action methods in my non-RESTful controller support, the default process is able to select methods to handle requests. To see the effect of the verb attributes, start the application, use the browser to navigate to the /Home/Today URL, and click the Get Day button. Unlike the error message displayed in Figure 22-4, the client will receive a 200 (OK) response and the requested data, as shown in Figure 22-5.

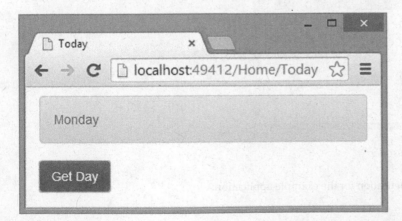

Figure 22-5. *The effect of applying HTTP verb attributes to a non-RESTful controller*

Understanding the RESTful/Non-RESTful Routing Problem

Before continuing to describe the `ApiController` dispatch process, I am going to switch topics and describe a common problem that I deliberately introduced into the example project, explain what causes it, and illustrate how it can be avoided.

Previously, I added a route to the `WebApiConfig.cs` file that specified an `action` variable so that I could target requests to the `Today` controller and, more recently, the `Custom` controller. At the time I noted that adding the route caused a problem, which I can describe now that I have explained how action methods are selected and how the RESTful naming convention works.

Understanding the Problem

To see the problem, start the application, use the browser to navigate to the `/Home/Index` URL, and click each of the Get All, Get One, and Post buttons in turn. The Get All and Post buttons will work as expected—the client will request the `/api/products` URL, and the HTTP verb will be used to select the (parameterless) `Get` method or the `Post` method. When the Get One button is clicked, the client will request the `/api/products/2` URL, and Web API will respond with a 404 (Not Found) error, as shown in Figure 22-6.

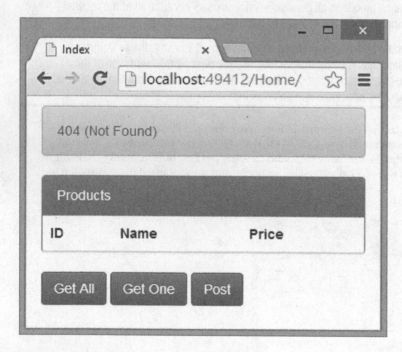

Figure 22-6. *A problem with a RESTful controller* ·

As a reminder, here is the routing configuration for the example application:

```
using System.Web.Http;

namespace Dispatch {
    public static class WebApiConfig {
        public static void Register(HttpConfiguration config) {
```

```
        config.Routes.MapHttpRoute(
            name: "ActionMethods",
            routeTemplate: "api/{controller}/{action}/{day}",
            defaults: new { day = RouteParameter.Optional }
        );

        config.Routes.MapHttpRoute(
            name: "DefaultApi",
            routeTemplate: "api/{controller}/{id}",
            defaults: new { id = RouteParameter.Optional }
        );
    }
  }
}
```

This is a common problem when mixing Web API controllers that follow the RESTful naming convention with those that don't. For RESTful controllers, the action method selection relies on the action method name starting with the HTTP verb that the action supports, using this routing template:

```
...
routeTemplate: "api/{controller}/{id}"
...
```

The non-RESTful controllers rely on the other route, which defines an action variable to match requests:

```
...
routeTemplate: "api/{controller}/{action}/{day}",
...
```

The non-RESTful route matches requests for RESTful controllers. A request for a URL such as /api/products works because the non-RESTful route template will match only three- or four-segment URLs and so the request is passed on to the RESTful route, which will match two- or three-segment URLs (the final segment for both templates is optional).

For a three-segment URL such as /api/products/2—which is what the client sends when the Get One button is clicked—the non-RESTful route matches the request and assigns 2 as the value of the action variable. The request is passed through the Web API dispatch process until it reaches the ApiControllerActionSelector class, which detects the presence of the action value in the route data (step 3 in Table 22-7) but can't match it to a method in the ProductsController class and returns the 404 (Not Found) result.

Solving the Problem with Route Specificity

There are two ways to solve this problem. The first is to create more specific routes, either by constraining convention-based routes or by using direct routes. This approach works well in applications that contain a lot of one kind of controller (RESTful or non-RESTful) and only a small number of the other kind. In Listing 22-8, you can see how I have narrowed the scope of the route for the non-RESTful controllers.

Listing 22-8. Narrowing the Non-RESTful Route in the WebApiConfig.cs File

```
using System.Web.Http;
using System.Web.Http.Routing.Constraints;

namespace Dispatch {
    public static class WebApiConfig {
        public static void Register(HttpConfiguration config) {

            config.Routes.MapHttpRoute(
                name: "ActionMethods",
                routeTemplate: "api/{controller}/{action}/{day}",
                defaults: new { day = RouteParameter.Optional },
                constraints: new { controller = new RegexRouteConstraint("today|custom")}
            );

            config.Routes.MapHttpRoute(
                name: "DefaultApi",
                routeTemplate: "api/{controller}/{id}",
                defaults: new { id = RouteParameter.Optional }
            );
        }
    }
}
```

I have added a constraint to the first route so that it will match only those requests whose second segment—the controller segment—is either today or custom. This ensures that requests for the RESTful Products controller won't be matched and will be routed correctly. To test the change, start the application, navigate to the /Home/Index URL with the browser, and click the Get One button. Rather than the error shown in Figure 22-6, you will see a Success response, and the client will display the details of a data object.

■ **Caution**   This problem cannot be solved by re-ordering the routes in the WebApiConfig.cs file, which just has the effect of changing the requests that are mismatched but doesn't address the underlying problem.

Solving the Problem with a Route Template Prefix

I do not like constraining routes in this way because it means that there is a list of controller names that has to be kept synchronized with the classes in the application—something that adds to the testing burden and that can cause problems once the application is deployed. Direct routes are a more elegant solution to the problem, but I prefer not to use them, as I explained in Chapter 20.

The approach I prefer to take is to create a separate prefix for one category of controller so that, for example, RESTful controllers are reached through URLs with the normal /api prefix and non-RESTful controllers are reached through a different prefix, such as /api/nonrest. Listing 22-9 shows the changes I made to the WebApiConfig.cs file to implement this change.

Listing 22-9. Changing the Non-RESTful Controller Route Template in the WebApiConfig.cs File

```
using System.Web.Http;

namespace Dispatch {
    public static class WebApiConfig {
        public static void Register(HttpConfiguration config) {

            config.Routes.MapHttpRoute(
                name: "ActionMethods",
                routeTemplate: "api/nrest/{controller}/{action}/{day}",
                defaults: new { day = RouteParameter.Optional }
            );

            config.Routes.MapHttpRoute(
                name: "DefaultApi",
                routeTemplate: "api/{controller}/{id}",
                defaults: new { id = RouteParameter.Optional }
            );
        }
    }
}
```

This change means that the non-RESTful route will match URLs with four or five segments and the RESTful route will match two- and three-segment URLs, ensuring that requests won't be matched by the wrong route. The drawback of this technique is that it requires the client to make requests with the right prefix, as shown in Listing 22-10.

Listing 22-10. Changing the URL Prefix in the today.js File

```
var response = ko.observable("Ready");
var gotError = ko.observable(false);

var sendRequest = function () {
    $.ajax("/api/nrest/custom/dayofweek/1", {
        type: "GET",
        success: function (data) {
            gotError(false);
            response(data);
        },
        error: function (jqXHR) {
            gotError(true);
            response(jqXHR.status + " (" + jqXHR.statusText + ")");
        }
    });
};

$(document).ready(function () {
    ko.applyBindings();
});
```

Understanding Filters

Having selected a method through the IHttpActionSelector interface, the ApiController classes executes the *filters* that have been applied to the method. As with the MVC framework, Web API filters inject additional logic into the request dispatch process and are used to implement *cross-cutting concerns*, which are functionality that is used throughout the application but doesn't fit neatly into the MVC pattern without breaking the separation-of-concerns principle.

■ **Tip** Filters support a design pattern called Aspect-Oriented Programming, which is described at http://en.wikipedia.org/wiki/Aspect-oriented_programming.

Web API filters are defined through the IFilter interface, which is defined in the System.Web.Http.Filters namespace. The IFilter interface isn't used directly but provides the base from which the interfaces that describe the five different kinds of Web API filter are defined, as described in Table 22-10.

Table 22-10. *The Web API Filter Types and Interfaces*

Filter Type	Interface	Description
Authentication	IAuthenticationFilter	This kind of filter is used to require users or clients to be authenticated before action methods can be executed.
Authorization	IAuthorizationFilter	This kind of filter is used to restrict access to action methods to specific users or groups.
Action	IActionFilter	This kind of filter is used to manipulate the request or response.
Exception	IExceptionFilter	This kind of filter is used to handle exceptions thrown by the action method or another kind of filer.
Override	IOverrideFilter	This kind of filter is used to tailor the behavior of other filters for individual action methods.

■ **Caution** The Web API filter interface names are the same as the equivalent interfaces in the MVC Framework. Be careful when creating filters because it is easy to get the namespaces mixed up and create an MVC filter rather than one for Web API.

I describe filters in detail in Chapters 23 and 24, but I wanted to introduce them in this chapter because they are part of the ApiController dispatch process. Filters are supported by the ApiController class and are not delegated to an interface like some of the other dispatch tasks, which means they are not available when you create a controller from the IHttpController interface.

Understanding the Action Method Execution Process

At this point, the ApiController—or its delegates—has selected an action method and prepared the filters that have been applied to it. The next step is to execute the action method and obtain the HttpResponseMessage object that will be passed back along the dispatch chain and used to send the response to the client.

Action method execution is delegated to an implementation of the IHttpActionInvoker interface, which is defined as follows:

```
using System.Net.Http;
using System.Threading;
using System.Threading.Tasks;

namespace System.Web.Http.Controllers {

    public interface IHttpActionInvoker {

        Task<HttpResponseMessage> InvokeActionAsync(HttpActionContext actionContext,
            CancellationToken cancellationToken);
    }
}
```

The IHttpActionInvoker interface defines the InvokeActionAsync method, which is required to asynchronously execute the action described by the HttpActionContext argument (which is the result of the selection process) and return an HttpResponseMessage that can be used to send the response to the client.

The HttpActionContext argument provides the means to execute the action method through its ActionDescriptor property, which returns an instance of the HttpActionDescriptor class. The HttpActionDescriptor, in turn, defines the ExecuteAsync method, which performs parameter and model binding, executes the selected action method, and generates the result.

The default implementation of the IHttpActionInvoker interface is the ApiControllerActionInvoker class, defined in the System.Web.Http.Controllers namespace. This class is responsible for converting the result of the action method into an HttpResponseMessage object and is the component that allows the ApiController class to support built-in C# types and the IHttpActionResult interface and its implementations, which I described in Chapter 11.

Customizing the Controller Dispatch Process

There are several ways in which the ApiController dispatch process can be customized, and I describe them in the following sections. The default behavior will suit most applications, but if you do perform customizations, then make sure you test thoroughly and that you really can't get what you need through other features, such as filters (which I describe in Chapters 23 and 24).

The ApiController class provides a set of properties that provide access to context objects that are useful for creating customizations. The ApiController context properties are described in Table 22-11.

Table 22-11. *The Context Properties Defined by the ApiController Class*

Name	Description
ActionContext	Returns an HttpActionContext object that describes the currently executing action and that provides many of the context objects that the ApiController class exposes through the properties in this table
Configuration	Returns the HttpConfiguration object that should be used to process the request
ControllerContext	Returns the HttpControllerContext for this request, as described in Chapter 19
ModelState	Returns the ModelStateDictionary object, used by the model validation process that I describe in Chapter 18
Request	Returns the HttpRequestMessage object that describes the current request
RequestContext	Returns the HttpRequestContext object for the request
User	Returns an implementation of the IPrincipal interface that identifies the user associated with the current request, as described in Chapters 23 and 24

You can use these properties in your action methods as well, but this isn't usually required since action methods in a web service controller are generally focused on getting data to or from the repository. Action methods don't usually interact directly with the HttpRequestMessage and HttpResponseMessage objects and instead rely on parameter/model binding and result conversion to get data from the request and create a result. Table 22-12 puts customizing the ApiController dispatch process into context.

Table 22-12. *Putting Customizing the ApiController Dispatch Process in Context*

Question	Answer
What is it?	The ApiController class relies on the IHttpActionSelector and IHttpActionInvoker interfaces to select and execute action methods. Custom implementations of these interfaces allow you to change the dispatch process.
When should you use it?	The built-in implementations are suitable for almost all web services, and custom implementations should be created with caution and tested thoroughly.
What do you need to know?	You can selectively apply custom implementations by creating a controller-specific configuration, as described in the "Creating a Controller-Specific Configuration" section.

Creating a Custom IHttpActionInvoker Implementation

The IHttpActionInvoker interface has two responsibilities: it executes the action method, and it converts the result it produces into an HttpResponseMessage object. There is no real value in changing the way that methods are invoked, but creating a custom implementation of the IHttpActionInvoker interface can be a useful way of providing special handling for return types. Listing 22-11 shows the contents of the CustomActionInvoker.cs class file that I added to the Infrastructure folder.

Listing 22-11. The Contents of the CustomActionInvoker.cs File

```
using System.Net.Http;
using System.Threading;
using System.Threading.Tasks;
using System.Web.Http;
using System.Web.Http.Controllers;

namespace Dispatch.Infrastructure {
    public class CustomActionInvoker : IHttpActionInvoker {

        public async Task<HttpResponseMessage> InvokeActionAsync(HttpActionContext
                actionContext, CancellationToken cancellationToken) {

            object result = await actionContext.ActionDescriptor.ExecuteAsync(
                actionContext.ControllerContext, actionContext.ActionArguments,
                cancellationToken);

            if (result is HttpResponseMessage) {
                return (HttpResponseMessage)result;
            } else if (result is IHttpActionResult) {
                return await ((IHttpActionResult)result).ExecuteAsync(cancellationToken);
            } else if ( actionContext.ActionDescriptor.ReturnType != typeof(string)) {
                return actionContext.ActionDescriptor.ResultConverter.Convert(
                    actionContext.ControllerContext, result);
            } else {
                return new ValueResultConverter<string[]>().Convert(
                    actionContext.ControllerContext, new string[] { (string)result });
            }
        }
    }
}
```

This implementation of the IHttpActionInvoker executes the action method and checks the result that the method produces. It handles four types of result type.

- If the action method result is an HttpResponseMessage object, then the CustomActionInvoker class returns the object without modification as the result of the InvokeActionAsync method.

- If the action method result is an implementation of the IHttpActionResult interface, then the CustomActionInvoker class calls the ExecuteAsync method to create an HttpResponseMessage object, which is returned as the result of the InvokeActionAsync method. (I described the IHttpActionResult interface and its ExecuteAsync method in Chapter 19.)

- If the result is a string, then the CustomActionInvoker class creates a string array with the result as the only element and uses a result converter to create the HttpResponseMessage that I need as the result of the InvokeActionAsync method.

- For all other result types, the CustomActionInvoker class uses the result converter provided by the HttpActionContext.ControllerContext property to create the HttpResponseMessage object.

At the heart of my custom implementation is the use of *result converters*, which take a result type and create an HttpResponseMessage that can be returned through the dispatch process. Result converters are defined by the IActionResultConverter interface.

```
namespace System.Web.Http.Controllers {
    public interface IActionResultConverter {
        HttpResponseMessage Convert(HttpControllerContext controllerContext,
            object actionResult);
    }
}
```

The Convert method accepts an HttpControllerContext object and the result from the action method and is required to return an HttpResponseMessage. There are two built-in Web API implementations of the IActionResultConverter interface, the ValueResultConverter and VoidResultConverter classes, both of which are defined in the System.Web.Http.Controllers namespace.

The built-in implementations are simple. The ValueResultConverter class calls the HttpRequestMessage.CreateResponse extension method I described in Chapter 11 to produce an HttpResponseMessage object with a 200 (OK) status code and, in doing so, encodes the result data using the media type formatters I described in Part 2.

The VoidResultConverter class also calls the CreateResponse extension method, but with a 204 (No Content) status code. As you might imagine from the name, the VoidResultConverter is used when action methods are defined with the C# void keyword.

The ValueResultConverter class is strongly typed, and that means I have to create an instance of ValueResultConverter<string[]> in my custom IHttpActionInvoker because the object returned by the HttpActionContext.ActionDescriptor.ResultConverter property has been set up to handle the declared result type of the action method.

```
...
return new ValueResultConverter<string[]>().Convert(
    actionContext.ControllerContext, new string[] { (string)result });
...
```

I have to create an instance only when I want an HttpResponseMessage that contains data of a type that is different from the one returned by the action method.

■ **Note** I am not going to register or test the CustomActionInvoker class until the "Creating a Controller-Specific Configuration" section, where I show you how to apply it to a single controller class.

Creating a Custom IHttpActionSelector Implementation

A custom implementation of the IHttpActionSelector interface allows you to take control of the way that requests are matched to an action method. Listing 22-12 shows the contents of the CustomActionSelector.cs file that I added to the Infrastructure folder.

Listing 22-12. The Contents of the CustomActionSelector.cs File

```
using System;
using System.Linq;
using System.Net;
using System.Reflection;
using System.Web.Http;
using System.Web.Http.Controllers;
```

```
namespace Dispatch.Infrastructure {
    public class CustomActionSelector : IHttpActionSelector {

        public ILookup<string, HttpActionDescriptor>
            GetActionMapping(HttpControllerDescriptor descriptor) {
            return descriptor.ControllerType.GetMethods()
                .Where(x => x.IsPublic
                    && !x.IsSpecialName
                    && x.GetCustomAttribute<NonActionAttribute>() == null)
                .Select(x => (HttpActionDescriptor)
                    new ReflectedHttpActionDescriptor(descriptor, x))
                .OrderBy(x => x.GetParameters().Count)
                .ToLookup(x => x.ActionName, StringComparer.OrdinalIgnoreCase);
        }

        public HttpActionDescriptor SelectAction(HttpControllerContext context) {
            if (context.RouteData.Values.ContainsKey("action")) {
                string actionName = (string)context.RouteData.Values["action"];
                return GetActionMapping(context.ControllerDescriptor)
                    [actionName].First();
            } else {
                throw new HttpResponseException(HttpStatusCode.NotFound);
            }
        }
    }
}
```

There are few compelling requirements for a custom implementation of the IHttpActionSelector interface, which is why the CustomActionSelector class does something that would not be useful in a real project: it selects action methods by name, and if there are multiple methods with the same name, then the one with the fewest parameters is used.

The IHttpActionSelector interface provides information about action methods through the abstract HttpActionDescriptor class. You can create a concrete implementation of HttpActionDescriptor, but it is simpler to use the ReflectedHttpActionDescriptor class, which performs all the reflection required to create and populate the HttpActionDescriptor properties.

I use the GetActionMapping method to create an enumeration of the action methods available in the specified controller and filter that enumeration in the SelectAction method based on the value of the action routing variable.

■ **Note** I don't implement the RESTful naming convention in my custom IHttpActionSelector implementation, which means that only requests that can be matched by a route template that has an action variable segment are supported.

Creating a Controller-Specific Configuration

The custom implementations of the IHttpActionInvoker and IHttpActionSelector interfaces that I created in the previous section are not especially useful. In fact, they work well only with the Custom controller, which has action methods that return string values (which is what I look for in the CustomActionInvoker class) and methods with the same name but different numbers of parameters (which is what the CustomActionSelector handles).

If I replaced the default implementations in the services collection with my custom classes in the WebApiConfig.cs file, they would be applied to all controllers. In the case of the CustomActionInvoker class, this means that requests to controllers relying on the RESTful naming convention would not be routed correctly.

I can resolve this problem by creating a configuration that uses my custom classes and applying it selectively to the controllers whose action method selection and execution I want to change. This is done by creating an attribute class that implements the IControllerConfiguration interface, defined as follows:

```
namespace System.Web.Http.Controllers {

    public interface IControllerConfiguration {

        void Initialize(HttpControllerSettings controllerSettings,
            HttpControllerDescriptor controllerDescriptor);
    }
}
```

The interface defines the Initialize method, which is used to populate an HttpControllerSettings object passed as a method parameter. The other parameter is an HttpControllerDescriptor object, which provides context information about the controller that is being processed (and which I described in Chapter 19). The HttpControllerSettings class is used to override configuration settings using the properties defined in Table 22-13.

Table 22-13. *The Properties Defined by the HttpControllerSettings Class*

Name	Description
Formatters	Returns the collection of media type formatters (see Part 2)
ParameterBindingRules	Returns the collection of parameter binding rules (see Part 2)
Services	Returns the collection of services (see Part 2)

Creating a Custom IControllerConfiguration Interface

There is no default implementation of the IControllerConfiguration, but it is easy to create one. Listing 22-13 shows the contents of the CustomControllerConfigAttribute.cs class file that I added to the Infrastructure folder.

Listing 22-13. The Contents of the CustomControllerConfigAttribute.cs File

```
using System;
using System.Web.Http.Controllers;

namespace Dispatch.Infrastructure {

    public class CustomControllerConfigAttribute : Attribute, IControllerConfiguration {

        public void Initialize(HttpControllerSettings controllerSettings,
                HttpControllerDescriptor controllerDescriptor) {

            controllerSettings.Services.Replace(typeof(IHttpActionSelector),
                new CustomActionSelector());
            controllerSettings.Services.Replace(typeof(IHttpActionInvoker),
                new CustomActionInvoker());
        }
    }
}
```

Custom implementations of the IControllerConfiguration interface are derived from the Attribute class so they can be applied to controller classes. My implementation of the Initialize method uses the HttpControllerDescriptor method to replace the default implementations of the IHttpActionSelector and IHttpActionInvoker interfaces with instances of my custom classes.

Listing 22-14 shows how I have applied the CustomControllerConfigAttribute attribute to the Custom controller.

Listing 22-14. Applying the CustomControllerConfigAttribute in the CustomController.cs File

```
using System;
using System.Web.Http;
using Dispatch.Infrastructure;

namespace Dispatch.Controllers {

    [CustomControllerConfig]
    public class CustomController : ApiController {

        [AcceptVerbs("GET", "HEAD")]
        public string DayOfWeek() {
            return DateTime.Now.ToString("dddd");
        }

        [HttpGet]
        [HttpHead]
        public string DayOfWeek(int day) {
            return Enum.GetValues(typeof(DayOfWeek)).GetValue(day).ToString();
        }

        [HttpGet]
        public int DayNumber() {
            return DateTime.Now.Day;
        }
    }
}
```

The effect of applying the CustomControllerConfig attribute is that the custom selector and invoker classes are used to handle requests that target the Custom controller, while other requests for other controllers will be handled by the default implementations.

■ **Tip** This is not specific to the ApiController class. Custom configurations can be applied to any IHttpController implementation.

Summary

In this chapter, I described how Web API controllers work and, in particular, the dispatch process that the default controller base class provides. I explained how action methods are selected and invoked, touched upon request filters, and demonstrated how the default dispatch process can be customized. In Chapter 23, I begin describing *filters*, which allow extra logic to be injected into the dispatch process.

■■■

CHAPTER 23

Filters Part I

I touched on filters in Chapter 20 so that I could describe the dispatch process that the ApiController class implements. In this chapter, I describe how filters work in depth and demonstrate how they can be used to add cross-cutting concerns to a Web API application. Table 23-1 summarizes this chapter.

Table 23-1. *Chapter Summary*

Problem	Solution	Listing
Add logic to the dispatch pipeline.	Define an action filter by defining an attribute that implements the IActionFilter interface. Apply the attribute to the action method or controller where the logic is required.	1–2
Create an action method without having to manage continuation functions.	Derive the class from the ActionFilterAttribute class.	3
Terminate the request handling process in a filter.	Create a short-circuiting filter that generates an HttpResponseMessage object rather than invoking the continuation function. If using the attribute base classes, then set the HttpActionContext.Response property.	4–6
List the filters that have been applied to an action method.	Enumerate the filter pipeline.	7, 8, 14
Apply a filter to all of the action methods in an application.	Define a global filter.	9, 10
Associate a user identity with a request.	Create an authentication filter.	11–13

Preparing the Example Project

I am going to continue using the Dispatch project I created in Chapter 19. No changes are required for this chapter.

Understanding Filters

Filters inject extra logic into the ApiController dispatch process and provide a simple and elegant mechanism to implement features that operate across multiple components in the MVC pattern, known as *cross-cutting concerns*. The most common uses for filters are applying authentication and authorization, handling errors, and measuring performance.

Filters are attributes that implement the IFilter interface, which is defined in the System.Web.Http.Filters namespace. Here is the definition of the interface:

```
namespace System.Web.Http.Filters {
    public interface IFilter {
        bool AllowMultiple { get; }
    }
}
```

The only member defined by the interface is the AllowMultiple property, which specifies whether more than one instance of a specific filter can be used. It is unusual to work directly with the IFilter interface because there is a set of interfaces, all of which are derived from IFilter, that define different kinds of filter. Table 23-2 lists these interfaces and describes how they are used.

Table 23-2. *The Web API Filter Types and Interfaces*

Filter Type	Interface	Description
Authentication	IAuthenticationFilter	This kind of filter is used to require users or clients to be authenticated before action methods can be executed.
Authorization	IAuthorizationFilter	This kind of filter is used to restrict access to action methods to specific users or groups. See Chapter 24 for details.
Action	IActionFilter	This kind of filter is used to manipulate the request or response.
Exception	IExceptionFilter	This kind of filter is used to handle exceptions thrown by the action method or another kind of filer. See Chapter 24 for details.
Override	IOverrideFilter	This kind of filter is used to tailor the behavior of other filters for individual action methods. See Chapter 24 for details.

■ **Note** Filters should *not* be used to perform tasks that belong in an action method, which essentially means not creating filters that process a request in order to interact with the repository and generate results. Using filters to replace or supplement action methods makes it harder to isolate specific functions for unit testing.

There are corresponding abstract attribute classes that implement each of the interfaces listed in the table, and they are the simplest way to get started with filters, although I will show you how to work directly from the filter interfaces as well. I describe action and authentication filters in this chapter and the other types in Chapter 24. Table 23-3 puts filters in context.

Table 23-3. *Putting Filters in Context*

Question	Answer
What are they?	Filters allow extra logic to be inserted into the dispatch process before and after the execution of the action method. Filters can also short-circuit the dispatch process to prevent action methods—and other filters—from being executed. See the "Creating a Short-Circuiting Action Filter" section for details.
When should you use them?	Filters should be used only to contain logic that doesn't belong in the controller or data model as described by the MVC pattern in Chapter 4.
What do you need to know?	Filters can be applied as attributes to action methods and controllers or applied globally through the WebApiConfig.cs file.

Working with Action Filters

Action filters allow extra logic to be executed before and after an action method has been executed. This means you have the opportunity to change the HttpRequestMessage and HttpResponseMessage objects or perform tasks that span the action method execution, such as timing the dispatch process, which is the standard example for action filters (although I'll show you some other uses later in the chapter). Action filters are defined by the IActionFilter interface, which is defined as follows:

```
using System.Diagnostics.CodeAnalysis;
using System.Net.Http;
using System.Threading;
using System.Threading.Tasks;
using System.Web.Http.Controllers;

namespace System.Web.Http.Filters {

    public interface IActionFilter : IFilter {

        Task<HttpResponseMessage> ExecuteActionFilterAsync(
            HttpActionContext actionContext,
            CancellationToken cancellationToken,
            Func<Task<HttpResponseMessage>> continuation);
    }
}
```

In the sections that follow, I'll show you how action filters work and the different ways to create action filters. In Figure 23-1, I have updated the dispatch process diagram to show the relationship between an action filter and the action method. (I have shown only part of the diagram in the figure, but I'll show the complete view of the process later in the chapter.)

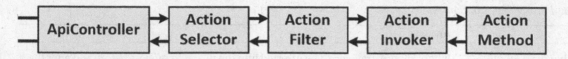

Figure 23-1. *Action filters and action methods in the ApiController dispatch process*

The important point to note about the diagram is that the action filter is invoked before the action method is invoked and afterward, when HttpResponseMessage has been created and is making its way back along the chain of components. Table 23-4 puts action filters into context.

Table 23-4. *Putting Action Filters in Context*

Question	Answer
What are they?	Action filters provide a mechanism to modify the HttpRequestMessage and HttpResponseMessage objects before and after the action method is executed.
When should you use them?	Action filters should be used with caution and only to perform tasks that do not contain business logic, operate on the data model, or perform authentication or authorization (which are handled by other filter types).
What do you need to know?	In Web API, action filters combine the functionality of action and result filters in the MVC framework.

Creating an Action Filter by Implementing IActionFilter

As I explained in the previous section, the IActionFilter interface defines one method: ExecuteActionFilterAsync. This method looks more complex than it really is because the goal of the interface is to let you define work to be performed before *and* after the action method is invoked. The best way to explain how this works is with an example, and Listing 23-1 shows the contents of the TimeAttribute.cs file, which I added to the Infrastructure folder.

Listing 23-1. The Contents of the TimeAttribute.cs File

```
using System;
using System.Diagnostics;
using System.Net.Http;
using System.Threading;
using System.Threading.Tasks;
using System.Web.Http.Controllers;
using System.Web.Http.Filters;

namespace Dispatch.Infrastructure {
    public class TimeAttribute : Attribute, IActionFilter {

        public async Task<HttpResponseMessage> ExecuteActionFilterAsync(
                HttpActionContext actionContext,
                CancellationToken cancellationToken,
                Func<Task<HttpResponseMessage>> continuation) {

            Stopwatch sw = Stopwatch.StartNew();

            HttpResponseMessage result = await continuation();
```

```
        long elapsedTicks = sw.ElapsedTicks;
        result.Headers.Add("Elapsed-Time", elapsedTicks.ToString());
        System.Diagnostics.Debug.WriteLine("Elapsed time: {0} ticks, {1} {2}",
            elapsedTicks, actionContext.Request.Method,
            actionContext.Request.RequestUri);
        return result;
    }

    public bool AllowMultiple {
        get { return false; }
    }
  }
}
```

The `TimeAttribute` class is an action filter: it is derived from the `Attribute` class, and it implements the `IActionFilter` interface. This filter uses the `StopWatch` class to measure the amount of time taken to execute the action method. (This is a simplification of what is really being measured, as I explain in the "Understanding Filter Scope" section.)

■ **Tip** The `StopWatch` class is a high-resolution timer that is useful for measuring small amounts of time, such as the invocation of a single method. The `elapsedTicks` property I read in Listing 23-1 returns the number of *ticks* since the timer was started, where a tick is the smallest duration that the `StopWatch` class can measure on the current system. The length of a tick will differ between systems, and the `Frequency` field tells you how many ticks there are per second on the current hardware. I am happy working with ticks in this chapter because my focus is on how filters work, but for more details of high-resolution timings, see

`http://msdn.microsoft.com/en-us/library/system.diagnostics.stopwatch.aspx`.

To perform my measurement, I need to take advantage of the opportunity to perform work before and after the action method is executed. Before the execution, I need to start a timer. After the execution, I need to read the value of the timer and report on the elapsed time, which I do by adding a header to the `HttpResponseMessage` object and by writing a message to the Visual Studio Ouput window.

The first thing you do when the `ExecuteActionFilterAsync` method is executed is to perform the work you want to do *before* the action. The filter in Listing 23-1 uses the `StopWatch` class to measure time, so the only work that I have to do is create and start a new instance of the timer, which I do in a single step like this:

```
...
Stopwatch sw = Stopwatch.StartNew();
...
```

Following the statements to be performed before the action method is invoked, you `await` the `Task` that the `Func<Task<System.Net.Http.HttpResponseMessage>>` parameter produces. This is a gnarly type: it is a function that, when invoked, returns a `Task` that yields an `HttpResponse` message. Or, to put another way, invoking the continuation parameter executes the action method, which the action filter invokes to get an `HttpResponse` message, like this:

```
...
HttpResponseMessage result = await continuation();
...
```

When the continuation Task has completed, the action filter can manipulate the response. For this action filter, that means adding a header to the HttpResponse message, as well as writing out a message to the Visual Studio Output window.

```
...
long elapsedMs = sw.ElapsedMilliseconds;
result.Headers.Add("Elapsed-Time", elapsedMs.ToString());
System.Diagnostics.Debug.WriteLine("Elapsed time: {0} ms, {1} {2}",
    elapsedMs, actionContext.Request.Method, actionContext.Request.RequestUri);
return result;
...
```

■ **Tip** The result returned by the ExecuteFilterAsync method is a Task that will yield an HttpResponseMessage object when it completes. I used the async and await keywords in my method implementation, which means I am able to return an HttpResponseMessage object and rely on the .NET runtime to convert it into a Task<HttpResponseMessage>.

If you need more information about the request, such as details of the controller, the action method, or its parameters, then you can obtain it through the HtpActionContext object that is passed as a parameter to the IActonFilter.ExecuteFilterAsync method. The HttpActionContext class defines the properties shown in Table 23-5. In the action filter, I use the Request property to get the HttpRequestMessage object so that I can get the HTTP verb and URL from the request.

Table 23-5. *The Properties Defined by the HttpActionContext ClassHttpActionContext Class*

Name	Description
ActionArguments	Returns a Dictionary<string, object> that maps the names of the action method arguments to their types.
ActionDescriptor	Returns an HttpActionDescriptor object that describes the action method that is going to be invoked.
ControllerContext	Returns an HttpControllerContext object that describes the controller in which the action method is defined.
ModelState	Returns a ModelStateDictionary object used in the model validation process, which I describe in Chapter 18.
Request	Returns the HttpRequestMessage object that describes the current request.
RequestContext	Returns the HttpRequestContext object that provides supplementary information about the request.
Response	Returns the HttpResponseMessage object that will be used to product the response to the client. This is only set during a *short-circuit* of the dispatch process, as described in the "Creating a Short-Circuiting Action Filter" section.

Applying an Action Filter

Action filters are applied as attributes, either to individual action methods or to a controller class. Applying a filter to a controller is equivalent to applying it to each and every action method in the controller, and you can see how I have applied the Time attribute from the previous section to the Products controller in Listing 23-2. (You can also apply filters globally, in which case they are applied to all action methods in all controllers—see the "Understanding Filter Scope" section for details.)

■ **Tip** I have applied the filter to a RESTful controller, but they work on any Web API controller that is derived from the ApiController class. Filters are not available when you create your own controllers directly from the IHttpController interface.

Listing 23-2. Applying a Filter to the ProductsController.cs File

```
using System.Collections.Generic;
using System.Linq;
using System.Web.Http;
using Dispatch.Models;
using Dispatch.Infrastructure;

namespace Dispatch.Controllers {

    [Time]
    public class ProductsController : ApiController {
        private static List<Product> products = new List<Product> {
                new Product {ProductID = 1, Name = "Kayak", Price = 275M },
                new Product {ProductID = 2, Name = "Lifejacket", Price = 48.95M },
                new Product {ProductID = 3, Name = "Soccer Ball", Price = 19.50M },
                new Product {ProductID = 4, Name = "Thinking Cap", Price = 16M },
        };

        public IEnumerable<Product> Get() {
            return products;
        }

        public Product Get(int id) {
            return products.Where(x => x.ProductID == id).FirstOrDefault();
        }

        public Product Post(Product product) {
            product.ProductID = products.Count + 1;
            products.Add(product);
            return product;
        }
    }
}
```

You can test the action filter by starting the application, navigating to the /Home/Index URL, and clicking each of the Get All, Get One, and Post buttons in turn. In addition to a header in the response, the action filter will write messages to the Visual Studio Output window, like this:

```
Elapsed time: 147 ticks, GET http://localhost:49412/api/products/
Elapsed time: 132 ticks, GET http://localhost:49412/api/products/2
Elapsed time: 89 ticks, POST http://localhost:49412/api/products/
```

You will see different durations displayed, based on how many ticks your hardware can measure each second and how fast requests can be processed.

Using the Convenience Action Filter Base Class

Not every developer is comfortable having the before and after statements defined in the same method. An alternative approach—and the most common way to create action filters—is to derive from the ActionFilterAttribute class, which implements the ExecuteActionFilterAsync to call separate before and after methods that allow you to separate your code statements. The ActionFilterAttribute class defines the methods described in Table 23-6.

Table 23-6. *The Methods Defined by the ActionFilterAttribute Class*

Name	Description
OnActionExecutingAsync	Invoked before the action method is executed
OnActionExecutedAsync	Invoked after the action method is executed

■ **Note** There are two additional methods, OnActionExecuting and OnActionExecuted, that are invoked by the base implementation of the methods shown in the table. These methods allow you to write filter code without having to worry about using Task objects and the async and await keywords. There is no advantage in using these pseudo-synchronous methods, and I strongly recommend you avoid their use.

In Listing 23-3, you can see how I have updated the TimeAttribute class so that it is derived from the ActionFilterAttribute class. (This is similar to the filter I created in Chapter 22.)

Listing 23-3. Deriving from the ActionFilterAttribute Class in the TimeAttrribute.cs File

```
using System.Diagnostics;
using System.Threading;
using System.Threading.Tasks;
using System.Web.Http.Controllers;
using System.Web.Http.Filters;

namespace Dispatch.Infrastructure {
    public class TimeAttribute : ActionFilterAttribute {
        private static readonly string propKey =
            "Dispatch.Infrastructure.TimeAttribute.StopWatch";

        public override Task OnActionExecutingAsync(HttpActionContext actionContext,
                CancellationToken cancellationToken) {
```

```
        return Task.Factory.StartNew(() => {
            actionContext.Request.Properties.Add(propKey, Stopwatch.StartNew());
        });
    }

    public override Task OnActionExecutedAsync(HttpActionExecutedContext
            actionExecutedContext, CancellationToken cancellationToken) {

        return Task.Factory.StartNew(() => {
            if (actionExecutedContext.Request.Properties.ContainsKey(propKey)) {
                Stopwatch sw =
                    ((Stopwatch)actionExecutedContext.Request.Properties[propKey]);
                long elapsedTicks = sw.ElapsedTicks;
                actionExecutedContext.Response.Headers.Add("Elapsed-Time",
                    elapsedTicks.ToString());
                System.Diagnostics.Debug.WriteLine(
                    "Elapsed time: {0} ticks, {1} {2}", elapsedTicks,
                        actionExecutedContext.Request.Method,
                        actionExecutedContext.Request.RequestUri);
            }
        });
    }
}
```

Deriving a filter from the `ActionFilterAttribute` class allows you to separate out the before and after code into separate methods, but it adds its own complexities.

■ **Tip** Working directly with the `IActionFilter` interface produces code that I think is simpler and more elegant, but in projects that other developers will maintain, I use the `ActionFilterAttribute` class because the use of before and after methods is a lot more approachable than the use of the async and await keywords, which are still not widely embraced or understood in corporate development teams.

To improve performance, instances of filters classes are used to handle multiple requests and may be used to handle requests concurrently. That means you must avoid using instance variables as state data if you need to pass context information from the `OnActionExecutingAsync` method to the `OnActionExecutedAsync` method. In my example action filter, the context that I need is the `StopWatch` object, which is started in `OnActionExecutingAsync` and read in `OnActionExecutedAsync`.

You can use the `HttpRequestMessage.Properties` property to access a collection that is used to store request-specific state data. The `HttpRequestMessage` object persists throughout the dispatch process, which means you can use it store objects before the action method is executed, like this:

```
...
actionContext.Request.Properties.Add(propKey, Stopwatch.StartNew());
...
```

and then retrieve them after the action method has been executed, like this:

```
...
Stopwatch sw = ((Stopwatch)actionExecutedContext.Request.Properties[propKey]);
...
```

The state data is available to any other Web API component that handles the request. This means you need to ensure that the key that you use to store the state data is unlikely to be duplicated elsewhere. I base my state data key names on the class that stores them, like this:

```
...
private static readonly string propKey =
    "Dispatch.Infrastructure.TimeAttribute.StopWatch";
...
```

STATE DATA PROBLEMS

The `HttpRequestMessage.Properties` collection is useful because the Web API programming model doesn't provide the state data features that are available in the legacy ASP.NET platform.

The `HttpRequestMessage` object isn't the only class that defines a `Properties` collection. Similar collections are available throughout the Web API class hierarchy, including the `HttpActionDescriptor`, `HttpControllerDescriptor`, and `HttpConfiguration` classes.

Using these property collections is fine when the state data is stored and retrieved by the same object, as is the case with the action filter in Listing 23-3. The other use for these collections is to pass data from one component to another—something I recommend you avoid.

The problem is that state data contained in properties collections creates a tight coupling between the component that stores the data and the component that retrieves it. In this situation, you have to use both components in your application—and that makes it difficult to create custom implementations of individual interfaces without figuring out the private meaning of the state data and re-creating or replacing it.

I recommend you avoid using this kind of state data unless it is contained within a single class. In fact, I think that using the property collections to coordinate components is such a dangerous technique that I have omitted the `Properties` property from all of the classes I describe in this book.

The `ActionFilterAttribute` class provides the `OnActionExecutedAsync` method with context information through the `HttpActionExecutedContext` class. In addition to the context available through the `HttpActionContext` class, the `HttpActionExecutedContext` class provides details of any exception that was thrown by the continuation class. I explain how to handle exceptions using filters in Chapter 24 and more broadly in Chapter 25. Table 23-7 shows the properties defined by the `HttpActionExecutedContext` class.

Table 23-7. *The Properties Defined by the HttpActionExecutedContext Class*

Name	Description
ActionContext	This returns the HttpActionContext that ApiController passes to the ExecuteActionFilterAsync method.
Exception	This property is set to any exception that occurs in executing the continuation task.
Request	This returns the HttpRequestMessage object associated with the response.
Response	This returns the HttpResponseMessage object that has been generated by the continuation task.

In the TimeAttribute class, I use the HttpActionExecutedContext.Request property to get the HttpRequestMessage and HttpResponseMessage objects. The HttpRequestMessage object gives me access to the StopWatch object I stored as state data and the request URL and verb that I include in the message written to the Visual Studio Output window. The HttpResponseMessage object allows me to add a header to the response.

```
...
actionExecutedContext.Response.Headers.Add("Elapsed-Time", elapsedTicks.ToString());
System.Diagnostics.Debug.WriteLine("Elapsed time: {0} ticks, {1} {2}",
    elapsedTicks, actionExecutedContext.Request.Method,
        actionExecutedContext.Request.RequestUri);
...
```

Creating a Short-Circuiting Action Filter

Action filters don't have to be passive observers of the dispatch process; they can also be active participants—although you must be careful not to use an action filter to perform work that should be defined in the action method. As a demonstration, I added the CounterAttribute.cs file to the Infrastructure folder and used it to define the action filer shown in Listing 23-4.

Listing 23-4. The Contents of the CounterAttribute.cs File

```
using System;
using System.Diagnostics;
using System.Net;
using System.Net.Http;
using System.Threading;
using System.Threading.Tasks;
using System.Web.Http.Controllers;
using System.Web.Http.Filters;

namespace Dispatch.Infrastructure {

    public class CounterAttribute : Attribute, IActionFilter {
        private static int counter = 0;
        private static int limit;

        public CounterAttribute(int requestLimit) {
            limit = requestLimit;
        }
```

```
public Task<HttpResponseMessage> ExecuteActionFilterAsync(
        HttpActionContext actionContext,
        CancellationToken cancellationToken,
        Func<Task<HttpResponseMessage>> continuation) {

    if (counter < limit) {
        Debug.WriteLine("Request {0} of {1}", counter, limit);
        counter++;
        return continuation();
    } else {
        HttpResponseMessage response = actionContext.Request.
            CreateErrorResponse(HttpStatusCode.ServiceUnavailable,
                "Limit Reached");
        return Task.FromResult<HttpResponseMessage>(response);
    }
}

public bool AllowMultiple {
    get { return false; }
}
    }
}
```

I have implemented this filter directly from the IActionFilter interface and defined a counter that specifies the maximum number of requests that are allowed, after which error messages are returned to the client. This isn't something you would do in a real project, but it lets me demonstrate some important action filter techniques. (I demonstrate how to create the same effect when deriving from the ActionFilterAttribute class in the "Deriving the Filter from the ActionFilterAttribute Class" section.)

■ **Caution** It can be tempting to patch up troublesome action methods by applying action filters. This is fine as a quick fix, but I recommend doing so sparingly and ensuring that you make the time to go back into the code and integrate the logic where it belongs: the action method or the model. Relying on action filters to perform work that belongs in the action method makes it harder to perform unit testing because you can no longer test just the action method—you must test the combined functionality of the filter and the action method together. It also makes the code harder for other developers to manage because understanding how a request is handled requires figuring out how the action method and the action filter interact.

In the ExecuteActionFilterAsync method, I check to see whether the current request exceeds the specified limit. If the limit has not been reached, then I invoke the continuation function to create the Task<HttpResponseMessage>, which I return as the method result. This is the normal request dispatch process, and it leads to the action method being invoked.

If the request has exceeded the limit, then I create an HttpResponseMessage object with the 503 (Service Unavailable) status code and return it as the result of the ExecuteActionFilterAsync method, without having invoked the continuation function. This is the *short-circuit*—the action generates the response for the request and, in doing so, prevents the action method from being invoked, as illustrated by Figure 23-2.

Figure 23-2. *Short-circuiting the dispatch process with an action filter*

When the request limit has been reached, the action filter starts to short-circuit the dispatch process and generates the HttpResponseMessage directly.

Testing the Short-Circuiting Filter

To test the filter, I need to apply it to the controller class, as shown in Listing 23-5.

Listing 23-5. Applying a Filter to the ProductsController.cs File

```
using System.Collections.Generic;
using System.Linq;
using System.Web.Http;
using Dispatch.Models;
using Dispatch.Infrastructure;

namespace Dispatch.Controllers {

    [Time]
    public class ProductsController : ApiController {
        private static List<Product> products = new List<Product> {
                new Product {ProductID = 1, Name = "Kayak", Price = 275M },
                new Product {ProductID = 2, Name = "Lifejacket", Price = 48.95M },
                new Product {ProductID = 3, Name = "Soccer Ball", Price = 19.50M },
                new Product {ProductID = 4, Name = "Thinking Cap", Price = 16M },
        };

        [Counter(3)]
        public IEnumerable<Product> Get() {
            return products;
        }

        public Product Get(int id) {
            return products.Where(x => x.ProductID == id).FirstOrDefault();
        }

        public Product Post(Product product) {
            product.ProductID = products.Count + 1;
            products.Add(product);
            return product;
        }
    }
}
```

I have applied the filter directly to the parameterless Get action method, rather than to the entire controller. To perform the test, start the application and use the browser to navigate to the /Home/Index URL. Click the Get All button four times, and you will see messages similar to these in the Visual Studio Output window:

```
Request 0 of 3
Elapsed time: 86870 ticks, GET http://localhost:49412/api/products/
Request 1 of 3
Elapsed time: 3196 ticks, GET http://localhost:49412/api/products/
Request 2 of 3
Elapsed time: 2220 ticks, GET http://localhost:49412/api/products/
Elapsed time: 7077 ticks, GET http://localhost:49412/api/products/
```

For the fourth and subsequent requests, the client will display the 503 (Service Unavailable) message, as illustrated by Figure 23-3.

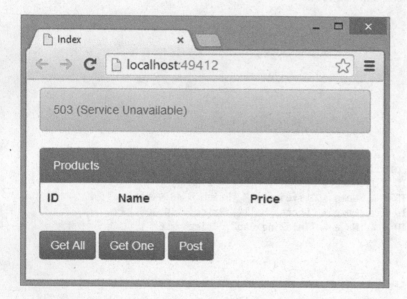

Figure 23-3. *The effect of a short-circuiting action filter*

Deriving the Filter from the ActionFilterAttribute Class

The technique for creating a short-circuiting filter that is derived from the ActionFilterAttribute class is slightly different because you are not responsible for executing the continuation function. Listing 23-6 shows how I revised the CounterAttribute class so that it is derived from ActionFilterAttribute.

Listing 23-6. Deriving from the ActionFilterAttribute Class in the CounterAttribute.cs File

```
using System;
using System.Diagnostics;
using System.Net;
using System.Net.Http;
using System.Threading;
```

```
using System.Threading.Tasks;
using System.Web.Http.Controllers;
using System.Web.Http.Filters;

namespace Dispatch.Infrastructure {

    public class CounterAttribute : ActionFilterAttribute {
        private static int counter = 0;
        private static int limit;

        public CounterAttribute(int requestLimit) {
            limit = requestLimit;
        }

        public override Task OnActionExecutingAsync(HttpActionContext actionContext,
                CancellationToken cancellationToken) {

            return Task.Factory.StartNew(() => {
                if (counter < limit) {
                    Debug.WriteLine("Request {0} of {1}", counter, limit);
                    counter++;
                } else {
                    actionContext.Response = actionContext.Request.CreateErrorResponse(
                        HttpStatusCode.ServiceUnavailable, "Limit Reached");
                }
            });
        }
    }
}
```

I only need to override the OnActionExecutingAsync method because I need to intercept requests before they get to the action method. To stop the action method from being executed, I create an HttpResponseMessage object and use it to set the HttpActionContext.Response method, like this:

```
...
actionContext.Response = actionContext.Request.CreateErrorResponse(
    HttpStatusCode.ServiceUnavailable, "Limit Reached");
...
```

The ActionFilterAttribute class implementation checks to see whether the HttpActionContext.Response property has been set after the OnActionExecutingAsync method has been called. If the Response property is null, then the OnActionExecutedAsync method is called as normal. If the Response property isn't null, then the HttpResponseMessage object to which it has been set is used as the result of its ExecuteActionFilterAsync implementation, which creates the short-circuit effect.

Understanding the Filter Pipeline

If you are especially sharp-eyed, you will have noticed something in the output from the two action filters in the previous section that gives a hint about the way in which filters are executed. Before I move on to describe the other kinds of filer, I am going to dig into the details of how filters are ordered into a *filter pipeline* when they are executed. Here is the output from the previous example:

```
Request 0 of 3
Elapsed time: 86870 ticks, GET http://localhost:49412/api/products/
Request 1 of 3
Elapsed time: 3196 ticks, GET http://localhost:49412/api/products/
Request 2 of 3
Elapsed time: 2220 ticks, GET http://localhost:49412/api/products/
Elapsed time: 7077 ticks, GET http://localhost:49412/api/products/
```

The clue is the highlighted statement, which shows that the Time filter is still processing requests even though the Counter filter is returning 503 (Service Unavailable) responses. This is because the Time filter appears before the Counter filter in the dispatch pipeline, as shown in Figure 23-4.

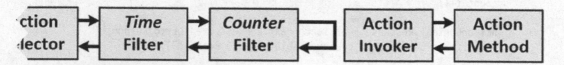

Figure 23-4. *The sequence of action filters in the request pipeline*

Filters are organized into a specific sequence, and the Time filter appears before the Counter filter in the filter pipeline. Even though the Counter filter is short-circuiting the dispatch process, the HttpResponseMessage object that it creates is passed back along the pipeline to the filters that appear before it. Table 23-8 puts the filter pipeline into context.

Table 23-8. *Putting the Filter Pipeline in Context*

Question	Answer
What is it?	The filter pipeline provides information about the filters that apply to an action method, sorted by scope.
When should you use it?	The filter pipeline is of interest only for diagnostic purposes or when adding support for filters to controllers that are derived directly from the IHttpController interface, rather than the ApiController class.
What do you need to know?	The filter pipeline takes into account the effect of scope on the order in which filters will be executed but not the way that the ApiController class organizes filters by type. I show you how to re-order the pipeline at the end of this chapter.

Displaying the Filter Pipeline

You can get insight into the filter pipeline through the HttpActionContext.GetFilterPipeline method, which returns an enumeration of FilterInfo objects. Each FilterInfo object provides the details of one filter using the properties shown in Table 23-9.

Table 23-9. *The Properties Defined by the FilterInfo Class*

Name	Description
Instance	Returns the filter object, which implements the IFilter interface.
Scope	Returns the scope of the filter, expressed using a value from the FilterScope enumeration. See the "Understanding Filter Scope" section for details.

The simplest way to examine the filter pipeline is to create a custom implementation of the IHttpActionSelector interface by deriving from the ApiControllerActionSelector class and overriding the SelectAction method to display information about the filters. Listing 23-7 shows the contents of the PipelineActionSelector.cs file, which I added to the Infrastructure folder.

Listing 23-7. The Contents of the PipelineActionSelector.cs File

```
using System.Collections.Generic;
using System.Diagnostics;
using System.Web.Http.Controllers;
using System.Web.Http.Filters;

namespace Dispatch.Infrastructure {
    public class PipelineActionSelector : ApiControllerActionSelector {

        public override HttpActionDescriptor SelectAction(HttpControllerContext
                controllerContext) {

            HttpActionDescriptor action = base.SelectAction(controllerContext);

            IEnumerable<FilterInfo> filters = action.GetFilterPipeline();

            foreach (FilterInfo filter in filters) {
                Debug.WriteLine("Scope {0} Type: {1}",
                    filter.Scope, filter.Instance.GetType().Name);
            }

            return action;
        }
    }
}
```

I still rely on the base implementation of the SelectionAction method, but I also write out a message that describes each filter. Listing 23-8 shows how I registered the PipelineActionSelector class as the implementation of the IHttpActionSelector interface that Web API will use.

Listing 23-8. Registering a Custom Action Selector in the WebApiConfig.cs File

```
using System.Web.Http;
using System.Web.Http.Controllers;
using Dispatch.Infrastructure;

namespace Dispatch {
    public static class WebApiConfig {
        public static void Register(HttpConfiguration config) {

            config.Routes.MapHttpRoute(
                name: "ActionMethods",
                routeTemplate: "api/nrest/{controller}/{action}/{day}",
                defaults: new { day = RouteParameter.Optional }
            );

            config.Routes.MapHttpRoute(
                name: "DefaultApi",
                routeTemplate: "api/{controller}/{id}",
                defaults: new { id = RouteParameter.Optional }
            );

            config.Services.Replace(typeof(IHttpActionSelector),
                new PipelineActionSelector());
        }
    }
}
```

To test the custom action selector and get details of the filter pipeline, start the application and use the browser to navigate to the /Home/Index URL. Click the Get All button, and you will see messages similar to these in the Visual Studio Output window:

```
Scope Controller Type: TimeAttribute
Scope Action Type: CounterAttribute
Request 0 of 3
Elapsed time: 87523 ticks, GET http://localhost:49412/api/products/
```

In the sections that follow, I'll explain why the filters are organized this way. As I continue to describe different kinds of filter, I'll revisit the pipeline and demonstrate how they are organized.

■ **Note** The filter pipeline doesn't completely reflect the order in which other types of filter are executed, but I will revise the code at the end of the chapter to sort the filters by type.

Understanding Filter Scope

There are three ways in which a filter can be applied, which determines the requests to which it is applied to, known as the filter's scope. The FilterScope enumeration defines a value for each scope, as described in Table 23-10.

Table 23-10. The Values Defined by the FilterScope Enumeration

Scope	Description
Global	The filter is executed for all requests.
Controller	The filter is executed for requests that target any action method defined by the controller to which it has been applied.
Action	The filter is executed for requests that target the action method to which it has been applied.

Filters are first ordered by type and then by scope. I listed the different filter types in Table 23-2, but here is the order in which the three most commonly used types are executed:

1. Authentication filters

2. Authorization filters

3. Action filters

This order is enforced by the ApiController class and cannot be changed by implementing he interfaces that I described in Chapter 22. Unlike the MVC framework, there is no way to control the execution order of filters of the same type with the same scope.

■ **Note**   There are two other kinds of filter—error filter and override filters—that operate differently and that I describe in Chapter 24.

In the dispatch process, the ApiController sorts the filters in the pipeline by type and then sorts them by scope. This is why the Time filter appears in the filter pipeline before the Counter filter—it is been applied to the controller, and controller-scoped filters take precedence over those that have been applied directly to an action method.

■ **Tip**   The effect of the scope precedence rules means that my Time filter isn't measuring just the execution of the action method; it is also measuring the amount of time it takes to execute any filters that appear subsequently in the filter pipeline.

Creating a Global Filter

I have demonstrated controller- and action method–scoped filters; to complete the set, I need to show you how to create a global feature. Listing 23-9 shows the contents of the SayHelloAttribute.cs file, which I added to the Infrastructure folder.

Listing 23-9. The Contents of the SayHelloAttribute.cs File

```
using System.Diagnostics;
using System.Threading;
using System.Threading.Tasks;
using System.Web.Http.Controllers;
using System.Web.Http.Filters;
```

```
namespace Dispatch.Infrastructure {
    public class SayHelloAttribute : ActionFilterAttribute {

        public string Message { get; set; }

        public override Task OnActionExecutingAsync(HttpActionContext actionContext,
            CancellationToken cancellationToken) {

            Debug.WriteLine("SayHello: {0}", (object)Message ?? "Hello");
            return Task.FromResult<object>(null);
        }
    }
}
```

This file contains a filter that simply writes a message to the Visual Studio Output window so that I can demonstrate filter precedence.

■ **Note** The fact is that there are not many general-purpose uses for action filters beyond logging and measuring performance. This is a feature that it is important to understand but becomes important only when you need to integrate functionality that doesn't fit neatly into the Web API/MVC model.

Global filters are registered in the WebApiConfig.cs file, as shown in Listing 23-10.

Listing 23-10. Registering a Global Filter in the WebApiConfig.cs File

```
using System.Web.Http;
using System.Web.Http.Controllers;
using Dispatch.Infrastructure;

namespace Dispatch {
    public static class WebApiConfig {
        public static void Register(HttpConfiguration config) {

            config.Routes.MapHttpRoute(
                name: "ActionMethods",
                routeTemplate: "api/nrest/{controller}/{action}/{day}",
                defaults: new { day = RouteParameter.Optional }
            );

            config.Routes.MapHttpRoute(
                name: "DefaultApi",
                routeTemplate: "api/{controller}/{id}",
                defaults: new { id = RouteParameter.Optional }
            );
```

```
        config.Services.Replace(typeof(IHttpActionSelector),
            new PipelineActionSelector());

        config.Filters.Add(new SayHelloAttribute { Message = "Global Filter" });
    }
  }
}
```

To test the global filter, start the application and use the browser to navigate to the /Home/Index URL. Click the Get All button, and you will see messages similar to the following in the Visual Studio Output window:

```
Scope Global Type: SayHelloAttribute
Scope Controller Type: TimeAttribute
Scope Action Type: CounterAttribute
SayHello: Global Filter
Request 0 of 3
Elapsed time: 83963 ticks, GET http://localhost:49412/api/products/
```

I have highlighted the important messages. The first shows that the SayHelloAttribute is the first filter in the pipeline, and the second confirms this by showing that output from the filter appears before the other filter messages.

■ **Tip** Although I created my global filter as an attribute, this is not required because the filter isn't being applied directly to a controller or action method. I prefer to create filter attributes, however, because it means that I can easily change the scope of a filter without having to modify its code.

Working with Authentication Filters

Authentication filters, as their name suggests, allow you to ensure that action methods are invoked only by clients that have been authenticated. Most Web API applications will use the ASP.NET Identity platform to perform authentication, and you saw how filters are used to apply ASP.NET Identity in Chapter 6. Table 23-11 puts authentication and filters in context.

Table 23-11. Putting Authentication Filters in Context

Question	Answer
What are they?	Authentication filters are responsible for inspecting an HTTP request and identifying the user identity associated with it. Requests with which no user can be associated are short-circuited.
When should you use them?	Apply an authentication filter when you want to restrict access to one or more action methods to requests made by users who are known to the application.
What do you need to know?	Authentication filters will allow access to all users as long as the request contains valid credentials. Use an authorization filter if you want to restrict access to specific users, as described in Chapter 24.

Authentication filters are invoked first irrespective of scope and before any other kind of filter and the action method. When authentication fails, the dispatch process is short-circuited, and an `HttpResponseMessage` is produced from the authentication filter without any other filter—or the target action method—being invoked.

■ **Caution**   In this section, I create some insecure filters solely to demonstrate how these types of filter work. Do not use these filters in a real project. More generally, think long and hard before creating your own authentication code—stick to the built-in support provided by ASP.NET unless you are truly an expert in writing secure code. It is all too easy to make a simple mistake that exposes your web service to attackers. I have been writing software for decades (certainly longer than I care to recount), and I *still* hesitate before writing custom security code. You should, too.

Preparing for Authentication

If your application needs to tailor the functionality and content delivered to different users, then you need some way of managing the users' identities and security credentials. This is usually handled through the ASP.NET Identity system (or its predecessor, ASP.NET Membership), but I don't want to get into the details of Identity beyond the description I gave for the SportsStore application, so for this chapter, I will define a user manager class that I will use to authenticate and authorize users using static data. Listing 23-11 shows the contents of the `StaticUserManager.cs` class file that I added to the `Infrastructure` folder.

Listing 23-11. The Contents of the StaticUserManager.cs File

```
using System.Collections.Generic;
using System.Linq;
using System.Security.Principal;

namespace Dispatch.Infrastructure {
    public class StaticUserManager {
        private static Dictionary<string, string[]> roles;

        static StaticUserManager() {
            roles = new Dictionary<string, string[]>();
            roles.Add("admin", new string[] { "admins", "users" });
            roles.Add("bob", new string[] { "users" });
        }

        public static IPrincipal AuthenticateUser(string user, string pass) {
            if (roles.ContainsKey(user) && pass == "secret") {
                return new StaticUser(user, roles[user]);
            }
            return null;
        }
    }

    public class StaticUser: IIdentity, IPrincipal {
        private string[] roles;
```

```
    public StaticUser(string name, string[] rolesList) {
        Name = name;
        AuthenticationType = "Basic";
        IsAuthenticated = true;
        roles = rolesList;
    }

    public string AuthenticationType { get; private set; }
    public bool IsAuthenticated { get; private set; }
    public string Name { get; private set; }

    public IIdentity Identity {
        get { return this; }
    }

    public bool IsInRole(string role) {
        return roles.Any(x => x == role);
    }
}
}
```

ASP.NET uses two interfaces to identity users, IPrincipal and IIdentity, both of which are defined in the System.Security.Principal namespace. The IIdentity interface is used to represent a specific user and defines the properties shown in Table 23-12.

Table 23-12. *The Properties Defined by the IIdentity Interface*

Name	Description
AuthenticationType	Returns a string that specifies the type of authentication used to create the identity
IsAuthenticated	Returns true if the user has been authenticated
Name	Returns the name of the user

The IPrincipal interface is a wrapper around an IIdentity object and provides information about the roles to which a user belongs (roles are used for authorization, as I explain in Chapter 24). The IPrincipal interface defines the property and method shown in Table 23-13.

Table 23-13. *The Properties Defined by the IPrincipal Interface*

Name	Description
Identity	Returns an implementation of the IIdentity interface that describes the user
IsInRole(role)	Returns true if the user has been assigned to the specified role and false otherwise

User management systems usually provide their own implementations of these interfaces, and in Listing 23-11, I have defined the StaticUser class, which implements both interfaces. The StaticUserManager class provides a static AuthenticateUser method that accepts a username and password as its parameters and returns an instance of the StaticUser class for known users. I have defined two users and some roles, creating the user set shown in Table 23-14. I use the roles in Chapter 24, when I describe authorization filters.

Table 23-14. *The Users, Passwords, and Roles Defined by the StaticUser Class*

User	Password	Roles
admin	secret	admins, users
bob	secret	users

■ **Caution** I have hard-coded the usernames, passwords, and roles into the StaticUserManager class, which is fine for a simple example but causes problems in a real project because it means you have to deploy a new version of the application each time there is a new user or a change to an existing one.

Understanding Authentication Filters

Authentication filters are responsible for establishing the identity of the user who has made the request. Web API doesn't specify how the user is identified, which means that authentication filters can be used to integrate any user management system into your web service. For most applications, the ASP.NET Identity system is the best way to handle authentication (and authorization, which I describe in Chapter 24), but even so, it is useful to be able to understand how the Web API authentication process works, especially when you don't get the results you expect in your own projects.

Authentication filters are defined by the IAuthenticationFilter interface, which is defined as follows:

```
using System.Threading;
using System.Threading.Tasks;

namespace System.Web.Http.Filters {

    public interface IAuthenticationFilter : IFilter {

        Task AuthenticateAsync(HttpAuthenticationContext context,
            CancellationToken cancellationToken);

        Task ChallengeAsync(HttpAuthenticationChallengeContext context,
            CancellationToken cancellationToken);
    }
}
```

Authentication filters are a little odd. The AuthenticateAsync method is called before the request is processed by other filters, and its job is to identify the user associated with the request or to create an IHttpActionResult object that reports an error to the client.

■ **Note** In an MVC Framework application, authentication failures are usually handled by redirecting the client to the login URL for the application. This technique doesn't work for HTTP web services, where the client cannot be assumed capable of parsing HTML or prompting the user for their credentials. Web services can be used to authenticate users—as I demonstrate in Chapter 24—but failed authentication should be handled by returning a 401 (Unauthorized) response to the client.

The oddity is that the `IHttpActionResult` produced by the `AuthenticateAsync` method isn't used to create the response sent to the client. Instead, that is the responsibility of the `ChallengeAsync` method, which is invoked after the request has been processed, even if the user has been properly authenticated. This will start to make sense with an example—but not entirely since, as I say, authentication filters are odd.

UNDERSTANDING BASIC HTTP AUTHENTICATION

The example authentication filter that I describe in this section uses the *basic authentication* mechanism that is defined as part of the HTTP specification. It is incredibly simple to implement but isn't widely used because it has some profound limitations, especially when used without SSL.

To authenticate itself, the client adds an `Authorization` header to the request, like this:

`Authorization: Basic YWRtaW46YWRtaW5TZWNyZXRY`

The value of the header is the word `Basic`, followed by a Base64-encoded string that contains the username and password separated by a colon (the : character). Decoding the string `YWRtaW46YWRtaW5TZWNyZXRY` reveals `admin:adminsecret`, meaning that the client is authenticating itself as the user `admin` with a password of `adminSecret`.

If the client sends a request without the `Authorization` header or with credentials that are incorrect (specifying either a nonexistent user or an invalid password), then the web service will return a 401 (Unauthorized) response that includes a `WWW-Authenticate` that specifies the Basic authentication mechanism, like this:

`WWW-Authenticate: Basic`

Basic authentication requires the client to send the user's credentials to the web service with every request in a format that is easily decoded. If you do find yourself using Basic authentication (and I sincerely hope that you do not), then ensure that all of your requests are handled through SSL.

Creating an Authentication Filter

To demonstrate how authentication filters operate, I created a class file called `CustomAuthenticationFilter.cs` in the `Infrastructure` folder and used it to create the filter shown in Listing 23-12.

■ **Caution**   This filter relies on the basic HTTP authentication scheme, which is wholly inadequate for use in real projects unless SSL is used. Use this example only to understand how the authentication filter mechanism works, and see Part 1 for details of how to use ASP.NET Identity to handle user authentication in real projects.

Listing 23-12.   The Contents of the CustomAuthenticationFilter.cs File

```
using System;
using System.Net;
using System.Net.Http;
using System.Net.Http.Headers;
using System.Text;
using System.Threading;
using System.Threading.Tasks;
using System.Web.Http.Filters;
using System.Web.Http.Results;
```

```
namespace Dispatch.Infrastructure {
    public class CustomAuthenticationAttribute : Attribute, IAuthenticationFilter {

        public Task AuthenticateAsync(HttpAuthenticationContext context,
                CancellationToken cancellationToken) {

            context.Principal = null;
            AuthenticationHeaderValue authentication =
                context.Request.Headers.Authorization;
            if (authentication != null && authentication.Scheme == "Basic") {
                string[] authData
                    = Encoding.ASCII.GetString(Convert.FromBase64String(
                        authentication.Parameter)).Split(':');
                context.Principal
                    = StaticUserManager.AuthenticateUser(authData[0], authData[1]);
            }

            if (context.Principal == null) {
                context.ErrorResult
                    = new UnauthorizedResult(new AuthenticationHeaderValue[] {
                    new AuthenticationHeaderValue("Basic") }, context.Request);
            }

            return Task.FromResult<object>(null);
        }

        public Task ChallengeAsync(HttpAuthenticationChallengeContext context,
                CancellationToken cancellationToken) {
            return Task.FromResult<object>(null);
        }

        public bool AllowMultiple {
            get { return false; }
        }
    }
}
```

There is a lot going on in this class, so I'll break down the details in the sections that follow. As I get into the details, the most important thing to remember is that the authentication filter is responsible for identifying the user from the request and *not* obtaining the credentials from the user.

■ **Tip** Do not implement an authentication filter in your projects until you have read Chapter 24, in which I explain how to create a message handler to authenticate requests and refactor the filter to consume the data that it generates.

Checking the Request

The job of the `AuthenticateAsync` method is to examine the request to see whether it contains the information that is required to identify a user. Information about the request is provided through an instance of the `HttpAuthenticationContext` class, which defines the properties shown in Table 23-15.

Table 23-15. *The Properties Defined by the HttpAuthenticationContext Class*

Name	Description
ActionContext	This property returns the `HttpActionContext` object that describes the action method that has been selected to execute the request.
ErrorResult	This is property is set to an implementation of the `IHttpActionResult` interface if the request cannot be authenticated.
Principal	This property is set to an implementation of the `IPrincipal` interface if the request has been authenticated. Setting the `Principal` property causes the `HttpContext.Principal` property to be set as well, which makes details of the authentication process available to other components—including the authorization filters I described in Chapter 24.
Request	This property returns the `HttpRequestMessage` object that describes the current request.

To create an effective authentication filter, the `AuthenticateAsync` must do one of the following:

- If the request is authenticated, set the `HttpAuthenticationContext.Principal` property to an implementation of the `IPrincipal` interface.

- If the request cannot be authenticated, set the `HttpAuthenticationContext.ErrorResult` property to an implementation of the `IHttpActionResult` interface that will produce a 401 (Unauthorized) result.

Web API doesn't specify the mechanism that the `AuthenticateAsync` method uses to authenticate users, but for web services, the most common techniques involve inspecting request cookies or headers. For HTTP basic authentication, I need to look for the `Authorization` header, which I do like this:

```
...
context.Principal = null;
AuthenticationHeaderValue authentication = context.Request.Headers.Authorization;
if (authentication != null && authentication.Scheme == "Basic") {
    string[] authData = Encoding.ASCII.GetString(Convert.FromBase64String(
                        authentication.Parameter)).Split(':');
    context.Principal = StaticUserManager.AuthenticateUser(authData[0], authData[1]);
}
...
```

The `Authorization` header is represented by the `AuthenticationHeaderValue` class, which parses the header value and presents `Scheme` and `Parameter` properties. The `Scheme` property returns `Basic` when HTTP basic authentication is used, and the `Parameter` property will return the Base64-encoded username and password, which I decode and pass to the `StaticUserManager` class to authenticate the user and obtain the `IPrincipal` object.

■ **Tip** Notice that I explicitly set the `HttpAuthenticationContext.Principal` property to `null` before attempting to authenticate the request. If a Web API application is running on the traditional ASP.NET platform, then the `Principal` property may already be set by the time that the `AuthenticateAsync` method is called to represent credentials from Windows or elsewhere. It is possible to locate and disable other sources of `IPrincipal` objects, but I find explicitly setting the `Principal` property to `null` to be more reliable.

Getting the right value for the `Principal` value is important because I use it to check to see whether I need to report an error through the `ErrorResult` property, like this:

```
...
if (context.Principal == null) {
    context.ErrorResult = new UnauthorizedResult(
        new AuthenticationHeaderValue[] { new AuthenticationHeaderValue("Basic") },
            context.Request);
}
...
```

If the call to the `StaticUserManager.AuthenticateUser` method hasn't produced an `IPrincipal` or if the method wasn't called because the request didn't contain the authentication information I require, then I set the `HttpAuthenticationContext.ErrorResult` property to an instance of the `UnauthorizedResult` class. The `UnauthorizedResult` class allows me to specify the `WWW-Authenticate` header, which tells the client which authentication scheme should be used to authenticate the user.

Adding the Response Challenge

The `ChallengeAsync` method is call for every request, but there are two scenarios that have to be dealt with. The first is that the `AuthenticateAsync` method has set a value for the `HttpAuthenticationContext.ErrorResult` property, which has the effect of short-circuiting the dispatch process and invoking the `ChallengeAsync` method without invoking any other filter or the action method.

The second scenario is that authentication succeeded, and the `ChallengeAsync` method is called so that the filter has the change to modify the `HttpResponse` object, usually to make it easier to authenticate subsequent requests.

For my HTTP basic authentication scheme, I don't have to take any action at all because I created the response needed for failed authentications in the `AuthenticateAsync` method, which is how I prefer to create authentication filters. You will sometimes encounter code where the `IHttpActionResult` is executed, checked for a status code, and then replaced by a new result, but that isn't really required. If you do need to modify the result, you can use the `HttpAuthenticationChallengeContext` parameter, which defines the properties shown in Table 23-16.

Table 23-16. *The Properties Defined by the HttpAuthenticationChallengeContext Class*

Name	Description
`ActionContext`	This property returns the `HttpActionContext` object that describes the action method that has been selected to execute the request.
`Request`	This property returns the `HttpRequestMessage` object that describes the current request.
`Result`	This property is used to specify the `IHttpActionResult` that will be executed to generate the `HttpResponseMessage` object for the request.

Applying and Testing the Authentication Filter

Authentication filters are applied just like any other filter and can be given global, controller, and action scope. Listing 23-13 shows how I applied my example filter to the Products controller.

Listing 23-13. Applying an Authentication Filter in the ProductsController.cs File

```
using System.Collections.Generic;
using System.Linq;
using System.Web.Http;
using Dispatch.Models;
using Dispatch.Infrastructure;

namespace Dispatch.Controllers {

    public class ProductsController : ApiController {
        private static List<Product> products = new List<Product> {
                new Product {ProductID = 1, Name = "Kayak", Price = 275M },
                new Product {ProductID = 2, Name = "Lifejacket", Price = 48.95M },
                new Product {ProductID = 3, Name = "Soccer Ball", Price = 19.50M },
                new Product {ProductID = 4, Name = "Thinking Cap", Price = 16M },
            };

        [Time]
        [Counter(3)]
        public IEnumerable<Product> Get() {
            return products;
        }

        [CustomAuthentication]
        public Product Get(int id) {
            return products.Where(x => x.ProductID == id).FirstOrDefault();
        }

        public Product Post(Product product) {
            product.ProductID = products.Count + 1;
            products.Add(product);
            return product;
        }
    }
}
```

I have applied the filter to the version of the Get method that takes a parameter. This has the effect of allowing every other action method that is defined by the controller to be targeted by any request but restricts the Get action to requests that have been authenticated.

■ **Tip** An authentication filter doesn't restrict access to specific users—that's the job of authorization filters, which I describe in Chapter 24. An authentication filter will grant access to *any* authenticated request, irrespective of the user identity associated with it.

To test the filter, start the application and use the browser to navigate to the /Home/Index URL. First, click the Get All or Post button to ensure that unauthenticated requests are handled correctly. To check the authentication process, click the Get One button.

The client-side code will respond to the button press by sending an Ajax request to the /api/products/2 URL, which the dispatch process will match to the Get method that accepts a parameter in the Products controller. The AuthenticateAsync method defined by the CustomAuthentication filter will be invoked and, failing to find the Authorization header, will return a 401 (Unauthorized) response to the client.

Almost all browsers have built-in support for basic authentication and will respond by prompting the user for credentials on receipt of a 401 (Unauthorized) response that contains a WWW-Authenticate header set to Basic, as illustrated by Figure 23-5.

Figure 23-5. *Chrome prompting the user for credentials*

Enter one of the usernames and passwords from Table 23-14 (either admin or bob with a password of secret), and Chrome will resend its Ajax request to the /api/products/2 URL, but this time with the required header. The result is that the authentication filter will set the IPrincipal object on the HttpRequestMessage object, and the dispatch pipeline will not be short-circuited. Alternatively, you can click the Cancel button, in which case the 401 status code is reported to the client-side JavaScript code, which will display the error.

Viewing the Filter Pipeline

If you look at the Visual Studio Output window, you will see that the PipelineActionSelector class that I created earlier in the chapter has been writing out the filter pipeline for requests. For a request that targets the Get method to which I applied the authentication filter, the output looks like this:

```
Scope Global Type: SayHelloAttribute
Scope Controller Type: TimeAttribute
Scope Action Type: CustomAuthenticationAttribute
```

There are three filters in the pipeline for this action method: the global SayHelloAttribute filter that I set up in the "Creating a Global Filter" section, the TimeAttribute filter I created in the "Working with Action Filters" section, and the CustomAuthenticationAttribute filter from the previous section.

The pipeline as returned by the HttpActionContext.GetFilterPipeline method takes into account the effect that scope has on the order of the filters but not the effect of the filter type. As I explained earlier, the filters are executed in this order:

1. Authentication filters

2. Authorization filters

3. Action filters

There are two special kinds of filter—*error* and *override* filters—that I describe in Chapter 24, but for now it is enough to focus on the three filter types in the list. Listing 23-14 shows how I have updated the PipelineActionSelector class to process the filter pipeline and sort it by filter type.

■ **Tip** Remember that the filter pipeline is a list of the filters that will be executed only if none of the filters elects to short-circuit the dispatch process.

Listing 23-14. Sorting the Pipeline by Filter Type in the PipelineActionSelector.cs File

```
using System.Collections.Generic;
using System.Diagnostics;
using System.Web.Http.Controllers;
using System.Web.Http.Filters;
using System.Linq;

namespace Dispatch.Infrastructure {
    public class PipelineActionSelector : ApiControllerActionSelector {

        public override HttpActionDescriptor SelectAction(HttpControllerContext
                controllerContext) {

            HttpActionDescriptor action = base.SelectAction(controllerContext);

            IEnumerable<FilterInfo> filters = action.GetFilterPipeline();

            IEnumerable<FilterInfo> orderedFilters =
                GetFilters<IAuthenticationFilter>(filters)
                .Concat(GetFilters<IAuthorizationFilter>(filters))
                .Concat(GetFilters<IActionFilter>(filters));

            foreach (FilterInfo filter in orderedFilters) {
                Debug.WriteLine("Scope {0} Type: {1}", filter.Scope,
                    filter.Instance.GetType().Name);
            }
```

```
        return action;
    }

    private IEnumerable<FilterInfo> GetFilters<T>(IEnumerable<FilterInfo> filters) {
        return filters.Where(f => f.Instance is T);
    }
  }
}
```

I used LINQ to arrange filters by type, which produces the following messages in the Visual Studio Output window when you start the application, navigate to the /Home/Index URL, and click the Get One button:

```
Scope Action Type: CustomAuthenticationAttribute
Scope Global Type: SayHelloAttribute
Scope Controller Type: TimeAttribute
```

Summary

In this chapter, I explained the role that filters play in the dispatch process and showed you two types of filters: action filters and authentication filters. I demonstrated how to read the filter pipeline and explained how scope and filter types are used to order filters for execution. In the next chapter, I continue describing the Web API support for filters and show you how authorization, exception, and override filters work.

■ ■ ■

CHAPTER 24

Filters Part II

In this chapter, I continue describing the Web API support for filters and demonstrate how authorization filters work. I also show you two kinds of special filters: exception filters and override filters. Table 24-1 summarizes this chapter.

Table 24-1. *Chapter Summary*

Problem	Solution	Listing
Create an authorization filter.	Implement the IAuthorizationFilter interface, derive from the AuthorizationFilterAttribute class, or use the Authorize attribute.	1, 5–9
Restrict access to an action method.	Apply an authorization attribute to the action method or its containing controller.	2–4
Handle an exception thrown by an action method or another filter.	Create an exception filter by implementing the IExceptionFilter interface or deriving from the ExceptionFilterAttribute class.	10–14
Disable the effect of a controller-wide or global exception filter for an action method.	Apply an override filter.	15–16

Preparing the Example Project

I am going to continue with the Dispatch project I created in Chapter 19 and have been building on throughout this part of the book. No preparatory changes are required for this chapter.

■ **Tip** You don't have to re-create the project from Chapter 19 and apply all of the changes I have described since. You can also download all of the source code organized by chapter from http://apress.com.

Reviewing Filters in the Dispatch Process

In Chapter 23, I explained how filters are wrapped around the action method so that they can execute logic before and after it is executed. This provides the means to alter the request processed by the action method or the response that will be sent to the client, and it allows for short-circuiting, where the dispatch process is terminated. The order in which filters are executed depends on the type of filter and its scope. Table 24-2 shows the different filter types in the order they are executed.

Table 24-2. *The Web API Filter Types and Interfaces*

Filter Type	Interface	Description
Authentication	IAuthenticationFilter	This kind of filter is used to require users or clients to be authenticated before action methods can be executed. See Chapter 23.
Authorization	IAuthorizationFilter	This kind of filter is used to restrict access to action methods to specific users or groups.
Action	IActionFilter	This kind of filter is used to manipulate the request or response. See Chapter 23.
Exception	IExceptionFilter	This kind of filter is used to handle exceptions thrown by the action method or another kind of filter.
Override	IOverrideFilter	This kind of filter is used to tailor the behavior of other filters for individual action methods.

In this chapter, I describe the last of the convention filters (the authorization filter) and explain how two special types of filters work (the exception and override filters). Authorization filters are executed after authentication filters and before action filters, as illustrated by Figure 24-1.

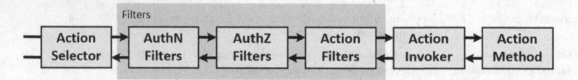

Figure 24-1. *Filters in the dispatch process*

■ **Tip** I have used two common contractions in Figure 24-1 to fit everything on the page. *AuthN* is a contraction of authentication, and *AuthZ* is a contraction of authorization.

Working with Authorization Filters

Authorization filters are used to restrict access to action methods to specific users. This may seem like a variation on the authentication filters that I described in Chapter 23, but as you will see, authorization works differently.

In most applications, you will simply apply the Authorize attribute to your controllers and action methods and rely on the ASP.NET Identity system to perform the authentication and authorization work, but in this section I go behind the scenes and explain how this important kind of filter works. Table 24-3 puts authorization filters into context.

Table 24-3. *Putting Authorization Filters in Context*

Question	Answer
What are they?	Authorization filters restrict action methods to specific users or the roles to which they have been assigned.
When should you use them?	The most common use for authorization filters is to prevent normal users from gaining access to administrative functionality.
What do you need to know?	Authorization filters generally rely on another component to authenticate requests and then inspect the authenticated user for role membership. The simplest way to perform authorization is to use the Authorize attribute.

Understanding Authorization Filters

Authorization filters are defined by the IAuthorizationFilter interface, which is defined in the System.Web.Http. Filters namespace and shares the same basic approach as action filters. Here is the IAuthorization interface:

```
using System.Diagnostics.CodeAnalysis;
using System.Net.Http;
using System.Threading;
using System.Threading.Tasks;
using System.Web.Http.Controllers;

namespace System.Web.Http.Filters {
    public interface IAuthorizationFilter : IFilter {

        Task<HttpResponseMessage> ExecuteAuthorizationFilterAsync(
            HttpActionContext actionContext, CancellationToken cancellationToken,
                Func<Task<HttpResponseMessage>> continuation);
    }
}
```

Web API doesn't enforce any kind of restrictions on how requests are authorized or how information about the user associated with the request is obtained. The most common approach is to read the value of the HttpRequestContext.Principal property to get an IPrincipal object that can be compared to an authorization policy. This approach allows authorization to be decoupled by authentication, meaning that the authentication mechanism can be changed without affecting authorization.

Creating an Authorization Filter

Authorization filters are required to enforce an authorization policy before the action method is executed. If a request complies with the policy—meaning that it is associated with a user who has been granted access to the action method—then action filter does nothing. If the request doesn't comply with the policy, the filter short-circuits the dispatch process and returns a 401 (Unauthorized) response to the client. To demonstrate how an authorization filter works, I added a class file called CustomAuthorizationAttribute.cs to the Infrastructure folder and used it to define the filter shown in Listing 24-1.

Listing 24-1. The Contents of the CustomAuthorizationAttribute.cs File

```csharp
using System;
using System.Linq;
using System.Net;
using System.Net.Http;
using System.Security.Principal;
using System.Threading;
using System.Threading.Tasks;
using System.Web.Http.Controllers;
using System.Web.Http.Filters;

namespace Dispatch.Infrastructure {

    public class CustomAuthorizationAttribute : Attribute, IAuthorizationFilter {
        private string[] roles;

        public CustomAuthorizationAttribute(params string[] rolesList) {
            roles = rolesList;
        }

        public Task<HttpResponseMessage> ExecuteAuthorizationFilterAsync(
                HttpActionContext actionContext,
                CancellationToken cancellationToken,
                Func<Task<HttpResponseMessage>> continuation) {

            IPrincipal principal = actionContext.RequestContext.Principal;
            if (principal == null || !roles.Any(role => principal.IsInRole(role))) {
                return Task.FromResult<HttpResponseMessage>(
                    actionContext.Request.CreateResponse(HttpStatusCode.Unauthorized));
            } else {
                return continuation();
            }
        }

        public bool AllowMultiple {
            get { return false; }
        }
    }
}
```

■ **Tip** You don't have to create a filter directly from the interface. There is a built-in attribute class that applies authorization, as I describe in the "Using the Authorize Attribute" section. The examples that follow explain how authorization works, but you can jump right to the built-in attribute section if you just want to see how to restrict access to your action methods.

The filter employs some of the techniques I described in Chapter 23 to authorize requests. The class constructor takes an array of roles that will be granted access and uses the IPrincipal.IsInRole method to check to see whether the authenticated user belongs to one of the permitted roles.

If the user is in a permitted role, then the filter invokes the continuation function and returns the result. This is often referred to as a *pass-through*, meaning that a request from an allowed user passes through the filter without any modification.

If the user is not in a permitted role, then the filter short-circuits the dispatch process and returns an HttpResponseMessage that yields a 401 (Unauthorized) status code to the client.

■ **Tip** For simple applications, you might be tempted to perform authorization using individual account names rather than roles, which you can do through the IIdentity associated with the IPrincipal object. Be careful, though: simple applications often live longer than initially inspected and grow in unexpected directions. Working with roles, even when there is only one user, often pays off in the long term.

Appling the Authorization Filter

Notice that the CustomAuthorizationAttribute in Listing 24-1 does not identity the user associated with the request but relies on the HttpContext.Principal property having been set. The cost of loosely coupling authentication and authorization is that authorization filters rely on there being another component to identify the user and create the IPrincipal associated with the request. In Listing 24-2, you can see how I have paired the authentication attribute from Chapter 23 with the authorization filter to restrict access to an action method defined by the Products controller.

Listing 24-2. Applying Authorization in the ProductsController.cs File

```
using System.Collections.Generic;
using System.Linq;
using System.Web.Http;
using Dispatch.Infrastructure;
using Dispatch.Models;

namespace Dispatch.Controllers {

    [Time]
    public class ProductsController : ApiController {
        private static List<Product> products = new List<Product> {
                new Product {ProductID = 1, Name = "Kayak", Price = 275M },
                new Product {ProductID = 2, Name = "Lifejacket", Price = 48.95M },
                new Product {ProductID = 3, Name = "Soccer Ball", Price = 19.50M },
                new Product {ProductID = 4, Name = "Thinking Cap", Price = 16M },
        };

        [Counter(3)]
        public IEnumerable<Product> Get() {
            return products;
        }

        [CustomAuthentication]
        [CustomAuthorization("admins")]
        public Product Get(int id) {
            return products.Where(x => x.ProductID == id).FirstOrDefault();
        }
```

```
        public Product Post(Product product) {
            product.ProductID = products.Count + 1;
            products.Add(product);
            return product;
        }
    }
}
```

The CustomAuthentication filter sets up the IPrincipal for the request, which is then assessed by the CustomAuthorization filter to make sure the user has been assigned to the admins role, which I specified as the constructor parameter.

Testing the Authorization Filter

To test the authorization filter, start the application and use the browser to navigate to the /Home/Index URL. Click the Get One button and, when prompted, enter the username **bob** and the password **secret**.

The browser will encode the credentials you have provided and resend the request to the server. The authentication filter will create an IPrincipal object that represents the user bob and allow the request to continue through the dispatch process. The authorization filter inspects the IPrincipal to see whether the user has been assigned to the admins role. Table 24-4 lists the users and roles I defined in Chapter 23 and shows that bob isn't part of the admin role and therefore isn't authorized to invoke the action method.

Table 24-4. *The Users, Passwords, and Roles Defined by the StaticUser Class*

User	Password	Roles
admin	secret	admins, users
bob	secret	users

The authorization filter short-circuits the request and returns a 401 (Unauthorized) response to the client. Browsers that deal with basic authentication directly intercept the 401 response before it is passed to jQuery, which means that you will be prompted for different credentials without ever seeing the error response.

■ **Note**   Browsers store HTTP basic authentication credentials even when the history cache is cleared. To switch from one user account to another, you will usually have to restart the browser, navigate to the /Home/Index URL, and click the Get One button again.

Restart the browser, navigate to the /Home/Index URL, and click the Get One button again. This time, enter the username **admin** and the password **secret**. These credentials are for a user who has been assigned to the admins role, which means that the authorization filter will allow the request to pass to the next stage of the dispatch process.

Removing the Authentication Filter

The type ordering of filters ensures that the authentication filter runs before the authorization filter, even when they have the same scope. (I explained filter scope in Chapter 23.) If you look at the Visual Studio Output window, you will see that the pipeline information written out by the PipelineActionSelector class I created previously confirms the authentication before authorization sequencing.

This ordering allows me to create an authorization filter that builds on the authentication process, without having to worry about where the IPrincipal objects are coming from. The drawback of depending on an authentication filter is that I have to make sure that I apply two filters every time I want to perform authorization.

A more common approach is to create a message handler that will perform authentication earlier in the dispatch process so that the authorization filter can be applied on its own, without needing an accompanying authentication filter. Listing 24-3 shows the contents of the AuthenticationDispatcher.cs file that I added to the Infrastructure folder and used to define an authenticating message handler.

Listing 24-3. The Contents of the AuthenticationDispatcher.cs File

```
using System;
using System.Net;
using System.Net.Http;
using System.Net.Http.Headers;
using System.Text;
using System.Threading;
using System.Threading.Tasks;

namespace Dispatch.Infrastructure {
    public class AuthenticationDispatcher : DelegatingHandler {

        protected override async Task<HttpResponseMessage> SendAsync(
                HttpRequestMessage request,
                CancellationToken cancellationToken) {

            AuthenticationHeaderValue authentication = request.Headers.Authorization;
            if (authentication != null && authentication.Scheme == "Basic") {
                string[] authData =
                    Encoding.ASCII.GetString(Convert.FromBase64String(
                        authentication.Parameter)).Split(':');
                request.GetRequestContext().Principal
                    = StaticUserManager.AuthenticateUser(authData[0], authData[1]);
            }

            HttpResponseMessage response = await base.SendAsync(request,
                cancellationToken);
            if (response.StatusCode == HttpStatusCode.Unauthorized) {
                response.Headers.Add("WWW-Authenticate", "Basic");
            }
            return response;
        }

    }
}
```

This filter uses the same basic code I applied in the authentication filter in Chapter 24 but arranged in a different way. I still check for the Authorization header and use it to authenticate the request if it is present, but I don't terminate the dispatch process for requests that cannot be validated. This allows requests to flow unhindered through the application to reach action methods open to anyone but still provides the authorization filter with the information it needs.

In addition to authenticating requests, the message handler inspects responses and adds a WWW-Authenticate header to 401 (Unauthorized) responses to give the client the information it needs to try again. Listing 24-4 shows how I registered the authenticating message handler in the WebApiConfig.cs file.

Listing 24-4. Registering a Message Handler in the WebApiConfig.cs File

```
using System.Web.Http;
using System.Web.Http.Controllers;
using Dispatch.Infrastructure;

namespace Dispatch {
    public static class WebApiConfig {
        public static void Register(HttpConfiguration config) {

            config.Routes.MapHttpRoute(
                name: "ActionMethods",
                routeTemplate: "api/nrest/{controller}/{action}/{day}",
                defaults: new { day = RouteParameter.Optional }
            );

            config.Routes.MapHttpRoute(
                name: "DefaultApi",
                routeTemplate: "api/{controller}/{id}",
                defaults: new { id = RouteParameter.Optional }
            );

            config.Services.Replace(typeof(IHttpActionSelector),
                new PipelineActionSelector());

            config.Filters.Add(new SayHelloAttribute { Message = "Global Filter" });

            config.MessageHandlers.Add(new AuthenticationDispatcher());
        }
    }
}
```

I can now remove the authentication filter from the action method in the Products controller and rely on just the authorization filter, as illustrated by Listing 24-5.

Listing 24-5. Removing the Authentication Filter from the ProductsController.cs File

```
...
//[CustomAuthentication]
[CustomAuthorization("admins")]
public Product Get(int id) {
    return products.Where(x => x.ProductID == id).FirstOrDefault();
}
...
```

■ **Tip** The authentication filter I created in Chapter 24 can still be useful because it restricts access to any authenticated user, which is a common requirement, especially for paid-for services. In the "Reworking the Authentication Filter" section, I revisit the authentication filter and rework it to take advantage of the message handler.

Retesting the Authorization Filter

The simplest way to test the effect of the message handler is to give the browser the basic credentials that you want to test as part of the URL. Start the application and use the browser to request the following URL, taking care to change the port number to correspond to the one your application is running on:

```
http://admin:secret@localhost:49412/Home/Index
```

The part of the URL that I have highlighted tells the browser to use the specified credentials if basic authentication is required. Click the Get One button, and the client-side jQuery code will send an Ajax request to the web service.

The request does not contain any credentials, so the authorization filter will short-circuit the dispatch process and return a 401 (Unauthorized) response, to which the authentication message handler will add a `WWW-Authenticate` header telling the client that basic authentication is required.

The browser will automatically resend the request using the credentials you provided in the URL without notifying jQuery. The message handler will process the `Authorization` header and create the `IPrincipal` object, which allows the authorization filter to validate the request.

To see the effect of a request from a user who is not allowed to access the action method, request the following URL:

```
http://bob:secret@localhost:49412/Home/Index
```

Clicking the Get One button will repeat the sequence of requests but still produce a 401 (Unauthorized) result because the bob has not been assigned to the admins role, which is the policy that the authorization filter enforces.

Using the Built-in Authorization Filter Attributes

Two built-in filter classes allow you to perform authorization without needing to implement a class directly from the `IAuthorizationFilter` interface. The first is the `AuthorizationFilterAttribute` class, defined in the `System.Web.Http.Filters` namespace; this class makes it possible to write a filter without worrying about continuations, much like the `ActionFilterAttribute` class I described in Chapter 23 does for action filters. The `AuthorizationFilterAttribute` class defines the method shown in Table 24-5.

Table 24-5. *The Method Defined by the AuthorizationFilterAttribute Class*

Name	Description
OnAuthorizationAsync	This method is overridden to implement the authorization policy.

There is little reason to use the `AuthorizationFilterAttribute` class because the other built-in class, which I describe in the next section, is simpler to work with; however, for completeness, Listing 24-6 shows how I have reworked the `CustomAuthorizationAttribute` class so that it is derived from `AuthorizationFilterAttribute`.

Listing 24-6. Deriving from AuthorizationFilterAttribute in the CustomAuthorizationAttribute.cs File

```
using System.Linq;
using System.Net;
using System.Net.Http;
using System.Security.Principal;
using System.Threading;
using System.Threading.Tasks;
using System.Web.Http.Controllers;
using System.Web.Http.Filters;

namespace Dispatch.Infrastructure {

    public class CustomAuthorizationAttribute : AuthorizationFilterAttribute {
        private string[] roles;

        public CustomAuthorizationAttribute(params string[] rolesList) {
            roles = rolesList;
        }

        public override Task OnAuthorizationAsync(HttpActionContext actionContext,
                CancellationToken cancellationToken) {

            IPrincipal principal = actionContext.RequestContext.Principal;
            if (principal == null || !roles.Any(role => principal.IsInRole(role))) {
                actionContext.Response =
                    actionContext.Request.CreateResponse(HttpStatusCode.Unauthorized);
            }
            return Task.FromResult<object>(null);
        }
    }
}
```

When deriving from the `AuthorizationFilterAttribute` class, the `OnAuthorizationAsync` method short-circuits the dispatch process by setting the `Response` property of the `HttpActionContext` parameter. For requests that pass the authorization policy, no response is set, and the request continues through the dispatch pipeline.

Using the Authorize Attribute

The reason that there is little reason to use the `AuthorizationFilterAttribute` class is because Web API includes an `Authorize` filter that has built-in support for creating a policy to restrict access to specific users and roles without needing any coding at all. The `Authorize` attribute defines the configuration properties shown in Table 24-6.

Table 24-6. *The Properties Defined by the Authorize Attribute*

Name	Description
Roles	A comma-separated list of roles that are allowed to access the action method
Users	A comma-separated list of users who are allowed to access the action method

The Authorize attribute works in the same way as the custom attributes I defined and relies on another—unspecified—component in the dispatch process to authenticate the requests. Listing 24-7 shows how I have replaced my custom authorization attribute with the built-in one in the Products controller.

Listing 24-7. Using the Built-in Authorize Attribute in the ProductsController.cs File

```
...
//[CustomAuthentication]
//[CustomAuthorization("admins")]
[Authorize(Roles="admins")]
public Product Get(int id) {
    return products.Where(x => x.ProductID == id).FirstOrDefault();
}
...
```

The effect is the same as for my custom filter but without the need to write any custom code.

■ **Note** You might be wondering why I have taken the long way around to reach the point where I demonstrate the simplest way to perform authorization checks. There are two reasons. First, the Authorize attribute relies on another component to perform authentication, and I wanted to explain how to achieve this before introducing the Authorize filter. Second, by understanding how authorization works behind the scenes, you are less likely to be caught out when the Authorize attribute doesn't work the way you expect, which is not uncommon when working with user management systems such as ASP.NET Identity. These systems are complex and often counterintuitive, and the more you understand about how they integrate into Web API, the less likely you are to encounter problems.

Reworking the Authentication Filter

I want to tidy up one loose end before moving on: when the authentication filter that I created in Chapter 23 is applied, authentication will be performed twice, once in the filter and again in message handler. Listing 24-8 shows how I have revised the CustomAuthenticationFilter class so that it only enforces the policy of restricting access to authenticated users and relies on the message handler to perform the authentication.

Listing 24-8. Revising the Authentication Policy in the CustomAuthenticationFilter.cs File

```
using System;
using System.Net.Http.Headers;
using System.Threading;
using System.Threading.Tasks;
using System.Web.Http.Filters;
using System.Web.Http.Results;
```

```
namespace Dispatch.Infrastructure {

    public class CustomAuthenticationAttribute : Attribute, IAuthenticationFilter {

        public Task AuthenticateAsync(HttpAuthenticationContext context,
                CancellationToken cancellationToken) {

            if (context.Principal == null
                    || !context.Principal.Identity.IsAuthenticated) {
                context.ErrorResult
                    = new UnauthorizedResult(new AuthenticationHeaderValue[] {
                        new AuthenticationHeaderValue("Basic") }, context.Request);
            }

            return Task.FromResult<object>(null);
        }

        public Task ChallengeAsync(HttpAuthenticationChallengeContext context,
                CancellationToken cancellationToken) {
            return Task.FromResult<object>(null);
        }

        public bool AllowMultiple {
            get { return false; }
        }
    }
}
```

The filter no longer has any knowledge of the mechanism used to authenticate users and simply relies on the IPrincipal objects that the message handler from Listing 24-3 associated with requests. Listing 24-9 shows how I have applied the revised filter to the Products controller.

Listing 24-9. Applying the Revised Authentication Filter to the ProductsController.cs File

```
using System.Collections.Generic;
using System.Linq;
using System.Web.Http;
using Dispatch.Infrastructure;
using Dispatch.Models;

namespace Dispatch.Controllers {

    [Time]
    [CustomAuthentication]
    public class ProductsController : ApiController {
        private static List<Product> products = new List<Product> {
                new Product {ProductID = 1, Name = "Kayak", Price = 275M },
                new Product {ProductID = 2, Name = "Lifejacket", Price = 48.95M },
                new Product {ProductID = 3, Name = "Soccer Ball", Price = 19.50M },
                new Product {ProductID = 4, Name = "Thinking Cap", Price = 16M },
            };
```

```
[Counter(3)]
public IEnumerable<Product> Get() {
    return products;
}

//[CustomAuthentication]
//[CustomAuthorization("admins")]
[Authorize(Roles="admins")]
public Product Get(int id) {
    return products.Where(x => x.ProductID == id).FirstOrDefault();
}

public Product Post(Product product) {
    product.ProductID = products.Count + 1;
    products.Add(product);
    return product;
}
    }
}
```

The combined effect of the authentication and authorization filters is that requests from any authenticated user can invoke Post and parameterless Get action methods, but only authenticated users who are assigned the admins role are able to invoke the Get action method that accepts a parameter.

Working with Exception Filters

Exception filters are executed only if, as their name suggests, an exception is thrown by the action method or another filter; they are used to translate that exception into a response that will be sent to the client. As I demonstrate, the default Web API is to treat exceptions as problems within the server, but that isn't always helpful. Table 24-7 puts exception filters into context.

Table 24-7. Putting Exception Filters in Context

Question	Answer
What are they?	Exception filters are executed when an exception is thrown by the action method or another filter.
When should you use them?	Exception filters are useful for replacing the default response with one that gives the client more information about the problem and what actions may be taken to remedy it.
What do you need to know?	Throwing an HttpResponseException bypasses the exception filters, as I explain in Chapter 25.

Understanding the Default Behavior

Before I get into the detail of exception filters, I need to create a source of exceptions. Listing 24-10 shows the modifications I made to the Products controller so that I can generate exceptions on demand. (I also removed the filters from earlier examples to simplify the code.)

Listing 24-10. Throwing Exceptions in the ProductsController.cs File

```
using System.Collections.Generic;
using System.Linq;
using System.Web.Http;
using Dispatch.Infrastructure;
using Dispatch.Models;

namespace Dispatch.Controllers {

    public class ProductsController : ApiController {
        private static List<Product> products = new List<Product> {
                new Product {ProductID = 1, Name = "Kayak", Price = 275M },
                //new Product {ProductID = 2, Name = "Lifejacket", Price = 48.95M },
                //new Product {ProductID = 3, Name = "Soccer Ball", Price = 19.50M },
                //new Product {ProductID = 4, Name = "Thinking Cap", Price = 16M },
                };

        public IEnumerable<Product> Get() {
            return products;
        }

        public Product Get(int id) {
            return products[id];
            //return products.Where(x => x.ProductID == id).FirstOrDefault();
        }

        public Product Post(Product product) {
            product.ProductID = products.Count + 1;
            products.Add(product);
            return product;
        }
    }
}
```

I have commented out several of the statements that define data objects and changed the version of the Get action method that accepts a parameter so that the value of the parameter is treated as an index into the data collection.

To see the effect of the change, start the application, navigate to the /Home/Index URL with the browser, and click the Get One button. The URL that the client requests when the Get One button is clicked is /api/products/2, which is out of the data collection bounds. The overall effect is that the client receives a 500 (Internal Server Error), as shown in Figure 24-2.

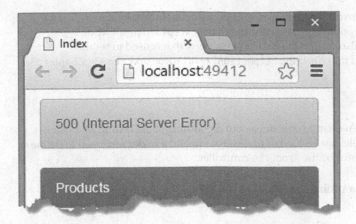

Figure 24-2. *The default error-handling behavior*

If you use the F12 developer tools, you will see that the response from the web service is a JSON object that contains details about the exception that was thrown, as follows:

```
{"Message" : "An error has occurred.",
"ExceptionMessage" : "Index was outside the bounds of the array.",
"ExceptionType":"System.IndexOutOfRangeException",
"StackTrace":"at Dispatch.Controllers.ProductsController.Get(Int32 id) in ..."}
```

I'll come back to the JSON object and explain its use in Chapter 25, but for this chapter, the key point to note is that the default behavior when an exception is thrown is to send a 500 (Internal Server Error) response.

Understanding Exception Filters

Treating all exceptions the same by sending a 500 (Internal Server Error) response is a catchall strategy that doesn't always make sense, especially if you are using code that uses exceptions to signal outcomes that are not server-side problems. In the case of Products controller in the previous section, the client is requesting a data object that doesn't exist, and returning a 500 (Internal Server Error) response isn't entirely helpful because it indicates that the request couldn't be processed because of some problem within the server, rather than a problem with the request. An exception filter can be used to override the default behavior and return a more meaningful and useful response to the client.

Exception filters are derived from the IExceptionFilter interface, which is defined in the System.Web.Http. Filters namespace. Here is the definition:

```
using System.Threading;
using System.Threading.Tasks;

namespace System.Web.Http.Filters {

    public interface IExceptionFilter : IFilter {

        Task ExecuteExceptionFilterAsync(HttpActionExecutedContext actionExecutedContext,
            CancellationToken cancellationToken);
    }
}
```

613

The ExecuteExceptionFilterAsync method is invoked when an exception has been thrown by the action method or by another filter. Details of the exception are accessed through the Exception property of the HttpActionExecutedContext parameter, which also defines the Response property that is used to set the HttpResponseMessage that will be sent to the client. (I described the HttpActionExecutedContext class in Chapter 23.)

Creating an Exception Filter

Exception filters can create a new response, modify an existing one, or elect to do nothing at all. Listing 24-11 shows the contents of the CustomExceptionAttribute.cs file that I added to the Infrastructure folder and used to define an exception filter that will handle the exception thrown by the Products controller.

Listing 24-11. The Contents of the CustomExceptionAttribute.cs File

```
using System;
using System.Net;
using System.Net.Http;
using System.Threading;
using System.Threading.Tasks;
using System.Web.Http.Filters;

namespace Dispatch.Infrastructure {
    public class CustomExceptionAttribute : Attribute, IExceptionFilter {

        public Task ExecuteExceptionFilterAsync(HttpActionExecutedContext
            actionExecutedContext, CancellationToken cancellationToken) {

            if (actionExecutedContext.Exception != null
                && actionExecutedContext.Exception is ArgumentOutOfRangeException) {
                    actionExecutedContext.Response =
                        actionExecutedContext.Request.CreateErrorResponse(
                            HttpStatusCode.BadRequest, "No data item");
            }
            return Task.FromResult<object>(null);
        }

        public bool AllowMultiple {
            get { return true; }
        }
    }
}
```

Unlike the other filter interfaces, there are no continuation functions or even method results required in the ExecuteExceptionFilterAsync method. When the method is called, I check that the HttpActionExecutedContext.Exception property has been set and that it is an instance of the exception that I am interested in: the ArgumentOutOfRangeException class.

I create an HttpResponseMessage using the HttpRequestMessage.CreateError message extension method and use it to set the HttpActionExecutedContext.Response property, which allows me to change the 500 (Internal Server Error) response to a more helpful 401 (Bad Request) response. Listing 24-12 shows how I applied the exception filter to the Products controller.

Listing 24-12. Applying an Exception Filter in the ProductsController.cs File

```
...
[CustomException]
public Product Get(int id) {
    return products[id];
    //return products.Where(x => x.ProductID == id).FirstOrDefault();
}
...
```

Exception filters are applied just like other filter types and can be used for specific action methods or an entire controller or registered as global filters so that they affect the entire application.

To see the effect, start the application, use the browser to navigate to the /Home/Index URL, and click the Get One button. The new response is shown in Figure 24-3.

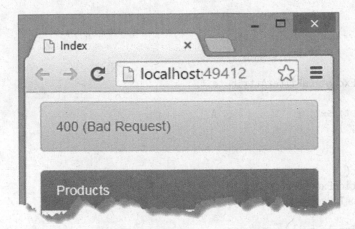

Figure 24-3. Using an exception filter to change the response

If you use the F12 developer tools, you will see that the string I passed to the CreateErrorResponse method like this:

```
...
actionExecutedContext.Request.CreateErrorResponse(HttpStatusCode.BadRequest,
    "No data item");
...
```

is used to create the JSON object that is included in the following response:

```
{"Message":"No data item"}
```

I return to the JSON object, and the broader Web API error handling, in Chapter 25.

Deriving the Filter from the ExceptionFilterAttribute Class

The ExceptionFilterAttribute class can be used as the base for exception filters, although since the IExceptionFilter interface doesn't require the use of continuation functions, the main benefit is consistency with other types of custom filter. The ExceptionFilterAttribute class defines the method shown in Table 24-8.

Table 24-8. *The Method Defined by the ExceptionFilterAttribute Class*

Name	Description
OnExceptionAsync	This method is overridden to handle exceptions thrown by the action method or by other filters.

Listing 24-13 shows how I have updated the custom exception filter class so that it is derived from ExceptionFilterAttribute. I have also made the class configurable so that it can be configured to map from exception types to HTTP results when it is applied.

Listing 24-13. Changing the Base Type in the CustomExceptionAttribute.cs File

```
using System;
using System.Net;
using System.Net.Http;
using System.Threading;
using System.Threading.Tasks;
using System.Web.Http.Filters;

namespace Dispatch.Infrastructure {
    public class CustomExceptionAttribute : ExceptionFilterAttribute {

        public HttpStatusCode StatusCode { get; set; }
        public Type ExceptionType { get; set; }
        public string Message { get; set; }

        public override Task OnExceptionAsync(
                HttpActionExecutedContext actionExecutedContext,
                CancellationToken cancellationToken) {

            if (actionExecutedContext.Exception != null
                && actionExecutedContext.Exception.GetType() == ExceptionType) {
                actionExecutedContext.Response
                    = actionExecutedContext.Request.CreateErrorResponse(StatusCode,
                        Message);
            }
            return Task.FromResult<object>(null);
        }
    }
}
```

The basic technique in this filter is the same as when I derived directly from the IExceptionFilter interface, except that I have extracted the exception type, the HTTP status code, and the message to be included in the JSON object into properties. Listing 24-14 shows how I have changed the application of the filter to the Products controller to set the property values.

Listing 24-14. Changing the Application of the Exception Filter in the ProductsController.cs File

```
using System.Collections.Generic;
using System.Linq;
using System.Web.Http;
using Dispatch.Infrastructure;
using Dispatch.Models;
```

```
using System.Net;
using System;

namespace Dispatch.Controllers {

    public class ProductsController : ApiController {
        private static List<Product> products = new List<Product> {
            new Product {ProductID = 1, Name = "Kayak", Price = 275M },
            //new Product {ProductID = 2, Name = "Lifejacket", Price = 48.95M },
            //new Product {ProductID = 3, Name = "Soccer Ball", Price = 19.50M },
            //new Product {ProductID = 4, Name = "Thinking Cap", Price = 16M },
        };

        public IEnumerable<Product> Get() {
            return products;
        }

        [CustomException(ExceptionType=typeof(ArgumentOutOfRangeException),
            StatusCode=HttpStatusCode.BadRequest, Message="No such index")]
        public Product Get(int id) {
            return products[id];
            //return products.Where(x => x.ProductID == id).FirstOrDefault();
        }

        public Product Post(Product product) {
            product.ProductID = products.Count + 1;
            products.Add(product);
            return product;
        }
    }
}
```

■ **Tip**   If you are dealing with a lot of exceptions, then consider using the *global error handling* feature, which I describe in Chapter 25.

Working with Override Filters

In Chapter 23, I explained that filters have scope. This is a useful feature that means you don't have to apply a filter to every single action method on which you want to apply. I also demonstrated how to create global filters that are applied to all the action methods in the application.

A *filter override* allows you to disable one or more filters for an action method. This allows you to still benefit from controller and global scopes but selectively disable filters to create different behaviors for specific action methods. Table 24-9 puts overriding filters in context.

Table 24-9. *Putting Overriding Filters in Context*

Question	Answer
What are they?	Override filters disable higher-scoped filters of a given type.
When should you use them?	Use an override when you want to vary the filter pipeline for a single action method so that controller-level and global filters won't be executed.
What do you need to know?	Override filters do not affect filters applied at the same scope, as demonstrated in the "Redefining Filter Policies" section.

Overriding Built-in Filter Types

Override filters implement the `IOverrideFilter` interface, which is defined in the `System.Web.Http.Filters` namespace. Here is the interface:

```
namespace System.Web.Http.Filters {

    public interface IOverrideFilter : IFilter {

        Type FiltersToOverride { get; }
    }
}
```

The `FiltersToOverride` propertyreturns the type of filter that is to be overridden. To apply an override, use one of the built-in filter classes that I have shown in Table 24-10. Each override filter attribute affects one type of filter.

Table 24-10. *The Built-in Override Filter Attributes*

Name	Description
OverrideAuthenticationFilters	Prevents authentication filters from being executed
OverrideAuthorizationFilters	Prevents authorization filters from being executed
OverrideActionFilters	Prevents action filters from being executed
OverrideExceptionFilters	Prevents exception filters from being executed

■ **Tip** Unlike the other filter types, there is no benefit in creating a custom override filter. This is because the class that ApiController uses to handle overrides (the FilterGrouping class) checks only for each filter type and not the types they are derived from. This means it is possible to override filters that implement the IExceptionFilter interface, for example, but not IFilter. The built-in override filter classes shown in the table encapsulate the complete range of functionality that the IOverrideFilter interface can be used for.

Listing 24-15 shows how I applied an authorization filter to the Products controller so that it applies to all of the action methods and then applies the OverrideAuthorizationFilters attribute to disable authorization for one of them. (The authentication for requests is still being handled by the HTTP Basic authentication message handler that I created earlier in the chapter.)

Listing 24-15. Overriding Controller-wide Authorization in the ProductsController.cs File

```
using System.Collections.Generic;
using System.Linq;
using System.Web.Http;
using Dispatch.Infrastructure;
using Dispatch.Models;
using System.Net;
using System;

namespace Dispatch.Controllers {

    [Authorize(Roles="admins")]
    public class ProductsController : ApiController {
        private static List<Product> products = new List<Product> {
                new Product {ProductID = 1, Name = "Kayak", Price = 275M },
                //new Product {ProductID = 2, Name = "Lifejacket", Price = 48.95M },
                //new Product {ProductID = 3, Name = "Soccer Ball", Price = 19.50M },
                //new Product {ProductID = 4, Name = "Thinking Cap", Price = 16M },
            };

        [OverrideAuthorization]
        public IEnumerable<Product> Get() {
            return products;
        }

        [CustomException(ExceptionType=typeof(ArgumentOutOfRangeException),
            StatusCode=HttpStatusCode.BadRequest, Message="No such index")]
        public Product Get(int id) {
            return products[id];
            //return products.Where(x => x.ProductID == id).FirstOrDefault();
        }

        public Product Post(Product product) {
            product.ProductID = products.Count + 1;
            products.Add(product);
            return product;
        }
    }
}
```

The effect of the Authorize attribute is to restrict all of the action methods in the Products controller so they can be accessed only by authenticated users who have been assigned to the admins role.

The effect of applying the OverrideAuthorization attribute to the parameterless version of the Get action method is to prevent execution of all authorization filters for that action method, which means that any request is able to invoke the action.

Redefining Filter Policies

The clever part of the override filters is that they affect filters only at the previous scope, which means you can apply attributes of the overridden type at the same level as the override, and they will be executed. As an example, Listing 24-16 shows how I have applied the Authorize attribute alongside the OverrideAuthorization attribute in the Products controller.

Listing 24-16. Redefining Authorization in the ProductsController.cs File

```
using System.Collections.Generic;
using System.Linq;
using System.Web.Http;
using Dispatch.Infrastructure;
using Dispatch.Models;
using System.Net;
using System;

namespace Dispatch.Controllers {

    [Authorize(Roles="admins")]
    public class ProductsController : ApiController {
        private static List<Product> products = new List<Product> {
                new Product {ProductID = 1, Name = "Kayak", Price = 275M },
                //new Product {ProductID = 2, Name = "Lifejacket", Price = 48.95M },
                //new Product {ProductID = 3, Name = "Soccer Ball", Price = 19.50M },
                //new Product {ProductID = 4, Name = "Thinking Cap", Price = 16M },
            };

        [OverrideAuthorization]
        [Authorize(Roles="users")]
        public IEnumerable<Product> Get() {
            return products;
        }

        [CustomException(ExceptionType=typeof(ArgumentOutOfRangeException),
            StatusCode=HttpStatusCode.BadRequest, Message="No such index")]
        public Product Get(int id) {
            return products[id];
            //return products.Where(x => x.ProductID == id).FirstOrDefault();
        }

        public Product Post(Product product) {
            product.ProductID = products.Count + 1;
            products.Add(product);
            return product;
        }
    }
}
```

I have applied the `Authorize` filter to the `Get` method, specifying that only authenticated users who have been assigned to the `users` role are allowed to invoke the action method. Without the `OverrideAuthorization` attribute, the filter pipeline would contain both `Authorize` attributes, and they would be executed one after the other, creating a combined effect of restricting access to those users who have been assigned to both the `admins` and `users` roles.

But *with* the `OverrideAuthorization`, the controller-scoped `Authorize` attribute is removed from the pipeline, meaning that only the `Authorize` filter applied directly to the action method will be used: the effect is to restrict access to the `users` role.

Summary

In this chapter, I finished describing the Web API support for filters by explaining how authentication and exception filters work. I also demonstrated how override filters can be used to prevent the execution of filters that have been applied at the global and controller scopes, allowing filtering to be disabled or redefined for an action method.

CHAPTER 25

■ ■ ■

Error Handling

In this chapter, I complete my description of the Web API dispatch process by showing how errors are handled. I'll show you the different ways you can deal with problems that you anticipate during development and what happens when unexpected problems arise. I explain how to control the response that is sent to the client and how to manage and log unhandled exceptions for the entire application. Table 25-1 summarizes this chapter.

Table 25-1. *Chapter Summary*

Problem	Solution	Listing
Trigger the default error handling policy.	Throw an exception from an action method or filter.	1–3
Throw an exception that generates a specific result status code.	Throw an instance of HttpResponseException.	4
Return a response for error that has been anticipated.	Return an implementation of the IHttpActionResult interface.	5
Control the additional data that is sent to the client when an error occurs.	Use an HttpError object.	6–9
Control how information is sent to the client for an unhandled exception.	Set the HttpConfiguration. IncludeErrorDetailPolicy property.	10
Receive additional error data at the client.	Read the jqXHR.responseJSON property to get a JavaScript object decoded from the response and display the Message property, if it exists, to the user.	11
Change the default policy for dealing with unhandled exceptions.	Create a global exception handler.	12–14
Log unhandled exceptions.	Create a global exception logger.	15–16

Preparing the Example Project

I am going to continue working with the Dispatch project I created in Chapter 19. To prepare for this chapter, I have the removed filters from the Products controller, as shown in Listing 25-1.

Listing 25-1. The Contents of the ProductsController.cs File

```
using System;
using System.Collections.Generic;
using System.Linq;
using System.Net;
using System.Web.Http;
using Dispatch.Infrastructure;
using Dispatch.Models;

namespace Dispatch.Controllers {

    public class ProductsController : ApiController {
        private static List<Product> products = new List<Product> {
                new Product {ProductID = 1, Name = "Kayak", Price = 275M },
                //new Product {ProductID = 2, Name = "Lifejacket", Price = 48.95M },
                //new Product {ProductID = 3, Name = "Soccer Ball", Price = 19.50M },
                //new Product {ProductID = 4, Name = "Thinking Cap", Price = 16M },
        };

        public IEnumerable<Product> Get() {
            return products;
        }

        [LogErrors]
        public Product Get(int id) {
            return products[id];
            //return products.Where(x => x.ProductID == id).FirstOrDefault();
        }

        public Product Post(Product product) {
            product.ProductID = products.Count + 1;
            products.Add(product);
            return product;
        }
    }
}
```

I have applied a LogErrors attribute to one of the Get action methods in the Product controller. This is the application of a simple exception filter that I defined by adding a LogErrorsAttribute.cs file to the Infrastructure folder and defining the class shown in Listing 25-2.

Listing 25-2. The Contents of the LogErrorsAttribute.cs File

```
using System;
using System.Diagnostics;
using System.Threading;
using System.Threading.Tasks;
using System.Web.Http.Filters;
```

```
namespace Dispatch.Infrastructure {
    public class LogErrorsAttribute : Attribute, IExceptionFilter {
        public Task ExecuteExceptionFilterAsync(HttpActionExecutedContext
            actionExecutedContext, CancellationToken cancellationToken) {

            Debug.WriteLine(string.Format(
                "Exception Type: {0}", actionExecutedContext.Exception.Message));
            Debug.WriteLine(string.Format(
                "Exception Message: {0}", actionExecutedContext.Exception.GetType()));

            return Task.FromResult<object>(null);
        }

        public bool AllowMultiple {
            get { return false; }
        }
    }
}
```

The filter writes out the message and type of exceptions that it is asked to process, which I will use to highlight differences in the way that some errors are processed. Finally, I have updated the WebApiConfig.cs file to comment out the custom classes that I added in earlier chapters. Listing 25-3 shows the revised configuration.

Listing 25-3. The Contents of the WebApiConfig.cs File

```
using System.Web.Http;
using System.Web.Http.Controllers;
using Dispatch.Infrastructure;

namespace Dispatch {
    public static class WebApiConfig {
        public static void Register(HttpConfiguration config) {

            config.Routes.MapHttpRoute(
                name: "ActionMethods",
                routeTemplate: "api/nrest/{controller}/{action}/{day}",
                defaults: new { day = RouteParameter.Optional }
            );

            config.Routes.MapHttpRoute(
                name: "DefaultApi",
                routeTemplate: "api/{controller}/{id}",
                defaults: new { id = RouteParameter.Optional }
            );

            //config.Services.Replace(typeof(IHttpActionSelector),
            //    new PipelineActionSelector());
            //config.Filters.Add(new SayHelloAttribute { Message = "Global Filter" });
            //config.MessageHandlers.Add(new AuthenticationDispatcher());
        }
    }
}
```

Dealing with Errors

All web services will run into problems, but what separates the good applications from the bad is the way that you deal with those problems and how you present them to the client and user.

In broad terms, there are two kinds of errors: the ones you anticipated during development and the ones that catch you by surprise in production. Careful coding and thorough testing can help minimize surprises, but you can't foresee every issue. It is important to have a plan to deal with the problems you anticipate *and* have a fallback position for responding to the ones you don't see coming. Web API provides features for dealing with both kinds of problem, as I explain in the sections that follow. Table 25-2 puts the Web API error handling support into context.

Table 25-2. *Putting Error Handling in Context*

Question	Answer
What is it?	Exception handling is the process of responding to problems and exceptions so that they are presented to clients via HTTP responses.
When should you use it?	You should handle as many problems as possible within action methods and filters and rely on the default behavior as little as you can.
What do you need to know?	You can change the default behavior by implementing a new global exception handler, as I describe in the "Responding to Errors Globally" section.

Relying on the Default Behavior

The simplest way to deal with problems is to ignore them and let the default behavior take care of generating a response for the client, which is to send a 500 (Internal Server Error) status code along with some diagnostic data.

To see the default behavior, start the application and use the browser to navigate to the /Home/Index URL. Click the Get One button to send the Ajax request that will invoke the Get action method. The value of the id parameter taken from the requested URL exceeds the number of data items available, which causes an exception to be thrown. The exception is expressed to the client as a 500 (Internal Server) response, as shown in Figure 25-1.

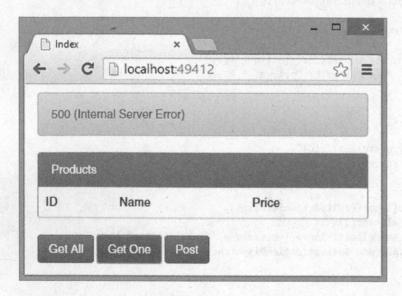

Figure 25-1. *The default Web API exception handling*

Relying on the default behavior is the least useful thing you can do, and it should be relied on only for unforeseen problems. The issue is that the 500 (Internal Server Error) status code conveys no useful information to the client except that the request could not be processed.

When I see a 500 status code, I am reminded of a car that my mother used to drive. It was an old Peugeot and had a red STOP light on the dashboard that came on whenever the car detected a problem. The light would come on for everything from an interior lightbulb blowing to a serious engine fault, and there was no way to tell whether it was safe to continue and fix the problem tomorrow or whether you should pull to the side of the road and call a fire truck. The 500 status code is like the STOP light: it doesn't convey any useful information beyond a problem having occurred. It does not explain what caused the problem, how severe the problem is, or how the problem might be resolved.

To deal with the lack of context, Web API includes additional data in the response body, like this:

```
{"Message":"An error has occurred.",
 "ExceptionMessage":"Index was out of range. Must be non-negative and less than the
      size of the collection.\r\nParameter name: index",
 "ExceptionType":"System.ArgumentOutOfRangeException",
 "StackTrace":"   at System.ThrowHelper.ThrowArgumentOutOfRangeException() at
      System.Collections.Generic.List`1.get_Item(Int32 index)\r\n   at
      Dispatch.Controllers.ProductsController.Get(Int32 id) in ..."}
```

I explain how this part of the response is created and formatted in the "Using the HttpError Class" section, but for now, it is enough to know that the client is sent four pieces of information.

- A message that describes the problem

- The message from the exception

- The .NET type of the exception

- The stack trace (which I have edited for brevity)

This appears more useful than it is in reality. The information is vague ("an error has occurred" is no more informative than the response status code) and contains information that is only of use to the web service developer.

Finally, as you would expect from having read Chapter 24, the LogErrors exception filter that I applied at the start of the chapter is executed, which produces the following messages in the Visual Studio Output window:

```
Exception Type: Index was out of range. Must be non-negative and less than the size of the collection.
Parameter name: index
Exception Message: System.ArgumentOutOfRangeException
```

Throwing a Special Exception

The default behavior is applied when an action method throws an exception (or fails to catch an exception thrown by code it calls), but there is one type of exception that does not trigger the default behavior: HttpResponseException. The constructor for the HttpResponseException class takes an HttpStatusCode parameter, which is used as the status code for the HTTP response. Listing 25-4 shows how I applied the HttpResponseException to the Get action of the Products controller.

Listing 25-4. Applying the HttpResponseException in the ProductsController.cs File

```csharp
using System;
using System.Collections.Generic;
using System.Linq;
using System.Net;
using System.Web.Http;
using Dispatch.Infrastructure;
using Dispatch.Models;

namespace Dispatch.Controllers {

    public class ProductsController : ApiController {
        private static List<Product> products = new List<Product> {
                new Product {ProductID = 1, Name = "Kayak", Price = 275M },
                //new Product {ProductID = 2, Name = "Lifejacket", Price = 48.95M },
                new Product {ProductID = 3, Name = "Soccer Ball", Price = 19.50M },
                new Product {ProductID = 4, Name = "Thinking Cap", Price = 16M },
        };

        public IEnumerable<Product> Get() {
            return products;
        }

        [LogErrors]
        public Product Get(int id) {
            Product product = products.Where(x => x.ProductID == id).FirstOrDefault();
            if (product == null) {
                throw new HttpResponseException(HttpStatusCode.BadRequest);
            }
            return product;
        }

        public Product Post(Product product) {
            product.ProductID = products.Count + 1;
            products.Add(product);
            return product;
        }
    }
}
```

I have taken a more nuanced approach to the implementation of the action method, using LINQ to try to locate a Product object with the ID specified by the client. If there is no match, then I throw a new HttpResponseException with the 400 (Bad Request) status code.

The way that HttpResponseException is handled by Web API is different from all other exceptions. Most importantly, exception filters are not executed. This is because the ApiControllerActionInvoker class (which is the default implementation of the IHttpActionInvoker interface, as I explained in Chapter 22) explicitly catches instances of HttpResponseException and processes them to create an HttpResponseMessage object before the normal error handling is executed.

Using an Implementation of the IHttpActionResult Interface

For problems you are expecting—especially those caused by a problem with the request—you can follow the standard approach available through the ApiController base class and return an object that implements the IHttpActionResult interface. Listing 25-5 shows how I reworked the Get action method in the Products controller to return this kind of result if the requested data object doesn't exist.

Listing 25-5. Returning an IHttpActionResult in the ProductsController.cs File

```
...
[LogErrors]
public IHttpActionResult Get(int id) {
    Product product = products.Where(x => x.ProductID == id).FirstOrDefault();
    if (product == null) {
        return BadRequest("No such data object");
    }
    return Ok(product);
}
...
```

I find this approach feels less natural than using an HttpResponseException because the result from the action method has to be IHttpActionResult in order to allow successful and error results to be produced, although this is mitigated a little by the convenience methods that the ApiController class provides for creating results, such as Ok and BadRequest. When you use convenience methods, such as BadRequest, the string argument is included in the body of the response sent to the client, like this:

```
{"Message":"No such data object"}
```

To see this data, start the application, use the browser to navigate to the /Home/Index URL, and click the Get One button. Using the F12 tools, you will be able to see that the response contains a JSON object with a Message property.

Using the HttpError Class

The content in the body of an error HTTP response is controlled by the HttpError class, which has been created and populated behind the scenes in the previous examples. You can get more direct control over the way in which errors are expressed to the client by creating an HttpResponseMessage object within the action method and providing an HttpError object with the information you want included in the response body.

■ **Tip** The HttpError object is subject to serialization through media type formatters, which I described in Part 2. This means the format will adapt to the client's preferences, which is why the HttpError objects I create in this chapter are all expressed as JSON. See Part 2 for how objects are serialized and how the client specifies which formats it prefers to deal with.

I am showing you how to use the HttpError object to send data to the client for completeness, but the data itself is of limited use. HTTP web service clients are required to deal only with the response status code, and there is no standard for the body data and how it should be used. You should take care to ensure that the response status code accurately reflects the nature of the problem and not rely on the client being able to parse and respond to any additional information you have chosen to include.

Additional data can be helpful during development when you are responsible for creating the web service and the client, but I find it more helpful to use the Visual Studio debugger and the browser F12 tools to figure out what is happening when things go wrong. Table 25-3 puts the HttpError object into context.

Table 25-3. *Putting the HttpError Class in Context*

Question	Answer
What is it?	The HttpError class is used to send additional data to the client when something goes wrong.
When should you use it?	The HttpError class is used automatically when Web API handles uncaught exceptions, but you can also create instances directly for use with HttpResponseMessage objects.
What do you need to know?	There is no agreed standard on how web services send error data to the client, and the default data sent by Web API is generally of use only to developers.

Using an Error Response and an HttpError Object

The HttpError class, which is defined in the System.Web.Http namespace, defines the properties shown in Table 25-4.

Table 25-4. *The Properties Defined by the HttpError Class*

Name	Description
ExceptionMessage	Gets or sets a descriptive string, usually used to hold the message from the exception that the HttpError represents.
ExceptionType	Gets or sets the type of the exception that the HttpError represents, expressed as a string.
InnerException	Gets or sets an HttpError that represents a nested error.
Message	Gets or sets the user-readable message that describes the problem the HttpError object represents, expressed as a string.
MessageDetail	Gets or sets a message intended for the client developer that describes the error the HttpError represents, expressed as a string.
ModelState	Gets an HttpError that contains details of model validation errors. To set this property, create a new instance of the HttpError class using the constructor that accepts a ModelStateDictionary object. See the "Including Model State Errors in the HTTP Response" section for a demonstration.
StackTrace	Gets the stack trace for the error that the HttpError object represents, expressed as a string.

To take control of the data includes in the response body, you create an instance of HttpError, set the properties you want to include, and then create an HttpResponseMessage that will convey the data back through the dispatch chain and to the client. Listing 25-6 shows the use of the HttpError object in the Get action method of the Products controller.

Listing 25-6. Creating an Error Response in the ProductsController.cs File

```
using System;
using System.Collections.Generic;
using System.Linq;
using System.Net;
using System.Web.Http;
using Dispatch.Infrastructure;
using Dispatch.Models;
using System.Net.Http;

namespace Dispatch.Controllers {

    public class ProductsController : ApiController {
        private static List<Product> products = new List<Product> {
                new Product {ProductID = 1, Name = "Kayak", Price = 275M },
                //new Product {ProductID = 2, Name = "Lifejacket", Price = 48.95M },
                new Product {ProductID = 3, Name = "Soccer Ball", Price = 19.50M },
                new Product {ProductID = 4, Name = "Thinking Cap", Price = 16M },
        };

        public IEnumerable<Product> Get() {
            return products;
        }

        [LogErrors]
        public HttpResponseMessage Get(int id) {
            Product product = products.Where(x => x.ProductID == id).FirstOrDefault();
            if (product == null) {
                return Request.CreateErrorResponse(HttpStatusCode.BadRequest,
                    new HttpError {
                        Message = "No such data item",
                        MessageDetail = string.Format("No item ID {0} was found", id)
                });
            }
            return Request.CreateResponse(product);
        }

        public Product Post(Product product) {
            product.ProductID = products.Count + 1;
            products.Add(product);
            return product;
        }
    }
}
```

In the listing, I use the CreateErrorResponse extension method on the HttpRequestMessage object to create an HttpResponseMessage. The version of the CreateErrorResponse method that I used takes an HTTP status code and an HttpError object, for which I set the Message and MessageDetail properties.

You can see how the property values I set in Listing 25-6 are processed by invoking the action method. Start the application, use the browser to navigate to /Home/Index, and click the Get One button. The URL that the client requests will trigger the creation of the error response, and you will see the following data in the response in the browser F12 tools:

```
{"Message":"No such data item","MessageDetail":"No item ID 2 was found"}
```

Adding Extra Information to the HttpError Object

Although the HttpError class defines the set of properties shown in Table 25-4, the class itself is derived from Dictionary<string, object>, which means you can add arbitrary data to the response sent to the client. Listing 25-7 shows how I have modified the Get method in the Product controller to send additional information through the HttpError object.

Listing 25-7. Adding Extra Error Information in the ProductsController.cs File

```
...
[LogErrors]
public HttpResponseMessage Get(int id) {
    Product product = products.Where(x => x.ProductID == id).FirstOrDefault();
    if (product == null) {
        HttpError error = new HttpError();
        error.Message = "No such data item";
        error.Add("RequestID", id);
        error.Add("AvailbleIDs", products.Select(x => x.ProductID));
        return Request.CreateErrorResponse(HttpStatusCode.BadRequest, error);
    }
    return Request.CreateResponse(product);
}
...
```

In this example, I set the Message property described in Table 25-4 and add two custom properties to provide additional information about the error. I include the requested product ID that was received by the action method (which can be useful to check to see whether there have been parameter/model binding errors as the request was processed) and return a list of the IDs of the data objects that are available. Here is the data included in the HTTP response:

```
{"Message":"No such data item","RequestID":2,"AvailbleIDs":[1,3,4]}
```

I don't recommend including lists of valid IDs in real projects because there can be a lot of them to deal with, but it provides a nice demonstration in this chapter of how you can pass arbitrary objects to the HttpError and leave them to be serialized as part of the response (in this case, an IEnumerable<int> that is expressed as an array of numeric values).

Including Model State Errors in the HTTP Response

In Chapter 18, I explained how data validation errors are expressed through model state. You can include model state data in an HttpError object, as shown by Listing 25-8.

Listing 25-8. Adding Model State Data to the Error in the ProductsControllers.cs File

```csharp
using System;
using System.Collections.Generic;
using System.Linq;
using System.Net;
using System.Web.Http;
using Dispatch.Infrastructure;
using Dispatch.Models;
using System.Net.Http;

namespace Dispatch.Controllers {

    public class ProductsController : ApiController {
        private static List<Product> products = new List<Product> {
                new Product {ProductID = 1, Name = "Kayak", Price = 275M },
                //new Product {ProductID = 2, Name = "Lifejacket", Price = 48.95M },
                new Product {ProductID = 3, Name = "Soccer Ball", Price = 19.50M },
                new Product {ProductID = 4, Name = "Thinking Cap", Price = 16M },
            };

        public IEnumerable<Product> Get() {
            return products;
        }

        [LogErrors]
        public HttpResponseMessage Get(int id) {
            Product product = products.Where(x => x.ProductID == id).FirstOrDefault();
            if (product == null) {
                HttpError error = new HttpError();
                error.Message = "No such data item";
                error.Add("RequestID", id);
                error.Add("AvailbleIDs", products.Select(x => x.ProductID));
                return Request.CreateErrorResponse(HttpStatusCode.BadRequest, error);
            }
            return Request.CreateResponse(product);
        }

        public HttpResponseMessage Post(Product product) {
            if (!ModelState.IsValid) {
                HttpError error = new HttpError(ModelState, false);
                error.Message = "Cannot Add Product";
                error.Add("AvailbleIDs", products.Select(x => x.ProductID));
                return Request.CreateErrorResponse(HttpStatusCode.BadRequest, error);
            }
            product.ProductID = products.Count + 1;
            products.Add(product);
            return Request.CreateResponse(product);
        }
    }
}
```

The HttpError class defines a constructor that accepts a ModelStateDictionary object, which can be obtained through the ApiController.ModelState property. The second constructor argument specifies whether details of the validation exceptions should be included in the HttpError object.

■ **Tip** Be careful not to include model state data unless there is a validation error; otherwise, you will send data to the client that simply confirms that the model state was valid. The purpose of error data is to explain what went wrong, not what worked as expected.

To test the changes I made to the Post action method, I added some validation attributes to the Product class, as shown in Listing 25-9 and which I described in Chapter 18.

Listing 25-9. Applying Validation Attributes in the Product.cs File

```
using System.Collections.Generic;
using System.ComponentModel.DataAnnotations;
using System.Web.Http;

namespace Dispatch.Models {

    public class Product {

        [HttpBindNever]
        public int ProductID { get; set; }

        [Required]
        public string Name { get; set; }

        [Range(20, 500)]
        public decimal Price { get; set; }
    }
}
```

To test the effect of adding validation errors to the HTTP response, start the application, use the browser to navigate to the /Home/Index URL, and click the Post button. The default Price value that the client sends is less than the lower bound I applied with the Range validation attribute, which ensures that the model state will be invalid.

Using the F12 tools to see the response sent from the web service will reveal the data from the HttpError object, as follows:

```
{"Message":"Cannot Add Product",
 "ModelState":{"product.Price":["The field Price must be between 20 and 500."]},
 "AvailbleIDs":[1,3,4]}
```

The properties that I set directly in the action method are sent alongside the validation errors that were detected.

Controlling Error Detail

Every predefined HttpError property except Message is considered to be detailed information and, as I explained at the start of this section, is generally useful only to developers. You can control whether properties other than Message are sent to the client through the HttpConfigutation.IncludeErrorDetailPolicy property, which is set to a value from the IncludeErrorDetailPolicy enumeration, as listed in Table 25-5.

Table 25-5. *The Values Defined by the IncludeErrorDetailPolicy Enumeration*

Name	Description
Always	All of the HttpError property values are sent to the client.
Default	Use the behavior defined by the customErrors configuration element in the Web.config file. Use this value only if your application is hosted by ASP.NET, and use the LocalOnly value for other hosts.
LocalOnly	All of the HttpError properties are sent to clients on the local machine, but only the Message property is sent to other clients.
Never	Only the Message property is sent, irrespective of where the client request originated or the host configuration.

Listing 25-10 shows how I set the detail policy in the WebApiConfig.cs file.

Listing 25-10. Setting the Exception Detail Policy in the WebApiConfig.cs File

```
using System.Web.Http;
using System.Web.Http.Controllers;
using Dispatch.Infrastructure;

namespace Dispatch {
    public static class WebApiConfig {
        public static void Register(HttpConfiguration config) {

            config.Routes.MapHttpRoute(
                name: "ActionMethods",
                routeTemplate: "api/nrest/{controller}/{action}/{day}",
                defaults: new { day = RouteParameter.Optional }
            );

            config.Routes.MapHttpRoute(
                name: "DefaultApi",
                routeTemplate: "api/{controller}/{id}",
                defaults: new { id = RouteParameter.Optional }
            );

            //config.Services.Replace(typeof(IHttpActionSelector),
            //    new PipelineActionSelector());
            //config.Filters.Add(new SayHelloAttribute { Message = "Global Filter" });
            //config.MessageHandlers.Add(new AuthenticationDispatcher());

            config.IncludeErrorDetailPolicy = IncludeErrorDetailPolicy.Never;
        }
    }
}
```

> ■ **Caution**   The `IncludeErrorDetailPolicy` setting affects the `HttpError` objects that Web API creates only when dealing with a regular unhandled exception. It doesn't have any effect on `HttpError` objects that you create directly, where you can control the data sent to the client explicitly.

Displaying HttpError Information in the Client

If you are responsible for writing the client that consumes the Web API web service, then you can take advantage of the `HttpError` information to increase the user's understanding of what caused a problem, beyond the basic characterization provided by the HTTP status code. Listing 25-11 demonstrates how to read the data from an error returned in response to a jQuery Ajax request.

> ■ **Caution**   You should display only the `Message` property to users and ensure that the messages you send to the client are meaningful and helpful to a typical end user. Keep technical details and information about the structure of your application to a minimum and limited to the `HttpError` properties intended for developers.

Listing 25-11. Processing Error Information in the dispatch.js File

```
...
error: function (jqXHR) {
    gotError(true);
    products.removeAll();
    if (jqXHR.responseJSON && jqXHR.responseJSON.Message) {
        response(jqXHR.status + " (" + jqXHR.responseJSON.Message + ") ");
    } else {
        response(jqXHR.status);
    }
}
...
```

jQuery makes the response body as a JavaScript object parsed from the JSON data, available through the argument passed to the `error` function. In this listing, I have replaced the status message text with the value of the `responseJSON.Message` property, which corresponds to the `HttpError.Message` property I set in Listing 25-8. Figure 25-2 shows the effect.

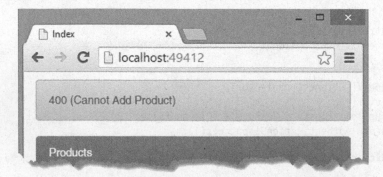

Figure 25-2. *Displaying additional error data*

Responding to Errors Globally

All the errors I have dealt with so far in this chapter have been generated by action methods, which are the source of most problems. However, you have seen just how many different ways there are to customize the way that Web API dispatches requests, and all of them have the potential to throw exceptions.

Web API defines two services that can be used to deal with exceptions wherever they occur in the application: the *global exception handler* and the *global exception logger*. I explain both in the sections that follow, and Table 25-6 puts them into context.

Table 25-6. *Putting the Global Error Services in Context*

Question	Answer
What are they?	The global error services allow you to change the default behavior for uncaught exceptions and to log those exceptions.
When should you use them?	Use the global exception handler when you want to change the response sent for exceptions. Use the global exception logger to record exceptions for future analysis.
What do you need to know?	Change the default fallback behavior with caution because sending a 500 (Internal Server Error) is usually the best approach for dealing with unforeseen problems.

Handling Exceptions

A global exception handler implements the IExceptionHandler interface, which is defined as follows:

```
using System.Threading;
using System.Threading.Tasks;

namespace System.Web.Http.ExceptionHandling {

    public interface IExceptionHandler {

        Task HandleAsync(ExceptionHandlerContext context,
            CancellationToken cancellationToken);
    }
}
```

The HandleAsync method is called when an exception is thrown and not handled elsewhere in the application. The HandleAsync method accepts an instance of the ExceptionHandlerContext class, which defines the properties described in Table 25-7.

Table 25-7. *The Properties Defined by the ExceptionHandlerContext Class*

Name	Description
CatchBlock	This property returns an ExceptionContextCatchBlock object, which describes where the exception originated. See Table 25-8 for details.
Exception	This property returns the Exception that has been thrown.
ExceptionContext	This property returns an ExceptionContext object, which provides access to the same objects as the ExceptionHandlerContext as well as the HttpActionContext and HttpControllerContext objects associated with the current request.
Request	This property returns the HttpRequestMessage object that represents the request being dispatched.
RequestContext	This property returns the HttpRequestContext object associated with the request being dispatched.
Result	This property is set by the exception handler to handle the exception and specify the IHttpActionResult that will be used to generate the response to the client.

A custom global exception handler can change the default Web API behavior by setting the ExceptionHandlerContext.Result property to an IHttpActionResult object, which is processed to create an HttpResponseMessage that can used to send a response to the client. If a custom global exception handler doesn't set the Result property, then Web API uses a fallback exception handler, which generates the standard 500 (Internal Server Error) response.

The CatchBlock property of the ExceptionHandlerContext class provides information about where the exception originated, expressed as one of the values in Table 25-8. There are additional values that are host-specific and that are used when an exception is encountered when sending a response to the client. I use the CatchBlock property in the "Creating a Custom Global Exception Logger" section later in this chapter.

Table 25-8. *The Values Used for the CatchBlock Property*

Name	Description
HttpServer	The exception originated from the SendAsync method of the HttpServer class.
HttpControllerDispatcher	The exception originated from the SendAsync method of the HttpControllerDispatcher class.
IExceptionFilter	The exception originated from the ExecuteAsync method of the controller.

Creating a Custom Global Exception Handler

Before you create a custom global exception handler, I recommend you take a moment and consider the problem you are trying to solve. Bear in mind that global exception handlers are used only for exceptions that are not handled elsewhere in the application and that the default behavior of sending a 500 (Internal Server Error) response is usually appropriate. After all, if there is a more appropriate response, then you should add code to your action methods that anticipate the problem and return the appropriate response to the client.

Global exception handlers are best used to make sweeping changes to all or most unhandled exceptions, and if you find yourself writing endless conditional statements to deal with specific exception and request types, then you should consider a different technique that pushes the logic closer to the action method, where it is easier to understand, test, and maintain.

To demonstrate the use of a global exception handler, I added a class file called CustomExceptionHandler.cs to the Infrastructure folder and used it to define the class shown in Listing 25-12.

Listing 25-12. The Contents of the CustomExceptionHandler.cs File

```
using System.Net;
using System.Threading;
using System.Threading.Tasks;
using System.Web.Http.ExceptionHandling;
using System.Web.Http.Results;

namespace Dispatch.Infrastructure {
    public class CustomExceptionHandler : IExceptionHandler {

        public Task HandleAsync(ExceptionHandlerContext context,
            CancellationToken cancellationToken) {

            context.Result = new StatusCodeResult(HttpStatusCode.InternalServerError,
                context.Request);
            return Task.FromResult<object>(null);
        }
    }
}
```

You can set the ExceptionHandlerContext.Result property to any implementation of the IHttpActionResult interface. I listed the built-in implementation classes from the System.Web.Http.Results namespace in Chapter 11, but you must instantiate them directly since the convenience methods I used in that chapter are implemented by the ApiController class and are not available to global exception handlers. In the listing, I use the ResponseMessageResult class, which lets me create the HttpResponseMessage within the scope of an IHttpActionResult.

The custom exception handler generates a standard 500 (Internal Server Error) response by creating an instance of the StatusCodeResult but doesn't include any of the additional data that comes from an HttpError object.

Registering and Testing a Custom Global Exception Handler

Global exception handlers are registered through the services collection in the WebApiConfig.cs file, as shown in Listing 25-13.

Listing 25-13. Registering a Global Exception Handler in the WebApiConfig.cs File

```
using System.Web.Http;
using System.Web.Http.Controllers;
using Dispatch.Infrastructure;
using System.Web.Http.ExceptionHandling;

namespace Dispatch {
    public static class WebApiConfig {
        public static void Register(HttpConfiguration config) {

            config.Routes.MapHttpRoute(
                name: "ActionMethods",
```

```
            routeTemplate: "api/nrest/{controller}/{action}/{day}",
            defaults: new { day = RouteParameter.Optional }
        );

        config.Routes.MapHttpRoute(
            name: "DefaultApi",
            routeTemplate: "api/{controller}/{id}",
            defaults: new { id = RouteParameter.Optional }
        );

        //config.Services.Replace(typeof(IHttpActionSelector),
        //    new PipelineActionSelector());
        //config.Filters.Add(new SayHelloAttribute { Message = "Global Filter" });
        //config.MessageHandlers.Add(new AuthenticationDispatcher());

        config.IncludeErrorDetailPolicy = IncludeErrorDetailPolicy.Never;

        config.Services.Replace(typeof(IExceptionHandler),
            new CustomExceptionHandler());
    }
  }
}
```

There can be only one global exception handler in an application, but the built-in handler is still used as a fallback so that it can apply the default behavior if the custom handler doesn't set the Result property of the ExceptionHandlerContext object.

Before I can test the custom handler, I need to create a reliable source of exceptions. Listing 25-14 shows how I have changed the Get action method in the Products controller to remove the error handling code and throw an exception when requests are received for data objects that don't exist.

Listing 25-14. Throwing Exceptions in the ProductsController.cs File

```
...
[LogErrors]
public Product Get(int id) {
    Product product = products.Where(x => x.ProductID == id).FirstOrDefault();
    if (product == null) {
        throw new ArgumentOutOfRangeException("id");
    }
    return product;
}
...
```

To test the handler, start the application, use the browse to navigate to /Home/Index, and click the Get One button. The changes that I made to the Get method mean that the URL that is requested will cause the action method to throw an exception, which will be passed to the custom global exception handler. You can see the result in Figure 25-3, but the effect is subtle because the only difference from the previous examples is the omission of the error message text.

Figure 25-3. *Using a custom global exception handler*

Logging Exceptions

The global exception logger allows you to record the exceptions that your application encounters. This isn't much help at runtime, but it can be useful when diagnosing recurring problems and planning maintenance and enhancements for future releases. Global exceptions loggers implement the IExceptionLogger interface in the System.Web.Http.ExceptionHandling namespace, which is defined as follows:

```
using System.Threading;
using System.Threading.Tasks;

namespace System.Web.Http.ExceptionHandling {

    public interface IExceptionLogger {

        Task LogAsync(ExceptionLoggerContext context,
            CancellationToken cancellationToken);
    }
}
```

The LogAsync method is called when there is an unhandled exception and receives an instance of the ExceptionLoggerContext class as a parameter, which defines the properties shown in Table 25-9.

Table 25-9. *The Properties Defined by the ExceptionLoggerContext Class*

Name	Description
CallsHandler	This property returns true if the exception can be handled by the IExceptionHandler to produce a response message. Some exceptions can occur after the response has started to be sent to the client, in which case this property will return false.
CatchBlock	This property returns an ExceptionContextCatchBlock object, which describes where the exception was caught.
Exception	This property returns the Exception to be logged.

(continued)

Table 25-9. (*continued*)

Name	Description
ExceptionContext	This property returns an ExceptionContext object, which provides access to the same objects as the ExceptionHandlerContext as well as the HttpActionContext and HttpControllerContext objects associated with the current request.
Request	This property returns the HttpRequestMessage object for the request being processed when the exception occurred.
RequestContext	This property returns the HttpRequestContext object associated with the request.

Creating a Custom Global Exception Logger

Unlike the global exception handler, there can be multiple global exception handlers, and each can choose which exceptions it records and how they are recorded. To demonstrate a simple exception logger, I added a class file called CustomExceptionLogger.cs to the Infrastructure folder and used it to define the class shown in Listing 25-15.

Listing 25-15. The Contents of the CustomExceptionLogger.cs File

```
using System.Diagnostics;
using System.Threading;
using System.Threading.Tasks;
using System.Web.Http.ExceptionHandling;

namespace Dispatch.Infrastructure {

    public class CustomExceptionLogger : IExceptionLogger {

        public Task LogAsync(ExceptionLoggerContext context,
            CancellationToken cancellationToken) {

            Debug.WriteLine("Log Exception Type: {0}, Originated: {1}, URL: {2}",
                context.Exception.GetType(),
                context.CatchBlock,
                context.Request.RequestUri);

            return Task.FromResult<object>(null);
        }
    }
}
```

The custom logger writes details of the exception, where it originated, and the requested URL to the Visual Studio Output window.

■ **Tip** Writing exceptions to the Visual Studio Output window isn't helpful for a production environment. If you do not have an existing logging system with which to integrate, then a good place to start is the open source package ELMAH. See https://code.google.com/p/elmah/ for details.

Registering and Testing a Custom Exception Logger

Custom exception loggers are registered with the services collection, as shown in Listing 25-16.

Listing 25-16. Registering a Custom Global Exception Logger in the WebApiConfig.cs File

```
using System.Web.Http;
using System.Web.Http.Controllers;
using Dispatch.Infrastructure;
using System.Web.Http.ExceptionHandling;

namespace Dispatch {
    public static class WebApiConfig {
        public static void Register(HttpConfiguration config) {

            config.Routes.MapHttpRoute(
                name: "ActionMethods",
                routeTemplate: "api/nrest/{controller}/{action}/{day}",
                defaults: new { day = RouteParameter.Optional }
            );

            config.Routes.MapHttpRoute(
                name: "DefaultApi",
                routeTemplate: "api/{controller}/{id}",
                defaults: new { id = RouteParameter.Optional }
            );

            //config.Services.Replace(typeof(IHttpActionSelector),
            //    new PipelineActionSelector());
            //config.Filters.Add(new SayHelloAttribute { Message = "Global Filter" });
            //config.MessageHandlers.Add(new AuthenticationDispatcher());

            config.IncludeErrorDetailPolicy = IncludeErrorDetailPolicy.Never;

            config.Services.Replace(typeof(IExceptionHandler),
                new CustomExceptionHandler());
            config.Services.Add(typeof(IExceptionLogger), new CustomExceptionLogger());
        }
    }
}
```

Notice that I used the Add method to register the logger, rather than the Replace method I used for the global handler. This is because there can be multiple loggers in an application, but only one handler and the service collection class will throw an exception if you try to Add a single-instance type.

To test the exception logger, start the application and use the browser to navigate to the /Home/Index URL. Click the Get One button, and the client will request a URL that will cause an exception to be thrown in the Get action method of the Products controller. The exception is unhandled and will be passed to the exception logger, producing the following message in the Visual Studio Output window:

```
Log Exception Type: System.ArgumentOutOfRangeException, Originated: IExceptionFilter,
    URL: http://localhost:49412/api/products/2
```

Summary

In this chapter, I explained how errors are handled by Web API. I showed you the default exception handling behavior and how to change it, how to use the HttpError class to control the additional data sent to a client, and, finally, how to log the unhandled exceptions that your application encounters.

CHAPTER 26

■ ■ ■

Using OWIN

In the other chapters in this part of the book, I showed you how the Web API dispatch process works and demonstrated how to customize it. In this, the last chapter of this book, I describe one final change to the dispatch process: changing the hosting environment that runs the Web API application itself.

■ **Caution**   For this chapter, you must have an edition of Visual Studio 2013 that is capable of creating console applications. The free Visual Studio Express 2013 for Web edition that I have been using in all the previous chapters does not include this support. You will need one of the paid-for versions or Visual Studio Express 2013 for Windows Desktop, which can be downloaded for free from `www.visualstudio.com`.

Understanding OWIN

The Open Web Interface for .NET (OWIN) is a standard that defines an interface for .NET web applications. The idea behind OWIN is to break the link between web applications and the application server—or, put another way, to allow .NET web applications to be run outside of the traditional IIS environment.

Microsoft has embraced OWIN as a way to free ASP.NET from the System.Web assembly, which is part of the main .NET Framework and which means that ASP.NET releases are synchronized with major .NET Framework and Windows Server releases. It is in the early days for OWIN, but there is the potential for more flexibility in how .NET web applications are hosted as OWIN support in ASP.NET matures, beyond today's choices of Azure and IIS running on Windows Server (although neither of these hosting options is going to go away).

Web API and SignalR are the first ASP.NET components to embrace OWIN and break away from the world of System.Web. This is why every Web API class and interface I have used in this book has been different from the ones you are familiar with in MVC framework development and why all of those types are contained in the System.Web.Http assembly, which is under the control of the ASP.NET development teams within Microsoft and not tied to the main .NET framework release schedule.

This is a short chapter because the range of OWIN hosting options is limited currently. The biggest limitation, however, is that only Web API and SignalR code can be run within OWIN. If you want to use the MVC framework to deliver static content, for example, then you will have to wait for MVC OWIN support, which will be introduced in MVC 6. Future editions of this book won't need to contain warnings about the different MVC and Web API namespaces because everything will use the System.Web.Http types I have been using to create web services, but for the moment, OWIN support and the alternative hosting options it leads to are little more than a curiosity and not much use beyond experimentation and tinkering for most developers.

> ■ **Note**   If you become interested in OWIN, you will quickly come across references to Katana. Katana is a Microsoft package that allows OWIN applications to be hosted by IIS or Azure—or, put another way, provides a mapping between the traditional System.Web functionality and the OWIN specification. Katana doesn't have any bearing on this book because, as I have demonstrated in previous chapters, Web API can already be hosted by IIS and Azure.

Creating a Self-hosted Web API Application

A self-hosted Web API application is a stand-alone process that receives and dispatches HTTP requests without relying on an application server. This means it is possible to embed Web API into other kinds of applications or to create small and simple Web API deployments that can run in constrained environments. In the sections that follow, I'll show you how to create a simple self-hosted Web API application that relies on the OWIN specification.

Creating the Project

As I noted at the start of this chapter, you need an edition of Visual Studio that is able to create console applications. I will be using Visual Studio Express 2013 for Windows Desktop, but any of the paid-for editions will work as well.

To create the project, select File ➤ New Project and select the Console Application from the Visual C# template section. (Visual Studio defaults to the Visual Basic template category, so be sure you get the C# template.) Set the name of the project to SelfHost and click the OK button. Visual Studio will create the project and add a class file to it called Program.cs.

Installing the Packages

Select Package Manager Console from the Visual Studio Tools ➤ NuGet Package Manager menu and enter the following command:

```
Install-Package Microsoft.AspNet.WebApi.OwinSelfHost -Version 5.1.1
```

This will install the Microsoft OWIN classes for self-hosting and the Web API assemblies required to create web services.

Creating the Model and Repository

To keep the example simple, I will create a repository that maintains a collection of data objects in memory, just like I did in Chapter 10. I added a Models folder to the project and created the Product.cs file within it. Listing 26-1 shows the model class I defined.

Listing 26-1. The Contents of the Product.cs File

```
namespace SelfHost.Models {
    public class Product {
        public int ProductID { get; set; }
        public string Name { get; set; }
        public decimal Price { get; set; }
    }
}
```

This is a simplified version of the model class that I created for the SportsStore application in Chapter 5. Listing 26-2 shows the contents of the Repository.cs class file that I added to the Models folder.

Listing 26-2. The Contents of the Repository.cs File

```csharp
using System.Collections.Generic;

namespace SelfHost.Models {
    public class Repository {
        private Dictionary<int, Product> data;
        private static Repository repo;

        static Repository() {
            repo = new Repository();
        }

        public static Repository Current {
            get { return repo; }
        }

        public Repository() {
            Product[] products = new Product[] {
                new Product {ProductID = 1, Name = "Kayak", Price = 275M },
                new Product {ProductID = 2, Name = "Lifejacket", Price = 48.95M },
                new Product {ProductID = 3, Name = "Soccer Ball", Price = 19.50M },
                new Product {ProductID = 4, Name = "Thinking Cap", Price = 16M },
            };

            data = new Dictionary<int, Product>();

            foreach (Product prod in products) {
                data.Add(prod.ProductID, prod);
            }
        }

        public IEnumerable<Product> Products {
            get { return data.Values; }
        }

        public Product GetProduct(int id) {
            return data[id];
        }

        public Product SaveProduct(Product newProduct) {
            newProduct.ProductID = data.Keys.Count + 1;
            return data[newProduct.ProductID] = newProduct;
        }

        public Product DeleteProduct(int id) {
            Product prod = data[id];
            if (prod != null) {
                data.Remove(id);
            }
```

```
            return prod;
        }
    }
}
```

My example repository populates an in-memory collection with Product objects and exposes them through a mix of properties and methods. Storing the data in memory means that the contents of the repository will be reset when the application is restarted. There is a static Current property that returns a shared instance of the Repository class, which I will use to obtain instances of the repository without having to implement dependency injection.

Defining the Configuration Classes

The configuration for OWIN-hosted applications is done through a class called Startup. I added a class file called Startup.cs to the example project and used it to define the class shown in Listing 26-3.

Listing 26-3. The Contents of the Startup.cs File

```
using Owin;
using System.Web.Http;

namespace SelfHost {
    public class Startup {

        public void Configuration(IAppBuilder appBuilder) {

            HttpConfiguration config = new HttpConfiguration();

            config.Routes.MapHttpRoute(
                name: "DefaultApi",
                routeTemplate: "api/{controller}/{id}",
                defaults: new { id = RouteParameter.Optional }
            );

            appBuilder.UseWebApi(config);
        }
    }
}
```

As you can see from the listing, the Startup class follows the same basic approach as the WebApiConfig.cs file that I have been relying on to configure IIS-hosted Web API applications in earlier chapters. The difference is that I have to create an instance of the HttpConfiguration class, which I described in Chapter 10, configure it for URL routing (as described in Chapters 20 and 21), and then call the UseWebApi method of the IAppBuilder parameter that is passed to the Configuration method.

The Startup class isn't the only class that is required to self-host a Web API application. I also need to add code to the Program.cs file so that it will initialize OWIN and use the Startup class for configuration. Listing 26-4 shows the changes I made to the Program.cs file.

Listing 26-4. Defining the Self-hosting Application in the Program.cs File

```
using Microsoft.Owin.Hosting;
using System;

namespace SelfHost {

    class Program {

        static void Main(string[] args) {
            WebApp.Start<Startup>("http://localhost:5000/");
            Console.ReadLine();
        }
    }
}
```

The call to the WebApp.Start<Startup> method specifies that I want to use the Startup class to configure Web API, and the method argument specifies the URL that will be used to listen for requests. The call to Console.ReadLine prevents the console application exiting—if you omit this statement, then the application will terminate before the first HTTP request is received.

Creating the Web API Controller

The final step is to create a Web API controller to define the web service. I added a Controllers folder to the project and created within it a new class file called ProductsController.cs, the contents of which are shown in Listing 26-5.

Listing 26-5. The Contents of the ProductsController.cs File

```
using SelfHost.Models;
using System.Collections.Generic;
using System.Linq;
using System.Web.Http;

namespace SelfHost.Controllers {
    public class ProductsController : ApiController {

        public IEnumerable<Product> GetProducts() {
            return Repository.Current.Products;
        }

        public Product GetProduct(int id) {
            return Repository.Current.Products
                .Where(p => p.ProductID == id).FirstOrDefault();
        }

        public Product PostProduct(Product product) {
            return Repository.Current.SaveProduct(product);
        }

        public Product DeleteProduct(int id) {
            return Repository.Current.DeleteProduct(id);
        }
    }
}
```

■ **Tip** There is no Visual Studio scaffolding support when creating self-hosted applications, and controllers have to be added by creating standard class files.

I have defined a RESTful controller that follows the same approach I used in Chapter 6. This controller lacks the features that I applied throughout Chapter 6, but it demonstrates the basic Web API mechanisms and exposes the contents of the repository to HTTP clients.

Testing the Self-hosted Web API Application

All that remains is to test the self-hosted application. I have not created a client application for the web service because that would require a separate non-Web API project, but it is easy to perform a test using Postman.

First, start the Web API application by selecting Start Debugging from the Visual Studio Debug menu. An empty console window will appear—do not close this because doing so will terminate the self-hosted application. Using Postman, send a GET request to the following URL:

```
http://localhost:5000/api/products
```

All of the Web API functionality I have described in this book is available in a self-hosted Web API application, and that includes, of course, URL routing. The URL route I defined in Listing 26-2 will map the request to the Products controller and the request verb, and the absence of data will target the GetProducts action method. Postman will display the following results, which correspond to the static data I defined in Listing 26-3:

```
[{"ProductID":1,"Name":"Kayak","Price":275.0},
 {"ProductID":2,"Name":"Lifejacket","Price":48.95},
 {"ProductID":3,"Name":"Soccer Ball","Price":19.50},
 {"ProductID":4,"Name":"Thinking Cap","Price":16.0}]
```

Summary

In this chapter, I gave you a brief overview of OWIN and the way it can be used to create self-hosted Web API applications that don't depend on IIS or Azure. It is early days for OWIN, and it remains a curiosity for the moment; however, it is an area of investment for Microsoft, and subsequent versions of Web API—and the MVC framework—will build on this slim foundation.

And that is all I have to teach you about ASP.NET Web API and how it can be used to create HTTP web services. I started by creating a simple application and then took you on a comprehensive tour of the different components in Web API, showing you how they can be configured, customized, or replaced entirely to create the web services you need. I wish you every success in your Web API projects, and I can only hope that you have enjoyed reading this book as much as I enjoyed writing it.

Index

▪ A, B

Action methods. *See* Controllers
Action results
    action result methods, 224
    custom action results, 228
    HttpResponseMessage, instantiating, 227
    IHttpActionResult interface, 222–223
    mapping ApiController methods to HTTP status
        codes, 226
    negotiable action results, 239
    returning model data, 230
        bypassing content negotiation, 238
        content negotiation process, 231
        ContentNegotiationResult class, 234
        custom content negotiator, 232
        default behavior, 230
        JsonMediaTypeFormatter class, 234
        ProductInfoValueHeader class, 235
    returning no result, 218
Ajax. *See* jQuery
ApiController. *See also* Controllers, Action results,
        Model validation
    action result methods, 224
        BadRequest method, 108
        context properties, 560
    dispatch process, 543
        HttpActionDescriptor classs, 548
        HttpControllerContext class, 547
        IHttpActionSelector, 547
    introduction to, 100
    mapping methods to HTTP status
        codes, 226
    methods that bypass content
        negotiation, 238
    model state (*see* Model validation)
        properties defined by, 183
    ResponseMessage method, 227
ApiControllerActionSelector class, 549

Application configuration, 187, 199
    callback method, 200
    Global.asax.cs file, 199
    GlobalConfiguration.Configure method, 199
    HttpConfiguration class, 201
    HttpConfiguration object, 200
    HttpMessageHandler, 200
    WebApiConfig.cs file, 201
ASP.NET Identity, 87. *See also* Examples, SportsStore
    access token, 136
    application cookie, removing, 97
    database creation, 173
    configuration, 92
    database context classes, 88
    manager classes, 90
    testing, 93
    user and role classes, 87
Asynchronous methods, 35, 42
    async keyword, 43
    await keyword, 43
    task creation, synchronous statements, 47–49
    Task.FromResult method, 229, 339
Authentication. *See* Security, ASP.NET Identity
Authorization. *See* Security, ASP.NET Identity
Azure
    ASP.NET Identity database creation, 173
    database configuration, 177
    preparing for deployment, 169
    publishing, 177
    publish profile, 175
    Web Site, creating, 175

▪ C

Configuration. *See* Application configuration
ContentNegotiationResult, properties defined by, 233
Context objects
    ExceptionHandlerContext, 186
    ExceptionLoggerContext, 186

Context objects (*cont.*)
    HttpActionContext, 186
    HttpActionDescriptor, 186
    HttpActionExecutedContext, 186
    HttpAuthenticationChallengeContext, 186
    HttpAuthenticationContext, 186
    HttpControllerContext, 185–186
    HttpControllerDescriptor, 186
    HttpParameterDescriptor, 186
    HttpRequestContext, 184, 186
    HttpRequestMessage, 184
    ModelBindingContext, 186
Controllers, 537. *See also* Action Results, Dispatch process
    Action method selection
        default action method selection, 549
        HTTP verbs, 551
        RESTful naming convention, 549
    ApiController class. *See also* ApiController
        BadRequest method, 108
        context properties, 560
        properties defined by, 183
    ApiController dispatch process, 543
        HttpActionDescriptor classs, 548
        HttpControllerContext class, 547
        IHttpActionSelector, 547
    built-in services and features, 541
    controller-specific configuration, 563
    creation, 20
    custom action results, 228
    custom controllers, 543
    Customization, 559
    ExecuteAsync method, 540
    filters (*see* Filters)
    IHttpController.ExecuteAsync method, 544
    IHttpController interface, 538
    Web API dispatch process, 537

D

Dependency injection, 202
    configuration, 209
    containers, 206
        Castle Windsor, 206
        Ninject, 121, 206, 208–209, 211, 213
        StructureMap, 206
        Unity, 206
    DependencyResolver property, 209
    IDependencyResolver.GetService
        method, 236
    IDependencyResolver interface, 204
    IDependencyScope interface, 205
    MVC framework, 211
    object scopes, 209
    preparation, 203
    request objects, 208
    scopes, 206

    singleton objects, 207
    transient objects, 207
Dispatchers and handlers, 189
Dispatch process. *See also* Controllers, Action Results,
    ApiController
    activating the controller, 465
    changing the controller suffix, 479
    controller selection, 463
    custom message handlers, 468
        diagnosing problems with message handlers, 474
        modifying requests or responses, 471
    executing the controller, 466
    extension methods, 467
    HttpControllerDispatcher class, 463
    HttpRoutingDispatcher class, 460
    HttpServer class, 459
    IAssembliesResolver interface, 464
    IHttpControllerTypeResolver interface, 464
    message handlers, 457
        chain, 457
        default implementation classes, 458
        SendAsync method, 457

E

Entity Framework
    checking schema, 86
    Code First, 75
    connection strings, 171
    context class, 77
    database context class, 77
    preventing database reset, 169
Error handling
    controlling error detail, 635
    dealing with errors, 626–627
    default error handling, 626
    global error handling, 637–638
        CatchBlock property, 638
        registering, 639
    handling exceptions, 637
        CatchBlock property, 638
        ExceptionHandlerContext class, 638
        IExceptionHandler interface, 637
    HttpError class, 629
        adding extra information, 632
        adding model state data, 632
        properties defined by, 630
    logging exceptions, 641
        creating a custom logger, 642
        ExceptionLoggerContext class, 641
        IExceptionLogger interface, 641
    using the IHttpActionResult interface, 629
Examples
    ExampleApp, 191
        browser client, 194
        HTTP web service, 193

Index.cshtml File, 195
model and repository, 192
testing with Postman, 198
PartyInvites project, 10
ASP.NET project type, 10
Data Repository, 13
GuestResponse.cs File, 12
MVC framework application, 12
NuGet packages, 11
TCP port and URL, 12
Primer, 35
Asynchronous methods, 42
MVC framework controller, 39
NuGet Packages, 37
project type, 36
Stopwatch Class, 39
TCP port and URL, 41
Web API controller, 37
web service testing, 41
Source Code Download, 5
SportsStore, 4
administration client, 159
administration controller, 159
Ajax code, 133
ASP.NET Identity (*see* ASP.NET Identity)
ASP.NET project type, 71
authentication controller, 136
Azure (*see* Azure)
checking database schema, 86
client-side model, 135
customer client, 145
customer controller, 146
database (*see* Entity Framework)
database initializer class, 77
data models, 75
Dependency Injection, 121
deployment, 169
JavaScript IntelliSense setup, 132
Model Validation, 118
MVC controller, 131
NuGet packages, 72
orders controller, 142
OWIN startup class, 74
Repository pattern, 77
RESTful controller, 99, 102
Security, 109
TCP port, 75

■ **F**

F12 browser tools. *See* Google Chrome
Filters
action filters, 569
ActionFilterAttribute class, 574
applying, 573

ExecuteActionFilterAsync method, 570
HttpActionContext class, 572
HttpActionExecutedContext class, 577
IActionFilter interface, 569
request dispatch process, 570
short-circuiting, 577
authentication filters, 587
AuthenticateAsync method, 590
Authorization request header, 593
creating, 591
HttpAuthenticationChallengeContext Class, 594
HttpAuthenticationContext class, 593
IIdentity interface, 589
IPrincipal interface, 589
removing, 604
authorization filters, 600
applying, 603
AuthorizationFilterAttribute class, 607
Authorize attribute, 608
creating, 601
IAuthorizationFilter interface, 601
exception filters, 611
creating, 614
default behavior, 611
ExceptionFilterAttribute class, 616
IExceptionFilter interface, 613
FilterInfo class, 583
filter pipeline, 582
global filters, 585
IFilter interface, 568
override filters, 617
IOverrideFilter interface, 618
override filter attributes, 618
overriding built-in filters, 618
redefining filter policies, 620
scope, 584–585
System.Web.Http.Filters namespace, 568
types and interfaces, 568
FromBody attribute, 401
FromUri attribute, 355

■ **G**

Google Chrome, 6
cache clearing and reloading, 19
debugging, 7
download link, 6
F12 tools, 19
Measuring Network Requests, 19

■ **H**

HTTP
Accept header, 245, 259
Content-Type header, 245

HttpActionContext class, 331, 572

HttpActionDescriptor class, 371, 420, 548

HttpControllerContext class, 538, 547. *See also* Context objects, HttpControllerContext

HttpControllerDispatcher class, 463

HttpParameterBinding, 334

HttpParameterDescriptor, 336

HttpRequestContext. *See* Context objects, HttpRequestContext)

HttpRequestMessage, 217. *See also* Context objects, HttpRequestMessage

HTTP requests dispatch, 4

HttpResponseMessage

    instantiating, 227

    properties defined by, 223

HTTP responses, 4

HttpRouteCollection class, 490

HttpRoutingDispatcher class, 460

HttpServer class, 459

HTTP status codes, 107

HTTP web services, 57

    native applications, 59

    RESTful web service (*see* RESTful web service)

    service applications, 60

    shared-model applications, 59

    simple web service

        client JavaScript code, 61

        tight coupling, 61

    single-page applications, 58

■ I

IContentNegotiator interface, 232

    IFilter interface, 568

IHttpActionResult, ExecuteAsync method, 223

IHttpActionResult interface, 222–223

IHttpController interface, 538

IHttpRouteConstraint interface, 504

IHttpRoute interface, properties and methods, 490

■ J

JavaScript Object Notation (JSON), 53. *See also* Media type formatters

jQuery, 35, 49

    $.ajax method, 52

    $.ajaxSetup method, 134

    Ajax configuration properties, 53

    Ajax requests, 50

    Ajax, required parameters, 134

    data formats, 251

        default binding behavior , 306

■ K, L

Knockout, 35, 54

    bindings, 55

    bindings activation, 56

    client-side validation, 158

    data-bind attribute, 54

    data bindings, 28

    ko.observable, 54

    ko.observableArray, 54

    model and bindings, 54

    observable arrays, 28, 54

■ M

Mapping Namespaces and Types to Web API, 181

Media type formatters

    BSON, 272

    CanReadType method, 247

    CanWriteType method, 247

    custom formatter, 252

        Accept-Charset header, 252

        Content-Type header, 256

        HttpContent.Headers property, 253

        HTTP response headers, 257

        ProductFormatter class, 252

        SelectCharacterEncoding methods, 253

        SetDefaultContentHeaders method, 255–256

        StreamWriter object, 253

        SupportedEncodings property, 252

        System.Text.Encoding class, 253

    features, 269

    formatter instance creation, 264

    FormUrlEncodedMediaTypeFormatter class, 403

    GetPerRequestFormatterInstance method, 263

    IFormatterLogger interface, 446

    Index method, 270

    JSON data

        configuration, 282

        DataContractJsonSerializer class, 282

        DefaultValueHandling setting, 291

        Indent property, 282

        JsonMediaTypeFormatter class, 281

        Microsoft date format, 288

        SerializerSettings properties, 284

        StringEscapeHandling enumeration, 289

    match-on-type feature, 273

        application/x.product format, 274

        CanWriteType method, 274

        constructor argument, 277

        custom format negotiator, 275

        DefaultContentNegotiator class, 276

MediaTypeFormattingCollection, 274
WebApiConfig.cs file, 274, 277
XmlMediaTypeFormatter class, 272–273
MediaTypeFormatterCollection class, 269–270
MediaTypeHeaderValue class, 247
negotiation process, 257, 262
AddRequestHeaderMapping extension
method, 263
AddUriPathExtensionMapping method, 263
mapping extension methods, 262
parameter and model binding (*see* Parameter and
model binding)
registration, 249
serializing model data, 248
formatting loops, 126
SupportedMediaTypes collection, 247
System.Net.Http assembly, 271
System.Net.Http.Formatting namespace, 245
validating with, 444
Web API configuration, 272
WriteToStreamAsync method, 248
XML data, configuration, 293
MediaTypeHeaderValue class, 233
Message Handlers. *See* Dispatch process, message
handlers
Model binding. *See* Parameter and model binding
ModelBindingContext class, properties defined by, 371
ModelError class, properties defined by, 438
Model state class, 438. *See also* Model validation
ModelStateDictionary Class, 436
Model validation, 106
Ajax POST request, 427
ApiController class, 437–438
binding control attributes, 439
built-in validation attributes, 441
common problems, 431
over-posting data, 433
under-posting data, 431
unusable data, 434
Data transfer object (DTO), 434
data validation attributes, 441
media type formatters
IFormatterLogger interface, 446
JSON Data, 448
validating with, 444
ModelError class, 438
ModelState Class, 436, 438
ModelStateDictionary Class, 436
self-validating model classes, 443
SportsStore Example, 118
validation attributes, 119
MVC framework
Mapping Namespaces and Types to Web API, 181

N
Namespaces
System.Net.Http, 100
System.Web.Http, 100
Ninject. *See* Dependency injection
Non-RESTful web service
model objects, 125
routing configuration, 124

O
Open Web Interface for .NET (OWIN)
definition, 645
limitation, 645
self-hosted Web API application, 646, 650
configuration, 648
controller, 649
model creation, 646
NuGet package installation, 646
startup class (*see* Examples, SportsStore)

P, Q
Parameter and model binding
binding arrays and lists, 365
binding complex types, 312
binding key-value pairs, 366
binding multiple objects, 356
binding nested objects, 358
binding objects, 355
binding rule
definition, 316
FromBody attribute, 317
FromUri attribute, 317
HttpParameterBinding object, 316
HttpParameterDescriptor object, 316
WebApiConfig.cs file, 316
binding simple types, 314
built-in media type formatters, 401
Content-Type request header, 402
creating complex types, 404, 412
DataMember attribute, 417
FormDataCollection class, 403
FormUrlEncodedMediaTypeFormatter class, 403
FromBody attribute, 401
built-in model binders, 354
classes, 355
FromUri attribute, 355
containsPrefix method, 330
custom action value binder, creation, 424
customizing the binding process, 420–421
custom media type formatters, 393

Parameter and model binding (*cont.*)
  formatter structure, 397
  model object, creation, 399
  ReadFromStreamAsync method, 397
  registering, 400
 custom model binders, 368
  getting model property values, 374
  HttpActionContext class, 371
  HttpActionDescriptor class, 371
  IModelBinder interface, 370
  loosely coupled binders, 372
  ModelBinder attribute, 377
  ModelBinderProvider class, 378
  ModelBindingContext class, 371
  parameter binding rule, creation, 380
  registering model binders, 378
  tightly coupled binders, 372
 custom provider
  FromBody attribute, 334
  FromUri attribute, 334
 default binding behavior, 302
  data values, 303
  HttpRequestMessage object, 312
  .NET primitive types, 303
  Numbers and Operation object, 311
 FromUri attribute, 340
 GetValue method, 330
 GetValueProviderFactories method, 340
 HeaderValueParameterBinding class, 345–346
 HttpActionBinding class, 421
 HttpActionContext class, 331
 HttpActionDescriptor class, 420
 HttpHeaders class, 328
 HttpParameterBinding class, 334
 HttpParameterDescriptor class, 336, 345
 HttpRequestMessage object, 321
 IActionValueBinder interface, 420
 IValueProvider interface, 330, 361
 JSON and XML formatting, 304
 ModelBinder attribute, 377
 ModelBinderProvider class, 378
 ModelBindingAttribute class, 338
 ParameterBindingAttribute class, 335, 338
 QueryStringValueProviderFactory
   class, 348
 RouteDataValueProviderFactory class, 348
 TryGetValues method, 321
 Type Converters, 382
  creating, 383
  TypeConverter class, 382
 ValueProvider attribute, 336
 ValueProviderFactory class, 330–331
 ValueProviderResult class, 331
PartyInvites. *See* Examples

Postman
  download link, 6
  HTTP Client, 6
  HTTP DELETE request, 109
  Interceptor extension, 7

■ R

Repository pattern, 77
Representational state transfer (REST). *See* RESTful
    web service
Request dispatching. *See* Dispatch process
RESTful naming convention, 549
RESTful web service
  action method convention, 103
  data discovery
    collection filtering, 66
    collection URL, 65
  design patterns, 62
  example API, 66
  HTTP verbs and URLs, 63
    GET and POST, 64
    safe and idempotent verbs, 65
  non-RESTful Web Service (*see* Non-RESTful
      web service)
  serialization configuration, 104
  simple dependency injection, 121
RouteAttribute class, 513

■ S, T

Security. *See also* ASP.NET Identity
  access restriction, 110
  authentication configuration, 113
  authentication provider, 112
  SportsStore example, 109
  testing authentication, 114
Serialization. *See also* Media type formatters
formatting loops, 126
Services, 187
  HttpConfig.Services.Replace method, 236
  multiple-instance services, 187
  ServicesContainer
    Extension Methods, 188
    methods defined by, 187
  single-instance services, 187
SimpleModelBinderProvider class, 378
Single-page application, 25
  client-side data model
    controller functions, 28
    knockout-specific features, 28–29
    observable array, 28
    PartyInvites example, 26–28
    properties, 27

data bindings, 32
JavaScript IntelliSense references, 26
non-JavaScript clients, 25
result summary, 33
SportsStore. *See* Examples
System.Net.Http namespace, 100
   System.Net.Http.Formatting namespace, 245
   System.Web.Http namespace, 100
   System.Web.Http.Filters namespace, 568

■ U

URL routing, 486
   controlling route matching, 499
      built-in constraints, 507
      default data values, 500
      IHttpRouteConstraint interface, 504
      optional segments, 501
      routing constraints, 504
      segment defaults, 500
   convention-based routing, 492
      custom templates, 496
      HTTP method attributes, 494
      route templates, 493
   customization
      custom constraints for direct routes, 529
      route-specific message handlers, 525
      route-wide custom constraints, 532
      using data tokens, 527
   defining routes, 490
   direct/attribute-based routing, 483
   direct routing, 512
      common prefix, 515, 521
      constraints, 519
      controller-wide routes, 523
      optional segments, 516

      Route attribute, 514
      RoutePrefix attribute, 515
      segment scoring, 522
      shorthand references for constraints, 520
   HttpRequestContext.RouteData property, 486
   HttpRouteCollection class, 490
      collection methods, 491
      extension methods, 492
      methods for defining routes, 490
   IHttpRoute interface, 490
   important classes and
      interfaces, 488
   RouteAttribute class, 513
   route attributes, 492

■ V

ValueProviderFactory, 331
ValueProviderResult, 331
Visual Studio, 6
   Empty project (*see* PartyInvites project)
   Empty template, 9
   features, 6
   JavaScript IntelliSense setup, 132
   NuGet, 6
   Project Templates, 6
   Selecting Controller Type, 14
   web version, 6

■ W, X, Y, Z

Web API
   comparing MVC framework and Web API
      application components, 57
   overview, 3
   System.Web.Http namespace, 22

Get the eBook for only $10!

> Now you can take the weightless companion with you anywhere, anytime. Your purchase of this book entitles you to 3 electronic versions for only $10.

This Apress title will prove so indispensible that you'll want to carry it with you everywhere, which is why we are offering the eBook in 3 formats for only $10 if you have already purchased the print book.

Convenient and fully searchable, the PDF version enables you to easily find and copy code—or perform examples by quickly toggling between instructions and applications. The MOBI format is ideal for your Kindle, while the ePUB can be utilized on a variety of mobile devices.

Go to www.apress.com/promo/tendollars to purchase your companion eBook.